Francesca Stavrakopoulou
King Manasseh and Child Sacrifice

Francesca Stavrakopoulou

King Manasseh and Child Sacrifice

Biblical Distortions of Historical Realities

Walter de Gruyter · Berlin · New York

♾ Printed on acid-free paper which falls within
the guidelines of the ANSI to ensure permanence and durability.

ISBN 3-11-017994-6

Library of Congress Cataloging-in-Publication Data

Stavrakopoulou, Francesca.
  King Manasseh and child sacrifice : biblical distortions of histori-
cal realities / Francesca Stavrakopoulou.
      p. cm. — (Beihefte zur Zeitschrift für die alttestamentliche
  Wissenschaft ; 338)
  Includes bibliographical references and indexes.
  ISBN 3-11-017994-6 (alk. paper)
  1. Manasseh, King of Judah. 2. Child sacrifice in the Bible. 3. Bible.
O.T. — Criticism, interpretation, etc.   4. Child sacrifice — Judaism.
I. Title. II. Series.
  BS580.M3S73   2004
  296.4'92 — dc22
                                                                 2004012835

Bibliographic Information published by Die Deutsche Bibliothek

Die Deutsche Bibliothek lists this publication in the Deutsche Nationalbibliografie; detailed
bibliographic data is available in the Internet at < http://dnb.ddb.de >.

Printed in Germany

Cover Design: Christopher Schneider, Berlin

Dedicated to Gweneth Janet Marie Jones

Acknowledgments

Though the only name to appear upon the title page of this volume is my own, there are several other people who have made this work possible, all of whom deserve recognition and thanks here.

This volume is a slightly revised form of my doctoral thesis, completed in the autumn of 2002 and examined at the beginning of 2003. Accordingly, my deepest thanks go to my doctoral supervisor, Paul M. Joyce, whose generosity in knowledge, time and support continues to prove limitless. I am also indebted to my doctoral examiners, John Barton and Adrian H.W. Curtis, for their careful and constructive critique of the arguments presented here. Their observations, both scholarly and practical, have been of immense benefit in preparing the work for publication. It is also a pleasure to acknowledge the generosity of the Arts and Humanities Research Board, whose postgraduate award made possible the research for this volume.

My special thanks go to Kevin J. Cathcart. Our conversations have inspired and clarified much of my thinking, and as such, they form the backdrop to many of the ideas explored in this book. His wisdom, friendship and support remain invaluable to me. I am also particularly grateful to Susan E. Gillingham, whose infectious passion for the biblical texts inspired my own love of the Hebrew Bible.

There are several others to whom I am indebted. To Anselm Hagedorn, Helenann Hartley, Jill Middlemas, Sharon Moughtin, Aulikki Nahkola, Henry Wansbrough and Molly Zahn, I offer my affectionate thanks—for their expertise, their time, and above all, their friendship. I also owe a debt of gratitude to Jonathan Benson, whose careful assistance, along with his good humour, enabled me to prepare the manuscript for publication. Needless to say, any errors remaining are my own.

Words cannot express the depth of my gratitude to my mother; her love and encouragement are boundless. I am also utterly beholden to Glenn, whose patient support and gentle teasing ensure that my feet remain rooted firmly to the ground. This book is dedicated to my grandmother, without whom my preoccupation with the people and practices of the past would never have begun.

Contents

Abbreviations

AASOR	Annual of the American Schools of Oriental Research
AB	Anchor Bible
ABD	*The Anchor Bible Dictionary* (6 vols. Edited by D.N. Freedman. New York: Doubleday, 1992).
ABRL	Anchor Bible Reference Library
ADAJ	Annual of the Department of Antiquities of Jordan
AJA	*American Journal of Archaeology*
AJBA	*Australian Journal of Biblical Archaeology*
AfR	*Archiv für Religionsgeschichte*
AfOB	Archiv für Orientforschung: Beiheft
AJSL	*American Journal of Semitic Languages and Literatures*
ANEP	*The Ancient Near East in Pictures Relating to the Old Testament* (Edited by J.B. Pritchard. Second edn. Princeton: Princeton University Press, 1969).
ANET	*Ancient Near Eastern Texts Relating to the Old Testament* (Edited by J.B. Pritchard. Third edn. Princeton: Princeton University Press, 1969).
AOAT	Alter Orient und Altes Testament
ArchOd	*Archaeology Odyssey*
ASOR	American Schools of Oriental Research
ASORMS	American Schools of Oriental Research Monograph Series
AulOr	Aula Orientalis
AP	*Aramaic Papyri of the Fifth Century BC* (Edited by A.E. Cowley. Oxford: Clarendon Press, 1923).
BA	*Biblical Archaeologist*
BAIAS	*Bulletin of the Anglo-Israel Archaeological Society*
BAR	*Biblical Archaeology Review*
BASOR	*Bulletin of the American Schools of Oriental Research*
BDB	*A Hebrew and English Lexicon of the Old Testament* (F. Brown, S.R. Driver and C.A. Briggs. Oxford: Clarendon Press, 1907).
BEAT	Beiträge zur Erforschung des Alten Testaments
BETL	Bibliotheca ephemeridum theologicarum lovaniensium

BHS	*Biblia Hebraica Stuttgartensia* (Edited by K. Elliger and W. Rudolph. Stuttgart: Deutsche Bibelstiftung, 1983).
Bib	*Biblica*
BibB	Biblische Beiträge
BibInt	*Biblical Interpretation*
BibOr	Biblica et orientalia
BN	*Biblische Notizen*
BO	*Bibliotheca orientalis*
BR	*Bible Review*
BZ	*Biblische Zeitschrift*
BZAW	Beihefte zur Zeitschrift für die alttestamentliche Wissenschaft
CAT	Commentaire de l'Ancien Testament
CB	Century Bible
CBET	Contributions to Biblical Exegesis and Theology
CB OTS	Coniectanea biblica. Old Testament Series
CBQ	*Catholic Biblical Quarterly*
CIS	*Corpus inscriptionum semiticarum*
CIS	Copenhagen International Seminar
COS	*The Context of Scripture* (3 vols. Edited by W.W. Hallo. Leiden: Brill, 1997-2002).
CRAIBL	*Comptes rendus de l'Académie des inscriptions et belles-lettres*
CR:BS	*Currents in Research: Biblical Studies*
CSA	Copenhagen Studies in Assyriology
CSF	Collezione di studi fenici
CTA	*Corpus des tablettes en cunéiformes alphabétiques découvertes à Ras Shamra-Ugarit de 1929 à 1939* (Edited by A. Herdner. Mission de Ras Shamra 10. Paris: Imprimerie nationale, 1963).
CTU	*The Cuneiform Alphabetic Texts from Ugarit, Ras Ibn Hani, and Other Places* (Edited by M. Dietrich, O. Loretz, and J. Sanmartín. Münster: Ugarit-Verlag, 1995).
DBSup	*Dictionnaire de la Bible: Supplément* (Edited by L. Pirot and A. Robert. Paris: Letouzey & Ané, 1928-).
DCH	*The Dictionary of Classical Hebrew* (5 vols. Edited by D.J.A. Clines. Sheffield: Sheffield Academic Press, 1993-2001).
DDD	*Dictionary of Deities and Demons in the Bible* (Edited by K. van der Toorn, B. Becking and P. W. van der Horst. Second extensively revised edition. Leiden: Brill, 1999).
DISO	*Dictionnaire des inscriptions sémitiques de l'ouest* (Edited by Ch.F. Jean and J. Hoftijzer. Leiden: Brill, 1965).

DNWSI	*Dictionary of North-West Semitic Inscriptions* (2 vols. J. Hoftijzer and K. Jongeling. Leiden: Brill, 1995).
DULAT	*A Dictionary of the Ugaritic Language in the Alphabetic Tradition* (2 vols. Edited by G. Olmo Lette and J. Sanmartín. Translated by W.G.E Watson. HdO 67. Leiden: Brill, 2003).
EI	*Eretz Israel*
ESHM	European Seminar in Historical Methodology
ET	English Translation
ETL	*Ephemerides theologicae lovanienses*
ExpTim	*Expository Times*
FRLANT	Forschungen zur Religion und Literatur des Alten und Neuen Testaments
GCT	Gender, Culture, Theory
GKC	*Gesenius' Hebrew Grammar* (Edited by E. Kautsch. Translated by A.E. Cowley. Second edn. Oxford: Clarendon Press, 1910).
HALOT	*The Hebrew and Aramaic Lexicon of the Old Testament* (4 vols. L. Koehler, W. Baumgartner and J.J. Stamm. Translated and edited under the supervision of M.E.J. Richardson. Leiden: Brill, 1994-1999).
HAR	*Hebrew Annual Review*
HAT	Handbuch zum Alten Testament
HdO	Handbuch der Orientalistik
HSM	Harvard Semitic Monographs
HTR	*Harvard Theological Review*
HUCA	*Hebrew Union College Annual*
ICC	International Critical Commentary
IEJ	*Israel Exploration Journal*
IES	Israel Exploration Society
Int	*Interpretation*
JA	*Journal Asiatique*
JANESCU	*Journal of the Ancient Near Eastern Society of Columbia University*
JAOS	*Journal of the American Oriental Society*
JBC	*Jerome Biblical Commentary*
JBL	*Journal of Biblical Literature*
JCS	*Journal of Cuneiform Studies*
JNES	*Journal of Near Eastern Studies*
JNSL	*Journal of Northwest Semitic Languages*
JPOS	*Journal of the Palestine Oriental Society*
JPSTCS	Jewish Publication Society Commentary Series

JSJ	*Journal for the Study of Judaism in the Persian, Hellenistic and Roman Period*
JSNTSup	Journal for the Study of the New Testament Supplement Series
JSOT	*Journal for the Study of the Old Testament*
JSOTSup	Journal for the Study of the Old Testament Supplement Series
JSS	*Journal of Semitic Studies*
JTS	*Journal of Theological Studies*
K	Ketib
KAI	*Kanaanäische und aramäische Inschriften* (H. Donner and W. Röllig. Second edn. Wiesbaden: Harrassowitz, 1964-1966).
KTU	*Die keilalphabetischen Texte Ugarit* (Edited by M. Dietrich, O. Loretz and J. Sanmartin. AOAT 24/1. Neukirchen-Vluyn: Neukirchener Verlag, 1976).
LCL	Loeb Classical Library
LXX	Septuagint
MT	Masoretic Text
MRS	Mission de Ras Shamra
NEA	*Near Eastern Archaeology*
NEAEHL	*The New Encyclopaedia of Archaeological Excavations in the Holy Land* (4 vols. Edited by E. Stern; Jerusalem: Magnes Press, 1993).
NCB	New Century Bible
NT	New Testament
OBC	*The Oxford Bible Commentary* (Edited by J. Barton and J. Muddiman. Oxford: Oxford University Press, 2001).
Or	*Orientalia* (Rome)
OrAnt	*Oriens antiques*
OrEx	*Orient Express*
OTL	Old Testament Library
OTP	*The Old Testament Pseudepigrapha* (2 vols. Edited by J.H. Charlesworth. New York: Doubleday, 1983).
OTS	Oudtestamentische Studiën
PEQ	*Palestine Exploration Quarterly*
Q	Qere
QDAP	*Quarterly of the Department of Antiquities in Palestine*
RB	*Revue biblique*
RES	*Répertoire d'épigraphie sémitique*
RHR	*Revue de l'histoire des religions*
RivB	*Rivista biblica*
RPARA	*Rendiconti della Pontifica Accademia Romana di Archeologia*

RS	Ras Shamra (tablet inventory number)
RSO	*Rivista degli studi orientali*
RSR	*Religious Studies Review*
RSF	*Rivista di studi fenici*
SAAB	*State Archives of Assyria Bulletin*
SBAB	Stuttgarter biblische Aufsatzbände
SBLDS	Society of Biblical Literature Dissertation Series
SBLMS	Society of Biblical Literature Monograph Series
SBLSP	*Society of Biblical Literature Seminar Papers*
SHANE	Studies in the History of the Ancient Near East
SJOT	*Scandinavian Journal of the Old Testament*
SS	Studi semitici
SSEJC	Studies in Scripture in Early Judaism and Christianity
SWBAS	Social World of Biblical Antiquity Series
TA	*Tel Aviv*
TBü	Theologische Bücherei
TDOT	*Theological Dictionary of the Old Testament* (8 vols. Edited by G.J. Botterweck and H. Ringgren. Translated by J.T. Willis, G.W. Bromiley and D.E. Green. Grand Rapids: Eerdmans, 1974-).
ThLZ	*Theologische Literaturzeitung*
TynBul	*Tyndale Bulletin*
UCOP	University of Cambridge Oriental Publications
UF	*Ugarit-Forschungen*
VT	*Vetus Testamentum*
VTSup	Vetus Testamentum Supplements
WBC	Word Biblical Commentary
WZKM	*Wiener Zeitschrift für die Kunde des Morgenlandes*
ZA	*Zeitschrift für Assyriologie*
ZAW	*Zeitschrift für die alttestamentliche Wissenschaft*
ZDMG	*Zeitschrift der deutschen morgenländischen Gesellschaft*
ZDPV	*Zeitschrift der deutschen Palästina-Vereins*

Introduction

The Hebrew Bible presents a religious history of a people called "Israel". As such, much of this collection of ancient texts is concerned with people and practices, conveying to the ancient reader a simple but powerful message: who you are and what you do necessarily defines whether you are to be included within or excluded from this people called "Israel". In seeking to explore the parameters of this biblical "Israel", it is necessary to examine the people and practices within the Hebrew Bible that ostensibly function as boundary markers, qualifying and defining the behaviour that allows or prohibits access to "Israel". In such a context, King Manasseh may be understood as the most reprehensible person in the biblical story of "Israel", and child sacrifice the most reprehensible practice. Yet archaeological, inscriptional and socio-scientific data indicate that historically, neither Manasseh nor child sacrifice were as deviant as the Hebrew Bible appears to insist. Thus one of the aims of this study is to reconstruct the likely reality of the historical figure of Manasseh, and the likely reality of the historical practice of child sacrifice. It is anticipated that these historical realities will contrast considerably with their biblical portrayals. Consequently, the other aim of this study is to discern how and why both Manasseh and child sacrifice are distorted into the reprehensible within the Hebrew Bible.

Underlying this discussion is the continuing debate concerning the use of the Hebrew Bible within historical reconstructions of ancient Israelite and Judahite societies and their religious beliefs and practices. The perceived historical reliability of the Hebrew Bible remains in a state of flux: though the tension between historical memory and literary fiction within the biblical texts is widely acknowledged, a consensus concerning the extent to which the Hebrew Bible preserves reliable historical information about the people, practices and events it describes has not emerged—nor is it likely to. Indeed, the seemingly Janus-like character of the Hebrew Bible pulls and pushes scholarship between its twin poles of history and ideology. As a result, absolute certainty about the past remains elusive. In one sense, the past may be distinguished from history, for the latter is an account of the former. This notion is succinctly described by Brettler:

> All history is created. Events transpire, but people tell and record, select and reshape
> them, creating historical texts.[1]

The gradual permeation of this recognition throughout scholarship renders uncertain the extent to which the biblical texts are considered to offer reasonably reliable accounts of the past. Indeed, the biblical story of "Israel" is increasingly perceived to be just that: *story*, rather than history.

Yet there remains an unwillingness to call off the search for the people and practices of the past altogether, for the possibility exists that the biblical texts may unwittingly reveal glimpses of the historical reality they attempt to re-image by means of their ideologies. "Ideology" is a designation frequently employed within biblical scholarship, yet rarely defined with precision, for it usefully embraces a range of literary, theological, political and sociological issues generally acknowledged to shape biblical texts. Its fluidity of usage thus mirrors its ambiguity in meaning. Yet as the importance of the social location of biblical writers and their corresponding world-views is increasingly accepted as a primary influence within their texts, a more precise understanding of the term "ideology" is demanded. Whilst a carefully considered definition of "ideology" would fulfil this perceived need for precision, it could also harbour the risk of stagnation in its immovability. Among the myriad discussions within biblical scholarship of the forms and functions of ideology,[2] certain key observations have arisen, which combine

---

1   M.Z. Brettler, *The Creation of History in Ancient Israel* (London: Routledge, 1995), 1.
2   See, for example, D. Jobling and T. Pippin (eds.), *Ideological Criticism of Biblical Texts* (Semeia 59; Atlanta: SBL, 1992); M. Sternberg, *The Poetics of Biblical Narrative: Ideological Literature and the Drama of Reading* (Bloomington: Indiana University Press, 1985); T. Pippin, "Ideology, Ideological Criticism, and the Bible", *CR:BS* 4 (1996), 51-78; J.E. Dyck, "A Map of Ideology for Biblical Critics", in M. Daniel Carroll R. (ed.), *Rethinking Contexts, Rereading Texts: Contributions from the Social Sciences to Biblical Interpretation* (JSOTSup 299; Sheffield: Sheffield Academic Press, 2000), 108-128; S. Fowl, "Texts Don't Have Ideologies", *BibInt* 3 (1995), 15-34; J. Barr, *History and Ideology in the Old Testament: Biblical Studies at the End of a Millennium* (Oxford: Oxford University Press, 2000); The Bible and Culture Collective, *The Postmodern Bible* (New Haven: Yale University Press, 1995), 272-308; G. Garbini, *History and Ideology in Ancient Israel* (trans. J. Bowden; London: SCM Press, 1988); Y. Amit, *History and Ideology: An Introduction to Historiography in the Hebrew Bible* (trans. Y. Lotan; BS 60; Sheffield: Sheffield Academic Press, 1999). For non-biblical discussions, see particularly C. Hampton, *The Ideology of the Text* (Milton Keynes: Open University Press, 1990); T. Eagleton, *Criticism and Ideology: A Study in Marxist Theory* (London: Verso, 1976); *idem.*, *Ideology: An Introduction* (London: Verso, 1991); S. Žižek (ed.), *Mapping Ideology* (London: Verso, 1994).

to offer an alternative, and perhaps more expedient, approach to understanding the nature of ideology.

In his nuanced and persuasive discussion of the nature, function and impact of ideologies, Clines draws particular attention to ideology as a collection of "large-scale ideas that influence and determine the whole outlook of groups of people".[3] As the title of his book makes plain, ideology can, and indeed does, shape the outlooks of both biblical writers and their readers.[4] In this context, the personal "ownership" of ideologies is occasionally articulated within modern scholarship: a biblical commentator, for example, may wish to acknowledge and to accept his or her potential biases and agendas in the presentation or interpretation of the ideas expressed.[5] Yet as Clines points out, ideologies are often assumed, "even without their adherents even knowing quite what they are assuming".[6] This in itself can present a particular danger for the biblical scholar, for there is inherent in religious writings an "ideological impulse"[7] which, if undetected or unacknowledged, can colour academic enquiry and cloud scholarly judgement.[8]

Mayes rightly emphasizes that an ideology exists within a dynamic context of opposition to other ideologies: it possesses an inherent polemic which simultaneously seeks to legitimize its own social context and perspectives, whilst discrediting the world-views of opposing ideologies.[9] Yet this is not to encourage a misunderstanding of ideology as an expression of social dominance or significance; rather, ideology also plays a crucial role among comparatively insignificant or inferior groups and individuals.[10] An important function of "ideology" is thus the delineation or construction of self-identity. In the Hebrew Bible, the contours of the self-identity of "Israel"

---

3   D.J.A. Clines, *Interested Parties: The Ideology of Writers and Readers of the Hebrew Bible* (JSOTSup 205/GCT 1; Sheffield: Sheffield Academic Press, 1995), 11-12.

4   Clines, *Interested Parties*, 16-23.

5   Cf. Pippin, "Ideology", 51; see also D. Penchansky, "Up For Grabs: A Tentative Proposal for Doing Ideological Criticism", in Jobling and Pippin, *Ideological Criticism of Biblical Texts*, 35-41.

6   Clines, *Interested Parties*, 12.

7   Penchansky, "Up For Grabs", 38.

8   See further, for example, K.W. Whitelam, *The Invention of Ancient Israel: The Silencing of Palestinian History* (London: Routledge, 1996), esp. 11-36; N.P. Lemche, *The Israelites in History and Tradition* (Library of Ancient Israel; Louisville: Westminster John Knox, 1998), ch. 5.

9   A.D.H. Mayes, "Deuteronomistic Ideology and the Theology of the Old Testament", *JSOT* 82 (1999), 57-82; cf. Eagleton, *Ideology*, 30.

10 Cf. Eagleton, *Ideology*, 6.

are primarily shaped by three important and related ideological concepts: nation, and its accompanying territorial concerns; ethnicity, with an emphasis upon genealogical continuity; and religion, and its strong tendency to denounce the beliefs and rituals it rejects. In this regard, ideology is often perceived most clearly in the form of conceptual boundaries, configuring the self-identity of "Israel". The following observations of Brett, though made with specific reference to ethnicity, are nevertheless illuminating in this broader context:

> ... the formulation of boundaries is crucial feature [*sic*] of self-definition. Who should be considered one of "us" and who should be considered "other"? ... But, as has frequently been observed, the most problematic social transactions occur precisely at the boundary, between "us" and those who are "like us".[11]

Brett's comments are also helpful in that, like many others, he focuses attention upon the *social* context of ideology: regardless of its medium of expression—whether, for example, literary, iconographic, dramatic or musical—ideology is a social expression, and cannot be divorced from its social context. This is true of all forms of ideology, including those articulated within the Hebrew Bible. As Eagleton comments, "Ideology is ... a question of who is saying what to whom for what purposes."[12]

Born of literary and sociological theories,[13] "ideological criticism" thus builds upon the widely-accepted premise that biases evident within the Hebrew Bible often reflect the biblical writers' self-definition, social contexts, and world-views. Locating and identifying the social and theological concerns of biblical writers offers a framework for discussion focused upon the ideological influences within biblical texts. But a cautionary note must be sounded, lest a complex issue is to be oversimplified: the recognition and acceptance of the ideological nature of the Hebrew Bible is not to overlook the biblical material as a varied and often contradictory collection of religious texts, texts with complex literary histories, which exhibit a dynamic range of themes and ideas. The Hebrew Bible is not an inherently coherent collection with a unified theological

---

11 M.G. Brett, "Interpreting Ethnicity: Method, Hermeneutics, Ethics", in M.G. Brett (ed.), *Ethnicity and the Bible* (Leiden: Brill, 2002), 3-22 (10).

12 Eagleton, *Ideology*, 9.

13 See further F. Jameson, *The Political Unconscious: Narrative as a Socially Symbolic Act* (Ithaca: Cornell University Press, 1981); R.P. Carroll, "Poststructuralist Approaches; New Historicism and postmodernism", in J. Barton (ed.), *The Cambridge Companion to Biblical Interpretation* (Cambridge: Cambridge University Press, 1998), 50-66.

agenda. But nor is it so incoherent as to be simply a disparate group of texts, loosely held together by their central focus upon a specific deity. In spite of its varied concerns—and indeed its many ideologies—the Hebrew Bible, on the whole, does project an overarching, unified ideological system: that of a monotheistic world-view, in which a creator god forges an exclusive relationship with "Israel", a relationship which is traceable through history and evidenced through the gift of land. This ideological theme pervades and unifies the texts of the Hebrew Bible, and in this sense, this discussion is justified in referring throughout to the "ideology of the Hebrew Bible". Yet where does this leave history?

Without aligning this discussion with a particular scholar or group of scholars,[14] the following observations are offered as a means of locating this study upon the figurative map of the debate concerning the historical reliability of the Hebrew Bible: firstly, and perhaps most importantly, the Hebrew Bible must be distinguished from the religious history it seeks to describe. To recognize the Hebrew Bible as a collection of religious and ideological literature is not to deny that information of an historical nature may be discerned in it. Yet in acknowledging that this sort of information may lie within the biblical texts, neither can the religious and ideological context of that information be disregarded. Nor can the possibility of historically-credible information verify the reliability of the Hebrew Bible as an historical source.

Secondly, given its nature as religious and ideological literature, the Hebrew Bible may reveal more about its writers than it can about the historical realities of the people, practices and events it seeks to describe. Therefore the perceived importance and role of the Hebrew Bible within historical reconstructions demands close delineation. Essentially, this entails the relative prioritization of biblical and non-biblical material employed within such reconstructions. For some scholars, the Hebrew Bible is

---

14 The volume of material discussing this issue is now vast. For a sampling of views, see for example, I.W. Provan, "Ideologies, Literary and Critical: Reflections on Recent Writing on the History of Israel", *JBL* 114 (1995), 585-606; P.R. Davies, "Method and Madness: Some Remarks on Doing History with the Bible", *JBL* 114 (1995), 699-705; E.A. Knauf, "From History to Interpretation", in D.V. Edelman (ed.), *The Fabric of History: Text, Artifact and Israel's Past* (JSOTSup 127; Sheffield: JSOT Press, 1991), 26-64; L.L. Grabbe (ed.), *Can a "History of Israel" Be Written?* (JSOTSup 245/ESHM 1; Sheffield: Sheffield Academic Press, 1997); W.G. Dever, *What Did the Biblical Writers Know and When Did they Know It? What Archaeology Can Tell Us about the Reality of Ancient Israel* (Grand Rapids: Eerdmans, 2001).

potentially a primary source able to provide, for example, a reasonably reliable insight into the religious character of the kingdoms of Israel and Judah, which may be supplemented or interpreted in the light of non-biblical literature, inscriptions, and artefacts. In contrast, others would relegate the Hebrew Bible to the role of a secondary source, assigning precedence instead to the potential evidence of non-biblical material to provide a reasonably reliable foundation upon which the religious characters of the kingdoms may be constructed. The present discussion will generally tend to favour the latter option. However, it is important to acknowledge that this process of prioritization is not rigidly immovable. Thus although the Hebrew Bible may not function as a primary source in the historical reconstruction of ancient Israel and Judah, its potential value as a source for discerning the ideological stance and socio-historical location of the biblical writers is greatly increased. Consequently, the Hebrew Bible is perhaps best understood as offering its own versions of the histories of Israel and Judah, just as modern scholarship offers its own multiple versions of those histories.

A notable reflex of this relative prioritization of non-biblical material over the biblical is what Edelman describes as a "paradigm shift" in the conceptualization of the historical realities of Israelite and Judahite religions.[15] A particular interest in the beliefs and practices of various social groups, such as families, women, priests, urban elites, and rural communities, has emphasized the internal diversity of Israelite and Judahite religious beliefs and practices.[16] Coupled with a renewed focus upon the plurality of deities, and their varied and localized manifestations throughout the land,[17] a picture has emerged of Israelite and Judahite religions as normatively polytheistic and internally pluralistic, and as such they are to be regarded as

---

15 D.V. Edelman, Review of J. Day, *Yahweh and the God and Goddesses of Canaan*, *BI* 10 (2002), 79-81.

16 See, for example, Z. Zevit, *The Religions of Ancient Israel: A Synthesis of Parallactic Approaches* (London/New York: Continuum, 2001); K. van der Toorn, *Family Religion in Babylonia, Syria, and Israel* (Leiden: Brill, 1996); E.S. Gerstenberger, *Theologies in the Old Testament* (trans. J. Bowden; Edinburgh: T&T Clark, 2002); R. Albertz, *Persönliche Frömmigkeit und offizielle Religion* (Stuttgart: Calwer Verlag, 1978); *idem.*, *A History of Israelite Religion in the Old Testament Period* (2 vols; trans. J. Bowden; Louisville: Westminster John Knox, 1994); G.W. Ahlström, *Royal Administration and National Religion in Ancient Palestine* (Leiden: Brill, 1982); L.G. Perdue, J. Blenkinsopp, J.J. Collins and C. Meyers, *Families in Ancient Israel* (FRC; Louisville: Westminster John Knox, 1997).

17 Van der Toorn, *Family Religion*, 236-265.

inherently coherent with the religious climate of the ancient Near East.[18] Closely related is the widespread recognition that Israelites and Judahites are best considered subsets of the native people of the land commonly designated "Canaan", thereby dispelling the biblically-based distinction between "Israelite" and "Canaanite".[19] This in itself is informed by the shifting sands of archaeology, which has now clearly established that Israel and Judah emerged from the indigenous population of Palestine, and did not originate outside the land.[20]

A further facet of this paradigm shift in the conceptualization of Israelite and Judahite religions reflects the gradual erosion of the sharp distinction frequently discerned between "official religion" and "popular religion". In essence, this distinction perceives a difference between an institutionalized religious system, commonly endorsed by the state, practised in its accompanying established sanctuaries, and commonly termed "official" or "formal" religion, and those religious beliefs and practices which do not have a place in this institutionalized religion, which are instead associated with the people living and worshipping away from the established sanctuaries, and as

---

18   See further K. van der Toorn, "Currents in the Study of Israelite Religion", *CR:BS* 6 (1998), 9-30; M.S. Smith, *The Early History of God: Yahweh and the Other Deities in Ancient Israel* (San Francisco: Harper & Row, 1990); O. Keel and C. Uehlinger, *Gods, Goddesses, and Images of God in Ancient Israel* (trans. T.H. Trapp; Edinburgh: T&T Clark, 1998); L.K. Handy, "The Appearance of Pantheon in Judah", in D.V. Edelman (ed.), *The Triumph of Elohim: From Yahwisms to Judaisms* (CBET 13; Kampen: Kok Pharos, 1995), 27-43; H. Niehr, "The Rise of YHWH in Judahite and Israelite Religion: Methodologiocal and Religio-Historical Aspects", in Edelman, *The Triumph of Elohim*, 45-72; F. Stolz, "Monotheismus in Israel", in O. Keel (ed.), *Monotheismus im Alten Israel und seiner Umwelt* (BibB 14; Freiburg: Schweizerisches Katholosches Bibelwerk, 1980).

19   See further, for example, N.P. Lemche, *The Canaanites and Their Land: The Tradition of the Canaanites* (JSOTSup 110; Sheffield: JSOT Press, 1991); T.L. Thompson, *Early History of the Israelite People: From the Written and Archaeological Sources* (SHANE 4; Leiden: Brill, 1994), 310-316; G.W. Ahlström, *Who Were the Israelites?* (Winona Lake: Eisenbrauns, 1986); cf. V. Fritz, "Israelites and Canaanites: You Can Tell Them Apart", *BAR* 28 (2002), 28-31, 63; W.G. Dever, "How to Tell a Canaanite from an Israelite", in H. Shanks (ed.), *The Rise of Ancient Israel* (Washington: Biblical Archaeology Society, 1992), 27-56; *idem., Who Were the Early Israelites and Where Did They Come From?* (Grand Rapids: Eerdmans, 2003).

20   See further I. Finkelstein, *The Archaeology of the Israelite Settlement* (Jerusalem: Israel exploration Society, 1988); *idem.,* "The Emergence of Israel: A Phase in the Cyclic History of Canaan in the Third and Second Millennia BCE", in I. Finkelstein and N. Na'aman (eds.), *From Nomadism to Monarchy: Archaeological and Historical Aspects of Early Israel* (Jerusalem: Israel Exploration Society, 1994), 150-178.

such are often described as "village religion", "folk religion", or even "superstition". It is not uncommon to find that discussions maintaining this distinction frequently slide into a further distinction, that of "legitimate" and "illegitimate" religious beliefs and practices, the former characterizing institutionalized religion, and the latter characterizing practices external to or rejected by the institutionalized religion. Yet in the light of compelling evidence for a normative and native plurality and variety of religions within the ancient Israelite and Judahite belief-systems, it is increasingly recognized that distinctions of this kind are frequently unhelpful, if not misleading and distorting.[21] Accordingly, the terms "official religion" and "popular religion", along with their synonyms, are best avoided.

The observations summarized here thus present a picture of the historical and religious realities of ancient Israel and Judah at odds with the biblical portrayal. In taking account of the strong ideological concerns of the biblical writers and the illuminating paradigm shift within the historical imaging of ancient Israelite and Judahite religions, it is essential to distinguish carefully between the Hebrew Bible and the probable historical realities of ancient Israel and Judah. In order to reaffirm this distinction, and secondarily as a trigger for the reader to recall these observations, this study will employ an appellative distinction between YHWH, the central character and god of the Hebrew Bible, and *Yhwh*, a deity worshipped in and around ancient Palestine.[22]

One of the primary aims of this study is the identification and demonstration of an ideological strategy employed within the Hebrew Bible. This strategy is the construction of conceptual boundaries which identify

---

21 For further discussion, see J. Berlinerblau, *The Vow and the "Popular Religious Groups" of Ancient Israel: A Philological and Sociological Inquiry* (JSOTSup 210; Sheffield: Sheffield Academic Press, 1996), ch. 1; *idem.*, "The 'Popular Religion' Paradigm in Old Testament Research: A Sociological Critique", *JSOT* 60 (1993), 3-26; M. Daniel Carroll R., "Re-Examining 'Popular Religion': Issues of Definition and Sources. Insights from Interpretative Anthropology", in M. Daniel Carroll R. (ed.), *Rethinking Contexts, Rereading Texts: Contributions from the Social Sciences to Biblical Interpretation* (JSOTSup 299; Sheffield: Sheffield Academic Press, 2000), 146-167; J. Gomes, "Popular Religion in Old Testament Research: Past, Present and Future", *TynBul* 54 (2003), 31-50; P. Vrijhof and J. Waardenburg (eds.), *Official and Popular Religion: Analysis of a Theme for Religious Studies* (Religion and Society 19; The Hague: Mouton, 1979).

22 This terminology is a modification of that offered by C. Uehlinger, "Anthropomorphic Cult Statuary in Iron Age Palestine and the Search for Yahweh's Cult Images", in K. van der Toorn (ed.), *The Image and the Book: Iconic Cults, Aniconism, and the Rise of Book Religion in Israel and the Ancient Near East* (Leuven: Peeters, 1997), 97-155.

"Israel" as the people of God. These boundaries qualify and define behaviour allowing or prohibiting access to the people "Israel". As stated at the outset, the biblical portrayals of King Manasseh and child sacrifice as the embodiments of religious deviancy thus serve as ideological "boundary markers" in this biblical, ideological context. In the close examination of King Manasseh and child sacrifice, this study will fall into two parts. The first may be considered a defence of the historical King Manasseh. The portrait of Manasseh within the Hebrew Bible and later traditions differs greatly depending upon the portrait-painter. For the Book of Kings,[23] Manasseh plays the role of the ultimate villain within its story of "Israel", for it is in direct response to his deliberate cultic mispractice that YHWH destroys Judah and Jerusalem and finally rejects his people. In contrast to this portrayal of Manasseh the "destructor", the Book of Chronicles casts Manasseh as the "constructor". He is the paradigmatic penitent, who returns to YHWH in prayer, purifies the cult, and fortifies his kingdom. Both perceptions of Manasseh are reflected within post-biblical traditions. Whereas the *Martyrdom of Isaiah* blames Manasseh for the gruesome execution of the prophet Isaiah, the Prayer of Manasseh presents Manasseh as the remorseful penitent. Rabbinic tradition also exhibits these conflicting impressions of Manasseh, presenting him both as an idolatrous prophet-slayer and as a repentant sinner and scriptural scholar.

Despite Manasseh's rehabilitation within some of these traditions, his villainous characterization is shared by all portrayals of this king. Moreover, most modern reconstructions of the historical kingdoms of Israel and Judah also adopt this negative portrayal, thereby perpetuating the portrait of Manasseh as a villain. This may find partial explanation in the apparent lack of interest within modern scholarship in locating and assessing the historical Manasseh. Rather, scholarly enquiry into Judah's kings tends to be dominated by those heroic characters the biblical writers wanted their audiences to remember, namely David, Hezekiah and Josiah.[24] This biblically-based bias is rarely—if ever—acknowledged within scholarship,

---

23 The label "Book of Kings", as well as that of "Book of Chronicles", should not be taken as indicative of a clumsy disregard of the traditional division of 1 and 2 Kings and 1 and 2 Chronicles each into two books; rather, this label reflects both the perceived unified, literary coherence of both Kings and Chronicles, and the necessary limitations of this study, preventing as they do any detailed discussion of the literary histories of these texts.

24 This bias is reflected in the fact that the modest number of studies concerning Manasseh is dwarfed by the huge volume of books, monographs and articles devoted to the subjects of David, Hezekiah and Josiah.

yet it must be recognized and rectified if the scholarly reconstruction of ancient Judahite societies and religious practices is to be even approximately representative of the probable historical reality.

In assessing biblical, post-biblical and scholarly presentations of King Manasseh, this discussion hopes to add to the small number of studies devoted to Manasseh, and to defend the Manasseh of history against the traditional and conventional charges of wickedness and apostasy. This may be achieved in three stages. Firstly, the biblical portrayals of Manasseh will be investigated in chapter 1. By this means, the role and function of Manasseh as a biblical character may be established, and the motivations for his villainous characterization discerned. Secondly, by examining archaeological, inscriptional and socio-scientific data, the discussion in chapter 2 will seek to construct a plausible profile of the historical Manasseh and his Judah, in which it will be argued that Manasseh was actually one of Judah's most successful monarchs. In chapter 3, this historical profile will be compared and contrasted with biblical, post-biblical and scholarly portraits of Manasseh, in order to clarify how and why the Manasseh of history has been distorted into the biblical epitome of the wicked, idolatrous apostate.

The second part of this study is essentially a reassessment of child sacrifice. The provocative nature of the subject of child sacrifice is clearly felt by both biblical writers and modern scholars. A cursory reading of the Hebrew Bible indicates not only that the practice was known, but also that the biblical writers felt that it was the particular practice of the "Canaanite" nations, and hence alien to YHWH-worship. However, the biblical writers concede that some idolatrous "Israelites" disobeyed YHWH's commands not to imitate the practices of the nations by causing their children "to pass over in the fire". Biblical scholarship has generally accepted—almost without question—the biblical picture in arguing that these texts refer or allude to a Canaanite deity named "Molek" to whom children were sacrificed, a practice adopted by idolatrous Israelites due to Canaanite influence. The advent of Eissfeldt's monograph in 1935 proclaiming the end of the god "Molek" in favour of Punic evidence for biblical מֹלֶךְ as a sacrificial term encouraged the academic abandonment of the concept of "Molek" as a deity.[25] However, Eissfeldt's theory has made less impact upon scholarship than is generally realised, for though he argued that children were sacrificed to *Yhwh*, the biblical insistence that such a practice was originally alien to Israel, imported by foreign nations, practised by idolatrous Israelites, and consistently

---

25 O. Eissfeldt, *Molk als Opferbegriff im Punischen und Hebräischen und das Ende des Gottes Moloch* (Halle: Niemeyer, 1935).

outlawed by YHWH, has persisted, not least in the wide-ranging consensus that foreign cultural influence upon Israel and Judah was to blame, a view recently rearticulated by Miller:

> The practice of child sacrifice may have had some continuing place in heterodox Yahwism, but it seems to have been a genuinely syncretistic practice brought in from outside in the assimilation of cults of other deities to the worship of Yahweh.[26]

This academic assertion has been made in spite of some highly ambiguous texts, such as the story of the sacrifice of Jephthah's daughter in Judg. 11:30-40, and texts which claim explicitly that YHWH demanded child sacrifice, such as the tale of the binding of Isaac in Gen. 22:1-19. A further example occurs in the book of Ezekiel. Though in this text child sacrifice is generally condemned within the context of the worship of foreign gods, in 20:25-26 it is claimed that YHWH deliberately demanded that his people sacrifice their firstborn children to him in order to punish them. Indeed, a closer examination of the Hebrew Bible suggests that the offering of the firstborn to YHWH may well have included the sacrifice of human babies along with the offering of animals and crops. In spite of these texts, the debate appears to have come full circle within modern scholarship with the relatively recent defence of the biblical concept of "Molek" as a foreign god of child sacrifice.[27] However, contrary to this view, this study will argue that the identification of child sacrifice as a foreign element within Judahite religious practice is based upon the distortion of the historical reality of child sacrifice within the Hebrew Bible. Furthermore, it will be argued that the academic acceptance of this biblical distortion as historical probability reflects a persistent and unself-critical ideological bias within modern scholarship. Unlike most other areas of academic enquiry, the subject of child sacrifice is particularly susceptible to misrepresentation within modern scholarship because of its sensitive nature. The historical reality of child sacrifice in ancient (and indeed modern) civilisations is an unpleasant reality, particularly, as van der Horst comments, if such a practice is attested within a culture that has played some role in the formation of one's personal world-

---

26 P.D. Miller, *The Religion of Ancient Israel* (Library of Ancient Israel; Louisville: Westminster John Knox, 2000), 59.

27 G.C. Heider, *The Cult of Molek: A Reassessment* (JSOTSup 43; Sheffield: JSOT Press, 1985); J. Day, *Molech: A god of human sacrifice in the Old Testament* (UCOP 41; Cambridge: Cambridge University Press, 1989).

view.[28] This may well account in part for the apparent reluctance within
biblical scholarship to apply the perspectives of ideological criticism to the
examination of the subject of child sacrifice and the Hebrew Bible. As
Bergmann suggests:

> We have a particular difficulty in understanding this phenomenon because the Judeo-
> Christian tradition has accustomed us to regard God as an ego-ideal. Therefore how
> could God tolerate human sacrifices?[29]

As observed above, ideological criticism suggests that ideology generally
exists within a dynamic context of opposition. In seeking to distinguish
between the biblical portrayal of child sacrifice and the historical reality of
this practice, this discussion will argue that the biblical material concerning
child sacrifice is generally opposed to the historical reality that children were
sacrificed to *Yhwh*, and that an "ideology of separateness"[30] governs the
biblical insistence that child sacrifice was a Canaanite practice. Moreover, it
will be argued that child sacrifice played an important role within the royal
Judahite cult, and that "Molek" is best understood as a biblical character
masking the historical reality of the sacrifice of children to *Yhwh*.

Accordingly, in discussing child sacrifice this study will follow a pattern
parallel to that applied to the subject of Manasseh. Thus in chapter 4, the
biblical portrayal of child sacrifice will be examined in order to identify the
specific role this sacrifice plays within the ideology of the Hebrew Bible.
This will be followed in chapter 5 by the construction of a plausible picture
of the nature and function of child sacrifice in Judah, based upon the
examination of archaeological, inscriptional and textual evidence. This
reconstruction will argue that child sacrifice was a native and normative
element of the historical reality of Judahite religious practice. In chapter 6, a
selective overview of some of the "afterlives" of the practice of child
sacrifice will be offered, demonstrating the enduring impact of this sacrifice

---

28 P.W. van der Horst, "'Laws that were not Good': Ezekiel 20:25 in Ancient Judaism and
    Early Christianity", in J.N. Bremmer and F. Garcia Martinez (eds.), *Sacred History and
    Sacred Texts in Early Judaism: A Symposium in Honour of A.S. van der Woude*
    (Kampen: Kok Pharos, 1992), 94-118.

29 M.S. Bergmann, *In the Shadow of Moloch: The Sacrifice of Children and Its Impact on
    Western Religions* (New York: Columbia University Press, 1992), 22.

30 Cf. P.M. Joyce, "Israelites and Canaanites, Christians and Jews: Studies in Self-
    Definition", in J.M. Soskice, *et al.*, *Knowing the Other: Proceedings of the Catholic
    Theological Association of Great Britain, Leeds, 1993, New Blackfriars*, Vol. 75, No.
    878 (1994), 31-38; E.S. Gerstenberger, *Levitcus: A Commentary* (trans. D.W. Stott;
    OTL; Louisville: Westminster John Knox, 1996), 255-57.

as a religious motif within Jewish and Christian traditions. It will be argued that the biblical distortion of child sacrifice as a "foreign" practice is a deliberate and ideologically-motivated attempt to disguise the historically-probable reality that children were sacrificed to *Yhwh* in Judah. Moreover, the failure of many scholars to recognize this biblical distortion will be underscored.

Biblical writers and modern scholars share a common interest in describing the people and practices of the past. None is immune from the danger of bias. A key method of this study, as Clines encourages, is thus "to try to reach beneath the surface of the text of the Hebrew Bible and the texts of biblical scholars and to expose what it is I think is 'really' going on underneath the claims and commands and statements of the biblical and scholarly texts".[31] As such, it is hoped that with a keen, self-critical rigour, and a careful process of historical contextualization, the admittedly tentative presentations of King Manasseh and child sacrifice in this study will redress some of the ideological imbalances and biased assumptions evident within biblical and non-biblical portrayals of this ancient person and this ancient practice.

---

31 Clines, *Interested Parties*, 12.

1 The Biblical Manasseh

Given that King Manasseh of Judah is presented as the longest reigning monarch within the biblical story of "Israel", it is remarkable that it takes less than two chapters and a few scattered verses within the biblical corpus to tell his story. Moreover, this story differs tremendously depending upon the storyteller. 2 Kgs 21:1-18 is the Kings account of Manasseh's reign, in which the idolatrous monarch is held personally responsible for the destruction of Judah and Jerusalem by misleading the people to do more evil than the nations, thereby provoking YHWH to bring punishment upon the people. This accusation is repeated in 2 Kgs 23:26-27 and 24:3-4, and also occurs in Jer. 15:4, in which YHWH claims, "I will make them a horror to all the kingdoms of the earth because of what King Manasseh, son of Hezekiah of Judah, did in Jerusalem". 2 Chr. 33:1-10 concurs almost exactly with Kings' portrayal of Manasseh as the villainous monarch who leads the people astray, yet makes a radical break from the Kings account in verses 11-20, in which the Assyrian king carries Manasseh off to Babylon, where he repents before YHWH, who thus restores him to the Judahite throne. The reformed Manasseh then purges the cult, implements an extensive building project, and strengthens Judah's military installations. Kings and Chronicles conflict so much in their presentation of Manasseh and his reign that scholars of what may be cautiously termed "the Judah of history" find themselves choosing between the two accounts based upon the supposed historical reliability of each. Consequently, though attempts have been made to demonstrate the historical plausibility of the Chronicler's report of Manasseh's captivity, the majority of scholars appear to dismiss the account in Chronicles as a fictitious theological vehicle, and favour instead Kings' portrait of Manasseh. Making this simplistic choice between Kings and Chronicles would appear to satisfy the academic appetite for critical questioning, for as Evans observes, many scholars continue to accept uncritically the negative portrait of Manasseh in 2

Kgs 21.[1] This position was particularly popular in the 'seventies and 'eighties: McKay states that "Manasseh himself positively encouraged [the] revival of heathenism", and is thus "rightly condemned" by the biblical writers.[2] Cogan describes the reign of Manasseh as "an age of unprecedented abandonment of Israelite tradition".[3] Though he acknowledges the theological bias of the Kings' account of Manasseh's reign, Jagersma claims that Assyrian influence upon Manasseh resulted in a syncretistic, religious decline during his reign.[4] Such value judgments are hardly the stuff of objective, academic investigation.[5] Yet despite the recent scholarly emphasis upon the polytheistic character of native and normative Judahite religion, Manasseh continues to be described as an idolatrous anti-monotheist. Day asserts that Manasseh allowed syncretism to run rampant,[6] whilst Milgrom claims:

> ... the difference in the state-endorsed religion of Judah between the eighth and the seventh century is largely summarized by a single word—rather, by a single person: Manasseh. By force majeure (2 Kgs 21:16), he reintroduced idolatry into Jerusalem and Judah, completely undoing the reform of his father, Hezekiah (2 Kgs 21:3), and, even exceeding the previous status quo, he installed idols in the Temple courtyards and in the sanctuary itself (2 Kgs 21:5, 7; 23:4-7).[7]

---

1   C.D. Evans, "Manasseh, King of Judah", *ABD*, vol. 4, 496-99 (497).

2   J.W. McKay, *Religion in Judah under the Assyrians, 732–609 BC* (SBT 26; London: SCM Press, 1973), 26-27.

3   M. Cogan, *Imperialism and Religion: Assyria, Judah, and Israel in the Eighth and Seventh Centuries BCE* (SBLMS 19; Missoula: Scholars Press, 1974), 113; though note Cogan's more circumspect stance in a recent article, "Into Exile: From the Assyrian Conquest of Israel to the Fall of Babylon", in M.D. Coogan (ed.), *The Oxford History of the Biblical World* (Oxford: Oxford University Press, 1998), 242-75, esp. 252-56.

4   H. Jagersma, *A History of Israel in the Old Testament Period* (London: SCM Press, 1982), 165-66.

5   Note R.P. Carroll's critique of such value judgements within modern scholarship, *Wolf in the Sheepfold: The Bible as a Problem for Christianity* (second edn; London: SCM Press, 1997).

6   J. Day, "The Religion of Israel", in A.D.H. Mayes (ed.), *Text in Context* (Oxford: Oxford University Press, 2000), 428-53 (434); see also his comments in *Yahweh and the Gods and Goddesses of Canaan* (JSOTSup 265; Sheffield: Sheffield Academic Press, 2000), 230.

7   J. Milgrom, *Leviticus 17–22: A New Translation with Introduction and Commentary* (AB 3A; New York: Doubleday, 2000), 1386.

In adopting the opinions of the biblical writers, many scholars have thus aligned the Manasseh of history with the Manasseh of Kings, perpetuating the distortion of the biblical writers further.

1.1 The Manasseh of Kings

As is well known, blame for the destruction of Judah and the exile of her people is placed almost entirely upon the figure of Manasseh within Kings. Yet despite the great importance of his role within Kings, Manasseh is relatively neglected within scholarship, which instead tends to focus upon the heroes of Kings: David, Hezekiah and Josiah.[8] The recent increase in publications dealing with the Manasseh account in Kings—though still disproportionate to those focusing upon other characters—appears to signal a growing interest in the figure of Manasseh. However, it is notable that many of these publications analyse the account of Manasseh's reign as a means of testing or demonstrating theories of Deuteronomistic composition and redaction, rather than focusing upon the characterization and function of Manasseh within Kings.[9] Though the question of the hypothesis of the Deuteronomistic History and its various modifications remains pertinent, the objective of this study is not to peel back hypothetical, literary layers of Deuteronomistic composition, but to move beyond the domination of Deuteronomistic scholarship to examine the portrayal of Manasseh within

---

8 See further 2.3.
9 Eg. B. Halpern, "Why Manasseh is Blamed for the Babylonian Exile: The Evolution of a Biblical Tradition", *VT* 48 (1998), 473-514; E. Eynikel, "The Portrait of Manasseh and the Deuteronomistic History", in M. Vervenne and J. Lust (eds.), *Deuteronomy and Deuteronomic Literature: Festschrift C.H.W. Brekelmans* (BETL 133; Leuven: Peeters, 1997), 233-61; P.S.F. van Keulen, *Manasseh through the Eyes of the Deuteronomists: The Manasseh Account (2 Kings 21:1-18) and the Final Chapters of the Deuteronomistic History* (OTS 38; Leiden: Brill, 1996); W.M. Schniedewind, "History and Interpretation: The Religion of Ahab and Manasseh in the Book of Kings", *CBQ* 55 (1993), 649-61; E. Ben Zvi, "The Account of the Reign of Manasseh in II Reg 21, 1–18 and the Redactional History of the Book of Kings", *ZAW* 103 (1991), 355-74.

Kings in its present form.[10] As such, the question of the Deuteronomistic History hypothesis merits only brief comment here.[11]

In presenting his celebrated hypothesis that the books of Deuteronomy, Joshua, Judges, 1 and 2 Samuel and 1 and 2 Kings comprise a self-contained historiography, Noth was keen to emphasize the coherence and unity of the Deuteronomistic History. Accordingly, he argued that the Deuteronomistic History was produced in the period of the exile by a single author/editor, who drew on a variety of older literary traditions to compose his history of "Israel", a history beginning with the acquisition of the land, and ending with the loss of the land.[12] Yet the theory of the essential unity of the

---

10 Although it should be noted that the discussion of issues concerning the text's composition or redaction will be addressed as and when required.

11 For a detailed discussion of the Deuteronomistic History, see T. Römer and A. de Pury, "Deuteronomistic Historiography (DH): History of Research and Debated Issues", in A. de Pury, T. Römer and J.-D. Macchi (eds.), *Israel Constructs Its History: Deuteronomistic Historiography in Recent Research* (JSOTSup 306; Sheffield: Sheffield Academic Press, 2000), 9-120; see also H.N. Rösel, *Von Josua bis Jojachin: Untersuchungen zu den deuteronomistischen Geschichtsbüchern des Alten Testaments* (VTSup 75; Leiden: Brill, 1999). For discussions concerning Kings and the Deuteronomistic History, see J.R. Linville, *Israel in the Book of Kings: The Past as a Project of Social Identity* (JSOTSup 272; Sheffield: Sheffield Academic Press, 1998), 38-73; G.N. Knoppers, "Rethinking the Relationship between Deuteronomy and the Deuteronomistic History: The Case of Kings", *CBQ* 63 (2001), 393-415; W.M. Schniedewind, "The Problem with Kings: Recent Study of the Deuteronomistic History", *RSR* 22 (1996), 22-27; S.L. McKenzie, *The Trouble with Kings: The Composition of the Book of Kings in the Deuteronomistic History* (VTSup 42; Leiden: Brill, 1991); idem., "The Book of Kings in the Deuteronomistic History", in S.L. McKenzie and M.P. Graham (eds.), *History of Israel's Traditions: The Heritage of Martin Noth* (JSOTSup 182; Sheffield: Sheffield Academic Press, 1994), 281-307; idem., "Deuteronomistic History", *ABD*, vol. 2, 160-168; M. Cogan, *I Kings: A New Translation with Introduction and Commentary* (AB 10; New York: Doubleday, 2000), 96-100.

12 M. Noth, *Überlieferungsgeschichtliche Studien*. I. *Die sammelnden und bearbeitenden Geschichtswerke im Alten Testament* (Tübingen: Niemeyer, 1943); ET *The Deuteronomistic History* (JSOTSup 15; Sheffield: JSOT Press, 1981) and *The Chronicler's History* (trans. H.G.M. Williamson; JSOTSup 50; Sheffield: JSOT Press, 1987); see also H.-D. Hoffmann, *Reform und Reformen: Untersuchungen zu einem Grundthema der deuteronomistischen Geschichtsschreibung* (ATANT 66; Zurich: Theologische, 1980), 315-318; G. Minette de Tillesse, "Martin Noth et la 'Redaktiongeschichte' des Livres Historiques", in C.H. Hauret (ed.), *Aux grands carrefours de la révélation et de l'exegese de l'Ancien Testament* (Recherches Bibliques

Deuteronomistic History, which remains popular, has been seriously challenged in the ensuing decades by considerable modifications of Noth's theory, which emphasize the authorial and/or editorial disunity of the Deuteronomistic History. Three positions may be discerned. The first argues with prominent reference to Kings that the Deuteronomistic History developed in two stages: a first edition was produced during the reign of Josiah, perhaps with reference to an older literary source,[13] and was then extended and redacted to a greater or lesser extent after the Babylonian destruction of Jerusalem.[14] A second position supports Noth's exilic dating of the composition of the Deuteronomistic History, but argues for at least three distinct, successive and thorough-going layers of redaction during this period.[15] Though a middle-ground between these two positions has been

---

8; Paris: Doornik, 1967), 51-75; J.G. McConville, "Narrative and Meaning in the Books of Kings", *Bib* 70 (1989), 50-73.

13 For a sampling of opinions on this issue, see for example, B. Halpern and D.S. Vanderhooft, "The Editions of Kings in the 7th–6th Centuries BCE", *HUCA* 62 (1991), 179-244; A.D.H. Mayes, *The Story of Israel between Settlement and Exile: A Redactional Study of the Deuteronomistic History* (London: SCM Press, 1983); I.W. Provan, *Hezekiah and the Books of Kings: A Contribution to the Debate about the Composition of the Deuteronomistic History* (BZAW 72; Berlin: de Gruyter, 1988); E. Eynikel, *The Reform of King Josiah and the Composition of the Deuteronomistic History* (OTS 33; Leiden: Brill, 1996).

14 For example, F.M. Cross, "The Themes of the Book of Kings and the Structure of the Deuteronomistic History", in *idem.*, *Canaanite Myth and Hebrew Epic: Essays in the History of the Religion of Israel* (Cambridge: Harvard University Press, 1973), 274-289; R.D. Nelson, *The Double-Redaction of the Deuteronomistic History* (JSOTSup 18; Sheffield: JSOT Press, 1981); R.E. Friedman, "From Egypt to Egypt: Dtr^1 and Dtr^2", in B. Halpern and J.D. Levenson (eds.), *Traditions in Transformation: Turning Points in Biblical Faith* (Winona Lake: Eisenbrauns, 1981), 167-192; *idem.*, *The Exile and Biblical Narrative: The Formation of the Deuteronomistic and Priestly Codes* (HSM 22; Atlanta: Scholars Press, 1981); Z. Zevit, "Deuteronomistic Historiography in 1 Kings 12–2 Kings 17 and the Reinvestiture of the Israelian Cult", *JSOT* 32 (1985), 57-73; J.D. Levenson, "Who Inserted the Book of the Torah?", *HTR* 68 (1975), 203-233.

15 R. Smend, "Das Gesetz und die Völker: Ein Beitrag zur deuteronomistischen Redaktionsgeschichte", in H.W. Wolff (ed.), *Probleme biblischer Theologie: G. von Rad zum 70. Geburtstag* (Munich: Chr. Kaiser Verlag, 1971), 494-509; W. Dietrich, *Prophetie und Geschichte: Eine redaktionsgeschichtliche Untersuchung zum deuteronomistischen Geschichtswerk* (FRLANT 108; Göttingen: Vandenhoeck & Ruprecht, 1972); T. Veijola, *Die ewige Dynastie: David und die Entstehung seiner Dynastie nach der deuteronomistischen Darstellung* (Helsinki: Suomalainen Tiedeakatemia, 1975); *idem.*, *Das Königtum in der Beurteilung der deuteronomistischen Historiographie: Eine redaktionsgeschichtliche Untersuchung* (Helsinki: Suomalainen Tiedeakatemia, 1977).

sought,[16] a consensus of opinion remains elusive. Moreover, a potentially fatal challenge to Noth's hypothesis has arisen. This represents the third position, and it draws notable strength from the lack of consensus concerning the Deuteronomistic History. Its primary emphasis falls upon the distinctive and often contradictory characteristics of each biblical book held to comprise the History, and whilst pointing to the increased identification of "Deuteronomistic" material elsewhere in the Hebrew Bible,[17] this position contests the very existence of a Deuteronomistic History.[18]

Given the range and variety of theories concerning the Deuteronomistic History and other supposedly Deuteronomistic material, it is increasingly difficult to employ the label "Deuteronomistic" with precision, as some scholars have observed.[19] Indeed, the term "Deuteronomistic" is potentially

---

16 This approach is particularly associated with the work of N. Lohfink; see further the collection of articles reprinted in his volumes entitled *Studien zur Deuteronomium und zur deuteronomistischen Literatur* (SBAB 8, 12, 20; Stuttgart: Katholisches Bibelwerk, 1990, 1991, 1995).

17 See particularly the discussion in R.R. Wilson, "Who Was the Deuteronomist? (Who Was Not the Deuteronomist?): Reflections on Pan-Deuteronomism", in L.S. Schearing and S.L. McKenzie (eds.), *Those Elusive Deuteronomists: The Phenomenon of Pan-Deuteronomism* (JSOTSup 268; Sheffield: JSOT Press, 1999), 67-82; see also T.C. Römer, "L'école deutéronomiste et la formation de la Bible hébraïque", in *idem.* (ed.), *The Future of the Deuteronomistic History* (BETL 147; Leuven: Peeters, 2000), 179-194, and the collection of essays in J.C. de Moor and H.F. van Rooy (eds.), *Past, Present, Future: The Deuteronomistic History and the Prophets* (OTS 44; Leiden: Brill, 2000).

18 E.A. Knauf, "Does 'Deuteronomistic Historiography' (DH) Exist?", in De Pury, Römer and Macchi, *Israel Constructs Its History*, 388-398; C. Westermann, *Die Geschichtsbücher des Alten Testaments: Gab es ein deuteronomistisches Geschichtswerk?* (TBü 87; Gütersloh: Chr. Kaiser Verlag, 1994); cf. Eynikel, *Reform*, 363; A.G. Auld, "The Deuteronomists and the Former Prophets, or What Makes the Former Prophets Deuteronomistic?", in Schearing and McKenzie, *Those Elusive Deuteronomists*, 116-126; see also J. Van Seters, "The Deuteronomistic History: Can it Avoid Death by Redaction?", in Römer, *The Future of the Deuteronomistic History*, 213-222; G.N. Knoppers, "Is There a Future for the Deuteronomistic History?", in Römer, *The Future of the Deuteronomistic History*, 119-134.

19 See also R. Coggins, "What Does 'Deuteronomistic' Mean?", in Schearing and McKenzie, *Those Elusive Deuteronomists*, 22-35; Wilson, "Who Was the Deuteronomist?", 78; W.B. Barrick, *The King and the Cemeteries: Toward a New Understanding of Josiah's Reform* (VTSup 88; Leiden: Brill, 2002), 13-14; Linville, *Israel in the Book of Kings*, 61-69. For a useful survey of opinions concerning the Manasseh account within the context of the Deuteronomistic History, see Van Keulen, *Manasseh*, ch. 1.

so slippery that it is rendered unhelpful within this study. Thus following Barrick's example,[20] the label "Deuteronomistic" will not be applied to the Books of Kings. Instead the Books of Kings will be treated as a single, unified work and called simply "Kings"; where appropriate, its writer shall be called the "Kings Writer".[21] It will be assumed that Kings in its present form is a post-monarchic composition, addressed to a post-monarchic audience.[22] It is important to acknowledge that whilst very similar ideologies pervade Deuteronomy and Kings, there are also considerable tensions between these texts. As such, the supposition of a generic relationship between them is not certain; nor is it central to the arguments of this discussion.[23] Consequently, it will be assumed that the Kings Writer and the author of Deuteronomy shared some similar world-views, and that Deuteronomy *in its present form* is also a post-monarchic composition addressed to a post-monarchic audience.[24]

Having established the methodological parameters required to deal with Kings, the discussion can now turn to the portrayal of Manasseh in Kings.

---

20 Barrick, *King and the Cemeteries*, 14.

21 This is in deliberate distinction to Barrick's preferred designations for the books and their author, namely the "Kings History" and the "Kings Historian", respectively (*King and the Cemeteries*, 14-15). Barrick's designations are suggestive of an assumed degree of historical reliability, which may not be justified. Note too that the use of terminology in the singular, such as "writer" and "author", does not preclude the possibility that the text derives from more than one hand. However, for simplicity's sake, the singular is to be preferred.

22 See the discussions in T.C. Römer, "Transformations in Deuteronomistic and Biblical Historiography: On 'Book-Finding' and other Literary Strategies", *ZAW* 107 (1997), 1-11; J.R. Linville, "Rethinking the 'Exilic' Book of Kings", *JSOT* 75 (1997), 21-42; *idem.*, *Israel in the Book of Kings*, 69-73.

23 See further Knoppers, "Rethinking the Relationship", 393-415; *idem.*, "Solomon's Fall and Deuteronomy", in L.K. Handy (ed.), *The Age of Solomon: Scholarship at the Turn of the Millennium* (SHCANE 11; Leiden: Brill, 1997), 392-410, esp. 403 n. 49.

24 See also, for example, G. Hölscher, "Komposition und Ursprung des Deuteronomiums", *ZAW* 40 (1922), 161-255; E. Würthwein, "Die Josianische Reform und das Deuteronomium", *ZTK* 73 (1976), 365-423. An innovative position regarding the dating of both Deuteronomy and Kings is not crucial to this discussion. Whilst the majority of scholars assume that versions of both texts existed in some form or another within the monarchic period, it is reasonable to assert that this majority would also agree that both texts achieved their present form in the post-monarchic period. Given that it is the present forms of Deuteronomy and Kings which, in the main, will be dealt with here, it is thus assumed that these are post-monarchic texts. This is not to deny the possibility of the existence of monarchic material within these texts, but this possibility will be addressed on the basis of specific examples only where necessary.

> The most striking feature of the Deuteronomists' portrait of Manasseh ... is that it is
> not the portrait of an individual at all.[25]

Lasine's comment is well-founded. As he observes, the Manasseh of 2 Kgs
21:1-18 is unlike any other king within the regnal history presented by
Kings. He makes no royal speeches, there are no descriptions of his
responses or emotions, and most interestingly, he does not interact with any
other characters: not a foreign nation, nor prophets, nor "the people", and
certainly not YHWH, yet these characters all appear in the story.[26] Moreover,
as Lasine comments further, the backdrop to the production is blank,
complementing the "faceless king",[27] for there is no mention of any
international event with which to anchor the period within the wider ancient
Near Eastern context. This is particularly notable given that most modern
interpretations of this account of Manasseh's reign are constructed upon the
assumed Assyrian domination of Judah during this period.[28] Yet according to
Kings, the Assyrians fled Judah after the miraculous deliverance of Zion
during Hezekiah's reign, apparently never to return (2 Kgs 19:32-37).

Given the fact that Manasseh plays what is arguably the most crucial role
within Kings in causing the destruction of Judah and the exile of her people,
this brief and flimsy characterization is surprising, presenting Manasseh as
little more than a man of straw. It is equally surprising that although most
commentators agree that this chapter is a heavily-stylized account of
Manasseh's reign, many remain convinced that it harbours, to a greater or a
lesser extent, reliable information about the historical Manasseh.[29] A closer
examination of the text demonstrates just how stylized this story is, and
reveals far more about the Kings Writer than about the Manasseh of history.

---

25 S. Lasine, "Manasseh as Villain and Scapegoat", in J.C. Exum and D.J.A. Clines (eds.),
    The New Literary Criticism and the Hebrew Bible (JSOTSup 143; Sheffield: JSOT
    Press, 1993), 163-183 (163).
26 Lasine, "Manasseh", 164-165.
27 Lasine, "Manasseh", 164.
28 See further below, 2.3.
29 See 2.3.

Translation: 2 Kgs 21:1-18

1 Manasseh was twelve[30] years old when he became king and he reigned fifty-five years in Jerusalem. His mother's name was Hephzibah. 2 He did evil in the eyes of YHWH just like the abhorrent practices of the nations whom YHWH had driven out before the Israelites.

3 He rebuilt the high places which his father Hezekiah had destroyed; he erected altars to Ba'al and he made an *asherah*[31] just like Ahab King of Israel had done. He bowed down to all the Host of Heaven and worshipped them, 4 and he built altars in the House of YHWH of which YHWH had said, "I will establish my Name in Jerusalem". 5 And he built altars to all the Host of Heaven in the two courtyards of the House of YHWH. 6 He made his son[32] pass over in the fire; he practised soothsaying[33] and divination[34] and he produced an ancestral ghost[35] and Knowers.[36] He did much evil in the eyes of YHWH to provoke (him) (to anger).[37]

---

30 Some Lucianic mss (19, 82, 108) read ten years.

31 LXX and Vulg. read a plural (cf. 2 Chr. 33:3), but the singular of MT is supported by 1 Kgs 16:32, which is itself supported by LXX[B] and Vulg.

32 LXX[B] and LXX[L] read a plural (cf. 2 Chr. 33:6).

33 The meaning of עֹנֵן is uncertain. It may be a cultic term referring to divinatory cloud-watching (so J. Gray, *I & II Kings: A Commentary* [OTL; third edn.; London: SCM Press, 1977], 707), or it may describe the activity of causing something to appear (*HALOT*, vol. 2, 857). Given this uncertainty, the usual rendering "soothsaying" is employed here.

34 נִחֵשׁ appears to refer to the seeking or giving of omens (*HALOT*, vol. 2, 690), though as R.D. Nelson (*Deuteronomy* [OTL; Louisville/London: Westminster John Knox, 2002], 233) suggests, Gen. 44:5, 15 may indicate divination by means of reading liquid surfaces.

35 The meaning and etymology of אוֹב is difficult to ascertain. Throughout the Hebrew Bible it occurs frequently in association with יִדְּעֹנִי (on which see the note below). אוֹב appears to refer to a ghost of the dead (e.g., Lev. 19:31; 20:26-27; Deut. 18:11; 1 Sam. 28:7-8; Isa. 8:19; 19:3; 29:1; 1 Chr. 10:13). This, along with the possibility that אוֹב is related to אָב ("father" or "ancestor"), is thus reflected in the translation "ancestral ghost". Supporting this interpretation are those ancient Near Eastern expressions for deified ancestral ghosts which are composed of the words for "god" and "father", listed in J. Tropper, "Spirit of the Dead", *DDD*, 806-809. Ancient Near Eastern cults of the dead appear to have shared a divinatory function, whereby dead ancestors were summoned and consulted for information; see further K. Spronk, *Beatific Afterlife in Ancient Israel and in the Ancient Near East* (AOAT 219; Neukirchen-Vluyn: Neukirchener Verlag, 1986), 253-254; H. Rouillard and J. Tropper, "Vom kanaanäischen Ahnenkult zur Zauberei. Eine Auslegungsgeschichte zu den hebräischen Begriffen *'wb* und *yd 'ny*", *UF* 19 (1987), 235-254. However, alternative interpretations abound. For example, H.A. Hoffner ("Second Millennium Antecedents to the Hebrew *'ôb*", *JBL* 86 [1967], 385-401), argues that the biblical term אוֹב denotes a ritual pit,

7 And he set the image of Asherah which he had made[38] in the House concerning which YHWH had said to David and to his son Solomon, "In this House and in Jerusalem, which I have chosen out of all the tribes of Israel, I will establish my Name forever. 8 And I will no more cause the feet of Israel to wander[39] from the land that I gave to their ancestors, if only they will be vigilant to do all that I commanded them, that is, according to all the Law which my servant Moses commanded them." 9 But they did not listen and Manasseh misled them so that they did more evil than the nations whom YHWH destroyed before the Israelites.

10   And YHWH spoke through his servants the prophets,[40] saying,   11 "Because Manasseh King of Judah has done these abhorrent practices, doing more evil than all which the Amorites did, who were before him, and has caused Judah also to sin by his dung-gods,[41] 12 therefore, thus says YHWH the God of Israel: behold, I am bringing such disaster upon Jerusalem and Judah that both ears of whoever hears[42] of it will tingle,   13 and I will stretch over Jerusalem the measuring line of Samaria and the plummet of the House of Ahab and I will wipe out Jerusalem just as one wipes a dish, wiping it and turning it over on its face. 14 And I will reject the remnant of my

---

whereas B.B. Schmidt (*Israel's Beneficent Dead: Ancestor Cult and Necromancy in Ancient Israelite Religion and Tradition* [FAT 11; Tübingen: J.C.B. Mohr, 1994; repr. Winona Lake: Eisenbrauns, 1996], 151-52) relates אוב to Arabic *ʾāba*, "to return", thus rendering אוב as "the One-who-returns". For further discussion of these views, see J. Tropper, *Nekromantie: Totenbefragung im Alten Testament* (AOAT 223; Kevelaer & Neukirchen-Vluyn: Neukirchener, 1989); idem., "Wizard", *DDD*, 907-908; J. Bottéro, "Les morts et l'au-delà dans le rituels en accadien contre l'action des 'revenants'", *ZA* 73 (1983), 153-203; J. Lust, "On Wizards and Prophets", in D. Lys *et al.*, *Studies on Prophecy* (VTSup 26; Leiden: Brill, 1974), 133-142; P.S. Johnston, (*Shades of Sheol: Death and Afterlife in the Old Testament* (Leicester: Apollos, 2002), 161-166.

36 Many mss have the singular. The ambiguous ידעני is probably derived from ידע, and is consequently rendered "Knowers" here (cf. Tropper, *Nekromantie*, 317-319), though it may refer to familiar spirits or known ancestors (Nelson, *Deuteronomy*, 233). This term always occurs in parallelism with אוב in the Hebrew Bible (Lev. 19:31; 20:6, 26-27; Deut. 18:11; 1 Sam. 28:3, 9; 2 Kgs 23:24; Isa. 8:19-20; 19:3). Tropper ("Wizard", 907-908) suggests that though the precise semantic nuance of the adjectival formation of the word is difficult to establish given its rarity in the Hebrew Bible, the emphatic pronunciation of the word, reflected in writing in the doubling of the middle radical, indicates that this word had a more intensive signification than ordinary adjectives. Thus this term is best understood as "extremely knowledgeable, all-knowing". This is reflected in this translation by the capitalization of the label "Knowers".

37 Reading להבעיסו, with Versional support (cf. 2 Chr. 33:6). As van Keulen observes (*Manasseh*, 57), the ו has probably been lost by haplography.

38 אשר עשה, "which he had made" is not reflected in LXX.

39 Or, "to be removed"; see M. Cogan and H. Tadmor, *II Kings: A New Translation with Introduction and Commentary* (AB 11; Garden City: Doubleday, 1988), 268; Eynikel, "Portrait of Manasseh", 247. This idiom occurs only here (cf. 2 Chr. 33:8).

40 MT ביד עבדיו הנביאים, literally, "by the hand of his servants the prophets".

41 On the designation גלולים, see 4.1.2.

42 Reading, with Versional support, Q שמעה (K שמעיו).

inheritance and I will deliver them into the hand of their enemies, and they will be plunder and spoil to all their enemies 15 because they have done evil in my eyes and they have been provoking me (to anger) from the day when their fathers came out of Egypt until this day."

16 Moreover, Manasseh shed so much innocent blood that he filled Jerusalem from end to end, as well as the sin he committed in causing Judah to do what was evil in the eyes of YHWH.

17 The rest of the deeds of Manasseh, and all that he did and the sin that he committed, are they not written in the Book of the Annals of the Kings of Judah? 18 And Manasseh slept with his ancestors and he was buried in the garden of his palace, in the Garden of Uzza, and Amon his son reigned after him.

The account of Manasseh's reign in 2 Kgs 21:1-18 falls into four distinct parts.[43] The first verse offers the standard introduction of a king, stating Manasseh's age upon his ascension to the throne, the duration of his reign, and reporting the name of his mother.[44] Verses 2-9 give a theological evaluation of the king's religious behaviour, listing the cult crimes Manasseh commits. Verses 10-16[45] form an anonymous prophetic judgement oracle against Judah and Jerusalem, and verses 17-18 conclude the Manasseh account in the standard way, citing the source from which the storyteller implies he has received his information, reporting the death and burial place

---

43 Cf. B.O. Long, *2 Kings* (FOTL 10; Grand Rapids: Eerdmans, 1991), 246-247. For alternative suggestions of subdivisions within 21:1-18, see for example K.A.D. Smelik, "The Portrayal of King Manasseh: A Literary Analysis of II Kings xxi and II Chronicles xxxiii", in *idem.*, *Converting the Past: Studies in Ancient Israelite and Moabite Historiography* (OTS 28; Leiden: Brill, 1992), 129-189, esp. 132-136; R.D. Nelson, *First and Second Kings* (Interpretation; Louisville: John Knox Press, 1987), 248; M.A. Sweeney, *King Josiah of Judah: The Lost Messiah of Israel* (Oxford: Oxford University Press, 2001), 54-57. There is no reason to doubt that 2 Kgs 21:1-18 was composed by a single author (cf. Hoffmann, *Reform und Reformen*, 155-167; T.R. Hobbs, *2 Kings* [WBC 13; Waco: Word, 1985], 300-301), though v. 16 appears almost as an after-thought. For various theories assuming a more complex compositional history of 2 Kgs 21:1-18, see for example Gray, *I & II Kings*, 705; Nelson, *Double Redaction*, 65-70; E. Würthwein, *Die Bücher der Könige: 1. Kön. 17—2. Kön. 25* (ATD 11, 2; Göttingen: Vandenhoeck & Ruprecht, 1984), 440.

44 For the role and status of the queen mother within the royal cult and court, see E.K. Solvang, *A Woman's Place is in the House: Royal Women of Judah and their Involvement in the House of David* (JSOTSup 349; Sheffield/New York: Sheffield Academic Press, 2003), and the literature cited there.

45 Verse 16 is a peculiar accusation levelled at Manasseh, sitting uncomfortably at the end of the judgement oracle. It is often taken as a secondary addition to the Kings account of Manasseh's reign. This verse is discussed further below.

of the monarch, and announcing the royal successor.[46] As Smelik comments, the account of Manasseh's reign initially appears rather dull, as the reader is presented with a list of evil deeds, rather than a narrative.[47] However, despite this initial impression, closer examination reveals that the regnal account is a complex, colourful construction that is far from dull.

Manasseh's prominent role within Kings is anticipated in the unique introduction to his reign. The opening accession formula introducing Manasseh's reign stands apart from those of other Judahite kings, for it includes only the name of his mother, and not her patronym nor place of origin.[48] This contrasts with the accession notices of Manasseh's successors, all of which offer these three pieces of information.[49] It also contrasts with the accession notices to his predecessors' reigns, which, with just two exceptions,[50] name either the queen mother's father or her place of origin.[51] The potential significance of this peculiar feature will be addressed in the following chapter.[52] A further curiosity of the introductory formula occurs in verse 2. Within the accession formula of every other Judahite monarch, the

---

46 R.H. Lowery, *The Reforming Kings: Cults and Society in First Temple Judah* (JSOTSup 120; Sheffield: JSOT Press, 1991), 171.

47 Smelik, "Portrayal", 132; cf. Nelson, *Kings*, 247.

48 Because the Kings Writer does not regard Athaliah as a legitimate monarch, the account of her reign does not contain any regnal formulae. On the regnal formulae employed throughout Kings, see S.R. Bin-Nun, "Formulas from the Royal Records of Israel and Judah", *VT* 18 (1968), 414-432; Cogan, *I Kings*, 89-90, 100-101; Eynikel, *Reform of King Josiah*, 122-135; W.H. Barnes, *Studies in the Chronology of the Divided Monarchy of Israel* (HSM 48; Atlanta: Scholars Press, 1991), 137-149; Halpern and Vanderhooft, "Editions of Kings", 179-24; cf. H. Weippert, "Die 'deuteronomistischen' Beurteilungen der Könige von Israel und Juda und das Problem der Redaktion der Königsbücher", *Bib* 53 (1972), 301-339.

49 2 Kgs 21:19; 22:1; 23:31, 36; 24:8, 18.

50 The mothers of neither Jehoram (2 Kgs 8:16-17) nor Ahaz (2 Kgs 16:1-2) are mentioned.

51 The father of the queen mother is named in the formulae introducing Abijam (1 Kgs 15:2), Asa (15:10), Jehoshaphat (22:42), Ahaziah (2 Kgs 8:26), Jotham (15:33), and Hezekiah (18:2). The queen mother's place of origin is included in the formulae introducing Rehoboam ("Naamah the Ammonite"; 1 Kgs 14:21), Jehoash (2 Kgs 12:1), Amaziah (14:2), and Azariah (15:2).

52 This fleeting yet precise focus upon the Judahite queen mothers stands in stark contrast to the accounts of the Israelite monarchs within Kings. Although preceded by a similar formulaic notice summarizing each reign, no reference is made to the mothers of the Israelite kings at all. This interesting contrast suggests that the naming of the mother of each Judahite king was of significance to the Kings Writer.

Kings Writer draws an explicit comparison between the newly-ascended king and one of his predecessors. The only exceptions are Jehoram, Ahaziah and Ahaz, all of whom are said to have behaved like the kings of Israel or the House of Ahab.[53] This in itself is an important observation, for in verse 3, Manasseh too is explicitly compared with Ahab, a point of comparison to which the discussion will return shortly. However, in verse 2, Manasseh is compared not with a previous king, but with the foreign nations who inhabited the land before the Israelites. This is striking, for it sets Manasseh apart from all his predecessors and successors, even the particularly sinful ones. Thus the accession formula deviates from the norm in two significant ways, each preparing the reader for a regnal account unlike any other within Kings.

The list of Manasseh's cult crimes (21:2-9) is the longest of any in Kings. Given that other Israelite and Judahite monarchs are accused of some of these cultic mispractices, the Kings Writer endeavours to present Manasseh as the worst of all royal cultic offenders by intensifying his crimes. Whereas previous Judahite monarchs had simply tolerated the *bamoth*,[54] Manasseh is portrayed as deliberately encouraging worship at the *bamoth* by rebuilding those Hezekiah had destroyed in his purge (v. 3; cf. 18:4).[55] According to Kings, Manasseh is the only Judahite king to erect altars to Ba'al and to make an *asherah* (v. 3). Though Ahab of Israel is also accused of these crimes (1 Kgs 16:32), he sets up only one altar, whereas Manasseh erects more than one. Similarly, whereas Ahab is accused of making an *asherah* (1 Kgs 16:33), Manasseh's crime surpasses that of Ahab as he not only makes an *asherah* (21:3), but sets[56] the image of Asherah in the temple (21:7-8).[57]

---

53 2 Kgs 8:18, 27; 2 Kgs 16:3. A further exception is Jehoash, who is not compared to any other character in the story because he is supervised by the priest Jehoiada (12:2). See also Van Keulen, *Manasseh*, 89-90.

54 The only exceptions are Solomon, who makes offerings at the *bamoth* before building the temple (1 Kgs 3:3) and builds *bamoth* for his foreign wives (11:7-8), Ahaz, who is accused of making offerings at the *bamoth* (2 Kgs 16:4), and Abijam, Jehoram and Ahaziah, in whose regnal accounts there is no explicit mention of the *bamoth*. With the exception of Josiah's destruction of the *bamoth*, notices about the *bamoth* are not included within the regnal accounts of Manasseh's successors.

55 See further W.B. Barrick, "On the Removal of the High Places in 1–2 Kings", *Bib* 55 (1974), 257-259.

56 The repetition of the verb שׂים, "set", "establish", in v. 7 makes explicit Manasseh's reversal of YHWH's actions in establishing his "Name" in the temple; see also Smelik, "Portrayal of King Manasseh", 147; Nelson, *First and Second Kings*, 250.

Moreover in doing so, Manasseh is again reversing the religious reforms of
Hezekiah.[58] A further crime of which Manasseh is accused is that of causing
his son to "pass over in the fire" (2 Kgs 21:6). This is best understood as a
biblical euphemism for a particular form of child sacrifice,[59] a crime of which
only one other king is accused: Ahaz (16:3). However, once again the Kings
Writer worsens Manasseh's cultic mispractice by adding that he also
participated in various divinatory practices associated with child sacrifice,[60]
something Ahaz did not do.[61] Moreover, Manasseh's participation within
these activities is emphasized in the language of this accusation: the activities
עָנַן ("soothsay") and נחש ("divine") are credited to Manasseh, and he does not
"appoint" an ancestral ghost and Knowers, but "makes" or "produces" (עשה)
them himself.[62]

Further cementing Manasseh's role as the ultimate idolater in Kings is the
accusation that he worshipped the Host of Heaven (21:3). No other king is

---

57 Cogan and Tadmor, *II Kings*, 267. Though it is now widely accepted that Asherah was a
    Semitic goddess, the term אֲשֵׁרָה appears to be used in two senses throughout the
    Hebrew Bible. Here in 21:3, it is claimed that Manasseh "made an *asherah*", and in v. 7
    it is stated that he set the "image of the *asherah* which he had made in the House of
    YHWH". MT v. 7 reads פֶּסֶל הָאֲשֵׁרָה, literally, "the (material) image of the *asherah*". The
    use of the relative clause אֲשֶׁר עָשָׂה, "which he made", in v. 7 seeks to identify the
    asherah of v. 7 as being the same *asherah* of v. 3 (Van Keulen, *Manasseh*, 103; Eynikel,
    "Portrait of Manasseh", 245). However, the use of the definite article is puzzling, given
    that v. 3 suggests that the *asherah* is an object, most probably a cult statue of some kind
    (as the verb עשה implies) yet v. 7 refers to a material image (פסל) of the *asherah*, which
    v. 3 suggests is itself a material image. This apparent confusion may be resolved by
    accepting, as here, that the term *asherah* has been used in two different ways within one
    literary unit. The *asherah* of v. 3 is best understood as a cult image (perhaps a statue or
    a stylized tree), whereas the *asherah* of v. 7 is the proper name of the goddess. Thus it is
    "the image of (the goddess) Asherah", which Manasseh made in v. 3, that is set in the
    temple (*pace* Smelik, "Portrayal of King Manasseh", 144 n. 39). In an attempt to debase
    the goddess, the biblical writer has used the definite article implying the goddess is
    nothing more than a man-made object. This is probably the Chronicler's reading of 2
    Kgs 21:7, as 2 Chr. 33:7 has הסמל, "the idol", instead of "the image of Asherah".
58 Cf. 18:4; Van Keulen, *Manasseh*, 95.
59 See chapters 4, 5, 6.
60 Eg. Deut. 18:10; Lev. 20:2-6; 2 Kgs 17:17. For various divinatory practices in Israel,
    Judah and the ancient Near East, see for example F.H. Cryer, *Divination in Ancient
    Israel and Its Near Eastern Environment: A Socio-Historical Investigation* (JSOTSup
    142; Sheffield: JSOT Press, 1994); A. Jeffers, *Divination in Ancient Palestine and Syria*
    (SHCANE, 8; Leiden: Brill, 1996).
61 Cf. Schmidt, *Beneficent Dead*, 244. Saul is the only other king associated with this type
    of cultic behaviour, but this story does not occur in Kings but Samuel (1 Sam. 28:3-25).
    Josiah is accredited with suppressing this practice (2 Kgs 23:24).
62 Cogan and Tadmor, *II Kings*, 267.

accused of this cult crime, although the Israelites of the Northern Kingdom are also said to participate in this practice (17:16).[63] This unique charge is further emphasized in the accusation that Manasseh built altars to the Host of Heaven in the temple complex (2 Kgs 21:5; cf. 23:12). Much has been made of the seemingly clumsy repetition of the charge that Manasseh built altars in verses 4 and 5.[64] However, following Smelik's suggestion, the Kings Writer intends to emphasize the sacrilegious nature of this act by employing a literary device Smelik terms "repetition with an increase in information":[65] in verse 4 it is claimed that Manasseh built altars in YHWH's temple, though the deities to whom the altars are dedicated are not named; in verse 5, the Kings Writer provides more detailed information about this cult crime by revealing that Manasseh built altars to all the Host of Heaven in the two courtyards of YHWH's temple. Moreover, as Van Keulen proposes, these verses also focus attention repeatedly upon the location of the altars,[66] thereby not only emphasizing that Manasseh's cultic mispractice occurred in YHWH's temple, but intensifying Manasseh's apparently sacrilegious attitude further.

The list of Manasseh's cult crimes is carefully crafted, for each of his transgressions is specifically prohibited in the Deuteronomic codes.[67] Significantly, each crime enumerated in verse 6 is described in 17:17 as a malpractice of the Kingdom of Israel, and is also outlawed in Deut. 18:9-14, which describes these offences as those of the nations (v. 9).[68] This in turn is

---

63 Cf. 23:56. Outside of Kings, worship of the Host of Heaven is associated with the Judahite kings in Jer. 8:1-2; 19:13; cf. Deut. 4:19; 17:3; Zeph. 1:5.

64 Many commentators assume that either verse 4 or verse 5 is a later addition, for example J.A. Montgomery and H.S. Gehman, *A Critical and Exegetical Commentary on the Books of Kings* (ICC; New York: Scribners, 1951), 519; H. Spieckermann, *Juda unter Assur in der Sargonidenzeit* (FRLANT 129; Göttingen: Vandenhoech & Ruprecht, 1982), 163-164; see also Van Keulen, *Manasseh*, 96-98.

65 Smelik, "Portrayal of King Manasseh", 145.

66 Van Keulen, *Manasseh*, 97.

67 Eg. Deut. 7:5 (cf. 12:3; 16:21); 12:29-31; 17:2-7; 18:9-14. See further Lowery, *Reforming Kings*, 182-185.

68 Much has been made of the possible interrelationship of Deut. 18:9-14; 2 Kgs 17:17 and 21:6. Most scholars regard Deut. 18:9-14 (or a version of it) as the prototype upon which the condemnations in 2 Kgs 17:17 and 21:6 were based. For many scholars of this group, this does assume an earlier date of composition for Deuteronomy rather than Kings. See the recent discussions in Barrick, *King and the Cemeteries*, 95-97; Eynikel, "Portrait of Manasseh", 244-245, 255; Van Keulen, *Manasseh*, 101; cf. Brettler, *Creation of History*, 123-124; Cogan and Tadmor, *II Kings*, 266; N. Lohfink, Review of

reminiscent of the introductory statement that Manasseh behaved like the foreign nations (2 Kgs 21:2). Thus each of Manasseh's crimes is a direct violation of "Mosaic Law", as the Kings Writer swiftly points out in verse 8.

The direct contrast with Mosaic Law is not the only comparison the narrator is keen to draw. Though the comparison of a king and another character is a regular feature of the regnal accounts within Kings,[69] in juxtaposing Manasseh with an array of characters from his story, the Kings Writer creates a portrait of a villainous, anti-YHWH king unlike any other. As Lasine comments, "Manasseh is not only like the worst monarchs but the exact opposite of the best".[70] He writes:

> Manasseh is the opposite of his father Hezekiah (v. 3), and like Ahab (v. 3; cf. v. 13). He is like Ahaz (v. 6; cf. 2 Kgs 16:3) and the opposite of Saul, who banished spirit mediums in accordance with ritual laws (v. 6; cf. 1 Sam. 28:3, 9; Lev. 19:31; 20:6; Deut. 18:11). He is the opposite of David and Solomon when it comes to temple policy (vv. 7-8; cf. vv. 4-5). Finally, he is like Jeroboam in seducing the people and causing them to sin with "his" idols (v. 9; cf. v. 11).[71]

To Lasine's list can also be added the accusation that Manasseh is not only like the nations whom YHWH had dispossessed before the Israelites (v. 2) but, in a further example of the intensification of Manasseh's sinful portrayal, he is also worse than the Amorites (v. 11), who are associated with idolatry in 1 Kgs 21:26.[72] The discussion will return to this interesting comparison. However, of this list, most explicit is the claim that Manasseh is like King Ahab of Israel (v. 3 cf. 13).

Manasseh's explicit comparison with Ahab is frequently discussed by commentators, many of whom seek to interpret the portrayal of Manasseh in Kings in light of the biblical presentation of Ahab,[73] particularly as the character of Ahab within Kings would appear to have more flesh about him

---

Von der politischen Gemeinschaft zur Gemeinde, by U. Rüterswörden, *TLZ* 113 (1988), 425-430; Lowery, *Reforming Kings*, 171, 183-185; *contra* Schmidt, *Beneficent Dead*, 243. For the view that Deut. 18:10-12 is an expansion on 2 Kgs 21:6, see Schmidt, *Beneficent Dead*, 182, 188-190. Note also H.L. Bosman, "Redefined Prophecy as Deuteronomic Alternative to Divination in Deut. 18:9-22", *Acta Theologia* 16 (1996), 1-23.

69   Van Keulen, *Manasseh*, 90.
70   Lasine, "Manasseh as Villain", 163.
71   Lasine, "Manasseh as Villain", 163-164.
72   Cf. Josh. 24:15, 18.
73   Eg. Sweeney, *King Josiah*, 29, 49-50, 52-54, 60; Lasine, "Manasseh as Villain", 167-170; Schniedewind, "History and Interpretation", 649-661.

than the one-dimensional Manasseh.[74] Ahab is presented as an idolatrous and murderous ruler: he establishes the royal cults of Ba'al and Asherah, and persecutes and slaughters YHWH's prophets. He is also portrayed as weak-willed, childish, and easily influenced by his powerful, Ba'al-worshipping foreign wife, Jezebel.[75] Consequently, Ahab's biblical reputation as an idolatrous, wicked king has led some scholars to describe the Manasseh of Kings as "Judah's Ahab"[76] or even the "Jezebel of the South".[77] The explicit comparison of Manasseh and Ahab in 2 Kgs 21:3 and their implicit comparison in 21:13 are certainly suggestive of the Kings Writer's intention to encourage such a view.

Van Keulen notes that the formula "he did evil in the eyes of YHWH", which is frequently applied to the Northern monarchs, is not only applied to Manasseh in verse 2 (cf. v. 6), but also occurs in the regnal evaluations of the Judahite kings Jehoram and Ahaziah, whose wickedness is attributed to their relationship with the House of Ahab (2 Kgs 8:18, 27).[78] In contrast, this phrase does not occur in the regnal accounts of Abijam and Ahaz (1 Kgs 15:1-9; 2 Kgs 16:1-20), both of whom are evaluated negatively but are not associated with Ahab.[79] However, as Van Keulen comments, the phrase appears to lose its associative charge after 2 Kgs 21:1-18, for it is applied to each of Manasseh's successors—with the exception of Josiah—without reference to Ahab.[80] This complements the portrayal of Manasseh's reign as the apex of evil, during which the fate of the kingdom was sealed, and the wickedness of her monarchs became inherent thereafter. Indeed, Manasseh is the only Judahite king accused of provoking YHWH to anger.[81]

---

74 Cf. Lasine, "Manasseh as Villain", 165.

75 1 Kgs 16:28–22:40.

76 Hobbs, *2 Kings*, 311; Long, *2 Kings*, 250; Smelik, "Portrayal of King Manasseh", 132.

77 Y. Kaufmann, *The Religion of Israel: From Its Beginnings to the Babylonian Exile* (trans. M. Greenberg; Chicago: University of Chicago, 1960), 141.

78 Van Keulen, *Manasseh*, 89-90. See also Smelik, "Portrayal of King Manasseh", 139-141.

79 Ahaz is accused of "walking in the way of the kings of Israel", probably because in the same verse he is said to cause his son to "pass over in the fire", a crime associated with the Northern Kingdom in 17:17. In contrast, S.A. Irvine (*Isaiah, Ahaz and the Syro-Ephraimitic Crisis* [SBLDS 123; Atlanta: Scholars Press, 1990], 76-79) argues that the expression "(to) walk in the way of the kings of Israel" in 16:3 was originally a political reference, subsequently interpreted in a religious sense.

80 Van Keulen, *Manasseh*, 90.

81 See further Van Keulen, *Manasseh*, 102.

The portrayal of Ahab as an idolatrous monarch seemingly continues to loom large throughout Kings, and thus provides a useful model for the portrayal of Manasseh.[82] Yet unlike the portrayal of Manasseh, Kings' portrait of Ahab is far from one-dimensional, for as Schniedewind demonstrates, the book presents three conflicting interpretations of Ahab's religious behaviour.[83] 1 Kgs 16:30-33 claims that Ahab built a temple to Baʿal in Samaria and worshipped him, thereby provoking YHWH, but 1 Kgs 20 depicts Ahab going to war against the Arameans in the name of YHWH, who delivers the enemy into Ahab's hand. Moreover, 2 Kgs 10:18 appears to diminish the significance of Ahab's Baʿal-worship in light of Jehu. The characterization of Ahab within Kings is thus far from coherent. Yet in describing the reign of Manasseh, the Kings Writer appears to have in mind his characterization of Ahab as an idolater. Schniedewind draws particular attention to the similarities between 1 Kgs 21:26 and 2 Kgs 21:11, in which the same language is employed (גלולים,[84] תעב), and an explicit comparison is drawn between the sins of the king and the sins of the Amorites.[85] This is a striking comparison, for it occurs only in these two texts of the Hebrew Bible. It may be that this comparison with the Amorites serves as a type of conceptual shorthand for communicating what for the Kings Writer is the very essence of evil apostasy.[86] Moreover, Van Keulen observes that whilst the Amorite motif in 1 Kgs 21:26 and 2 Kgs 21:11 seeks to parallel Manasseh and Ahab further, it simultaneously signals a difference between the two monarchs: 1 Kgs 21:26 claims that Ahab matched the Amorites in idolatry, yet 2 Kgs 21:11 accuses Manasseh of outdoing the Amorites in committing evil.[87]

---

82 Cf. Mic. 6:16. T. Ishida ("The House of Ahab", *IEJ* 25 [1975], 135-137) argues that the "House of Ahab" became the symbolic name of the Northern Kingdom's most evil dynasty soon after its fall.

83 Schniedewind, "History and Interpretation", 649-661.

84 See further 4.1.2.

85 Schniedewind, "History and Interpretation", 654-655; cf. O. Steck, *Überlieferung und Zeitgeschichte in den Elia-Erzählungen* (WMANT 2; Neukirchen-Vluyn: Neukirchener Verlag, 1968), 39-40.

86 See further J. Van Seters, "The terms 'Amorite' and 'Hittite' in the Old Testament", *VT* 22 (1972), 64-81 (esp. 72-74); cf. also Eynikel, "Portrait of Manasseh", 251. Schniedewind ("History and Interpretation", 654, n. 15) links the sins of the Amorites with the references to the "gods of the Amorites" in Judg. 6:10 and Josh. 24:15 (cf. Gen. 15:16).

87 Van Keulen, *Manasseh*, 125.

But why is the author of the Manasseh account keen to align Manasseh so specifically with Ahab? The portrayal of Ahab as an apparent prophet-persecutor within the peculiar Elijah and Elisha stories might go some way to explain his infamous reputation within Kings.[88]   More significant though is the biblical claim that Ahab "did more evil in the eyes of YHWH than all who were before him" (1 Kgs 16:30, 33) and that "there was no one like Ahab, who sold himself to do what was evil in the eyes of YHWH" (1 Kgs 21:25, cf. 20).[89] These summary comments complement the stories of Ahab's antagonism of YHWH's prophets, thereby eclipsing his portrayal as a YHWH-warrior in 1 Kgs 20, leaving the reader with the overarching impression of Ahab as an idolatrous Northern king, the worst of all the kings of Israel, worse even than Jeroboam ben Nebat (1 Kgs 16:31-33). However, though Ahab is depicted as the ultimate Northern idolater, at no point in Kings is he accused of bearing sole responsibility for the fall of the Northern Kingdom. In contrast, both Manasseh and King Jeroboam I of Israel carry the blame for the destruction of their respective kingdoms.[90] Jeroboam is accused of "leading the people to sin". The Kings Writer underscores the irreversibility of this crime by presenting it as the pervading inheritance of Jeroboam's

---

88 Ahab is better understood as a naive accessory to these crimes against YHWH, for it is Jezebel, not Ahab, who is said to be killing off YHWH's prophets (1 Kgs 18:4) and who personally threatens Elijah's life (19:1-3). Indeed, seeking to remedy the drought and famine that have besieged his kingdom at Elijah's command, Ahab obeys Elijah's instruction to assemble the prophets of Baʿal and Asherah "who eat at Jezebel's table" at Mount Carmel (18:19-20). Furthermore, it is Jezebel who orchestrates the execution of the innocent Naboth (21:7-15); Ahab humbles himself before YHWH upon realising the gravity of his queen's actions and Elijah's condemnation of his house (21:17-29).

89 Sweeney (*King Josiah*, 172-173) suggests that Manasseh's alignment with Ahab demonstrates the continuing influence of the Omride dynasty within the Davidic monarchy, for from Ahaziah onwards, all Judahite kings are descendants of the House of Omri. However, though possible, one would expect the Kings Writer to draw more attention to this feature within the Manasseh account (as he does in the cases of Jehoram and Ahaziah in 2 Kgs 8:18, 27) as it would enhance his comparison of Manasseh with Ahab.

90 1 Kgs 14:16; 2 Kgs 17:21-23; cf. 21:10-15; 23:26-27; 24:3-4. See further C.D. Evans, "Naram-Sin and Jeroboam: The Archetypal *Unheilsherrscher* in Mesopotamian and Biblical Historiography", in W.W. Hallo, J.C. Moyer and L.G. Perdue (eds.), *Scripture in Context, II: More Essays on the Comparative Method* (Winona Lake: Eisenbrauns, 1983), 114-124; P.S. Ash, "Jeroboam I and the Deuteronomistic Historian's Ideology of the Founder", *CBQ* 60 (1998), 16-24; McKenzie, *The Trouble with Kings*, 56-58; Sweeney, *King Josiah*, 78-79.

successors, for this formulaic critique is applied to all but three Northern kings.[91] It is thus significant that Manasseh is also accused of leading the people to sin (2 Kgs 21:9, 11), particularly in view of the fact that this accusation is not levelled at any other Southern king. Nelson's description of Manasseh as "Judah's Jeroboam" is thus well-founded.[92] The deliberate parallelling of the fall of Israel and the pending fall of Judah is indicated further by 2 Kgs 23:26-27, which asserts that Manasseh provokes YHWH to resolve, "I will remove Judah also out of my sight, as I have removed Israel". This threat is seen to be carried out in 24:2-4:

> YHWH sent against him bands of the Chaldeans, bands of the Arameans, bands of the Moabites, and bands of the Ammonites; he sent them against Judah to destroy it, according to the word of YHWH that he spoke through his servants the prophets. Surely this came upon Judah at the command of YHWH, to remove them out of his sight, for the sins of Manasseh, for all that he had committed, and also for the innocent blood that he[93] had shed; for he filled Jerusalem with innocent blood, and YHWH was not willing to pardon.

This text cites the judgement oracle of 21:10-15 in order to correlate the attacks on Judah with the sins of Manasseh. Thus 24:2-4 seeks to demonstrate the fulfilment of the prophecy of 21:10-15, just as 17:23 makes it plain that the fall of the Kingdom of Israel is the fulfilment of the prophecy spelt out in 1 Kgs 14:15-16. As Van Keulen rightly comments, both the prophecy and its fulfilment notice intimate that, "Manasseh's sins meant for

---

91   1 Kgs 14:16; 15:26, 30, 34; 16:13, 19, 26; 2 Kgs 3:3; 10:29, 31; 13:2, 6, 11; 14:24; 15:9, 18, 24, 28; 17:21-23. The only exceptions are Ahab, Shallum, and Hoshea. Shallum is portrayed as a political usurper who reigns for only a month before he is assassinated (2 Kgs 15:10-15), perhaps accounting for the absence of this standard critique. Ahab probably escapes this standard critique because his role as the ultimate Northern idolater renders this formulaic expression impotent (1 Kgs 16:31-33). Also, he is held personally responsible for his own sin (21:20-22; 22:38). As the last reigning king of Israel, Hoshea is explicitly distanced from the evil of his predecessors in order to emphasize that it is the sin of Jeroboam I that caused the collapse of the kingdom (2 Kgs 17:2 cf. 7-8). For an analysis of this formula, see T.E. Mullen, "The Sins of Jeroboam: A Redactional Assessment", *CBQ* 49 (1987), 212-232.

92   Nelson, *First and Second Kings*, 247-249.

93   LXX ms 243 includes the name of Manasseh here, whereas LXX^L has Ιωακιμ (Jehoiakim); cf. LXX 2 Chr. 36:5c-d. See further 39-40.

Judah what Jeroboam's sins meant for Israel."[94] Van Keulen also makes an important observation, frequently overlooked by other commentators:

> As part of a design to describe the ends of Israel and Judah as parallel events, the comparison with Jeroboam aims at bringing out the decisive negative importance Manasseh's reign had for Judah. The comparison with Ahab ... primarily means to characterize Manasseh as an utterly wicked king. Its main purpose is to fill in the portrait of Manasseh.[95]

Yet although the Kings Writer seeks to parallel the approaching destruction of Judah with the fall of the Kingdom of Israel, the judgement oracle against Manasseh's Judah in 2 Kgs 21:10-15 associates the fall of the Northern kingdom not with Jeroboam, but with Ahab:

> I will stretch over Jerusalem the measuring line of Samaria and the plummet of the House of Ahab and I will wipe out Jerusalem just as one wipes a dish, wiping it and turning it over on its face.[96]

To associate Jeroboam with the fall of the city of Samaria would be inappropriate, for according to Kings, Samaria did not exist during the reign of Jeroboam; rather, it is Ahab's father Omri who founds the city as the capital of the Kingdom of Israel.[97] But though Omri is typically condemned for committing more evil than his predecessors, following in the way of Jeroboam and causing Israel to sin with idols,[98] the suspicious silence concerning this monarch precludes the Kings Writer from associating Omri with the fall of the city.[99] But the question remains, why does the Kings

---

94 Van Keulen, *Manasseh*, 148-150 (150).

95 Van Keulen, *Manasseh*, 152.

96 2 Kgs 21:13. Though מחה, "wipe out", is fairly common in Biblical Hebrew, it occurs only twice within Kings (here and 2 Kgs 14:27), and four times within Deuteronomy (Deut 9:14; 25:6, 19; 29:20). Within other biblical texts, it is usually employed of sin or transgression, e.g. Isa. 43:25; 44:22; Pss. 51:3, 11; 109:14; Prov. 6:3; Neh. 4:5; cf. Lowery, *Reforming Kings*, 179.

97 1 Kgs 24.

98 1 Kgs 16:25-26.

99 The brief biblical account of Omri is surprising given his apparent historical significance: the Mesha Inscription concedes that "Omri humbled Moab for many years." (*ANET*, 320). Moreover, the annals of the Assyrian king Tiglath-pileser III, approximately a century and a half later, refer to Israel as *Bit Ḫu-um-ri-a*, "the House of Omri", suggesting that Omri's reputation and influence extended well beyond his reign (*ANET*, 284).

Writer select Ahab, who, like Manasseh, died long before the fall of his kingdom? Schniedewind suggests that Ahab is associated with the destruction of his kingdom here because his sins are connected with the eventual fall of his kingdom.[100] However, as has been seen, nowhere in Kings is it claimed that it is specifically Ahab's sins that bring destruction upon the kingdom. Rather, the explicit mention of Ahab in the judgement oracle of the Manasseh account is better explained in terms of his particularly close association with Samaria. Though the judgement oracle of 2 Kgs 21:10-15 warns of Judah's impending disaster, the oracle's focus is inverted: it looks back to the past in order to make plain the future by referring to the fall of Samaria (v. 13).[101] This inverted focus is emphasized further in verse 15, which locates the beginning of the people's evil as far back as their ancestors' departure from Egypt. Thus looking again at the language of 21:10-15 suggests that the phrase בית אחאב, "House of Ahab", is intended to refer not to the Omride dynasty,[102] which reached its end well before the fall of the kingdom, but to the city of Samaria itself as the royal residence.[103] This is suggested by the language of material construction in verse 13: קו, "measuring line", and משקלת, "plummet".[104] Given Omri's marginal role within the biblical story of Israel, Samaria is portrayed as the city of the infamous "King Ahab of Samaria" (1 Kgs 21:1). Furthermore, for the Kings Writer, Ahab remains the most suitable model of comparison with Manasseh because as van Keulen comments, although Jeroboam, like Manasseh, is depicted as the king who caused the downfall of his people, "Ahab is undisputably presented as a more idolatrous king than Jeroboam," as 1 Kgs

---

100 Schniedewind, "History and Interpretation", 659. In light of his adherence to the dual-redaction theory of the Deuteronomistic History, Schniedewind argues that "...the exilic redactor reinterpreted Ahab's religious practices and cast him in the mold of Manasseh as a worshipper of foreign deities" (657).

101 Lowery, Reforming Kings, 185; Noth, Deuteronomistic History, 115.

102 Most other occurrences of the phrase בית אחאב in Kings tend to designate Ahab's family (e.g., 2 Kgs 8:18, 27; 9:7-9; 10:10); Eynikel, "Portrait of Manasseh", 252.

103 See also Van Keulen, Manasseh, 130-131; Eynikel, "Portrait of Manasseh", 252. For Samaria as a royal city, see D. Ussishkin, "Jezreel, Samaria, and Megiddo: Royal Centres of Omri and Ahab", in J.A. Emerton (ed.), Congress Volume Cambridge, 1995 (VTSup 66; Leiden: Brill, 1997), 351-364.

104 In light of this verse, the emphasis upon Ahab's role as a constructor in 1 Kgs 22:39 takes on an ironical tone. Instruments of construction are often employed as YHWH's tools of destruction throughout the Hebrew Bible: Amos 7:7-9; Isa. 28:17; 34:11; Lam. 2:8; Zech. 1:16; Job 38:5.

16:31 indicates.[105] According to the Kings Writer, idolatry leads to expulsion from the land. Moreover, Manasseh's comparison with a Northern king, rather than an idolatrous Southern king such as Ahaz,[106] serves not only to parallel the shared fates of the kingdoms, but also seeks to explain just how a Davidic monarch could cause the destruction of the kingdom. The discussion will return to this important point.[107]

The cult crimes of which Manasseh is accused are portrayed throughout Kings as the behaviour of the foreign nations, behaviour which had led to YHWH's expulsion of the nations from the land in the first place. This is made absolutely plain in the introduction to the cult crime list (v. 2):

> He did evil in the eyes of YHWH just like the abhorrent practices of the nations whom YHWH had dispossessed before the Israelites.

In order to account for YHWH's decision to bring disaster upon Judah, the Kings Writer has to depict Manasseh as "a sinner of unparalleled dimensions."[108] Thus as has been seen, Manasseh not only sins, but he magnifies his sin: he not only replaces the *bamoth* (21:3a) but he also builds altars for Ba'al (21:3b); he not only makes an *asherah*, (21:3b) but he sets it in YHWH's temple (21:7); he not only serves the Host of Heaven (21:3c) but he builds altars to them in the courtyards of YHWH's temple (21:5). He not

---

105 Cf. 1 Kgs 21:26. Van Keulen, *Manasseh*, 154.

106 Manasseh and Ahaz are mentioned in the same breath in the account of Josiah's cultic purge (2 Kgs 23:12) but they are not compared. It is necessary for the Kings Writer to mention these kings here in order to present Josiah's purge as being as comprehensive as possible.

107 See 1.3 below. There are three important differences between the portrayals of Ahab and Manasseh in Kings. The first is that Ahab's sins lead to the fall of his dynasty, whereas Manasseh's do not (so too Schniedewind, "History and Interpretation", 659). The second is that Ahab repents, whereas Manasseh does not (Linville, *Israel in the Book of Kings*, 175). The third important difference is the role ascribed to their queens: the foreign Jezebel is not only portrayed as an idolatress and murderess, but is also held equally responsible for Ahab's idolatry (1 Kgs 16:31; 18:13, 19; 19:1-3; 21:5-16, 23-25; 22:52; 2 Kgs 3:2, 13; 9:7, 10, 22, 30-37). Many commentators have drawn attention to the apparently non-Judahite origin of Manasseh's queen Meshullemeth (2 Kgs 21:19) and some even suggest her influence lies behind Manasseh's cult crimes (e.g., McKay, *Religion in Judah*, 23-25; Schniedewind, "History and Interpretation", 660 n. 26). However, the Kings Writer makes no such claim, unlike in the case of Jezebel. On Meshullemeth, see 2.3.

108 Van Keulen, *Manasseh*, 156.

only sacrifices his son (21:6a), but he participates in a variety of divinatory practices. The conclusion to the cult crime list magnifies Manasseh's sins further by stating that Manasseh misled the people so much that they did even *more* evil than the nations had done (21:9, cf. 11). In this way, the Kings Writer sets Manasseh up for the biggest fall in Judahite history: the fall of the kingdom.

The Kings Writer is explicit in holding Manasseh personally responsible for the fall of the kingdom: the oracle of judgement against Jerusalem and Judah (21:10-15) accounts for the approaching destruction with the opening words, "Because King Manasseh of Judah has committed these abominations" (v. 11). This accusation is repeated in two important texts elsewhere in the book. The first of these is 23:26-27. This text interrupts the regnal account of Josiah, falling between the lengthy account of his cultic purge and the curious notice of his death. In employing language which intentionally recalls the description of Manasseh's reign in 21:1-18, such as כעס (23:26; cf. 21:6, 15) and בחר (23:27; cf. 21:7), along with the explicit reference to the divine Name (שם) in the temple in Jerusalem (23:27; cf. 21:7),[109] the Kings Writer ensures that Manasseh is held inextricably responsible for YHWH's destructive anger against Judah. The point of this ideologically-loaded assertion is transparent: *despite* Josiah's apparently orthodox cult policies, the fall of the Judahite Kingdom remains inevitable, just as the fall of Israel remained inevitable long after Jeroboam's death.[110]

The second text offering a "Manasseh alone"[111] explanation for the fall of Judah is 24:1-4. Here, Manasseh's behaviour is cited as the reason for the initial Babylonian conquest of Judah. A particularly striking feature of this text is the repetition of the charge that Manasseh shed innocent blood, a crime first detailed in 21:16: "Manasseh shed so much innocent blood that he filled Jerusalem from end to end". The repetition of this charge in explicit relation to the claim that Manasseh alone is responsible for provoking the attacks upon Judah is striking. It not only suggests that the crime of shedding

---

109 On this "centralization formula", see Nelson, *Deuteronomy*, 152-153, and the literature cited there; see also T.C. Römer, "Du Temple au Livre: L'idéologie de la centralisation dans l'historiographie deutéronomiste", in S.L. McKenzie and T.C. Römer (eds.), *Rethinking the Foundations: Historiography in the Ancient World and in the Bible: Essays in Honour of John Van Seters* (BZAW 294; Berlin/New York, 2000), 207-225.

110 1 Kgs 14:16; 2 Kgs 17:21-23.

111 Lowery, *Reforming Kings*, 172-175; see also Van Keulen, *Manasseh*, 183-184; Provan, *Hezekiah and the Books of Kings*, 151 n. 62.

innocent blood is instrumental in confirming Manasseh's culpability, but it also has the obverse effect of diminishing the impact of Manasseh's cultic crimes and highlighting instead this one misdemeanour. This stands in notable contrast to the careful formulation of the regnal account, which provides a lengthy and detailed breakdown of Manasseh's cultic crimes, and only a brief mention of his shedding innocent blood, almost as an afterthought, before the death and burial formula.[112] This incongruity is perhaps remedied in arguing that the accusation that Manasseh shed innocent blood in 21:16 draws a further parallel with the northern apostate Ahab, recalling the slaughter of YHWH's prophets and Naboth (1 Kgs 18-21).[113] However, Ahab is not *explicitly* accused of shedding innocent blood; rather, it is his foreign wife, Jezebel, who is seen to instigate the killings (1 Kgs 21:19; 2 Kgs 9:7, 26). Moreover, the language of 2 Kgs 21:16 is vague and ambiguous—a stark contrast to the specific accusations against Manasseh in the cult crime list (21:3-8). Indeed, so peculiar is 21:16 that many commentators argue it is a later addition to the account of Manasseh's reign.[114] Indeed, this view is encouraged by the possibility that the same charge against him in 24:4 might not have referred originally to Manasseh. Rather, it may be that in the tradition underlying 24:4 Jehoiakim, whose death-notice immediately follows in vv. 5-6, was held responsible for this particular crime.[115] The phrase in MT 24:4, "the innocent blood which he shed", is rendered in 4 Kingdoms Lucianic 24:4 as, "the innocent blood which Jehoiakim shed". This reading is complemented by the possibility that in MT Jer 22:17, Jehoiakim is similarly accused of shedding innocent blood,[116] and that in 2 Paralipomena 36:5c-d Jehoiakim is said to have shed innocent blood. Thus in the Lucianic version of 2 Kgs 24:3-4, Manasseh and Jehoiakim are held jointly responsible for the Babylonian invasion. This may suggest that the charge of shedding innocent blood was originally levelled at Jehoiakim in the *Vorlage* of 24:4, and only secondarily ascribed to Manasseh,

---

112 As Eynikel observes ("Portrait of Manasseh", 253), the accusation is introduced by םגו, as if this crime had been overlooked in vv. 3-8.

113 This appears to have been a favoured interpretation among ancient commentators; cf. Cogan and Tadmor, *II Kings*, 270. See also 3.1 below.

114 See the discussion in Eynikel, "Portrait of Manasseh", 253, 258.

115 Noted also by Halpern, "Why Manasseh is Blamed", 506.

116 It is uncertain as to whether this accusation is levelled against Jehoiakim or perhaps Shallum (Jehoahaz) here. For the important association of this crime with child sacrifice, see 4.1.2.

as reflected in MT.[117] This would support those suggesting that the same
charge against Manasseh in 21:16 is an awkward, later addition. Indeed, the
theological motif of shedding innocent blood appears to have gained a
particularly prominent ideological significance within certain prophetic
literary traditions, and it is not impossible that the Manasseh account in
Kings has been modified to reflect this prophetic interest.[118] If this is correct,
the subsequent addition of this crime to Manasseh's charge sheet would
demonstrate his deliberate and continued vilification further. However, it is
equally possible that the association of Jehoiakim with the shedding of
innocent blood in 4 Kingdoms Lucianic 24:3-4 and 2 Paralipomena 36:5c-d
reflects "an exegetical innovation of later origin",[119] intended to denigrate
Jehoiakim's reputation by means of his association with Manasseh.
Jehoiakim is closely aligned with Manasseh in death, for in 4 Kingdoms
Lucianic 24:6, Jehoiakim is said to be buried in the "garden of Oza" (κηπω
Οζα), whilst in 2 Paralipomena 36:8, Jehoiakim's burial place is named
"Ganoza" (Γανοζα); the former is a translation and the latter a transliteration
of עזא גן, "Garden of Uzza", the burial place of Manasseh and Amon (MT 2
Kgs 21:18, 26).[120] This, along with the charge that Jehoiakim shed innocent
blood in 4 Kingdoms Lucianic 24:3-4 and 2 Paralipomena 36:5c-d, might
thus suggest a later vilification of Jehoiakim,[121] crafted upon the Manasseh
paradigm presented in Kings.

A subsequent addition to Manasseh's biblical portrayal or not, the crime
of shedding innocent blood in 2 Kgs 21:16 and 24:3-4 serves an important
theological purpose. Given that it is the only one of Manasseh's crimes which
Josiah is not seen to remedy, it may be that on one level it seeks to address
the failure of Josiah's cultic reform to halt the impending collapse of the
kingdom.[122] Similarly, it may be that the Kings Writer also implicates

---

117 Halpern, "Why Manasseh is Blamed", 506.
118 Cf. 4.1.2. Notice also that both Manasseh and Jehoiakim are accused of killing prophets:
    Manasseh executes Isaiah (*Martyrdom of Isaiah*; cf. 3.1, below) and Jehoiakim kills
    Uriah (Jer. 26:20-23).
119 S. Delamarter, "The Vilification of Jehoiakim (a.k.a. Eliakim and Joiakim) in Early
    Judaism", in C.A. Evans and J.A. Sanders (eds.), *The Function of Scripture in Early
    Jewish and Christian Tradition* (JSNTSup 154/SSEJC 6; Sheffield: Sheffield Academic
    Press, 1998), 190-204.
120 Delamarter, "Vilification of Jehoiakim", 196-198.
121 So Delamarter, "Vilification of Jehoiakim", 201-204.
122 On another level, it also serves an important ideological purpose, as discussed in 1.3 and
    2.3 below.

Manasseh in the sudden death of his hero Josiah: Manasseh's culpability for the destruction is reiterated in 23:26-27, prefacing both the death notice and the brief account of Josiah's assassination at the hands of the Egyptian king.[123]

In holding Manasseh wholly and personally responsible for the destruction of the kingdom, 23:26-27 and 24:3-4 fulfill the prophetic judgement oracle of the Manasseh account (21:10-15). However, it would appear that the "Manasseh alone"[124] explanation is not the only interpretation of the fall of Judah offered within Kings. Further explanations are evident. One holds the Davidic dynasty collectively responsible for the disaster. After the death of Josiah, the narrative picks up more momentum as the approaching disaster hurtles towards Judah. A consequence of this is evident in the accession notices of Josiah's initial successors, which are more generalized than those of his predecessors. Rather than comparing each king to a particular predecessor, the accession notices of Jehoahaz and Jehoiakim describe each king as doing evil in the eyes of YHWH just as *all* his ancestors had done.[125] These statements are unqualified: the Kings Writer makes no exceptions, so that even David, Hezekiah and Josiah are seemingly blackballed. Spieckermann suggests that the use of Manasseh's title "King of Judah" in the judgement oracle of 21:10-15 is intended to draw the Davidic monarchy as a whole into the foreground of culpability.[126] However, it may be that a further interpretation of the destruction of Judah is offered. Though the accession notice of Jehoiachin maintains the generalized tone evident in those of the king's two predecessors, it loses the pluralization of guilt in the assertion that he did evil in the eyes of YHWH just as his father (Jehoiakim) had done (24:9). Similarly, the accession notice of the last king of Judah, Zedekiah, also compares the king's evil behaviour to that of Jehoiakim:

> He did what was evil in the sight of YHWH, just as Jehoiakim had done. Indeed, Jerusalem and Judah so angered YHWH that he expelled them from his presence.[127]

---

123 So too Halpern, "Why Manasseh is Blamed", 507-508; Lowery, *Reforming Kings*, 172. See also S.B. Frost, "The Death of Josiah: A Conspiracy of Silence", *JBL* 87 (1968), 369-382. H.G.M. Williamson, "The Death of Josiah and the Development of the Deuteronomic History", *VT* 32 (1982), 242-248.

124 Lowery, *Reforming Kings*, 171.

125 Jehoahaz (23:32); Jehoiakim (23:37).

126 Spieckermann, *Juda unter Assur*, 168.

127 2 Kgs 24:19-20.

Given that this is the Kings Writer's final theological comment on the eventual collapse of Judah, it would appear that the fall of the city is specifically attributed to the combined evil of Jehoiakim and Zedekiah,[128] not to the evil of the Davidic monarchy as a whole, and importantly, not to the sins of Manasseh.[129]

A further explanation for the Babylonian exile(s) is the collective guilt of "the people". Significantly, this explanation is evident within Kings' account of Manasseh. In employing a series of plural forms throughout 21:7-9, the Kings Writer implicates the community in contributing to the evil which will eventually cause the destruction of Judah and the exile of the people:

> "I will no more cause the feet of Israel to wander from the land that I gave to their ancestors if only they will be vigilant to do all that I commanded them, that is, according to all the Law which my servant Moses commanded them." But they did not listen and Manasseh misled them so that they did more evil than the nations whom YHWH destroyed before the Israelites.

This is reminiscent of Kings' lengthy theological reflection upon the fall of the Kingdom of Israel in 2 Kgs 17, in which the *collective* guilt of the Northern Kingdom, as well as the sins of Jeroboam, are flagged up as reasons for the disaster.[130] Similarly, the Kings Writer emphasizes the corporate responsibility of the people and Manasseh. As Lasine comments, "the narrator is telescoping the 'Israel' to whom Yahweh had referred at the beginning of the monarchical period with the 'they' who were still not listening when Manasseh caused them to wander astray. Taken together, these verses imply that if 'they' had hearkened to what Yahweh told the kings who governed their ancestors, Manasseh's cultic reforms would not have been able to mislead them". [131]

The corporate responsibility of the people is the popular explanation for the Babylonian conquest of Judah more generally attested in other biblical texts. Yet despite these alternative explanations for the Babylonian conquest

---

128 Given that Jehoiakim and Zedekiah are portrayed as the ruling monarchs upon the occasions of the Babylonian attacks in 597 and 587 BCE, their castigation in Kings is not altogether surprising.

129 Cf. M. Smith, "The Veracity of Ezekiel, the Sins of Manasseh, and Jeremiah 44:18", *ZAW* 87 (1975) 11-16 [14]; cf. Halpern, "Why Manasseh is Blamed", 507.

130 See further 1.3 below.

131 Lasine, "Manasseh as Villain", 170.

of Judah, the figure of Manasseh characterized as the arch-villain of Kings casts a long and dark shadow over the rest of the story, eclipsing any other interpretation the text might allow.[132]

One of the flaws within the Kings Writer's schema blaming Manasseh for the destruction of Judah and the exile of the people is that Manasseh himself appears to go unpunished. In fact, he is the longest reigning monarch in Kings, which theologically suggests that Manasseh not only went unpunished, but was blessed with longevity. This stands in contrast with the particularly idolatrous monarchs of the Northern Kingdom, who are personally punished for their sins: Jeroboam's child cannot be prevented from dying, and his dynasty is thus brought to an end;[133] Ahab is killed in battle, and his queen is killed upon the instruction of Jehu, and eaten by dogs.[134] Given that the biblical ideology of the perpetuation of the Davidic dynasty seems to inform the Kings Writer's portrayal of the Jerusalem kings, the extermination of a Judahite king's dynastic line would be an inappropriate punishment by YHWH. This is exemplified in the case of Manasseh's ancestor Jehoram:

> He walked in the way of the kings of Israel, as the House of Ahab had done, for the daughter of Ahab was his wife. He did what was evil in the eyes of YHWH, yet YHWH would not destroy Judah, for the sake of his servant David, since he had promised to give a lamp to him and to his descendants forever.[135]

However, even the favourite monarchs of the Kings Writer, Hezekiah and Josiah, who purge the Jerusalem cult of idols and tear down the high places, are plagued by misfortune. Hezekiah is besieged by the Assyrians (2 Kgs 18:9-19:37) and comes close to death with illness (20:1-7). Josiah, the Kings

---

132 Eynikel ("Portrait of Manasseh", 257) discusses whether the tension between blaming Manasseh alone and blaming the people for the approaching disaster is evidence of different redactors; see also Lowery, *Reforming Kings*, 171.

133 1 Kgs 14:9-11, 16.

134 1 Kgs 21:20-22; 22:29-38; 2 Kgs 9:6-10, 30-37.

135 2 Kgs 8:18-19; cf. 1 Kgs 11:34-36; 15:4 (cf. 2:3-4). Ahaziah is also accused of walking in the way of the house of Ahab as he is the son of Jehoram and Athaliah and (8:25-27). Athaliah's reign is depicted as simply interrupting the rule of the Davidic monarchy, for she fails to kill Jehoash (Joash) the son of Jehoram (2 Kgs 11:1-20).

Writer's David *redivivus*,[136] is embarrassingly killed by Pharaoh (23:29-30). Given these precedents, and the grave nature of Manasseh's sin, the reader naturally expects Manasseh to receive some sort of divine retribution, yet none occurs: his reign is unremarkable in political terms, he experiences no personal misfortune, and it is intimated that he dies a natural death at a ripe old age (21:18). It would appear that although in places Manasseh is held solely responsible for bringing disaster upon his kingdom, he goes wholly unpunished by YHWH. It would thus seem that the villainous Manasseh of Kings has the last laugh. Yet it may be that the Kings Writer metes out a subtle, sardonic punishment of his own. Manasseh's burial notice signals a sudden shift within the formulaic expression concluding the account of his reign. The standard death and burial formula applied to each of Manasseh's predecessors states that the king slept with his ancestors and was buried in the City of David with his ancestors.[137] Yet Manasseh's burial notice is very different, for though it is said that Manasseh "slept with his ancestors", Manasseh's burial place is located "in the garden of his house in the garden of Uzza" (21:18). Though previous scholarship has sought to explain this curious reference to the mysterious "Garden of Uzza" in a variety of ways,[138]

---

136 A. Laato, *Josiah and David Redivivus: The Historical Josiah and Messianic Expectations of Exilic and PostExilic Times* (CB OTS 33; Stockholm: Almqvist & Wiksell, 1992).

137 This formula occurs in 1 Kgs 2:10; 11:43; 14:31; 15:8; 15:24; 22:50; 2 Kgs 8:24; 9:28; 12:21; 14:20; 15:7, 38; 16:20; 20:21 with only minor variations: the subclause "(buried) with his ancestors" is not included in the formula applied to David (1 Kgs 2:10), Solomon (11:43) and Abijam (15:8), and Hezekiah is not said to be buried in the City of David (2 Kgs 20:21).

138 Scholars tend to align themselves to one of three proposals: the first is that the name Uzza is a variant of the name of the diseased Judahite king Uzziah (also called Azariah in the Hebrew Bible) and that his personal garden was used for the burials of Manasseh and Amon; e.g. S. Yeivin, "The Sepulchers of the Kings of the House of David", *JNES* 7 (1948), 30-45, esp. 33-35. A second proposal suggests that the garden is named after the unfortunate Uzza ben Abinadab, who was killed when he touched the Ark to steady it on its procession to Jerusalem (2 Sam. 6:3-8; 1 Chr. 13:7-11); e.g., Provan, *1 & 2 Kings*, 269. A third alternative is offered by McKay (*Religion in Judah*, 24-25, 95), who suggests that the garden of Uzza was a cult place dedicated to an Arabian god in honour of Manasseh's wife Meshullemeth, whom McKay argues unconvincingly was Arabian. Schmidt (*Beneficent Dead*, 252-254) offers the alternative suggestion that the Kings Writer here refers to the reburial of royal ancestors in a royal garden, a concept modelled upon Mesopotamian practice. He further suggests that Hezekiah engineered this move in

the essential function of Manasseh's burial notice appears to have been overlooked: in locating Manasseh's final resting place away from the ancestral tomb in the City of David, Manasseh is in death displaced from his ancestral line, and hence dislocated from his rightful place within his ancestral cult.[139] That an ancient audience would have recognized the damning implications of this is suggested by the careful observation that despite being killed at Megiddo, Josiah was buried in his own tomb in Jerusalem (23:30), seemingly fulfilling Huldah's oracle that YHWH would gather Josiah to his ancestors and his tombs (22:20). Similarly, both Amaziah and Ahaziah are killed away from Jerusalem, and are brought back to the city to be buried with their ancestors (9:27-29; 14:19-20). Notable also is the vitriolic crowing of the poet in Isa. 14:12-20 over the battlefield death of Sargon II of Assyria,[140] in which vv. 18-20 in particular reveal both the horror and theological judgement implicit in a king's corpse lying away from his tomb. Thus in hurling this final insult at Manasseh, the Kings Writer indicates that the villainous Manasseh did not go altogether unpunished.[141] However, though the Chronicler probably recognized the significance of Manasseh's burial away from his ancestors, this was not punishment enough for Manasseh's behaviour. Consequently, in his own account of Manasseh's reign, the Chronicler ensures that the theological repercussions of disobedience to YHWH's law, statutes and ordinances are both explicit and fitting.

---

readiness for the Assyrian siege, Manasseh is apparently held responsible for the garden tomb in Kings.

139 E. Bloch-Smith (*Judahite Burial Practices and Beliefs about the Dead* [JSOTS, 123; Sheffield: JSOT Press, 1992], 117) also recognizes the ideological function that the burial notices can have, briefly stating: "Ending the record of a king's reign with the fact of burial with his predecessors in the City of David emphasizes descent from David with its official divine sanction of maintaining the Davidic dynasty". However, she does not apply the possibility of an ideological interpretation to the notice of Manasseh's burial place, suggesting instead that it reflects an historical change in the burial locations of Judahite monarchs (119).

140 M.A. Sweeney, *Isaiah 1–39: with an Introduction to Prophetic Literature* (FOTL 16; Grand Rapids: Eerdmans, 1996), 232-233. On the curse of non-burial and tomb-desecration in biblical and non-biblical texts, see Barrick, *King and the Cemeteries*, 178-179.

141 Given that Manasseh's successor Amon is said to do "what is evil in the eyes of YHWH, just as his father Manasseh had done" by serving and worshipping his father's idols, he too is consigned to the Garden of Uzza, away from the ancestral tomb and cult (21:20-22, 26).

1.2 The Manasseh of Chronicles

The Book of Chronicles seems to be particularly problematic for modern scholarship. The problem with Chronicles is not the fact that it offers an account of Israel's past alongside that of Kings, nor even that this story of the past can, in places, differ from and even contradict the version offered by Kings. Rather, the problem with Chronicles is that these differences and contradictions occur despite the great probability that the Chronicler has composed his history using as his weightiest sources versions of the books of Samuel and Kings.[142] This is problematic for some scholars for it casts into doubt the historicity of the Chronicler's story and that of his sources, which often appear to be manipulated, distorted and even disregarded by the Chronicler.[143] But this should not be seen as a problem. Rather, the freedom with which the Chronicler appears to employ his source material emphasizes the tendentious nature of all biblical texts, reminding the reader that both Kings and Chronicles are not history writing in the modern sense, but rather

---

142 It is widely accepted that the Chronicler knew and used something similar to the so-called "Deuteronomistic History" as his primary source for his work. He may also have used material from other biblical books and extra-biblical sources (now lost). For useful discussions of the Chronicler's likely sources, see H.G.M. Williamson, *1 and 2 Chronicles* (NCB; London: Marshall, Morgan & Scott, 1982), 17-23, and Williamson's introduction to the English translation of M. Noth, *The Chronicler's History* (trans. H.G.M. Williamson; JSOTSup 50; Sheffield: JSOT Press, 1987), 11-26. See also S. Japhet, *I & II Chronicles: A Commentary* (London: SCM Press, 1993), 14-23; A.F. Rainey, "The Chronicler and His Sources—Historical and Geographical", in M.P. Graham, K.G. Hoglund and S.L. McKenzie (eds.), *The Chronicler as Historian* (JSOTSup 238; Sheffield: Sheffield Academic Press, 1997), 30-72. An alternative view of the interrelationship of Kings and Chronicles is offered by Auld, who argues that the books of Kings and Chronicles each independently supplemented a shared inherited text telling the story of the Davidic monarchy from David to the fall of Jerusalem; A.G. Auld, *Kings Without Privilege: David and Moses in the Story of the Bible's Kings* (Edinburgh: T&T Clark, 1994); *idem.*, "What if the Chronicler did use the Deuteronomistic History?", *BibInt* 8 (2000), 137-150. In the case of the Manasseh account, Auld (*Kings Without Privilege*, 73-88) argues that the Chronicler has used the Solomon narratives as a source with which to rework the shorter, shared story of Manasseh's reign.

143 On the debate concerning the historicity of the Chronicler, see K. Peltonen, *History Debated: The Historical Reliability of Chronicles in Pre-Critical and Critical Research* (2 vols. PFES 64; Helsinki/Göttingen: Finnish Exegetical Society/Vandenhoeck & Ruprecht, 1996).

are ideological stories of the past told in order to account for the present and to advise for the future. Thus the potential compromising of their historicity (the extent to which they can reliably inform about the past they seek to describe) is not actually especially problematic, for the question of historicity is in effect a secondary issue dominated by conjecture and possibility.[144] Thus the Chronicler "is no evil fictionalizer trying to mislead his audience"[145] but a theologian, offering a presentation of the history of God's relationship with the earthly realm and his people. As such, Chronicles is best understood as "theocentric historiography",[146] or as a "theological essay".[147]

The Second Temple context of the Chronicler's history is widely-accepted,[148] yet despite the apparent consolidation of Jerusalem's new socio-

---

144 Defining the nature of the Books of Chronicles appears to have posed a problem for some of its ancient readers and translators, as its various designations demonstrate. Whereas its Hebrew name is a straightforward description of its contents, דברי הימים ("the happenings of the days"), the Greek translators seem to have regarded it more as a supplement to the other biblical histories, entitling it παραλειπομενων ("things left out").

145 K.G. Hoglund, "The Chronicler as Historian: A Comparativist Perspective", in Graham, Hoglund, McKenzie, *Chronicler as Historian*, 19-29 (29).

146 S. Japhet, *The Ideology of the Book of Chronicles and its Place in Biblical Thought* (trans. A. Barber; BEATAJ 9; Frankfurt am Main: Peter Lang, 1997), 11.

147 W. Johnstone, "Guilt and Atonement: The Theme of 1 and 2 Chronicles", in J.D. Martin and P.R. Davies (eds.) *A Word in Season: Essays in Honour of William McKane* (JSOTSup 42; Sheffield: JSOT Press, 1986), 113-138 (116); cf. P.R. Ackroyd, "The Theology of the Chronicler", in *idem.*, *The Chronicler in His Age* (JSOTSup 101; Sheffield: JSOT Press, 1991), 273-289. See further I. Kalimi, "Was the Chronicler a Historian?", in Graham, Hoglund, McKenzie, *The Chronicler as Historian*, 73-89; W.M. Schniedewind, "History or Homily: Toward Understanding the Chronicler's Purpose", in *Proceedings of the Eleventh World Congress of Jewish Studies* (Jerusalem: World Union of Jewish Studies, 1994), 92-93; cf. M. Fishbane, *Biblical Interpretation in Ancient Israel* (Oxford: Clarendon Press, 1985), 385-403.

148 A more precise context for the dating of Chronicles has not been firmly established. Cross's identification of a provisional edition in 520 BCE represents an early suggestion for the date of composition (F.M. Cross, "A Reconstruction of the Judean Restoration", *JBL* 94 [1975], 4-18; see also D.N. Freedman, "The Chronicler's Purpose", *CBQ* 23 (1961), 436-442). Williamson (*1 and 2 Chronicles*, 16-17) locates the Chronicler in or around Jerusalem in the mid-fourth century, arguing he was probably a Levite; cf. *idem.*, *Israel in the Books of Chronicles* (Cambridge: Cambridge University Press, 1977), 7-70. Japhet (*I & II Chronicles*, 23-28) argues for a date at the end of the fourth century, thus placing the Chronicler in the late Persian, or more preferably the early Hellenistic period. H.P. Mathys ("1 and 2 Chronicles", *OBC*, 267-308) locates the Chronicler in the Hellenistic period, arguing that Chronicles is intended to counter the histories of civilization offered by Ptolemaic and Seleucid historiographers Manetho, Hekataios and

religious apparatus, the Chronicler's history offers a retrospective thesis seeking to define what it is to be "Israel", a concern the Chronicler shares with the Kings Writer. As Japhet comments:

> By reformulating Israel's history in its formative period, the Chronicler gives new significance to the two components of Israelite life: the past is explained so that its institutions and religious principles become relevant to the present, and the ways of the present are legitimized anew by being connected to the prime source of authority—the formative period in the people's past.[149]

Yet the past the Chronicler presents has a particularly precise focus: despite setting his history within a genealogical context beginning with Adam, the story passes fleetingly over foundation stories such as the call to Abraham, the Exodus, settlement in the land, and the period of the Judges.[150] Instead, the Chronicler concentrates upon the unique role of the Jerusalem temple cult as the expression of God's relationship with his people. The central place of the Davidic monarchy within this schema is firmly established in David's crucial role in the organizing of the temple and its worship,[151] and consequently reaffirmed throughout the story, thereby emphasizing the continued legitimacy of the Davidic dynasty further. Mathys observes, "Once the Davidic monarchy has been installed, the temple constructed, and the cult accommodated, nothing more of fundamental importance occurs".[152]

The role of the Northern Kingdom also appears unimportant in Chronicles. Though this has been interpreted in a variety of ways,[153] this feature of Chronicles essentially reflects the Chronicler's view that the

---

Berossos; cf. Hoglund, "Chronicler as Historian", 19-29; P. Welten, *Geschichte und Geschichtsdarstellung in den Chronikbüchern* (Neukirchen-Vluyn: Neukirchener Verlag, 1973), 199-200. See also M.J. Selman, *1 Chronicles* (TOTC; Leicester: Inter-Varsity Press, 1994), 65-75.

149 Japhet, *I & II Chronicles*, 49.

150 Mathys, "1 and 2 Chronicles", 267.

151 See further H.G.M. Williamson, "The Temple in the Books of Chronicles", in W. Horbury (ed.), *Templum Amicitiae: Essays on the Second Temple Presented to Ernst Bammel* (JSNTSup 48; Sheffield: JSOT Press, 1991), 15-31.

152 Mathys, "1 and 2 Chronicles", 267.

153 See for example the discussions in Japhet, *Ideology of the Book of Chronicles*, 308-324, 325-334; Williamson, *1 and 2 Chronicles*, 24-26; *idem.*, *Israel in the Books of Chronicles*, 87-140; H.H. Rowley, "Sanballat and the Samaritan Temple", *BJRL* 38 (1955-56), 166-198; R.L. Braun, "A Reconsideration of the Chronicler's Attitude toward the North", *JBL* 96 (1977), 59-62; R.J. Coggins, "The Old Testament and Samaritan Origins", *ASTI* 6 (1967-68), 35-42; F.M. Cross, "Aspects of Samaritan and Jewish History in Late Persian and Hellenistic Times", *HTR* 59 (1966), 201-211; G.H. Jones, *1 & 2 Chronicles* (OTG; Sheffield: JSOT Press, 1993), 49-51, 99-103.

Davidic monarchy is the only theologically legitimate monarchy, therefore the Northern Kingdom is illegitimate and hence unimportant.[154] The most telling illustration of this is the Chronicler's fleeting reference to the fall of the North (2 Chr. 30:6-9) in comparison with the lengthy treatise of Kings (2 Kgs 17). Yet despite this apparent disregard for the Northern Kingdom, the Chronicler recognizes the heritage of the Northern tribes as "Israelites", and thus crucially allows for the rehabilitation of the Northern peoples on the proviso that they accept the Jerusalem temple as the locus of the one legitimate cult of YHWH.[155] Consequently, this has interesting implications for the Chronicler's portrayal of Manasseh.

Like the Kings narrative about the reign of Manasseh, the Chronicler's account of Manasseh is heavily stylized, reflecting the narrator's key theological themes.[156] The narrative falls into contrasting halves: the first, 2 Chr. 33:1-9, depicts Manasseh the reprobate; the second, 33:10-20 portrays Manasseh the repentant.[157]

Translation: 2 Chr. 33:1-20

1 Manasseh was twelve years old when he became king and he reigned fifty-five years in Jerusalem. 2 And he did evil in the eyes of YHWH just like the abhorrent practices of the nations whom YHWH had dispossessed before the Israelites.

3 He rebuilt the high places which his father Hezekiah had broken down; he erected altars[158] for (the) Baʿals[159] and he made *asheroth*.[160] He bowed down to all the Host of Heaven and worshipped them 4 and he built altars in the House of YHWH of which YHWH had said, "In Jerusalem shall be my Name forever".[161] 5 And he built altars to all the Host of Heaven in the two courtyards of the House of YHWH; 6 and he[162] made his sons[163] pass over in the fire in the Valley of Ben Hinnom[164] and he

---

154 See for example Japhet, *I & II Chronicles*, 17; Jones, *1 & 2 Chronicles*, 49-51.
155 See for example Japhet, *Ideology of the Book of Chronicles*, 308-324; Mathys, "1 and 2 Chronicles", 268
156 Lowery, *Reforming Kings*, 185.
157 W. Johnstone, *1 and 2 Chronicles,* vol. 2, 222.
158 MT מזבחות, "altars"; LXX reads στηλας, "monuments".
159 MT has a singular form in 2 Kgs 21:3.
160 MT has a singular form in 2 Kgs 21:3.
161 לעולם does not occur in 2 Kgs 21:4.
162 והוא העביר may be intentionally more emphatic than the use of והעביר in 2 Kgs 21:6.
163 Syr. has a singular, as does MT 2 Kgs 21:6.
164 בני בן הנם does not occur in MT 2 Kgs 21:6.

practiscd soothsaying and divining and sorcery[165] and he produced an ancestral ghost and Knowers.

7 And he set the image of the idol[166] which he had made in the House of God[167] of which God had said to David and to his son Solomon, "In this House and in Jerusalem, which I have chosen out of all the tribes of Israel, I will set my Name forever, 8 and I will not again remove[168] the foot of Israel from upon[169] the land that I appointed[170] to your fathers[171] if only they will be vigilant to do all that I commanded them, that is, according to all the Law and the statutes and the ordinances (given) through the hand of Moses." 9 But Manasseh misled Judah and the inhabitants of Jerusalem to do more evil than the nations whom YHWH destroyed before the Israelites. 10 And YHWH spoke to Manasseh and to his people but they did not pay attention.

11 And so YHWH brought in upon them the commanders of the army of the King of Assyria and they captured Manasseh with hooks and they bound him with (fetters of) bronze[172] and took him to Babylon. 12 And when he was in distress he begged the favour[173] of YHWH his god and he humbled himself greatly before the god of his fathers 13 and he prayed to him and he entreated him and (YHWH) heard his supplication and he returned him to Jerusalem to his kingdom and Manasseh (then) knew that YHWH was God.

14 Afterwards he built an outer wall for the City of David west of Gihon in the valley and for the entrance into the Fish Gate and around Ophel and raised it exceedingly (high) and he set commanders of the army in all the fortified cities in

---

165 וכשף does not occur in MT 2 Kgs 21:6.

166 הסמל, "the idol", appears to stand in place of MT 2 Kgs 21:7 האשרה, "the Asherah"; cf. Williamson, *1 and 2 Chronicles*, 391; G.W. Ahlström, *Royal Administration and National Religion in Ancient Palestine* (SHANE 1; Leiden: Brill, 1982), 76, n. 3.

167 On the Chronicler's use of the divine name אלהים see Japhet, *Ideology of the Book of Chronicles*, 11-41.

168 סור (*hiphil*), "remove"; compare נוד (*hiphil*), "cause to wander", in 2 Kgs 21:8.

169 על does not occur in 2 Kgs 21:8, which has only מן.

170 העמדתי, "I appointed", cf. MT 2 Kgs 21:8, נתתי, "I gave"; reflected in LXX, Syr., Vulg.

171 אבתיכם is syntactically clumsy, given that Israel is referred to in the third person singular, and differs from 2 Kgs 21:8 which reads אבותם, "their fathers" (reflected in LXX, Syr. and Vulg.). Theologically, אבתיכם may be intended to convey a stronger attachment to the land (so Japhet, *I & II Chronicles*, 1007-1008).

172 MT נחשתים and נחושתים. S. Dalley ("Yabâ, Atalyā and the Foreign Policy of Late Assyrian Kings", *SAAB* 12 [1998], 83-98), notes that an Akkadian equivalent to נחתם could be rendered "spittle", and that verbs of binding may be associated with bewitching, leaving open the possibility that Manasseh was enticed in this manner (93). In support of this, she observes that rituals involving sympathetic magic formed a part of oath-taking ceremonies, the implication being that in his captive state, Manasseh may have sworn an oath of obedience to the Assyrian king before being restored to his throne.

173 Cf. 2 Chr. 7:14.

Judah. 15 And he put away the foreign gods and the idol from the House of YHWH
and all the altars which he had built on the Mountain of the House of YHWH and in
Jerusalem and he threw them outside the city. 16 And he built[174] the Altar of YHWH
and he offered upon it sacrifices of peace and thanksgiving and he told Judah to serve
YHWH the God of Israel. 17 However the people were still sacrificing at the high
places, but only to YHWH their god.

18 And the rest of the deeds of Manasseh, and his prayer to his god, and the words
of the seers who spoke to him in the name of YHWH the God of Israel, behold, they
are in the Annals of the Kings of Israel; 19 and his prayer and his entreaty to God, and
all his sin and his unfaithfulness, and the sites on which he built high places and set
up the *asherim* and the images, before he humbled himself, behold, they are written in
the Words of the Seers.[175]

20 And Manasseh slept with his fathers and he was buried in his house[176] and
Amon his son reigned after him.

As Japhet comments, the Chronicler's reworking of Kings' regnal account of
Manasseh is essentially evident in the loss of the "absolute one-sidedness" of
the portrayal of Manasseh in 2 Kgs 21.[177] Yet Manasseh's repentance and
reform is surprisingly not anticipated in the regnal introduction. Rather, the
first half of the Chronicler's account (33:1-9) appears to follow that of Kings
almost exactly. However, there are some interesting differences which
contribute to the Chronicler's distinctive portrayal of Manasseh.

One of the most notable differences is that the Chronicler does not refer
to the Queen Mother at all. Moreover, from this point on, the Chronicler
ceases to refer to any Queen Mother. Johnstone suggests that the Chronicler
has referred only to those Queen Mothers who appear to have been native-
born in order to prevent his audience from blaming the queens for exerting
foreign influences within the Judahite cult.[178] Similarly, McKay, followed by
Williamson, argues that the mothers of Manasseh, Amon and Josiah are non-

---

174 Reading ויבן (K), rather than ויבן (Q).

175 MT חוזי, "Hozai", or "my seer", but LXX suggests החזים, leading some to conclude that
the original text may have read חוזיו, "his seers", the final ו having been lost through
haplography; cf. E.L. Curtis and A.A. Madsen, *A Critical and Exegetical Commentary
on the Books of Chronicles* (ICC; Edinburgh: T&T Clark, 1910), 500; Williamson, *1 and
2 Chronicles*, 395. However, in arguing that v. 19 is a later gloss, Japhet (*I & II
Chronicles*, 1012) suggests that the proper name "Hozai" reflects דברי החזים in v. 18,
which was mistakenly read by the glossator as the title of a prophetic work; see further
Schniedewind, "Source Citations", 459.

176 MT ביתו; some commentators choose to read with 2 Kgs 21:18, בגן ביתו.

177 Japhet, *I & II Chronicles*, 1001.

178 Johnstone, *1 and 2 Chronicles*, vol. 2, 15.

Judahites, thus their names are omitted from the Chronicler's regnal accounts so they cannot be held responsible for introducing foreign cults.[179] However, in the case of Manasseh's mother, this is pure conjecture, for there is nothing within the biblical accounts to suggest that she was foreign.[180] Rather, the biblical material would suggest the opposite, for Manasseh's mother is named Hephzibah (2 Kgs 21:1) which means "my delight is in her", a name which occurs only here and in Isa. 62:4, in which YHWH employs it as an alternative name for Zion.[181] Given that the Chronicler does not name the mothers of any of Manasseh's successors, it may be either that there is nothing of particular theological significance in this apparent omission, or that this detail was not included in his *Vorlage*.[182]

Though the Chronicler's list of Manasseh's cult crimes initially appears to duplicate that in Kings, a closer examination reveals there are some significant differences. Of initial interest is the apparent pluralization of cult crimes in verse 3: Manasseh erects altars to the Baʿals and makes *asherim* (the text has the alternative form אשרות), whereas the Manasseh of Kings builds altars to Baʿal alone, and makes just one *asherah* in the equivalent verse. As Williamson comments, it may be that the Chronicler seeks to heighten Manasseh's apostasy in this way.[183] Similarly, the charge of child sacrifice in verse 6 also appears to be worsened in the pluralization of the crime, for Manasseh sacrifices more than one son. The Chronicler locates the sacrifice in the Valley of Ben Hinnom, a detail unmentioned in 2 Kgs 21:6 but occurring in the Kings' account of Josiah's reform in 23:10. Moreover, Manasseh's divination practices are also intensified in the addition of a third

---

179 The Chronicler omits any reference to the Asherah-worshipping Maacah, the mother of Asa (2 Chr. 14:1-16 cf. 1 Kgs 15:9-24). Cf. McKay, *Religion in Judah*, 23-25; Williamson, *1 and 2 Chronicles*, 390; *contra* Japhet, *I & II Chronicles*, 1004.

180 As noted above, the Kings Writer provides neither her patronym nor her place of origin.

181 B. Halpern ("The New Names of Isaiah 62:4: Jeremiah's Reception in the Restoration and the Politics of 'Third Isaiah'", *JBL* 117 [1998], 623-643) suggests that the prophet deliberately selects the name of Manasseh's mother in his renaming of Zion as a part of setting up an elaborate pun founded upon the monarchic association of the city with the queen mother.

182 Cf. S.L. McKenzie, *The Chronicler's Use of the Deuteronomistic History* (HSM 33; Atlanta: Scholars Press, 1984), 174-175; Barnes, *Studies in the Chronology*, 141-142.

183 Williamson, *1 and 2 Chronicles*, 390. Note however the equally reasonable suggestion that the pluralization of Manasseh's cult crimes may reflect their generalization, rather than intensification, at the hands of the Chronicler; cf. Smelik, "Portrayal of King Manasseh", 174 n. 147, and bibliography cited there.

crime of practising sorcery (קשׁף) to the charges of soothsaying and divination in 2 Chr. 33:6, an addition which parallels the charges more closely with Deut. 18:10.[184]

In contrast to the Kings' account of Manasseh, the Chronicler's portrayal does not parallel Manasseh with Ahab. Given the significance of this ideologically-motivated comparison for the Kings Writer, its absence within the Chronicler's account is notable. Though the Chronicler exhibits only a limited interest in the Northern kings, three Judahite monarchs are compared with their Northern counterparts: Jehoram and Ahaziah are accused of walking in the ways of the House of Ahab[185] and Jehoram and Ahaz are accused of walking in the ways of the kings of Israel.[186] All of these comparisons are perhaps best understood as an echo of the Chronicler's *Vorlage*.[187] Yet it is thus surprising that Manasseh's explicit comparison with Ahab in 2 Kgs 21 is disregarded by the Chronicler. Several suggestions have been offered: perhaps the Chronicler considers Ahab's influence to have ceased by the time of Joash (2 Chr. 24);[188] alternatively, in his intensification of Manasseh's sins in verse 3, the Chronicler diminishes the parallel between Ahab and Manasseh, thereby rendering it redundant;[189] perhaps the Chronicler simply perceives the comparison with Ahab to be immaterial to his portrayal of Manasseh, particularly in view of the reference to Ahab's sin in connection with Jehoram and Ahaziah[190], who are, respectively, husband and son to Ahab's daughter Athaliah; or perhaps the parallelling of Ahab and Manasseh is unhelpful because the Chronicler does not include an extensive account of Ahab's reign in his story.[191] Indeed, the Chronicler's negative attitude towards the Northern kings is neither as expansive nor as vitriolic as that of the Kings Writer.[192] Thus the parallelling of Manasseh and Ahab

---

184 Japhet, *I & II Chronicles*, 1006.
185 2 Chr. 21:6, 13 (Jehoram); 22:3, 4 (Ahaziah).
186 2 Chr. 21:13; 28:2.
187 See 2 Kgs 8:18, 27; 16:3.
188 Johnstone, *1 and 2 Chronicles*, Vol. 2, 223.
189 McKay, *Religion in Judah*, 91; Williamson, *1 and 2 Chronicles,* 390.
190 Japhet, *I & II Chronicles*, 1006.
191 Curtis and Madsen, *Chronicles*, 497.
192 The Chronicler's limited interest in the illegitimate Northern kings is governed only by those occasions in his story when they come into contact with their legitimate, Southern counterparts. As Jones comments, "Ties and alliances, clashes and war, brought the two kingdoms into contact, and it is only because they could be introduced in such a context that these kings of the northern kingdom have been mentioned." (*1 & 2 Chronicles,* 50-

cannot have the same polemical impact within the Chronicler's narrative as it does within Kings, and therefore does not feature within the portrayal of Manasseh in Chronicles.[193] However, the apparent censoring of Ahab from the Chronicler's portrayal of Manasseh renders Ahaz's explicit comparison with the kings of Israel all the more surprising, as the reader would expect either Ahaz's comparison with the Northern kings to be eliminated altogether, or the same accusation to be levelled at Manasseh. However, the absence of any comparison with Northern kings within the Manasseh account is essentially founded upon the fact that, within Chronicles, Manasseh is not the worst of all Judahite kings; rather, that role is played by Ahaz. Not only does Ahaz commit more cult crimes than Manasseh, but in receiving military punishment at the instigation of YHWH, he does not repent, instead he sacrifices to the gods of Damascus and requests help from the Assyrian king (2 Chr. 28).[194] This stands in contrast to Manasseh, whom in punishment duly repents. In the Chronicler's eyes then, Ahaz is the worst of all Judahite kings, and thus merits the accusation that he walked in the ways of the kings of Israel.

Though there are some differences between the two accounts of Manasseh's cult crimes, the disobedience of Judah and Jerusalem is attested within the narrative, yet the ultimate responsibility for the people's sin remains with Manasseh (v. 9). However, the Chronicler's radical departure from the account in Kings transforms the characterization of Manasseh. As discussed above, the Kings Writer appears to leave a loose theological end hanging in his portrayal of Manasseh, for the archvillain of the Davidic

---

51). This stands in contrast to the Northern Kingdom's primary role as the "foreign" antagonist to Judah within Kings, as shall be discussed in 1.3.

193 B.E. Kelly (*Retribution and Eschatology in Chronicles* [JSOTSup 211; Sheffield: Sheffield Academic Press, 1996], 222), asserts that the Chronicler's presentation of Manasseh is instead modelled upon the idolatrous Davidic king Ahaz (2 Chr. 28:2-4), whose crimes are also emphasized in their apparent pluralization. However, though this is possible, Ahaz is not mentioned explicitly within the Chronicler's account of Manasseh, whereas Ahab is referred to within the presentation of Manasseh in Kings.

194 See further K.A.D. Smelik, "The Representation of King Ahaz in 2 Kings 16 and 2 Chronicles 28", in J.C. de Moor (ed.), *Intertextuality in Ugarit and Israel: Papers read at the Tenth Joint Meeting of the Society for Old Testament Study and Het Oudtestamentisch werkgezelschap in Nederland en Belgie (Oxford 1997)* (OTS 40; Leiden: Brill, 1998), 143-185; P.R. Ackroyd, "The Biblical Interpretation of the Reigns of Ahaz and Hezekiah", in W.B. Barrick and J.R. Spencer (eds.), *In the Shelter of Elyon: Essays on Ancient Palestinian Life and Literature in Honour of G. W. Ahlström* (JSOTSup 31; Sheffield: JSOT Press, 1984), 247-259. Note also the useful chart comparing the Chronicler's portrayal of the sins of Manasseh and the sins of Ahaz in Smelik, "Portrayal of King Manasseh", 183.

monarchy is not seen to have received any personal punishment throughout his long reign, even though he is held responsible for the divine punishment wrought upon Judah. Consequently, the Chronicler seems to redress this apparent imbalance of divine justice, demonstrating Manasseh's personal and immediate punishment for his crimes in verse 11:

> And YHWH spoke to Manasseh and to his people, but they did not pay attention. And so YHWH brought in upon them the commanders of the army of the King of Assyria and they captured Manasseh with hooks and they bound him with (fetters of) bronze and took him to Babylon.

The theological motif of immediate and direct retribution plays a vital role within the Chronicler's history.[195] As Smelik observes, this results in a more specific appraisal of each king than is found in Kings: for example, in 1 Kgs 15:23 Asa is diseased in his feet, despite his piety; in 2 Chr. 16:7-12, Asa is plagued with the illness because he imprisons a prophet and disobeys YHWH. Similarly, though Uzziah of 2 Kgs 15:3 is a pious king, he becomes leprous; in 2 Chr. 26:16-21, Uzziah rebukes and disobeys YHWH's priest, and thus becomes a leper.[196] Thus for the Chronicler, Manasseh's cult crimes are punished in his capture and brief exile. Moreover, the threat of impending national destruction is also averted because the king himself is punished. The Chronicler's Manasseh is the most thorough and effective illustration of a repeated ideological schema pervading the Chronicler's history, in which sin and punishment are closely aligned. Other examples include the explanation of the fall of Saul (1 Chr. 10:13-14), the disobedience of Rehoboam (2 Chr. 12:1-8) and the story of Hezekiah's illness (2 Chr. 32:24-26; cf. 2 Kgs 20:1-19; Isa 38–39).

However, establishing theological parity is not the Chronicler's primary motivation for his exiling of Manasseh. As Williamson points out, the Chronicler makes no explicit reference to the idea that Manasseh's capture is a punishment for his sins, nor that his long reign is a reward for his

---

195 For a survey and critique of research into the Chronicler's key theme of divine retribution, see Kelly, *Retribution and Eschatology*, 29-45; see also Japhet, *Ideology of the Book of Chronicles*, 165-176; Williamson, *1 and 2 Chronicles*, 31-33. For further discussion of the issue of longevity, see A. Malamat, "Longevity: Biblical Concepts and some Ancient Near Eastern Parallels", in H. Hirsch and H. Hunger (eds.), *Vorträge gehalten auf der 28. Recontre Assyriologique Internationale am Wein, 6-10 Juli 1981* (CRRAI 28/AfOB 19; Horn: F. Berger & Söhne, 1982), 215-224.

196 Smelik, "Portrayal of King Manasseh", 179-181.

subsequent repentance.[197] Moreover, if this were the primary reason behind the Chronicler's transformation of the Manasseh story of Kings, would it not have been easier for him simply to alter the length of the king's reign?[198] Though several scholars have attempted to demonstrate the historicity of the exile of Manasseh, or at least to identify some small kernel of historical probability underlying the story, their arguments are not convincing.[199] Indeed, for these scholars a particularly problematic element of the Chronicler's account is Manasseh's exile to Babylon, rather than to Nineveh, the royal seat of Assyrian imperial power. However, this problem is eradicated in the recognition that the Chronicler's Manasseh functions as a direct symbol of the punished, repentant, restored and newly-blessed Israel.[200] In stating that the Assyrians bound Manasseh in (fetters of) bronze and took him to Babylon (33:11), the Chronicler intentionally anticipates the account of Jehoiakim's capture and exile during the Babylonian conquest of Judah in 36:6. Moreover, both texts recall the description of Zedekiah's Babylonian capture and exile in Kings, who is likewise described as being bound in (fetters of) bronze and taken to Babylon (2 Kgs 25:7).[201] Thus in composing his account of the capture and exile of Manasseh, the Chronicler is keen to draw a direct parallel with the Babylonian exile some generations later. Indeed, this is made explicit in the anachronistic reference to Babylon as the place of Manasseh's exile. Manasseh's Babylonian exile is thus not coincidental. Rather, it is a fictitious theological device, engineered to cast

---

197 Williamson, *1 and 2 Chronicles,* 393.

198 Japhet recognizes that the Chronicler could either account for Manasseh's long reign or shorten it, yet comments: "Although the latter would involve only a negligible literary and textual change, the Chronicler never avails himself of this expedient, and systematically refrains from tampering with these hard-core chronological data, even in the face of the most embarrassing theological questions" (*I & II Chronicles,* 1002). For a discussion of the Chronicler's literary rather than "historical" use of dates see M. Cogan, "The Chronicler's Use of Chronology as Illuminated by Neo-Assyrian Royal Inscriptions", in J.H. Tigay (ed.), *Empirical Models for Biblical Criticism* (Philadelphia: University of Pennsylvania Press, 1985), 197-209.

199 See the discussion in 2.3 below.

200 R. Mosis, *Untersuchungen zur Theologie des chronistischen Geschichtswerkes* (Freiburg: Herder, 1973), 192-194; Williamson, *1 and 2 Chronicles,* 389-390; Kelly, *Retribution and Eschatology,* 223; Schniedewind, "Prophets and Prophecy in Chronicles", in Graham, Hoglund, McKenzie, *Chronicler as Historian,* 204-224; Schniedewind, "Source Citations", 451-455.

201 Cf. Jer. 39:7; 52:11. See also Schniedewind, "Source Citations", 452; Johnstone, *1 and 2 Chronicles,* vol. 2, 227; Williamson, *1 and 2 Chronicles,* 393.

Manasseh as the paradigm for the restored Israel. The Chronicler seeks to demonstrate to his audience that despite their sinful cult crimes of the past, Israel's humbling and repentance can indeed lead to divine forgiveness and restoration. This pattern of sin-repentance-forgiveness complements the Chronicler's fondness for reversing the fortunes of his characters. As Japhet observes, the reigns of Rehoboam, Joash, Amaziah and Uzziah are all composed of two opposite periods in which the king is transformed from a good monarch into a bad monarch. In the case of Manasseh, this is itself reversed.[202]

Consequently, the Chronicler's repentant and restored Manasseh carries out a cult reform, joining the Chronicler's other reforming monarchs: Jehoshaphat, Jehoash, Hezekiah and Josiah. Moreover, unlike the Manasseh of Kings, who is the "destructor" of Judah, the Chronicler's Manasseh is the "constructor" of Judah: the emphasis upon Manasseh's building projects and military fortifications are, for the Chronicler, appropriate and important activities for a blessed Davidic monarch (33:14).[203] Another essential task of the blessed Davidic king is religious administration, which the restored Manasseh undertakes piously, directing his subjects accordingly: he purges the cult, builds an altar of YHWH upon which he offers sacrifices, and instructs the people to serve YHWH (33:15-16). The Chronicler's account of Manasseh's cult reform is expressed in general terms, and not all of his cult crimes are remedied.[204] Indeed, none of the crimes of verse 6 are addressed in this brief account of Manasseh's purge.[205] Moreover, the claim that Manasseh's son Amon worshipped all the idols that his father had made (v. 22) could contradict the Chronicler's assertion that Manasseh destroyed his foreign gods and images. Yet the measured tone of the acknowledgement that the people continued to use the *bamoth* to worship YHWH alone maintains the

---

202 Japhet, *I & II Chronicles*, 1001.

203 Johnstone, *1 and 2 Chronicles*, Vol. 2, 227; see further Welten, *Geschichte und Geschichtsdarstellung*, 31-34, 72-75; Japhet, *Ideology of the Book of Chronicles*, 428-444; Williamson, *1 and 2 Chronicles*, 240-242; E. Ben Zvi, "The Chronicler as Historian: Building Texts", in Graham, Hoglund and McKenzie, *Chronicler as Historian*, 132-149.

204 As Halpern observes ("Why Manasseh is Blamed", 506), the ambiguous accusation that Manasseh shed innocent blood goes unmentioned, and hence unreversed, in Chronicles.

205 Nor are they remedied elsewhere in the Chronicler's story.

expediency of Manasseh's religious authority whilst allowing for Josiah's now limited cult reforms.[206]

In employing his usual notice of the burial place of the king, the Chronicler offers a final theological comment at the close of his regnal account of Manasseh. In deference to his rehabilitated Manasseh, the Chronicler's burial notice deviates from Kings' insistent emphasis that Manasseh was dislocated from the ancestral cult by means of burial in the "Garden of Uzza". Thus instead of following his presumed *Vorlage*, the Chronicler simply concludes with the neutral statement that Manasseh "slept with his ancestors" and was buried "in his palace" (v. 20), reflecting Manasseh's reign as a period of both deliberate idolatry and pious reform.[207]

The Chronicler's portrayal of Manasseh is thus a carefully balanced theological paradigm, designed to encourage and direct his audience that YHWH will forgive and rehabilitate even the most sinful if they humble themselves and beg his help. There is no need for Manasseh to be held responsible for the destruction of Judah and the exile of her people: for the Chronicler, sins are punished immediately, and the focus of his history is not the exile, but the future of his "Temple community".[208] Therefore Manasseh is held accountable only for his own behaviour in his own time. Moreover, the rehabilitation of Manasseh may also function as a realistic (rather than idealistic) symbol of the rehabilitation of the Davidic monarchy and its descendants within the eyes of certain sections of the post-exilic community.[209] As a biblical king, the Chronicler's Manasseh is thus a colourful personality. Yet as an ideological motif, the figure of Manasseh in

---

206 Josiah's climactic role within Kings is depreciated considerably within Chronicles. Though he remains an important figure, he is theologically eclipsed by Hezekiah, who assumes the hero's role in the eyes of the Chronicler; see further Smelik, "Portrayal of King Manasseh", 177, 185-186.

207 *Pace* Japhet (*I & II Chronicles*, 1012-13), who asserts that Manasseh's burial place indicates an historical change in the location of the royal tombs, and Williamson (*1 and 2 Chronicles*, 395), who in following McKay's proposal that the "Garden of Uzza" in 2 Kgs 21:18 refers to a cult site dedicated to an Arabian deity, suggests that the Chronicler deletes this reference to the garden in conformity with his positive appraisal of Manasseh; so too Johnstone, *1 and 2 Chronicles*, Vol. 2, 229.

208 See also Halpern, "Why Manasseh is Blamed", 474-485; Smelik, "Portrayal of King Manasseh", 175, 187.

209 See further Albertz, *A History of Israelite Religion*, vol. 2, 554; cf. D.F. Murray, "Dynasty, People, and the Future: The Message of Chronicles", *JSOT* 58 (1993), 71-92; Japhet, *Ideology of the Book of Chronicles*, 460-491, 493-504.

Chronicles is as one-dimensional as that of Kings, for despite the major difference between the two accounts, the character of Manasseh functions paradigmatically in both Kings and Chronicles. As Auld comments:

> The doomed Manasseh of the Book of Kings is quite as representative of the nation and especially of the kings of Judah in that book as Chronicles' penitent and restored Manasseh is of the other book.[210]

1.3 The Scapegoating of Manasseh

Having examined the biblical traditions concerning King Manasseh of Judah, it is apparent that both the Kings Writer and the Chronicler "hijack" this figure as a vehicle for their own ideological and theological purposes. The Chronicler adapts the Manasseh tradition of Kings, transforming its paradigmatic portrayal of the most dangerous threat to orthodox YHWH-worship into the model of continuing hope for the newly-restored people of YHWH.

For the Kings tradition holding Manasseh responsible for the fall of Judah, Manasseh is a scapegoat.[211] Lasine draws attention to Girard's sociological theory of the "anti-sovereign", which is attractive in view of the Kings Writer's characterization of Manasseh.[212] Girard explains that communities often regain stability and coherence during political and religious crises by unanimously selecting a scapegoat whom all can affirm to be the locus of guilt.[213] Lasine makes the valuable point that in narrative terms, this sociological theory can be seen, for example, in modern detective stories: a fictional villain is responsible for crime and disorder, not the prevailing social structure of which *the reader* is a part. The fictional villain thus functions as a scapegoat for the real audience.[214] In this way, all factions within the group behind the scapegoating of Manasseh, "the people", the

---

210 Auld, *Kings Without Privilege*, 80.
211 Lasine, "Manasseh as Villain", 166-167; Sweeney, *King Josiah*, 52; see also McKenzie, *Trouble with Kings*, 142-143.
212 Lasine, "Manasseh as Villain", 176-178.
213 R. Girard, *Violence and the Sacred* (trans. P. Gregory; Baltimore: Johns Hopkins University Press, 1977), 77-78, 96-99, 107-109, 302-306.
214 Lasine, "Manasseh as Villain", 174-175.

literate elite and other community leaders, could avoid the heavy burden of guilt if they could agree that a specific individual from a distant generation was to blame for their crisis situation. Thus on one level, the accusation that Manasseh "shed innocent blood" (2 Kgs 21:16; 24:4) may be intentionally vague, functioning as an ideological device designed to scapegoat Manasseh further, for as Lasine explains:

> These texts allow the audience to identify with their innocent ancestors whose blood was shed by Manasseh, and hence to view themselves as secondary victims of the evil king ... For an audience coping with catastrophe and exile, a royal scapegoat-villain provides a more comforting explanation for their plight than one based on the assumption that they and their ancestors are fundamentally corrupt.[215]

The total absence of Assyria within the Kings story after Hezekiah's reign also contributes to the scapegoating of Manasseh, for his cult crimes are presented as his own innovations, rather than as symbols of Assyrian vassalage.[216] As Barrick observes, "the Manasseh of Kings lives in a world without Assyria, and in that world his religious 'reform', the anti-type of Josiah's, is the product solely of his own religious perversity".[217]

However, the portrayal of Manasseh as the archvillain of Judah functions very differently for the Chronicler. He is not interested in "scapegoating" the king; indeed, his Manasseh account lacks any reference to the shedding of innocent blood. Absent also are the explicit comparisons with Ahab. Instead the Chronicler utilizes the imperial presence of Assyria for his own theological purpose. The Chronicler's Manasseh is not a scapegoat for his audience, but serves instead as a paradigm for them. It is the humbling of Manasseh and YHWH's subsequent forgiveness, restoration and blessing of the repentant king that interests the Chronicler, intimating to his audience that despite the past, they too can repent and be forgiven and restored. However, despite his theological rehabilitation, it is essential to note that the Chronicler's portrait of the repentant Manasseh necessarily remains wholly dependent upon Kings' portrayal of Manasseh as the most villainous of all kings.

But one important question demands further attention: why does the Kings Writer select Manasseh to play the role of the scapegoat, rather than

---

215 Lasine, "Manasseh as Villain", 166-167.
216 See also Sweeney, *King Josiah*, 54.
217 Barrick, *King and the Cemeteries*, 6.

another monarch? Indeed, blaming one of Josiah's successors could solve some of the tensions concerning Josiah's reform and the irrevocable exile. Moreover, the capture and exile of Jehoahaz (2 Kgs 23:33-34), Jehioachin (24:12-15) and Zedekiah (24:20; 25:6-7) would provide the Kings Writer with the theological scope to scapegoat one—or all—of them, as would Jehioakim's rebellion against Babylon (24:1). Yet the Kings Writer scapegoats a king who lived and died several generations before the disastrous events for which he is held personally responsible.

On a literary level, the majority of commentators offer as their only explanation for Manasseh's vilification the heroic portrayal of Josiah, arguing that Manasseh's idolatry acts as a foil to his grandson's aggressive piety.[218] Yet this explanation is not particularly persuasive: its only merit is the length of Manasseh's reign, which may allow for the speculation that the long period of his idolatry was impossible to remedy within Josiah's shorter reign. Yet alternatively, Amon could have functioned as a suitable foil to Josiah, particularly as his reign is ended with his assassination and a subsequent revolt.[219] Consequently, most scholars account for the vilification of Manasseh by accepting uncritically the portrait of Manasseh within Kings and thus attributing to it a considerable degree of historical reliability. Therefore because Manasseh is portrayed as an idolatrous monarch within Kings, many scholars argue that historically, he must have introduced "foreign" deity-worship into the Jerusalem cult, or have been a violent tyrant, or, less conservatively, Manasseh must have been a fervent supporter of traditional Judahite polytheism.[220]

However, it is not necessary to accept this picture of Manasseh in order to be able to explain why the Kings Writer selects him as his scapegoat. Rather, a far more persuasive explanation lies in the king's name. The name מְנַשֶּׁה is widely held to mean "he who makes forget", a name probably alluding to the death of a prior child,[221] or perhaps attesting that the pain of labour is

---

218 E.g., Sweeney, *King Josiah*, 62, 175; Lowery, *Reforming Kings*, 185; Cogan and Tadmor, *II Kings*, 271.

219 *Pace* Smith ("Veracity of Ezekiel", 14) who suggests that Amon's two year reign is too brief to allow for the possibility that he could be responsible for Josiah's death and the fall of the kingdom.

220 For all these opinions, see 2.3 and 3.2, below.

221 C.H.J. de Geus, "Manasseh (Place)", *ABD*, vol. 4, 494-496; G.J. Wenham, *Genesis 16–50* (WBC 2; Dallas: Word, 1994), 397-398.

forgotten in the joy of birth.[222] A handful of scholars have commented upon
the theological irony of Manasseh's name: according to the biblical
traditions, Manasseh "makes (the people) forget" the law of Moses given to
their ancestors (2 Kgs 21:8,15; 2 Chr. 33:8).[223] But there is a further, more
profound and hitherto unnoticed reason why Manasseh's name facilitates his
scapegoating at the hands of the Kings Writer.

As observed above, the Kings account of Manasseh deliberately parallels
the fall of Judah with the fall of the Northern Kingdom. Consequently, the
role of Manasseh in the punishment of Judah is set alongside the role of
Jeroboam in the events of c. 721 BCE. Both kings are held directly
responsible for the destruction of their kingdoms. Moreover, Manasseh's cult
crimes are explicitly compared with those of Ahab, thereby emphasizing
further the similarities between Manasseh and the worst Northern kings. Thus
as Auld correctly comments, the Kings Writer intends his reader to recognize
Manasseh as "the southern scoundrel dressed in northern colours".[224]
However, this discussion would carry Auld's observation further in
proposing that the Kings Writer deliberately characterizes Manasseh as a
"Northern" type of king because he bears a *Northern* name: Manasseh is the
only biblical king of Judah or Israel to share his name with a Northern tribal-
territory. Thus it is Manasseh's northern name which provokes his portrayal
as a quasi-Northern king and seals his fate as the chosen scapegoat of Kings.
This new proposal demands careful attention.

The biblical story describing Israel as an ethnic body comprising twelve
tribes to whom YHWH gave his land is best understood as a foundation myth,
yet it is a myth lying at the heart of the biblical concept of "Israel".[225]
According to the biblical story of Israel, the tribes became a kingdom united
around the ark of YHWH which King David placed in his capital Jerusalem.
Manasseh was one of the ten tribes located in the north of the land who

---

222 Johnstone, *1 and 2 Chronicles,* vol. 2, 223.
223 Eg. Johnstone, *1 and 2 Chronicles,* vol. 2., 223.
224 Auld, *Kings Without Privilege,* 85. Note also Sweeney's passing comment (*King Josiah,*
    62) that, "Manasseh ... reverts to northern patterns of evil behaviour".
225 See the useful discussion about the twelve tribe system in N.P. Lemche, *The Israelites in
    History and Tradition* (Louisville: Westminster John Knox Press, 1998), 97-107. For a
    sociological exploration of the so-called "tribal" period see J.D. Martin, "Israel as a
    tribal society" in R.E. Clements (ed.), *The World of Ancient Israel: Sociological,
    Anthropological and Political Perspectives* (Cambridge: Cambridge University Press,
    1989), 95-117.

rebelled against the Davidic house and established a rival kingdom with YHWH-sanctuaries of their own. Thus for the Kings Writer, Manasseh is a name inextricably associated with the rebellious, apostate Northern Kingdom. The Kings Writer therefore draws deliberate attention to the name shared by the idolatrous Judahite king and the northern tribe by alluding to the tribal period of Israel within the indictment of King Manasseh: 2 Kgs 21:7-9 describes Manasseh placing the carved image of Asherah in the temple of YHWH in Jerusalem, the place chosen by YHWH "out of all the tribes of Israel"; in verses 8-9 (cf. v. 2) the reader is reminded of YHWH's conditional gift of the land to the tribes:

> "I will no more cause the feet of Israel to wander from the land that I gave to their ancestors, if only they will be vigilant to do all that I commanded them, that is, according to all the Law which my servant Moses commanded them." But they did not listen, and Manasseh misled them so that they did more evil than the nations whom YHWH destroyed before the Israelites.

The judgement oracle of 21:10-15 also alludes to the tribal past in referring to the escape from Egypt: "they have done what is evil in my sight and have provoked me to anger, since the day their ancestors came out of Egypt, even to this day". The allusions to the so-called tribal period of "Israel" within the Manasseh narrative of Kings thus intimate the Kings Writer's intentional connection of the name of the king and the Northern tribal-territory of the same name.

However, the scapegoating of Manasseh on the basis of his Northern name is wholly dependent upon the extensive vilification of the Northern kingdom within Kings. Closer examination of this anti-Northern polemic reveals that it performs a very specific and vital function within the Kings Writer's schematizing of the catastrophes of 597 and 587 BCE and is essential to the pivotal role ascribed to Manasseh within that theological and ideological schema.

Throughout much of the Hebrew Bible, the kingdoms of Israel and Judah are primarily presented as being closely interrelated. The nature of this interrelation receives its most coherent treatment within Kings in its portrayal of the kingdoms as two halves of one whole: Israel and Judah are "sister-states", born of the disintegration of the Davidic-Solomonic kingdom which had emerged from one demographic and cultural body called Israel.

Accordingly, the Kings Writer narrates the stories of the kingdoms alongside each other, thereby emphasizing their close interrelationship.[226] However, this interrelationship harbours a tense ideological negativity, for a distinct anti-Northern polemic pervades Kings.[227] This polemic is most explicitly and systematically articulated in 2 Kgs 17, which is best described as a "theological justification"[228] of the fall of the Northern Kingdom of Israel.[229] This text presents the twin ideological foundations upon which the anti-Northern polemic of Kings is constructed: the first is the explicit portrayal of the separateness of the Israelite and Judahite kingdoms, and the second is the insistence that the possession of YHWH's land is directly related to the cult practices of the people.

Within 2 Kgs 17 the Kings Writer justifies his anti-Northern polemic by appealing to his story of the northern tribes' rejection of the Davidic-Zion monarchy in favour of the kingship of Jeroboam ben Nebat and his royal sponsorship of the YHWH-cults at Bethel and Dan (1 Kgs 12–13). Jeroboam's selection of Bethel and Dan as his kingdom's central YHWH sanctuaries in place of Judahite Jerusalem is judged within Kings as a religious crime against YHWH, a crime perpetuated by successive generations of the people of the kingdom, inevitably leading to the exile of the people of

---

226 Note Linville's assertion (*Israel in the Book of Kings*, 171) that this interwoven history implies that neither Israel nor Judah can really exist without the other.

227 On the presentation of the Northern Kingdom in Kings, see Sweeney, *King Josiah*, 77-92; Brettler, *Creation of History*, 112-134.

228 M. Brettler, "Ideology, History and Theology in 2 Kings XVII 7-23", *VT* 39 (1989), 268-282.

229 For further discussions of this important chapter in Kings, see Hoffmann, *Reform und Reformen*, 127-139; Linville, *Israel in the Book of Kings*, 202-224; P. Viviano, "2 Kings 17: A Rhetorical and Form-Critical Analysis", *CBQ* 49 (1987), 548-559; Cogan and Tadmor, *II Kings*, 195-214; Nelson, *Double Redaction*, 55-62; B. Becking, "From Apostasy to Destruction: A Josianic View on the Fall of Samaria (2 Kings 17, 21-23)", in Vervenne and Lust, *Deuteronomy and Deuteronomic Literature*, 279-297; *idem.*, "From Exodus to Exile: 2 Kgs 17, 7-20 in the Context of Its Co-Text", in G. Galil and M. Weinfeld (eds.), *Studies in Historical Geography and Biblical Historiography Presented to Zecharia Kallai* (VTSup 81; Leiden: Brill, 2000), 215-231; M. Cogan, "Israel in Exile: The View of the Josianic Historian", *JBL* 97 (1978), 40-44; Mayes, *Story of Israel*, 125-127; B. Oded, "2 Kings 17: Between History and Polemic", *Jewish History* 2 (1987), 37-50; S. Talmon, "Polemics and Apology in Biblical Historiography—2 Kings 17:24-41", in *idem.*, *Literary Studies in the Hebrew Bible: Form and Content—Collected Studies* (Leiden: Brill, 1993), 134-159.

the Kingdom of Israel. This is alluded to in 2 Kgs 17:16, and explicitly stated in vv. 21-22:

> When he had torn Israel from the house of David, they made Jeroboam son of Nebat king. Jeroboam drove Israel from following YHWH and made them commit great sin. The people of Israel continued in all the sins that Jeroboam committed; they did not depart from them.

This polemical portrayal of the Kingdom of Israel in this chapter is heightened by the emphasis upon the separateness of rebellious Israel from Judah: "YHWH was very angry with Israel and removed them out of his sight; none was left but the tribe of Judah alone" (17:18). The language of this verse deliberately recalls Kings' account of the division of the kingdoms, in which it is made plain that the continued separateness of Israel and Judah is the direct consequence of Israel's formation of her own kingdom: "So Israel has been in rebellion against the house of David to this day ... There was no one who followed the house of David, except the tribe of Judah alone" (1 Kgs 12:19, 20b).

Closely related to this emphasis upon the separateness of Israel and Judah is a second ideological foundation central to the anti-Northern polemic of 2 Kgs 17. This is the insistence that YHWH exiled the Northern Kingdom as a punishment for following the cult practices of the foreign nations (17:7-9; cf. 11, 15, 22-23). The heavy emphasis upon the idea that foreign cult practices result in the dispossession of the land is a distinctive characteristic of the ideology of separateness that shapes the Kings Writer's definition of "correct" YHWH-worship. The language of 2 Kgs 17 intentionally recalls the prohibitions of Deuteronomy, which is very specific in its ideology of land possession, as illustrated by Deut 18:9-10, 12:

> When you come into the land that YHWH your god is giving you, you must not learn to imitate the abhorrent practices of those nations. No one shall be found among you who makes a son or a daughter pass over in the fire, or who practises divination, or is a soothsayer, or a diviner, or a sorcerer, or who casts spells, or who consults ghosts or spirits, or who seeks oracles from the dead. For whoever does these things is abhorrent to YHWH; it is because of such practices that YHWH your god is driving them out before you.

Thus the text plainly states that because of their abhorrent practices, YHWH cast out the foreign nations and gave the land to the Israelites. The implication of this is therefore clear: if the Israelites imitate the practices of the nations, they too will be cast out of the land. 2 Kgs 17 makes it perfectly plain that this is indeed what has happened to the Northern Kingdom. Verses 7-18 comprise a list of those cult practices committed by the people of the

North, each of which is specifically outlawed within Deuteronomy because they are the cult practices of the nations, and are thus "foreign" to YHWH-worship.

The chapter's emphasis upon the separateness of Israel and Judah may thus be seen as an ideologically-motivated attempt to distance Judah from the quasi-foreign Israel. This anti-Northern polemic reaches its most remarkable expression in the extraordinary claim of 17:19-20 that Israel has not only caused her own exile, but is even responsible for Judah's sin and, by implication, her exile:

> Judah also did not keep the commandments of YHWH their god but walked in the customs that Israel had established. YHWH rejected all the descendants of Israel; he punished them and gave them into the hand of the plunderers, until he had banished them from his presence.

Thus Judah is distanced not only from Israel, but to a certain degree she is also distanced from the responsibility for her own fate in the accusation that Israel introduced the foreign practices that lead inevitably to exile.

It is thus particularly significant that a similar ideological process of separation and distance lies at the heart of the portrayal of King Manasseh in Kings. As previously stated, Manasseh is held personally responsible for the fall and exile of Judah. Given the Kings Writer's ideology of land dispossession, it is unsurprising that the Judahite exile is explained as the direct result of the "foreign" cult practices of Manasseh. It is equally unsurprising that the cult crimes of which Manasseh is accused are virtually identical to those which led to the exile of the Northern Kingdom, rituals which are outlawed in Deuteronomy.[230] The understanding that these outlawed cult practices had already led to the foreign nations' dispossession of the land later inherited by the Israelites is in full view in the introduction to the cult crime list, in which it is stated that Manasseh "did evil in the eyes of YHWH just like the abhorrent practices of the nations whom YHWH had dispossessed before the Israelites" (21:2; cf. 17:8, 11, 15). This is reinforced further by the conclusion to the cult crime list, which magnifies Manasseh's sins in stating that he misled the people so much that they did even more evil than the nations had done (v. 9, cf. 11). Indeed, Manasseh's crimes are so great that not even the cult reforms of the heroic Josiah can avert the

---

230 So Dietrich, *Prophetie und Geschichte*, 45; Brettler, *Creation of History*, 123.

inevitability of the exile, as 23:25-27 asserts. It is thus plain that both 2 Kgs 17 and 21 interpret the loss of the land as the direct result of "foreign" cult practices.[231] Similarly, within both chapters the fall of the Kingdom of Israel is set alongside the fall of Judah (17:18-20; 21:11-13).

In the light of the anti-Northern polemic of 2 Kgs 17 and its emphasis upon the separateness of Israel and Judah, it is reasonable to assert that the Manasseh narrative of Kings is not simply paralleling the fall of the South with that of the North, but is deliberately distancing Judah from direct responsibility for her crimes. Manasseh is intentionally portrayed as behaving like the rebellious and apostate Northern kingdom. Therefore his cult crimes are exactly the same as those attributed to the fallen Northern Kingdom in 2 Kgs 17. In committing these cult crimes the Northern kingdom is thus implicitly understood to be "foreign", and thereby separate and distant from the supposedly orthodox Judahites. Given Manasseh's portrayal as a quasi-Northern king committing cult crimes of the Northern Kingdom and the foreign nations, he too is implicitly presented as "foreign". Thus Judah is effectively distanced from responsibility for her exile in the accusation that Manasseh's "foreign" cult crimes led to the destruction and exile of the kingdom. This way of distancing Judah from direct responsibility for her exile complements the assertion of 17:19-20 which claims that Judah was disobedient and subsequently exiled because she followed the foreign customs which Israel introduced.

Thus Manasseh is scapegoated *because* of his Northern name. The Kings Writer exploits Manasseh's Northern name in order to hold him personally responsible for the destruction of Judah and Jerusalem. In itemizing Manasseh's cult crimes and blaming the king for the resulting exile, the Kings Writer thus poses a simple but powerful rhetorical question: what more could Judah have expected from a quasi-Northern king? In this way, the Kings Writer achieves two important goals: firstly, he distances the Davidic monarchy, to whom the eternity of the dynasty was promised, from being held directly responsible for the exile by casting Manasseh as a typically rebellious, idolatrous "Northern" king. Secondly, Judah is distanced from direct responsibility for the Babylonian catastrophe by placing the blame for the exile solely upon Manasseh: "*Because* King Manasseh of Judah has committed these abhorrent practices ..." the kingdom will fall and her people

---

231 See Schniedewind's useful chart parallelling the cult crimes of the North in 2 Kgs 17 with those of Manasseh in 2 Kgs 21 ("History and Interpretation", 657).

will go into exile. By placing the blame for the fall of the South squarely upon the shoulders of an individual, this accusation, which is repeated throughout Kings and again in Jeremiah, effectively distances Judah from the idolatrous practices of the "Northern" king Manasseh. Thus the ancestors of the Kings Writer and his audience are distanced from the cult crimes prompting the fall of the Judahite kingdom, clearing Judah of direct responsibility, and leaving the "Northern" king Manasseh to take the fall.[232]

1.4 Anti-Manasseh Polemic in the Hebrew Bible

Given the prominent role of Manasseh within both Kings and Chronicles, it is particularly curious that he is mentioned only once by name elsewhere in the Hebrew Bible. The opening verses of Jer. 15 insist upon the irrevocable nature of the impending Babylonian destruction, and, in step with Kings, Manasseh is blamed for the conquest and exile of the people in verse 4:

> And I will make them a horror[233] to all the kingdoms of the earth because of all that[234] Manasseh son of Hezekiah, king of Judah, did in Jerusalem."

The blaming of Manasseh here is unexpected, for within Jeremiah it is usually the collective guilt of the people which is said to have induced the Babylonian destruction.[235] Indeed, many commentators prefer to view the reference to Manasseh and the clause in which it occurs as a secondary addition.[236] Though this is possible, the shared ideological and literary

---

232 As Williamson notes (*1 and 2 Chronicles*, 361), for the Chronicler, the designations "Ephraim and Manasseh" are almost synonymous with the people of the (former) Kingdom of Israel. Consequently, if the Chronicler recognized any significance in Manasseh's name, it may be that in depicting the restoration of the king with a Northern name to Jerusalem, the Chronicler signals that the people of the former Kingdom of Israel can also be restored to Jerusalem.

233 K זְוָעָה, cf. Jer. 24:9; 29:18; 34:17; Isa. 38:19.

234 Reading כל אשר, with Versional support

235 R.P. Carroll, *Jeremiah: A Commentary* (OTL; London: SCM Press, 1986), 321; W.L. Holladay, *Jeremiah 1: A Commentary on the Book of the Prophet Jeremiah, Chapters 1–25* (Hermeneia; Philadelphia: Fortress Press, 1986), 440.

236 E.g., Holladay, *Jeremiah 1*, 426, 440.

affinities of Jeremiah and Kings are widely recognized,[237] and as Carroll comments, the blaming of Manasseh in this text may be suggestive of the settling of an old score.[238] Moreover, the wider context of this verse includes references to other figures from the past, namely Moses and Samuel (15:1), and so the reference to Manasseh is not wholly incongruous here. A secondary addition or not, this brief text exhibits an awareness of the tradition scapegoating Manasseh for the Babylonian destruction and exile, though it does not elaborate on this claim. Though the specific misdeeds of Manasseh are not provided, in referring directly to what Manasseh "did in Jerusalem", this verse may allude to the accusation that Manasseh filled Jerusalem with innocent blood (2 Kgs 21:16; 24:3-4).[239] The fleeting and generalized nature of the accusation that Manasseh is responsible for the provocation of national punishment suggests for many commentators that because Manasseh's crimes were so well known, further elaboration was unnecessary. If so, it is curious that King Manasseh is not mentioned, nor even alluded to, anywhere else in the Hebrew Bible.[240] Indeed, given that Manasseh is presented as the longest reigning of all Israelite and Judahite monarchs, it is particularly surprising that he is not mentioned in any other biblical texts outside of Kings, Chronicles and Jer. 15:4;[241] he is not even referred to in the frequent chronological superscriptions included within

---

237 See the bibliography cited in K.M. O'Connor, "Jeremiah", *OBC*, 487-528.

238 Carroll, *Jeremiah*, 321.

239 Carroll (*Jeremiah*, 321) also appears to make this connection, though he does not state it explicitly.

240 *Pace* B. Oded ("Judah and the Exile", in J.H. Hayes and J.M. Miller [eds.], *Israelite and Judaean History* [London: SCM Press, 1977], 435-488), who suggests that Zeph. 1:4-6; 3:1-4 allude to Manasseh's crimes (452), and W. Dietrich ("1 and 2 Kings", *OBC*, 232-266), who states, "Prophetic resistance to Manasseh's [religious and political] policy is ... made tangible for us through figures such as Nahum and Habakkuk" (262); see further, *idem.*, "Der Eine Gott als Symbol politischen Widerstands: Religion und Politik im Juda des 7. Jahrhunderts", in W. Dietrich and M. A. Klopfenstein, *Ein Gott allein? JHWH-Verehrung und biblischer Monotheismus im Kontext der israelitischen und altorientalischen Religionsgeschichte* (OBO 139; Göttingen: Vandenhoeck and Ruprecht, 1994), 463-490.

241 Noted also by E. Nielsen, "Political Conditions and Cultural Developments in Israel and Judah during the Reign of Manasseh", in *Fourth World Congress of Jewish Studies, Papers*, vol. 1 (Jerusalem: Union of Jewish Studies, 1967), 103-106.

prophetic books.[242] Moreover, if Manasseh was as notorious as the regnal accounts in both Kings and Chronicles insist, or even if he were taken captive as the Chronicler claims, the reader of the Hebrew Bible would expect to find further theological comments about Manasseh and the events of his reign. This remarkable textual silence is perhaps suggestive of the exclusion, or even censorship, of Manasseh from biblical texts. This raises the possibility that alongside the villainous portrayal of Manasseh in Kings, 2 Chr. 33:1-10 and Jer. 15:4 there exists an anti-Manasseh polemic in the Hebrew Bible. In turning to consider the portrayal of other Manassehs in the Hebrew Bible, this possibility is heightened further.

Despite the likelihood that the personal name Manasseh was fairly common, there are very few characters named Manasseh within biblical literature. However, of those who are called Manasseh, the possibility that the name carries polemical undertones appears likely. This would appear to be the case in Judg. 18:30. In this text, the polemical use of the name Manasseh is evident in the Masoretic application of the name to one of the ancestors of the idolatrous Jonathan. As will be argued below, it would appear that the name Moses (משה) has been deliberately distorted into the name Manasseh (מנשה) by means of a superimposed נ, probably in an attempt to distance Moses from the idolatry of his descendant Jonathan.[243]

The biblical portrayal of the eponymous ancestor of the Manasseh tribe may also exhibit indications of an anti-Manasseh polemic. As a reflection of the biblical presentation of Manasseh as the firstborn of Joseph and thus the elder brother of Ephraim,[244] the name Manasseh tends to precede the name Ephraim.[245] However, in several texts this order is often reversed.[246] Though

---

242 Some scholars have used the lack of prophetic opposition to Manasseh in the Hebrew Bible to support the ancient claim that, historically, Manasseh persecuted and killed prophets; see further below, 2.3 and 3.2.

243 See 3.1 below.

244 Gen. 41:50-52; 48:14, 18; Josh. 17:1.

245 E.g., Gen. 46:20; 48:1; Num. 26:28-34; Josh. 14:4; 16:4; 2 Chr. 34:6; cf. Ps. 60:9; cf. 108:9. Manasseh and Ephraim appear only in some of the biblical tribal lists. In his volume *The Tribes of Israel: An Investigation into Some of the presuppositions of Martin Noth's Amphictyony Hypothesis* (Assen and Amsterdam: Van Gorcum, 1976), C.H.J. de Geus argues that lying behind these lists are two tribal systems, one based upon patronyms which includes Joseph and Levi but omit Manasseh and Ephraim, and an older system based on geographical divisions, which omits Levi and divides Joseph into Manasseh and Ephraim. See further N.P. Lemche, *Early Israel: Anthropological and Historical Studies on the Israelite Society before the Monarchy* (VTSup 37; Leiden:

the usurpation of the elder brother by the younger brother is a common biblical motif,[247] the possibility that the reversal of Manasseh and Ephraim is a secondary and deliberate emendation may be attested in Josh. 16 and 17, as De Geus argues.[248] Related to this is a further illustration of the intentional status reversal of Manasseh and Ephraim, the well known story of their blessing by their grandfather Jacob in Gen. 48:8-20. This text seeks to explain why Ephraim receives the blessing of the firstborn which should have been Manasseh's by right of birth, and as such is often regarded as an aetiology reflecting the historical supremacy of Ephraim as the dominant northern territory,[249] or, less frequently, the cultic superiority of Ephraimite Bethel over Manassite Shechem in the premonarchic period.[250] However, recent demographic and archaeological research appears to confirm earlier proposals that the geographical area identified with the tribal territory of Manasseh developed more rapidly and remained more prosperous and powerful than that of Ephraim, indicating that historically, Manasseh was the dominant territory in the North.[251] In view of the strength of this research, the biblical relegation of Manasseh in favour of Ephraim cannot be explained

---

Brill, 1985), 284; cf. A.D.H. Mayes, "The Period of the Judges and the Rise of the Monarchy", in Hayes and Miller, *Israelite and Judaean History*, 285-322. For a more recent discussion of the biblical systems of the twelve tribes, see Z. Kallai, "The Twelve-Tribe System of Israel", *VT* 47 (1997), 53-90.

246 E.g., Gen. 48:5, 8-22; Num. 1:10, 32-35; 2:20; Deut. 34:2; Judg. 12:4.

247 E.g., E. Fox, "Stalking the Younger Brother: Some Models for Understanding a Biblical Motif", *JSOT* 60 (1996), 45-68; see also the literature cited below, 180, n. 156.

248 De Geus, *The Tribes of Israel*, 79-80.

249 E.g., De Geus, "Manasseh", 494; see also A. Alt, "Israels Gaue unter Salomo", *BWAT* 13 (1913), 1-39; cf. B. Mazar, "Die westliche Linie des Meerweges", *ZDPV* 58 (1935), 79-84.

250 E.g., E.C. Kingsbury, "He Set Ephraim Before Manasseh", *HUCA* 38 (1967), 129-136.

251 A. Zertal, "The Heart of the Monarchy: Pattern of Settlement and Historical Considerations of the Israelite Kingdom of Samaria", in A. Mazar (ed.), *Studies in the Archaeology of the Iron Age in Israel and Jordan* (JSOTSup 331; Sheffield: Sheffield Academic Press, 2001), 38-64; *idem.*, "Israel enters Canaan: Following the Pottery Trail", *BAR* 17/5 (1991), 28-50; *idem.*, "'To the Land of the Perizzites and the Giants': On the Israelite Settlement in the Hill-Country of Manasseh", in Na'aman and Finkelstein, *From Nomadism to Monarchy*, 37-70; I. Finkelstein, *The Archaeology of the Israelite Settlement* (Jerusalem: Israel Exploration Society, 1988); Thompson, *Early History*, 221-239; A. Lemaire, "La haute Mesopotamie et l'origine de Bene Jacob", *VT* 34 (1985), 95-101; *idem.*, "Les Bene Jacob", *RB* 85 (1978), 321-337; see also W.F. Albright, "The Site of Tirzah and the topography of Western Manasseh", *JPOS* 11 (1931), 241-251; A. Lemaire, "Aux origines d'Israël: La montagne d'Éphraïm et le territoire de Manassé (XIII-XIC av. J.-C.)", in J. Briend, A. Caquot, H. Cazelles, A. Kempinski, E.-M. Laperrousaz, A. Lemaire, D. Valbelle, J. Yoyotte, *La Protohistoire d'Israël : De l'exode à la monarchie* (Paris: Les Éditions du Cerf, 1990), 183-292.

by the assertion that Ephraim became the superior region. Rather, it may be that the subordination of the Manasseh tribal territory within the biblical stories is a further example of an anti-Manasseh polemic within the Hebrew Bible.

The remaining biblical occurrences of the name Manasseh appear in the Book of Ezra, in which the name appears twice in a long list of returned exiles who are censured by Ezra for marrying foreign women (10:30, 33; cf. 1 Esdr. 9:31, 33). In view of the seemingly intentional association of Manasseh with "foreignness" in Kings, it may initially seem unsurprising that this name should appear in this context. However, little weight can be placed upon this, as several other names with both royal and tribal or patriarchal associations occur within this list,[252] and the fleeting nature of these references precludes any further discussion in this context. But it is worth noting in passing that if this list does contain historical information about the post-exilic community, as many commentators have argued, the continued occurrence of the name Manasseh alongside other patriarchal names may suggest that those members of the community who did not share certain ideological perceptions of what was considered "foreign" (hence their marriages to so-called foreigners), neither adopted the polemical attitude to the name Manasseh, perhaps much like the Chronicler.

Given the evidence examined here, it thus seems probable that a distinct anti-Manasseh polemic pervades the Hebrew Bible. This polemic is to be related to the scapegoating of King Manasseh in 2 Kgs 21:1-18; 23:26-27; 24:3-4 and Jer. 15:4. In reconstructing an historically plausible picture of King Manasseh, his reign and his kingdom, it may be that the origins and function of this biblical anti-Manasseh polemic may be discerned with more precision. It is to this task that the discussion will now turn.

---

252 Cf. J. Blenkinsopp, *Ezra-Nehemiah: A Commentary* (OTL; London: SCM Press, 1988), 199.

2 The Historical Manasseh

In demonstrating the tendentious, ideological and largely created nature of the biblical accounts of King Manasseh, doubt is necessarily cast upon the extent to which these accounts may be employed in the construction of a plausible picture of the historical King Manasseh. In the light of both this observation and the methodological parameters outlined in the Introduction, the construction of a plausible portrait of the historical King Manasseh will be founded upon the primary evidence available to modern scholarship. Essentially, primary evidence directly related to King Manasseh is sparse, comprised as it is of only two references within Assyrian texts, and a possible seal inscription. However, other primary data can be employed, composed of socio-scientific data, including archaeological and artefactual evidence and demographic and settlement patterns, in order to reconstruct the likely geo-political and socio-religious milieu of Manasseh's kingdom. In picturing Manasseh's Judah, it may be that a plausible image of the king will emerge. Moreover, in unpacking the possible historical roots of the ideologies that shape the polemical portrayals of the biblical Manasseh, this image of the historical king may come into sharper focus.

It is clear that the negative portrait of King Manasseh is not only a biblical caricature, but is directly related to the overtly critical—and hostile—presentation of the northern Kingdom of Israel. Investigating the Manasseh of history thus demands a closer look at the relationship of the kingdoms of Israel and Judah, given his portrayal as a quasi-Northen king. It will be argued that this anti-Northern polemic is rooted within the historical separateness of Israel and Judah as neighbouring but essentially unrelated Palestinian territories. Furthermore, it will be proposed that the blackballing of King Manasseh as "foreign" within Kings is closely related to the deliberate distortion of the historical reality of the relationship of Israel and Judah. Moreover, the investigation of the rise of Judah as a fully-blown state and as an Assyrian vassal will suggest that, in contrast to his character in Kings, who caused the ultimate destruction of Judah, the King Manasseh of history may well have masterminded the transformation of his floundering city-state into a strengthened and prospering kingdom.

2.1 The Separateness of Judah and Israel

The frequently hostile presentation of the northern tribes and the Northern
Kingdom within the Hebrew Bible is often held to reflect a pro-Judahite
ideology prompted by the Assyrian conquest and destruction of Samaria in c.
721 BCE. Though the biblical portrayal of the separateness of Judah and
Israel is frequently noted by commentators, the former unity of the kingdoms
under David and Solomon is conventionally assumed.[1] However, in contrast
to this conventional view, it may be that the biblical distinction between
Judah and Israel, and particularly the hostility of the presentation of the
Kingdom of Israel in Kings, is ultimately rooted in the original historical
separateness of Israel and Judah as neighbouring but wholly unrelated
Palestinian territories.

Physical indications of the separateness of Israel[2] and Judah are well-
known. For example, Campbell describes a social and cultural fracture line of
long duration dividing north and south just north of Jerusalem, which is
reflected in settlement patterns.[3] Dever also draws attention to archaeological
signs of the north-south divide:[4] the so-called pillar figurines, inscribed
sheqel-weights and the royal stamped jar handles of late eighth and seventh
centuries which are so prevalent in Judah are rarely found in the north.[5] He
also cites Amiran's classification of Iron Age pottery into northern and

---

1 See the discussions in E. Lipiński, "Juda et 'tout Israël': Analogies et contrastes", in E.
   Lipiński (ed.), *The Land of Israel—Cross-Roads of Civilisations* (OLA 19; Leuven:
   Peeters, 1985), 93-112; E.F. Campbell Jr., "A Land Divided: Judah and Israel from the
   Death of Solomon to the Fall of Samaria", in Coogan, *Biblical World*, 206-241; J.A.
   Soggin, *An Introduction to the History of Israel and Judah* (trans. J. Bowden; third edn;
   London: SCM Press, 1999)., 50-51; Z. Kallai, "Judah and Israel—A Study in Israelite
   Historiography", *IEJ* 28 (1978), 251-261.
2 With regard to the designation "Israel" as the name of the so-called Northern Kingdom,
   note P.R. Davies' passing comment (*In Search of "Ancient Israel"* [JSOTSup 148;
   Sheffield: JSOT Press, 1992], 64, n. 9): "I wonder whether, without the biblical
   literature, historians would now call this kingdom "Israel" at all, rather than "Omri-
   land"... even in the biblical literature, "Ephraim" and "Samaria" are common alter-
   natives. "Israel" predominates only from later preference, and may not have been the
   name by which the state was most commonly known during its existence."
3 Campbell, "A Land Divided", 206.
4 Dever, *Biblical Writers*, 129-130.
5 See further R. Kletter, "Pots and Polities: Material Remains of Late Iron Age Judah in
   Relation to Its Borders", *BASOR* 314 (1999), 19-54.

southern "families".[6] The distribution of these material remains points to the separateness of Israel and Judah. As Dever comments, "Thus there exists just north of Jerusalem, along the Gezer-Bethel line, what archaeologists would call a 'shatter-zone', implying a cultural and thus a *political* border at that point".[7] Despite these indications of the long-standing separation of north and south, the united monarchy of David and Solomon has been viewed as one of the most certain periods of the historical Israel. As Knoppers observes,[8] virtually all modern histories of ancient Israel include or begin with a reconstruction of the monarchy of David and Solomon.[9] This scholarly confidence in the historicity of the united-then-divided monarchy may be accredited to a combination of two primary factors: first, the biblical traditions about the united monarchy have been commonly related to some form of "court history" originating in monarchic Jerusalem, which thereby has been seen to render the biblical traditions of the united monarchy historically tenable.[10] Second, the biblical account of tribal Israel's transformation into a monarchic society is assumed to have left traces in the archaeological record.[11] Therefore the results of the big tel excavations

6 R. Amiran, *Ancient Pottery of the Holy Land* (Jerusalem: Masada, 1969), 191-265; cited in Dever, *Biblical Writers*, 129-130.

7 Dever, *Biblical Writers*, 130.

8 G.N. Knoppers, "The Vanishing Solomon: The Disappearance of the United Monarchy from Recent Histories of Ancient Israel", *JBL* 116 (1997), 19-44.

9 E.g., G.W. Ahlström, *The History of Ancient Palestine* (Minneapolis: Fortress Press, 1993), 429-542; H. Cazelles, "The History of Israel in Pre-Exilic Times", in G.E. Anderson (ed.), *Tradition and Interpretation* (Oxford: Clarendon Press, 1979), 274-319; J. Bright, *A History of Israel* (third edn; Philadelphia: Westminster, 1981), 183-228; J.A. Soggin, "The Davidic-Solomonic Kingdom", in J.H. Hayes and J.M. Miller (eds.), *Israelite and Judaean History* (London: SCM Press, 1977), 131-186; *idem.*, *An Introduction to the History of Israel and Judah* (trans. J. Bowden; third edn; London: SCM Press, 1999), 49-93; *idem.*, "King David's State", in W.B. Barrick and J.R. Spencer (eds.), *In the Shelter of Elyon: Essays on Ancient Palestinian Life and Literature in Honor of G.W. Ahlström* (JSOTSup 31; Sheffield: JSOT Press, 1991), 261-275.

10 As noted by M.M. Gelinas, "United Monarchy—Divided Monarchy: Fact or Fiction?", in E.W. Holloway and L.K. Handy (eds.), *The Pitcher is Broken: Memorial Essays for Gösta W. Ahlström* (JSOTSup 190; Sheffield: Sheffield Academic Press, 1995), 227-237. For a recent, detailed defence of the essential historicity of the biblical texts relating to the united monarchy, see B. Halpern, *David's Secret Demons: Messiah, Murderer, Traitor, King* (Grand Rapids: Eerdmans, 2001).

11 Knoppers, "Vanishing Solomon", 21; C. Meyers, "Kinship and Kingship: The Early Monarchy", in M.D. Coogan (ed.), *The Oxford History of the Biblical World* (Oxford: Oxford University Press, 1998), 165-205, esp. 169-175; *idem.*, "David as Temple Builder", in P.D. Miller, P.D. Hanson and S.B. McBride (eds.), *Ancient Israelite*

dominating the modern period of scholarship are held by many to verify further the biblical accounts. In particular, the remains of monumental architecture have been directly related to the emergence of the monarchy, essentially dated on the basis of the biblical chronology[12] to about the tenth century BCE.[13] The biblical claim that Solomon embarked upon extensive building projects is a useful illustration of this reasoning. 1 Kgs 9:15-17 states that Hazor, Megiddo and Gezer were rebuilt by Solomon. Excavations appeared to reveal that defence systems constructed at these sites exhibited almost identical architectural features. From this sprang the supposition that one central authority must have been responsible for these seemingly parallel fortification patterns. Given the biblical material, Solomon was thus widely accredited with instigating these tokens of statehood.[14] Consequently, as Gelinas observes,[15] many modern histories, though recognizing the theological and apologetic nature of the biblical material, tend to read like a paraphrase of the narratives of Samuel and Kings, portraying a biblically-based picture of a vast Davidic-Solomonic empire.[16] The following quotation from Soggin illustrates the conviction with which many scholars continue to maintain the historicity of the united monarchy:

Religion: Essays in Honor of Frank Moore Cross (Philadelphia: Fortress Press, 1987), 357-376; Gelinas, "United Monarchy", 228; N.K. Gottwald, *The Hebrew Bible: A Socio-Literary Introduction* (Philadelphia: Fortress Press, 1986), 293-404.

12 See Lemche, *Israelites in History and Tradition*, 77- 78.

13 Eg. W.G. Dever, "Monumental Architecture in Ancient Israel in the Period of the United Monarchy", in T. Ishida (ed.), *Studies in the Period of David and Solomon and Other Essays* (Winona Lake: Eisenbrauns, 1982), 269-306; Meyers, "Kinship and Kingship", 187-189; A. Mazar, *Archaeology of the Land of the Bible, 10,000–586 BCE* (New York: Doubleday, 1990), chs. 9, 11.

14 See most recently Halpern, *David's Secret Demons,* 433-450. See also Y. Yadin, "Solomon's City Wall and Gate at Gezer", *IEJ* 8 (1958), 82-86; W.G. Dever, "Solomon and the Assyrian 'Palaces' at Gezer", *IEJ* 35 (1985), 217-230; *idem.*, "Monumental Architecture", 269-306; J.S. Holladay, "The Kingdoms of Israel and Judah: Political and Economic Centralization in the Iron IIA-B", in T.E. Levy (ed.), *The Archaeology of Society in the Holy Land* (London: Leicester University Press, 1995), 368-398. For a critical discussion of this view, see Lemche, *Israelites in History and Tradition*, 79-80; Thompson, *Early History*, 10-26; Mazar, *Archaeology*, 32-33.

15 Gelinas, "United Monarchy", 227.

16 E.g., Bright, *History of Israel*, 184-228; Soggin, "Davidic-Solomonic Kingdom", 332-380.

Where, then, does a history of Israel and Judah begin? In other words, is there a time after which the material in the tradition begins to offer verifiable accounts ... ? I feel it necessary to indicate that the answer should be the empire of David and Solomon, an empire which, according to the sources, would also have included, in one way or another, a large part of the neighbouring nations.[17]

However, new surveys and recent reviews of archaeological data have prompted a re-evaluation of the evidence which, when set alongside increasing socio-scientific research, suggests that the biblical concept of Israel and Judah as one people divided into two may be historically inaccurate.

The debate between "maximalists", who support the basic historicity of the biblical accounts of the monarchic period, and "minimalists", who are far more reluctant to do so, is well known.[18] Closely tied to this debate is the continuing controversy over the "Tenth Century". From amongst the minimalists a new voice has emerged, often designated "nihilist"[19] by its opponents, challenging the conventional adherence to the concept of the historicity of the united monarchy. This new voice argues that the idea of an historical Israel composed of northern and southern constituencies and governed by a single monarch is an ideological, literary fiction of later centuries.[20] Scholars maintaining this position draw strength from three

---

17 Soggin, *History*, 32. Soggin's seemingly tempered language contrasts with the confidence of his earlier assertion that the united monarchy is "a datum point from which the investigation of Israel's history can be safely begun" ("Davidic-Solomonic Kingdom", 332).

18 See especially Z. Zevit, "Three Debates about Bible and Archaeology", *Bib* 83 (2002), 1-27. See also the discussions by P.R. Davies, W.G. Dever and A. Mazar and J. Camp in *BAR* 26/2 (2000); Dever, *Biblical Writers*, 1-22, 23-52; *idem.*, "Archaeology, Ideology, and the Quest for an 'Ancient' or 'Biblical' Israel", *NEA* 61 (1998), 39-52; *idem.*, "Histories and Nonhistories of 'Ancient Israel'", *BASOR* 316 (1999), 89-105; N.P. Lemche, "Early Israel Revisited", *CR:BS* 4 (1996), 9-34; N.K. Gottwald, "Triumphalist versus Anti-Triumphalist Versions of Early Israel", *CR:BS* 5 (1997), 15-42; B. Halpern, "Erasing History: The Minimalist Assault on Ancient Israel", *BR* 11/6 (1995), 26-35, 47; Grabbe, *Can a "History of Israel" Be Written?*. Note also Halpern's observation (*David's Secret Demons*, 427) that "the United Monarchy has been the site of a symbolic battle over the reliability of biblical historiography".

19 Knoppers ("Vanishing Solomon", 20) labels these scholars "historical nihilists"; in several publications, Dever calls them "new nihilists", so, *idem.*, "'Will the Real Israel Please Stand Up?' Archaeology and Israelite Historiography: Part I", *BASOR* 297 (1995), 61-80; "Histories and Nonhistories", 89-105; *What did the Biblical Writers Know?*, 23-24.

20 As observed by Knoppers, "Vanishing Solomon", 20. Scholars arguing for the non-historicity of the united monarchy include I. Finkelstein and N.A. Silberman, *The Bible*

significant developments within scholarship: the reevaluation of archaeological evidence, the considerable contribution of social-scientific investigations, and the increasing opinion arguing for the later dating of the biblical texts, all of which have undermined the assumption of the basic historicity of the biblical description of the united-then-divided monarchy. However, before summarizing this evidence, the purpose and parameters of the discussion demand immediate and close delineation: first, the debate concerning the existence or non-existence of a united monarchy is not central to the historical reconstruction of King Manasseh: it merely furnishes that reconstruction with a useful and intentionally broad historical context. Second, the question addressed is whether or not the northern and southern Palestinian territories were unified as a single state system[21] under the central political and administrative direction of Jerusalem. As such, the discussion must be prefaced with a basic understanding of both what "statehood" is, and how ancient statehood may be detected in the archaeological record. Yet it may be difficult to distinguish the properties of a state from those of an alternative, often earlier political entity.[22] Most historical scholars of Israel and Judah work within the confines of mainstream socio-political and anthropological research relating to early civilizations. Within this context, a modified version of Finkelstein's summary[23] (which is representative of the opinions of the majority of scholars of Israelite and Judahite histories) is useful: a full-blown state is a well-stratified, complex society directed by a specialized administration. This administration is led by a ruling elite extending beyond the kinship circle of the ruler, who is usually separated from the general populace by several hierarchical levels.[24] Characteristics of

---

Unearthed: Archaeology's New Vision of Ancient Israel and the Origin of Its Sacred Texts (New York: Free Press, 2001), 149-168; Lemche, *Israelites in History and Tradition*, 35-64, 77-85; T.L. Thompson, *The Bible as History: How Writers Create A Past* (London: Pimlico, 2000); *idem.*, *Early History*, 306-307, 415-423; Gelinas, "United Monarchy", 227-237; Davies, *In Search of "Ancient Israel"*, 16-48, 69; see also Garbini, *History and Ideology*, 1-21, 22-33.

21 For a useful discussion of the nature of state systems see Meyers, "Kinship and Kingship", 165-205.

22 I. Finkelstein, "State Formation in Israel and Judah: A Contrast in Context, A Contrast in Trajectory", *NEA* 62 (1999), 35-52 (39). See further *idem.*, "The Emergence of the Monarchy in Israel and the Environmental and Socio-Economic Aspects", *JSOT* 44 (1989), 43-74; F.S. Frick and P.R. Davies, *The Origin of the Ancient Israelites States* (JSOTSup 228; Sheffield: Sheffield Academic Press, 1996); and the literature cited in Meyers, "Kinship and Kingship", 203-205.

23 Finkelstein, "State Formation", 39. Note also the useful table of archaeologically-discernable characteristics of a state in Holladay, "Kingdoms", 373.

24 Meyers, "Kinship and Kingship", 187.

a full-blown state include writing systems, organized, intensive industrial and agricultural production, trade with neighbouring regions, the distribution of luxury goods,[25] and the erection of public monumental structures serving both practical and legitimizing functions within regional or national, rather than domestic or local, contexts.[26]

Though indications of pre-monarchic monumental architecture exist,[27] it remains widely-held that monumental architecture in ancient Palestine demonstrates the existence of a centralized state. However, as noted above, considerable disagreement now pervades the interpretation of many such material remains. Whereas architectural features from several sites such as Megiddo, Hazor, and Gezer were formerly understood to reflect a shared and unified process of development and fortification within the tenth century, their reinterpretation now challenges this view: as Knoppers observes,[28] the similarities and dates of the monumental six-chambered gates are questioned;[29] the prevalence of four-chambered gates at several sites challenges the relevance of six-chambered gates further;[30] and the citing of the casemate wall as an indicator of tenth century fortification is disputed.[31] These architectural features thus no longer signify what they once did. Their testimony to the existence of a common, centralized political power in the tenth century is not indisputable. In challenging the conventional interpretation of this data, the bedrock of archaeological evidence supporting

25 Finkelstein and Silberman, *Bible Unearthed*, 158-159.
26 Finkelstein, "State Formation", 39; see also K.W. Whitelam, "The Symbols of Power: Aspects of Royal Propaganda in the United Monarchy", *BA* 49 (1986), 166-173.
27 The temple of El-berith at Shechem is frequently offered as an example.
28 Knoppers, "Vanishing Solomon", 27-29.
29 See for example D. Milson, "The Designs of the Royal Gates at Megiddo, Hazor, and Gezer", *ZDPV* 102 (1986), 87-92; D. Ussishkin, "Was the 'Solomonic' City Gate at Megiddo Built by King Solomon?", *BASOR* 239 (1980), 1-18; Lemche, *Israelites in History and Tradition*, 79. See also H.M. Niemann, "Megiddo and Solomon: A Biblical Investigation in Relation to Archaeology", *TA* 27 (2000), 61-74; B. Halpern, "The Gate of Megiddo and the Debate on the 10th Century", in A. Lemaire and M. Sæbø (eds.), *Congress Volume Oslo, 1998* (VTSup 80; Leiden: Brill, 2000), 79-121.
30 See Z. Herzog, *Das Stadtor in Israel und in den Nachbarländen* (Mainz-am-Rhein: Phillip von Zabern, 1989), 89-134; cited in Knoppers, "Vanishing Solomon", 28 n. 56. See also Halpern, *David's Secret Demons*, 439-450.
31 Ahlström, *History of Ancient Palestine*, 525-526; Y. Aharoni, "Excavations at Tel Beer-Sheba", *BA* 35 (1972), 111-127 (117).

the united monarchy therefore does not appear as firm as previously thought.[32]

Closely related to this reinterpretation of monumental architecture is Finkelstein's extensive argument for the re-dating of many of the archaeological strata at several Palestinian sites, including Megiddo, Hazor and Gezer.[33] His proposal of an alternative, "low chronology" is based upon a more comprehensive classification of strata discernible across the board among the major tel sites, and is supported by the dating of Philistine pottery and refined methods in carbon 14 dating.[34] This new chronology has the overall effect of lowering the dating of some strata at sites that were previously held to be eleventh, tenth, or ninth century. It does not effect eighth century strata, thus maintaining the current dating of most material remains known from the Kingdoms of Israel and Judah. [35] Accordingly, Finkelstein rejects the traditional identification of material remains with a supposed Davidic-Solomonic kingdom of the tenth century, and instead relocates most of the monumental architecture, fortifications and public buildings previously dated to the tenth century to the ninth century.[36] Consequently, Finkelstein argues for the formation of the states of Israel and Judah as distinct occurrences, separated both chronologically and geographically.[37] Though Finkelstein's low chronology has as yet won only

---

32 In relation to this is the redating to later periods of the so-called "fortresses" (a designation now often deemed inappropriate) in the Negev; see Knoppers, "Vanishing Solomon", 30-31, and the bibliography cited there.

33 Finkelstein, "State Formation", 35-52; idem., "The Date of the Settlement of the Philistines in Canaan", TA 22 (1995), 213-139; idem., "The Archaeology of the United Monarchy: An Alternative View", Levant 28 (1996), 177-187; idem., "Bible Archaeology or Archaeology of Palestine in the Iron Age? A Rejoinder", Levant 30 (1998), 167-174; idem., "The Stratigraphy and Chronology of Megiddo and Beth-Shan in the 12th–11th Centuries BCE", TA 23 (1996), 170-184; idem., "Hazor and the North in the Iron Age: A Low Chronology Perspective", BASOR 314 (1999), 55-70; idem., "Hazor XII-XI with an Addendum on Ben-Tor's Dating of Hazor X-VII", TA 27 (2000), 231-247. See also the summary and assessment of Finkelstein's views in Zevit, "Three Debates", 19-26.

34 Finkelstein, "State Formation", 36-39; Finkelstein and Silberman, Bible Unearthed, 141-142; see also Zevit, "Three Debates", 20-21.

35 Finkelstein, "State Formation", 39.

36 Finkelstein and Silberman (Bible Unearthed, 180-186) recognize the architectural similarities of many northern sites, but liken them to Samaria and accredit them to the building programmes of the Omrides.

37 Note however Finkelstein's earlier acceptance of a limited, brief and failed united monarchy in "The Great Transformation: The 'Conquest' of the Highlands Frontiers and the Rise of the Territorial States", in Levy, Archaeology of Society, 349-363.

limited support,[38] the breadth and depth of his arguments symbolize another breech in the security of the historicity of the united monarchy.[39] Moreover, his conclusion that Israel and Judah were always separate entities complements the findings of other studies.

Settlement patterns in Palestine have been examined for clues pertaining to the development of Israel and Judah. Surveys appear to indicate that until the eighth century, the settlement system in the Judaean highlands was neither extensive nor developed, consisting of only a few poor, small sites, thereby negating the possibility that Judah was a state in the tenth and ninth centuries.[40] Indications of some form of an advanced state would include medium and large sites alongside the small ones evident in the Judaean hills at this time.[41] Importantly, though this does not preclude the possibility that a small Jerusalemite kingdom could have existed in the tenth and ninth centuries,[42] it does argue against the "statehood" of the larger Judahite region

---

38 D. Ussishkin, "Jerusalem in the Period of David and Solomon: The Archaeological Evidence", in A. Faust and E. Baruch (eds.), *New Studies on Jerusalem: Proceedings of the Third Conference December 11th 1997* (Ramat-Gan: Bar-Ilan University Faculty of Jewish Studies, 1997), 57-58 (Hebrew); cited in Lemche, *Israelites in History and Tradition*, 78, 196, n. 54; T.L. Thompson, quoted in H. Shanks, "Face to Face: Biblical Minimalists Meet Their Challengers", *BAR* 23/4 (1997), 26-42, 66 (34-35). For a critique of Finkelstein's proposal, see A. Mazar, "Iron Age Chronology: A Reply to I. Finkelstein", *Levant* 29 (1997), 157-167, and the literature cited in Dever, *Biblical Writers*, 43, n. 40; Zevit, "Three Debates", 22, n. 36. See also the discussion in Halpern, *David's Secret Demons*, 451-478. For a recent response to Finkelstein's article "State Formation", see A.F. Rainey, "Stones for Bread: Archaeology versus History", *NEA* 64 (2001), 140-149.
39 Indeed, though Finkelstein has been incorrectly labelled a "minimalist", he has not participated directly within the debate between "maximalists" and "minimalists"; see further Zevit, "Three Debates", 24.
40 E.A. Knauf, "From History to Interpretation", in Edelman, *Fabric of History*, 26-64 (39); Gelinas, "United Monarchy", 229; Finkelstein, "State Formation", 42; Thompson, *Early History*, 288-292, 312-313; see also A. Ofer, "'All the Hill Country of Judah': From a Settlement Fringe to a Prosperous Monarchy", in Finkelstein and Na'aman, *From Nomadism to Monarchy*, 92-121.
41 Finkelstein, "State Formation", 42.
42 M. Steiner, "Jerusalem in the Tenth and Seventh Centuries BCE: From Administrative Town to Commercial City", in A. Mazar (ed.), *Studies in the Archaeology of the Iron Age in Israel and Jordan* (JSOTSup 331; Sheffield: Sheffield Academic Press, 2001), 280-288 (283); A. Ofer, "The Monarchic Period in the Judaean Highland: A Spatial Overview", in Mazar, *Studies in the Archaeology of the Iron Age*, 14-37 (27); Finkelstein, "Bible Archaeology", 172-173; cf. Thompson, *Early History*, 312. See also E.A. Knauf, "Jerusalem in the Late Bronze and Early Iron Ages: A Proposal", *TA* 27 (2000), 75-90.

invested with the political and economic clout necessary to control the northern territory. Thus the notion of the "united monarchy" is again challenged.

Archaeological evidence from Jerusalem—or rather, the lack of it—supports this conclusion further. As Gelinas observes, "the archaeological evidence for the biblical Davidic and Solomonic period in Jerusalem, the 'state' capital or seat of governance, is rather scarce and at best fragmentary.[43] The few architectural features recovered from tenth and ninth century Jerusalem are ambiguous.[44] In particular, the large stepped-stone defensive structure, popularly identified with the *millo* of the biblical united monarchy,[45] has been reinterpreted or re-dated to the Late Bronze Age, rendering its association with the united monarchy untenable.[46] In general, the increasing opinion is that in the tenth and ninth centuries BCE, Jerusalem was a small, poor and remote highland stronghold with little, if anything to distinguish it from other fortified settlements in the Palestinian highlands.[47] Also adhering to this view is Steiner, whose interpretation of a few building fragments found by Kenyon suggests that public buildings of some sort may have existed in ninth century BCE Jerusalem.[48] However, as Steiner comments, "It seems ... unlikely that this Jerusalem was the capital of a large state, the capital of the United Monarchy of biblical history. Compared to other towns of the tenth and ninth centuries, Jerusalem was not very

---

43 Gelinas, "United Monarchy", 228; see also H.J. Franken and M.L. Steiner, "Urusalim and Jebus", *ZAW* 104 (1992), 110-111; J.M. Cahill and D. Tarler, "Excavations Directed by Yigal Shiloh at the City of David, 1978–1985", in H. Geva (ed.), *Ancient Jerusalem Revealed* (Jerusalem: Israel Exploration Society, 1994), 30-45. Note, however, the criticisms of this attitude in Dever, *Biblical Writers*, 130-131; N. Na'aman, "The Contribution of the Amarna Letters to the Debate on Jerusalem's Political Position in the Tenth Century BCE", *BASOR* 304 (1996), 17-27; *idem.*, "Cow Town or Royal Capital? Evidence for Iron Age Jerusalem", *BAR* 23/4 (1997), 43-47, 67.

44 Mazar, *Archaeology*, 374.

45 See 2 Sam. 5:9; 1 Kgs 9:15, 24; 11:27; 1 Chr. 11:8.

46 Finkelstein, "State Formation", 40. See further J.M. Cahill and D. Tarler, "Respondents", in A. Biran and J. Aviram (eds.), *Biblical Archaeology Today* (Jerusalem: Israel Exploration Society, 1993), 625-626; L.E. Stager, "The Archaeology of the East Slope of Jerusalem and the Terraces of Kidron", *JNES* 41 (1982), 111-124; Y. Shiloh, "Jerusalem", *NEAEHL*, vol. 2, 705-708. For a recent reiteration of a tenth-to-ninth century date for the stepped-stone structure, see Steiner, "Jerusalem", 281-282; *idem.*, "Redating the Terraces of Jerusalem", *IEJ* 44 (1994), 13-20.

47 Finkelstein, "State Formation", 40; Steiner, "Jerusalem", 283; Na'aman, "Contribution", 17-27; Lemche, *Israelites in History and Tradition*, 78; Ussishkin, "Jerusalem", 57-58.

48 Steiner, "Jerusalem", 282-283.

different."[49] This evidence suggests that if a small, royal settlement did exist in Jerusalem in this early period, it probably arose sometime in the ninth century BCE; not before.[50]

It would appear that it is not until late in the eighth century that Jerusalem expanded quite rapidly, and became surrounded by wide, fortified walls.[51] This concurs with the results of Jamieson-Drake's extensive socio-archaeological analysis of Judah.[52] In his assessment of the cultural nature and political status of this region, Jamieson-Drake argues that the production of luxury items is a fair indication of a centralized political structure, reflecting a developed and complex economic system.[53] When set alongside his analysis of demographic patterns and archaeological evidence, he argues persuasively that unambiguous evidence for developed statehood in Judah cannot be found before the eighth century BCE, complementing the conclusions of many other scholars. He writes, "There is little evidence that Judah began to function as a state at all prior to the tremendous increases in population, building, production, centralization and specialization which began to appear in the 8th century".[54]

In contrast, the development of the northern region appears to have been markedly different. By the early ninth century, fortified settlements with public buildings had arisen in the north, including Samaria, Jezreel and Megiddo.[55] Settlement patterns of the period spanning the tenth to the eighth centuries BCE demonstrate an increasingly high population density, with a variety of sites of different sizes in both the highlands and lowlands, indicating a hierarchical settlement system suggestive of fully-developed "statehood".[56] Indeed, during the ninth century, several major fortified

---

49   Steiner, "Jerusalem", 283.
50   So too Lemche, *Israelites in History and Tradition*, 78.
51   M. Steiner, "A Note on the Iron Age Defence Wall on the Ophel Hill of Jerusalem", *PEQ* 118 (1986), 27-32; N. Avigad, *Discovering Jerusalem* (Nashville: Thomas Nelson, 1983), 28; Finkelstein, "State Formation", 40.
52   D.W. Jamieson-Drake, *Scribes and Schools in Monarchic Judah: A Socio-Archaeological Approach* (SWBAS 9/JSOTSup 109; Sheffield: JSOT Press, 1991).
53   Jamieson-Drake, *Scribes and Schools*, 107-135.
54   Jamieson-Drake, *Scribes and Schools*, 138-139; see also Knauf, "History to Interpretation", 39; *idem.*, "The Migration of the Script, and the Formation of the State in South Arabia", *PSAS* 19 (1989), 79-91 (esp. 79-80, 82-83); Na'aman, "Contribution", 25; Finkelstein, "State Formation", 39-48; Thompson, *Early History*, 407-412; Lemche, *Israelites in History and Tradition*, 77-85; Davies, *In Search of "Ancient Israel"*, 64.
55   Finkelstein, "State Formation", 40.
56   Finkelstein, "State Formation", 42. Finkelstein also draws attention to the rapid increase in olive oil production, the major industrial activity of the region, which testifies further

centres emerged, characterized by public buildings and limited residential areas (probably taken up by the elites).[57] As is well known, the use of ashlar masonry is indicative of affluence, and it is far more prevalent in northern sites (including Hazor, Megiddo, Gezer, Dan, Taʿanach) than in the south. However, it is in Samaria that the most impressive examples of ashlar masonry are found.[58] Indeed, the archaeological record testifies to the high status and affluence of Samaria.[59] Of all the major centres, this city was the largest, with an estimated dependent population of about 17,000 during the life of the kingdom: despite the co-existence of other major centres, Samaria appears to have remained the formal and actual capital of the kingdom.[60]

Samaria was located within the settlement and economic heartland of the north, the territory designated Manasseh within the biblical texts. This is obviously significant to this discussion. The importance of Manasseh within the early history of Israel is well known.[61] In a comprehensive article, Zertal demonstrates that this region rapidly became the heartland of a well-organized state: Samaria appears to have controlled the main roads crossing the region, and concentrated efforts to fortify the highways, cities and regional borders are evident in the remains of fortresses, military posts and towers, all indicating the political and economic strength of the territory.[62] The eighth century saw a settlement peak in Manasseh, accompanied by the foundations of new sites in the desert fringes. Interestingly, these new settlements appear to have been part of a deliberate attempt to establish or expand the borders of the kingdom, for not only do new settlements spring up

---

to the developed statehood of the north. Large numbers of ninth and eighth century sites specializing in mass oil production have been located. In contrast, olive oil production in the south was dominated by local, private households in the ninth and eighth centuries; it was only in the seventh century that the state assumed greater control over oil production; see also D. Eitam, "Olive-Oil Production during the Biblical Period", in M. Heltzer and D. Eitam (eds.), *Olive Oil in Antiquity* (Haifa: University of Haifa, 1987), 16-36; L.E. Stager and S.R. Wolff, "Production and Commerce in Temple Courtyards: An Olive Press in the Sacred Precinct at Tel Dan", *BASOR* 243 (1981), 95-102; R. Frankel, *Wine and Olive Oil Production in Antiquity in Israel and Other Mediterranean Countries* (ASORM 10; Sheffield: Sheffield Academic Press, 1999); Ahlström, *History of Ancient Palestine*, 623-624; P.J. King and L.E. Stager, *Life in Biblical Israel* (Library of Ancient Israel; Louisville: Westminster John Knox, 2001), 96-98, 194.

57   Finkelstein, "State Formation", 46.
58   King and Stager, *Life in Biblical Israel*, 22; Finkelstein, "State Formation", 40, 46-47.
59   King and Stager, *Life in Biblical Israel*, 204.
60   Zertal, "Heart of the Monarchy", 49.
61   See the literature cited above, 72, n. 252.
62   Zertal, "Heart of the Monarchy", 40-41, 51-58.

in previously uninhabited areas, but the number of desert sites doubled within a century.[63]

These summary observations indicate that the kingdoms of Israel and Judah developed independently, and at different rates. As Finkelstein and Silberman comment, while Judah was still economically backward and marginal, Israel was booming.[64] Israel probably emerged as a state at least a century earlier than Judah: the northern region appears to have attained monarchic statehood by the ninth century, growing rapidly into a prospering and powerful kingdom by the eighth century BCE, whereas during the ninth century the Judahite region was little more than a collection of rural, isolated settlements and a few scattered strongholds, one of which was Jerusalem. Though this small fortified settlement probably had a king, it was not until at least the eighth century that the economic and political power of the Jerusalemite monarchy attained regional domination in Judah.[65]

The combined weight of this evidence thus strongly suggests that the kingdoms of Israel and Judah arose independently, and maintained this essential separation throughout their histories. Yet this observation also amounts to a powerful challenge to the notion of a united monarchy. Though similar challenges have been answered by the witness of inscriptions, epigraphic material contributes little to either side. The non-mention of Jerusalem in the Karnak relief inscription describing the Palestinian campaign of Shoshenq[66] (biblical Shishak)[67] is notable in view of the listing of Megiddo, Ta'anach and Beth-shan as conquered sites, prompting Thompson's suggestion that the inscription is indicative of the non-existence of a Jerusalem-based united monarchy.[68] However, the silence of the inscription could also be interpreted as supporting the existence of a united monarchy based in Jerusalem which did *not* fall to the Egyptian king.[69] As such, it cannot offer conclusive evidence for or against the historicity of the

---

63 Zertal, "Heart of the Monarchy", 42-43; Thompson, *Early History*, 412.

64 Finkelstein and Silberman, *Bible Unearthed*, 158.

65 For the environmental and topographic factors contributing to the separateness of Israel and Judah, see Finkelstein and Silberman, *Bible Unearthed*, 155-158.

66 *ANET*, 263-264.

67 1 Kgs 14:25-28.

68 Thompson, *Early History*, 306-307; see also Gelinas, "United Monarchy", 230.

69 See also the response to Thompson by D.V. Edelman, "Solomon's Adversaries Hadad, Rezon and Jeroboam: A Trio of 'Bad Guy' Characters Illustrating the Theology of Immediate Retribution", in Holloway and Handy, *Pitcher Is Broken*, 166-191 (188, n. 47).

united monarchy.[70] Conversely, the controversial Tel Dan inscription has found particular favour among those seeking to defend the existence of the united monarchy.[71] Though the authenticity of this Aramaic inscription from a victory stela has been questioned,[72] it is generally held to be a genuine though fragmentary inscription of the late ninth/early eighth century BCE.[73] Its significance is found in its mention of a "king of Israel" and a possible reference to the "House of David" in lines 8 and 9 respectively. This latter phrase is generally understood to refer to the dynastic name of the state of Judah.[74] However, though the reference to a "king of Israel" is fairly secure, the rendering of the phrase *bytdwd* as "House of David" is disputed,[75] not least because it occurs without the expected word dividers, which are employed elsewhere throughout the inscription.[76] As such, this fragmentary text cannot bear the weight of arguments heaped upon it concerning the historicity of the early monarchy. Moreover, even if the inscription is best interpreted as referring to the "House of David", it testifies neither to the historicity of David nor to the co-existence of the kingdoms of Israel and Judah in the ninth century BCE. Rather, the designation "House of David"

---

70 Noted also by Knoppers, "Vanishing Solomon", 36.

71 A. Biran and J. Naveh, "An Aramaic Fragment from Tel Dan", *IEJ* 43 (1993), 81-98; *idem.*, "The Tel Dan Inscription: A New Fragment", *IEJ* 45 (1995), 1-18.

72 G. Garbini, "L'iscrizione aramaica di Tel Dan", *Atti della Accademia Nazionale dei Lincei* 391 (1994), 461-471; cf. N.P. Lemche and T.L. Thompson, "Did Biran Kill David? The Bible in Light of Archaeology", *JSOT* 64 (1994), 3-22; N.P. Lemche, "'House of David': The Tel Dan Inscription(s)", in Thompson, *Jerusalem in Ancient History and Tradition*, 46-67. For a defence of the authenticity of the inscription, see A. Lemaire, "The Tel Dan Stela as a Piece of Royal Historiography", *JSOT* 81 (1998), 3-14.

73 Lemche (*Israelites in History and Tradition*, 39-43), contests that the fragments form a unified inscription, suggesting instead that they derive from separate sections of a larger inscription: he argues that the lines of each fragment do not match and that the style of writing on one fragment differs from that on the other.

74 E.g., Dever, *Biblical Writers*, 128-129; Knoppers, "Vanishing Solomon", 36-40; N. Na'aman, "Beth-David in the Aramaic Stela from Tel Dan", *BN* 79 (1995), 20-21.

75 Alternative interpretations of *bytdwd* include the interrelated renderings of *dwd* as a toponym (e.g., F.H. Cryer, "On the Recently Discovered "House of David" Inscription", *SJOT* 8 [1994]: 3-19; *idem.*, "A '*betdawd*' Miscellany: dwd, dwd' or dwdh?", *SJOT* 9 [1995]: 52-58; P.R. Davies, "'House of David' Built on Sand", *BAR* 20/4 [1994]: 54-55; *idem.*, "*Bytdwd* and *Swkt Dwyd*: A Comparison", *JSOT* 64 [1994]: 23-24; Lemche, *Israelites in History and Tradition*, 43) or a divine name or epithet (e.g., E.A. Knauf, A. de Pury and T.C. Römer, "**BaytDawīd* ou **BaytDōd*? Une relecture de la nouvelle inscription de Tel Dan", *BN* 72 [1994]: 60-69; R.G. Lehmann and M. Reichel, "Dod und Ashima in Tell Dan", *BN* 77 [1995]: 29-31).

76 Lemche, *Israelites in History and Tradition*, 43.

may refer simply to the ruling family of the small, fortified settlement of Jerusalem and its dependent villages whose (perhaps legendary) founder was believed to be named David or "Beloved".[77] It does not logically lead to the assumption that David was an historical figure,[78] nor that he and his son reigned over a Palestinian empire. Moreover, the mention of the "House of David" within an inscription which also mentions a king of Israel need not indicate the paralleling of their political stature, nor the fully-fledged statehood of the "House of David".[79] Indeed, as Knoppers himself suggests, the reconstructed claim in line 6 of the inscription that the military victor killed seventy kings complements the probability that there were many local and regional powers in Palestine.[80] Most importantly, however, is the consideration that if this inscription does refer to a king of Israel and the House of David, it clearly distinguishes them as separate entities, underscoring further the evidence accumulated here.

In conclusion, the essential and long-standing separateness of Israel and Judah as unrelated, neighbouring Palestinian territories appears to be confirmed within the archaeological record. Though the kingdoms came to share common features, such as *Yhwh*-worship and similarities in language, Israel and Judah appear to have arisen independently, the former eclipsing the latter in political, economic and territorial stature. Indeed, the Kingdom of Israel may have earned the hatred evident within the traditions of the Hebrew Bible precisely because she was an economically and politically dominant player on the Syro-Palestinian stage.[81] However, it is not only the contrast between the growth and character of the states of Judah and Israel that is striking, but, crucially, the contrast between the historical separateness of Israel and Judah and the biblical concept of Israel and Judah as sister-states born of a united monarchy. There is no trace of this within the historical landscape of Palestine, yet the biblical traditions appear insistent that the two are interrelated as one people split into two kingdoms. Significantly, it is the heavily-stylized anti-Northern polemic of 2 Kgs 17 that may reveal, albeit

---

77 For the title "Beloved", see further 5.5.
78 *Pace* Knoppers, "Vanishing Solomon", 39; Finkelstein and Silberman, *Bible Unearthed*, 129-130.
79 See also Lemche, *Israelites in History and Tradition*, 42. See further B. Halpern, "The Stela from Dan: Epigraphic and Historical Considerations", *BASOR* 296 (1995), 67-68; G. Rendsburg, "On the Writing *bytdwd* in the Aramaic Inscription from Tel Dan", *IEJ* 45 (1995), 22-25; E. Ben Zvi, "On the Reading '*bytdwd*' in the Ramaic Stele from Tel Dan", *JSOT* 64 (1994), 29-32.
80 Knoppers, "Vanishing Solomon", 40.
81 See also Finkelstein and Silberman, *Bible Unearthed*, 170-171.

unintentionally, what is likely to have been the true nature of the relationship between Judah and Israel—that of separateness. This separateness, and the Kingdom of Israel's perceived economic and territorial success, may thus account in significant part for the hostility behind the anti-Northern polemic of Kings, which in turn has distorted the biblical presentation of King Manasseh.

2.2 The Fall of Samaria and the Non-Fall of Jerusalem

Despite the separateness of Israel and Judah, the fates of the kingdoms were closely aligned in the last decades of the eighth century, for the eventual demise of Israel at the hands of the Assyrians had a major and enduring impact upon the subsequent development of Judah.

For much of the ninth and eighth centuries, the Kingdom of Israel had enjoyed relative security and increased prosperity. However, the persistent advance of Assyria within the wider region had necessitated military coalitions among Israel and her neighbours in repeated attempts to defend against aggressive Assyrian expansionist policies.[82] The Kurkh Monolith Inscription lists chariots and foot soldiers belonging to "Ahab the Israelite" among a coalition of armed forces defeated by the Assyrian king Shalmaneser III at Qarqar in about 853 BCE.[83] By about 841 BCE, indications that Israel's independence was to disappear began to emerge: the success of Shalmaneser's renewed campaigns in Syria appears to have prompted the Israelite king Jehu to pay tribute to the Assyrian king, as may be depicted upon the Black Obelisk from Nimrud.[84] Jehu's acknowledgment of Assyrian dominance was probably intended to demonstrate the kingdom's political alignment with Assyria in the hope of staving-off attack from the imperial army.[85] Indeed, in order to avoid military attack, an independent

---

82 See further J.K. Kuan, *Neo-Assyrian Historical Inscriptions and Syria-Palestine: Israelite/Judean-Tyrian-Damascene Political and Commercial Relations in the Ninth-Eighth Centuries BCE* (Hong Kong: Alliance Bible Seminary, 1995). As Ahlström (*History of Ancient Palestine*, 602-603) suggests, Assyria's expansionist policies were born of her own geographical and geological limitations, prompting the need to acquire the resources and raw materials of other territories.

83 *COS*, vol. 2, 261-264; *ANET*, 278-279.

84 Ahlström, *History of Ancient Palestine*, 592-594; *ANET*, 280-281; *ANEP*, 355. It is uncertain whether it is Jehu or another (possibly Israelite) prisoner depicted.

85 Cogan and Tadmor, *II Kings*, 121; Ahlström, *History of Ancient Palestine*, 594.

state on the border of a rapidly expanding Assyrian empire had little option but to become a voluntary, tributary vassal-state.[86] It is possible that Israel also came under the political subjugation of Aram-Damascus, during a period of temporary Assyrian weakness in Syria,[87] and archaeological evidence suggests that the northern areas of the kingdom suffered military attacks.[88] Yet the resurgence of Assyrian hegemony in Syria and northern Palestine resulted in the subduing of Aram-Damascus and a further Israelite tribute payment to Assyria came in about 796 BCE,[89] offered by King Joash (Jehoash) "of Samaria" in a major military campaign in southern Syria.[90] Israel appears to have benefited from this repeated act of submission, for archaeological evidence suggests that the kingdom flourished.

The inevitable slide towards full vassalage, annexation and eventually the destruction of the kingdom began in earnest with the reign of Tiglath-pileser III (746–727 BCE).[91] The Assyrian king was occupied with putting down revolts within the vassal-states of the empire. As Becking comments, the payment of tribute often provoked anti-Assyrian feelings among the populations of vassal-states, and the power vacuum created by the death of an Assyrian king encouraged rebellions against the imperial overlords.[92] As a result of an anti-Assyrian coalition of vassal-states, in c. 738 BCE the borders of Tiglath-pileser's empire were brought closer to Israel through the annexation of rebellious states in Syria and Phoenicia.[93] The Israelite king

---

86 B. Becking, *The Fall of Samaria: An Historical and Archaeological Study* (SHANE 2; Leiden: Brill, 1992), 1-2.

87 See further Ahlström, *History of Ancient Palestine*, 604-612.

88 Finkelstein and Silberman, *Bible Unearthed*, 201-205; see also S. Yamada, "Aram-Israel Relations as Reflected in the Aramaic Inscription from Tel Dan", *UF* 27 (1995), 611-625.

89 The date of this payment is not certain; see further the bibliography in Cogan and Tadmor, *II Kings*, 152 n. 6.

90 S. Page, "A Stela of Adad-nirari III and Nergal-ereš from Tell al Rimah", *Iraq* 30 (1968), 139-153; H. Tadmor, "The Historical Inscriptions of Adad-nirari III", *Iraq* 35 (1973), 141-150.

91 For the successive stages of the transformation of independent states into Assyrian provinces see H. Donner, "The Separate States of Israel and Judah", in Hayes and Miller, *Israelite and Judaean History*, 381-434, esp. 418-420.

92 Becking, *Fall of Samaria*, 2.

93 The role of Judah within this anti-Assyrian coalition is often mistakenly supposed on the basis of an apparent reference to Azariah/Uzziah the king of Judah in a fragmentary text incorrectly ascribed to the Assyrian annals. Rather, the fragment belongs to a text dated to 701 BCE, and refers to a rebellious king from Hamath. See further N. Na'aman, "Sennacherib's 'Letter to God' on His Campaign to Judah", *BASOR* 214 (1974), 25-38;

"Menahem of Samaria" is listed among those paying voluntary tribute to the Assyrian king during this campaign.[94] Despite extremely fragmentary evidence from Assyrian sources, the historicity of the biblical account of the so-called Syro-Ephraimite alliance against Assyria (and Jerusalem)[95] is generally assumed and held accountable for the subsequent Assyrian annexation of Israelite territory in the Galilee and Transjordan.[96] What is more certain is the testimony of Assyrian sources: frequent but ultimately unsuccessful rebellions in Syria and Palestine appear to have occurred.[97] Three inscriptions summarize a campaign against the Philistine cities in about 734 BCE;[98] the inclusion of Jehoahaz (Ahaz) of Judah within a list of tribute-payers at about this time is thus unsurprising.[99] Shortly afterwards, in about 733–732 BCE, and despite her history of economic and political strength, Tiglath-pileser conquered and depopulated much of Israel, reducing the kingdom to a "rump state" consisting of the highlands of Samaria.[100] The annexed territory became Assyrian provinces: Du᾿ru, Magidu and probably Gal᾿a(d)a.[101] In his annals the Assyrian king claims to have carried off to Assyria the inhabitants of "Omri-Land" (Israel), and to have replaced the fallen king Pekah with Hoshea, from whom he received financial tribute.[102] The portrayal of Hoshea as an imperially-approved king upon the throne of a butchered kingdom suggests that Israel had lost virtually all independence. Within about ten years, the Kingdom of Israel would cease to exist altogether. The non-biblical sources employed to illuminate this final period

---

Becking, *Fall of Samaria*, 2-3; Donner, "Separate States", 424-425; Cogan and Tadmor, *II Kings*, 165 n. 1.

94 *ANET*, 283; see also Becking, *Fall of Samaria*, 4 n. 12.

95 Isa. 7:1-9.

96 *Contra* R. Tomes, "The Reason for the Syro-Ephraimite War", *JSOT* 59 (1993), 55-71. For a discussion of the biblical and non-biblical material relating to the "Syro-Ephraimite" issue, see for example S.A. Irvine, *Isaiah, Ahaz, and the Syro-Ephraimitic Crisis* (SBLDS 123; Atlanta: Scholars Press, 1990).

97 Kuan, *Historical Inscriptions*, 186-192.

98 Becking, *Fall of Samaria*, 8-19.

99 *ANET*, 282. The absence of Pekah of Israel, Rezin of Aram-Damascus and Hiram of Tyre within this tribute list suggests to some commentators that these states were attempting to resist Assyrian hegemony; see further Kuan, *Historical Inscriptions*, 161-164.

100 See further Becking, *Fall of Samaria*, 15-20. Interestingly, Becking highlights internal conflict between the "Gileadites" and "Manassites" as a contributing factor to the political, economic and territorial losses of Israel at the hands of the Assyrians.

101 Becking, *Fall of Samaria*, 20.

102 *COS*, vol. 2, 288; *ANET*, 284; cf. Cogan and Tadmor, *II Kings*, 335; Kuan, *Historical Inscriptions*, 177.

of Israel's history are complex, uncertain, and seemingly contradictory. In the Mesopotamian inscriptions, both the Assyrian king Shalmaneser V (c. 727–722 BCE) and his successor Sargon II (c. 722–705 BCE) claim to have conquered Samaria.[103] That Samaria rebelled and was subdued more than once is possible.[104] However, what is more certain is that by 720 BCE, Samaria had been attacked, besieged, defeated, and had become the centre of an Assyrian province called Samerina. The deportations of many of her people and her gods occurred during this period,[105] as Sargon later boasts on the Nimrud Prism:

> [The inhabitants of Sa]merina, who agreed [and plotted] with a king [hostile to] me, not to do service and not to bring tribute [to Aššur] and who did battle, I fought against them with the power of the great gods, my lords. I counted as spoil 27, 280 people, together with their chariots, and gods, in which they trusted. I formed a unit with 200 of [their] chariots for my royal force. I settled the rest of them in the midst of Assyria. I repopulated Samerina more than before. I brought into it people from countries conquered by my hands. I appointed my eunuch as governor over them. And I counted them as Assyrians.[106]

The impact of these events upon the fledgling state of Judah was profound. In political terms, Judah was already an Assyrian vassal of sorts, as an Assyrian inscription of Tiglath-pileser III records the tributary payment of Jehoahaz (Ahaz) of Judah.[107] In geographical terms, the Assyrian annihilation of the

---

103 Becking, *Fall of Samaria*, 21.
104 For a detailed evaluation of the non-biblical and biblical sources, and reconstructions of the events leading to the fall of Samaria, see Becking, *Fall of Samaria*, 21-60; J.H. Hayes and J.K. Kuan, "The Final Years of Samaria (730–720 BC)", *Bib* 72 (1991), 153-181; N. Na'aman, "The Historical Background to the Conquest of Samaria (720 BC)", *Bib* 71 (1990), 206-225; H. Tadmor, "The Campaigns of Sargon II of Assur: A Chronological-Historical Study", *JCS* 12 (1958), 33-40.
105 See further K.L. Younger, "The Deportations of the Israelites", *JBL* 117 (1998), 201-227.
106 *COS*, vol. 2, 295-296. On the Assyrian provinces in the former Kingdom of Israel, see E. Stern, *Archaeology of the Land of the Bible. Volume II: The Assyrian, Babylonian, and Persian Periods, 732–332 BCE* (ABRL; New York: Doubleday, 2001) 42-57.
107 See above, n. 99; for further discussion, see Younger, "Deportations", 211-215, 218-221; S. Dalley, "Foreign Chariotry and Cavalry in the Armies of Tiglath-pileser III and Sargon II", *Iraq* 47 (1985), 31-38. On the reliability of large numbers (of deportees) in Assyrian inscriptions, see A.R. Millard, "Large numbers in the Assyrian Royal Inscriptions", in M. Cogan and I. Eph'al (eds.), *Ah, Assyria ... Studies in Assyrian History and Ancient Near Eastern Historiography presented to Hayim Tadmor* (Scripta Hierosolymitana 33; Jerusalem: Magnes, 1991), 213-222. For the iconographic depictions of Sargon II's campaigns in the west, including his treatment of the

Kingdom of Israel meant that Judah now shared a border with the imperial aggressors, which undoubtedly influenced foreign policy to a certain degree.[108] Yet in economic terms, this close proximity to Assyria was beneficial for Judah, for it offered increased trading opportunities.[109] In demographic terms, Jerusalem underwent a massive population surge in the wake of the Assyrian conquest of the Kingdom of Israel, a surge most probably composed of refugees from the defeated northern territories.[110] Archaeological excavations indicate that by the end of the eighth century, Jerusalem was filled with public buildings, shops and houses. Her residential areas had expanded rapidly onto the western hill, and were protected by a huge, broad defensive wall.[111] Finkelstein and Silberman describe Jerusalem's sudden growth within just a few decades from a small highland town of about ten or twelve acres to a city of 150 acres as a transformation: "The royal citadel of Jerusalem was transformed in a single generation from the seat of a rather insignificant local dynasty into the political and religious nerve center of a regional power".[112] The city's outlying rural areas also testify to this sudden demographic increase: new farming settlements sprang up, and towns evolved from villages.[113] Related to this is evidence for the beginnings of the centralized management of the regional economy—such as

---

Samarians, see N. Franklin, "A Room with a View: Images from Room V at Khorsabad, Samaria, Nubians, the Brook of Egypt and Ashdod", in Mazar, *Studies in the Archaeology*, 257-277.

108 The Assyrian resettlement of foreign deportees within the territories of the former Kingdom of Israel contributed further to the geographical confusion within Palestine. See further B. Oded, *Mass Deportations and Deportees in the Neo-Assyrian Empire* (Wiesbaden: Reichert, 1979); N. Na'aman and R. Zadok, "Population Changes in Palestine Following Assyrian Deportations", *TA* 20 (1993), 104-124.

109 Cogan, "Into Exile", 245-246; Finkelstein and Silberman, *Bible Unearthed*, 246; see further J.N. Postgate, "The Economic Structure of the Assyrian Empire", in M.T. Larsen (ed.), *Power and Propaganda: A Symposium on Ancient Empires* (CSA 7; Copenhagen: Akademisk Forlag, 1979), 193-221.

110 Halpern dismisses this common suggestion, proposing instead that Jerusalem's population expanded suddenly as a result of Hezekiah's emergency urbanization of rural communities in preparation for his rebellion against Assyria; B. Halpern, "Sybil, or the Two Nations? Archaism, Kinship, Alienation, and the Elite Redefinition of Traditional Culture in Judah in the 8th–7th Centuries BCE", in J.S. Cooper and G.M. Schwartz (eds.), *The Study of the Ancient Near East in the 21st Century: The William Foxwell Albright Centennial Conference* (Winona Lake: Eisenbrauns, 1996), 291-338.

111 M. Broshi, "The Expansion of Jerusalem in the Reigns of Hezekiah and Manasseh", *IEJ* 24 (1974), 21-26; Steiner, "Note on the Iron Age Defence Wall", 7-32; Avigad, *Discovering Jerusalem*, 31-60.

112 Finkelstein and Silberman, *Bible Unearthed*, 243.

113 Ofer, "Monarchic Period", 28; Finkelstein and Silberman, *Bible Unearthed*, 245.

the production and distribution of olive oil, wine, textiles, artefacts and luxury goods—which arises in the eighth century and accelerates in the seventh.[114]

The socio-cultural matrix of Judah probably underwent a profound transformation also. With the maturing of the state came the rise of a national or, perhaps better, a Jerusalemite, elite, as suggested by the use of increasingly elaborate bench tombs as the virtually exclusive method of burial in Jerusalem, and their overwhelming use elsewhere in Judah from the late eighth century.[115] Alongside the probable influx of refugees from Palestinian territories ravaged by Assyria were merchants and elements of the rural Judahite population. It is impossible to ascertain how Judah responded to the fall of Samaria and the eradication of the Kingdom of Israel. However, in the light of the separateness of the two kingdoms and the former political and economic dominance of Israel within the region, it is likely that the loss of the kingdom was not necessarily mourned in Judah. Rather, as will be seen, the fall of the Kingdom of Israel impacted upon the religious ideology of Judah in such a way that the collapse of the Kingdom in the north is likely to have played a formative and positive role within the religious self-definition of Judah.

In essence, the fall of the Kingdom of Israel and the expansion of Assyria in Palestine prompted the emergence of Judah as a mature, though still a vassal, state, with a large royal capital, several urban administrative centres, many towns and villages, an extensive rural population, and a booming trade in oil, wine and other goods. However, this brief period of sudden growth and increased prosperity came to a sudden halt with the somewhat foolhardy actions of Judah's king, Hezekiah. The death of Sargon II in battle and the accession of Sennacherib prompted internal upheaval in Assyria and a renewed outbreak of rebellions throughout the west and Babylonia.[116] Among

---

114 Jamieson-Drake, *Scribes and Schools*, esp. 133-135, Halpern, "Sybil, or the Two Nations", 304-305.

115 Finkelstein and Silberman, *Bible Unearthed*, 245-246; Bloch-Smith, *Judahite Burial Practices*, 48, 51-52, 137, 147-148; see also I. Yezerski, "Burial-Cave Distribution and the Borders of the Kingdom of Judah toward the End of the Iron Age", *TA* 26 (1999), 253-270; Barrick, *King and the Cemeteries*, 154-159. On tomb inscriptions dating to this period, see K.A.D. Smelik, *Writings from Ancient Israel: A Handbook of Historical and Religious Documents* (trans. G.I. Davies; Edinburgh: T&T Clark, 1991), 72-75; *COS*, vol. 2, 177-182.

116 W.C. Gwaltney, "Assyrians", in A.J. Hoerth, G.L. Mattingly and E.M. Yamauchi (eds.), *Peoples of the Old Testament World* (Grand Rapids: Baker, 1994), 77-106 (94-96); B.

the western vassals to rebel were the kings of Tyre-Sidon, Ashkelon, Ekron, and Hezekiah of Judah.[117] Hezekiah appears to have taken advantage of the new Assyrian king's preoccupation with campaigns in the east in making careful preparations for rebellion, including the strengthening of fortresses, the construction of a water tunnel to supply Jerusalem,[118] and perhaps an urbanization policy drawing the rural populations into towns and forts, designed to shelter the rural communities or to maximize manpower in the event of attack.[119] Despite Hezekiah's preparations, the inevitable Assyrian attack in 701 BCE was catastrophic for Judah.[120] As is well known, Sennacherib claims:

> As for Hezekiah, the Judaean, I besieged forty-six of his fortified walled cities and surrounding smaller towns, which were without number. Using packed-down ramps and applying battering rams, infantry attacks by mines, breeches, and siege machines, I conquered (them). I took out 200,150 people, young and old, male and female, horses, mules, donkeys, camels, cattle, and sheep, without number, and counted then as spoil. He himself, I locked him up within Jerusalem, his royal city, like a bird in a

---

Oded, "Judah and the Exile", in Hayes and Miller, *Israelite and Judaean History*, 435-488 (446).

117 It is widely agreed that these vassal kings conspired with each other. Hezekiah's prominent role within the rebellions of the western kings is indicated in the Assyrian claim that the people of Ekron handed over their king Padi to Hezekiah, who imprisoned the displaced monarch in Jerusalem (*ANET*, 287). For a discussion of Hezekiah's possible motivations for rebellion, see W.R. Gallagher, *Sennacherib's Campaign to Judah: New Studies* (SHANE 18; Leiden: Brill, 1999), 263-274.

118 See further, for example, Ahlström, *History of Ancient Palestine*, 697-707; Halpern, "Jerusalem and the Lineages", 19-28; Finkelstein and Silberman, *Bible Unearthed*, 255-259. For the possible relationship between Hezekiah's rebellion and the supposed cult reforms, see O. Borrowski, "Hezekiah's Reforms and the Revolt against Assyria", *BA* 58 (1995), 148-155; A.G. Vaughn, *Theology, History, and Archaeology in the Chronicler's Account of Hezekiah* (Atlanta: Scholars Press, 1999). For a useful summary of Jerusalem's water systems, see King and Stager, *Life in Biblical Israel*, 213-223. For the debate concerning the dating of the Siloam Tunnel and its inscription, see P.R. Davies and J. Rogerson, "Was the Siloam Tunnel Built by Hezekiah?", *BA* 59 (1996), 138-149; R.S. Hendel, "The Date of the Siloam Inscription: A Rejoinder to Rogerson and Davies", *BA* 59 (1996), 233-237; J.A. Hackett, "Defusing Pseudo-Scholarship: The Siloam Inscription Ain't Hasmonean", *BAR* 23 (1997), 41-50, 68; *COS*, vol. 2, 145-146.

119 See further Halpern, "Jerusalem and the Lineages", 18-27; *idem.*, "Sybil, or the Two Nations", 213-321.

120 For the discussion concerning whether Sennacherib campaigned once or twice in Judah, see J. Goldberg, "Two Assyrian Campaigns against Hezekiah and Later Eighth Century Biblical Chronology", *Bib* 80 (1999), 360-390; M. Cogan, "Sennacherib's Siege of Jerusalem—Once or Twice?", *BAR* 27/1 (2001), 40-45, 69; Gallagher, *Sennacherib's Campaign*, 1-20; W.H. Shea, "Sennacherib's Second Palestinian Campaign", *JBL* 104 (1985), 410-418.

cage. I surrounded him with earthworks, and made it unthinkable for him to exit by the city gate. His cities which I had despoiled I cut off from his land and gave them to Mitinti, king of Ashdod, Padi, king of Ekron, and Ṣilli-bel, king of Gaza, and thus diminished his land. I imposed dues and gifts for my lordship upon him, in addition to the former tribute, their yearly payment.[121]

The Assyrian inscriptions indicate that the siege of Jerusalem ended with the capitulation of Hezekiah and a massive tribute payment sent to Nineveh which included his daughters, palace women, male and female singers, armed forces, chariots, gold, silver and expensive furniture.[122] Hezekiah's rebellion was a failure. Rather than freeing his kingdom from its imperial shackles, Hezekiah's actions brought the military might of Assyria upon Judah. Physically, the kingdom was decimated: archaeological surveys confirm the Assyrian portrayal of the devastation of the Judahite settlements outside of Jerusalem;[123] the annexing of territories to neighbouring Assyrian vassals rendered the kingdom little more than a city-state centred around Jerusalem. Politically, Judah had been drawn firmly into the Assyrian empire as a closely-monitored vassal. Economically, Judah was crippled, not only by the tribute payments, which would undoubtedly continue at least annually, but by the deportation of many of her people[124] and the loss of her territories and the resources therein.[125] Sennacherib's intention was to weaken and break Judah,

---

121 *COS*, vol. 2, 303; *ANET*, 287-288.

122 *COS*, vol. 2, 303; *ANET*, 287-288.

123 See for example I. Finkelstein, "The Archaeology of the Days of Manasseh", in M.D. Coogan, J.C. Exum and L.E. Stager (eds.), *Scripture and Other Artifacts: Essays on the Bible and Archaeology in Honor of Philip J. King* (Louisville: Westminster John Knox, 1994), 169-187, esp. 172-176. Excavations at Lachish and the famous wall relief from Sennacherib's palace in Nineveh provide an extraordinarily vivid account of the Assyrian ravaging of Judah in 701 BCE; see further D. Ussishkin, *The Conquest of Lachish by Sennacherib* (Tel Aviv: Tel Aviv University, 1982); W.H. Shea, "Sennacherib's Description of Lachish and of its Conquest", *AUSS* 26 (1988), 171-180.

124 Halpern ("Jerusalem and the Lineages", 32) observes, "Sennacherib's appetite for manpower was voracious, and the high pitch of his deportations reflects this." See also Oded, *Mass Deportations*, 90.

125 Indeed, the olive-pressing industry at the Philistine city-state Ekron (Tel Miqne) which came to dominate olive oil production and trade in the region appears to boom after c. 701 BCE, suggesting that Judahite lands given to Ekron by Sennacherib benefited production. See further S. Gitin, "Ekron of the Philistines, Part II: Olive Oil Suppliers to the World", *BAR* 16/2 (1990), 32-42, 59; *idem.*, "Tel Miqne-Ekron: A Type Site for the Inner Coastal Plain in the Iron Age II Period", in S. Gitin and W.G. Dever (eds.), *Recent Excavations in Israel: Studies in Iron Age Archaeology* (AASOR 49; Winona Lake: Eisenbrauns, 1989), 23-58; A. Mazar, "The Northern Shephelah in the Iron Age: Some

rendering her impotent, thereby allowing his successors to dominate the western territories without being threatened by local rulers.[126] He clearly achieved this goal in Judah.

Though in political and economic terms Hezekiah's rebellion had been an utter failure, the events of c. 701 BCE were probably interpreted as a success for the city of Jerusalem, which was left standing amid the extensive destruction. Indeed, the siege of Jerusalem had a formative and persevering impact upon the socio-religious self-definition of the Jerusalemites. Given Jerusalem's restricted existence as little more than a self-contained royal fortress before the eighth century, it is likely that the royal dynasty and its accompanying elites had always been particularly insular in their religious ideology and self-definition. However, this insularity appears to have reached new levels in the wake of the siege and the subsequent isolation of Jerusalem in c. 701 BCE. Given the city's hilltop location, ancient myths and traditions concerning the function of the hill as a sacred mountain and chosen dwelling place for the principal god(s) probably dominated the royal cult before c. 701 BCE.[127] However, the non-fall of Jerusalem during the Assyrian onslaught in c. 701 BCE prompted traditions of the city's miraculous deliverance from destruction, as biblical texts attest.[128] In particular, traditions concerning

---

Issues in Biblical History and Archaeology", in Coogan, Exum and Stager, *Scripture and Other Artifacts*, 247-267.

126 So Na'aman ("Forced Participation", 96), against those who argue that Sennecherib's Judahite campaign was a failure because he did not take Jerusalem. Dalley's recent proposal ("Yabâ, Atalyā and the Foreign Policy of Late Assyrian Kings", *SAAB* 12 [1998], 83-98) that Tiglath-pileser III and his son Sargon II were both married to Judahite princesses (Yabâ and Atalyā, respectively) may offer a further explanation as to why Sennacherib, as the son of Sargon and Atalyā, did not destroy Jerusalem, but permitted Hezekiah to remain on the throne.

127 The interrelationship of the Zion and David ideologies is well known, but see for example, J.D. Levenson, *Sinai and Zion: An Entry into the Jewish Bible* (Minneapolis: Winston, 1985), esp. § 2; *idem.*, "Zion Traditions", *ABD*, vol. 4, 1098-1102; J.J.M. Roberts, "The Davidic Origin of the Zion Tradition", *JBL* 92 (1973), 329-344; *idem.*, "Zion in the Theology of the Davidic-Solomonic Empire", in Ishida, *Studies in the Period of David and Solomon*, 93-108; J.H. Hayes, "The Tradition of Zion's Inviolability", *JBL* 82 (1963), 419-426; B.C. Ollenburger, *Zion the City of the Great King: A Theological Symbol of the Jerusalem Cult* (JSOTSup 41; Sheffield: JSOT Press, 1987), esp. 59-66; P.K. McCarter, "Zion", *DDD*, 940-941; see also Ahlström, *Royal Administration and National Religion*, 1-9. On the common ancient Near Eastern motif of the sacred mountain, see the summary discussion offered by H. Niehr, "Zaphon", *DDD*, 927-929.

128 E.g., 2 Kgs 18:13–19:37; Isa. 36–39. See further S.B. Parker (*Stories in Scripture and Inscriptions: Comparative Studies on Narratives in Northwest Semitic Inscriptions and the Hebrew Bible* [Oxford: Oxford University Press, 1997], 105-130), who examines 2

Zion's inviolability and divine protection, evident in the Hebrew Bible,[129] probably received formative expression in the aftermath of the Assyrian siege. Though these traditions may have very ancient antecedents,[130] and despite many scholars explicitly associating them with the supposed establishment of the ark in David's Jerusalem, it is entirely possible that the traditions concerning the divine inviolability of Zion attained their comprehensive expression and fundamental place within the royal Jerusalem cult in the wake of the non-fall of the city in about 701 BCE.[131]

This probability is strengthened further in view of the fall of Samaria just over twenty years before. Given the political, economic and geographical superiority of the Kingdom of Israel in Palestine, its Assyrian annihilation probably received a mixed response in Judah: though unsettling and frightening, the Judahites probably interpreted the destruction of the kingdom in the north as resulting from the defeat of the local gods by the Assyrian deities, or as the deliberate divine abandonment of the royal sanctuary in Samaria. That this is a possibility is suggested by Sargon II's boast that he counted as spoil the gods in whom the Samaritan people trusted,[132] indicating that the Samaritan temple was looted of its cult statues.[133] Included within this group of looted cult statues was probably that of the primary deity[134] of

---

Kgs 18:13-19:37 and other biblical texts in light of ancient Near Eastern texts telling of miraculous deliverances from a siege.

129 E.g., Pss. 2; 46; 48; 125; Isa. 8:5-10; 25:6-12; 26:1-7; 33:5-6, 14-24; 37:33-38.

130 See for example Levenson, "Zion Traditions", 1101-1102.

131 So too R.E. Clements, *Isaiah and the Deliverance of Jerusalem: A Study of the Interpretation of Prophecy in the Old Testament* (JSOTSup 13; Sheffield: JSOT Press, 1980); cf. B.G. Ockinga, "The Inviolability of Zion: A Pre-Israelite Tradition?", *BN* 44 (1988), 54-60.

132 See the quotation above, 93.

133 This was not an uncommon act within ancient Near Eastern warfare, for it carried the dual function of demonstrating the defeat of the local gods, and providing booty in the form of the precious metals and jewels cladding the statues. See further Cogan, *Imperialism and Religion*, 9-21, 119-127; Spieckermann, *Juda unter Assur*, 347-354; T. Jacobsen, "The Graven Image", in Miller, Hanson, McBride, *Ancient Israelite Religion*, 15-32; H. Niehr, "In Search of YHWH's Cult Statue in the First Temple", in K. van der Toorn (ed.), *The Image and the Book: Iconic Cults, Aniconism, and the Rise of Book Religion in Israel and the Ancient Near East* (CBET 21; Leuven: Peeters, 1997), 73-95; B. Becking, "The Gods, In Whom They Trusted ... Assyrian Evidence for Iconic Polytheism in Ancient Israel", in B. Becking, M. Dijkstra, M.C.A. Korpel and K.J.H. Vriezen, *Only One God? Monotheism in Ancient Israel and the Veneration of the Goddess Asherah* (BS 77; London: Continuum, 2001), 151-163.

134 On non-biblical evidence attesting to *Yhwh*'s primary status in Samaria, see H. Niehr, "The Rise of YHWH in Judahite and Israelite Religion: Methodological and Religio-

the Kingdom of Israel, "*Yhwh* of Samaria", a title known from the famous inscription from Kuntillet ʿAjrud.[135] Given that the Jerusalemites worshipped their own version of *Yhwh*,[136] the capturing of the cult statues of the capital of the formerly powerful Kingdom of Israel is likely to have had a profound effect upon them, particularly in view of evidence collated by Schmitt suggesting that the people of the Kingdom of Israel had maintained a belief in the divine inviolability of Samaria.[137] However, in light of the non-fall of Jerusalem just a couple of decades after the fall of Samaria, the defeat or desertion of *Yhwh* of Samaria is likely to have been imbued with a new ideological significance: whereas *Yhwh* of Samaria had failed to protect his capital from the Assyrians, *Yhwh* of Jerusalem had succeeded in defeating Assyria. The mood in Jerusalem after the non-fall of Jerusalem is perhaps captured in a cave inscription from Khirbet Bet-Lei, eight km east of Lachish, dated by some scholars to around 700 BCE:

> Yahweh is the god of the whole earth. The highlands of Judah belong to the god of Jerusalem.[138]

With the destruction of other Judahite settlements and the defeat or desertion of their local gods, Jerusalem stood alone but undefeated with the protection

---

Historical Aspects", in D.V. Edelman (ed.), *The Triumph of Elohim: From Yahwisms to Judaisms* (Kampen: Kok Pharos, 1995), 45-72, esp. 55-58.

135 *COS*, vol. 2, 171-173. For recent treatments of the inscriptions from Kuntillet ʿArjud, see M. Dijkstra, "I have Blessed you by YHWH of Samaria and his Asherah: Texts with Religious Elements from the Soil Archive of Ancient Israel", in Becking, Dijkstra, Korpel, Vriezen, *Only One God?*, 17-39; J.M. Hadley, *The Cult of Asherah in Ancient Israel and Judah: Evidence for a Hebrew Goddess* (UCOP 57; Cambridge: Cambridge University Press, 2000).

136 *Yhwh* of Samaria and *Yhwh* of Jerusalem were separate deities with separate cults, and should not be identified; so too, for example, Niehr, "Rise of YHWH", 52; G.W. Ahlström, "The Role of Archaeological and Literary Remains in Reconstructing Israel's History", in Edelman, *Fabric of History*, 128-129.

137 J.J. Schmitt, "Samaria in the Books of the Eighth-Century Prophets", in Holloway and Handy, *Pitcher Is Broken*, 355-367.

138 *COS*, vol. 2, 179-180. See further S. Mittmann, "A Confessional Inscription from the Year 701 BC Praising the Reign of Yahweh", *Acta Academica* 21 (1989), 15-38; J. Naveh, "Old Hebrew Inscriptions in a Burial Cave", *IEJ* 13 (1963), 235-256; A. Lemaire, "Prières en temps de crise: Les inscriptions de Khirbet Beit Lei", *RB* 83 (1976), 558-568; Keel and Uehlinger, *Gods, Goddesses*, 312; F.M. Cross, "The Cave Inscriptions from Khirbet Beit Lei", in J.A. Sanders (ed.), *Near Eastern Archaeology in the Twentieth Century: Essays in Honor of Nelson Glueck* (Garden City: Doubleday, 1970), 299-306; P.D. Miller, "Psalms and Inscriptions", in J.A. Emerton (ed.), *Congress Volume Vienna, 1980* (VTSup 32; Leiden: Brill, 1981), 311-332.

of the royal patron deity, *Yhwh* of Jerusalem. Thus in the light of the fall of Samaria, the non-fall of Jerusalem took on an ideological significance of huge proportions: *Yhwh* of Jerusalem and his accompanying deities had proved stronger than the gods of Samaria and the gods of Assyria. This probably increased the insularity of the Jerusalemite elites and their socio-religious self-definition further, a characteristic that would dominate the worship of *Yhwh* in Jerusalem for centuries.

Thus on the eve of Manasseh's accession to the throne, the kingdom of Judah was little more than a small vassal city-state centred around Jerusalem, the kingdom having been decimated politically, economically and geographically by Assyria. However, in ideological terms, Jerusalem had perhaps proved herself stronger than the former Kingdom of Israel and Assyria. What then are the implications of this reconstruction of the historical Judah and Israel for the quest for the Manasseh of history?

2.3 King Manasseh of Judah

Attempting to reconstruct the historical figure of Manasseh is inherently problematic. There are two primary and related reasons for this. First, as has been seen, the biblical presentations of Manasseh in 2 Kgs 21:1-18 and 2 Chr. 33:1-20 are both highly-stylized theological tracts which are extremely difficult to evaluate in terms of their potential historicity. The second reason, which is also an unfortunate consequence of the first, is that very little research has been carried out into the location and assessment of the historical Manasseh. This lack of academic interest springs directly from the fact that most scholars continue to accept the biblical presentation of Manasseh as a syncretistic, and thus essentially anti-YHWH, pro-Assyrian vassal. Consequently, scholarly enquiry into monarchic Judah tends to be dominated by those heroic characters the biblical writers wanted their audiences to remember, namely Hezekiah and Josiah. This biblically-based bias towards the so-called "reformer" kings is inadequately acknowledged within scholarship.[139] This imbalance must be acknowledged and addressed if the scholarly reconstruction of ancient Judahite society and its religious

---

139 Eynikel ("Portrait of Manasseh", 234) makes a similar observation in relation to the scholarly attention given to the Kings material concerning Josiah rather than Manasseh in studies concerning the so-called Deuteronomistic History.

practices is to be even approximately representative of the probable historical reality.

The dearth of research focusing upon the historical figure of Manasseh, combined with the problematic nature of the biblical material, thus inevitably limits the parameters of this discussion. Therefore this investigation must rely to a certain extent upon a balance between cultural contextualization and historical probability. However, this process in itself harbours the risk of misinterpretation or over-interpretation, albeit unintentional. In seeking to draw attention to this problem nearly twenty years ago, Nelson pointed out that historical reconstructions of seventh century Judah invariably interpret the biblical accounts of this period strictly in terms of the assumed Assyrian political and cultural domination of Judah.[140] Consequently, the same assumptions tend to dominate so-called historical reconstructions of Manasseh's reign: primarily, religious policy tends to be understood as reflecting loyalty or disloyalty to Judah's Assyrian overlords. Thus Manasseh is held to be pro-Assyrian in his alleged sponsorship of "foreign" cult practices, whereas Hezekiah and Josiah are frequently regarded as anti-Assyrian. As Nelson observes,[141] this leads to the implicit judgement that Manasseh was an "unpatriotic weakling" willing to disregard his national heritage in favour of his pro-Assyrian stance, in contrast to the often explicit opinion that Hezekiah and Josiah were staunch nationalists and loyal *Yhwh*-worshippers, willing to risk their lives to shake off Assyrian domination and restore Judah's past greatness.[142] Nelson thus sought a re-evaluation of these assumptions in light of comparative data. However, though there is now a greater use of non-biblical methodologies and materials within historical surveys of this period, nearly two decades on, these same academic assumptions continue to undergird the majority of historical reconstructions of monarchic Judah. The reason for this, as Na'aman asserts, is that the assumption of the biblical history's fundamental correctness persists within

---

140 R. Nelson, "Realpolitik in Judah (687–609 BCE)", in W.W. Hallo, J.C. Moyer and L.G. Perdue (eds.), *Scripture in Context, II: More Essays on the Comparative Method* (Winona Lake: Eisenbrauns, 1983), 177-189.

141 Nelson, "Realpolitik", 177.

142 E.g., Tadmor and Cogan, *II Kings*, 291; Laato, *Josiah and David Redivivus*, 45-46, 75-80; Bright, *History of Israel*, 316-325; Noth, *History of Israel*, 272-279; F.M. Cross and D.N. Freedman, "Josiah's Revolt against Assyria", *JNES* 12 (1953), 56-58; N. Lohfink, "The Cult Reform of Josiah of Judah: 2 Kings 22–23 as a Source for the History of Israelite Religion", in Miller, Hanson, McBride, *Ancient Israelite Religion*, 459-476 (466-468).

scholarship.[143] Consequently, non-biblical data relating to this period can be misinterpreted, over-emphasized, or even ignored in favour of reconstructions slanted towards biblical versions of events. This can only result in a distorted picture of the historical reality of the reign of Manasseh. Though any modern reconstruction of Manasseh and his reign is inevitably skewed given the distance of time separating current scholarship from monarchic Judah, a reasonably plausible picture of this period may be sketched by building upon the foundations laid by Nelson and Na'aman. Both caution against the interpretation of non-biblical data in light of biblical testimony. Though obvious, this methodological principle is frequently ignored, and therefore cannot be overstated.

Thus far the discussion has reconstructed the backdrop against which the figure of the historical Manasseh may be set. This backdrop depicts Judah at a crucial point in her history, as Ben Zvi emphasizes:

> The combined effect of the destruction of most of Judah—except Jerusalem—at the end of the eighth century and the integration into the neo-Assyrian system in the seventh century resulted in the creation of a "new" Judah, quite different from the one that existed before 701 BCE.[144]

As such, Manasseh's reign represents a crucial turning point in the history of Judah, particularly in view of the probability that it spanned just over half of the seventh century BCE.[145] Thus Manasseh's reign demands the careful and detailed evaluation more usually accredited to the reigns of Hezekiah and Josiah.

Establishing the chronological parameters of Manasseh's reign with precision is problematic. As will be seen, the location of Manasseh within the first half of the seventh century is confirmed by direct references to him in Assyrian texts from the reigns of Esarhaddon and his successor Assurbanipal. This evidence, like Assyrian references to other Judahite kings, thus at least broadly supports the biblical chronology. Yet the biblical chronology is problematic in its details, for it is incoherent: essentially, it is difficult to reconcile the lengths of the reigns of the kings from Ahaz to Josiah with events dated to certain years during their reigns, such as the accessions of

---

143 N. Na'aman, "The Debated Historicity of Hezekiah's Reform in Light of Historical and Archaeological Research", *ZAW* 107 (1995), 179-195.

144 E. Ben Zvi, "Prelude to a Reconstruction of the *Historical* Manassic Judah", *BN* 81 (1996), 31-44 (32).

145 Ben Zvi, "Prelude to a Reconstruction", 31; Finkelstein, "Days of Manasseh", 169.

Israelite kings or interaction with foreign nations.[146] Consequently, a consensus is yet to be established concerning the chronologies of the kings of Judah and Israel. This results in a range of proposals for Manasseh's reign,[147] including the suggestion that in 696/95 BCE Manasseh ascended the throne as co-regent with Hezekiah until the latter's death some ten or eleven years later.[148] Given that a detailed assessment of these proposals is beyond the scope of this study, it will suffice to posit a reign of about 55 or 56 years to Manasseh—without a period of co-regency—spanning the period from about 698 to 642 BCE.[149]

The Assyrian references are the only known and uncontested non-biblical data directly related to King Manasseh. The annals of Esarhaddon (680–669 BCE) refer to "Manasseh, king of the city(-state)[150] of Judah" within a list of

---

146 See further G. Galil, *The Chronology of the Kings of Israel and Judah* (SHANE 9; Leiden: Brill, 1996); Barnes, *Studies in the Chronology*; J.H. Hayes and P.K. Hooker, *A New Chronology for the Kings of Israel and Judah and Its Implications for Biblical History and Literature* (Atlanta: John Knox, 1988); N. Na'aman, "Hezekiah and the Kings of Assyria", *TA* 21 (1994), 235-254; G. Larsson, "The Chronology of the Kings of Israel and Judah as a System", *ZAW* 114 (2002), 224-235. See also V.P. Long, "How Reliable are Biblical Reports? Repeating Lester Grabbe's Comparative Experiment", *VT* 52 (2002), 367-384.

147 Different proposals include 699–644 BCE (Hayes and Hooker, *New Chronology*, 80, 109-111); 697/6-642/1 BCE (Galil, *Chronology of the Kings*, 147); 697–642 BCE (J.M. Miller and J.H. Hayes, *A History of Ancient Israel and Judah* (London: SCM Press, 1986), 363; Jones, *1 & 2 Kings*, 28; Barnes, *Studies in the Chronology*, 154); 696/5–642/1 BCE (N. Na'aman, "Historical and Chronological Notes on the Kingdoms of Israel and Judah in the Eighth Century BC", *VT* 36 [1986], 71-92, esp. 90-92; Ben Zvi, "Prelude to a Reconstruction", 31); and 694–640 BCE (J. Hughes, *Secrets of the Times: Myth and History in Biblical Chronology* [JSOTSup 66; Sheffield: JSOT Press, 1990], 223).

148 See the discussions in Na'aman, "Historical and Chronological Notes", 90; R.E. Thiele, *The Mysterious Numbers of the Hebrew Kings* (third edn; Grand Rapids: Zondervan, 1983), 173-178; Evans, "Foreign Policy", 166; S.H. Horn, "The Chronology of King Hezekiah's Reign", *AUSS* 2 (1964), 40-52.

149 M. Cogan, "Chronology", *ABD*, vol. 1, 1002-1111; see also *idem.*, *I Kings*, 100-103, plus Appendix II; Cogan and Tadmor, *II Kings*, 341.

150 Although it is often supposed that the lack of the determinative for "land" may reflect the reduced territory of Judah after c. 701 BCE (eg. Ahlström, *History of Ancient Palestine*, 732), R. Gane ("The Role of Assyria in the Ancient Near East during the Reign of Manasseh", *AUSS* 35 [1997], 21-32) points out that the determinative for "city" is applied to all the western states listed here, and that in other versions of the same text, "Judah" and other western vassals are preceded by the determinative for "land", thereby indicating that a distinction between city-states and larger states is not made in these historical lists.

twenty-two western vassal kings of Syro-Palestine and Cyprus who are required to provide and transport building materials for the rebuilding of the royal palace or arsenal[151] at Nineveh:

> ... all these I sent out and made them transport under terrible difficulties, to Nineveh, the town where I exercise my rulership, as building material for my palace: big logs, long beams and thin boards from cedar and pine trees, products of the Sirara and Lebanon mountains.[152]

Though the year of this event is not provided, the absence of Sidon within the list of vassal kings suggests that Manasseh's provision of resources and transportation occurred sometime after the destruction of Sidon in about 677 BCE.[153]

A further reference to "Manasseh, king of (the land) of Judah" occurs within the annals of Assurbanipal (c. 668–627 BCE), the successor of Esarhaddon. In a description of Assurbanipal's first campaign against Egypt in about 667–666 BCE, Assyrian texts[154] state that twenty-two vassal kings paid tribute and homage to the new Assyrian king, and joined the imperial army on the journey to Egypt:

> I called up my mighty armed forces which Ashur and Ishtar have entrusted to me and took the shortest road to Egypt and Nubia. During my march twenty-two kings from the seashore, the islands and the mainland ... [including] Manasseh, king of Judah ... servants who belong to me, brought heavy gifts to me and kissed my feet. I made these kings accompany my army over the land as well as over the sea-route with their armed forces and their ships ...[155]

This text testifies to the importance of the Syro-Palestinian vassal states for Assyria's smooth passage to and from Egypt, and the necessity for their provisions, resources and transportation for a successful campaign.[156] Though these are the only extant references to Manasseh within Assyrian texts, it is possible that a text mentioning a tribute payment from Judah and collective references to the vassal kings of Syro-Palestine also speak indirectly of Manasseh.[157] Regardless, these Assyrian inscriptions clearly

---

151 Gane, "Role of Assyria", 22 n. 6.
152 *ANET*, 291.
153 Gane, "Role of Assyria", 22.
154 See further Evans, "Foreign Policy", 167; Gane, "Role of Assyria", 26.
155 *ANET*, 294.
156 Gane, "Role of Assyria", 26-27.
157 *ANET*, 290, 301; see further R.H. Pfeiffer, "Three Assyriological Footnotes to the Old Testament", *JBL* 47 (1928), 185; Gane, "Role of Assyria", 27-30.

depict Manasseh as a vassal king involved in both Assyrian military and construction projects.

Yet what is particularly significant for this discussion is the fact that these Assyrian texts also verify the historicity of Manasseh's name. The primary argument of this study is that the biblical characterization of King Manasseh is prompted by, and deliberately constructed around, his name. The confirmation of Manasseh's name within the Assyrian inscriptions thus supports the hypothesis that the scapegoating of Manasseh is facilitated by the very fact of his name, and thereby dispels any possibility that the Kings Writer has retrospectively labelled this idolatrous king with the name for polemical purposes.

Additional pieces of non-biblical evidence relating to King Manasseh have been offered in the form of seal inscriptions, which could also verify the historicity of Manasseh's name.[158] Though three inscriptions have been published, only one has been widely accepted as an authentic Hebrew inscription. Of the others, one is suggested to be Moabite,[159] whilst the authenticity of the other is uncertain.[160] The authentic Hebrew seal is described by Avigad and Sass as an oval scaraboid shaped from a dark brown stone with pink and white veins.[161] It has a single-line border around its edges, with two horizontal double-lines dividing the seal into three registers. In the top register is a two-winged beetle, flanked by a dot on either side. The hindlegs of the beetle are not depicted, but in its forelegs the beetle holds

---

158 On employing seals and seal inscriptions, see B. Becking, "Inscribed Seals as Evidence for Biblical Israel? Jeremiah 40.7-41.15 par example", in Grabbe, *Can a "History of Israel" be Written?*, 65-83. N. Avigad, "The Contribution of Hebrew Seals to an Understanding of Israelite Religion and Society", in Miller, Hanson, McBride, *Ancient Israelite Religion*, 195-208.

159 A seal bearing the legend *lmnšh bn hmlk* was published and identified as Hebrew by Avigad thirty years ago ("A Seal of 'Manasseh Son of the King'", *IEJ* 13 [1963]: 133-136); however, it has subsequently been suspected as being Moabite (J. Naveh, "The Scripts of Two Ostraca from Elath", *BASOR* 183 [1966]: 27-30 [29 n. 24]; *idem.*, *Early History of the Alphabet* [Jerusalem: Magnes, 1982], 101).

160 In a recent article concerning a well-known antiquities collector, photographs and a brief description of an extraordinary seal were published (H. Shanks, "Is Oded Golan a Forger?", *BAR* 29/5 [2003], 34-37). The seal sits in a lavish gold setting, which appears to comprise a winged sun disc, topped with a hollow, circular disc through which a cord might be threaded. The inscription is translated, "Belonging to Manasseh, son of Hezekiah, King of Judah", but its authenticity is uncertain. Moreover, the seal's provenance and current whereabouts are reportedly unknown.

161 N. Avigad and B. Sass, *Corpus of West Semitic Stamp Seals* (Jerusalem: Israel Exploration Society, 1997), 55 no. 16.

a ball, suggesting this scarab is a representation of a dung beetle. The two lower registers bear the inscription *lmnšh bn hmlk*, "(Belonging) to Manasseh, (the) son of the king". The winged scarab is a common motif within the symbol systems of the ancient Near East. It is generally considered that the scarab pushing the ball of dung represents the movement of the rising of the sun, probably symbolizing divine protection. This solarized emphasis in combination with the two or four-winged scarab is a common feature of the seal iconography of both the Kingdom of Israel and eighth-to-seventh century BCE Judah, and is probably a symbol of high-status.[162] Indeed, it may be associated particularly with royalty in Judah.[163]

The presence of possibly royal iconography upon the first seal, combined with the explicit title "son of the king", may suggest that this seal belonged to Hezekiah's heir Manasseh. Though the increasing number of seals bearing the legend "PN, (the) son of the king" could suggest that this title was borne by officials of the royal court, rather than princes directly related to the monarch, it is generally acknowledged that some members of the royal family may have functioned as officials within the court, and as such may have possessed their own seals.[164] Indeed, Avigad notes that some of these royal officials may have been proper sons of the king, yet he questions whether this would be a possibility in the case of Manasseh, given his presumably tender age whilst his father Hezekiah remained upon the

---

162 Keel and Uehlinger, *Gods, Goddesses*, 256-257, 275-279, 353. For a Judahite tendency to solarize *Yhwh*, see J.G. Taylor, *Yahweh and the Sun: Biblical and Archaeological Evidence for Sun Worship in Ancient Israel* (JSOTSup 111; Sheffield: JSOT Press, 1988); Day, *Yahweh*, 151-163.

163 R. Deutsch, *Messages from the Past: Hebrew Bullae from the Time of Isaiah through the Destruction of the First Temple—Shlomo Moussaieff Collection and an Updated Corpus* (Tel Aviv: Archaeological Center Publications, 1999), 51; Y. Yadin, "A Note on the Nimrud Bronze Bowls", *EI* 8 (1965), 6. This motif also appears on a seal arguably belonging to Hezekiah; see M. Lubetski, "King Hezekiah's Seal Revisited", *BAR* 27/4 (2001), 44-51, 59; F.M. Cross, "King Hezekiah's Seal bears Phoenician Imagery", *BAR* 25/2 (1999), 42-45, 60; cf. N. Avigad, *Hebrew Bullae from the Time of Jeremiah* (Jerusalem: Israel Exploration Society, 1986), 110, no. 199. It may be that a later biblical interpretation of the idea expressed in this type of symbol system is found in Mal. 3:20 (ET 4:2): "For you who revere my name, the sun of righteousness shall rise with healing in its wings" (Cross, "Hezekiah's Seal", 45). For further discussion of the winged scarab motif, see for example B. Sass and C. Uehlinger, *Studies in the Iconography of Northwest Semitic Inscribed Seals* (Fribourg: University of Fribourg Press, 1992); Keel and Uehlinger, *Gods, Goddesses*, 256-257; R. Hestrin and M. Dayagi, "A Seal Impression of a Servant of King Hezekiah", *IEJ* 24 (1974), 27-29.

164 See the discussions in Smelik, *Writings from Ancient Israel*, 104-142; A. Lemaire, "Note sur le titre *bn hmlk* dans l'ancien Israël", *Semitica* 29 (1979), 59-65.

throne.[165] For those positing a period of co-regency, Manasseh's young age would not be a problem. However, if this is a seal originally belonging to the royal Manasseh, it is reasonable to assume both that a royal prince would have his own seal and that he may have held some official position and title within the royal court, regardless of his age. Indeed, Avigad concedes that as a young prince, Manasseh may have owned property, and as a custodian he may have used the seal.[166] Despite these possibilities, it is important to note that there is no direct evidence to confirm that the owner of this seal was the royal Manasseh, for the name Manasseh was not unique throughout Syro-Palestine, and the seal may have belonged to a court official who coincidentally shared the same name as the royal Manasseh.[167] However, it is intriguing to note that if the seal's owner could be identified with the royal Manasseh, it may offer evidence that Hezekiah chose the name Manasseh for his son, rather than it being selected as a throne-name by Manasseh himself upon his accession. The discussion will return to examine the possible implications and historical significance of Manasseh's name.

Given that the only known non-biblical data directly related to Manasseh consists of passing references in the Assyrian texts and a possible seal inscription, reconstructing the Manasseh of history becomes a process of historical contextualization. However, as Finkelstein observes, it is difficult to pinpoint the reign of a specific king archaeologically.[168] Significantly, this is a good indication of the success of Manasseh's reign, for it was a peaceful period with no great destructions identifiable to modern archaeologists.[169] As Finkelstein and Silberman comment, the days of Manasseh "were peaceful times for Judah. Yet what was good for the people of Judah is, ironically, bad for archaeologists. We do not have even one stratum that can be safely dated to his days".[170] Consequently, an archaeological survey of the general characteristics of the first half of the seventh century is necessary to provide an historical context in which the historical figure of Manasseh may be located. This task is made a little easier by the presence of material remains of Assyrian attacks on Judahite settlements in c. 701 BCE, which provide archaeologists with a corroborative combination of archaeological and

---

165 Avigad, "Contribution", 202.
166 Avigad, "Contribution", 202.
167 A point noted also by Avigad, "Contribution", 202-203.
168 Finkelstein, "Days of Manasseh", 169.
169 Finkelstein, "Days of Manasseh", 171.
170 Finkelstein and Silberman, *Bible Unearthed*, 346; cf. Hoffmann, *Reform und Reformen*, 165.

historical data from this year.[171] Yet given the propensity for historical reconstructions of the reigns of Hezekiah and Josiah within modern scholarship, the most useful studies upon which the following sketch is essentially based are few, and are those of Halpern,[172] Ben Zvi,[173] Finkelstein,[174] and Finkelstein and Silberman.[175]

Demographically, Manasseh's Judah was markedly different from the Judah that existed before 701 BCE. Among the major demographic alterations were the loss of the Shephelah, resulting in a decrease of at least fifty per cent of the population of Judah, and the concentration of almost all the remaining Judahite inhabitants in the hill country, which underwent a population explosion in the early seventh century—probably due to the influx of refugees from former Judahite territories.[176] Indeed, a notable intensification of agricultural settlements around Jerusalem is apparent at this time.[177] However, a sudden expansion of settlements into the arid areas to the east and south of the Judahite hill country is accredited to a deliberate resettlement policy of Manasseh's reign: all sedentary sites in the desert region—previously virtually empty—were established in the first half of the seventh century, and clusters of small sites sprang up in ecological niches better suited to cultivation than other areas of the desert.[178] Moreover, an extensive building programme constructing or repairing forts, including those of Ḥorvat ʿUza, Radum, Tel ʿIra and Arad, occurred during Manasseh's reign, attesting to the existence of a new, sophisticated administration within the region.[179] The population of these arid zones increased ten fold within the

---

171 However, these data have their own limitations; see Finkelstein, "Days of Manasseh", 170-171.

172 Halpern, "Jerusalem and the Lineages", 60-77.

173 Ben Zvi, "Prelude to a Reconstruction", 31-44.

174 Finkelstein, "Days of Manasseh", 169-181.

175 Finkelstein and Silberman, *Bible Unearthed*, 264-274, 345-346.

176 Finkelstein, "Days of Manasseh", 173-177; Finkelstein and Silberman, *Bible Unearthed*, 265-266; Broshi, "Expansion", 21; D. Bahat, "The Wall of Manasseh in Jerusalem", *IEJ* 28 (1978), 235-236.

177 Finkelstein and Silberman, *Bible Unearthed*, 266.

178 Finkelstein, "Days of Manasseh", 175-176; Finkelstein and Silberman, *Bible Unearthed*, 266.

179 Finkelstein, "Days of Manasseh", 177; L. Tatum, "King Manasseh and the Royal Fortress at Ḥorvat ʿUsa", *BA* 54 (1991), 136-145. See also Stern, *Archaeology*, 151-163; Halpern, "Jerusalem and the Lineages", 60; Gane "Role of Assyria", 29-30; Ben Zvi, "Prelude to a Reconstruction", 32. Note also I. Beit-Arieh and B.C. Cresson, "Ḥorvat ʿUza: A Fortified Outpost on the Eastern Negev Border", *BA* 54 (1991), 126-135.

seventh century.[180] This evidence is thus suggestive of a programme of expansion and cultivation in the various pockets of viable farming land in these regions. With the loss of the Shephelah, Judah lost the majority of her grain-producing farmland. Archaeological evidence indicates that Judahites moved into the arid zones in an ultimately successful attempt to exploit the potential of its more fertile areas, in order to compensate for the loss of the Shephelah. Finkelstein estimates that, with efficient, state-controlled organization, the Beersheba valley alone could supply up to a quarter of Judah's overall grain needs.[181] As well as exploiting the arid zones left to Judah, the resettlement programme also may have eased the swollen proportions of Jerusalem. It is thus a reasonable assumption that these changes in the first half of the seventh century took place under the direction of Manasseh.[182]

Directly related to this policy of expansion are the increased trading opportunities made available to an expanded Judah. Manasseh appears to have taken full advantage of this situation, as demonstrated by the presence in Judah of spices, incense, balms and sesame from the south. Moreover, Arabian, Greek and Cypriot merchants and goods are also evidenced in the region, whilst the mass production of cash crops, such as wine, oil and herbs for perfume, is also attested in the archaeological record.[183] Needless to say, this economic recuperation and settlement expansion into the hills and the southern and eastern regions could not have occurred without the approval of Assyria, who continued to dominate the trading routes throughout Palestine.[184] Indeed, it is most probable that Judah's economic recovery was a direct result of her further integration into the Assyrian empire in c. 701 BCE.[185] Seventh century Palestinian pottery found in Nineveh complements Assyrian pottery of the same date located in Palestine, suggesting that the imperial overlords participated within commercial relations with their

---

180 Finkelstein and Silberman, *Bible Unearthed*, 266.
181 Finkelstein, "Days of Manasseh", 177-178; Finkelstein and Silberman, *Bible Unearthed*, 266-267; see also Z. Herzog, "The Beer-Sheba Valley: From Nomadism to Monarchy", in Finkelstein and Na'aman, *From Nomadism to Monarchy*, 122-149.
182 Halpern, "Jerusalem and the Lineages", 64; Finkelstein and Silberman, *Bible Unearthed*, 267; Finkelstein, "Days of Manasseh", 178.
183 Halpern, "Jerusalem and the Lineages", 61-64; Finkelstein, "Days of Manasseh", 178-179; Finkelstein and Silberman, *Bible Unearthed*, 267-270.
184 Finkelstein, "Days of Manasseh", 178.
185 Ben Zvi, "Prelude to a Reconstruction", 32-33; Halpern, "Jerusalem and the Lineages", 63; Nielsen, "Political Conditions", 106.

Palestinian vassals.[186] As Halpern comments, it is perhaps no great surprise that Manasseh's name occurs second after that of Ba'lu, king of Tyre, in the Assyrian list of western vassals.[187] It is likely that Assyria allowed, and even encouraged, Judah's economic recovery because Manasseh's small kingdom served as an increasingly strong and useful buffer against Egypt.[188]

As has been seen, the non-fall of Jerusalem in c. 701 BCE encouraged the religious verification of the traditional Jerusalemite elite, which probably intensified with the rapid expansion of the city. The Assyrian policy of economic tolerance or encouragement towards Judah during Manasseh's reign is likely to have contributed to this intensification, for as both Gane and Ben Zvi emphasize, a pre-existing local, socio-political and economic centre was useful for the imperial overlords. Local elites would quickly realize that the advantages of imperial inclusion far outweighed the risks in resisting; thus they were more easily integrated into the Assyrian hegemonic system, thereby securing the stability of the region whilst sparing the costs of creating new centres of power.[189] In highlighting archaeological features suggestive of smaller family units (such as a decrease in the average sizes of cooking pots and ovens) Halpern argues that a major characteristic of Manasseh's reign was the widespread social dislocation of many rural Judahites from their ancestral land.[190] Contributing factors to this social dislocation could be the influx of refugees from the former Kingdom of Israel, Hezekiah's urbanization schemes, the Assyrian attack on Judah in c. 701 BCE, and perhaps Manasseh's resettlement policies. If Halpern is correct, it may be that the traditional ideological insularity of the Jerusalemite elites, which was relatively unchanged given the non-fall of the city, intensified further,

---

186 Gane, "Role of Assyria", 29.

187 Halpern, "Jerusalem and the Lineages", 63; *ANET*, 291.

188 Nielsen, "Political Conditions", 104; Gane, "Role of Assyria", 23; Finkelstein, "Days of Manasseh", 180; Finkelstein and Silberman, *Bible Unearthed*, 265.There is some suggestion that during the latter half of Manasseh's reign some of the Shephelah and hill terrain lost in c. 701 BCE was restored to Judah, perhaps as a reward for imperial loyalty (Evans, "Foreign Policy", 168; Ahlström, *Royal Administration*, 77-78; Lowery, *Reforming Kings*, 169; Barrick, *King and the Cemeteries*, 151). However, it is important to note that there is no direct evidence for this within Assyrian texts, nor within the archaeological record (Finkelstein, "Days of Manasseh", 181). Rather, these suggestions are undergirded by the supposition of the basic historicity of 2 Chr. 33:11-17, a text which will be discussed below.

189 Gane, "Role of Assyria", 23-24; Ben Zvi, "Prelude to a Reconstruction", 33.

190 Halpern, "Jerusalem and the Lineages", 64-65, 70; Halpern, "Sybil, or the Two Nations?", 326-328; Barrick, *King and the Cemeteries*, 154-159.

thereby heightening the contrast between the dislocated rural population of Judah and the city-dwelling elites in Jerusalem.[191]

Thus it was under the direction of Manasseh that Judah not only recovered from the devastation of c. 701 BCE, but positively flourished; the kingdom was transformed from a wasteland into a highly developed state.[192] It is no exaggeration to describe Manasseh's reign as "the climax of Judah's monarchic history".[193] In populating what was left of the rural areas, maximizing the production of cash crops, drawing Judah into the profitable trade markets of the empire, and strengthening her fortifications, Manasseh is perhaps better considered the "constructor" of Judah, rather than its "destructor", as the Kings Writer claims.

Given the scarcity of non-biblical evidence directly relating to Manasseh, further discussion becomes admittedly more dependent upon the biblical material than is methodologically preferable. However, despite this discomfort, and in an attempt to avoid distortion as far as possible, the heavy bias of the biblical texts may be counter-balanced by the recognition of biblical polemic and its ideological agenda outlined in the previous chapter, combined with a careful process of historical contextualization and probability.

Locating potential fossils of historicity within the biblical accounts of Manasseh's reign is hugely problematic given the ideological and tendentious nature of the texts. There is a temptation to superimpose upon the historical profile of Manasseh's Judah details from the biblical accounts. Illustrative of this is the suggestion that the biblical claim that Hezekiah dismantled the *bamoth* is to be related to non-biblical evidence for his urbanization programme, which shut down the countryside in preparation for rebellion against Assyria.[194] The corresponding assumption, then, is that in repopulating what was left of Judah's countryside, Manasseh restored the *bamoth*, as is claimed in the Hebrew Bible.[195] Though theoretically possible, the specific and direct association of Manasseh's supposed cult crimes listed in Kings with the historical profile of Judah is best avoided given the polemical nature of the account. As Ben Zvi similarly comments, "equating

---

191 Note also Barrick, *King and the Cemeteries*, 150, and the literature cited there.
192 Finkelstein and Silberman, *Bible Unearthed*, 273. Halpern ("Jerusalem and the Lineages", 60) describes Manasseh as accomplishing "an astonishing revival" of Judah.
193 F. Sawah, "Jerusalem in the Time of the Kingdom of Judah", in Thompson, *Jerusalem in Ancient History and Tradition*, 114-144 (133).
194 Halpern, "Jerusalem and the Lineages", 26-28; Barrick, *King and the Cemeteries*, 149-150.
195 Halpern, "Jerusalem and the Lineages", 64-70; Barrick, *King and the Cemeteries*, 193.

the historical Judahite cult in the Manassic era with the report in Kings is simplistic, and most likely misleading".[196] However, it is important to note that even if the cultic practices accredited to Manasseh are representative of the religious milieu of the historical Manasseh's Judah, they should not be considered as foreign, non-*Yhwh*istic acts of worship,[197] but rather, as part and parcel of the normative and native polytheism of Judah, in which *Yhwh*-worship played an important role.[198] This will be illustrated in the examination of child sacrifice in later chapters.

Though the majority of the accusations levelled at Manasseh by the Kings Writer may thus be discounted as historically unreliable given their function as ideological polemic, many scholars have argued for the historicity of one particular crime of which Manasseh is accused: that of his shedding copious amounts of innocent blood (2 Kgs 21:16; 24:3-4). This peculiar accusation has prompted some to argue that Manasseh systematically eliminated any opponents. Oded identifies these opponents as rival factions within Judah, perhaps those opposing Manasseh's supposed pro-Assyrian policies.[199] Ahlström tentatively suggests that Manasseh could have "neutralized" disruptive elements within the state, such as civil servants, military or cultic personnel.[200] However, there is no evidence to support the assumption that "innocent bloodshed" should be understood as referring to the murder of establishment figures. Alternatively, others have sought to identify Manasseh's "innocent victims" with *Yhwh*'s prophets: stepping blindly from the Kings Writer's account of Manasseh's reign, these scholars tend to combine the textual comparison between Manasseh and Ahab, the notorious persecutor of YHWH's prophets, with the apparent lack of prophetic material from this period within the Hebrew Bible, thereby surmising that Manasseh's shedding of innocent blood refers to his murderous suppression of *Yhwh*'s prophets.[201] However, this is pure conjecture. Nielsen suggests that the

---

196 Ben Zvi, "Prelude to a Reconstruction", 37.
197 E.g., Hoffman, *Reform und Reformen*, 144, 164-166; B. Peckham, "Israel and Phoenicia", in F.M. Cross, W.E. Lemke and P.D. Miller (eds.), *Magnalia Dei: The Mighty Acts of God: Essays on the Bible and Archaeology in Memory of G. Ernest Wright* (Garden City: Doubleday, 1976), 224-248 (238); Oded, "Judah and the Exile", 453, 463; McKay, *Religion in Judah*, 67; Kaufmann, *Religion of Israel*, 430.
198 See also Ahlström, *Royal Administration*, 75-81.
199 Oded, "Judah and the Exile", 453-454.
200 Ahlström, *History of Ancient Palestine*, 737-738.
201 Eg. Cogan, "Into Exile", 255; Soggin, *Introduction*, 269; M. Rehm, *Das zweite Buch der Könige: Ein Kommentar* (Würzburg: Echter Verlag, 1982), 210; Gray, *I & II Kings*, 709; Montgomery and Gehman, *Kings*, 521.

apparent absence of prophecy during Manasseh's reign may be indicative of the Assyrian domination of Judahite politics, during which there were no major political crises to provoke a response from the prophets.[202] Yet as observed above, the lack of prophetic material related to Manasseh's reign coheres with the lack of any other allusions to Manasseh and his reign outside of Kings, Chronicles and Jer. 15:4. Thus a more plausible means of accounting for the lack of prophetic texts from Manasseh's reign is that additional material relating to Manasseh has been deliberately excluded, or censored, from the biblical story of Israel.

Rather than alluding to an historical feature of Manasseh's reign, the mysterious reference to "innocent blood" is better understood as an ideological tool. As has been seen, Lasine argues that this charge against Manasseh seeks to distance both the Kings Writer and his audience from the sinful Judahites whom Manasseh supposedly led astray. The Kings Writer's intended audience thus identifies its ancestors with the "innocent blood" shed by Manasseh, not with the people following in Manasseh's idolatrous footsteps, who brought punishment upon Judah and Jerusalem.[203] The deliberate vagueness of the charge in 21:16 and its clumsy appearance at the close of the Manasseh narrative suggest that this detail is not an echo from history, but a false memory. As Lasine explains, the vagueness of the accusation leaves room for the "innocent" readers to find their ancestors among Manasseh's victims.[204] Crafted through ideological motivation, this verse thus seeks to remedy the spiritual ills of a displaced, post-monarchic audience who are concerned to identify with their monarchic ancestors without inheriting the legacy of their apparent idolatry.

The account of Manasseh's reign in Kings thus reveals more about its author than it can about the historical Manasseh. But can the account in Chronicles add anything to the historical survey? Some scholars argue that it can.[205] The most significant difference between the Manasseh narratives in Kings and Chronicles is the fact that the theological judgement of the Manasseh of Kings differs fundamentally from that of the Chronicler. As has

---

202 Nielsen, "Political Conditions", 104-105.

203 Lasine, "Manasseh as Villain", 182.

204 Lasine, "Manasseh as Villain", 182.

205 For discussions favouring the basic historicity of the Chronicler's distinctive material concerning Manasseh, see B. Kelly, "Manasseh in the Books of Kings and Chronicles (2 Kings 21:1-18; 2 Chron 33:1-20)", in V. Philips Long, D.W. Baker and G.J. Wenham (eds.), *Windows into Old Testament History: Evidence, Argument, and the Crisis of "Biblical Israel"* (Grand Rapids: Eerdmans, 2002), 131-146; Cogan, "Into Exile", 253-254; Japhet, *I & II Chronicles*, 1003-1004); Tatum, "King Manasseh", 136-145.

been seen, the first half of the Chronicler's account of Manasseh's reign follows the Kings presentation almost exactly. Manasseh is once again depicted as the archvillain of the Davidic house: he reverses the reforms of Hezekiah, he introduces astral cults into the Temple, he practises soothsaying, divining and sorcery, and he sacrifices his son (2 Chr. 33:3-7). However, whereas the Manasseh of Kings pursues this idolatrous lifestyle for the entirety of his reign without incurring punishment, of neither a personal nor a national nature, the Chronicler's Manasseh is suddenly taken captive by the Assyrians, and exiled to Babylon. There, the idolatrous king repents and is duly restored to his throne in Judah, where he purges the cult and carries out an extensive building project and military activities (33:11-17). The two accounts thus diverge so fundamentally that many scholars simply select the story they feel is the more historically reliable, and then accept uncritically its presentation of Manasseh. Consequently, most supposedly historical reconstructions of the Judahite monarchy portray Manasseh either as an idolatrous, syncretistic villain courting the religious affections of Assyria, or as a repentant, reforming vassal who was simply the victim of Assyrian supremacy. It has already been argued that the Kings account has little historical value. But given that the Chronicler's version of events is so different, could it be that parts of this account can be given historical credence?

The material unique to the Chronicler is often held to be theologically-crafted, rather than historically reliable. As has been seen, the reference to Manasseh's exile to Babylon is most persuasively argued to be a deliberate typological motif within the Chronicler's narrative. By having Manasseh exiled by the Assyrians to Babylon, rather than to the Assyrian capital Nineveh, the Chronicler sets up a theological paradigm of sin-repentance-restoration for his post-exilic audience, demonstrating that the punished, idolatrous Israel can, like Manasseh, repent and be restored. However, some scholars argue for the historicity of the Chronicler's account of Manasseh's exile.

A range of possible contexts for Manasseh's deportation and reinstatement have been offered.[206] Among the most popular is the suggestion that during the period 652–648 BCE, King Asshurbanipal was busy putting down a rebellion led by his younger brother, Shamash-shumukin, king of Babylon, thereby providing Assyria's vassals with an opportunity to revolt. But Asshurbanipal defeated his brother, and in 648

---

206 See Oded, "Judah and the Exile", 455.

BCE was thus in Babylon, from where he directed the suppression of smaller revolts in his empire.[207] The supposition then is that Manasseh was among a group of western kings arrested for plotting against Assyria, and was taken to the Assyrian king who remained in Babylon. However, Manasseh was pardoned, or his innocence accepted, and reinstated upon the Judahite throne as a loyal vassal.[208] Thus the reference to Babylon in 2 Chr. 33:11 is held to authenticate the Chronicler's account of Manasseh's deportation. It is further supported by Assyrian texts describing the reinstallation of Necho as an Egyptian king after his collusion with other Egyptian vassals to expel Assurbanipal's Assyria from Egypt.[209] This therefore provides a favourable point of historical comparison for the Chronicler's account of Manasseh's capture and reinstatement. However, despite a degree of plausibility, these hypotheses are purely speculative, for there is no non-biblical evidence for Manasseh's plotting, rebellion, or exile.[210] Rather, the extant Assyrian texts relating to Manasseh, or to Judah in the period of his reign, consistently portray him as an obedient vassal. Given the devastating results of Hezekiah's rebellion in c. 701 BCE, which Manasseh would have witnessed as a child, and the probability that Jerusalem lay only a day's march away from Assyria's borders, it is unlikely that Manasseh would have risked rebellion.[211] Indeed, archaeological evidence for the continued presence of Assyrian troops in southern Palestine suggest the likelihood that, as Nelson comments, Manasseh "may have had some sort of Assyrian high commissioner watching over his shoulder".[212] Moreover, even if Manasseh were taken captive by the Assyrians, it is odd that the Kings Writer does not make theological use of such an event, as indeed Nielsen remarks: "even a transitory deportation of the Judean king should have been regarded by the Deuteronomists as a punishment, and it is therefore difficult to maintain that

---

207 Gwaltney, "Assyrians", 98-100.
208 E.g., A.F. Rainey, "Manasseh, King of Judah, in the Whirlpool of the Seventh Century BCE", *TA* 1 (1993), 147-164 (160-162); E.L. Ehrlich, "Der Aufenthalt des Königs Manasse in Babylon", *ThZ* 21 (1965), 281-286; McKay, *Religion in Judah*, 25-26. Also supporting the basic historicity of Manasseh's brief deportation are Cogan, *Imperialism and Religion*, 67-69; *idem.*, "Into Exile", 254; Bright, *History of Israel*, 311-314; Japhet, *I & II Chronicles*, 1003-1004.
209 *ANET*, 294-295; see also Gane, "Role of Assyria", 24-25, and the literature cited there.
210 See further Ben Zvi, "Prelude to a Reconstruction", 39-41.
211 Ben Zvi, "Prelude to a Reconstruction", 39.
212 Nelson, "Realpolitik", 179.

such a tradition should have been suppressed by them, had they any knowledge of it."[213]

Though the Chronicler's account of Manasseh's captivity is not historically credible, other aspects of his unique material have been deemed historical. Ahlström cannot dismiss the Chronicler's report as a complete invention. He argues that the account of Manasseh's building projects (33:14) reflects an historical period of expansion. His loyalty as a vassal was rewarded, Ahlström proposes, with the return of several of the territories lost in the events of c. 701 BCE. Consequently, fortifying regained territories would have been a priority for Manasseh. Moreover, evidence for the construction of an outer wall in Jerusalem during Manasseh's reign appears to cohere with the Chronicler's account.[214] Similarly, Tatum argues that archaeological evidence for the (re)construction of forts in Judah is to be directly related to the Chronicler's account of Manasseh's building and military projects.[215] Rainey claims that the Kings Writer has deliberately suppressed information about Manasseh's cultic, military and building programmes in order to hold him responsible for the destruction of the kingdom.[216] However, though the information in 33:14 coheres with archaeological evidence indicating that Manasseh did carry out extensive building projects and military fortifications, it is circumstantial rather than conclusive.[217] Moreover, this historical evidence cannot verify the Chronicler's account of Manasseh's reign. As Ben Zvi comments:[218]

> ... archaeological data pointing to building activities during the seventh century are irrelevant to the question of the historicity of the account in Chronicles. True ... new settlements were established and Jerusalem grew larger ... But what do these developments tell us about the existence or non-existence of historically reliable sources underlying the Chronicler's account of Manasseh? An appeal to the archaeological data to answer this question is reasonable only if one accepts beforehand the existence of sources connecting between building activities that took place in the monarchic account and the Chronicler's account. This being the case, such an appeal represents a clear case of circular thinking, because it assumes what it is to prove.[219]

---

213 Nielsen, "Political Conditions", 104; so too Evans, "Manasseh", 499.
214 Ahlström, *Royal Administration*, 75-81; *idem.*, *History of Ancient Palestine*, 733-737.
215 Tatum, "King Manasseh", 136-145.
216 Rainey, "Chronicler and his Sources", 54.
217 Particularly in view of the theological significance the Chronicler attaches to royal construction, military and cultic activities, as discussed above, 1.2.
218 See further Ben Zvi, "Prelude to a Reconstruction", 41-43.
219 Ben Zvi, "Prelude to a Reconstruction", 43.

It would thus appear that relatively little can be discerned about the historical Manasseh from the biblical accounts of his reign. Yet the portrayals of Manasseh in Kings and Chronicles do offer one piece of historically reliable information about Manasseh that is of primary importance: his name. As has been seen, it is Manasseh's Northern name that provokes his scapegoating in Kings. In Chronicles, Manasseh's name does not appear to be as divisive as it is in Kings, though it is possible that Manasseh's repentance and restoration in Jerusalem could be seen to offer a theological model to the people of the former Northern Kingdom. The question thus remains whether the historical Manasseh's name carried any ideological significance, and if so, whether the nature of this significance may be discerned in order to shed a little more light upon the Manasseh of history.

In considering this question, the first point of emphasis is that for the sake of clarity, the discussion will assume that Manasseh was named at birth, though it is not impossible that he assumed the name Manasseh as a throne-name upon his accession.[220] The second point of emphasis must be that although Manasseh's name is of ideological significance within the biblical portrayals of his reign,[221] it is quite possible that the historical Manasseh's name may not have carried ideological overtones at all. Indeed, the name Manasseh, meaning "he who makes forget", may have been appropriate: some scholars have expressed doubts that Manasseh was Hezekiah's firstborn son, for according to the biblical chronology as it stands, Hezekiah was in his early forties when Manasseh was born. This makes it unlikely that Manasseh was Hezekiah's first child. However, it may be that Manasseh was Hezekiah's (only) surviving son and heir.[222] If this were the case, Manasseh's

---

220 Cf. 2 Sam. 12:24-25; 2 Kgs 23:34; 24:17. For the possibility of the Judahite kings (including Manasseh) possessing private names and throne names, see A.M. Honeyman, "The Evidence for Regnal Names among the Hebrews", *JBL* 67 (1948), 13-25. If the seal inscription discussed above can be related to the royal Manasseh, it might offer confirmation of Manasseh being given his name as a child, before his accession.

221 As argued in 1.3.

222 A further possibility is that Manasseh's older siblings were passed over in favour of his accession (Cogan and Tadmor, *II Kings*, 266). Schmidt (*Beneficent Dead*, 238) suggests that the Assyrians selected Manasseh over his older brothers (note also Barrick, *Kings and the Cemeteries*, 150). Barrick considers it more likely that Hezekiah was Manasseh's grandfather, his father—Hezekiah's son and heir—having been killed during the Assyrian attacks in 701 BCE (*idem.*, "Genealogical Notes on the 'House of David' and the 'House of Zadok'", *JSOT* 96 [2001]: 29-58; *idem.*, *King and the Cemeteries*, 144 n. 3, 150; *idem.*, "Dynastic Politics, Priestly Succession, and Josiah's Eighth Year", *ZAW* 112 [2000]: 564-582).

name would appropriately reflect the joy of the birth of a new royal prince, easing the pain of the loss of his older sibling(s).[223]

An alternative suggestion accounting for the significance of Manasseh's name is briefly proposed by Lubetski, who argues that Hezekiah chose the name Manasseh for his son as a sign of his political alliance with Egypt:

> [Hezekiah] chose a name that originated on Egyptian soil. Manasseh was the name Joseph gave to his own firstborn—from his Egyptian wife, daughter of the priest of "'Ôn" (Genesis 41:50-51), hence a grandson to an Egyptian rē or priest ... the king who renewed his interest in Judah's southwestern neighbor chose to revive a name for his only son and heir to the throne that evoked an association with Egypt.[224]

However, though it is possible that Hezekiah did align himself with Egypt at times during his reign, it is unlikely that he named his son Manasseh as an allusion to this political stance, for the assumed Egyptian connection is somewhat opaque. Rather, one would expect a name with a more explicit association with Egypt, such that borne by Manasseh's successor, Amon.[225]

A further possibility is offered by Oded, who proposes that in naming his son Manasseh after one of the most powerful northern tribes, Hezekiah alluded to his political ambition to reunite all the "tribes of Israel" under the reign of the Davidic dynasty.[226] However, as this study has argued, the conventional view of the original unity of the north and south—be it in terms of a "tribal" system or a burgeoning monarchy—is highly unlikely.[227] Yet it remains notable that a Judahite king should share a name with the powerful Northern territory. Manasseh's name may thus cohere with the conventional view that during the eighth and seventh centuries, the royal house of Judah sought some sort of reunification with the (former) Kingdom of Israel.[228]

---

223 The interesting anomaly that Manasseh's name does not exhibit a theophoric element derived from the name of the patron deity of the monarchy, *Yhwh* (unlike most other Judahite monarchs), may further suggest that he was not the heir to the throne when he was named.

224 Lubetski, "King Hezekiah's Seal", 48.

225 Lubetski ("King Hezekiah's Seal", 48) proposes that Amon's Egyptian name demonstrates Judah's pro-Egyptian stance; *contra* D. Rudman, "A Note on the Personal Name Amon (2 Kings 21, 19-26//2 Chr 33, 21-25)", *Bib* 81 (2000), 403-405, who argues that Manasseh named his son and heir Amon to commemorate Assurbanipal's capture of the capital city known in Hebrew as נא אמון (Egyptian Ni').

226 Oded, "Judah and the Exile", 444; Williamson, *1 and 2 Chronicles*, 361.

227 See 2.1 above.

228 See for example, Oded, "Judah and the Exile", 445-446, 463-468; Braun, "A Reconsideration", 59-62; Cross and Freedman, "Josiah's Revolt", 56-58; H.H. Rowley, *Men of God: Studies in Old Testament History and Prophecy* (London: Nelson, 1963),

However, rather than signifying hope for a *re*unification—which is
historically improbable given both the original separateness of Israel and
Judah and the total assimilation of the territories of the former Kingdom of
Israel into the Assyrian empire—it may be that Manasseh's name reflects the
perhaps covert ambitions of the royal Judahite house to exert some sort of
influence, whether in terms of territory or trade, within the affluent heartland
of the former Kingdom of Israel.

Moreover, it may be that Manasseh did have a special connection with
the Northern territory of the same name. If the biblical texts providing the
names, patronyms and origins of the Judahite Queen Mothers are accepted,
then this connection may be alluded to in 2 Kgs 21:19. This text introduces
Amon as Manasseh's son and heir, and names the new king's mother as
Meshullemeth, daughter of Haruz of Jotbah. The implication then is that
Meshullemeth is one of Manasseh's wives.[229] Though the location of Jotbah
is disputed, it is likely that Meshullemeth came from the town called Jotbah
in the Manassite territory of the new Assyrian empire (formerly the Kingdom
of Israel).[230] This likelihood is strengthened in view of Judah's post-701 BCE
status as an obedient Assyrian vassal, which would necessarily infer Assyrian
approval of any royal marriages.[231] This marriage may thus reflect a political
relationship between the royal house of Judah and an important Manassite
family of the former Kingdom of Israel, now part of Assyria.[232]

However, although Manasseh's northern name and his possible northern
marriage may suggest a special connection with the territory of the same
name, it is equally possible that his name did not signal a political

---

98-132; M. Weinfeld, "Cult Centralization in Israel in the Light of a Neo-Babylonian
  Analogy", *JNES* 23 (1964), 202-212; D.C. Greenwood, "On the Jewish Hope for a
  Restored Northern Kingdom", *ZAW* 88 (1976), 376-385.

229 Though note Barrick's suggestion ("Dynastic Politics", 566). that Manasseh is Amon's
  grandfather, thereby rendering Meshullemeth his daughter-in-law, rather than wife.

230 So too Dalley, "Yabâ, Atalyā", 93; Barrick, "Dynastic Politics", 566; *pace* Gray, *I & II
  Kings*, 711, and Ahlström (*History of Ancient Palestine*, 734), who suggest
  Meshullemeth was an Edomite; cf. Num. 33:33-34; Deut. 10:7.

231 Barrick, "Dynastic Politics", 566.

232 On the marriages between the royal house of Judah and the former Kingdom of Israel,
  see W.F. Albright, *The Biblical Period* (Oxford: Blackwell, 1952), 45. It has been
  suggested that Meshullemeth may have been a particularly powerful Queen Mother, on
  the premise that cultic reforms are often seen to occur after the tenure of such Queen
  Mothers, so K. Spanier, "The Northern Israelite Queen Mother in the Judaean Court:
  Athaliah and Abi", in M. Lubetski, C. Gottlieb and S. Keller (eds.), *Boundaries of the
  Ancient Near Eastern World: A Tribute to Cyrus H. Gordon* (JSOTSup 273; Sheffield:
  Sheffield Academic Press, 1998), 143, n. 36. For literature concerning the possible
  status and role of the Queen Mother, see above 25, n. 44.

relationship or an ideological programme. Instead, the name Manasseh may simply reflect the prestigious and long-lived reputation of the territory of the same name, which, despite the Assyrian take-over of the Kingdom of Israel, remained economically and politically powerful.[233] As such, perhaps the name Manasseh had become synonymous with power, prestige and affluence—a suitable designation for a royal prince, particularly for a prince born in the boom years of Judah.

It is impossible to ascertain the reasons motivating the selection of the historical Manasseh's name. However, as this study has argued, what is more certain is that it is the very fact of Manasseh's name that has provoked his scapegoating in Kings as the idolatrous and murderous monarch who caused the destruction of his kingdom. However, this portrayal of Manasseh is far removed from the probable historical reality. The real king Manasseh of Judah was a successful monarch, who rebuilt the decimated kingdom he inherited into a flourishing state. Modern accusations and implications that Manasseh was pro-Assyrian and anti-nationalistic must be dismissed as misleading. As Nelson comments, "Are we to believe that any king of Judah was ever pro-Assyrian in the sense that he would go one single step beyond the national self-interest in supporting Assyrian policy?"[234] Yet despite his success as a monarch, the portrayal of Manasseh within biblical and post-biblical traditions and within modern scholarship has been distorted almost beyond recognition. It is to this distortion that that the discussion will now turn.

---

233 On the material development of the Assyrian provinces in the former Kingdom of Israel, see for example Stern, *Archaeology*, 42-57.
234 Nelson, "Realpolitik", 178; cf. Soggin, *History*, 268.

3 The Distortion of Manasseh

In the light of the discussions of the preceding chapters, it is reasonable to assert that the biblical Manasseh bears little resemblance to the Manasseh of history. As has been seen, the deliberate biblical distortion of one of Judah's most successful monarchs serves an important ideological function. It is well-known that the aftermath of the Babylonian conquest of Judah and the destruction of Jerusalem was likely to have been theologically and socially disorienting. Consequently, the Kings Writer and his audience sought a theologically comprehensive explanation for the disaster that not only maintained both the potency of YHWH as the patron deity of Judah and the people's divinely-ordained claim upon their land, but also functioned as a socio-religious blueprint for a potentially new "Israel". In simple terms, this careful balance appears to have been achieved in three related stages: first, the destruction and loss of the land was interpreted as a punishment from YHWH; second, the punishment was understood to result from "foreign" cult practices offensive to YHWH; third, a scapegoat was personally blamed for promoting the "foreign" cult practices that led inevitably to exile. For the Kings Writer, Manasseh was the ideal scapegoat: in bearing a name equated with the hated and exiled Northern Kingdom, he was labelled as "foreign" and accused of leading his subjects astray with his "foreign" cult practices. Moreover, Manasseh's lengthy reign may also have been taken to account for both the magnitude and pervading affects of his cult crimes, which thereby disabled the intended function of Josiah's brief reform.

The biblical distortion of the Manasseh of history was also effected in other ways within the Hebrew Bible. Though the foundation text for this distortion was the portrayal of Manasseh in Kings, increasing distortions mutated this figure further, to the point at which the Chronicler employed Manasseh as a paradigm of the newly blessed and restored "Israel". The distortion of the figure of Manasseh was thus begun within the Hebrew Bible, yet it continued unabated within several post-biblical traditions, and is even perpetuated by modern scholarship. It is to some of these "afterlives" of Manasseh that the discussion will now turn.

3.1 Afterlives of Manasseh

Like the Hebrew Bible, rabbinic traditions exhibit both negative and positive portraits of King Manasseh. Whilst some of these post-biblical "afterlives" may be direct elaborations upon the biblical stories of Manasseh, others exhibit little relation to the biblical accounts. One afterlife which may be rooted within the Kings Writer's portrait of Manasseh as a Law-breaker (2 Kgs 21:8) is the tradition portraying him as the violator of Torah: he is accused of examining the Scriptures in order to prove them worthless;[1] he is said to have removed the divine name from the Torah;[2] and it is claimed that as a youth Manasseh was brought to the "house of learning" where he poked fun at his pious father.[3] Rabbinic tradition exaggerates further the biblical portrayals of Manasseh as an idolater in claiming that he destroyed the altar in the Jerusalem temple and set in its place an idol with four faces, so that whichever way one entered the Temple, the face of an idol would always be visible. He is also said to have constructed an idolatrous image weighing as much as one thousand men, whom it would kill each day.[4] This rabbinic accusation against Manasseh appears to draw upon the biblical portrayal of Manasseh as both an arch-idolater and shedder of copious amounts of innocent blood.

Manasseh's infamous afterlife as a prophet-killer may also be rooted within the biblical accusation that he shed innocent blood (2 Kgs 21:16). Several traditions depict Manasseh as the murderer of Isaiah. These traditions appear in various forms within rabbinic midrashim[5] and in the *Ascension of Isaiah*, the first part of which is known as the *Martyrdom of Isaiah*, widely-held to date to the first century CE.[6] Given this variety, it may be that the

---

1   *b. Sanh.* 99b.

2   See further A. Shemesh, "King Manasseh and the Halakhah of the Sadducees", *JJS* 52 (2001), 27-39.

3   *b. Ber.* 10a. Like some modern commentators, the rabbis relate Manasseh's name to his sinful behaviour, deriving the name from *nšh* "forget", because Manasseh "forgot" his God and the ways of his father Hezekiah (so *b. Sanh.* 102b); see also Johnstone, *1 and 2 Chronicles*, vol. 2, 223; J. Jarick, *1 Chronicles* (Sheffield: Sheffield Academic Press, 2002), 59.

4   *b. Sanh.* 103b. Manasseh's persistent, ambitious apostasy and lawlessness is ascribed to his strengthening by Satan in *Mart. Isa.* 2:4-5, which enabled him to increase the practice of witchcraft, magic, divination, fornication, adultery and the persecution of the righteous throughout Israel.

5   *b. Sanh.* 103b; *b. Yev.* 49b; *y. Sanh.* 10.28c; *Targ. Isa.* 66:1; *Pesiq. Rab.* 4:3.

6   See M.A. Knibb, "Martyrdom and Ascension of Isaiah", *OTP*, vol. 2, 143-176.

underlying legend telling that Manasseh killed Isaiah is very early indeed.[7] One version relates the killing of Isaiah to the graven image Manasseh sets in the temple. In rebuking Manasseh, Isaiah prophesies that the temple will be destroyed and that Judah will fall to the Babylonians. The prophet then hides within a tree which Manasseh saws into two.[8] A second version of the story describes Manasseh entrapping the prophet on a charge of heresy. In attempting to escape Manasseh, Isaiah utters the Divine Name and is promptly swallowed by a cedar tree, in which he is killed.[9] Like other Jewish stories about martyred prophets, one of the primary functions of the Isaiah legend is to account for the sudden disappearance of Isaiah from the biblical story.[10] Yet it is also a further example of the scapegoating of Manasseh, for setting the prophet—and his death—within a reign of utter wickedness and idolatry creates an ideal context in which the disappearance of the prophet from the scriptures could be explained. The further scapegoating of Manasseh is also evident in rabbinic claims that Manasseh murdered a family member, for Isaiah is rendered Manasseh's maternal grandfather. Though this has no parallel in the Hebrew Bible, this tradition creates the story that Manasseh is the son born of the marriage of Hezekiah and Isaiah's daughter.[11] The rabbinic charges that Manasseh not only raped married women,[12] but also committed incest by sexually violating his sister, heighten the defamation of Manasseh's character further.[13]

Despite this villainous characterization of Manasseh, rabbinic tradition also exhibits positive portrayals of Manasseh. The same tradition portraying Manasseh as the violator of Torah also depicts him as a brilliant scholar, who interpreted the laws regarding priesthood within the book of Leviticus in fifty-five different ways, corresponding to each year of his reign.[14] Manasseh is also presented as a great interpreter of the Law in the story of his appearance in a dream to Rabbi Rav Ashi, in which he teaches the rabbi the

---

7   See further B.H. Amaru, "The Killing of the Prophets: Unraveling a Midrash", *HUCA* 54 (1983), 153-180, esp. 172. The legend is also alluded to in Heb. 11:37.
8   *b. Sanh.* 103b; *y. Sanh.* 10.28c; *y. Taʿan.* 4.68d; *Targ. Isa.* 66:1; *Targ. 2 Kgs* 21:16.
9   *b. Yev.* 49b; *Mart. Isa.* 3:1-12.
10 Amaru, "Killing of the Prophets", 175.
11 *y. Sanh.* 10.28c. This tradition is perhaps encouraged by the oracle associated with the prophet Isaiah concerning the naming of Jerusalem as "Hephzibah" (Isa. 62:4), which is given as the name of Manasseh's mother in 2 Kgs 21:1.
12 *2 Bar.* 64:2-3.
13 *b. Sanh.* 103b.
14 *b. Sanh.* 103b; cf. *b. Sukk.* 52a.

answers to highly technical, theological questions.[15] Rabbinic traditions concerning Manasseh's repentance and restoration are probably based upon the Chronicler's account, although suspicion of this king clearly persisted as the integrity of his repentance was contested.[16] Talmudic tradition asserts that Jeroboam, Ahab and Manasseh are so wicked that despite all Israelites being granted a share in the world to come, these three kings have forfeited their share. However, the pious Rabbi Judah bar Ilai objects to this divine rejection of Manasseh because Scripture attests that the wicked king repented before God.[17] The third century rabbi Johanan also discusses Manasseh's repentance, claiming that whoever denies Manasseh his share in the world to come weakens the power of repentance.[18] Similarly, another tradition states that when the angels begged God not to accept Manasseh's repentance, God answered that if he rejected Manasseh, God himself would be denying the chance for repentance to all sinners. God then causes a wind to arise to carry Manasseh back to Jerusalem from his captivity in Babylon.[19]

Manasseh's rabbinic "afterlives" as both idolatrous villain and penitent sinner clearly complement the biblical portrayals of Manasseh. Indeed, these traditions are probably best identified as elaborations and interpretations of the portrayals of Manasseh in Kings and Chronicles, demonstrating the ease with which the figure of Manasseh has been adopted and adapted to serve particular functions. This process of adoption and adaptation is also clearly visible within the writings of Josephus. Despite his claim that he has not added to or subtracted from Scripture in his retelling of the story of Israel (*Ant.* I.17) Josephus appears to embellish or omit scriptural material from his account of Israel's past.[20] In his *Antiquities*, Josephus' portrayal of Manasseh (*Ant.* X.3) would seem to draw upon both biblical and rabbinic traditions, for it is moulded upon the Chronicler's account, supplemented by details from

---

15 *b. Sanh.* 102b.

16 Amaru, "Killing of the Prophets", 174.

17 *m. Sanh.* 10.1-2.

18 *b. Sanh.* 103a.

19 *y. Sanh.* 10.2.28c; *Pesiq. Rab. Kah.* 24.11; cf. *Deut. Rab.* 2.20.

20 H. Feldman, "Josephus' Portrait of Manasseh", *JSP* 9 (1991), 3-20; *idem.*, "Use, Authority and Exegesis of Mikra in the Writings of Josephus", in M.J. Mulder and H. Sysling (eds.) *Mikra: Text, Translation, Reading and Interpretation of the Hebrew Bible in Ancient Judaism and Early Christianity* (CRINT 2.1; Assen: Van Gorcum, 1988), 466-470.

Kings, and coloured by traditions which are found recorded in later rabbinic material.[21]

Like the Chronicler's version, Josephus' account of Manasseh's reign falls into two contrasting halves: a period of wickedness and impiety is followed by a period of piety and construction. However, one of the most striking features of Josephus' narrative is that unlike both biblical versions, it does not dwell upon the particularities of Manasseh's idolatry, but instead briefly summarizes the biblical lists of his cult crimes (2 Kgs 21:2-9; 2 Chr. 33:2-9) in just a few words:

> [Manasseh] broke away from his father's practices and took the opposite course, exhibiting every form of wickedness in his conduct and leaving no impious act undone, but imitating the lawless deeds of the Israelites wherein they sinned against God and so perished. He even dared to pollute the temple of God as well as the city and the entire country.[22]

One of the most striking features of Josephus' account is that Manasseh's impious behaviour is not likened to that of foreigners—the Amorites (2 Kgs 21:11) and the nations (2 Kgs 21:2, 9; 2 Chr. 33:2, 9)—but as that of the Israelites. Yet Josephus is writing primarily for non-Jews, and his main concern is the response of his audience. As Feldman argues, throughout *Antiquities* Josephus seeks to refute the gentile charge that the Jews are misanthropists and hostile to foreigners.[23] Consequently, Josephus deliberately shifts the focus away from the biblical claim that Manasseh's sins are those of the foreign nations, and instead makes the more general statement that Manasseh was wicked in every way, and committed every impious act, thereby avoiding a perceived attack upon the beliefs and practices of non-Jewish peoples.

Another striking feature of Josephus' account of Manasseh's reign is his accusation that Manasseh regularly massacred the prophets and the righteous, crimes which Josephus implies were prompted by Manasseh's disdain for God:

---

21 The possibility that Josephus drew upon these oral rabbinic traditions is suggested not only by his selection of material, but also by his testimony of his education in Jerusalem (*Life* VIII–IX) during which, he claims, he far excelled his peers in Jewish learning (*Ant.* XX.263).

22 *Ant.* X.37, following the translation of R. Marcus in *Jewish Antiquities IX–XI* (LCL 326; London: Harvard University Press, 1937), 179.

23 Feldman, "Josephus' Portrait", 8-10.

> ... setting out with a contempt of God, he killed all the righteous men among the Hebrews, nor did he spare even the prophets, some of whom he slaughtered daily, so that Jerusalem ran with blood.[24]

This passage is clearly reminiscent of the Kings Writer's repeated claim that "Manasseh shed very much innocent blood until he had filled Jerusalem from end to end" (2 Kgs 21:16; cf. 24:3-4). Moreover, Josephus appears to have elaborated upon this biblical accusation by means of the rabbinic traditions of Manasseh's murderous persecution of the prophets surveyed above. Similarly, Josephus also includes and elaborates upon the biblical claims that Manasseh and his people were warned by the prophets of the disastrous consequences of their behaviour:

> God, being wrathful at these things, sent prophets to the king and the people, and through these threatened them with the same calamities which had befallen their Israelite brothers when they outraged him. They were not, however, persuaded by these words, from which they might so have profited as not to experience any misfortune, but had to learn from deeds the truth of what the prophets said.[25]

This text states explicitly what the Kings Writer made implicit: that the Law-breaking behaviour of Manasseh and his people will lead to the destruction of the kingdom just as the same behaviour led to the destruction of the Northern Kingdom. It is thus clear that Josephus, or the tradition on which he is drawing, has understood the ideological motifs of land dispossession planted throughout Kings. It is perhaps with his gentile audience in mind that Josephus appears to deviate from the Chronicler's account of Manasseh's exile in two significant ways. First, he describes the antagonist as the king of Babylonia and Chaldea, not Assyria, presumably to remedy the Chronicler's assertion that Manasseh was taken to Babylon.[26] Second, he asserts that Manasseh was captured by cunning, presumably to negate the assumption that Manasseh was militarily weak.[27] Interestingly, this last difference may reflect the magical overtones of the Chronicler's language, as noted in the preceding chapter.[28]

Another way in which Josephus adopts and adapts his inherited Manasseh traditions is the distinctive way in which he describes the process of

---

24 *Ant.* X.38.
25 *Ant.* X.39.
26 *Ant.* X.40; cf. 2 Chr. 33:11.
27 *Ant.* X.40.
28 See above, 50, n. 172.

Manasseh's repentance. If Josephus has drawn upon a version of the Chronicler's account—which is most likely—he has expanded 2 Chr. 33:12 in stating that Manasseh not only prays to God, but realizes that it is his own behaviour that has caused his plight. Josephus emphasizes that Manasseh's repentance is a continuous process, for even upon his return to Jerusalem, Manasseh remains anxious to maintain his repentance and forget his former sins against God. Indeed, Josephus claims:

> [Manasseh] sanctified the temple and purified the city, and thereafter his only care was to show gratitude to God for having been saved, and to keep his favour throughout his whole life. And he taught the people to do the same, having learned how close he had been to disaster because of following the opposite way of life.[29]

Similarly, the use of the imperfect ἐδίδασκε, "taught" carries a sense of Manasseh's repeated and continuous teaching of his people. Manasseh is so repentant that "from the time of his return to piety towards God, he was deemed a blessed and enviable man".[30]

Perhaps the most striking feature of Josephus' portrayal of Manasseh is his characterization of this king. Unlike the one-dimensional portrayals of Manasseh offered by the Hebrew Bible, Josephus' elaboration of his received scriptural traditions has enabled him to flesh out the character of Manasseh. It may be his use of the colourful rabbinic traditions that has enabled him to do so.

King Manasseh of Judah is not the only Manasseh discussed by Josephus. In book XI of *Antiquities*, Manasseh is also the name of the first high priest of the Samaritan temple on Mount Gerizim. He is described as "sharing the high priesthood" in Judah,[31] perhaps because his brother Jaddua is said to be the high priest of Jerusalem. Moreover, Manasseh is said to have married Nicaso, the daughter of the Samaritan governor Sanballat.[32] Josephus tells his readers that Manasseh's marriage to a foreigner prompted an angry ultimatum from the Jerusalem elders: divorce, or expulsion from the Jerusalem priesthood. Yet according to Josephus, Manasseh's father-in-law Sanballat offered a solution:

---

29 *Ant*. X.42-43.
30 *Ant*. X.45.
31 *Ant*. XI.306, n. c.
32 *Ant*. XI.302-305.

Sanballat promised not only to preserve the priesthood for him but also to procure for him the power and office of high priest and to appoint him governor of all the places over which he ruled, if he were willing to live with his daughter; and he said that he would build a temple similar to that in Jerusalem on Mount Garizein—this is the highest of the mountains near Samaria—and undertook to do these things with the consent of King Darius.[33]

Josephus testifies not only that Manasseh accepted Sanballat's offer, but also that the defection to the north caused a great disturbance in Jerusalem, as a number of priests and Levites deserted with Manasseh to Samaria, where Sanballat gave them houses, land and money.[34]

This tradition is thus far known only in Josephus. Given its setting within the period of Alexander the Great, scholars tend to doubt the historical credibility of Josephus' story, assuming it to be a fabrication of Neh. 13:28. Set within the context of the prohibition of intermarriage, this text alludes to the marriage of a daughter of the Samaritan governor Sanballat to a member of the high priestly family in Jerusalem. This figure is expelled from Jerusalem because of his foreign marriage:

... one of the sons of Jehoiada, son of the high priest Eliashib, was the son-in-law of Sanballat the Horonite; I chased him away from me.

Sanballat the Horonite features frequently throughout the book of Nehemiah as the governor of the province of Samaria and the enemy of Nehemiah. A reference to a Sanballat of Samaria in the Elephantine papyri appears to confirm the historicity of this figure within the fifth century BCE.[35] Yet Josephus' story of Sanballat and Manasseh the High Priest is set within the fourth century BCE. In his comprehensive reconstruction of the Persian period, Cross argues that both events, that of Neh. 13:28 and *Ant.* XI, are historically credible.[36] However, in the light of the discussions of the

---

33   *Ant.* XI.310-311.
34   *Ant.* XI.312.
35   *Elph.P.* 30.29.
36   F.M. Cross, "A Reconstruction of the Judean Restoration", *JBL* 24 (1975), 4-18; *idem.*, "The Discovery of the Samaria Papyri", *BA* 26 (1963), 110-121; *idem.*, "Papyri of the Fourth Century BC from Dâliyeh: A Preliminary Report on their Discovery and Significance", in D.N. Freedman and J.C. Greenfield (eds.), *New Directions in Biblical Archaeology* (Garden City: Doubleday, 1969), 41-62; *idem.*, "Aspects of Samaritan and Jewish History in Late Persian and Hellenistic Times", *HTR* 59 (1966), 201-211. His arguments are based upon the double occurrence of the name Sanballat within the Wadi ed-Dâliyeh papyri, indicating that there may have been more than one governor of Samaria named Sanballat. Cross argues that the governorship was hereditary, allowing

preceding chapters, it is perhaps more than a striking coincidence that another
Manasseh is portrayed as participating within the supposedly deviant cult of
the apostate foreigners in the North. Indeed, what better way to slander the
rival Samaritan temple than to name its first high priest after the arch-
apostate of the Scriptures? Moreover, this would also carry ironical
undertones, for the Samaritans apparently identified themselves as the
descendants of the tribes of Ephraim and Manasseh. Thus following Grabbe,
it would appear that Josephus' story is an expanded form of the fleeting
tradition found in Neh. 13:28, in which the previously anonymous apostate
priest has been named Manasseh after the idolatrous king as a clear symbol
of his religious villainy.[37] The possibility that Josephus is thus drawing upon
an early Jewish, antagonistic tradition concerning the founding of the
Samaritan temple is underscored further by a brief text in Judges.

Judg. 18:30 gives the genealogy of the corrupt priest Jonathan, and
appears to trace Jonathan's ancestry back to Moses. However, a slightly
elevated נ has been employed to transform the name "Moses" (משׁה) into the
name "Manasseh" (מנשׁה):

ויקימו להם בני־דן את־הפסל ויהונתן בן־גרשם בן־מֹ֯שׁה הוא ובניו היו
כהנים לשבט הדני עד־יום גלות הארץ

This would appear to be an ancient scribal alteration, as attested by some
Septuagint manuscripts and the Vulgate, which preserve the original reading
"Moses". Commentators are thus agreed that this suspended נ serves to
prevent the reputation of Moses from being sullied by his association with the
wayward Jonathan, a Levitical priest who abandons his Judahite home to

---

the possibility that Sanballat I governed in the time of Nehemiah, and that a Sanballat III
could have been the father-in-law of Manasseh. However, Cross's arguments are
weakened by his dependence upon the theory of papponymy (naming a child after its
grandfather); see further G. Widengren, "The Persian Period", in Hayes and Miller,
Israelite and Judaean History, 489-538 (506-509); L.L. Grabbe, "Josephus and the
Reconstruction of the Judean Restoration", *JBL* 106 (1987), 231-246; *idem., Judaism
from Cyrus to Hadrian* (London: SCM Press, 1992), 112-114; R.J. Coggins, *Samaritans
and Jews* (Oxford: Blackwell, 1975), 106-107; H.G.M. Williamson, "Early Post-Exilic
Judaean History", in *idem., Studies in Persian Period History and Historiography* (FAT
38; Tübingen: Mohr Siebeck, 2004), 3-24.

37 Grabbe, "Josephus", 237-238. Though Grabbe briefly recognizes within the story the
idolatrous associations of the name Manasseh as both the name of a wicked king and a
name associated with the former Northern kingdom, he does not connect this with a
distinct and fundamental anti-Manasseh and anti-Northern polemic pervading biblical
and post-biblical traditions.

serve as a priest for the idolatrous Micah, and later for the tribe of Dan (Judg. 17–18). This textual corruption has existed at least since the rabbinic period, as ancient texts testify.[38] The majority of commentators, both ancient and modern, have long presumed that the Manasseh who is artificially grafted into the genealogy of Jonathan is intended to be understood as King Manasseh of Judah (in spite of its anachronistic implications) given his biblical reputation for promoting idolatry. Indeed, this verse may allude to King Manasseh's religious crimes in employing the term פסל, which is used of King Manasseh's cult statue in 2 Kgs 21:7 and 2 Chr. 33:7.

However, building upon a passing observation made by Moore in 1895, Weitzman has constructed a plausible case arguing that the Manasseh superimposed in Judg. 18:30 was not originally intended to be understood as King Manasseh, but Manasseh the High Priest of the Samaritan temple.[39] Indeed, Josephus' story of the apostasy of Manasseh the High Priest bears a striking resemblance to that of Jonathan in Judg. 17–18. Jonathan is a Levite who leaves Judah to hold office as a priest in the idolatrous YHWH temple constructed by Micah on the mountain of Ephraim. This detail further favours the parallelling of Jonathan and the high priest Manasseh, for their temples encourage close identification given the Samaritans' claimed Ephraimite and Manassite heritage.[40] Consequently, the suspended נ in Judg. 18:30 functions on several levels: first, it distances the figure of Moses from the idolatry of Jonathan; second, in his association with an apostate biblical priest, the first high priest of the Samaritan temple, Manasseh the apostate Jew, is discredited; and third, it further denigrates the High Priest Manasseh by emphasizing the idolatrous connotations of his imposed name in employing the language of idolatry associated with the biblical King Manasseh (פסל). The fusion of these interrelated polemics within one verse neatly summarizes the existence of an anti-Manasseh polemic pervading biblical and post-biblical traditions.

The deliberate and theologically-loaded use of the name "Manasseh" is also demonstrated in a more positive way in the "Prayer of Manasseh". This short pseudepigraphal text is best described as an individual lament of personal sin,[41] in which the penitent appeals for forgiveness. Establishing the

---

38 See *b.B. Bat.* 109b.

39 S. Weitzman, "Reopening the Case of the Suspiciously Suspended *Nun* in Judges 18:30", *CBQ* 61 (1999), 448-460; G.F. Moore, *A Critical and Exegetical Commentary on the Book of Judges* (ICC; second edn; Edinburgh: T&T Clark, 1898), 400-402.

40 Josh. 21:21 cf. 1 Chr. 6:52.

41 J.H. Charlesworth, "Manasseh, Prayer of", *ABD*, vol. 4, 499-500.

provenance of the Prayer is problematic. The text is preserved primarily in Greek and Syriac, and it is notable that neither an Aramaic nor Hebrew version has yet been recovered.[42] This has led to a general division of scholarly opinion, with some arguing for the prayer's original composition in Greek,[43] and others supporting the idea that the original language of the prayer was Semitic.[44] However, as Charlesworth observes, the text itself is too short, and the history of the transmission of both the Greek and Syriac versions too unclear, to support any firm conclusions.[45] In spite of these uncertainties, the prayer is probably best regarded as Jewish, for as Cross notes, it exhibits a "thoroughly Jewish theology".[46]

Although the name Manasseh does not occur at all within the text, the ascription of the prayer to Manasseh may be an original feature of its composition, for it makes several allusions to the Chronicler's account of the reign of Manasseh, which itself claims that Manasseh offered up a prayer during his Babylonian captivity (2 Chr. 33:13, 18).[47] The prayer is addressed to the "Lord, God of our fathers, God of Abraham, Isaac and Jacob" (1:1) recalling the Chronicler's claim that the captured Manasseh "humbled himself greatly before the god of his fathers" (2 Chr. 33:12). The language of idolatry employed by the Kings Writer and adopted by the Chronicler is also in view within the prayer, as is the allusion to the Chronicler's account of the capture and binding of Manasseh (1:10):

---

42 G.W.E. Nickelsburg ("Prayer of Manasseh", *OBC*, 770-773) and F.M. Cross ("The Prayer of Manasseh", *ECB*, 859-861) note that fragments of a prayer ascribed to Manasseh occur within a Qumran text (4Q381, frag. 33, 8-11) but it is not certain that it is related to the Prayer of Manasseh; see further E.M. Schuller, *Non-Canonical Psalms from Qumran: A Pseudepigraphic Collection* (HSS 28; Atlanta: Scholars Press, 1986), 151-162; W.M. Schniedewind, "A Qumran Fragment of the Ancient 'Prayer of Manasseh'", *ZAW* 108 (1996), 105-107.

43 E.g. L.H. Brockington, *A Critical Introduction to the Apocrypha* (London: SCM Press, 1961), 101; L. Rost, *Judaism Outside the Hebrew Canon: An Introduction to the Documents* (trans. D.E. Green, Nashville: Abingdon, 1976), 95; H.H. Rowley, *The Origin and Significance of the Apocrypha* (rev. edn; London: SPCK, 1967), 8; M.E. Stone, "Apocryphal Notes and Readings", *Israel Oriental Studies* 1 (1971), 123-131.

44 E.g. W.O.E. Oesterley, *An Introduction to the Books of the Apocrypha* (London: SPCK, 1935), 298.

45 Charlesworth, "Manasseh, Prayer of", 499.

46 Cross, "Prayer of Manasseh", 859.

47 Two early Christian handbooks (*Didascalia Apostolorum* and *Apostolic Constitutions*) dating to the third and fourth centuries CE set the prayer within a narrative context which conflates elaborations of the biblical accounts of Manasseh's reign in 2 Kgs 21:1-19 and 2 Chr. 33:1-20; see further Nickelsburg, "Prayer of Manasseh", 770.

> And I am bent by a multitude of iron chains,[48]
> so that I cannot lift up my head;
> for I do not deserve to lift up my eyes
> and look and see the height of heaven,
> Because I did evil things before you[49]
> and I provoked your fury[50]
> and I set up idols[51] and multiplied defilement.

Indeed, it may be that the poet intends to supply the prayer repeatedly attributed to Manasseh in 2 Chr. 33:13-19 (cf. *2 Bar.* 64–65),[52] particularly in view of the Chronicler's claim (33:18-19) that Manasseh's prayer is recorded elsewhere:

> ... the rest of the deeds of Manasseh, and his prayer to his god, and the words of the seers who spoke to him in the name of YHWH the God of Israel, behold, they are in the Annals of the Kings of Israel. And his prayer and his entreaty to God, and all his sin and his unfaithfulness, and the sites on which he built high places and set up the *asherim* and the images, before he humbled himself, behold, they are written in the Words of the Seers.

However, despite the text's implication that King Manasseh is the author, establishing the likely date and provenance of the prayer is extremely problematic, particularly in view of the difficulties in establishing its original language of composition. Given that the prayer is probably an expansion of 2 Chr. 33:1-20, it must postdate Chronicles (fourth century BCE) and predate the *Didascalia* (third century CE) quite considerably, given its extant inclusion within this collection.[53] In the light of other early Jewish prayers and hymns, which exhibit many similarities to the Prayer of Manasseh,[54] it is most likely that the Prayer was composed sometime before the destruction of the temple in 70 CE.[55] Interestingly, an early date of composition, and the

---

48 Cf. 2 Chr. 33:11. The translations of the Prayer of Manasseh are those of Charlesworth, "Prayer of Manasseh", 635-637. He observes that the earliest extant version of the prayer occurs in the Syriac *Didascalia*, and it is possible that all extant versions, Syriac and Greek, are based upon this version.

49 Cf. 2 Chr. 33:2, 6.

50 Cf. 2 Chr. 33:6.

51 Cf. 2 Chr. 33:3, 7, 15; cf. 2 Kgs 21:7.

52 So too Nickelsburg, "Prayer of Manasseh", 770.

53 Nickelsburg, "Prayer of Manasseh", 770-771; Charlesworth, "Prayer of Manasseh", 627.

54 See further Charlesworth, "Prayer of Manasseh", 627.

55 Charlesworth, "Prayer of Manasseh", 627; see also Nickelsburg, "Prayer of Manasseh", 770-771; Rost, *Judaism Outside the Hebrew Canon*, 95.

Prayer's original attribution to Manasseh, would seem to be complemented by Josephus' claim that the forgiven and restored Manasseh's only care was "to show his gratitude to God for having been saved, and to keep his favour throughout his whole life."[56] This is reminiscent of the final verse of the Prayer of Manasseh, in which the penitent vows, "I will praise you continually all the days of my life" (1:15).[57]

In developing the tradition of Manasseh's repentance, both the Prayer of Manasseh and Josephus' portrayal of the king are testimony to the powerful portrait the Chronicler created in his account of the wicked king's penitent remorse. However, neither the Chronicler, nor Josephus, nor the poet of the Prayer of Manasseh succeed in rehabilitating Manasseh, for their texts necessarily depend upon the continued potency of the popular imaging of Manasseh as the ultimate sinner. The pervasive nature of Manasseh's villainous reputation is also demonstrated within the plethora of rabbinic traditions elaborating on his misdeeds further, culminating in the accusations of rape, incest and propheticide. Perhaps most striking of all is the Jewish tradition denigrating the Samaritan temple by naming its first high priest Manasseh, and thereby setting up in just one name a host of preconceptions about the religious character of peoples living in the North. All of these traditions may be traced with some certainty to the biblical portrayals of King Manasseh as the arch-idolater and villain of "Israel", who provoked YHWH to destroy his city, Jerusalem, and exile his people. Yet perhaps the most notable feature of these afterlives of Manasseh is that the figure of Manasseh continued to be distorted. Post-biblical characterizations of this king or those bearing his name appear to be more developed than the portrayals of Manasseh within the Hebrew Bible. This may reflect an implicit dissatisfaction with the one-dimensional portrayals of Manasseh within both Kings and Chronicles, prompting the need to flesh-out this character within post-biblical traditions. Consequently, the figure of Manasseh is distorted further.

---

56 *Ant.* X.42.

57 *Contra* Charlesworth ("Prayer of Manasseh", 632), who asserts that, "Josephus displays no cognizance of the content of or traditions in our prayer".

3.2 Distorting Manasseh

In seeking to distinguish between the Manasseh of history and the Manasseh of tradition, this discussion has revealed the increasing distortion of the figure of Manasseh throughout biblical and post-biblical literature. Indeed, an examination of the portrayal of Manasseh within the texts reveals not a portrait, but a caricature. In blaming Manasseh, the Kings Writer seeks to distance Judah from direct responsibility for the destruction of Jerusalem and the exile of her people. Rather than blaming Jehoiakim, Jehoiachin or Zedekiah, the last Judahite kings, for the Babylonian destruction of Judah, the Kings Writer deliberately selects Manasseh as his scapegoat, despite Manasseh having been dead for at least half a century before the Babylonian conquest in c. 597 BCE. This scapegoating of Manasseh is facilitated by his name. Sharing his name with the dominant Manasseh territory of the neighbouring Kingdom of Israel singled the Judahite king out as a "foreigner". This is the feature insidiously exaggerated by the Kings Writer in his caricature of Manasseh as the villainous "foreign" king leading Judah astray.

The portrayal of Manasseh is distorted further by the Chronicler's rehabilitation of Manasseh as the paradigmatic repentant. However, this rehabilitation relies wholly upon the misrepresentation of Manasseh adopted from the Kings account. Thus the Chronicler's contradiction of Kings' portrait of Manasseh does not undermine the characterization of Manasseh as a villain, but instead reinforces it. The vilification of Manasseh is picked up by the Chronicler, yet radically transformed to suit his own ideological purposes. The Chronicler has no need to scapegoat an individual in order to explain the exile, for his History is constructed upon a sin-repentance-restoration paradigm. Consequently, Manasseh is the typological Israel: the wicked sinner is duly exiled as punishment for his disloyalty to YHWH, but his repentance brings restoration and blessing, just as the Chronicler's newly restored "Israel" has experienced. Thus the Kings Writer's efforts to distance and separate the Judahite exiles from Manasseh are turned on their head by the Chronicler, who seeks to identify Manasseh with the newly-restored exiles. This transformation is itself indicative of the relative ease with which traditions can be adopted and adapted to serve different purposes and to suit different audiences.

The villainous portrayal of Manasseh casts a long shadow over the remainder of the Hebrew Bible. The deliberate distortion of the name Moses into Manasseh in Judg. 18:30 is not only further evidence of the scapegoating of Manasseh, but testifies also to the polemical tradition evidenced in

Josephus, in which the first high priest of the hated Samaritan temple has acquired the name Manasseh. Further illustrating the anti-Manasseh polemic identified within this discussion are biblical traditions concerning the tribe of Manasseh: not only is the eponymous ancestor of the tribe of Manasseh, the firstborn of Joseph, deliberately eclipsed by that of Ephraim, as demonstrated in the blessing story of Gen. 48:12-20, but within many texts the sequential listing of Manasseh and Ephraim appears artificially reversed. Moreover, the surprising lack of references, positive or negative, to King Manasseh or to the period of his reign outside of 2 Kgs 21–24; 2 Chr. 33:1-20 and Jer. 15:3-4 is suggestive of the deliberate censoring of Manasseh from other texts. This is particularly striking in view of the frequent attestation of prophetic polemic against Judahite kings, leaders and their "improper" cult practices clearly evident within most of the prophetic literature.[58] This curious silence concerning Manasseh has also been noted by Nielsen, who comments:

> ... the historical traditions of Manasseh which were known to the composers of the biblical works of history must have been censored and shortened by them rather drastically before these traditions were allowed to be handed over to later generations, neatly arranged as starting points for pieces of theological instruction.[59]

The biblical caricature of Manasseh as a villain has endured within Jewish traditions, despite his rehabilitation in Chronicles, the Prayer of Manasseh, and in the work of Josephus.   Indeed, within post-biblical traditions Manasseh is even accused of crimes unmentioned in the Hebrew Bible. The charges of massacre, incest, prophet-persecution and the murder of Isaiah represent a further stage in the distortion of Manasseh. Like Josephus' characterization of Manasseh within his development of the Chronicler's account, these elaborate stories flesh out the figure of Manasseh, perhaps indicating that later tradition recognized the biblical portrayal of Manasseh as a caricature. However, in adding character to the caricature, the image of Manasseh is mutated further.

This process of distortion is compounded even more by some scholars, who accept unquestioningly the biblical portrayal of Manasseh as a villainous, anti-YHWH idolater in their reconstructions of Judahite history. Particularly illustrative of the continued distortion of the image of Manasseh within scholarship is the work of Haran. In attempting to account for the

---

58 Ben Zvi ("Prelude to a Reconstruction", 37, n. 26) notes that the lack of attestations to Manasseh's reign within the superscriptions to prophetic books may reflect the belief that Manasseh executed all prophets.

59 Nielsen, "Political Conditions", 103.

biblical silence concerning the fate of the ark of the covenant, Haran speculates that King Manasseh removed the ark from the Jerusalem temple and destroyed it in order to make way for his image of Asherah.[60] Like the rabbis, Haran accuses the Manasseh of history of crimes of which not even the biblical character of Manasseh is accused. So too does Bird, who claims that Manasseh's introduction of the cult image of Asherah into the Temple was accompanied by his conversion of storehouses into workshops dedicated to the goddess,[61] whilst Oded accuses Manasseh of concealing the so-called "book of the covenant" in the Temple.[62] Manasseh's biblical portrayal as an idolater is also likely to underlie the suggestion that the worship of the Host of Heaven and the Queen of Heaven reached its zenith under Manasseh.[63] This opinion is probably rooted in the supposition that in his vassalage, Manasseh enthusiastically promoted Assyrian cultural and religious interests within Judah, just as Hezekiah and Josiah are commonly perceived as fierce nationalists crusading against foreign influences.[64] In spite of the re-evaluation of Assyrian religious influence within Judah and the emerging consensus that Judahite religion differed very little from that of the surrounding cultures, many commentators continue to presume that the cult crimes of which Manasseh stands accused within the Hebrew Bible were essentially alien to the native religion of Judah. This presumption is probably itself founded upon the fundamental assumption of the basic historicity of the biblical texts. Thus the historical Manasseh continues to be mistakenly depicted according to his biblical portrayal. Indeed, even within more recent studies which acknowledge the severe biases of the biblical text, there prevails an assumption of historicity in the charges against Manasseh, as the following quotation from Van Keulen illustrates:

---

60 M. Haran, "The Disappearance of the Ark", *IEJ* 13 (1963), 46-58; *idem.*, *Temples and Temple-Service in Ancient Israel* (Oxford: Clarendon Press, 1978), 276-288. For an equally presumptive, but more nuanced, discussion of Manasseh and "his Asherah", see Milgrom, *Leviticus 17–22*, 1390-1391.

61 P.A. Bird, "The End of the Male Cult Prostitute: A Literary-Historical and Sociological Analysis of Hebrew *Qādēš-Qĕdēšîm*", in J.A. Emerton (ed.), *Congress Volume Cambridge, 1995* (VTSup 66; Leiden: Brill, 1997), 37-80.

62 Oded, "Judah and the Exile", 463.

63 M. Weinfeld, "The Worship of Molech and of the Queen of Heaven and its Background", *UF* 4 (1972), 133-154 (149); M. Rose, *Der Ausschliesslichkeitsanspruch Jahwes: Deuteronomische Schultheologie und die Volksfrömmigkeit in der späten Königszeit* (BWANT 106; Berlin: de Gruyter, 1975), 213-268.

64 See 2.1.

... in view of the extreme bias of the Manasseh account [2 Kgs 21:1-18], the assessment of its value as a historical source must be negative. Yet, some notes in the account may have preserved historically reliable information, and it seems that the picture drawn of Manasseh as a king who introduced foreign cult in Judean religion is basically correct.[65]

Even Lowery, who describes Manasseh's cultic policy as a return to Judah's traditional values, cannot help but temper his view with the assertion that the resulting royal religion was a syncretistic cult enhanced by Assyrian practice and belief.[66] Similarly, Schmidt describes Manasseh as a traditional, polytheistic "yahwist" who adopted a radically new and foreign element into the Judahite cult in the form of Mesopotamian necromancy.[67] In contrast, some scholars are keen to distance Manasseh's cult crimes from Assyrian influence, yet emphasize his personal and intentional responsibility for the supposed decline in Judahite religious practice: for Albertz, Manasseh's cult crimes thus reflect his personal stance, rather than state policy;[68] similarly, Cogan and Tadmor describe Manasseh's religious behaviour as a rejection of his father's piety,[69] whilst Wiseman confidently claims that Manasseh's sin in reversing his father's policies was his own decision.[70] Indeed, for some scholars, there is no excusing Manasseh at all. Tigay states:

> In the case of Solomon and Ahab, tolerance of polytheism was probably motivated by the same political conditions which led to their marriages with foreign princesses. In the case of Manasseh, the polytheism may have been the king's personal idiosyncracy.[71]

---

65 Van Keulen, *Manasseh*, 212.

66 Lowery, *Reforming Kings*, 169-170; see also Dietrich, "1 and 2 Kings", 262; Spieckermann, *Juda Unter Assur*, 84-111, 270-295. Note too the survey in H. Donner, *Geschichte des Volkes Israel und seiner Nachbarn in Grundzügen. Teil 2: Von der Königszeit bis zu Alexander dem Gro en mit einem Ausblick auf die Geschichte des Judentums bis Bar Kochba* (Göttingen: Vandenhoeck & Ruprecht, 1986), 329-338.

67 Schmidt, *Beneficent Dead*, 292, n. 47, see also 141.

68 Albertz, *History of Israelite Religion*, vol. 2, 398, n. 100; cf. Cogan, *Imperialism and Religion*, 113.

69 Cogan and Tadmor, *II Kings*, 273.

70 D.J. Wiseman, *1 and 2 Kings* (TOTC; Leicester: Inter-Varsity Press, 1993), 290.

71 J.H. Tigay, *You Shall Have No Other Gods: Israelite Religion in the Light of Hebrew Inscriptions* (HSS 31; Atlanta: Scholars Press, 1986), 39. This comment also raises the interesting issue of the biblical blaming of foreign women for supposedly illegitimate religious practices, a notion that is often historicized within modern scholarship, as McKay's accounting for the "Garden of Uzza" illustrates (above, 44, n. 138).

These attitudes can only distort the Manasseh of history further. Yet Manasseh's personal villainy is also assumed by many commentators seeking to understand the curious biblical assertion that Manasseh shed copious amounts of innocent blood (2 Kgs 21:16; 24:3-4). Dietrich asserts, "Manasseh was Assyria's servant ... There is not the slightest indication that he resisted his masters. This is precisely the reason for his length of reign. Manasseh represented and reproduced Assyrian violence".[72] Manasseh's supposed collusion with Assyria is also assumed by Cogan and Tadmor, who assert that Manasseh ruthlessly slaughtered his opponents with the support of the Assyrian army.[73] However, as has been seen, the biblical accusation that Manasseh shed innocent blood is more likely to be a deliberate fiction designed to scapegoat him, and allowing the Kings Writer and his intended audience to identify their direct ancestors with the innocents slaughtered by Manasseh, thereby absolving them from responsibility for being led astray by Manasseh.

The scapegoating of Manasseh is not simply an ancient phenomenon: of all the crimes of which the historical Manasseh is accused within modern scholarship, the most prevalent and the most serious is that of promoting and participating within child sacrifice. This is well-illustrated by the recent comments of Anderson and Freedman:

> It is possible that the sin of Manasseh, who filled Jerusalem from one side to the other with "innocent blood"... a sin that the LORD would not pardon, was human sacrifice on a considerable scale.[74]

In associating the Manasseh of history with this shocking practice, scholars continue to scapegoat Manasseh for what amounts to an uncomfortable reality within the history of Judahite religion. Yet as shall be argued, whether historical or not, the biblical charge of child sacrifice seeks to underscore Manasseh's imaging as a "foreigner". In blaming Manasseh for this and the other cult crimes of which he is accused, scholars reinforce and perpetuate the distorted portrayal of Manasseh as a villainous idolater, a portrayal initiated in the Hebrew Bible and furthered within post-biblical tradition.

Needless to say, this is all a far cry from the reconstructed image of the King Manasseh of historical probability. Behind the distorted caricature of

---

72 Dietrich, "1 and 2 Kings", 262.
73 Cogan and Tadmor, *II Kings*, 276.
74 F.I. Anderson and D.N. Freedman, *Micah: A New Translation with Introduction and Commentary* (AB 24E; New York: Doubleday, 2000), 532.

tradition is the shadowy figure of a seventh century king of Jerusalem, standing in the midst of a rapidly expanding kingdom. Though subject to Assyrian domination, it was during the reign of Manasseh that Jerusalem emerged as the economic and political centre of the Judahite region, a period which perhaps saw the consolidation of certain Zion ideologies born of the non-fall of the city in c. 701 BCE. Thus the Manasseh of history is perhaps best imagined as the "constructor" of Judah, rather than resorting to the caricature of Manasseh as the "destructor" of Judah.

4 The Biblical Portrayal of Child Sacrifice

The practice of child sacrifice is well-known throughout the Hebrew Bible. It is the subject of two extensive narratives—Abraham's attempt to sacrifice Isaac (Gen. 22:1-19) and Jephthah's sacrifice of his daughter (Judg. 11:29-40). It also forms the climax to the Kings Writer's account of war against Moab, as King Mesha sacrifices his firstborn son (2 Kgs 3:26-27), and in the story of the reconstruction of Jericho, the city is founded upon the sacrifice of Hiel's firstborn and lastborn sons (1 Kgs 16:34; cf. Josh. 6:26). Yet in view of these texts, it is surprising to find that scholarly discussion of the subject of child sacrifice is dominated by the so-called "cult of Molek", particularly as there are only eight occurrences of the term מֹלֶךְ in the MT. This imbalance is all the more striking given the frequent association of child sacrifice with YHWH; indeed, many texts designate YHWH as the recipient of the offerings. In examining the biblical portrayal of child sacrifice, this study will argue that this imbalance within scholarly debate is fundamentally bound up with the biblical attempts to insist that child sacrifice is a foreign practice alien to "Israel" and her god YHWH.

But the examination of the biblical material must be prefaced with some methodological observations and remarks. A primary observation is that in essence, the study of child sacrifice in the Hebrew Bible is complicated by two closely related factors: the varying terminology of the biblical texts, and divergent interpretations of this terminology. Of the seven expressions of action employed within those texts most commonly held to refer to child sacrifice,[1] only two verbs indicate beyond reasonable doubt that the described practices are intended to be understood as lethal: שׁחט, "slaughter" (Gen.

---

1   Gen. 22:1-19; Lev. 18:21; 20:2-5; Deut. 12:31; 18:10; Josh. 6:26; Judg. 11:30-40; 1 Kgs 16:34; 2 Kgs 3:27; 16:3; 17:17, 31; 21:6; 23:10; 2 Chr. 28:3; 33:6; Ps. 106:37-38; Isa. 57:5; Jer. 7:31; 19:5; 32:35; Ezek. 16:20-21; 20:26, 31; 23:37, 39; Mic. 6:7. It is important to reiterate that this list should not be taken as an exhaustive catalogue of biblical texts referring to child sacrifice. Rather, it comprises those texts widely accepted as describing the practice. Additional texts which may allude to or describe, or relate to or refer to child sacrifice, are discussed below.

22:10; Isa. 57:5; Ezek. 16:21; 23:39)[2] and זבח, "sacrifice" or "ritual slaughter" (Ps. 106:37, 38; Ezek. 16:20).[3] In addition to these are the verbs אכל, "eat" (Ezek. 16:20; cf. 23:37), עלה hiphil, "offer up" (Gen. 22:2; Judg. 11:31; 2 Kgs 3:27), and שרף, "burn" (Deut. 12:31; 2 Kgs 17:31; Jer. 7:31; 19:5), all of which may also be taken as suggestive of the deadly nature of the described practices. But by far the most common verbs associated with child sacrifice in the Hebrew Bible are עבר hiphil, "(cause to) pass over"[4] (Lev. 18:21; Deut. 18:10; 2 Kgs 16:3; 17:17; 21:6; 23:10; Jer. 32:35; Ezek. 16:21; 20:26, 31;[5] 23:37; 2 Chr. 28:3;[6] 33:6) and נתן, "give" or "donate" (Lev. 18:21; 20:2, 3, 4; Ezek. 16:21;[7] Mic. 6:7), yet neither of these can be taken to refer unambiguously to ritual killing. The compounding of the verbs שרף and עבר hiphil with באש, "in (the) fire" (Deut. 12:31; 18:10; 2 Kgs 16:3; 17:17, 31; 21:6; 23:10; 2 Chr. 28:3[8]; 33:6; Jer. 7:31; 19:5; Ezek. 20:31[9]) may be taken as a much more certain indication of the deadly nature of the practice to which the biblical texts refer. Complicating the matter, though, is the possibility that the inseparable preposition in the expression העביר באש is better rendered "through", rather than "in", thereby complementing the sense of motion that העביר can have, and yet heightening further the ambiguity of the expression העביר באש. More secure is the rendering of שרף באש as "burn in (the) fire", though as will be seen, for some commentators this need not imply lethal incineration, but scorching, an interpretation distancing the phrase שרף באש from a more literal frame of reference.

The variation and ambivalence of the biblical terminology thus leaves open several possibilities. One is that distinct rituals are to be perceived within the texts, of which all or only some may reflect perceived forms of child sacrifice; perhaps some of these rituals are intended to be understood as death-inducing, whilst others are to be regarded as more harmless. Another possibility is that the ambivalent language is either representative of the technical terminology of ritual, or is intentionally euphemistic, perhaps

---

2   *HALOT*, vol. 4, 1459.
3   *HALOT*, vol. 1, 262.
4   This is more usually rendered "pass through" or "transmit"; however, the (perhaps more literal) rendering "pass over" is to be preferred in this discussion.
5   The phrase בהעביר בניכם באש is often deleted as a secondary gloss, as will be seen below.
6   Reading, with Versional support, ויעבר rather than MT ויבער (cf. 2 Kgs 16:3).
7   Cf. Ezek. 20:26, 31.
8   See n. 5 above.
9   See n. 5 above.

reflecting the biblical writers' discomfort with the subject-matter. A further possibility is that the language of killing is not to be interpreted within a context of sacrifice, but is better understood as referring to non-ritual slaughter and infanticide. It could even be suggested that the language is purely metaphorical, and that to accept any literal interpretation is to misunderstand the biblical writers, their use of language, and their purposes. All of these uncertainties are compounded further by the general lack of comment or detail within the biblical texts concerning the practices to which they refer. Indeed, it is rare to find the biblical writers or their characters offering a direct opinion on the matter.

Interpretations of these texts thus have the potential to range widely. Most significant is the minority opinion that, on the whole, the biblical references do not refer to actual sacrifice. This is a view which has persisted throughout pre-modern and modern biblical study, especially with regard to the vexed issue of the so-called "Molek" practice. The force of the argument turns upon the interpretation of the expression (למלך) העביר באש. Snaith has argued with some vigour that the sexual context of the prohibition of this practice in Lev. 18:21 testifies strongly against the idea that the "Molek" references in the Hebrew Bible speak of sacrifice.[10] Instead, he follows the Talmud in arguing that these biblical texts refer to a dedicatory practice in which children were passed between rows of fire and handed over to become temple prostitutes.[11] Weinfeld, followed by Albertz, similarly opts for a non-sacrificial interpretation of the practice to which these biblical texts refer.[12] Building upon the observations of Deller,[13] Weinfeld argues that the phrase העביר באש does not refer to actual burning but to an Assyrian-style dedicatory or initiation ritual in which children were passed between rows of

---

10 N.H. Snaith, "The Cult of Molech", *VT* 16 (1966), 123-124.

11 *b. Sanh.* 64a. See also Wilke, who argued that the dedication of children to sacred prostitution was accompanied by a fire ritual, F. Wilke, "Kinderopfer und kultische Preisgabe im 'Heiligkeitsgesetz'", *Festschrift der 57. Versammlung deutscher Philologen und Schulmänner in Salzburg, 1929* (Vienna: Rudolf M. Rohrer, 1929), 138-151.

12 M. Weinfeld, "The Worship of Molech and of the Queen of Heaven and its Background", *UF* 4 (1972), 133-154; Weinfeld, "Burning Babies in Ancient Israel: A Rejoinder to Morton Smith's Article in *JAOS* 95 (1975), pp. 477-479", *UF* 10 (1978), 411-413; *idem.*, "The Moloch Cult in Israel and Its Background", *Proceedings of the Fifth World Congress of Jewish Studies* (Jerusalem: World Union of Jewish Studies, 1969), 133-154 (Hebrew), 227-228 (English abstract); Albertz, *A History of Israelite Religion* , vol. 1, 190-194.

13 K. Deller, Review of *Les sacrifices de l'Ancien Testament*, by R. de Vaux, *Orientalia* 34, NS (1965), 182-186.

fire.[14] He too draws upon early Jewish writings in which the outlawed practice is explained as a dedication of some sort.[15] Yet crucially, Weinfeld is compelled to concede that some biblical texts do speak of actual sacrifice, though these he dismisses as unreliable polemic. Instead, he relies upon the accounts within the Torah and Kings which, he claims, preserve "laws and historical information which generally relate to actual conditions". Accordingly, Weinfeld argues that these texts speak simply of a dedicatory ritual.[16]

In more recent years, a non-sacrificial interpretation of the biblical terminology has been especially encouraged by two marked developments within the wider field of study. The first is the increased interest in the forms and functions of divinatory practices, both as portrayed in the Hebrew Bible and as might be reconstructed historically—though it is notable that within many discussions this distinction is not always clear. The biblical association of the expression העביר באש with allusions to divinatory practices in Deut. 18:10-11, 2 Kgs 17:17 and 21:6 (par. 2 Chr. 33:6) is for some commentators suggestive of a divinatory function of the practice more usually understood as a type of sacrifice.[17] This view is reminiscent of those of Snaith and Weinfeld, for it allows for the possibility that a child could be "passed through fire" without incurring his or her death. As Nelson remarks, "perhaps the survival or death of the child indicated a yes or no answer".[18] However, it is important to note that Nelson, like others, perceives a distinction between העביר באש, which he regards as referring to a divinatory ritual, and שרף באש, which he takes to refer to child sacrifice.[19] Barrick goes further, however, in suggesting that שרף באש need not refer to the intentional, ritualized death of a child. Rather, he draws a conceptual—though not an explicitly semantic—distinction between burning and incineration, suggesting that "a painful

---

14 See also D. Plataroti, "Zum Gebrauch des Wortes *MLK* im Alten Testament", *VT* 28 (1978), 286-300; Cogan, *Imperialism and Religion*, 77-83; Tropper, *Nekromantie*, 235-236.

15 Weinfeld, "Worship of Molech", 141; cf. T.H. Gaster, *Myth, Legend, and Custom in the Old Testament* (London: Duckworth, 1969), 586-588.

16 Weinfeld, "Worship of Molek", 140-141. Note Morton Smith's challenge to Weinfeld's theory in "A Note on Burning Babies", *JAOS* 95 (1975), 477-479; and Weinfeld's response, "Burning Babies in Ancient Israel. A Rejoinder", *UF* 10 (1978), 411-413.

17 Eg., H.F. Fuhs, "ʿābar", *TDOT*, vol. 10, 408-425; Barrick, *King and the Cemeteries*, 84-86, 91-92. J.H. Tigay, *Deuteronomy* (JPSTC; Philadelphia: Jewish Publication Society, 1996), 465.

18 Nelson, *Deuteronomy*, 233.

19 Nelson, *Deuteronomy*, 161, n. 20; see also Barrick, *King and the Cemeteries*, 84.

singeing at the least" would have occurred, which would not have necessarily resulted in the death of the child.[20] A second and related development which is beginning to influence the interpretation of the pertinent biblical texts lies amidst the archaeological sites of the ancient Phoenician and Punic worlds. As shall be seen in the following chapter, vast sacred sites containing the burnt and buried remains of infants and young animals have become the subject of a conservative reassessment, which has re-identified these sacrificial precincts as baby-burial grounds.[21] This reassessment has begun to impact upon the contextualization of biblical references and allusions to the burning of children,[22] resulting in a small but growing opinion that these texts do not speak of sacrifice at all. These two developments thus encourage the view that the biblical expressions העביר באש and even שרף באש do not refer to a deadly practice, but rather to a non-lethal dedicatory or divinatory ritual.

However, contrary to this opinion, it seems quite clear that the Hebrew Bible does indeed portray these practices as sacrificial rituals, and that the language is intentionally sacrificial. As has been noted, שחט and זבח are reasonably secure in their association with sacrifice and death. The more contentious expressions are העביר (באש), שרף באש, and the term נתן and its derived forms. But the book of Ezekiel offers compelling evidence for a sacrificial interpretation of some of these expressions. References and allusions to the cultic "offering" of children occur in three clusters of texts: Ezek. 16:20-21; 20:25-26, 31; 23:37-39. Within these texts, שחט and זבח are employed to describe the sacrifice of children to "dung-gods".[23] However, this terminology is complemented by the accusations that these children are "given" (נתן)[24] and "made to pass over" (העביר)[25] to the same deities, to be devoured by them as food (employing forms of אכל),[26] and thus suggesting that נתן and העביר are also employed in a sacrificial sense. Indeed, the cultic usage of נתן as a sacrificial term is well-established,[27] and it is both perfectly

---

20 Barrick, *King and the Cemeteries*, 83; cf. Jeffers, *Magic and Divination*, 124; Zevit, *Religions of Ancient Israel*, 550.
21 For a discussion of the importance of these sites to the appropriate contextualization of child sacrifice in Syro-Palestine, and for a refutation of their recent reassessment, see below, 5.2.
22 E.g., V. Fritz, *1 & 2 Kings* (trans. A. Hagedorn; Continental; Minneapolis: Fortress Press, 2003), 340, 407.
23 For this designation, see further below, 4.1.2.
24 Ezek. 16:21; 20:26, 31.
25 Ezek. 16:21; 20:26, 31; 23:37.
26 Ezek. 16:20; 23:37.
27 See, for example, H.-J. Fabry, "*nātan*", *TDOT*, vol. 10, 90-109.

reasonable and widely accepted to affirm that forms of this term are employed in a sacrificial sense in the pertinent texts in Ezekiel. Of particular note is the designation of the sacrificed children as "gifts" to the divine recipients in 20:26, 31 (cf. Mic. 6:7). Interestingly, in the MT, this latter verse parallels the offering of gifts with the expression העביר בניכם באש,[28] which is suggestive of an intended, sacrificial interpretation of this formula. This may also be the case in 20:26, in which the action of "passing over" all the firstborn (העביר כל פטר רחם) may be interpreted as a ritual designed to "devastate" (שמם) its practitioners. As such, העביר in this context must refer to the lethal offering of children, rather than a more harmless dedication or divination practice.[29] The semantic spectrum of this terminology in Ezekiel is thus suggestive of its sacrificial meaning in the book.

A sacrificial interpretation of this language also finds some support in Jeremiah. As has been noted, the expression שרף באש is held by some to refer to a non-lethal ritual, yet its usage in Jeremiah confirms its deadly and sacrificial meaning: in 19:5 the expression is followed by עלות לבעל, "burnt offerings to Baʿal". Though this may be a secondary addition,[30] the use of עלות attests to a sacrificial understanding of שרף באש both here and in 7:31. Moreover, it recalls the use of the verb עלה to describe the sacrifice of Jephthath's daughter (Judg. 11:31), Mesha's son (2 Kgs 3:27) and the near-sacrifice of Isaac (Gen. 22:2), along with the designation of each of them in these texts as an עלה. Despite the wider textual complexities associated with the book of Jeremiah, it is almost universally agreed that 7:31, 19:5 and 32:35 are closely related. As such, the sacrificial expression שרף in 7:31 and 19:5 appears to parallel העביר in 32:35, just as the expressions seem to complement one another in Deut. 12:31 and 18:10. Furthermore, both העביר באש and שרף באש are parallelled with "burning (offerings)"[31] in the Valley of Ben Hinnom in 2 Chr. 28:3 and Jer. 19:4-5, respectively, thereby offering increased support for their reference to the same sacrificial practice. For some commentators, the sacrificial sense of העביר may also be bolstered further by the "devastating" connotations of the terminology as it occurs in Ezek. 20:26. Moreover, this interpretation is additionally strengthened by Num. 31:23, a

---

28 See n. 5, above.
29 On this important text, see 4.2.1.
30 עלות לבעל is not reflected in the LXX.
31 קטר appears to refer to making smoke, and so most frequently infers cultic burning of offerings (*HALOT*, vol. 3, 1094-1095), perhaps specifically food offerings, so D.V. Edelman, "The Meaning of *qiṭṭēr*", *VT* 35 (1985), 395-404.

text in which the phrase העביר באש functions as a cultic expression literally referring to burning *in* the fire,[32] often rendered "to plunge into fire".[33] This text not only weakens the view that העביר באש should be taken to refer to a ritual in which children were merely "passed through" fire,[34] but also offers an intriguing—though opaque—association with death by means of its contextualization within a directive concerning post-mortem rites.[35] For now, a final point of interest remains. The similarities in function and context of העביר and שרף testify against their distinct usage in reference to a dedication or divinatory practice, and a cult of child sacrifice, respectively. Rather, the two terms appear to share a context of child sacrifice. Some commentators have identified a polemical application of the expression שרף באש to "non-Israelite" practitioners of child sacrifice in Deut. 12:31 (cf. 18:10) and 2 Kgs 17:31 (cf. 17:17; 21:6);[36] indeed, this is an intriguing possibility which may indicate that שרף באש and העביר באש are employed to describe different sacrificial practices, or perhaps to signal differences between the practitioners themselves. This will be explored in the following pages.

In the light of these observations, it thus seems reasonable to refute the objections raised against a sacrificial interpretation of the biblical terminology conventionally understood to refer to child sacrifice. The biblical writers employ a varied vocabulary to refer or allude to child sacrifice, including both relatively transparent terminology, such as זבח, שחט, and העלה, and more obtuse—or perhaps euphemistic—expressions, including העביר, נתן, and שרף. However, it is vital to acknowledge that, despite its

---

32 Also noted by, among others, Smith, "Burning Babies", 478; J. Day, *Molech: A god of human sacrifice in the Old Testament* (UCOP 41; Cambridge: Cambridge University Press, 1989), 20; Barrick, *King and the Cemeteries*, 83. The Chronicler may also have understood העביר באש as referring to literal burning in fire, for the expression in 2 Chr. 28:3 (following the Versions) is preceded by a reference to burning offerings (incense or sacrifices) in the Valley of Ben Hinnom; cf. Jer. 19:4-6.

33 B.A. Levine, *Numbers 21–36* (AB 4A; Garden City: Doubleday, 2000), 458.

34 Indeed, defenders of a sacrificial interpretation have frequently noted that if, like Weinfeld, one were to suppose that all these texts refer to a harmless ritual in which children were passed between rows of fire, one would most usually expect בין rather than ב to follow העביר.

35 This context recalls the post-mortem rituals in view in 1 Sam. 31:12, in which the term שרף is employed to describe the destruction of the corpses of Saul and his sons.

36 Weinfeld, "Worship of Molech", 141; P.G. Mosca, "Child Sacrifice in Canaanite and Israelite Religion: A Study in *Mulk* and מלך" (Unpublished Ph.D. dissertation; Harvard University, 1975), 173-177; cf. G.C. Heider, *The Cult of Molek: A Reassessment* (JSOTSup 43; Sheffield: JSOT Press, 1985), 266-268, 339-340.

collective treatment here, this biblical vocabulary of child sacrifice should not be assumed to refer to one practice. Indeed, in the following chapters it will be argued that up to three possible forms of child sacrifice may have impacted upon biblical traditions.

4.1 Child Sacrifice as a Foreign Practice

Having established that the biblical terminology does indeed impart a sacrificial context of meaning, the focus of discussion now moves to an assessment of the role and function of child sacrifice in the Hebrew Bible.

> When the LORD your god has cut off before you the nations whom you are about to enter to dispossess them, when you have dispossessed them and live in their land, take care that you are not snared into imitating them, after they have been destroyed before you: do not inquire concerning their gods, saying, "How did these nations worship their gods? I also want to do the same." You must not do the same for the LORD your god, because every abhorrent thing that the LORD hates they have done for their gods. They would even burn their sons and their daughters in the fire to their gods.

This prohibition in Deut. 12:29-31 is important in three ways: first, it formalizes the biblical idea that gaining possession of the land harbours the danger of adopting the cultic practices of the original inhabitants of that land (cf. 2 Kgs 17:25-28).[37] Second, in naming child sacrifice explicitly (and not any other practice), child sacrifice is not only presented as the most abhorrent of all forms of foreign deity worship, but it appears to function here as a conceptual shorthand for all that is repugnant to YHWH. And third, child sacrifice is portrayed as a rejected YHWH-ritual, for the prohibition seeks to impose limitations upon YHWH-worship—rather than outlaw the worship of foreign deities—as the expression "you must not do the same for YHWH your god" indicates.[38] But the essence of this prohibition is quite clear: it states perfectly plainly that child sacrifice is a foreign practice which leads to expulsion from the land.

Closely related to this text are the regulations of Deut. 18:9-14, verses which exhibit similar ideological contours. Again, in preparing the ground for Israel's possession of the land, the warning concerning the hazardous risk of the adoption of foreign cult practices is clearly articulated; indeed, it is

---

37 Nelson, *Deuteronomy*, 158.
38 See also Heider, *Molek*, 268.

additionally emphasized in the command to remain wholly faithful to YHWH
(v. 13). These verses also refer to child sacrifice as a means of illustrating
foreign forms of worship (v. 10), yet in distinction to 12:29-31, child
sacrifice is accompanied by a detailed inventory of divinatory and magical
practices which are also portrayed as foreign (vv. 10-11), and thereby they
too are prohibited (v. 14).[39] Given the location of these verses within a
chapter dealing with the Levitical priest and the Mosaic prophet, the
prohibitions appear to be concerned primarily with regulating acceptable
means of communication with YHWH. Yet the ideological force of the
prohibition is constructed upon the idea that possession of the land is wholly
dependent upon cultic behaviour. As such, then, 18:9-12 insist that YHWH is
to expel the nations from the land because of their abhorrent practices,
including child sacrifice, and that Israel will also be expelled from the land if
they imitate the practices of the foreign nations.[40]

The practice of child sacrifice is thus condemned not because it is
ethically untenable, but because it is foreign. Consequently, because it is
foreign, it is forbidden. Within the Hebrew Bible, participation in this
practice is thus *theoretically* limited to the idolatrous—foreigners and
disobedient YHWH-worshippers, such as King Mesha of Moab (2 Kgs 3:26-
27); the Sepharvites (2 Kgs 17:31); King Ahaz (2 Kgs 16:3); King Manasseh
(2 Kgs 21:3-6); the Northern Kingdom (2 Kgs 17:17); and apostate Judahites
(e.g., Jer. 7:30-32). However, closer examination of these and other child
sacrifice texts suggests that this biblical theory is not as coherent as it may
initially appear.

4.1.1 Sacrifice "to Molek"

There are only eight occurrences of the term מֹלֶךְ in the MT. In all of these
instances, מֹלֶךְ appears to be understood as the proper noun "Molek",
indicating that it functions as the name or title of a god (Lev. 18:21; 20:2, 3,
4, 5; 1 Kgs 11:7; 2 Kgs 23:10; Jer. 32:35). This is one of the least
controversial points within the discussion of the so-called "Molek cult". The
issue becomes more complicated in attempting to establish whether the pre-
Masoretic, consonantal versions of the biblical texts originally understood the

---

39 Cf. Lev. 20:5-6; 2 Kgs 17:17; 21:6; 2 Chr. 33:6.
40 Cf. Deut. 9:4-5. These verses emphasize the theological premise that Israel is to gain the
    land because of the expulsion of the inhabitants' wickedness, rather than Israel's
    comparative righteousness.

term מלך as the name or title of a god. Essentially, modern scholars tend to divide into two camps. One supports Eissfeldt, who in 1935 argued that מלך in these verses—with the exception of 1 Kgs 11:7[41]—was originally a technical term for a type of sacrifice, analogous with the terminology employed within Punic dedicatory inscriptions relating to the practice of child sacrifice.[42] Thus in the biblical verses in question, מלך is understood to have referred originally to a practice in which children were not made to pass over "to Molek" but were rather made to pass over "as a *mlk*-sacrifice".[43] In opposition to this theory is the traditional view maintaining that מלך was always intended to be understood as the name or title of a deity in these verses. Defenders of this position rely upon the interpretation of Lev. 20:5. This text is usually rendered, "I myself will set my face against him and against his family, and will cut him off from among his people, him and all who follow him in whoring after the Molek (אחרי המלך)". Day[44] argues that מֶלֶךְ in this passage cannot be translated "*mlk*-offering", because within the Hebrew Bible, Israelites unfaithful to YHWH do not whore after types of sacrifices, but only after other gods.[45] However, though Day's argument is reasonable on this point,[46] it is clear that in the remaining six occurrences of מֶלֶךְ in the Hebrew Bible the text can be rendered "*mlk*-offering" just as

---

41 This text refers to "Molek the abomination of the Ammonites", but it is almost universally agreed that this should be emended to "Milkom", the national god of Ammon, who is described in the same way in v. 5.

42 Note especially Mosca, "Child Sacrifice in Canaanite and Israelite Religion: A Study in *Mulk* and מלך"; see also S. Ackerman, *Under Every Green Tree: Popular Religion in Sixth-Century Judah* (HSM 46; Atlanta: Scholars Press, 1992); S.M. Olyan, *Asherah and The Cult of Yahweh in Israel* (SBLMS 34; Atlanta: Scholars Press, 1988); S.M. Olyan and M.S. Smith, Review of *The Cult of Molek: A Reassessment*, by George C. Heider, *RB* 94 (1987), 273-275; H-P. Müller, "*mōlek*", *TDOT*, vol. 8, 375-388; W.F. Albright, *Yahweh and the Gods of Canaan* (London: Athlone Press, 1968), 236.

43 This assumed biblical term is variously vocalized as "*molk*" or "*mulk*", corresponding to the reconstructed vocalization of the Punic term *mlk*. In this discussion, the unvocalized form *mlk* will be employed whenever possible, for the sake of clarity.

44 Day, *Molech*, 10-12; idem., *Yahweh*, 209-201; see also Heider, *Molek*, 242-252.

45 Eg. Exod. 34:15-16; Lev. 17:7; Deut. 31:16; Judg. 2:17; 8:33; Jer. 3:1, 2, 6, 8-9; Ezek. 6:9; 16:15-17, 26, 28, 30-31, 33-36, 41; 20:30; 23:3, 5, 19, 43-44; Hos. 1:2; 2:7 (ET 5); 4:12; 5:3; Mic.1:7.

46 The use of the definite article written consonantally before מלך occurs only here; the implications of this are examined in 5.3.

easily as "Molek".[47] For example, מֹלֶךְ occurs three times in the verses immediately preceding Lev. 20:5, and as verse 3 demonstrates, may be understood as a type of sacrifice: "Any of the people of Israel, or of the aliens who reside in Israel, who give any of their offspring as a *mlk*-offering (לַמֹּלֶךְ) shall be put to death". It is essential to recognize the ambiguity of the biblical terminology. Though the MT clearly understands the term מֹלֶךְ within these verses to be the name of a deity distinct from YHWH, it is unclear whether this was the *original* understanding of the term within the earliest history of some of the biblical texts. Moreover, it may be that the original meaning of this term within literary traditions differs from its use and meaning within the socio-religious climate of the historical Judah. The scarcity of attestations of MT מֹלֶךְ is problematic in itself; combined with a relative lack of extra-biblical evidence for a deity named "Molek", the original vocalization of biblical מלך within the verses is questionable. Indeed, some scholars have long-doubted the existence of a Hebrew word מֹלֶךְ.[48] Instead, many continue to support an hypothesis advanced by Geiger nearly a hundred and fifty years ago. On the basis of the Septuagint's translation of מלך in Lev. 18:21 and 20:2-5 with ἄρχων, "ruler", Geiger proposed that the MT's מֹלֶךְ is a secondary creation of post-biblical tradition amalgamating the vowels of בֹּשֶׁת "shame" and the consonants of an original מֶלֶךְ, "king".[49] Many arguing against Eissfeldt's rendering of מֹלֶךְ as "*mlk*-sacrifice" tend to cite Geiger's dysphemism theory as support for a deity whose name originally derived from the title מֶלֶךְ. All of these possibilities and their implications will be discussed at length in the following chapters. For now, though, in examining the biblical portrayal of child sacrifice, it is enough to reiterate the ambiguity of the biblical term מֹלֶךְ. Though it is uncertain as to whether מלך in these verses originally referred to a god, be it YHWH or "Molek", or to a type of sacrifice, there are indications that some of those who have had a hand in the shaping and transmission of the biblical material have deliberately sought to interpret the term as the name of a foreign god. Essentially, this interpretation

---

47 Cf. Ackerman, *Under Every Green Tree*, 107-110; K.A.D. Smelik, "Moloch, Molekh or Molk-Sacrifice? A Reassessment of the Evidence concerning the Hebrew Term Molekh", *SJOT* 9 (1995), 133-142.

48 E.g., H.H. Rowley, Review of *De Molochdienst*, by K. Dronkert, *BO* 10 (1953), 195-196; R. de Vaux, "Bulletin", *RB* 52 (1955), 609-610; *idem.*, *Studies in Old Testament Sacrifice* (translated from the French; Cardiff: University of Wales Press, 1964), 87-90.

49 A. Geiger, *Urschrift und Übersetzungen der Bibel in ihrer Abhängigkeit von der innern Entwickelung des Judenthums* (Breslau: Verlag von Julius Hainauer, 1857), 299-308.

is founded upon the portrayal of the מֹלֶךְ ritual as a foreign practice. Yet before turning to examine this portrayal, an overview of the instances and contexts of the term מֹלֶךְ is instructive.

Of the seven uncontested attestations of מֹלֶךְ, five occur in the book of Leviticus: once in 18:21, and four times, in a cluster, in 20:2-5. The remaining two occurrences are found in 2 Kgs 23:10 and Jer. 32:35. Thus from the outset, the biblical field of study is somewhat restricted. The term is accorded a sacrificial context by its accompanying language: העביר (Lev. 18:21; 2 Kgs 23:10; Jer. 32:35) and נתן (Lev. 20:2, 3, 4),[50] though Lev. 20:5 offers an exception, for this verse does not speak of sacrifice, but of metaphorical whoring (זנה). Within these Levitical texts, the sacrificial victims are designated "offspring" or "seed" (זרע), whilst in 2 Kgs 23:10 and Jer. 32:35 בן and בת are employed. Supplementing these texts are several others which, whilst they do not include the term מֹלֶךְ, are widely-held to refer to the same practice. As discussed above, these include verses employing the expressions העביר באש (Deut. 18:10; 2 Kgs 16:3; 17:17; 21:6; 2 Chr. 28:3;[51] 33:6; Jer. 32:35; Ezek. 20:31) and שרף באש (Deut. 12:31; 2 Kgs 17:31; Jer. 7:31; 19:5).[52] The Levitical texts appear to associate the practice with YHWH's sanctuary (20:3), whereas 2 Kgs 23:10 and Jer. 32:35 locate the site of the מֹלֶךְ ritual in the Valley of Ben Hinnom, at a place labelled תפת (MT תֹּפֶת), the term also employed in Jer. 7:31, 32; 19:6, 11, 12, 13, 14. An apparent variant, תפתה (MT תָּפְתֶּה), is employed in Isa. 30:33. Despite the relative frequency with which the term תפת occurs, discerning its meaning is hugely problematic, not least because it occurs only in biblical Hebrew and related rabbinic commentaries.[53] Moreover, with the exception of the Isaianic form תפתה, its use is restricted to Jeremiah and 2 Kgs 23:10. The cultic associations of תפת are suggested in the book of Jeremiah, in which תפת is described as a במה (7:31; cf. 19:5; 32:35), and the prophet himself is even said to have been sent by YHWH to prophesy at the תפת (19:14). Though numerous etymologies of תפת have been proposed,[54] a

---

50 Language earlier argued to be sacrificial, 143-148.
51 See n. 6, above.
52 See above, 141-148.
53 P.C. Schmitz, "Topheth", *ABD*, vol. 6, 600-601. The Versions transliterate the term תפת variously, for example, ταφεθ (LXX), θοφθα (LXX^A), θυφθ (Aquila), θαφεθ (Symmachus).
54 See the overviews of etymological suggestions in Heider, *Molek*, 346-350; Day, *Molech*, 24-28.

satisfactory consensus is yet to be reached. Whilst the Masoretic vocalization may reflect בֹּשֶׁת, "shame", or imitate the term תֻּפָּה, "spit" (Job 17:6),[55] Day finds attractive the proposal that the word is likely derived from יְפֶה, "bake" (cf. Lev. 6:14), which, if correct, would cement further the sacrificial, rather than dedicatory, nature of the fiery practice.[56] However, though the combined contexts of the biblical attestations of the term imply that תֹּפֶת is a fiery cult place, the sheer ambiguity surrounding this term, as well as its restricted range of occurrences (mainly Jer. 7 and 19), warns against drawing a firm conclusion regarding its etymology.[57] The most that can be stated, therefore, is that the biblical contexts are suggestive of תֹּפֶת as the biblical name of a site at which children were burned as sacrifices.

A handful of texts locate תֹּפֶת in the Valley of Ben Hinnom (2 Kgs 23:10; Jer. 7:31, 32; 19:6), which complements the association of this valley with the practice of child sacrifice elsewhere (2 Chr. 28:3; 33:6; Jer. 32:35). The reworked nature of much of this material might equally suggest, though, a degree of deliberate textual harmonization, bringing the Valley of Ben Hinnom and תֹּפֶת into closer alignment. Indeed, it is possible that the Valley of Ben Hinnom attained a particular symbolic significance within certain post-monarchic prophetic circles, for the book of Jeremiah renames this valley גיא ההרגה, "the Valley of Slaughter" (7:32; 19:6),[58] and the coded language of Ezek. 39:11 may allude to the passing over (העביר) of children in Ben Hinnom in the designation גי העברים, "the Valley of those who Passover" (39:11).[59]

A cursory reading of this material combines to present what appears to be a relatively detailed and informative picture of the מֹלֶךְ practice: a ritual in which children, both sons and daughters, were sacrificed in fire in a cult place known as תֹּפֶת in the Valley of Ben Hinnom. This is primarily achieved by the repetition of specific phrases, most notably שרף באש, העביר באש, and תֹּפֶת. Yet this detailed biblical picture is illusory, for not only do the pertinent references occur in fairly unvarying, concentrated clusters, but very little can be discerned concerning the perceived function of this sacrifice. Rather, the primary emphasis of the biblical portrayal of this cult of child sacrifice falls

---

55 Schmitz, "Topheth", 601; J.A. Dearman, "The Tophet in Jerusalem: Archaeology and Cultural Profile", *JNSL* 22 (1996), 59-71 (60 n. 4).
56 Day, *Molech*, 24-28.
57 So too Heider, *Molek*, 346-349.
58 On this designation, see below, n. 76.
59 See below, 4.2.3.

upon the notion that it is a foreign practice. This is the ideological thrust of the portrayal of the מֹלֶךְ ritual in Kings, in which it is included as one of several foreign practices (2 Kgs 17:17, 31, 23:10), fated to cast its practitioners out from the land (2 Kgs 16:3; 17:17; 21:6). This is also the perspective of Leviticus, which paints the מֹלֶךְ ritual as a defiling practice of the foreign nations that leads to exile (18:21, 24), and as a practice which results in socio-religious expulsion from the community (20:2-5), and by implication, from the land (20:22-24).[60] Indeed, in the book of Jeremiah YHWH's condemnation of the מֹלֶךְ practice occurs within the explicit context of the Babylonian invasion and conquest (32:28-35). These texts clearly complement Deut. 18:9-12, in which child sacrifice is regarded as a foreign practice alien to correct YHWH-worship. This text makes it plain that because of their abominable practices, YHWH cast out the foreign nations and gave the land to Israel.[61] The implication of all these texts is thus plain: if the Israelites imitate the practices of the nations, they too will be cast out of the land. This cause-and-effect schema of land dispossession, which is central to the biblical ideology of separateness, is deliberately and emphatically demonstrated throughout the history of Israel and Judah set out in Kings, particularly in 2 Kgs 17 and 21, which detail the exile-inducing cult crimes of the Northern Kingdom and King Manasseh, respectively. Given the portrayal of the fiery cult of child sacrifice as a foreign practice, it is no surprise to find that the crime העביר באשׁ appears upon the charge sheets of both the Northern Kingdom (17:17) and Manasseh (21:6).

The biblical portrayal of the מֹלֶךְ practice as a foreign ritual is also evident elsewhere within Kings. It is asserted in 2 Kgs 17:24 that the Assyrian king replaced the exiled population of Israel with a variety of foreign peoples. In a condensed account of the cultic behaviour of these peoples (17:25-34) the Sepharvites are singled out in verse 31 as burning (שׂרף) their children or sons (בנים) in the fire (באשׁ) to the gods of Sepharvaim, called Adrammelek (אדרמלך) and Anammelek (ענמלך).[62] The מלך- component of these divine names is obviously intriguing, yet attempts to elucidate them, as well as the location of Sepharvaim, remain unpersuasive.[63] It may be that Fritz is correct in postulating that the names

---

60 E.S. Gerstenberger, *Leviticus: A Commentary* (trans. D.W. Stott; OTL; Louisville: Westminster John Knox, 1996), 291-292.

61 Cf. Deut. 9:4; 12:29-31.

62 Q, אלהי ספרוים.

63 For a sampling of views, see A.R. Millard, "Adrammelech", *DDD* (1999), 10-11; "Anammelech", *DDD* (1999), 34-35; A. Pohl, "Zu 4 Könige 17,31", *Bib* 22 (1941), 35-

are artificial creations, designed to add credibility to the description of foreign peoples and cults in 2 Kgs 17:24-34.[64] Indeed, here the fiery sacrifice of children is clearly portrayed as a foreign practice in honour of foreign gods, which is entirely in keeping with the other biblical texts surveyed here.

It may be that the biblical association of the מֹלֶךְ practice with the foreign nations accounts for the apparent misvocalization of the name of the Ammonite god in 1 Kgs 11:7. The MT is usually rendered, "Then Solomon built a high place for Kemosh the abomination of Moab, and for Molek the abomination of the Ammonites on the mountain east of Jerusalem". However, there are good reasons for most commentators to amend ולמלך in this verse to ולמלכם, "and for Milkom": the Septuagint reads Μελχομ here; in verse 5, Milkom is described as שׁקץ עמנים, "the abomination of the Ammonites" (cf. 11:33; 2 Kgs 23:13);[65] and in the story of Josiah's reforms the Kings Writer appears to distinguish between the cult place of Milkom and that of מֹלֶךְ (2 Kgs 23:10, 13).[66]

A further illustration of the foreign portrayal of the practice associated with מֹלֶךְ is the biblical assertion that Ahaz also participated in child sacrifice. 2 Kgs 16:3-4 reads:

> He walked in the way of the kings of Israel and also made his son[67] pass over in the fire according to the abominations of the nations whom YHWH had dispossessed before the children of Israel. He sacrificed and burned offerings[68] on the *bamoth*, on the hills and under every green tree.

37; Becking, *Fall of Samaria*, 99-102; Olyan, *Asherah*, 67-69; Heider, *Molek*, 291-94; Day, *Molech*, 44-46, and the literature cited therein. Doyle suggests that the designation ספרוים may be intended to play aurally upon שׂרף; R. Doyle, "Molek of Jerusalem?", in R.S. Hess and G.J. Wenham (eds.), *Zion, City of Our God* (Grand Rapids: Eerdmans, 1999), 171-206 (200, n.102).

64 Fritz, *1 & 2 Kings*, 355-56. This is also the case in the account of Josiah's reform in 2 Kgs 23, which is peppered with the names and locations of idolatrous practices, and the details of their destruction; cf. Nelson, *First and Second Kings*, 258.

65 Though note the slight variation in v. 5, which has עמון rather than עמון. Scholars choosing to emend ולמלך to ולמלכם include Eissfeldt, *Molk*, 31; Noth, *Könige I. 1-16*, 241; De Vaux, *Studies*, 73-74; Mosca, "Child Sacrifice", 121-122; *contra* E. Dhorme ("Le Dieu Baal et le Dieu Moloch dans la tradition biblique", *Anatolian Studies* 6 [1956], 59-60); Wiseman, *1 and 2 Kings*, 135. These commentators argue that a god "Molek" or "Melek" is to be identified with the Ammonite deity Milkom.

66 Heider, *Molek*, 278-279.

67 LXX[L] reads a plural here (cf. MT 2 Chr. 28:3).

68 On the meaning of קטר, see n. 31 above. On the possible interrelation of this practice with העביר באש, see 161.

Alongside Manasseh, Ahaz is the only other king to be accused of this practice. Moreover, he is the sole monarch to be charged with worshipping at the *bamoth*, which combined with the formulaic but theologically-loaded crimes of high hill and green tree,[69] amounts to a significant invective against the king. Indeed, this list of cult crimes, like that ascribed to Manasseh, is carefully crafted, for the crimes of high hill and green tree are also associated with child sacrifice in Ezek. 20:25-31 and Isa. 57:5.[70] Further compounding this association is the shared application of the language of whoring and adultery to child sacrifice (Lev. 20:5; Ps. 106:37-39; Isa. 57:3; Ezek. 23:37-39) and the crimes of high hill and green tree (Jer. 2:20; 3:6-9, 13; Hos. 4:12-14).[71] Given the prominent function of the Kings Writer's portrayal of Manasseh, it is at first puzzling as to why Ahaz is singled out alongside Manasseh as having sacrificed his son, particularly as Ahaz is not accused of the other cult crimes comprising the Kings Writer's pet hates: making an *asherah*, bowing down to all the Host of Heaven, serving Ba'al, and practicing divination and augury.[72] The key to understanding this selection is Ahaz's biblical reputation as an imitator of the foreign nations. Following the explicit assertion that Ahaz walked in the way of the kings of Israel (16:3), the focal point of the account of his reign is the story of his copying of the Damascus altar for the YHWH temple in Jerusalem (16:10-18). Though the

---

69 Deut. 12:2 and 1 Kgs 14:23 portray these crimes as those of the foreign nations; for a detailed discussion of this expression, see W.L. Holladay, "On Every High Hill and Under Every Green Tree", *VT* 11 (1961), 170-76.

70 The association of child sacrifice and the crimes of the high hill and green tree may also occur in Jer. 2:20-23. The elusive rebuke of the people's "way in the valley" (v. 23) is often taken as an allusion to the practice of child sacrifice in the Valley of Ben Hinnom. This view is encouraged by 7:31-32; 19:2-6, 11-12 and the Septuagint's rendering of אֲיְ as "cemetery" in 2:23 and 19:6. See particularly J.A. Soggin, "'Your Conduct in the Valley': A Note on Jeremiah 2, 23a", in *idem.*, *Old Testament and Oriental Studies* (BibOr 29; Rome: Biblical Institute Press), 78-83 = "'La tua condotta nella Valle', Nota a Geremia ii, 23a", *RSO* 36 (1961), 207-11; W. McKane, "Jeremiah II 23-25: Observations on the Versions and History of Exegesis", *OTS* 17 (1972), 73-88.

71 On the use of this metaphorical language of whoring and adultery, see particularly 4.1.2 and 5.3, 6.1.

72 The Chronicler appears to remedy this abbreviated inventory of cult crimes by accusing Ahaz of making cast images for the Ba'als, sacrificing more than one son in the fire (2 Chr. 28:2-3), sacrificing to foreign gods (28:23) and constructing *bamoth* for foreign gods (28:25). It is important to note that the Chronicler can afford to worsen Ahaz's reputation because he has not invested responsibility for the exile with Manasseh. See further K.A.D. Smelik, "The Representation of King Ahaz in 2 Kings 16 and 2 Chronicles 28", in J.C. de Moor (ed.), *Intertextuality in Ugarit and Israel* (OTS 40; Leiden: Brill, 1998), 143-185.

Kings Writer refrains from commenting directly upon Ahaz's refurbishment of the temple, his disapproval is implicit in the acknowledgement of the foreign influence upon Ahaz: "He did this because of the King of Assyria" (16:18). It is thus striking that in seeking to portray a king who not only follows the practices of the Northern Kingdom, but who is also under the influence of a foreign nation (Assyria) and imitates a foreign nation (Damascus), the Kings Writer accuses Ahaz of causing his son to "pass over in the fire". It is also particularly significant that alongside the generalized and non-specific crimes of worshipping at the *bamoth*, on the high hills and under every green tree, this is the only specific cult practice employed to signal the grave nature of Ahaz's foreign behaviour, just as it appears to do so in Deut. 12:29-31.

Despite the uncertainty surrounding the biblical term מֹלֶךְ—uncertainty which will be explored and assessed more closely in the following chapter—the examination of texts employing this term or alluding to its associated practice offers a seemingly coherent picture of its nature and function. The biblical texts appear to speak of a sacrificial cult in which children were "passed over" in the fire, apparently to a deity named "Molek". The biblical literature intentionally presents this fiery rite of child sacrifice as a foreign practice, a practice which provokes YHWH's anger and leads to the loss of the land. As such, the biblical presentation of the מֹלֶךְ practice is perhaps best understood as one of the ideological boundaries defining the biblical "Israel". Those participating in the practice are deemed to be outside of the biblical Israel, and thus risk expulsion from YHWH's land. Therefore along with Ahaz and Manasseh, the Canaanites (Deut. 12:31), the Northern Kingdom (2 Kgs 17:17) the former Judahites (2 Kgs 23:10; Jer. 7:31; 19:5; 32:35; Ezek. 16; 23) and the new inhabitants of the former Northern Kingdom (2 Kgs 17:31-34), are defined as outside of the biblical Israel—and thus dispossessed of their land—on the basis of the sacrifice of their children.

4.1.2 Sacrifice to other Deities, Dung-Gods, Demons, and the Dead

This chapter has thus far focused upon biblical attempts to portray the fire sacrifice as a practice devoted to a deity named "Molek". Despite the scarcity of occurrences of the term מֹלֶךְ, the biblical portrait of the מֹלֶךְ practice is generally taken to be fairly coherent. However, this biblical portrayal is severely undermined by a glaring inconsistency: in several texts, the divine recipient of the sacrifice appears to be confused with other deities, or is apparently unknown to the biblical writers. Moreover, alongside this inconsistency, there are strong indications that traditions concerning other forms of child sacrifice were known and employed by the biblical writers. These factors combine to present a more nuanced portrait of child sacrifice in the Hebrew Bible, in which the מֹלֶךְ ritual is but one among many biblical presentations of child sacrifice. This amounts to a challenge to both the biblical portrayal of an idolatrous god named "Molek", and the all-too-frequent scholarly assumption that this portrayal is historically credible.

Jer. 19:4-6 offers the first illustration of this inconsistency in the biblical portrait of child sacrifice. These verses seek to condemn child sacrifice as a foreign practice, and in doing so, employ language and details reminiscent of 32:35, and elsewhere associated with the מֹלֶךְ practice: שרף באש, חפת, and גיא בן הנם. Yet despite this vocabulary, and in contrast to 32:35, the recipient of the sacrifices is named as Baʿal, rather than "Molek":

> Because the people have abandoned me, and have profaned this place by burning offerings in it to other gods whom neither they nor their ancestors nor the kings of Judah have known, and because they have filled[73] this place with innocent blood and have kept building the *bamoth* of Baʿal to burn (שרף) their sons in the fire as burnt offerings to Baʿal[74], which I did not command or decree,[75] nor did it enter my mind. Thus behold! The days are coming, declares YHWH, when this place shall no more be called "Topheth" or "Valley of Ben Hinnom", but "Valley of Slaughter".[76]

This text clearly seeks to condemn child sacrifice as a foreign practice, yet naming Baʿal as the recipient deity is inconsistent not only with the

---

73 It is interesting to note that Holladay (*Jeremiah*, vol. 1, 534, 540), reads מלאו with the Septuagint, thus rendering the Judahite kings the sole subjects of the verb, and so holding them responsible for having "filled this place with innocent blood". He explicitly relates his interpretation to the specific crimes of Ahaz (child sacrifice), Manasseh (child sacrifice and shedding innocent blood), and Jehoiakim (shedding innocent blood) in 2 Kgs 16:3; 21:6, 16; 24:4 and Jer. 22:17; cf. McKane, *Jeremiah*, vol. 1, 451-453. For the accusation against Jehoiakim, see above, 39-40.

74 עלות לבעל is often deleted as a secondary insertion, for it is not reflected in the LXX, nor in MT 7:31. However, whether it is secondary or not, it testifies to a sacrificial understanding of the phrase שרף באש, as noted above.

75 ולא דברי is not reflected in LXX, nor in MT 7:31, and is thus frequently deleted as a secondary gloss.

76 The label גיא ההרגה is derived from הרג ("kill", "slaughter"). In employing this vocabulary, the biblical writer appears to allude to the ritual killing carried out in the valley, but intentionally desacralizes the practice by employing הרג rather than the sacrificial term שחט, which is used of child sacrifice in Gen. 22:10; Isa. 57:5; Ezek. 16:21; 23:39.

remainder of texts describing or alluding to the practice of העביר/שרף באש,
but it is also at odds with the biblical portrayal of Baʿal,[77] a deity clearly
distinguished from "Molek" elsewhere in the Hebrew Bible.[78] As Heider
observes, this discrepancy is particularly well-illustrated by comparing this
text with 32:35, in which the cult place of the fiery sacrifice is also described
as the high places of Baʿal in the Valley of Ben Hinnom, but here the MT
names "Molek" as the divine recipient of the sacrifices. The confusion
concerning the identity of the recipient deity is heightened further by the
preceding verse, in which burning offerings to other gods (אלהים) seems to
parallel the burning of children for Baʿal. As observed above, the alignment
of these activities is also evident in 2 Chr. 28:3, in which burning offerings in
the Valley of Ben Hinnom is directly associated with the practice described
as העביר באש. It would thus appear that there is considerable confusion in
Jer. 19:4-6 concerning the identity of the god(s) to whom these sacrifices are
offered.[79] Significantly, the Greek version of this text does not include the
reference to Baʿal as the recipient of the offerings,[80] raising the possibility
that the confusion evident in MT is the result of a later gloss—probably
encouraged by במות בעל—naming Baʿal as the god for whom children were
burned. This suggestion concerning the Hebrew text is encouraged by the
closely aligned 7:31, in which the reference to Baʿal is similarly absent:

> [The people of Judah] keep building the *bamoth*[81] of Topheth, which is in the Valley
> of Ben Hinnom, to burn (שרף) their sons and their daughters in fire, which I did not
> command, nor did it come into my mind.

---

77 Nowhere else in the Hebrew Bible is Baʿal explicitly associated with child sacrifice.
    However, biblical traditions concerning Baʿal of Peor connect this deity with sacrifices
    offered to the dead (Num. 25:3; 31:16-17; Deut. 4:3; Ps. 106:28). The possibility that
    these traditions may also be loosely associated with child sacrifice will be explored in
    the following pages. Yet the point remains that the association of Baʿal with the ritual
    elsewhere related to "Molek" undermines the coherence of the biblical picture of this
    practice.

78 Heider, "Molech", *DDD*, 581-585 (584); though note Milgrom's suggestion that in Jer.
    19:5, "Baʿal" functions as an epithet for YHWH (*Leviticus 17–22*, 1562).

79 Zevit (*Religions of Ancient Israel*, 550) seeks to smooth this confusion by speculating
    that these verses testify to the existence of a (now unknown) mythology which clarified
    the relationship between YHWH, Baʿal, and "Molek", and upon which the burning
    rituals were founded. However, this assumes a great deal more than the biblical texts are
    able to support.

80 As noted above, n. 74.

81 LXX and Targ. read a singular here, probably encouraged by the inference of the
    singular in the designation תפה.

Heightening the suspicion that Baʿal did not originally feature as the designated recipient of sacrificed children in 19:5[82] is the opening observation of this argument, that in 32:35 it is "Molek" who is seemingly cast in the role of a god of child sacrifice.[83] Indeed, this is in spite of the association of the Valley of Ben Hinnom with the *bamoth* of Baʿal in 32:35, an association shared with 19:5. There are thus two important implications of this confusion evident in the material in the book of Jeremiah. The first is that the coherence of the biblical portrayal of "Molek" is undermined by the peculiar naming of Baʿal as the god to whom children are sacrificed in the Valley of Ben Hinnom in Jer. 19:5. As will be seen in the following chapter, this represents one step towards the weakening of the biblical and scholarly case for a god of child sacrifice known as "Molek". This is to be related to the second implication of the confusion apparent in Jeremiah: that the sacrifice of children was not a foreign practice, but commanded by YHWH. This requires unpacking. If the phrase עלות לבעל in 19:5 is indeed a secondary gloss, the verse would cohere more closely with 7:31, which already infers that the sacrifice of children may have been understood as a practice dedicated to YHWH, as the claim "which I did not command, nor did it come into my mind" might suggest, a statement repeated in 19:5 and 32:35. Indeed, as Smelik remarks, such a defensive claim is comprehensible only if

---

82 *Pace* Edelman ("Biblical *Molek* Reassessed", *JAOS* 107 [1987], 727-731, esp. 730-731), who proposes that Jer. 2:32, 3:24, 19:5, and 32:35 all indicate that the divine recipient of the sacrifices *was* a form of Baʿal ("Baʿal Melek" or "Baʿal Molek"). She supports her suggestion with reference to the Ugaritic myth of Baʿal's sojourn in the underworld (*KTU* 1.5). However, this view is not persuasive given that it depends upon an interpretation of מֹלֶךְ as a divine epithet or title. This counter-argument can also be applied to those seeking to relate Zeph. 1:5 to "Molek" worship; cf. A. Berlin, *Zephaniah: A New Translation with Introduction and Commentary* (AB 25A; Garden City: Doubleday, 1994), 75-77; A.S. Kapelrud, *The Message of the Prophet Zephaniah: Morphology and Ideas* (Oslo: Universitets, 1975), 23-24; Heider, *Molek*, 332-336; Weinfeld, "Worship of Molek", 149. For alternative arguments against the identification of "Molek" with Baʿal, see Day, *Molech*, 34-36. For the opinion that Jer. 19:5 and 32:35 are scribal, theological reflections upon 7:31, see O. Kaiser, "Den Erstgeborenen deiner Söhne sollst du mir geben. Erwägungen zum Kinderopfer im Alten Testament", in *idem.* (ed.), *Denkender Glaube: Festschrift Carl Heinz Ratschow* (Berlin: de Gruyter, 1976), 24-48; repr. in O. Kaiser (ed.), *Von der Gegenwartsbedeutung des Alten Testaments: gesammelte Studien zur Hermeneutik und zur Redaktionsgeschichte* (Göttingen: Vandenhoeck & Ruprecht, 1984), 142-166, esp. 156-158.

83 Though notice that the Septuagint also reflects confusion, offering Μολοχ βασιλει for מֹלֶךְ.

it were believed that YHWH had commanded this practice.[84] Certainly, this recalls the explicit claim in Ezek. 20:25-26 that YHWH commanded all the firstborn to be sacrificed to him. In the light of this and the repeated insistence in Jeremiah that YHWH did not demand this type of sacrifice, it would appear that there existed a belief that the sacrifice of children was divinely-ordained by YHWH.[85] The writer of Jeremiah attempts to rebuff this belief; the writer of Ezekiel accepts it, though at the cost of its theological integrity, as will be seen.[86] In view of these observations, it would thus appear that attempts in the book of Jeremiah to portray child sacrifice as a foreign practice are not as convincing as they may initially appear. Despite the (possibly secondary) inclusion of עלות לבעל in 19:5 and the occurrence of למלך in 32:35, the insistent denials in these texts and in 7:31 that YHWH had ever commanded the sacrifice of children suggests a perceived association of YHWH with the practice. Certainly, if עלות לבעל is omitted from 19:5—as is frequently the case in the commentaries—and if למלך in 32:35 is rendered "as a *mlk* sacrifice"—as Eissfeldt and others suggest—then YHWH's association with the practice in the book of Jeremiah is brought into even sharper focus. These possibilities will be addressed in the following chapters. For now, though, it suffices to reiterate that the book of Jeremiah seeks, albeit tenuously, to dismiss child sacrifice as a foreign practice, alien to YHWH-worship.

The book of Ezekiel contains a number of verses which appear to be more successful in portraying child sacrifice as a foreign practice: 16:20-21, 36; 20:31 and 23:37-39. These texts are frequently held to allude to the cult of "Molek", for they all employ language elsewhere associated with this fiery sacrifice, including נתן (16:21, 36), העביר (16:21; 23:37); העביר באש (20:31). Alongside this terminology, these verses also use the verbs זבח (16:20) and שחט (16:21; 23:39) to describe the sacrifice of children. However, the common scholarly assumption that all these verses refer to the "Molek" practice rests upon uncertain ground, for these texts do not include the term מלך, nor do they refer to תפת or the Valley of Ben Hinnom. Moreover, the only phrase referring to the sacrifice of children in fire, העביר

---

84 Smelik, "Moloch, Molekh", 139; so too J.D. Levenson, *The Death and Resurrection of the Beloved Son: The Transformation of Child Sacrifice in Judaism and Christianity* (New Haven: Yale University Press, 1993), 4-5; Day, *Molech*, 68; Olyan, *Asherah*, 13; Carroll, *Jeremiah*, 223; G.B. Gray, *Sacrifice in the Old Testament* (Oxford: Clarendon Press, 1925), 87-88.

85 So too Holladay, *Jeremiah 1*, 268.

86 See 4.2.1.

בניכם באש (20:31), is of dubious authenticity given its absence in the Septuagint, and is widely held to be a secondary, interpretative gloss.[87] The case against an association with "Molek" is also supported by the fact that a specific deity to whom the children are sacrificed is not named; rather the recipients of the sacrifices are named as "dung-gods"[88] (20:31; 23:37, 39), one of the preferred, disparaging label employed in Ezekiel to refer to cult images of foreign and outlawed deities.[89] This generalized identification may be fleshed out a little more in 16:20-21, in which the recipients of the sacrifices appear to be the צלמי זכר, "male images" or "images of a male", which the whore Jerusalem constructs in the preceding verses, and to which she makes offerings of food and incense. Yet the gods to whom the children are sacrificed remain frustratingly intangible.

Further colour is added to the portrayal of child sacrifice by means of the graphic use of blood imagery in these texts. This is an unusual characteristic, for most other biblical texts relating to child sacrifice offer—perhaps intentionally—flat and spartan accounts of the practice, avoiding the more emotive details of the physical acts of killing and dying.[90] But as a reflection of the priestly matrix of the book, blood imagery is a powerful and dominant metaphor in Ezekiel, most usually describing social and political misdemeanours.[91] However, in chapters 16 and 23, the imagery symbolizes

---

87 See further W. Zimmerli, *Ezekiel 1* (trans. R.E. Clements; Hermeneia; Philadelphia: Fortress Press, 1979); 402; D.I. Block, *The Book of Ezekiel* (2 vols. NICOT; Grand Rapids: Eerdmans, 1997, 1998), vol. 1, 645.

88 The term גלולים is a polemical designation, probably derived from גלל, "be round", "roll", and related to גללים, "faeces"; its vocalization may reflect שקוץ, "abhorrent" (*HALOT*, vol. 1, 192). As such, more accurate (though vulgar) renderings of this term include "shitgods" (D. Bodi, "Les *gillûlîm* chez Ezéchiel et dans l'Ancien Testament, et les différentes practiques cultuelles associées à ce terme", *RB* 100 [1993], 481-510) and "pieces of shit" (T. Krüger, *Geschichtskonzepte im Ezechielbuch* [BZAW 108; Berlin: de Gruyter, 1989]). The more polite expression "dung-gods" is employed here, though this admittedly softens the powerful impact of the Hebrew term.

89 The term occurs 39 times in the book of Ezekiel, six times in Kings (1 Kgs 15:12; 21:26; 2 Kgs 17:12; 21:11, 21; 23:24) and a further three times elsewhere (Lev. 26:30; Deut. 29:16; Jer. 50:2). The frequency of its occurrence in Ezekiel has encouraged the speculation that the prophet coined the term himself (*contra* Block, *Ezekiel*, vol. 1, 226). See further Bodi, 'Les *gillûlîm* chez Ezéchiel", 481-510; M.I. Gruber, 'Gillulim', *DDD* (1999), 346-347.

90 A notable exception is Isa. 30:27-33, discussed in 4.1.3, below. The references to "innocent blood" in Jer. 19:4 and Ps. 106:38 are also examined below.

91 A. Mein, *Ezekiel and the Ethics of Exile* (Oxford: Oxford University Press, 2001), 160-161. On Jerusalem as a bloody city, see J. Galambush, *Jerusalem in the Book of Ezekiel: The City as Yahweh's Wife* (SBLDS 130; Atlanta: Scholars Press, 1992).

cultic deviancy,[92] and as such it appears within the context of child sacrifice. In these chapters, the priestly perception of blood as the very essence of life impacts upon the charges of child sacrifice, not only emphasizing the killing of the children (16:36), but bringing to the fore the characterization of child sacrifice as a defiling practice. This is spelt out most clearly in 23:37-39:

> For they have committed adultery, and blood is on their hands; with their dung-gods they have committed adultery, and they have passed over (העביר) to them[93] as food the very children they have borne to me. More than this they have done to me: on the same day[94] they defiled my sanctuary and desecrated my sabbaths. And while they were slaughtering their children for their dung-gods, on the same day[95] they came into my sanctuary to desecrate it. Behold—this is what they did inside my house.

The close alignment of child sacrifice and bloodstained hands in these verses also marks an important theological point in the chapter, for both child sacrifice and bloodied hands are presented as metaphorical adultery. The metaphor of adultery, which is often confused with allusions to literal adultery, occurs infrequently in the Hebrew Bible.[96] As such, its use in the book of Ezekiel is especially noteworthy, particularly given that it is the metaphor of whoring which is more regularly employed in chapters 16 and 23. As such, the synthesis of metaphorical adultery with child sacrifice in 23:37-39 is significant.[97] The metaphor is informed by the claim that the sacrificed children are YHWH's own offspring, borne to him by his wives Oholah (Samaria) and Oholibah (Jerusalem);[98] a very similar claim also made in 16:20-21. The children are thus indicative of the consummation of YHWH's

---

92 Mein, *Ezekiel and the Ethics of Exile*, 161.
93 MT להם. On the seemingly incorrect use of masculine suffixes in vv.37-39, see M. Greenberg, *Ezekiel 1–20* (AB 22; Garden City, Doubleday, 1983), 485.
94 ביום ההוא is not reflected in the Septuagint. Its inclusion in MT here and in v. 39 probably serves to emphasize the serious nature of the cult crimes described; cf. L.C. Allen, *Ezekiel 20–48* (WBC 29; Dallas: Word, 1990), 44.
95 See the note above.
96 See further G. Baumann, *Love and Violence: Marriage as Metaphor for the Relationship between YHWH and Israel in the Prophetic Books* (trans. L.M. Maloney; Collegeville: Liturgical Press, 2003), 152-153; S. Moughtin, "Death of a Metaphor; Birth of New Meaning: An Exploration of Sexual and Marital Metaphorical Language in the Prophetic Books of the Hebrew Bible" (Unpublished D.Phil. dissertation; University of Oxford, 2004), 104, 171-173.
97 Moughtin, "Death of a Metaphor", 171.
98 For the ideological function of women as biblical symbols, see most recently G.A. Yee, *Poor Banished Children of Eve: Woman as Evil in the Hebrew Bible* (Minneapolis: Fortress Press, 2003).

marital relationships with his wives,[99] and as such, the wives' religious crimes are rendered not simply as prostitution (as in 16:20-21), but as adultery (23:37). The metaphor recurs in 23:45, in which YHWH describes the fate of Oholah and Oholibah, saying, "Righteous judges shall declare them guilty of adultery and of bloodshed; because they are adulteresses and blood is on their hands". The context of this verse demands the identification of the bloodied hands with the actions described in verses 37-39, in which the sisters' bloodstained hands signals their sacrifice of their children.[100] This recalls YHWH's condemnation of his adulterous and whoring wife in chapter 16, whose sacrifice of her children (vv. 20-21, 36) is said to bring down upon her YHWH's punishment: "I will judge you as women who commit adultery and shed blood are judged, and bring blood upon you in wrath and jealousy" (v. 38). The interrelation of child sacrifice, blood, and adultery in chapters 16 and 23 is probably founded upon the perception that all three threaten the perpetuation of the bloodline,[101] a key ideological concern evident throughout the Hebrew Bible, and of particular importance within the exilic setting of the book of Ezekiel. The interrelation of child sacrifice and adultery is also evident in the punishment of stoning, which is inflicted upon YHWH's wives (16:40; 23:47) and legislated for both adultery and child sacrifice in Lev. 20:2, 10. Their close occurrence in Leviticus and Ezekiel is probably no coincidence, for child sacrifice and adultery also appear together in Isa. 57:3-13, as will be seen.

In view of the graphic portrayal and vehement condemnation of child sacrifice in chapters 16 and 23, it remains surprising that the identity of the divine recipients is so vague. This may be indicative of the stereotypical usage of the biblical language of child sacrifice in these chapters, rather than, say, the reflections of an eye-witness to the practice. Yet the vagueness of the labels "dung-gods" and "male images" conflicts with the heavy emphasis upon YHWH's central role in the passages: he is father to the sacrificed children, husband to the perpetrators, divine host of the defiled sanctuary, and divine punisher of the offenders. It may be that the book of Ezekiel's extreme theocentric perspective[102] disallows the fuller characterization of the "dung-gods" and the "male images". Yet the vague sketch of these recipients of

---

99 Block, *Ezekiel*, vol. 1, 736.
100 Notice also the association of "innocent blood" with child sacrifice in Jer. 19:5 and Ps. 106:38; this association is discussed below.
101 So too Moughtin, "Death of a Metaphor", 105.
102 See further P.M. Joyce, *Divine Initiative and Human Response in Ezekiel* (JSOTSup 51; Sheffield: JSOT Press, 1989), 89-105.

sacrificed children stands in stark contrast to 20:25-26, in which the divine and willing recipient of the sacrificed firstborn is explicitly named as YHWH.[103] As a result, the portrayal of child sacrifice as a foreign practice in Ezek. 16 and 23 is at once confused and undermined by the startling claim of 20:25-26, an important text discussed in the following section. In their keenness to support the condemnation of child sacrifice in Ezekiel, commentators are too hasty in their identification of the sacrifices described in 16:20-21; 20:25-26, 31; 23:37-39 with offerings to "Molek"; the evidence is not strong enough to support this assumption. However, though most of these texts certainly seek to present child sacrifice as a practice alien to YHWH, discerning the intended identity of the recipient deities remains problematic.

More convincing in its portrayal of child sacrifice as a foreign practice is Ps. 106:34-39:

34	They did not destroy the peoples, as the LORD had said to them.
35	They mingled with the nations, and learned to do as they did.
36	They worshipped their images and they became a snare to them.
37	They sacrificed (זבח) their sons and their daughters to the שדים,
38	they shed innocent blood, (the blood of their sons and their daughters, whom they sacrificed [זבח] for the images of Canaan)[104] and the land was polluted with blood.
39	They became unclean by their acts, and they prostituted (זנה) themselves in their deeds.

---

103 On this text, see 4.2.1.

104 The clause in parenthesis is often deleted by commentators as a later interpolation, for it disrupts the meter of the poetry (so H.-J. Kraus, *Psalms 60–150: A Commentary* [trans. H.C. Oswald; Minneapolis: Augsburg, 1989, 316). However, many commentators allow this clause to stand, for example, M. Dahood (*Psalms 101–150* [AB 17A; Garden City: Doubleday, 1970], 74) sees a wordplay on כנען and יבנעו in v. 42; L.C. Allen (*Psalms 101–150* [WBC 21; Waco: Word, 1983], 53) argues for an original, extended chiastic pattern interweaving vv. 34-40; whilst N.H. Richardson ("Psalm 106: Yahweh's Succoring Love Saves from the Death of a Broken Covenant", in J.H. Marks and R.M. Good [eds.], *Love and Death in the Ancient Near East: Essays in Honor of Marvin H. Pope* [Guildford: Four Quarters, 1987], 191-203 [199-200]) prefers to view v. 37 as a later gloss on v. 38, and אשר זבחו לעצבי כנען in v. 38 as an editorial expansion.

The psalm in which these verses occur offers a selection of scenes depicting YHWH's relationship with "Israel", moving from Egypt, to the wilderness, to the gaining of the land, and to the close of the exile. The biblical ideology of separation, argued in this study to colour the portrayal of child sacrifice in several texts, is clearly in view in these verses. A sharp distinction is drawn between "Israel" on the one hand, and the "peoples" (עמים) and the "nations" (גוים), on the other. The purpose of this divinely-ordained separation (v. 34) is made apparent in the repercussions resulting from its disregard: the adoption of foreign practices, followed by the resulting pollution of the land and the defilement of "Israel" (vv. 35-39). Significantly, and in spite of the preceding catalogue of exile-inducing sins, the focus thus falls upon child sacrifice as the catalyst for YHWH's eventual expulsion of his people from the land (vv. 40-47). Interestingly, the portrayal of child sacrifice as a foreign practice leading irrevocably to exile particularly parallels that in Deut. 12:29-31.[105]

The language of child sacrifice employed in this poetic piece is explicit: the term זבח is twice used of the practice (vv. 37, 38), whilst the lethal nature of the ritual is given a heavy emphasis in the repetitious references to "blood" in verse 38. Yet the blood imagery also serves another purpose, for it seems to represent cultic defilement, which contaminates both the land (v. 38) and the people themselves (v. 39). This is reminiscent of the presentation of child sacrifice in the book of Ezekiel, in which the explicit term זבח is employed of the practice (16:20), and in which the powerful use of blood imagery is also attested (16:36, 38; 23:37-39, 45), similarly emphasizing the polluting nature of child sacrifice. However, the use of blood imagery here is made more complex by the inclusion of the biblical expression דם נקי, "innocent blood". This phrase carries ethical connotations, for it tends to refer to the blood of a person wrongfully or violently killed or oppressed within a social or political context,[106] and as such, it implies the correlated biblical notion that the shedder of innocent blood incurs bloodguilt, which in its turn demands vengeance or expiation.[107] In view of this broader biblical context, the inclusion of the expression דם נקי in a specific, cultic context here is

---

105 Cf. Deut. 18:9-12; 2 Kgs 17:17-18; 21:2-15.

106 G. Warmuth, "nāqâ", TDOT vol. 9, 553-563 (558). Warmuth lists 20 other occurrences of this expression: Deut. 19:10, 13; 21:8, 9; 27:25; 1 Sam. 19:5; 2 Kgs 21:16; 24:4 [twice]; Isa. 59:7; Jer. 2:34; 7:6; 19:4; 22:3, 17; 26:15; Joel 4:19 [ET 3:19]; Jon. 1:14; Ps. 94:21; Prov. 6:17.

107 Cf. Deut. 19:13; 21:8-9. In the context of child sacrifice, this may also be implied in Ezek. 16:38.

potentially confusing. Indeed, this appears to have been a concern for a later glossator, who has sought to eliminate any potential misunderstanding by pointedly identifying the דם נקי with the blood of the sacrificed children.[108] Yet the apparent blurring of a socio-political and cultic context of blood imagery in these verses is a clever confusion, for the parallelling of child sacrifice with the shedding of innocent blood functions in a significant way: it not only underscores the perceived illegitimacy of the sacrifice of sons and daughters, but it also transforms a cult crime into a social sin. As such, in Ps. 106 child sacrifice is not only portrayed as a foreign cult crime, but as a social crime, carrying with it serious theological consequences for the wider community, as is made plain in the charge that the people became unclean (v. 39) and came under foreign oppression (vv. 40-42) and were exiled (v. 46-47) as a result. The eradication of any boundary between cultic crime and social sin is perhaps best-illustrated in the book of Leviticus; as such, child sacrifice is presented as both a foreign practice which leads to exile (18:21, 24), and as a social sin which pollutes the community and is thus punishable by the community (20:2-5).

It may be that the book of Jeremiah also seeks to align child sacrifice with social transgression, for in 19:4-5 it is claimed that the people of Judah and Jerusalem have "filled this place with innocent blood (דם נקים) and have kept building the high places of Baʿal to burn their sons in the fire". However, in view of the fact that the biblical phrase דם נקי is most usually associated with illegal and violent killing or oppression, there is some debate concerning the appropriate interpretation of the phrase המקום הזה, for it is uncertain as to whether it refers to the cult site of child sacrifice, or to a distinct location, and hence a separate, social crime. Though the majority of commentators appear to favour the latter opinion,[109] many allow for the possibility that the תפת is intended here.[110] In the light of the close alignment of the phrase דם נקי with child sacrifice in Ps. 106:37-38, in addition to the dynamic application of blood imagery to the practice in Ezek. 16 and 23—a motif often overlooked in this context—it is not unreasonable to understand דם נקים in Jer. 19:4 as an allusion to sacrifice of children in the following verse. Indeed, like the poet of Ps. 106, the writer of Jer. 19 views the cult crime of child sacrifice as prompting both foreign domination (military oppression in 19:7) and social disaster (cannibalism in 19:9). As has been seen, the complex of theological

---

108 See n. 105 above.
109 See, for example, the discussion in McKane, *Jeremiah*, vol. 1, 452
110 See, for example, the discussion in Carroll, *Jeremiah*, 388.

ideas carried by the expression נקי דם is also evidenced in the account of King Manasseh's reign in 2 Kings. In the light of this discussion, it is unsurprising that Manasseh too is charged with shedding innocent blood (21:16). Though it is uncertain as to whether this ought to be understood as a reference to child sacrifice, the shedding of innocent blood here functions in a way strongly reminiscent of Ps. 106, for it is a crime which causes the wider community of Judah to sin (2 Kgs 21:16) and leads irrevocably to exile (24:1-4). Similarly, both texts appear to identify the punishment of these crimes with the experiences of later generations. However, there is one important difference which sets the charge against Manasseh in 2 Kgs 21 and 24 apart from that in Ps. 106. In the latter text, the socio-cultic crimes of shedding innocent blood and sacrificing children is a communal sin, perpetrated by the "ancestors"; in the former texts, it is Manasseh alone who commits the crimes,[111] though the repercussions are felt by the whole nation. In all these texts—2 Kgs 21:6, 16; 24:3-4; Ps. 106:34-39; Jer. 19:4-5; Ezek. 16:35, 38; 23:37-39, 45—the shedding of (innocent) blood and child sacrifice function as ideological motifs, signalling foreignness and impurity within both the cult and the community. Their fusion thus appears to be symptomatic of a people wholly alien to YHWH and undeserving of his land. These motifs thus form a powerful component of the ideology of separateness dominating the biblical story of "Israel".

In returning to focus more closely upon the portrayal of child sacrifice in Ps. 106, further parallels with Ezek. 16 and 23 become apparent. Alongside the powerful use of blood imagery, Ps. 106 also shares with Ezek. 16 and 23 the association of child sacrifice with metaphorical whoring (זנה) in verses 38-39. As has been seen, this metaphorical language is particularly characteristic of the condemnation of personified Jerusalem and Oholah and Oholibah in Ezek. 16 and 23, but it also occurs in other prophetic texts, most usually with reference to the adoption of foreign religious behaviour.[112] In this text, the language of whoring is associated with child sacrifice, though it is uncertain as to whether this association is triggered by explicit mention of the practice itself, or whether it arises more generally from the portrayal of child sacrifice as a ritual dedicated to foreign gods. On balance, it is more

---

111 The Lucianic version of 2 Kgs 24:3-4 accuses Jehoiakim of shedding innocent blood; see above, 39-40.

112 For further discussion, see P.A. Bird, "'To Play the Harlot': An Inquiry into an Old Testament Metaphor", in P.L. Day (ed.), *Gender and Difference in Ancient Israel* (Minneapolis: Fortress Press, 1989), 75-94, along with the literature cited above in nn. 98, 100.

likely that the language of whoring is encouraged by specific reference to the practice of child sacrifice, for neither זנה nor its derivatives occur elsewhere in this psalm, despite the fact that it describes other outlawed practices (vv. 19-20) and the worship of a foreign god (v. 28).[113]

A further feature shared with the portrayal of child sacrifice in Ezekiel also gives rise to a significant difference. Like Ezek. 16:20-21 and 23:37-39, Ps. 106 disparagingly presents the recipients of the sacrificed children as a plurality of manufactured deities, designated in verse 36 as "images" (עצבים) and in verse 38 as "images of Canaan" (עצבי כנען).[114] However, unlike the author of Ezek. 16:20-21 and 23:37-39, the psalmist also identifies these images with more precision, labelling them שדים. On the basis of the Akkadian term *šēdu*, which in its singular form tends to refer to a benevolent spirit, or in its plural form a malevolent demon,[115] the biblical term שֵׁדִים is commonly taken as a cognate, rendered as "demons", as most commentaries will attest. However, as will be seen in the following chapter, there are good reasons to follow Hackett in her revocalization of שֵׁדִים as שַׁדַּיִם,[116] thereby rendering the term as the designation "*šaddayyim*" or "*šadday*-gods". This revocalized form is, of course, to be related to the biblical YHWH's epithet שׁדי (*šadday*), and as such raises some intriguing possibilities.[117] Indeed, the potential association of the unpointed form שדים to שדי may have encouraged the apparent gloss in verse 38, in which it is made clear that the "images of Canaan" are to be understood as the שדים of verse 37, thereby avoiding any association with the biblical שׁדי. Similarly, the שדים to whom sacrifices are offered in Deut. 32:17 are also clearly distinguished from divine names associated with the biblical YHWH elsewhere; the discussion will return to this intriguing text in due course.[118]

In Ps. 106 child sacrifice is thus presented as a bloody and foreign practice, engendering the defilement of the community and the land, and thus leading to foreign domination and exile. It is a ritual performed by the apparently idolatrous "Israel", and dedicated to a group of alien gods, who

---

113 It may be that a specific context of child sacrifice has also prompted the application of the metaphorical language of whoring in Lev. 20:5 and Isa. 57:3, as will be argued below.

114 On the designation עצבים, see further Zevit, *Religions of Ancient Israel*, 577-578.

115 *HALOT*, vol. 4, 1417-1418. See further below, 5.4.5.

116 J.A. Hackett, *The Balaam Text from Deir ʿAllā* (HSM 31; Chico: Scholars Press, 1984), followed by Richardson, "Psalm 106", 200.

117 See further 5.4, 5.5.

118 See further 5.5.

are presented as malleable images and identified as שׁדִּים; it is also a practice to which the metaphorical language of whoring is applied in the description of its practitioners as those who have "prostituted themselves in their deeds" (v. 39). As has been seen, this portrayal in many ways parallels that in Ezek. 16 and 23, though this is widely overlooked, probably in view of the ascription of sacrifices to the שׁדים in Deut. 32:17, a text which rightly plays an important role in discussions of Ps. 106:37, but which also tends to overshadow other biblical parallels.

An important text contributing to the biblical portrayal of child sacrifice is Isa. 57:3-13, a lengthy but problematic poem—primarily due to its difficult vocabulary—condemning the practice.[119] Though this pericope will be examined in greater detail in the following chapter, verses 5-6c in particular demand consideration here:

> 5 You who warm yourselves among the (great) trees
> under every green tree;
> slaughtering children in the wadis,
> under the clefts of the rocks.
> 6 With the dead[120] of the wadi is your portion,
> they, indeed they are your lot;
> even to them you have poured out a drink offering,
> you have offered up a grain offering.

Perhaps the most striking feature of these verses is their explicit terminology. The use of שׁחט, "slaughter", is a far cry from the euphemistic language

---

119 Most commentators regard Isa. 57:3-13 as a poetic unit, discernible from the surrounding (though related) material in its contrasting grammatical forms and subject-matter.

120 MT חלקי is widely held to derive from the verb חלק "be smooth", and is thus usually translated "smooth (stones)". However, the parallelling of the Ugaritic adjectives ḥlq and mt suggests that a further meaning of חלק is "die", "perish" (DULAT, vol. 1, 393-394). Thus חלקי in this verse is better translated "dead" or "perished"; so too W.H. Irwin, "The Smooth Stones of the Wady? Isaiah 57:6", CBQ 29 (1967), 31-40; J. Blenkinsopp, Isaiah 56–66: A New Translation with Introduction and Commentary (AB 19B; New York: Doubleday, 2003), 153, 158; M. Dahood, "Hebrew-Ugaritic Lexicography II", Bib 45 (1964), 393-412, esp. 408; S. Ackerman, "Sacred Sex, Sacrifice and Death: Understanding a Prophetic Poem", BR 6 (1990), 38-44, esp. 41-42; idem., Under Every Green Tree, 103, n. 8, 146-148; T.J. Lewis, "Death Cult Imagery in Isaiah 57", HAR 11 (1987), 267-284; idem., The Cult of the Dead in Ancient Israel and Ugarit (HSM 39; Atlanta: Scholars Press, 1989), 148; Schmidt, Israel's Beneficent Dead, 255, 258; P.S. Johnston, Shades of Sheol: Death and Afterlife in the Old Testament (Leicester: Apollos, 2002), 176.

employed of child sacrifice elsewhere in the Hebrew Bible, such as העביר
and נתן. But as has been seen, this term is used of the practice in Ezek. 16:21
and 23:39.[121] As in Ezek. 16:21 and 23:39, the bluntness of שחט offers a
terminological emphasis upon the killing of the children, which may be
intended to desensitize the perceived sacredness of the practice. The
sacrifices are said to occur בנחלים, "in the wadis". The term נחל in this
context is often taken as a reference to the Valley of Ben Hinnom, the biblical
location of the supposed cult of "Molek".[122] This is particularly encouraged
by the occurrence of מלך in verse 9. Yet this is a misinterpretation, for the
term נחל is never used of the Valley of Ben Hinnom, which instead is
labelled גיא or גי.[123]

The sacrificing of children "in the wadis" is closely associated with
offerings to "the dead of the wadi" (v. 6). It is unclear whether these are to be
identified as the recipients of the sacrificed children, or even, as Irwin
suggests, the dead children themselves.[124] The biblical association of child
sacrifice with some sort of death cult certainly recalls the association of the
practice with sorcery and the consultation of the dead in Deut. 18:9-12, 2 Kgs
21:6 and 2 Chr. 33:6 (cf. Lev. 20:5-6). It is perhaps no coincidence that at the
beginning of this poem, the practitioners are described as "sons of a
sorceress" (v. 3). Yet in spite of these uncertainties, identifying the divine
recipient of the sacrifices is, for some commentators, an easy task, for the
occurrence of מֶלֶךְ in 57:9 is taken as a reference to "Molek", and frequently
revocalized accordingly. Whether מלך in this verse is understood as a divine
name or as a type of sacrifice, most commentators are agreed that it alludes to
the practice of child sacrifice. But the precise activity described is opaque,
primarily due to the difficulty of the language. More certain is the context of
death, evident in the reference to descent into Sheol, though it is notable that
Sheol is not associated with child sacrifice in any other biblical text. No
matter how מלך is interpreted here, the poem as a whole clearly condemns
child sacrifice as a practice at odds with the correct worship of YHWH.
Moreover, in verses 7-8 the practitioners appear to be the wayward YHWH-
worshippers who offer sacrifices on Zion, as the phrase הר גבה ונשא (v. 7)

121 Cf. Gen. 22:10.
122 For example, Schmidt, *Israel's Beneficent Dead*, 258; Mosca, "Child Sacrifice", 234;
     Ackerman, *Under Every Green Tree,* 140-141.
123 E.g., Josh. 15:8; 18:16; 2 Kgs 23:10; 2 Chr. 28:3; 33:6; Neh. 11:30; Jer. 7:31, 32; 19:2,
     6; 32:35.
124 Irwin, "Smooth Stones", 37-39; cf. Blenkinsopp, *Isaiah 56–66,* 158-159.

would suggest.[125] If this interpretation is correct, the association of child sacrifice and offerings on Zion in these verses is reminiscent of the assertion in Ezekiel that those sacrificing children also worship in YHWH's sanctuary (Ezek. 23:39). It also recalls the Levitical prohibition of making offerings to "Molek" in YHWH's sanctuary (Lev. 20:3), and is reminiscent of the implication in Jeremiah that some YHWH-worshippers sacrificed their children because they believed that YHWH had commanded them to do so (Jer. 7:31; 19:5; 32:35).[126]

The heavy emphasis upon the practitioners of child sacrifice in Isa. 57:3-13 contrasts with the surprising lack of any clear focus upon the deity to whom the children are offered. This would also be true if מלך in verse 9 were interpreted as a reference to the divine recipient, for it could offer itself only fleetingly and indirectly as the name of the deity associated with the sacrifices in the wadi. The divine recipient of child sacrifice thus remains, somewhat curiously, in the shadows, whilst the focus of the poem is fixed upon the Jerusalemite YHWH-worshippers, and the illegality of their religious activity. This focus is established from the start in the disparaging name-calling of the opening verse of the poem (v. 3), which significantly employs the language of adultery and whoring. This is highly significant, for this type of language has already been encountered in association with other biblical references to child sacrifice. Its closer examination is thus appropriate.

Unfortunately, MT of verse 3 appears to be corrupt, offering a confusion of forms. Most problematic is ותזנה, which can be read as a third person feminine singular ("and she whores") or as a second person masculine ("and you whore").[127] Most attempts to smooth the text emend this tricky term, reading with the Versions the noun זנה. In adopting this common emendation, this verse may be translated:

> But you, come here,
> sons of a sorceress,
> seed of an adulterer and a whore!

---

125 Blenkinsopp, *Isaiah 56–66*, 159; P.D. Hanson, *The Dawn of Apocalyptic* (rev. edn; Philadelphia: Fortress Press, 1979), 199-200.

126 Noted also by Blenkinsopp, *Isaiah 56–66*, 159.

127 The possibility that ותזנה should be understood as a participle form or a relative clause with the relative אשר omitted is discussed by J.J. Scullion, "Some Difficult Texts in Isaiah cc. 55-66 in the Light of Modern Scholarship", *UF* 4 (1972), 105-128. Ackerman (*Under Every Green Tree*, 102, n. 4), reconstructs an original participle form with a prefixed conjunction (וזנה), which was subsequently corrupted.

Another possibility is to emend the masculine מנאף to the feminine מנאפת,[128] thus reading the verse as a series of insults defaming the character of the mother of the group under attack from the poet. Emendation is certainly one option. But there is an alternative possibility. The awkwardness of ותזנה may be a reflection of its secondary nature, perhaps, as Moughtin suggests, as a gloss on מנאף.[129] This is certainly plausible. As has been seen, the metaphorical language of adultery is closely associated with child sacrifice in Ezek. 16 and 23.[130] It is perhaps no coincidence, therefore, that this language should also occur in this poem, reflected in the accusation that the practitioners of child sacrifice are "seed of an adulterer". But it is the language of metaphorical whoring which is more frequently associated with child sacrifice in Ezek. 16 and 23 (cf. Lev. 20:5), and as such, this may have encouraged the addition of ותזנה as a gloss on מנאף in Isa. 57:3, as Moughtin speculates. This finds support in the fact that the deletion of ותזנה in 57:3 would place in parallel "sons of a sorceress" and "seed of an adulterer", anticipating the parallelism of "sons of transgression" and "seed of deceit" in the following verse.[131]

The possibility that ותזנה may be a secondary gloss on מנאף is attractive. It also has interesting, though admittedly speculative, implications. Blenkinsopp speaks of the poem's portrayal of a "dysfunctional family", composed of wayward children, a whoring sorceress and an adulterous father, as presented in this opening verse.[132] These characters are frequently held to be drawn upon paradigms set out in other prophetic literature, especially Ezek. 16, in which the sexual and religious deviancy of the woman derives from her Amorite father and Hittite mother. Indeed, a cursory reading of this text alongside Hos. 1–3 and Ezek. 23 would support their close association with the imagery and language of Isa. 57:3-13, as several scholars have observed. However, the specific context of child sacrifice, shared by this poem and Ezek. 16 and 23, skews the neat paralleling of the "dysfunctional family" among these texts. As has been seen, Ezek. 16 and 23 do indeed portray a family group gathered around a whoring mother, but there are notable differences: the children in these texts are not the transgressors of Isa.

---

128 For example, C. Westermann, *Isaiah 40–66* (trans. D.M.G. Stalker; OTL; London: SCM Press, 1969), 321; Ackerman, *Under Every Green Tree*, 102.

129 Moughtin, "Death of a Metaphor", 134-135.

130 It is particularly noteworthy that references to child sacrifice and literal adultery appear in close proximity in Lev. 20:2-10 (see further 5.3).

131 Moughtin, "Death of a Metaphor", 135.

132 Blenkinsopp, *Isaiah 56–66*, 156.

57:3-13, but the "innocent" whose blood is shed by their mother(s), whilst their father is not the adulterer of Isa. 57:3-13, but YHWH himself. Indeed, this family portrait would be further altered if the reader were to disregard the difficult ותזנה in verse 3, as supported here, rendering the mother not a whore, but a sorceress alone. In that case, it is only the father of the group who is labelled a sexual transgressor, and neither he nor his crime is mentioned again in the poem. The result is that the "adultery" spoken of in verse 3 is not set within a sexual context, but symbolizes instead religious infidelity, as the sacrifice of children in the remainder of the poem is portrayed. This may be reflected in the allusion in verse 8 to the cutting of a covenant,[133] rivalling that made with YHWH, as the "covenantal" terminology may suggest.[134]

The metaphorical language of adultery and whoring in the opening verse of the poem has had significant, though unfortunate, interpretative repercussions. Many commentators offer a literal interpretation of this metaphorical language, and consequently make much of the presumed sexual imagery of the poem, envisaging contexts of ritual sexual intercourse and cultic prostitution.[135] Yet these commentators are mistaken. The language of adultery and whoring is metaphorical, and is not to be taken literally.[136] Accordingly, the only cultic practice in view in this poem is that of child sacrifice.[137] In returning to focus upon the explicit reference to child sacrifice in verse five of this poem, the margin for interpretative error is thrown into view. The expression הנחמים is frequently rendered, "You who burn with lust", or "you who become aroused", and such like.[138] Yet this is to overload the expression with a sexual connotation which is not inherent in the Hebrew

---

133 MT ותכרת. This interpretation admittedly assumes an ellipsis of ברית here (so, for example, Scullion, "Some Difficult Texts", 111-112). For further discussion, see Ackerman, *Under Every Green Tree*, 105, n. 12.

134 This language may originally have been intended to allude to the adulterer of v. 3, as suggested by MT ותכרת (m.sg.), which is commonly emended to ותכרותי (f.sg.), reading with 1QIsaᵃ.

135 Examples include Westermann, *Isaiah 40–66*, 324; J.N. Oswalt, *The Book of Isaiah Chapters 40-66* (Grand Rapids: Eerdmans, 1998), 478-481; Ackerman, "Sacred Sex", 38-39, 42.

136 Lewis, *Cult of the Dead*, 157-158.

137 So too Schmidt, *Beneficent Dead*, 254, n. 516.

138 For example, B. Schramm, *The Opponents of Third Isaiah: Reconstructing the Cultic History of the Restoration* (JSOTSup 193; Sheffield: Sheffield Academic Press, 1995), 128; Westermann, *Isaiah 40–66*, 321; Ackerman, *Under Every Green Tree*, 102; cf. also J.L. McKenzie, *Second Isaiah: Introduction, Translation and Notes* (AB 20; Garden City: Doubleday, 1968), 156.

terminology. The majority of commentators derive הנחמים from חמם,[139] which is employed to describe the heat of animal conception in Gen. 30:38-39. However, in all other biblical occurrences, חמם is used in the context of being or becoming warm or hot by means of fire, natural heat, or clothing. Its assumed connotation of lust is unattested elsewhere.[140] Given this semantic range, הנחמים is more plausibly rendered, "You who warm yourselves", and any sexual interpretation is best acknowledged as a forced and false reading.[141] Such a reading may well be encouraged by the reference to every "green tree" (עץ רענן) in the same verse,[142] a motif frequently accompanying sexual metaphorical language in the Hebrew Bible. Indeed, its close proximity to this type of language in verse three probably accounts in part for its inclusion here, functioning as a metaphorical device to signal the illicit nature of the cult and its sacred spaces ("under every green tree ... under the clefts of the rocks"). But it is also a motif accompanying references to child sacrifice, as has been seen, and as such cannot be assumed to allude to ritualized sexual deviancy nor cultic prostitution.

The literal interpretation of the metaphorical sexual language of Isa. 57:3-13 is not restricted to the verses described here. Indeed, several other key terms and phrases in the poem are all too frequently misinterpreted in the light of an assumed context of fertility rituals. These will be discussed, along with a full translation and interpretation of the poem, in the following chapter. Yet for now, the important point remains that Isa. 57:3-13 condemns child sacrifice in terms familiar from other biblical texts. It is presented as a practice rejected by YHWH, though it is YHWH's worshippers who are portrayed as its practitioners. This casts a different light upon the allusion to

---

139 Some commentators follow the Peshitta and Vulgate in rendering הנחמים as "comforting yourselves" (נחם niphal). This translation is often accompanied by the interpretation of אלים as "gods" or "shades of the dead", following the Septuagint and other Versions (so M. Weise, "Jesaja 57,5-6", *ZAW* 72 [1960], 25-32; Lewis, *Cult of the Dead*, 49-51; J.D.W. Watts, *Isaiah 34–66* [WBC 25; Waco: Word, 1987], 252-254; Blenkinsopp, *Isaiah 56–66*, 157-158; Zevit, *Religions of Ancient Israel*, 529). This is an attractive alternative, supported particularly by the use of נחם in the following verse. However, though the ambiguities of אלים are probably intentional, the parallel reference to the "green tree" encourages the more conventional translation "(great) trees" here, though with admitted caution.

140 Interestingly, none of the Versions support this modern interpretation, translating variously, "who call upon" (LXX) "who serve" (Targ.) "comfort yourselves" (Syr.; Vulg.).

141 *Pace* Johnston, *Shades of Sheol*, 177.

142 So too Moughtin, "Death of a Metaphor", 136.

the people making offerings on Zion, for it would appear to associate child sacrifice with these rituals, thereby unsettling the poet's attempts to disassociate YHWH from this practice.

This is reminiscent of other biblical descriptions and allusions to child sacrifice which have been examined here. Jer. 19:4-6; Ezek. 16:20-21, 36; 20:31; 23:37-39 and Ps. 106:34-39 all attempt to portray child sacrifice as a foreign practice. And a cursory reading would suggest that these texts are successful in doing so. However, a closer reading of this material reveals that the efforts of the biblical writers to present child sacrifice as a foreign practice are consistently complicated—and even undermined—by an implicit or explicit association of child sacrifice with YHWH. The book of Jeremiah's over-emphatic denial that YHWH ever commanded the sacrifice of children rings hollow in view of the confusion concerning the supposed recipient of the sacrifices. Indeed, the integrity of the claim in 19:5 that children were offered to Baʿal is undermined by its absence in the Septuagint.[143] The vagueness of Ezekiel's repeated claim that children were sacrificed to "dung-gods" jars with his specific assertion in 20:25-26 that YHWH demanded the sacrifice of the firstborn, as will be seen in the following pages.[144] Similarly, the designation of the mysterious recipients of child sacrifice as שׁדים sits uncomfortably alongside YHWH's epithet שׁדי,[145] despite the psalmist's equation of these deities with the "images of Canaan".

It is notable that despite the fact that all of these texts seek to portray child sacrifice as a foreign practice, they all speak of YHWH's people performing these sacrifices. In view of this characteristic feature, the only biblical text which succeeds in portraying child sacrifice as a foreign practice occurs at the end of a narrative describing the Israelite, Judahite and Edomite war against Moab. 2 Kgs 3:26-27 describes King Mesha of Moab sacrificing his firstborn son:

> When the king of Moab saw that the battle was becoming harder for him, he took with him seven hundred swordsmen to break through to the king of Edom, but they could not. Then he took his son, the firstborn (בכור) who would become king after him, and offered him up as a burnt offering (ויעלהו עלה) upon the wall and a great wrath came upon Israel, so they withdrew from him and returned to their own land.

---

143 See further below, 6.2.
144 Ezek. 16:20-21, 36; 20:31; 23:37-39. The remarkable claim in 20:25-26 is examined below.
145 See further 5.4, 5.5.

It is precisely because the practitioner is clearly foreign that the text may be seen to depict the sacrifice as a foreign ritual. Yet in contrast to the texts already examined, 2 Kgs 3:26-27 does not appear to be preoccupied with presenting the sacrifice in this way. In fact, the text does not appear to be overly concerned with the sacrifice at all,[146] for the narrator offers no theological judgement nor critique. Yet the sacrifice may be considered an effective ritual here, for it appears to end the war, leaving Moab undefeated. The implication, therefore, is that Kemosh, the Moabite god, has defeated the combined military forces of Israel, Judah and Edom—and their respective deities, too.[147] But this implication remains just that, for as Burns comments, the Hebrew Bible is "notoriously evasive when it comes to acknowledging the power of foreign gods".[148] In contrast to the other texts surveyed above, ranging from the excessive denials in Jeremiah, the graphic language of the book of Ezekiel, and the intriguing שׁדים of Ps. 106, 2 Kgs 3:26-27 is thus remarkable for presenting this story of sacrifice in such an unremarkable manner. However, this is not to suggest that this text is unimportant. Rather, it will become increasingly noteworthy during the course of this discussion, as it shares many common features with other biblical texts portraying child sacrifice not as a foreign practice, but as a YHWH-practice.

Yet before turning to examine these intriguing texts, there remains a final and crucial observation. As has been seen, the biblical portrayal of child sacrifice as a "foreign" practice is frequently effected by means of employing

---

146 *Pace* N.H. Tur-Sinai (*The Language and the Book*, vol. 1 [Jerusalem: Mosad Bialik, 1954], 84-91 [Hebrew]), who seeks to read **mōlk ʾādām* ("sacrifice of a man") in place of MT *melek ʾĕdôm*, thereby correlating this verse to Amos 2:1; cf. Albright, *Yahweh and the Gods of Canaan*, 209.

147 Though elsewhere קֶצֶף can refer to human frustration or anger (e.g., Qoh. 5:16; Esth. 1:18), it is most usually employed of divine anger (e.g., Num. 17:11 [ET 16:46]; Deut. 29:27; 2 Chr. 19:2; 29:8; 32:26; Jer. 21:5; 32:37; 50:13; Zech. 7:12). However, it is important to note that here, the divine recipient of the sacrifice is not named, nor indeed is the source of the wrath indicated; various ancient and modern suggestions of the latter include Kemosh, YHWH, Israel, Moab, or the Edomite king. See the commentaries for further discussions.

148 J.B. Burns, "Why Did the Besieging Army Withdraw (2 Reg 3:27)?", *ZAW* 102 (1990), 187-194 (193). On 2 Kgs 3:26-27 more generally, see the discussions in Parker, *Stories in Scripture and Inscriptions*, 124-127; P.D. Stern, "Of Kings and Moabites: History and Theology in 2 Kings 3 and the Mesha Inscription", *HUCA* 64 (1993), 1-14; J.R. Bartlett, "The 'United' Campaign against Moab in 2 Kings 3:4-27", in J.F.A. Sawyer and D.J.A. Clines (eds.), *Midian, Moab and Edom: The History and Archaeology of Late Bronze and Iron Age Jordan and North-West Arabia* (JSOTSup 24; Sheffield: JSOT Press, 1983), 135-145.

key motifs and metaphorical language. Particularly notable in this regard is the association or equation of child sacrifice with the shedding of "innocent blood" in several texts. Ideologically, this motif is important, for it functions to overturn the perceived sacredness and acceptability of the sacrifice by recasting its infant offerings as the murdered victims of an illegal ritual. In this way, its practitioners are characterized as religious deviants who, in behaving in a manner contrary to YHWH's will, pollute both cult and community, with a devastating result: the destruction of the nation. It has already been noted that this is also one of the ways in which the shedding of "innocent blood" functions in the Kings Writer's vilification of Manasseh. In 2 Kgs 21:16 and 24:1-4, Manasseh is accused of shedding copious amounts of "innocent blood", so that YHWH's expulsion of the nation is inevitable. Through its association with both Manasseh and child sacrifice, the motif of "innocent blood" acts as an ideological marker, signalling behaviour deemed to be alien to the biblical YHWH-community. Given that Manasseh and child sacrifice are characterized respectively as the most deviant person and the most abhorrent practice in the biblical story of "Israel", it is perhaps unsurprising to find that the motif of "innocent blood" is included in their biblical portrayals. Yet it is particularly striking to find that the close, ideological alignment of Manasseh and child sacrifice is demonstrated more implicitly in one text in particular: Jer. 19:1-13. As has been seen, this text condemns child sacrifice as a foreign practice which is explicitly rejected by YHWH, and appears to identify or associate the victims of the practice with "innocent blood". Indeed, the text employs language directly echoing the charge against Manasseh in Kings, as it tells of "this place"[149] being "filled" (מלא) with "innocent blood" (דם נקי), just as Manasseh is said to have shed so much "innocent blood" that Jerusalem was "filled" (מלא) with it (2 Kgs 21:16; 24:3-4). However, elsewhere in the book of Jeremiah, the charge of shedding innocent blood appears to be levelled not at Manasseh, but Jehoiakim (22:17). Though it is likely that the naming of this particular monarch is a secondary feature of the text,[150] it may reflect an alternative tradition in which Jehoiakim was especially associated with this crime. In spite of this, it remains entirely possible that the charge in Jer. 19:4 is related more directly to the defamatory presentation of Manasseh's reign in Kings, for in the immediately preceding verse of the Jeremiah text, language is

---

149 The label המקום in Jer. 19:4 is widely understood as a reference to Jerusalem and/or Judah in this context, though it is uncertain whether it may alternatively refer to the specific cult places of the Temple or תפה; see the commentaries for further discussion.

150 Carroll, *Jeremiah*, 427-428.

employed which is strongly reminiscent of the account of Manasseh's reign in 2 Kgs 21. Both texts present an oracle of judgement, in which YHWH vows that he is "bringing such evil" (מביא רעה) upon Judah and Jerusalem (labelled המקום in Jer. 19:3)[151] that אזניו [152]שתי תצלנה [153]כל שמעה, "the (two) ears of everyone who hears of it will tingle" (2 Kgs 21:12; Jer. 19:3).[154] In this way, then, Jer. 19 offers a striking and concise illustration of the manner in which extreme religious deviancy can be imaged in the language of the Hebrew Bible. As such, the parallels between this chapter and 2 Kgs 21 emphasize effectively some of the biblical methods employed to demonstrate the perceived "foreign" nature of both Manasseh and child sacrifice.

4.2 Child Sacrifice as a YHWH-Practice

Despite its repeated attempts to portray child sacrifice as a foreign practice alien to "Israel" and her god YHWH, the Hebrew Bible contains a considerable volume of material directly associating YHWH with the sacrifice of children. Within some of this material, YHWH is depicted as a silent and passive recipient; however, in many other biblical texts, not only is YHWH's willing acceptance of the offerings clearly indicated, but YHWH is also portrayed as demanding these sacrifices. As such, the Hebrew Bible appears unintentionally to overturn its own insistence that child sacrifice is a foreign practice, for it offers, both implicitly and explicitly, a vivid portrayal of YHWH as a god of child sacrifice.

4.2.1 The Firstborn Sacrifice

It is no exaggeration to suggest that perhaps the best-known but most controversial of biblical texts concerning child sacrifice are those dealing with the donation of the firstborn to YHWH. The special status of the firstborn child is a theme which reverberates throughout the Hebrew Bible. Though a

---

151 See n. 151.
152 2 Kgs 21:12 includes the term שתי, which, though absent, is naturally implicit in the expression in Jer. 19:3.
153 Reading in 2 Kgs 21:12, שמעה for שמעיו.
154 Cf. 1 Sam. 3:11.

common מלאה motif of many biblical stories is the seeming subversion of this special status,[155] there are many texts which legislate for both the social and cultic recognition of the valuable status of the firstborn. Among these are legal formulations suggesting that, in some cultic circles, the human firstborn was perceived in a manner akin to that in which the animal firstborn was seen: as a sign of divinely-endowed fecundity, and as such, as a potential sacrificial offering to YHWH. The most striking of these is Exod. 22:28-29 (ET 29-30):

> You shall not delay (to make offerings) from your fullness (of the grape harvest)[156] and from your outflow (of the presses).[157] The firstborn of your sons you will give to me, just as you will do with your oxen and with your sheep. Seven days he/it shall remain with his/its mother; on the eighth day you shall give he/it to me.

This text has proved contentious throughout many generations of critical scholarship. The claim that both the human and animal firstborn (בכור) are to be donated (נתן) to YHWH is loaded with sacrificial implication. Indeed, this would appear to be the plain understanding of the text. Yet the majority of commentators are agreed that whilst it allows for the dedication of the human firstborn, it is to be distinguished nevertheless from the sacrificial nature of the dedication of the animal firstborn. This view often claims support from other biblical texts in which the commanded donation of the human and animal firstborn is swiftly followed by the specification that the human firstborn are to be redeemed.[158] However, it is the very absence of any redemption clause in this text which undermines this view.[159] In 22:28-29, human and animal firstborn are distinguished, but not differentiated. Thus as Fishbane comments, "there is no *textual* reason for assimilating Exod. 22:28-29 to those articulations of the law where redemption by compensation is

---

155 See further R. Syrén, *The Forsaken Firstborn: A Study of a Recurrent Motif in the Patriarchal Narratives* (JSOTSup 133; Sheffield: JSOT Press, 1993); G.N. Knoppers, "The Preferential Status of the Eldest Son Revoked?", in S.L. McKenzie and T. Römer (eds.), *Rethinking the Foundations: Historiography in the Ancient World and in the Bible* (BZAW 294; Berlin/New York: de Gruyter, 2000), 117-126.

156 מלאה, "fullness", occurs only here and in Num. 18:27 and Deut. 22:9. Its meaning is uncertain, though in Num. 18:27 it appears to be related to the grape harvest.

157 דמע may be rendered "(trickling) juice", and in this context would appear to allude to the pressing of grapes.

158 Exod. 13:12-13; 34:19-20; Num. 18:15-18.

159 So too Levenson, *Beloved Son*, 4.

envisaged and specified".[160] This may suggest that this text reflects a law demanding the sacrifice of firstborn to YHWH. Fishbane observes that a notable, common feature of the various biblical prescriptions regarding the firstborn is the generalized statement that *all* firstborns, human and animal, are to be donated to YHWH.[161] The precise nature of this dedication is not made explicit, though it is clear that the human and animal firstborn are to be treated in exactly the same way. This is illustrated in its starkest form in Exod. 13:1-2, in which YHWH says to Moses, "Consecrate (קדשׁ) to me all the firstborn; whatever is the first-birth of every womb among the Israelites, of humans and animals, is mine". Like Exod. 22:28-29, this text makes no subsequent qualification of a means of the redemption of the human child; nor is any distinction drawn between the human firstborn and the animal firstborn. Indeed, the language of verse 2 is explicit in repeatedly encompassing both the human and animal firstborn: as Van Seters observes, in this chapter the term פטר, "first-birth", is primarily used of the firstborn of animals, whilst בכור, "firstborn", is employed of the human firstborn.[162] The verse speaks not only of the firstborn of humans and animals (באדם ובבהמה) but employs the terms פטר and בכור to refer to them. In contrast, Exod. 13:13 and 34:20 demand the donation of human and animal firstborn to YHWH, but add that the human child is to be redeemed or rescued (פדה). However, the manner in which this redemption is to be effected is not specified. This is curious given that both texts instruct that the firstborn of a donkey is to be redeemed either with a sheep (13:13; 34:20) or by having its neck broken (34:20). But no such specification is made for the redemption of the human firstborn. Attempts to remedy the ambiguity of the redemption clause within the laws of Exodus may be found in the book of Numbers, though inconsistencies are evident within these texts also. Num. 18:13-18 concerns the Aaronite priesthood's acquisition of the firstfruits and firstborn donated to YHWH. Verses 15-16 specify that the human firstborn and the firstborn of unclean animals are to be redeemed financially. This stands in contrast to Num. 3:12-13 and 8:16-19, which do not employ the term פדה,

---

160 M. Fishbane, *Biblical Interpretation in Ancient Israel* (Oxford: Clarendon Press, 1985), 181-182; see also Smith, "Note on Burning Babies", 477-478; B. Erling, "First-Born and Firstlings in the Covenant Code", *SBLSP* 25 (1986), 470-478, especially 473.
161 Fishbane, *Biblical Interpretation*, 182.
162 J. Van Seters, "The Law on Child Sacrifice in Exod 22, 28b-29", *ETL* 74 (1998), 364-372 (369).

but do claim that YHWH has taken the Levites in place of all the human firstborn.[163]

In view of the existence of the unqualified rule concerning the firstborn in Exod. 13:1-2 and 22:28-29, the suggestion that the qualifications specifying the redemption of the firstborn are secondary expansions is attractive. After all, and as Levenson also observes, the existence of the redemption clause within these texts simply emphasizes, by contrast, the absence of any such clause within the law of the firstborn in Exod. 22:28-29.[164] Indeed, Fishbane discerns two literary strata in Exod. 22:28-29, arguing that the unqualified law of the firstborn is a formulation older than the qualified law. He proposes that the expression כן תעשה is used in legal material to introduce extensions to legal clauses. In this text, כן תעשה appears to function in this way, serving to introduce the specification concerning oxen and sheep (v. 29a). Moreover, this extension appears to disrupt the syntax linking verses 28b and 29b. Fishbane contends that this is evident in the awkward way in which verse 29b follows: "he/it will stay seven days ... on the eighth day you shall give him/it to me". The singular pronouns jar with the plural antecedents ("oxen" and "sheep"). Thus according to Fishbane, it would appear that verse 29a is a secondary extension to this text, and that the phrase "Seven days he will remain with his mother ... on the eighth day you will give him to me" actually refers back to the human firstborn of verse 28b.[165] Exod. 22:28-29 would thus appear to comprise an original formulation demanding the donation of firstborn human males, and an extension of this law to include firstborn animals, harmonizing this text with the other legal formulations noted earlier. However, as Van Seters observes, the singular pronouns in verse 29a are

---

163 Neh. 10:35-39 contains a further reference to the law of the firstborn which is frequently overlooked. Though the language of this text (בוא hiphil) is not explicitly sacrificial—indeed, it may be intentionally ambiguous—it is of interest to note that despite its differentiation of the various types of firstfruits, it does not contain nor allude to a redemption clause concerning the human firstborn. However, it does state that the firstfruits and firstborn (בכור) will be brought to the temple, "just as it is written in the Torah", leaving open the possibility that the legal formulations which do contain the redemption clauses are in view here. Fishbane (*Biblical Interpretation*, 213-216) and G. Brin (*Studies in Biblical Law* [JSOTSup 176; Sheffield: JSOT Press, 1994], 211) propose that the law envisaged here is Num. 18:15. Williamson (*Ezra, Nehemiah*, 337) suggests that Exod. 13:13; 34:20 and Num. 18:15 are presupposed in Neh. 10:37; whereas Van Seters ("Law on Child Sacrifice", 371) argues the reference to the firstfruit and firstborn law in Neh. 10:37 reflects a conflation of Exod. 22:28-29 and Deut. 15:19.

164 Levenson, *Beloved Son*, 4.

165 Fishbane, *Biblical Interpretation*, 183-184.

entirely appropriate in referring to the animal firstborn, for it is the firstborn
animal of each oxen and sheep which is the subject of the legislation, not the
oxen and sheep themselves.[166] Moreover, underlying Fishbane's proposal
appears to be an assumption that an unqualified law specifying the dedication
of the human and animal firstborn to YHWH would necessarily be an older
formulation than regulations allowing for the redemption of the human
firstborn. However, this need not be the case. As Van Seters suggests, the
biblical laws dealing with the dedication of the human and animal firstborn,
and the possibility of their redemption, may reflect distinct traditions;[167] it
may be that some of Fishbane's "extended" laws reflect a process of textual
harmonization, rather than secondary theological correction. Indeed, it is
possible that laws requiring the dedication of the human firstborn may have
co-existed with regulations allowing for the redemption of the human
firstborn, as will be seen in chapter 5.

In spite of these observations, discerning the precise nature of the
donation of the human firstborn remains problematic. The language of the
biblical material is ambiguous, and open to a variety of interpretations, as the
use of קדש, "dedicate" or "consecrate", in Exod. 13:2 illustrates.[168] The
terminology of Exod. 13:12 (ET 11) is slightly more precise, as the Israelites
are told "and you will pass over (העביר) every firstborn of the womb to
YHWH". Similarly, the firstborn are to be "given" or "donated" (נתן) to YHWH
(Exod. 22:28; Num. 8:16, 18; 18:7). As has been argued above, the terms
העביר and נתן can carry a sacrificial interpretation, as their use in texts
dealing with the מלך practice testify. However, despite the potential
ambiguity of these terms within the laws of the firstborn, the sacrificial
context of the regulations is suggested by the emphatic language of many of
the redemption clauses. Num. 18:15 declares that, "Every first-birth of all
kinds which is offered to YHWH, human and animal, will be yours; however
you must surely redeem the human male".[169] It is possible that פדה in some

166 Van Seters, "Law on Child Sacrifice", 364-372; see also Kaiser, "Den Erstgeborenen",
164; cf. Erling, "First-Born and Firstlings", 470-478.
167 Van Seters, "Law on Child Sacrifice", 364-372.
168 Note however Heider, who comments that within the firstborn laws of Exod. 13:2; Lev.
27:26; Num. 3:13; 8:17; Deut. 15:19, קדש is synonymous with the sacrificial meanings
of העביר and נתן. Heider, *Molek*, 255 n. 515. Milgrom (*Leviticus 17–22*, 1587-1591)
agrees that קדש and נתן within the firstborn laws are indeed to be equated, but argues
instead that נתן is neutral, and in no way implies that the offering "given" is to be
sacrificed. However, his arguments are not persuasive.
169 Fishbane, *Biblical Interpretation*, 184.

of these texts might be taken in an optional sense, just as it appears to be in Exod. 13:13 and 34:20, in which allowance is made for alternative means of dealing with the firstborn of a donkey: "the firstborn of a donkey you may redeem with a sheep, or if you will not redeem it, you shall break its neck" (34:20). This optional sense of פדה might then account for its emphatic usage in Num. 18:15b, in which any optional interpretation is sternly rejected: "however, you must surely redeem (פדה תפדה) the human male".[170] This regulation is thus keen to prevent its interpretation as allowing for the possibility of the cultic offering of the human firstborn. It may be, therefore, that this reflects a perception of legal traditions which were believed to legislate for precisely this sort of practice.

The variety of biblical firstborn laws, as well as the broad range of their scholarly interpretations, is itself testimony to the complex nature and interrelations of the texts. It is thus difficult to ascertain with any confidence the literary histories of these laws, let alone the historical matrices from which they may have emerged. However, their wider biblical contextualization may offer another perspective from which to view these traditions. As such, the possibility that the Hebrew Bible reflects a legal formulation demanding the sacrifice of the firstborn becomes a probability in the light of other texts. Ezek. 20:25-26 reads:

> Moreover, I gave them no-good decrees and laws by which they could not live. I defiled them through their gifts, in their passing over (העביר) every first-birth of the womb (פטר רחם), in order that I might devastate them, so that they might know I am YHWH.[171]

The explicit assertion that YHWH commanded the sacrifice of the firstborn is striking. The expression למען אשמם makes plain the sacrificial meaning העביר that can have,[172] and leaves little room for doubt that YHWH was believed to have legislated for child sacrifice. The combination of the explicit references to the first-birth of the womb, YHWH's decrees and laws, and the use of sacrificial language shared with the firstborn laws, renders it likely that the book of Ezekiel here refers specifically to laws requiring the sacrifice of the firstborn, laws perhaps reflected in the traditions of the Pentateuch.[173]

---

170 See further 5.6.

171 MT's למען ידעו אשר אני יהוה is not reflected in several versions, including LXX.

172 So too Day, *Molech*, 19.

173 It is notoriously difficult to ascertain the precise relationship between sections of Ezekiel and Pentateuchal texts and traditions. For further discussions, see C. Patton, "'I Myself

Indeed, this text does not employ the more usual בכור to refer to the firstborn, but instead employs the terminology shared by the firstborn laws of Exod. 13:2, 12 and 34:19, for it describes the sacrificed child as the פטר רחם, "the first-birth of the womb".[174] Interestingly, Ezek. 20:25-26 makes no mention of redemption provisions, yet it does offer the closest expression of an ethical condemnation of child sacrifice in the Hebrew Bible. The practice is not rejected in this text because it is "foreign"; rather, it is accepted as a ritual native to YHWH-worship, yet designed to defile and to devastate its practitioners. Though the cultic connotations and implications of exile are clear, the theological tone of these particular verses hints at a uniquely ethical condemnation of child sacrifice in the Hebrew Bible.[175]

But whilst it is clear that this text seeks to condemn child sacrifice as an untenable practice, its negative portrayal of the ritual as a divinely-legislated sacrifice designed to lead its practitioners to death raises several theological difficulties. It is not surprising then to find that this text has provoked a vast array of scholarly discussions and proposals, both ancient and modern.[176] A common response to this difficult text is the tendency to render שמם as "horrify", rather than the more usual "devastate", in an attempt portray the "no-good" law as a divine shock-tactic, designed to rouse the people into obedience to YHWH.[177] Yet this is to ignore the plain meaning of שמם in these verses, which speak pointedly of YHWH intentionally devastating his people by leading them to death through their very obedience to divine legislation. A further and notable response is the suggestion that 20:25-26 is best viewed through the lens of traditions concerning YHWH's punishment of Egypt: as such, the portrayal of child sacrifice as an "anti-gift" commanded by YHWH is to be related to the presentation of YHWH's hardening of Pharaoh's heart,

---

Gave Them Laws that Were Not Good': Ezekiel 20 and the Exodus Traditions", *JSOT* 69 (1996), 73-90; I. Knohl, *The Sanctuary of Silence: The Priestly Torah and the Holiness School* (Philadelphia: Fortress Press, 1995), and the literature cited there.

174 Van Seters ("Law on Child Sacrifice", 368) prefers to relate the language of Ezek. 20:25-26 with Exod. 13:12 alone, whereas De Vaux (*Studies*, 72) and Zimmerli (*Ezekiel*, vol. 1, 411) associate the practice to which Ezekiel refers with Exod. 22:28-29; see also Greenberg, *Ezekiel 1–20*, 368-370. W. Eichrodt (*Ezekiel* [trans. C. Quin; OTL; Philadelphia: Westminster, 1970; German original, 1966], 270) and Mein (*Ezekiel and the Ethics of Exile*, 117-118) identify Exod. 34:19 as the law underlying Ezek. 20:25-26.

175 Cf. Mein, *Ezekiel and the Ethics of Exile*, 118-119; see further 191.

176 See further Van der Horst, "I gave them laws that were not good", 106-118; Block, *Ezekiel*, vol. 1, 637-639, and the literature cited there.

177 See further Block, *Ezekiel*, vol. 1, 637, 639.

which led to the death of the Egyptian firstborn, in the book of Exodus.[178] In this way, the theological assertion of 20:25-26 is rendered a comprehensible reapplication of a tradition of divine punishment.[179] Though this is a reasonable proposal, it nevertheless softens the startling theological impact of 20:25-26. This text undermines the presentation of child sacrifice elsewhere in the book, for whilst the practice is presented in a negative light, YHWH remains the deity demanding the sacrifice of children; accordingly, these verses conflict with the portrayal of the practice as a ritual performed in honour of foreign "dung-gods" in 16:20-21, 36; 20:31; 23:37-39. Moreover, this stands in sharp contrast to Jer. 7:31; 19:5 and 32:35, in which the notion that YHWH commanded child sacrifice is repeatedly rejected. Instead, the clear acceptance of YHWH's divine legislation for the ritual in 20:25-26 undermines the portrayal of child sacrifice as a foreign practice elsewhere in the Hebrew Bible. However, though this text both accepts and affirms the belief that YHWH legislated for the sacrifice of children, it does so at the cost of the theological integrity of pre-exilic divine legislation. As Patton observes, the "no-good" law of 20:25-26 is portrayed as but one of many pre-exilic law codes divinely-designed to lead to death, as suggested by the plural forms חֻקִּים and מִשְׁפָּטִים.[180] As such, child sacrifice is condemned, yet it "called into question the nature of the whole pre-exilic legal tradition".[181]

Ezekiel's startling assertion that YHWH deliberately demanded the sacrifice of the firstborn in order to defile the people is reminiscent of the biblical tradition of the reconstruction and resettlement of Jericho, which also portrays child sacrifice as an intentionally "no-good" decree from YHWH. Josh. 6:26 reads:

> Joshua pronounced this oath, saying, "Cursed before YHWH be anyone who tries to build this city—this Jericho! At the cost of his firstborn (MT בְּכֹרוֹ) he shall lay its foundation, and at the cost of his youngest he shall set up its gates!"

The high socio-religious status of the firstborn is clearly in view in this text, yet so too is the valuable nature of the youngest child, a theological motif employed in several biblical texts. The temptation felt by scholars of generations past to discuss foundation sacrifices in relation to this text is

---

178 G.C. Heider, "A Further Turn on Ezekiel's Baroque Twist in Ezek 20:25-26", *JBL* 107 (1988), 721-724.

179 Heider, "Ezekiel's Baroque Twist", 724.

180 Patton, "Laws that Were Not Good", 79.

181 Patton, "Laws that Were Not Good", 79.

sensibly resisted by most modern commentators.[182] Rather, focus falls upon the fulfillment of this curse in 1 Kgs 16:34:

> In his [Ahab's] days Hiel[183] of Bethel built Jericho; he laid its foundation at the cost of Abiram his firstborn (MT בכר), and with Segub[184] his youngest son he set up its gates, according to the word of YHWH, which he spoke by Joshua bin Nun.

This text notably reiterates that the children were sacrificed at the explicit command of YHWH. However, the possibility that some transmitters of this tradition felt uncomfortable with this emphasis may be suggested by the absence of this verse in the Lucianic recension of the Septuagint. Indeed, the phrase לפני יהוה in MT Josh. 6:26 is not reflected in several Greek manuscripts, which may also testify to a theological sensitivity in this context.[185] The location of the fulfilment of YHWH's curse "in the days of Ahab" is no surprise, given the theologically dubious nature of the curse itself. The Kings Writer thus predictably presents this example of child sacrifice with a polemical twist: it is in the "foreign" climate of Ahab's reign that the curse is fulfilled[186] (indeed, the notice occurs immediately after the introduction of Ahab as the worst king of Israel) and the sacrificer is said to be from Bethel, a sanctuary which, for the Kings Writer, is loaded with inflammatory connotations.[187] This text also contains a remarkable feature: the names of the sacrificed children, אבירם (Abiram), "My Father is Exalted" and שגוב (Segub),[188] "Exalted", echo the name Abram, "Exalted Father", the original name of Abraham, who also sought to sacrifice his son, as shall be explored below.[189]

Despite the fact that Josh. 6:26; 1 Kgs 16:34 and Ezek. 20:25-26 all present child sacrifice as a practice leading to doom, it escapes condemnation as a foreign ritual because it remains a practice decreed by YHWH. It is thus significant that elsewhere in the book of Ezekiel, the sacrifice of children is

---

182 E.g., Fritz, *1 & 2 Kings*, 180; Kaiser, "Den Erstgeborenen", 150-151.

183 LXX Αχειηλ; on this name, see further Cogan, *I Kings*, 421.

184 Reading with Q.

185 For the interrelation of these Greek variants and the implications for understanding the formation and transmission of the traditions underlying MT Josh. 6:26 and 1 Kgs 16:34, see L. Mazor, "The Origin and Evolution of the Curse upon the Rebuilder of Jericho: A Contribution of Textual Criticism to Biblical Historiography", *Textus* 14 (1988), 1-26.

186 Cf. Wiseman, *1 and 2 Kings*, 163; Cogan, *I Kings*, 423.

187 See 1 Kgs 12:29-33; 2 Kgs 10:29; 23:4, 15-19 cf. 17:28.

188 See n. 185.

189 Gen. 17:1-8; 22:1-19.

condemned; however, and as has been demonstrated, this condemnation
always occurs within the context of the worship of foreign deities, most
usually described as "dung-gods". Yet even in this context, child sacrifice is
not wholly alien to YHWH-worship, for the practitioners do not appear to
perceive any incongruity in sacrificing children and worshipping YHWH,[190] as
23:39 illustrates: "While they were slaughtering their children for their dung-
gods, on the same day they came into my sanctuary to desecrate it. Behold—
this is what they did inside my house". Moreover, in the light of 20:25-26, it
might be attractive to suggest that in this text YHWH is not condemning child
sacrifice in itself, but rather is complaining that the children should be
sacrificed to him, not to other gods. Indeed, it could even be argued that in
16:20-21 and 23:37, YHWH's claim upon the children as sacrificial victims is
brought into sharp focus, for here YHWH complains that the children passed
over to be devoured by the "dung-gods" and "male images" are those borne
for him:

> "You took your sons and your daughters, whom you had borne for me and these you
> sacrificed (זבח) to be eaten. As if your whorings were not enough. You slaughtered
> (שחט) my sons and gave (נתן) them up to be passed over (העביר) to them".[191]

However, this is to stretch the plain meaning of the text beyond the bounds of
reasoned interpretation. Instead, it is more sensible to view the prioritization
of YHWH's claim upon the children as springing from the extended marriage
metaphor characterizing YHWH's relationship with Jerusalem throughout
chapter 16. As Block explains, the marriage of YHWH and Jerusalem
naturally produced offspring, offspring imaged as both gifts from YHWH to
the woman Jerusalem, and as YHWH's own children.[192] Yet Jerusalem is
portrayed as squandering the divine gift of children by sacrificing them to the
"male images", just as she has already offered the "male images" all of the
sacred gifts YHWH has given her as his bride: garments, jewels, oil, incense,
bread, flour and honey (16:16-19). Child sacrifice is thus presented at the
climax of this list as the most abhorrent of cult crimes (16:20-21), a notion in
keeping with several other biblical texts.[193] However, the point remains that
the portrayal of child sacrifice as a "foreign" practice in Ezek. 16 and 23 is

190 Mein, *Ezekiel and the Ethics of Exile*, 117-118; cf. Zevit, *Religions of Ancient Israel*,
      565, 567.
191 Ezek. 16:20-21.
192 Block, *Ezekiel*, vol 1, 489-490.
193 E.g., Deut. 12:29-31; 2 Kgs 16:3; 17:17.

bound up with the theme of religious infidelity to YHWH; its apparent condemnation is not motivated by a moral disdain for the ritual itself.[194] This is in contrast to the presentation of the sacrifice of the firstborn in 20:25-26. As has been seen, rather than associating child sacrifice with the worship of foreign gods, this text depicts the sacrifice of firstborn children as a YHWH-practice, and its condemnation appears to be couched in ethical terms. Theologically, then, this text functions very differently from 16:20-21 and 23:37-39. Yet despite this significant difference, all of the child sacrifice texts in Ezekiel agree that YHWH's worshippers participated in this practice, either as a part of the cult of YHWH (the sacrifice of the first-birth of the womb in 20:25-26), or in conjunction with it (worship in YHWH's temple follows or accompanies the ritual slaughter of children in 23:39), or alongside it (the sacrificed children are those borne to YHWH in 16:20-21).

It is notable that these texts associating YHWH and his worshippers with child sacrifice stand in stark contrast to the repeated claims in Jeremiah that YHWH did not ask the people to sacrifice their children, neither to him nor to any other god, as illustrated in 19:5, in which YHWH claims that the people have "kept building the *bamoth* of Ba'al to burn (שׂרף) their sons in the fire as burnt offerings to Ba'al, which I did not command or decree, nor did it enter my mind". Yet this text creates more problems for the biblical portrayal of child sacrifice than it seeks to solve. It has already been noted that its attribution of the fiery sacrifice to the cult of Ba'al is an inconsistency weakening the biblical case for a deity named "Molek". Moreover, there are good reasons to doubt the textual integrity of this attribution.[195] Perhaps, as Levenson comments, the three-fold denial that YHWH ever commanded the practice of child sacrifice suggests that "the prophet doth protest too much".[196]

Though the books of Ezekiel and Jeremiah may disagree as to whether or not YHWH commanded the people to sacrifice their children to him, these prophetic texts do reflect the view that some parents did sacrifice their children to YHWH. This is further supported by Mic. 6:6-7:

---

194 *Pace* Mein, *Ezekiel and the Ethics of Exile*, 118.
195 Indeed, this inconsistency may well be a later interpolation; see further 6.2.
196 Levenson, *Beloved Son*, 4; see also A.R.W. Green, *The Role of Human Sacrifice in the Ancient Near East* (ASORDS 1; Missoula: Scholars Press, 1975), 178.

6   With what shall I enter the presence of YHWH;
         (with what) shall I bow myself down before God on high?
         Shall I come before him with burnt offerings,
         with calves a year old?
7   Will YHWH be pleased with thousands of rams,
         with ten thousands of rivers of oil?
         Shall I give (נתן) my firstborn (בכור) for my transgression,
         the fruit of my body for the sin of my soul?

The use of בכור in parallelism with פרי בטני leaves no doubt that the offering of a human firstborn to YHWH is envisioned in this text. The sacrificial nature of this offering is indicated by the occurrence of נתן in verse 7, language employed frequently elsewhere in a sacrificial context, and the generic use of עולות in verse 6, which encompasses all the offerings listed here.[197] Yet the apparent function of the offering in these verses contrasts with that in other biblical texts,[198] for here the firstborn sacrifice is portrayed as a means of atoning for sin. This might suggest that the text is distanced from any secure knowledge of this type of sacrifice, encouraging the interpretation of these verses as satirical hyperbole. Thus as de Vaux argues, the wider context of the text is the disobedience of the people, who "in their disarray ... pass from possible offers to impossible offers" in attempting to win YHWH's favour.[199] However, de Vaux's argument is rightly overturned by Mosca, who instead suggests that the list of offerings within this oracle depicts a progression from the valuable (עולות and עגלים, v.6) to the more valuable (אלפי אילים and רבבות נחלי שמן, v.7a) to the most valuable (פרי בטן, בבר, v.7b) because the people are seeking to repent.[200] Indeed, as Levenson points out, if the poet considered the offering of the firstborn to be an abomination, it is strange that

---

197 Anderson and Freedman, *Micah*, 532. Indeed, other biblical texts describe the sacrifice of the firstborn as an עלה (Gen. 22:2, 6, 8, 13; Judg. 11:32; 2 Kgs 3:37).

198 For example, Jephthah sacrifices his daughter in fulfilment of a vow (Judg. 11:30-31, 39) and Mesha offers up his son in an attempt to stave off military defeat (2 Kgs 3:26-27), whilst the firstborn sacrifice, like that of the firstfruits, in the Pentateuch, appears to have functioned as a thanksgiving offering.

199 De Vaux, *Studies*, 68-69; cf. W. McKane (*Micah: Introduction and Commentary* [Edinburgh: T&T Clark, 1998], 180), who comments, "The questions [in these verses] bear on the distinction between offering sacrifices to Yahweh, asked with exaggeration, and the practice of true religion".

200 Mosca, "Child Sacrifice", 225; followed more recently by T.C. Römer, "Le sacrifice humain en Juda et Israël au premier millénaire avant notre ère", *AfR* 1 (1999), 16-26 (21); see also Eissfeldt, *Molk*, 49-50; Anderson and Freedman, *Micah*, 538; cf. Heider, *Molek*, 317-319.

it would form the climax of a list of sacrifices which YHWH accepts.[201] Thus the list in 6:6-7 is best understood as a series of legitimate and increasingly valuable offerings which are ultimately fruitless for the present purpose of the poet; that is, in seeking to atone for sin.[202]

Given the material surveyed above, it would appear that the Hebrew Bible may indeed contain cultic and legal traditions reflecting the sacrifice of the human firstborn to YHWH. However, despite the strength of this case, many scholars remain unconvinced. Weinfeld in particular objects to the sacrificial interpretation of Exod. 22:28-29. He concedes that the *implication* of the text is that the human firstborn, like the animals, are to be killed, but on the basis of Num. 3:11-13 and 8:16, argues that the children were "given" to the Temple as officiators, a role later inherited by the "given ones", the Levites. He writes, "the 'giving' and the 'making to pass' do not in themselves imply a sacrifice but denote rather a transference to sacred authority".[203] Weinfeld's objection is inadequate, however, for the substitution of the Levites for the firstborn is generally considered to be a late reformulation of the firstborn laws related to the role and function of the Levites within the Hebrew Bible.[204] Weinfeld even claims that Ezek. 20:25-26, 31 refers to dedication, not sacrifice.[205] But why would the dedication of the firstborn to the Temple-service of YHWH be described as a "no good law" designed to "devastate" the people?

It is more reasonable to suggest that the sacrifice of the firstborn is a core element of some of the traditions underlying the Hebrew Bible. This is clearly indicated in the firstborn legislation of Exod 13:1-2 and 22:28-29, and is further supported by the sacrificial language these texts share with the claim in Ezek. 20:25-26 that YHWH demanded the sacrifice of the firstborn. Mic. 6:7 exhibits a belief that YHWH accepted the firstborn as a sacrifice; this is complemented by Jer. 7:31; 19:5; 32:35 and Ezek. 23:39, in which the perception that child sacrifice was a legitimate element of YHWH-worship is reflected. Moreover, the prominence of the firstborn sacrifice within biblical traditions is demonstrated within those texts which articulate the primary ideology of separateness defining the biblical Israel, as will now be seen.

---

201 Levenson, *Beloved Son*, 11.
202 Anderson and Freedman, *Micah*, 523.
203 Weinfeld, "Worship of Molech", 154.
204 Cf. Fishbane, *Biblical Interpretation*, 181-186.
205 Weinfeld, "Worship of Molech", 154.

4.2.2 Child Sacrifice in the Foundation Myths

In describing the narratives of the origins, exile and return of the biblical Israel, Lemche employs the designation "foundation myths".[206] This designation is usefully employed here, for the primary "foundation myths" of biblical Israel, that of the Ancestors and that of the Exodus, articulate the YHWH-ideology of separateness that shapes the biblical story of "Israel". These foundation myths define the nature of "Israel" purely in terms of her role as YHWH's chosen people. It is thus striking that a prominent motif of both myths is the role of YHWH as child-slayer. This is powerfully illustrated in the Aqedah, in which YHWH says to Abraham:

> Because you have done this, and have not withheld your son, your only son,[207] I will indeed bless you, and I will make your offspring as numerous as the stars of heaven and as the sand on the seashore. And your offspring shall possess the gate of their enemies, and by your offspring shall all the nations of the earth gain blessing for themselves, because you have obeyed my voice.[208]

It is within the explicit context of child sacrifice that YHWH blesses Abraham, the father of the biblical Israel and paradigmatic alien in a foreign land, promising to make his descendants a great nation. Conventionally, scholarship has understood the Aqedah (Gen. 22:1-19) as a polemic directed against child sacrifice, functioning aetiologically to legitimate the substitution of animal for human sacrifice, demonstrated in the substitution of a ram for Isaac (vv. 13-14).[209] However, this is a misinterpretation of the narrative. After all, none of the sacrifice texts specifying substitution for the firstborn child mention Abraham nor allude to the Aqedah. Moreover, the story begins with the deity[210] specifically commanding Abraham to sacrifice (העלה לעלה) his son to him. As Levenson comments, "Genesis 22:1-19 is

---

206 Lemche, *Israelites in History and Tradition*, 86-93.
207 Perhaps read with the Versions, for added emphasis, יחידך ממני (cf. v. 12).
208 Gen. 22:16-18.
209 E.g., T. Veijola, "Das Opfer des Abraham—Paradigma des Glaubens aus dem nachexilischen Zeitalter", *ZTK* 85 (1988), 165-198; see also Weinfeld, "Worship of Molech", 134; Smith, "Burning Babies", 478; Erling, "First-Born and Firstlings", 477-478.
210 Two divine names are used within this narrative: אלהים (vv. 1, 8, 9, 12) and יהוה (vv. 11, 14, 15, 16). For a detailed discussion of this text, see O. Kaiser, "Die Bindung Isaaks: Untersuchungen zu Eigenart und Bedeutung von Genesis 22", in *idem., Zwischen Athen und Jerusalem: Studien zur griechischen und biblischen Theologie, ihrer Eigenart und ihrem Verhältnis* (BZAW 320; Berlin/New York: de Gruyter, 2003), 199-223.

frighteningly unequivocal about YHWH's ordering of a father to offer up his son as a sacrifice ... it is passing strange to condemn child sacrifice through a narrative in which a father is richly rewarded for his willingness to carry out that very practice".[211] The blessing of descendants is brought about only because Abraham is willing to sacrifice the son destined to beget them: Abraham is not commanded to sacrifice the ram, but he is commanded to sacrifice his son; Abraham does not receive YHWH's blessing of descendants because he slays the animal, rather, he is blessed precisely *because* he is willing to sacrifice Isaac to YHWH.[212] Though the biblical story is primarily concerned to portray Abraham as the paradigm of faithfulness to YHWH,[213] the sacrifice of the firstborn to YHWH[214] may underlie this tradition.

Within the sacrificial laws of the Hebrew Bible, it would appear that it is the mother's first child which is identified as the firstborn. Exod. 13:2, 12, 15; 34:19; Num. 3:11-13; 8:13-18; and 18:15 all specify the firstborn as the one who opens the womb (פטר רחם).[215] Indeed, Exod. 13:15 implies that a father may have more than one firstborn. However, Deuteronomic law does not mention the פטר רחם but instead makes it plain that there can only be only one firstborn son (בכר) who is defined in relation to the father, not the mother (Deut. 21:15-17). The implications of this difference are striking. Whereas the Deuteronomic laws are primarily concerned with the firstborn's material birthright, the sacrificial laws of the firstborn focus upon the fertility of the mother. The implications of this observation will be discussed in greater detail below. For now, it is enough to note that the status of the firstborn as the chosen one, established within the sacrificial laws, remains

---

211 Levenson, *Beloved Son*, 12-13.

212 J.A. Hackett, "Religious Traditions in Israelite Transjordan", in Miller, Hanson, McBride, *Ancient Israelite Religion*, 125-136; C. Delaney, *Abraham on Trial: The Social Legacy of Biblical Myth* (Princeton: Princeton University Press, 1998). It may be that the biblical story contains traces of a tradition in which Abraham does sacrifice Isaac, for in Gen. 22:19 Abraham appears to return from the mountain without Isaac; cf. H. Moltz, "God and Abraham in the Binding of Isaac", *JSOT* 96 (2001), 59-69 (64).

213 But see O. Boehm, "The Binding of Isaac: An Inner-Biblical Polemic on the Question of 'Disobeying' a Manifestly Illegal Order", *VT* 52 (2002), 1-12, who argues that in an earlier form of the story, Abraham disobeyed the command to sacrifice Isaac by offering the ram instead.

214 It has been proposed that the מֹלֶךְ practice underlies the Aqedah, on the basis of the reference to the מלאך in vv. 11, 15; so A. Michel, *Gott und Gewalt gegen Kinder im Alten Testament* (FAT 37; Tübingen: Mohr Siebeck: 2003), ch. 4. Regrettably, Michel's study did not become known to the author in time for its findings to be considered in this discussion.

215 Cf. Ezek. 20:25-26.

firmly embedded within the other legal traditions of the Hebrew Bible. It is the status of the firstborn as the chosen one, YHWH's portion, that lies behind the narrative of the Aqedah. Though Isaac is not described as Abraham's firstborn, he is the first child of Sarah (Gen. 16:1; 17:19; 21:1-12) and as such his special status and high value as firstborn is evident within the Aqedah in the repeated reference to Isaac as Abraham's "only-begotten" child (יחיד; 22:2, 12, 16). Indeed, in Zech. 12:10, the יחיד and the firstborn appear to be equated:

> And I will pour out upon the House of David and upon the inhabitants of Jerusalem a spirit of compassion and supplication, so that when they look upon the one they have pierced, they shall mourn for him, as one mourns for an only-begotten child (יחיד) and weep bitterly [216] over him, as one weeps over a firstborn (בכור).[217]

It is significant that the label יחיד is also applied to Jephthah's daughter, who is sacrificed by her father to YHWH in fulfilment of a vow (Judg. 11:29-40).[218] The narrator is keen to emphasize her high status as Jephthah's only-begotten child: "She was his only-begotten child (יחידה); apart from her he had no son or daughter" (v, 34b). Another feature common to both stories is that the only-begotten is to be offered up to YHWH as a עולה, a burnt offering (Gen. 22:2, 6, 8, 13; Judg. 11:32), just as Mesha offered up his firstborn as a burnt offering (2 Kgs 3:37).[219] However, whereas a ram is sacrificed in place of Isaac (Gen. 22:13) no such substitution occurs for Jephthah's daughter, for Jephthah "did with her according to the vow he had made" (Judg. 11:39).

In the light of the earlier discussion concerning the biblical language of child sacrifice, it is particularly striking that the verb עבר, associated with both the firstborn sacrifice and the so-called "Molek" ritual, is employed three times to describe Jephthah's movements immediately before he makes

---

216 Reading והמרו for והמר (so BHS).

217 Cf. Amos 8:10; Jer. 6:26; 31:15; Deut. 33:12.

218 The significance of the title יחיד with regard to the practice of child sacrifice will be discussed in the following chapter. On the literary features and possible redaction-history of the story of Jephthah's sacrifice, see the overview in D. Marcus, *Jephthah and his Vow* (Lubbock: Texas Technical Press, 1986), 20-21.

219 Notice that the language of YHWH's command to Abraham in Gen. 22:2 is near-identical to that of Jephthah's vow (Judg. 11:31) and that describing Mesha's sacrifice (2 Kgs 3:27).

his vow. Moreover, the text implies that Jephthah's actions may be prompted by the descent of the spirit of YHWH (רוח יהוה) upon him (11:29).[220]

Given that both Jephthah and Abraham are consistently depicted as heroic figures faithful to YHWH, it is highly significant that in neither story is the practice of child sacrifice condemned, nor even remarked upon, by the narrator. Rather, it is the function of the sacrifice that appears to receive the narrator's attention. Both the Aqedah and the story of Jephthah's daughter present the sacrifice of a child to YHWH as an action bringing divine blessing. Moreover, this blessing appears to be bound up with fertility, for Gen. 22:1-19 and Judg. 11:29-40 portray the only-begotten child as a symbol of potential fertility. This is clear in the example of Isaac. Because Abraham is willing to sacrifice his son, YHWH will bless him with a multitude of descendants, a blessing made possible in both its bestowing and realization through Isaac. The fertility context of Jephthah's sacrifice is initially obscured, however, by its apparent function as an action bringing blessing in the form of military success (Judg. 11:30-33, 36), reminiscent of the function of Mesha's sacrifice of his firstborn. But a closer reading of the text reveals the story's association of the sacrifice with some sort of fertility custom, for before Jephthah sacrifices his daughter, she spends two new moons with her female companions "upon the mountains"[221] weeping on account of her status as בתולה (11:37-38). Peggy Day has convincingly demonstrated that this label, applied twice to Jephthah's daughter (11:37, 38) is used within the Hebrew Bible to refer specifically to a female who had reached puberty but had not yet given birth to her first child.[222] Thus as בתולה, Jephthah's daughter is, like Isaac, a clear symbol of potential fertility.

This focus upon fertility is common to all the texts relating to the firstborn sacrifice, indicating that the biblical portrayal of the firstborn-sacrifice to YHWH is clearly bound up with human fertility: the sacrificial

---

220 T.C. Römer, "Why Would the Deuteronomists Tell about the Sacrifice of Jephthah's Daughter?", *JSOT* 77 (1998), 27-38 (28-29); see also W. Richter, "Die Überlieferungen um Jephtah. Ri 10,17–12,6", *Bib* 47 (1966), 485-556.

221 On the expression וירדתי על־ההרים as an ironical allusion to a theophany, see Römer, "Why Would the Deuteronomists Tell?", 37.

222 P.L. Day, "From the Child is Born the Woman: The Story of Jephthah's Daughter", in *idem.*, (ed.), *Gender and Difference in Ancient Israel* (Minneapolis: Fortress Press, 1989), 58-74. The term בתולה is usually, and inaccurately, rendered "virgin", given the qualification here and elsewhere (Gen. 24:16; Judg. 21:12; Joel 1:8) that the girl had not known a man. But as Day argues, if בתולה meant "virgin", there would be no need to qualify the term. Moreover, the use of בתולה in Joel 1:8 (cf. Esth. 2) demonstrates that this label could also be applied a married women.

laws emphasize that the firstborn is the first to open the womb (פטר רחם) rather than the father's rightful heir. This special status of the firstborn is also attested in the title יחיד, the only-begotten child. This coheres with the biblical depiction of the firstfruits as the best portion of the harvest belonging to YHWH, and YHWH's claim that "whatever is the first to open the womb among the Israelites, of humans and animals, is mine" (Exod. 13:2). Thus the firstborn child is YHWH's by right, perhaps prompting qualifications of the firstborn law to allow for the redemption of the child in order to keep his life.[223]

The firstborn sacrifice is also evident within the foundation myth of the Exodus, as 13:15 suggests: "When Pharaoh stubbornly refused to let us go, YHWH killed all the firstborn (בכור) in the land of Egypt, from human firstborn to the firstborn of animals. Therefore I sacrifice to YHWH every male that first opens the womb (פטר רחם), but every firstborn (בכור) of my sons I redeem". Chapters 11–13 of the book of Exodus describe YHWH's deliverance of his people from oppression in Egypt, marking the beginning of the journey to the promised land. YHWH's act of deliverance takes the form of killing the firstborn of the oppressors by "passing over" (עבר) the land.[224] The Israelites are able to protect their firstborn from being killed by YHWH by sacrificing a lamb and marking their homes with its blood (Exod. 12:1-13). As has been seen, the assertion that the Passover is directly related to the law of the firstborn-sacrifice is explicit in 13:15. This is also indicated by the common terminology (עבר) and the sacrifice of a lamb preventing the Israelite firstborn from being slain. Moreover, it is evident in the repeated insistence that both the human and animal firstborn of Egypt were killed by YHWH.[225] This complements 22:28-29, which also specify that the firstborn of both humans and animals are to be given to YHWH.[226]

The interrelation of the Passover and the firstborn-sacrifice is emphasized further by the presence of the law of the firstborn-sacrifice at the heart of the Exodus story, forming a narrative bridge between the Passover and the journey to the promised land: "That very day YHWH brought the Israelites out of the land of Egypt, company by company. YHWH said to Moses, 'Consecrate to me all the firstborn; whatever is the first to open the womb

---

223 Levenson, *Beloved Son*, 59.
224 Is it Jephthah or YHWH who similarly "passes over" (עבר) various territories before the sacrifice of Jephthah's daughter (Judg. 11:29)?
225 Cf. Exod. 11:5; 12:12, 29; Num. 3:13; 8:17.
226 Cf. Exod. 13:2; Num. 3:41; 18:14-15.

among the Israelites, of human and animals, is mine'".[227] In this myth of
Israel's origins, YHWH's act of deliverance demonstrates that the people have
been chosen by YHWH, who thus has an absolute claim upon their firstborn.
Within the ideology of the Hebrew Bible, YHWH's role as a divine destroyer
is transformed into that of divine deliverer, celebrated in the ritual of the
Passover lamb. This may find support in the books of Jeremiah, Ezekiel, and
Deuteronomy, and in the so-called Holiness Code (Lev. 17–26), all of which
share exodus traditions, but none of which make reference to the slaying of
the Egyptian firstborn and the apparently apotropaic effect of the slaughter of
the lambs.[228]

A key element within the biblical ideology of separateness is the
covenant of circumcision. This is closely bound to both foundation myths.
Within the Exodus narratives, a circumcision myth concerning Moses lies
embedded within a Passover tradition, which argues strongly for the
probability that circumcision was bound up with the firstborn-sacrifice.
Exod. 4:24-26 reads:

> And it was on the way, at a place where they spent the night, YHWH[229] encountered
> him and he sought to kill him. But Zipporah took a flint and cut off her son's foreskin,
> and touched his genitalia with it, and said, "Truly you are a bridegroom of blood to
> me". So he left him alone. It was then she said, "A bridegroom of blood by
> circumcision".

This curious passage immediately follows YHWH's promise to Pharaoh that
he will kill the Egyptian firstborn because בני בכרי ישראל, "Israel is my
firstborn son", and Pharaoh has refused to release Israel (vv. 22-23). This at
the very least indicates that the writer who placed this text here clearly
understood it to relate to YHWH's killing of the firstborn. Indeed, in spite of
the frequent assertion that this text is disconnected from its context, Sarna has
highlighted several literary features of the text which illustrate its integral
interrelation with the surrounding material.[230]

The primary problem in deciphering the text is that it is difficult to
discern who is seeking to kill whom, and whose genitalia Zipporah touches.
Most commentators cast Moses as the subject of YHWH's apparent

---

227 Exod.12:51-13:2.
228 Levenson, *Beloved Son*, 45.
229 Several LXX mss, Targ. and Targ. Ps.-J reflect a tradition in which an "angel (of the
   Lord)", rather than YHWH, is the protagonist here. These readings may have arisen
   from a theological discomfort with the subject-matter.
230 N.M. Sarna, *Exodus* (JPSTC; Philadelphia: Jewish Publication Society, 1991), 24-25.

aggression, and consequently infer that it is Moses' genitalia which are daubed with the blood of the foreskin. This is probably based upon the premise that חתן, "bridegroom", is commonly related to Arabic *ḥatana*, "circumcise".[231] As such, this text is widely held to reflect traditions constructed upon a matriarchal marriage rite in which a young man sacrificed part of his penis to the goddess in order to appease her potential anger at his invasion of her body (in the form of the bride).[232] If YHWH is understood to be the assailant, this coheres with the apotropaic function of circumcision within some ancient cultures.[233] However, the wider context in which this passage occurs is the killing of the firstborn. This could suggest that YHWH is seeking to kill Moses' son. Hall argues that emending בדרך, "in/on the way", to בכרך, "your firstborn", renders the text, "his firstborn son was at the lodging and YHWH met him and he sought to kill him", thereby making sense of the child's circumcision and its function as a substitution for his sacrifice.[234] However, though Hall's interpretation is attractive, Maccoby offers an alternative suggestion which is more secure as it leaves the consonantal text unchanged. He proposes that it is Moses who seeks to kill his son.[235] On the basis of his argument, the following interpretation of the text is to be favoured:

> And it came to pass on the way at the overnight lodging that YHWH encountered him [Moses] and he [Moses] sought to kill him [the child]. And Zipporah took a flint and cut off her son's foreskin and touched his [Moses'] genitalia with it, and said, "Truly you are a bridegroom of blood to me". So he [YHWH] withdrew from him [Moses]. It was then that she said, "A bridegroom of blood by circumcision".

This interpretation may thus suggest that the circumcision of the child has protected him from being sacrificed by his father, Moses, as though it functions as a substitution ritual. In this context, it is notable that Arabic

---

231 De Vaux, *Ancient Israel*, 47; *HALOT*, vol. 1, 364.

232 H. Maccoby, *The Sacred Executioner: Human Sacrifice and the Legacy of Guilt* (London: Thames & Hudson, 1982), 92. See also M.V. Fox, "The Sign of the Covenant", *RB* 81 (1974), 557-596.

233 R.G. Hall, "Circumcision", *ABD*, vol. 1, 1025-1031.

234 Hall, "Circumcision", 1027; see further W.H. Propp, "That Bloody Bridegroom", *VT* 43 (1993), 495-518; B.S. Childs, *Exodus: A Critical, Theological Commentary* (OTL; Philadelphia: Westminster, 1974), 90-107; B.P. Robinson, "Zipporah to the Rescue", *VT* 36 (1986), 447-461; H. Kosmala, "The 'Bloody Husband'", *VT* 12 (1962), 14-28; L. Kaplan, "'And the Lord Sought to Kill Him': (Exod. 4:24) Yet Once Again", *HAR* 5 (1981), 65-74.

235 Maccoby, *Sacred Executioner*, 88-90.

ḥatana, "circumcise" has been related to Akkadian *ḥatānu*, "protect".[236] Moreover, the wider context of this story is the slaying of the Egyptian firstborn and the saving of the Israelite firstborn during the Passover, one biblical term for which is פסח, "protect".[237] Significantly, an alternative term employed of the Passover is עבר, a verb which occurs in the *hiphil* in numerous texts describing child sacrifice, as has been seen, including that of the firstborn (for example, Ezek. 20:25-26).

The theme of circumcision reappears within the Passover narrative in the immediate aftermath of the escape from Egypt. Exod. 12:43-51 specifies who is permitted to participate within the Passover ritual. Significantly, it is only the circumcised who may eat the Passover meal. The reason for this is made explicit: the uncircumcised are foreign, and "no foreigner shall eat of it" (v. 43). Circumcision defines who "Israel" is, and thus who may partake of her rituals of self-identity, as verses 47-48 make plain:

> The whole gathering of Israel shall perform it. If an alien residing with you shall perform the Passover (פסח) to YHWH all his males shall be circumcised and then he may approach to perform it; he shall be as a native of the land; but all the uncircumcised will not eat it.[238]

This passage is immediately followed by the law of the firstborn sacrifice, Exod. 13:1-2. Though there are variations of terminology within 12:43–13:2, this text strikingly combines the themes of Passover, circumcision and the firstborn sacrifice and locates them within the overarching biblical ideology of the separation of "Israel" from "foreignness".

The fundamental place circumcision is given within the biblical ideology of the separateness of Israel is also evident in its association with Abraham. Its obvious fertility associations are also seen within the circumcision tradition of Gen. 17:1-27. Usually ascribed to the Priestly writers, this narrative tells the story in which El Šadday binds himself to Abram ("Exalted Father") by renaming him Abraham (here, "Father of a Mutitude") and promising him that he will be made "exceedingly fruitful" as "the father of a multitude of nations" (vv. 5-6), parallelling the divine blessing Abraham

---

236 *HALOT*, vol. 1, 364.

237 Noted also by Sarna, *Exodus*, 25. On the complex literary traditions and narratives concerning Passover, see the useful overview in B.M. Levinson, *Deuteronomy and the Hermeneutics of Legal Innovation* (Oxford: Oxford University Press, 1998), ch. 3.

238 The close interrelation of the themes of Passover and circumcision is also evident in Josh. 5:2-11.

receives in the Aqedah. The covenant binds not only Abraham but his descendants to El Šadday:

> This is my covenant which you shall keep between me and you and your offspring after you: every male among you shall be circumcised. You shall circumcise the flesh of your foreskins, and it shall be a sign of the covenant between me and you. Throughout your generations every male among you shall be circumcised when he is eight days old ... Any uncircumcised male who is not circumcised in the flesh of his foreskin shall be cut off from his people; he has broken my covenant.[239]

The allusion to the firstborn-sacrifice laws is evident in the specification that the baby boy be circumcised at eight days old, the same period of time that the male firstborn remains with his mother before being sacrificed (cf. Exod. 22:28-28). This could indicate a further connection between the circumcision rite and the sacrifice of the firstborn. The language of the covenant in Gen. 17:9-14 parallels that of circumcision, as the cutting of the foreskin (מול) prevents the breaking of the covenant and the subsequent cutting off (כרת) from the community; this recalls the unexpected use of כרת, rather than מול, for the cutting of the child's foreskin in Exod. 4:25.[240]

The beginning of the story of Abraham's covenant of circumcision in Gen. 17:1-27 may reveal another association with the firstborn sacrifice: "YHWH appeared to Abram, and said to him, "I am El Šadday; walk before me, and be blameless. And I will make my covenant between me and you, and will make you exceedingly numerous" (vv. 1b-2). The term תמים occurs frequently throughout the Hebrew Bible, and is usually rendered "blameless" when applied to humans.[241] However, תמים occurs most frequently in a sacrificial context, in which it is used to describe animal offerings as "whole", "complete", "without physical fault".[242] The implication in Gen. 17:1-27 therefore is that Abra(ha)m's circumcision will render him as a sacrificial victim offered to the deity, revealing another possible association of circumcision and the sacrifice of the firstborn.

It has been seen that circumcision is directly related to Moses and Abraham, two great figures crucial to the self-definition of the biblical Israel. Circumcision is also directly related to the sacrifice of the firstborn, as are Moses and Abraham independently of their circumcision stories. It is thus

---

239 Gen. 17:10-12a, 14.
240 Cf. Sarna, *Exodus*, 25.
241 For example, Gen. 6:9; Deut. 18:13; 32:4; see also the brief discussion in Wenham, *Genesis 16–50*, 23-24.
242 *HALOT*, vol. 4, 1749; *BDB*, 1071.

reasonable to conclude that the firstborn-sacrifice holds a fundamental place within the biblical story of Israel. As such, the biblical portrayal of the sacrifice of the firstborn child is not only depicted as an acceptable component of past YHWH-worship, but is given a prominent place in the imaging of YHWH's relationship with his people Israel.

4.2.3   YHWH the Divine Sacrificer

Though the biblical portrayal of child sacrifice as a YHWH-practice is explicit in some texts, such as the "no-good" law of Ezek. 20:25-26, the sacrifice of Jephthah's daughter in Judg. 11:30-40, and the near-sacrifice of Isaac in Gen. 22:2-19, in others it is admittedly more opaque, such as the association of YHWH with the practice in Jer. 7:31; 19:5; 32:35. However, this stands in stark contrast to Isa. 30:27-33, a poem which, in describing YHWH's destruction of Assyria, employs language laden with the imagery of the fiery cult of child sacrifice, and even depicts YHWH as the divine sacrificer participating in the ritual. It reads:

27	Look! The name of YHWH comes from far away,
	blazing his anger,
	ominous his pronouncement;[243]
	his lips full of anger,
	his tongue like a devouring fire;
28	his breath like an overflowing torrent
	that reaches up to the neck;
	to yoke the nations with the yoke of destruction,[244]
	(to place) on the jaws of the peoples a bridle leading them astray.
29	Yet for you there will be singing
	as on a night of holy pilgrimage;
	and gladness of heart
	as when one processes with the flute;
	to go to the mountain of YHWH
	to the Rock of Israel.
30	YHWH will make his glorious voice heard
	he will show the downward-blows of his arm
	in heated anger and a flame of devouring fire,
	cloudburst and torrent and hailstones.

---

243 Following Mosca, "Child Sacrifice", 201, 203.

244 The verb נוף and the noun נפה are best rendered "yoke" here; see further J. Blenkinsopp, *Isaiah 1–39: A New Translation with Introduction and Commentary* (AB 19; New York: Doubleday, 2000), 422-423.

31   Yes, at the voice of YHWH
        Assyria will be seized with terror,
        he will be struck with the rod;
32   every stroke of the stick of punishment
        which YHWH lays on them
        will be to the sound of timbrels and lyres and dancing;[245]
        with brandishing arm he will fight him.
33   For תפתה is long-prepared
        he himself is prepared למלך
        (YHWH) has made his firepit deep and wide
        with fire and wood in abundance.
        The breath of YHWH,
        like a torrent of sulphur,
        sets it ablaze.

Isa. 30:27-33 is often considered the earliest biblical text relating to the fiery sacrifice. Yet it is also acknowledged as a textually-problematic passage, with opinions varying considerably on the thematic, compositional and redactional coherence of the piece. However, despite these problems, the imagery of the fiery sacrifice of children in this text seems to be secure.[246] Verse 33, in particular, provides a vivid illustration of the practice and its cult place in its description of the firepit here called תפתה, an apparent variant of the more usual biblical term תפת. Unsurprisingly, this verse is also held to offer decisive textual evidence by nearly all sides in the debate over מֹלֶךְ. For those defending the existence of a god "Molek", MT מֶלֶךְ can be revocalized מֹלֶךְ; for those adhering to Geiger's theory that the vowels of בֹּשֶׁת have been applied to an original מֶלֶךְ, it can be left unaltered in its apparent preservation of the deity's name ("King"),[247] whilst supporters of Eissfeldt's proposal prefer to render למלך as "as a *mlk*-victim".[248] However, irregardless of these possibilities is the fact that not only do these verses portray the cult place of this fiery sacrifice, but notably, they also present YHWH as the recipient of the offering. Indeed, YHWH's association with this practice is unquestionable: the sacrifice is depicted as the climax to a festival at YHWH's mountain, with singing, music and dancing (vv. 29, 32). Moreover, the focus upon YHWH's lips, tongue and breath, set in direct relation to a consuming fire (vv. 27-28),

---

245 Reading וּבִמְחֹלוֹת, "and with dancing", for וּבְמִלְחֲמוֹת, "and with battles".
246 A notable voice of dissent is that of Oswalt (*Isaiah 1–39*, 568), who argues that the imagery is not sacrificial, but funerary.
247 So Day, *Molech*, 17.
248 Heider (*Molek*, 323) chooses not to emend, for he reads מלך as a reference to the Assyrian king who is to be destroyed by YHWH, not as a reference to "Molek".

lips, tongue and breath, set in direct relation to a consuming fire (vv. 27-28), alludes to YHWH's devouring of the sacrifice, recalling Ezek. 16:20-21 and 23:37, which refer to the recipient deity eating sacrificed children. This explicit connection of YHWH with the תפת and its sacrifices is striking. As Schmidt comments, even if this connection were unintentional, one would expect a disclaimer to that effect.[249] Yet perhaps the most striking feature of this text is its portrayal of YHWH as the divine sacrificer, for it is YHWH who is depicted as preparing and setting alight the sacrificial firepit, having defeated and beaten the personified Assyria (vv. 31-33). The imaging of Assyria as the sacrificial victim of YHWH's תפת creates a powerful polemic against the might of Assyria, here portrayed as a helpless baby.[250]

Interestingly, just a few verses on from this oracle, the destruction of Assyria is again brought into focus. In 31:9, the defeat of the personified Assyria is pictured in images reminiscent of those of 30:27-33:

> "His rock will pass away from terror,
> his officers desert the standard in panic"—
> oracle of YHWH, whose fire is in Zion,
> and whose furnace is in Jerusalem.

The convergence of fire imagery with YHWH's cult place in this verse is certainly suggestive in view of the preceding discussion. Though the language of fire and burning (אור and תנור) in this verse is not employed in 30:27-33, the unusual reference to YHWH's תנור seems more than coincidental in view of its proximity to the foregoing oracle of Assyria's sacrificial destruction in תפת, and may therefore allude to the fiery sacrificial cult located in Jerusalem.[251] Moreover, the use of סלע, "rock", a term apparently employed to refer to the defeated Assyrian, sets up a literary contrast with its biblical synonym צור, the designated cult place of YHWH in 30:29.[252] Viewed from this perspective, it may be that the imagery of the

---

249 Schmidt, *Beneficent Dead*, 183.
250 Cf. Heider, *Molek*, 322.
251 If this language is to be taken as an allusion to the so-called "Molek" practice, it would cohere with the association of the practice with YHWH's sanctuary in Lev. 20:3 and Isa. 57:7, and the interrelation of YHWH-worship with child sacrifice in Ezek. 23:38-39.
252 Though a common divine title and metaphor in the Hebrew Bible, the designation צור occurs with surprising frequency in texts associated with child sacrifice and its related traditions (Exod. 4:25; Deut. 32:17-18; Isa. 30:29; 51:1-2; 57:5; cf. Ps. 89:26-29; compare also the use of אבן in contexts of human fertility: Gen. 49:24-25; Jer. 2:26-27). M.C.A. Korpel ("Rock", *DDD*, 709-710) argues that the tenor of the biblical metaphor

fiery sacrifice in 30:27-33 has permeated into this verse as a motif of YHWH's destructive power; as such, the occurrence of the verb עבר, used in the *hiphil* form to describe the sacrifice of children in several biblical texts, reverberates with a faint terminological symbolism.

In returning to the sacrificial destruction of the personified Assyria in Isa. 30:27-33, it is significant to find an intriguing parallel to this text in Ezek. 38–39.[253] In these chapters, the annihilation of Gog, the personification of the enemy from the north,[254] is similarly depicted as a sacrificial victim of YHWH. Irwin highlights several similarities between Isa. 30:27-33 and Ezek. 38–39.[255] In both texts the unusual word גפרית, "sulphur", "brimstone" occurs as a component of the sacrificial rite. Both Gog (Ezek. 38:4) and Assyria (Isa. 30:28) are described as having a restraining device placed in their jaws (לחי). As the victim of the sacrifice in Isa. 30:27-33, Assyria is installed in the firepit of תפה which is "deep and wide" (30:33) whilst Gog is buried in a broad valley (Ezek. 39:11).[256] The Gog narrative also draws considerably upon language derived from other texts describing or alluding to the so-called מלך practice. Of particular significance is the wordplay employed in the description of Gog's burial place: the site is named גיא המון גוג, "the Valley of the Horde of Gog" (Ezek. 39:11), which clearly plays on the name of the biblical location of the מלך sacrifices, גיא בן הנם, the Valley of Ben Hinnom.[257] Furthermore, in 39:11-20 the burial-valley is described in

צור may be summarized as "protection". In the following chapter, it will be argued that child sacrifice may have functioned as a ritual safeguarding the existence of its practitioners and their descendants by bestowing fertility or perhaps preventing disaster. As such, the title צור may be a most suitable epithet for a god of child sacrifice (cf. J.C. de Moor, "Standing Stones and Ancestor Worship", *UF* 27 [1995], 1-20). On the titles צור and אבן more generally, see I. Gruenwald, "God the "Stone/Rock": Myth, Idolatry, and Cultic Fetishism in Ancient Israel", *JR* 76 (1996), 428-449; M.P. Knowles, "'The Rock, His Work is Perfect': Unusual Imagery for God in Deuteronomy XXXII", *VT* 39 (1989), 307-322; M.C.A. Korpel, "Stone", *DDD*, 818-820.

253 For a useful overview of the literary features and theological interpretations of the Gog pericope, see further Block, *Ezekiel*, vol. 2, 424-432, and the literature cited there.

254 On this motif, see further D.J. Reimer, "The 'Foe' and the 'North' in Jeremiah", *ZAW* 10 (1989), 223-232.

255 B.P. Irwin, "Molek Imagery and the Slaughter of Gog in Ezekiel 38 and 39", *JSOT* 65 (1995), 93-112. Though Irwin supports the view that "Molek" is to be regarded as a god of child sacrifice, distinct from YHWH, many of his observations remain instructive.

256 Irwin, "Molek Imagery", 95-96.

257 Irwin, "Molek Imagery", 96; Block, *Ezekiel*, vol. 2, 469, 472. The underworld connotations of the Ben Hinnom Valley in the Hebrew Bible were originally examined by J.A. Montgomery ("The Holy City and Gehenna", *JBL* 27 [1908], 24-47; see also L.R. Bailey: "Gehenna: The Topography of Hell", *BA* 49 [1986], 187-191). However, it

terms akin to those employed in association with the תֹפֶת and the Valley of Ben Hinnom in Jer. 7:31-33, including its filling with corpses, upon which birds and animals will feed (Ezek. 39:4, 17-20).[258] Moreover, the language of child sacrifice shared by both the מֹלֶךְ texts and the firstborn laws also occurs in Ezek. 39:11 in the original name of Gog's death-valley, גֵי הָעֹבְרִים, "the Valley of those who Passover"[259] and in the prediction that Gog's burial will block the way of הָעֹבְרִים, "the Ones who Passover" (39:11, 15), each recalling the prominent use of הֶעֱבִיר in biblical references to child sacrifice.[260] Yet perhaps the most striking aspect of this text is that in the sacrificial imaging of the destruction of Gog, YHWH is presented as the divine sacrificer: it is YHWH who prepares the sacrificial feast for consumption at his table (39:17, 19, 20).[261]

In summary, then, it would appear that the Hebrew Bible is brimming with references to child sacrifice, many of which present this rite negatively as a "foreign" practice outlawed by YHWH. However, having examined these texts, it has become clear that the majority associate YHWH with child sacrifice, both explicitly—such as the Aqedah, the story of Jephthah's daughter, the firstborn laws, Ezekiel's "devastating" assertion, and the Jericho sacrifices—and implicitly, such as the Levitical prohibition of 20:3 and Jeremiah's overly insistent denials. Moreover, it is apparent that the scholarly preoccupation with the so-called "Molek" cult disproportionately outweighs the scarce number of direct references to the biblical term מֹלֶךְ. Indeed, this discussion has argued that the association of the fiery cult of child sacrifice with YHWH is far more prevalent throughout the Hebrew Bible than is its association with the term מֹלֶךְ. References to this deity are

---

is an adjoining valley which has the strongest connection with Sheol, as it is called the valley of the Rephaim (probably, "shades of the dead") in Josh. 15:8; 18:16. Isa. 17:5 appears to connect this valley with fertility; M.H. Pope ("Notes on the Rephaim Texts from Ugarit", in M. de Jong Ellis [ed.], *Essays on the Ancient Near East in Memory of Jacob Joel Finkelstein*, [Hamden: Archon, 1977], 163-182) argues for an ancient association of the three Jerusalem valleys (Ben Hinnom, Rephaim, and Kidron) within a complex of fertility and netherworld myths and functions. The biblical material certainly credits the Valley of Ben Hinnom with an association with death.

258 Irwin, "Molek Imagery", 96-98.

259 This notable parallel renders redundant the frequent revocalization of MT הָעֹבְרִים, "those who Passover", to הָעֲבָרִים, "Abarim", a place-name occurring in Num. 27:12 and Jer. 22:20 (e.g., Allen, *Ezekiel 20–48*, 201; Eichrodt, *Ezekiel*, 528).

260 Irwin, "Molek Imagery", 104-105; see also S. Ribichini and P. Xella, "La Valle dei Passanti (Ezechiele 39.11)", *UF* 12 (1980), 434-437; cf. Pope, "Notes on the Rephaim Texts", 163-182.

261 Cf. Isa. 34:6-8; Zeph. 1:7.

suspiciously scarce in comparison with the number of texts dealing with the practice itself. Despite the impression that child sacrifice was originally alien to Israel, imported by foreign nations, practiced by idolatrous Israelites, and consistently outlawed by YHWH, closer inspection of this biblical picture reveals an entirely different glimpse of child sacrifice. Its underlying portrayal locates the ritual securely within the bounds of YHWH-worship. Indeed, it can even be claimed that some biblical texts image YHWH as a god of child sacrifice.

5 The Historical Reality of Child Sacrifice

The contradictory nature of the biblical portrayal of child sacrifice casts into doubt biblical claims that child sacrifice was a practice alien to YHWH-worship. It also raises the suspicion that the god "Molek" may indeed be a fictitious biblical character. Consequently, it is essential to read the biblical material in the light of non-biblical evidence for child sacrifice within Judahite religious practice. This necessarily includes the selection and assessment of archaeological data pertaining to non-Judahite cultures. Admittedly, there are potential hazards in employing the material remains of one culture to illuminate another. Yet by means of careful contextualization and self-critical rigour, the utilization of a comparative methodology may offer plausible and persuasive proposals, however tentative.

5.1 *Mlk* as an Ancient Near Eastern God of Child Sacrifice

The rejection of Eissfeldt's proposal that מֹלֶךְ should be understood as a sacrificial term like Punic *mlk* rather than as the proper name of a deity has won increasing favour within recent scholarship.[1] Its main protagonists, Heider[2] and Day,[3] have spearheaded a return to the traditional concept of an ancient Near Eastern deity named "Molek" or "Melek" to whom idolatrous

---

1   E.g., T.J. Lewis, "How Far Can Texts Take Us? Evaluating Textual Sources for Reconstructing Ancient Israelite Beliefs about the Dead", in B.M. Gittlen (ed.), *Sacred Time, Sacred Place: Archaeology and the Religion of Israel* (Winona Lake: Eisenbrauns, 2002), 169-217 (185); Milgrom, *Leviticus 17–22*, 1384-1385, 1586-1591; Anderson and Freedman, *Micah*, 532-539; Doyle, "Molek of Jerusalem?", 171-206; Levenson, *Beloved Son*, 18; Tropper, *Nekromantie*, 233-235.

2   G.C. Heider, *The Cult of Molek: A Reassessment* (JSOTSup 43; Sheffield: JSOT Press, 1985).

3   J. Day, *Molech: A God of Human Sacrifice in the Old Testament* (UCOP 41; Cambridge: Cambridge University Press, 1989).

Israelites burned their children as a sacrifice.[4] This shift within scholarship is surprising for two reasons: first, the wealth of archaeological evidence supporting the association of Punic *mlk* with the sacrifice of children has greatly increased in the last three decades, bolstering further the arguments of Eissfeldt's 1935 monograph. Secondly, the majority of Eissfeldt's critics continue to accept almost unquestioningly his interpretation of Punic *mlk* as a technical term for a type of offering.[5] Instead, their objections are concentrated upon Eissfeldt's argument that מֹלֶךְ is cognate with Punic *mlk*, and his related assertion that Israelite *mlk* sacrifices of children were offered to *Yhwh*.[6]

As has been established above, the ambiguity of the biblical term מֹלֶךְ, set alongside its sheer infrequency throughout the Hebrew Bible, cautions against placing too much weight upon the function of the biblical term alone. Yet the strongest refutation of Eissfeldt's proposal has been based essentially upon his interpretation of Lev. 20:5, which Day describes as "forced".[7] This text warns that anyone who whores after "(the) Molek" will be cut off from his people. Day argues that מֹלֶךְ in this passage cannot be translated, "as a *mlk*-offering", because within the Hebrew Bible, Israelites unfaithful to YHWH do not whore after types of sacrifices, but after other gods.[8] However, as demonstrated above, the remaining six occurrences of מֹלֶךְ in the Hebrew

---

4   Before Heider and Day's publications, criticism of Eissfeldt's theory was led by De Vaux, whom reluctantly found himself moving towards an acceptance of much of Eissfeldt's hypothesis. Compare his review of *Molk als Opferbegriff* in *RB* 45 (1936), 278-282, and his modified view in his *Studies*, 73-90. Though "Molek" has commanded much attention within scholarship for centuries, the publications by Heider and Day certainly mark a further stage in the debate. For a thorough overview of the history of scholarship, see Heider's survey in *Molek*, 1-92.

5   The notable exceptions are Weinfeld, "Worship of Molech", and A. Cooper, "Divine Names and Epithets in the Ugaritic Texts", in S. Rummel (ed.), *Ras Shamra Parallels*, vol. 3 (Rome: Pontifical Biblical Institute, 1981), 333-469, both of whom argue that Punic *mlk* is not a sacrificial term but simply "king". These scholars follow the lead of R. Charlier, "La nouvelle série de stèles puniques de Constantine et la question des sacrifices dits 'molchomor', en relation avec l'expression 'BŠRM BTM'", *Karthago* 4 (1953), 1-48; and M. Buber, *Kingship of God* (trans. R. Scheimann; third edn; London: George Allen and Unwin, 1967), 178-179.

6   The reader is reminded of the distinction drawn in this study between YHWH, the god of the biblical writers and principal character of the Hebrew Bible, and *Yhwh*, the deity worshipped in and around ancient Palestine; see above, 8.

7   Day, *Molech*, 10.

8   E.g., Exod. 34:15-16; Lev. 17:7; Deut. 31:16; Judg. 2:17; 8:33; Jer. 3:1, 2, 6, 8-9; Ezek. 6:9; 16:15-17, 26, 28, 30-31, 33-36, 41; 20:30; 23:3, 5, 19, 43-44; Hos. 1:2; 2:7(ET 5); 4:12; 5:3; Mic.1:7; cf. Day, *Molech*, 10-13.

Bible, prefixed with ל, may be clearly rendered, "as a *mlk*-offering", just as easily as "for/to Molek".[9] Day's other textual objection is that verbs associated with מֹלֶךְ, such as עבר *hiphil*,"pass over", נתן, "give" and שרף, "burn", are well attested elsewhere in the Hebrew Bible with the particle ל plus a divine name, but nowhere else do these verbs occur with ל and a sacrificial term alone.[10]

In contrast, Heider's refutation of Eissfeldt's thesis rests primarily upon the supposed dependency of Eissfeldt's argument upon alleged Phoenician cultural influence within Israel. Eissfeldt's assumption that the Punic *mlk*-offerings were derived from the Phoenician motherland, and hence easily acquired by Israel, is a point of weakness for Heider, who has continued to argue that there remains a "missing link" of material or literary evidence for child sacrifice within Phoenicia which would facilitate the relationship of the practice between the Punic colonies and Israel.[11] Moreover, Heider acknowledges the serious challenge slowly gaining ground that the Punic material has been widely misinterpreted as evidence of a cult of child sacrifice.[12] He thus continues to defend his original suggestion that the sacrificial sense of *mlk* may be an intra-Punic development.[13]

Upon the perceived strength of these objections, both Heider and Day have sought to dislocate the biblical term מֹלֶךְ from the context of Punic archaeological and epigraphic evidence in their quest to locate and identify the deity they believe lies behind the biblical מֹלֶךְ texts. Consequently, their arguments for a deity of child sacrifice named "Molek" or "Melek" will be considered independently of the Phoenician and Punic material, which will itself be assessed in detail in the following section.

Both Heider and Day understand the name "Molek" to be derived from the common west Semitic stem *mlk*, meaning "rule" or "be king". Day argues that it is a proper noun, מֶלֶךְ, meaning "king", the vocalization of which has been deliberately distorted by the Masoretic substitution of the vowels of

---

9 Cf. Ackerman, *Under Every Green Tree*, 107-110; Smelik, "Moloch, Molekh?", 133-142.
10 Day, *Molech*, 10-12; *idem.*, *Yahweh*, 209-210.
11 Heider, "Molech", 582; *idem.*, *Molek*, 196-203; Heider's rejection of the so-called Nebi Yunis inscription and the testimony of the classical and patristic writers will be discussed below, along with more recently published evidence for the existence of the *mlk* practice in Phoenicia itself.
12 This material, and its interpretation, will be dealt with in the next section.
13 Heider, *Molek*, 196-203; 401; *idem.*, "Molech ", 582.

בֹּשֶׁת, "shame".[14] This view, initially proposed by Geiger,[15] is supported by the argument that the word בֹּשֶׁת appears to replace the name Baʿal within some biblical texts, and that its vowels may distort the name Astarte (Ashtart) into Ashtoreth within others.[16] Geiger's theory could also account for the apparent rarity of occurrences of מֹלֶךְ throughout the Hebrew Bible. In arguing that מֹלֶךְ is an artificial construction, Day is clearly seeking to put as much philological distance between Punic *mlk* and biblical מֹלֶךְ as possible, a tactic Eissfeldt anticipated of his critics.[17] Heider, however, rejects Geiger's dysphemism theory,[18] admittedly persuaded by the arguments of Mosca, who in turn suggests that מֹלֶךְ is "a perfectly good Hebrew word", which may have occurred in the Hebrew *Vorlage* of the Septuagint text far more frequently than the MT would indicate.[19] Instead, Heider suggests מֹלֶךְ is a "frozen" participle form functioning as the epithet "Molek", meaning "the Reigning One".[20]

Given that several ancient Near Eastern deities' names are related to the Semitic word *mlk*, the possibility that "Molek" may have evolved from the name of one of these "king-gods" has prompted many scholars to offer various "god-profiles" in support of the explicit identification of "Molek" with deities such as Milkom[21] or Adad-milki.[22] Additionally, the fact that *mlk*

---

14 Day, *Molech*, 46.

15 Geiger, *Urschrift und Übersetzungen der Bibel*, 299-308.

16 M. Tsevat ("Ishbosheth and congeners: the names and their study", *HUCA* 46 [1975], 71-87) questions this view, arguing that there is no evidence for the distortion of the vowels of the divine name Astarte into those of Ashtoreth, and that בֹּשֶׁת does not mean "shame" when it occurs in personal names, but "dignity, pride", suggesting that the term מֹלֶךְ does not reflect a deliberate misvocalization.

17 Eissfeldt, *Molk*, 33-45. Day's attraction to Geiger's hypothesis also enables him to place the weight of his argument for "Molek" ("Melek") as an underworld god of child sacrifice upon MT Isa. 57:9, which, he asserts, preserves the original vocalization of this god's name as "Melek" (Day, *Molech*, 50-52). However, this text cannot bear the weight of Day's reconstruction, as demonstrated below (5.3).

18 Heider, *Molek*, 84-85, 224-226;

19 Mosca, "Child Sacrifice", 122-134; see further below, n. 206.

20 Heider, *Molek*, 226-227. This hypothetical form is problematic, not least because the expected form would be מֹלֵךְ; see further 5.3, and Edelman, "Biblical *Molek*", 727-731; S.M. Olyan and M.S. Smith, Review of *The Cult of Molek: A Reassessment*, by G.C. Heider, *RB* 94 (1987), 273-275; Day, *Molech*, 58.

21 E.g. G.C. O'Ceallaigh, "And *so* David did to *all the cities* of Ammon", *VT* 12 (1962), 185-189. See also D.I. Block, *The Gods of the Nations. Studies in Ancient Near Eastern National Theology* (second edn; Grand Rapids: Baker Academic, 1988), 51-55.

functions as an epithet for many ancient Near Eastern deities raises the possibility that "Molek" could be derived from the common divine title "King". However, the titles "Melek" or "Molek" are unlikely to function in place of the name of one of these gods, particularly given the insufficient evidence connecting them to child sacrifice.

Thus convinced that "Molek" is a deity distinct from any other, and seeking to distance biblical "Molek" from Eissfeldt's thesis, both Heider and Day have looked independently to Mesopotamia and Syria-Palestine for a clue to the identity of "Molek". Consequently, their defence of a god "Molek" rests somewhat precariously upon evidence for a West Semitic underworld deity named *mlk*. It is this god, they believe, who lies behind the biblical references to "Molek".

In an exhaustive examination of personal names at Ebla (third millennium BCE) Heider locates the divine name "Malik" as a theophoric element, though he can adduce nothing about the character of this deity from its use in these names, nor find any other material from Ebla relating to Malik. Amorite personal names from Mari (second millennium BCE) include the elements *malik*, *milku/i*, *malki*, and *muluk*. Sometimes these names can occur with the divine determinative, but sometimes they also appear without it, indicating that *malik*, *milku/i*, *malki*, and *muluk* may function as the common noun "king" as well as a divine name.[23] However, Heider maintains that all three are various vocalizations of the same divine name or epithet. Yet Edelman correctly comments that the equation of all three terms and their restriction to a single god is unwisely "premature", given that so little is currently known about the religious climate of Mari, and that the participial epithet *malik* ("advisor") appears in Standard Babylonian as the epithet of many different deities,[24] a fact Heider briefly acknowledges in a footnote.[25] Indeed, as Smith and Olyan point out, no form of a divine name related to *malik* occurs within the various pantheon lists from Mari, as Heider also recognizes.[26] Regardless, in an attempt to bolster his thesis that these terms could function as a divine name, Heider points to texts from Mari attesting to the *maliku*, who receive funerary offerings in the *kispum* ritual.[27] However, that the *maliku* are likely

---

22 E.g. Deller, Review, 382-386; Weinfeld, "Worship of Molech", 144-149; Cogan, *Imperialism and Religion*, 81-83.
23 Heider, "Molech", 582; see also Day, *Molech*, 47-49.
24 Edelman, "Biblical Molek", 728; see also Ackerman, *Under Every Green Tree*, 131-133.
25 Heider, *Molek*, 240, n.332.
26 Olyan and Smith, Review, 273; Heider, *Molek*, 111.
27 Heider, *Molek*, 108-111; but note his contradictory position on the nature of the *mlkm* later in his discussion, 128-133.

to be the shades of dead royalty, rather than fully-fledged gods, is suggested by their apparent equation with the *mlkm* in a bilingual Akkadian-Ugaritic god list,[28] a group which appears in the Ugaritic royal cult of the dead with the *rpum*, the shades of the dead.[29]

For both Heider and Day, the strongest evidence arguing for a distinctive deity named *mlk* is found within two Ugaritic snake-bite cures which appear to refer to a divine being called *mlk*.[30] The first text refers to *mlk 'ttrth* and the second to *mlk b 'ttrt*. Both references occur within a list of divine names and residences, indicating to Heider and Day that a deity *mlk* resides at a place called *'ttrt*, "Ashtaroth". Heider argues that the snake-bite cures establish an underworld character for *mlk* by following Pope's proposal that *mlk* is to be equated with the netherworld god *rpu*. Pope proposes that *KTU* 1.108:1-3 locates *rpu* at *'ttrt*,[31] the same residence, Heider points out, at which the snake-bite cures place *mlk*.[32] However, Pope's translation of the text does not stand up to criticisms suggesting alternative renderings, in which it is El, not *rpu*, who is said to dwell in Ashtaroth,[33] or that the text speaks of El sitting with Astarte (Ashtart) and Hadad,[34] or that the term *mlk* in these snake-bite texts functions as an epithet of another deity.[35] Furthermore, if *'ttrt* is a place name, it can be identified with Ashtaroth in Bashan mentioned in the Hebrew Bible (Deut. 1:4; Josh. 9:10; 12:4; 13:12, 31), now identified as Tell 'Ashtarah.[36] This has important implications affecting the argument that *mlk* is a distinct deity, for Day chooses to identify

28 *RS* 20.24.
29 A difficulty Heider recognizes in a subsequent article (Heider, "Molech", 583; cf. Cooper, "Divine Names", 333-469; see also Olyan and Smith, Review, 273). Note, however, the careful objections to the identification of these two plural groups in M.S. Smith, *The Origins of Biblical Monotheism: Israel's Polytheistic Background and the Ugaritic Texts* (Oxford: Oxford University Press, 2001). He comments, "As with so many aspects of Ugaritic studies, the evidence supports little more than conjectures" (68).
30 *KTU* 1.100.41; 1.107.42.
31 Pope, "Notes", 169-172; see also Smith, *Origins*, 68-69.
32 Heider, *Molek*, 123.
33 B.A. Levine and J.-M. de Tarragon, "Dead Kings and Rephaim: The Patrons of the Ugaritic dynasty", *JAOS* 104 (1984), 649-659.
34 Cf. A.J. Ferrara and S.B. Parker, "Seating Arrangements at Divine Banquets", *UF* 4 (1972), 37-39.
35 Olyan and Smith, Review, 273; *contra* Schmidt, *Beneficent Dead*, 94 n. 231.
36 N. Wyatt, *Religious Texts from Ugarit: The Words of Ilimilku and his Colleagues* (BS 53; Sheffield: Sheffield Academic Press, 1998), 383, n. 23; 396, n. 8; M.C. Astour, "Two Ugaritic Serpent Charms", *JNES* 27 (1968), 13-36; *contra* Heider, "Molech", 583.

ttrt with biblical Ashtaroth, but does not take particularly seriously the consequence that this Transjordanian location could suggest a relation with Milkom, the god of the Ammonites.[37] He dismisses this possibility on the basis that in the Hebrew Bible, "Molek" and Milkom are distinct deities.[38] However, as has been seen, there is a high probability that the two have been confused in MT 1 Kgs 11:7, which describes "Molek" as "the abomination of the Ammonites", and is usually emended to read "Milkom".[39] Furthermore, the evidence of the snake-bite cures is itself extremely uncertain. In *KTU* 1.107.42, the expression *mlk b ʿttrt*, if taken as a divine name and address, occurs here as an oddity in the midst of a list of paired deities, none of whom are given any residential location in this text.[40] This suggests that the expression *mlk b ʿttrt* may be of a very different nature than the surrounding references to the deities. In the light of this, it could be argued that these Ugaritic cures for snake-bite associate *mlk* not with a place, but with the well-known goddess Ashtart, though admittedly this argument has its own weaknesses.[41] However, it remains that the Ugaritic snake-bite cures are extremely problematic for the arguments of Heider and Day, not the least because, as Smith comments, there is nothing to indicate that this *mlk* was connected with child sacrifice, nor indeed that the term *mlk* in these texts should be equated with a god called "Molek" or "Melek".[42]

For both Heider and Day, further evidence in support of their argument is the apparent equation of the god Malik with the Mesopotamian god of the underworld, Nergal, whose name may mean "king",[43] in two Akkadian god-lists from the Old Babylonian period, which, they argue, establishes a chthonic character for Malik.[44] Day claims, "there was a god Malik who was equated with Nergal and who therefore seems to have been an underworld

---

37 Cf. Wyatt, *Religious Texts*, 383, n. 22.

38 Day, *Molech*, 47.

39 Cf. J. Trebolle Barrera ("La transcripción *mlk=MOLOX*: Historia del texto e historia de lac lengua", *Aula Orientalis* 5 [1987], 125-128), who argues on the basis of the LXX that מֶלֶךְ originally read "Milkom".

40 M. Dietrich, O. Loretz, and J. Sanmartín, "Einzelbemerkungen zu RS 24, 251", *UF* 7 (1975), 127-131.

41 Cf. S. Ribichini, "Un 'ipotesi per Milkʿaštart", *RSO* 50 (1976), 43-55.

42 M.S. Smith, *The Early History of God: Yahweh and the Other Deities in Ancient Israel* (San Francisco: Harper & Row, 1990), 136.

43 P. Jensen, "Die Götter כמוש und מלך und die Erscheinungsformen *Kamush* und *Malik* des assyrisch-bablonischen Gottes *Nergal*", *ZA* 42 (1934), 235-237; *contra* J.J.M. Roberts, "Erra—Scorched Earth", *JCS* 24 (1972), 11-16. See also A. Livingstone, "Nergal", *DDD*, 621-622.

44 Day, *Molech*, 48-49; Heider, "Molech", 895.

deity. That this Malik is the same as the Old Testament Molech, and that there is not simply a coincidence of names, is indicated by the fact that Molech was likewise an underworld god."[45] However, Day's assertion is seriously flawed. First, it is Resheph, rather than Malik, with whom Nergal is more usually associated in god-lists,[46] a fact Day admits in a footnote but appears to dismiss.[47] Second, the weight both Heider and Day place upon the evidence of these two god-lists contradicts Heider's cautionary words, which, though crucial to this discussion, both scholars clearly ignore:

> ... the mere fact that a god is of a chthonic character and even of the highest rank in the underworld does not necessarily imply equation with all gods of that description.[48]

Third, as has been seen, it is by no means certain that the *mlk* of the Ugaritic snake-bite cures is given an underworld location. Lastly, Day's identification of "Molek" with Malik depends upon establishing an underworld context for "Molek", evidence for which hinges upon just one biblical verse, Isa. 57:9. Day repeatedly asserts that this text is the most important piece of evidence, for it equates journeying to "Molek" (MT מֶלֶךְ) with going down to Sheol.[49] However, this equation is by no means clear: the usual translation "journeyed" is far from certain,[50] and parallelism within biblical Hebrew verse need not imply equation. Moreover, this text is widely held to be post-exilic, which increases the chronological distance between the Akkadian god-lists, the Ugaritic snake-bite cures and the biblical evidence even further, thereby weakening the plausibility of their correlation even more. Indeed, it may be that this biblical verse, and the poem in which it occurs, has far more in common with Phoenician-Punic child sacrifice than it does with a shadowy Ugaritic *mlk*, as will be argued in detail below.

It is clear that Day's thesis that Molek is the equivalent of Ugaritic *mlk*, who in turn is the equivalent of Akkadian Malik, is not strong enough to support the biblical portrait of a god Molek to whom children were

---

45 Day, *Molech*, 50.

46 J. Healey, Review of J. Day, *Molech*, *ExpTim* 102 (1990), 54; H.G.M. Williamson, Review of J. Day, *Molech*, *EpRev* 18 (1991), 92-93.

47 Day, *Molech*, 49 n. 74.

48 Heider, *Molek*, 139.

49 Day, *Molech*, 50, 52, 84. Day asserts that Isa. 28:15, 18 also establishes an underworld context for "Molek"/"Melek" (*Molech*, 58-64), but this interpretation is entirely dependent upon its perceived association with the "Molek" practice and with 57:9, for 28:15, 18 does not make any reference to מֶלֶךְ/מֹלֶךְ but rather to death and to Sheol.

50 See the discussion in 5.3 below.

sacrificed. The evidence for a Ugaritic god *mlk* is too scant and there is nothing to associate either *mlk* or Malik with child sacrifice. Heider seeks to reconstruct a similar equation, but in an attempt to bridge the gap between Punic child sacrifice and biblical "Molek" posits a further identification with Phoenician Melqart, thus arguing that "Molek" is the equivalent of Ugaritic *mlk*, who is the equivalent of Akkadian Malik, who in turn is the equivalent of Phoenician Melqart.[51] Heider suggests that the sacrifice of a child "to the Ruler" in Phoenicia was subsequently misunderstood within the Punic colonies, evolving into the *mlk* sacrifice.[52] However, there is not sufficient evidence of child sacrifice within Melqart-worship. Thus as Müller observes, "perhaps the meaningful consistency of an Oriental god wandering from age to age and from one culture to another, who ... is named by an appellative noun of a somewhat common meaning at least in North-west Semitic languages, is easily over-estimated."[53]

Essentially, the defence of the existence of a god "Molek" or "Melek" is very difficult to sustain, for it rests upon insufficient non-biblical evidence and relies too heavily upon the biblical texts, which, as will be demonstrated, exhibit signs of an ideological distortion that should not be taken as historically reliable. Rather, as Eissfeldt and his supporters have long argued, the biblical term מֹלֶךְ may be better understood in light of the evidence for a Phoenician-Punic cult of child sacrifice. Moreover, Heider's principal objection that there is a lack of evidence for the *mlk* practice in mainland Phoenicia may now be addressed in view of recent discoveries.

5.2 *Mlk* as a Sacrificial Rite in the Phoenician and Punic Worlds

The now familiar claims of Eissfeldt's 1935 monograph sought to solve the problem of biblical מֹלֶךְ by arguing that the term is not the proper name of a deity, but related to Punic *mlk*, a technical term for a type of sacrifice. Accordingly, Eissfeldt understood the Hebrew Bible to refer to children being "passed over in the fire as a *mlk*-sacrifice" to YHWH.

---

51 Heider, *Molek*, 175-176, 404-405; cf. Albright, *Archaeology*, 79, who proposes that the name Melqart means "King of the (underworld) city".
52 In some ways, this assertion is surprising, given Heider's repeated criticism (*Molek*, 404) of Eissfeldt's thesis that there is a lack of evidence connecting mainland Phoenicia with the Punic *mlk* sacrifices.
53 H.-P. Müller, "Malik", *DDD*, 540.

His thesis was based upon a combination of Punic, Neo-Punic and Latin inscriptions dating from the late eighth century BCE to the third century CE. Hundreds of stelae excavated from several Phoenician-Punic sites in north Africa and the western Mediterranean bear inscriptions regularly naming Tanit and/or her consort Baʿal-Ḥammon as the recipients of *mlk*-sacrifices, and indicate that these sacrifices were usually offered in fulfilment of a vow.[54] The sacrificial context of these inscriptions appears to be confirmed in the archaeological evidence from several of these sites at Carthage[55] and Sousse (Roman Hadrumetum)[56] in North Africa, Motya in Sicily,[57] Nora,

---

54 Stelae have been found at sites at Carthage, Cirta and Sousse (Roman Hadrumetum) in modern Tunisia, Motya and Lillibeum in Sicily, and Tharros, Sulcis, Monte Sirai and Nora in Sardinia. See the useful archaeological summaries in S. Brown, *Late Carthaginian Child Sacrifice and Sacrificial Monuments in their Mediterranean Context* (JSOT/ASORMS 3; Sheffield: JSOT Press, 1991), 37-75. On the extent of Phoenician and Punic expansion, see H.G. Niemeyer, "Expansion et colonisation", in V. Krings (ed.), *La civilisation phénicienne et punique: Manuel de recherché* (Handbuck der Orientalistik, Section I: Near and Middle East, vol. 20; Leiden: Brill, 1995), 247-267.

55 See particularly L.E. Stager, "Carthage: A View from the Tophet", in H.G. Niemeyer (ed.), *Phönizier im Westen* (Madrider Beiträge 8; Mainz: Zabern, 1982), 155-166; *idem.*, "Excavations at Carthage 1975. Punic Project: First Interim Report", *AASOR* 43 (1978), 151-190; *idem.*, "The Rite of Child Sacrifice at Carthage", in J. Pedley (ed.), *New Light on Ancient Carthage* (Ann Arbour: University of Michigan Press, 1980), 1-11; M.E. Aubet, *The Phoenicians and the West: Politics, Colonies, and Trade*, (trans. M. Turton; second edn; Cambridge: Cambridge University Press, 2001), 245-256; J. Ferron, *Mort-dieu de Carthage: ou les stèles funéraires de Carthage* (Paris: Librairie orientaliste Paul Geuthner, 1975); S. Moscati, "Il sacrificio dei fanciulli: Nuove scoperte su un celebre rito cartaginese", *Rendiconti della Pontificia Accademia Romana di Archeologia* 38 (1965–1966), 61-68; L.E. Stager and S.R. Wolff, "The Rite of Child Sacrifice at Carthage—Religious Rite or Population Control?", *BAR* 10/1 (1984), 30-51; H. Benichou-Safar, *Les tombes puniques de Carthage: Topographie, structures, inscriptions et rites funéraires* (Paris : Éditions du Centre national de la recherche scientifique, 1982).

56 A. Berthier and R. Charlier, *Le sanctuaire punique d'El Hofra à Constantine* (2 vols ; Paris: Arts et métiers graphiques, 1955); R. Charlier, "La nouvelle série de stèles puniques de Constantine et la question des sacrifices dits 'Molchomor' en realtion avec l'expression 'BSRM BTM'", *Karthago* 4 (1953), 1-48; P. Cintas, "Le sanctuaire punique de Sousse", *Revue africaine* 91 (1947), 1-80; L. Foucher, *Hadrumetum* (Paris: Presses Universitaires de France, 1964).

57 See A. Ciasca (ed.) *Mozia I* (SS 12; Rome: University of Rome, 1964); *Mozia II* (SS 19; Rome: University of Rome, 1966); *Mozia VI* (SS 37; Rome: Consiglio nazionale delle ricerche, 1970); *Mozia VIII* (SS 45; Rome: Consiglio nazionale delle ricerche, 1973); V. Tusa, "Sicily", in S. Moscati (ed.), *The Phoenicians* (second edn; New York: Rizzoli, 1997), 231-253.

Sulcis, Monte Sirai and Tharros in Sardinia,[58] and possibly Amathus in Cyprus,[59] where thousands of urns containing the charred remains of babies and young children have been found buried beneath stelae bearing *mlk* inscriptions. Whereas earlier interpreters had understood the *mlk* component of these inscriptions as the name or title of a deity, verbs such as Punic *ytn* ("give") *zbh* ("sacrifice") and *nš ʾ* ("present, offer") seem to confirm Eissfeldt's understanding of Punic *mlk* and Latin *molc[h]* as a type of sacrifice, as this example demonstrates:

> *lʾdn lbʿl ḥmn ndr ʾš nʿdr ʾdnbʿl bn ʿbdʾšmn mlk ʾdm bšrm bnʿ tm šmʿ qlʾ brkʾ*

(Presented to) the Lord Baʿal-ḥammon is the vow that Idnibal son of Abdešmūn vowed, the *molk* sacrifice of a person of his own flesh; he heard his voice (and) he blessed him.[60]

However, despite the widespread acceptance of Punic *mlk* as a sacrificial term, controversy continues to surround the likely meaning of this word. Eissfeldt's suggestion that Punic *mlk* should be related to Syriac *mĕlak*, "promise",[61] is contested by his otherwise staunch supporter Mosca, who follows Albright in arguing that the term is derived from *mlk*, "royal".[62] In an effort to consolidate further his distancing of the biblical מֹלֶךְ from the Punic term *mlk*, Day adopts von Soden's argument that the Punic noun *mlk* is is a performative-*m* noun derived from *hlk*, "go", and is thus best rendered

---

58 See F.G. Fedele, "Tharros: Anthropology of the Tophet and Paleoecology of a Punic Town", in P. Bartoloni (ed.), *Atti del I Congresso internaionale di studi fenicie punici: Roma, 5–10 novembre 1979* (Rome: Consiglio nazionale delle ricerche, 1983), 637-650; F. Fedele and G.V. Foster, "Tharros: Ovicaprini sacrificali e rituale del Tofet", *RSF* 16 (1988), 46; S. Moscati and M.L. Uberti, *Scavi al tofet di Tharros. I monumenti lapidei* (CSF, 21; Rome: Consiglio nazionale delle ricerche, 1985); Mosca, "Child Sacrifice", 46-48; E. Acquaro, "Sardinia", in Moscati, *Phoenicians*, 259-278; and literature listed in Day, *Molech*, 6, n. 11.

59 V. Karageorghis, "A Tophet at Amathus in Cyprus", *OrExp* (1991), 11.

60 *KAI* 107.1/5; following the translation of C.R. Krahmalkov, *Phoenician-Punic Dictionary* (Studia Phoenicia 15; Leuven: Peeters, 2000), 287.

61 Eissfeldt, *Molk*, 4; see also J.-B. Chabot, "Note complémentaire de M. J.-B. Chabot", *CRAIBL* (1931), 27.

62 Mosca, "Child Sacrifice", 273; Smith, *Early History*, 135-136; Albright, *Yahweh*, 210; *idem.*, "A Case of Lèse Majesté in Pre-Israelite Lachish, with Some Remarks on the Israelite Conquest", *BASOR* 87 (1942), 32-38 (35 n. 20) and literature cited there; *idem.*, *Archaeology*, 162-163.

"offering".[63] It is unlikely that this question will ever be settled. Most are agreed,[64] however, that Punic *mlk* is a sacrificial term directly associated with child sacrifice.

The inscriptions tend to follow a stereotypical votive pattern, in which the divine recipient(s) is addressed, reference is made to the vow promised (*'š* plus the verb *ndr*—"which he vowed"), the offerant's name is given, followed by a genealogy, and the formulaic phrase "he heard his voice, he blessed him" concludes the inscription.[65] It is striking that in spite of the personal tone of the inscriptions—evident in the inclusion of the personal names and genealogies of the parent(s)—the name of the offered child is absent. This may find partial explanation in evidence suggesting that at times animal offerings may have substituted for human sacrifices, animals which are unlikely to have borne personal names themselves. Many inscriptions compound *mlk* with another element, resulting in constructions which include *mlk 'dm* (probably "*mlk* sacrifice of a blood [relation]"),[66] *mlk b'l* (probably "*mlk* sacrifice consisting of an infant")[67] and *mlk bš'ry/m* (possibly "*mlk* sacrifice consisting of his flesh").[68] The least controversial of these phrases is

---

63　W. von Soden, Review of Eissefeldt, *Molk als Opferbegriff*, *ThLZ* 61 (1936), col. 46; cited in Day, *Molech*, 8. Weinfeld ("Worship of Molech", 135-140) argues that Punic *mlk* is best rendered "king"; but this is problematic, as Day (*Molech*, 4-7) demonstrates.

64　Weinfeld ("Worship of Molech", 135-140) argues that Punic *mlk* is best rendered "king", but this is problematic, as Day (*Molech*, 4-7) demonstrates.

65　P.G. Mosca, "The Punic Inscriptions", Appendix to L.E. Stager, "Excavations at Carthage 1975. Punic Project: First Interim Report", *AASOR* 43 (1978), 186-190; Brown, *Child Sacrifice*, 29-35; Mosca, "Child Sacrifice", 55-103; see also M.H. Fantar, "Formules propitiatoires sur des stèles puniques et néo-puniques", in J. Quaegebeur (ed.), *Ritual and Sacrifice in the Ancient Near East* (Leuven: Peeters, 1993), 125-133.

66　F.M. Cross, "A Phoenician Inscription from Idalion: Some Old and New Texts Relating to Child Sacrifice", in Coogan, Exum, Stager, *Scripture and Other Artifacts*, 93-107 (100); see also J.G. Février, "Molchomor", *RHR* 143 (1953), 8-18; *idem.*, "Le vocabulaire sacrificiel punique", *JA* 243 (1955), 49-63; contested by J. Hoftijzer, "Eine Notiz zum punischen Kinderopfer", *VT* 8 (1958), 288-292. Alternative suggestions include Eissfeldt ("sacrifice of a man" or "sacrifice by a commoner"), *Molk*, 13-21; modified by Mosca ("sacrifice of a commoner"), "Child Sacrifice", 65, 76-77; cf. Stager, "Rite", 6; Stager and Wolff, "Child Sacrifice", 45-47.

67　Cross, "Phoenician Inscription", 100; see also Février, "Molchomor", 16; *contra* Mosca, who prefers the translation "sacrifice of a child of high birth" ("Child Sacrifice", 74-77, 99-101; see also Stager, "Rite of Child Sacrifice", 6; Stager and Wolff, "Child Sacrifice", 45-47). Krahmalkov renders "sacrifice to Ba'al (hammon)", in *Phoenician-Punic Dictionary*, 287-288. Day suggests "offering instead of a child" (*Molech*, 6, n. 13).

68　Cross, "Phoenician Inscription", 98-99; Krahmalkov, *Phoenician-Punic Dictionary*, 287; *contra* Müller, "instead of flesh" ("*mōlek*", 380). Some scholars may prefer the

the frequently attested compound form *mlk* ʾ*mr*, an expression widely rendered "*mlk* sacrifice of a lamb".[69] The depiction of lambs upon stelae beneath which were found the burned and buried remains of lambs—remains treated in exactly the same way as those of human babies—suggests that animals may have been offered in place of a child.[70] Further support for this appears in the form of several stelae from a late second/early third century CE sanctuary dedicated to Saturn in N'gaous in Algeria.[71] Most bear Latin votive inscriptions which include variations of the phrase *morchomor*, widely regarded to be transcriptions of the Phoenician-Punic term *mlk* ʾ*mr*.[72] The inscription upon stela III offers an intriguing insight into the possible function of the offering:

> Q(uod) b(onum) et f(austum) f(actum) s(it) d(omino) s(ancto) S(aturno) s(acrum) m(agnum)/nocturnum, anima pr[o]/anima, sang(uine) pro sang(uine)/vita pro vita, pro con[ces]/-s c (am) salutem ex viso et voto [sa]/crum reddiderunt molc[ho]/mor Felix et Diodora l(ibentes)/animo agnum pro vika(rio).[73]

> Prosperity and salvation! To the holy lord Saturn a great nocturnal sacrifice—breath for breath, blood for blood, life for life for the salvation of Concessa—on account of a vision and a vow, Felix and Diodora have offered a sacrifice, (namely) a *molchomor* with joyful hearts, a lamb as a (vicarious) substitute.[74]

This inscription enabled epigraphists to reconstruct and translate a damaged inscription upon an earlier stela (stela IV) discovered in the same area. Stela

---

translation "instead of flesh" because some stelae appear to occur without urns beneath them. However, the extent to which specific urns and stelae may be related is in many cases uncertain, for there is evidence at almost every site that older urns and stelae were displaced, relocated or removed in order to make room for further burials and stelae; see further Brown, *Child Sacrifice*, 72-75.

69 Cf. Krahmalkov, *Phoenician-Punic Dictionary*, 287; *contra* Weinfeld, "Worship of Molech", 135-137.

70 See the examples in Brown, *Child Sacrifice*, 269-283, figs. 27, 28, 29, 32, 41 (Carthage); 296 fig. 54 (Cirta).

71 J. and P. Alquier, "Stèles votives à Saturne découvertes près de N'gaous (Algérie)", *CRAIBL* (1931), 21-26; J. Carcopino, "Survivances par substitution des sacrifices d'enfants dans l'Africa romaine", *RHR* 106 (1932), 592-599; J.G. Février, "Le rite de substitution dans les textes de N'gaous", *JA* 250 (1962), 1-10; Mosca, "Child Sacrifice", 55-61; Day, *Molech*, 8-9; Brown, *Child Sacrifice*, 29-32.

72 Carcopino, "Survivances", 592-599; Eissfeldt, *Molk*, 3-4; Mosca, "Child Sacrifice", 55-61; Day, *Molech*, 8-9; but note the objections of E. Lipiński, "North Semitic Texts from the first millennium BC", in W. Beyerlin (ed.), *Near Eastern Religious Texts Relating to the Old Testament* (Philadelphia: Westminster, 1978), 227-268 (234-235).

73 Reconstructed by J. and P. Alquier, "Stèles votives", 24.

74 Following the translation of Cross, "Phoenician Inscription", 102.

IV also describes a "great nocturnal sacrifice", speaks of a lamb for a substitute, contains a variation of the seemingly formulaic expression "breath for breath, life for life, blood for blood", and includes the term *[m]orcomor*.[75] These inscriptions complement the depiction of a bearded figure—perhaps a god—holding a knife over a ram upon several of the stelae.[76] This cumulative evidence appears to suggest that a lamb could substitute for a child in some cases. In summary, the specific epigraphic contexts of these compounded elements, combined with the archaeological and iconographic evidence, strongly suggests that the term *mlk* is best understood as designating a very specific type of sacrifice, in which a child or an animal was burned.[77]

Though the archaeological data varies between locations, the differences are negligible in view of the great number of similarities exhibited throughout the sites and finds in North Africa, Sicily and Sardinia, similarities which are widely regarded as characteristic of the same practice.[78] Excavations have revealed unroofed, walled precincts[79] dating from as early as the eighth century BCE until, in some instances, the second century CE, in which were buried, in small, stone-lined niches, urns containing the calcinated remains of children and young animals (usually lambs, kids and birds).[80] Urns containing human remains were also frequently found to hold coloured beads and small amulets.[81] At the Carthaginian site, which currently offers the most extensive evidence for the rite, the vast majority of urns

---

75 J. and P. Alquier, "Stèles votives", 24
76 Eissfeldt, *Molk*, pl. I, nos. 1-3.
77 So Mosca, "Child sacrifice", 97-103, 271-274; Smelik, "Moloch, Molekh" , 136; Stager and Wolff, "Child Sacrifice", 47; *contra* Day, who suggests that Punic *mlk* is a general sacrificial term subsequently qualified by an accompanying word; Day, *Molech*, 7-9.
78 Note that *mlk* inscriptions have also been found in Malta and Turkey, though related sacred burial precinct have yet to be found; see further Mosca, "Child Sacrifice", 61; Heider, *Molek*, 199; H. Shanks, "Who—or what—was Molech? New Phoenician Inscription may Hold Answer", *BAR* 22/4 (1996), 13; Milgrom, *Leviticus 17–22*, 1556-1557.
79 Scholars commonly employ the biblical designation "tophet" to label these precincts, indicating the great extent to which these historical sites are readily identified with the biblical practice. However, given that this discussion seeks to examine and reconstruct the likely historical reality of this practice, the biblically-derived label "tophet" will be avoided as far as possible.
80 Precincts containing the remains of children have been found at Carthage and Sousse (Roman Hadrumetum) in modern Tunisia, Motya in Sicily, and Tharros, Sulcis and Nora in Sardinia. Hundreds of stelae commonly associated with the rite have also been found at Cirta in North Africa, Lillibeum in Sicily and Monte Sirai in Sardinia. See the useful archaeological summaries in Brown, *Child Sacrifice*, 37-75.
81 E.g. Stager and Wolff, "Child Sacrifice", 44; E. Acquaro, "Scarabs and Amulets", in Moscati, *Phoenicians*, 445-455.

dating to the seventh and sixth centuries were found to contain the charred remains of individual newborns, usually two to three months old. However, the majority of urns dating from the fourth century contains the remains of not just one, but usually two children from the same family; one a newborn, and the other aged between two and four years old.[82] Stager and Wolff estimate that between 400 and 200 BCE, as many as twenty thousand urns containing the charred remains of children were buried in the Carthaginian precinct, averaging out to about one hundred urns being buried each year, the equivalent to just less than one every three days.[83] Statistical analysis of the proportion of human and animal remains within the urns confirms the epigraphic data, suggesting that animal sacrifice co-existed with child sacrifice, the former probably substituting for the latter.[84] But animal sacrifices appear to have *decreased* over time. Of urns dating to the seventh century BCE, one out of every three contain animal, rather than human, remains. Of urns dating to the fourth century BCE, only one out of ten contain animal remains.[85] However, complicating the issue is the evidence from Tharros where thirty-five to forty per cent of the thousands of urns recovered were found to contain the mixed remains of infants and young animals.[86] Moreover, there appeared to be an absence of urns containing only animal remains, suggesting either that animal substitution did not occur in the Tharros cult, or that excavations have yet to find evidence for the practice.[87]

A fixed location for a place of ritual or burning has been difficult to locate within the precincts, for neither a permanent altar nor an area

---

82 Stager, "Rite of Child Sacrifice", 4-5.

83 Stager and Wolff, "Child Sacrifice", 31-51. It is interesting to note that during the earlier periods at the Carthage precinct (designated Tanit I [750/725 BCE] and Tanit II [600BCE–3rd century BCE]) the urns tended to be decorated, but by the later period (Tanit III [3rd century–146 BCE]) the urns are plain and of a smaller, standardized form, suggesting their mass-production. Stager and Wolff, "Child Sacrifice", 36.

84 So too E. Lipiński, "Sacrifices d'enfants à Carthage et dans le monde sémitique oriental", in *idem.*, (ed.), *Carthago. Acta Colloquii Bruxellensis habiti diebus 2 et 3 Maii anni 1986* (Studia Phoenicia 6/OLA 26; Leuven: Peeters, 1988), 151-185 (151).

85 Stager and Wolff, "Child Sacrifice", 38-40. Archaeological evidence suggests that the precinct at Carthage underwent both expansion and levelling at least two or three times in its history in order to make room for new urn burials. At many other precincts, older stelae appear to have been removed and buried in trenches or recycled as components of an enlarged outer wall. See Brown, *Child Sacrifice*, 72-73.

86 Brown comments that the mixing of human and animal remains raises questions concerning the sometimes poorly preserved or excavated evidence from other sites, and suggests that the intentional mixing of human and animal remains may have been a common practice. Brown, *Child Sacrifice*, 69.

87 Fedele, "Tharros", 641.

containing consistent ash layers within the precinct has been identified with
certainty.[88] This would also suggest that the babies and animals were
cremated away from their specific burial plots.[89] However, the soil of the
burial sanctuaries is generally found to be filled with charcoal, probably from
the sacrificial pyres.[90] This evidence is consistent with that from Tharros,
which indicates that pyres were lit on the ground.[91] Brown suggests that
unused sections of the precinct may have been employed as the place of
burning, which was then regularly moved as the number of burials
increased.[92]

Despite many scholars' near exclusive association of urns and stelae,
archaeological evidence suggests that the setting up of stelae over the sites of
buried urns was a subsequent development within the practice, a
development characteristic of the majority of sites around the Mediterranean.
The earliest burials (eighth century BCE) were not marked at all, whilst those
dating from the late eighth to the seventh centuries tended to be marked only
by cairns of stones. In later periods (seventh to the sixth century) the buried
urns began to be commemorated with cippi or with stelae, which may be
plain or decorated. By the sixth to the fifth centuries onwards, stelae almost
exclusively dominate the sacrificial precincts, bearing inscriptions,
iconography, or both.[93] However, it should be emphasized that not every urn
was marked with a burial monument, and that several urns could be buried
beneath just one monument.[94] This may indicate that the erection of a
monument over an urn did not become an established requirement of the
sacrifice—although it may have become popular—so that the remains of
babies could continue to be buried without being commemorated with a
burial marker as in the earlier history of the practice. However, inscribed
monuments appear to have functioned as public announcements,
demonstrating that the parents' pact with the gods had been fulfilled.[95]

---

88 Though J. Février has argued for the identification of a fixed burning pit at Sousse
    ("Essai de reconstruction du sacrifice Molek", *JA* 248 [1960], 167-187, esp 174).
89 Brown, *Child Sacrifice*, 72.
90 At Carthage, the charcoal was predominantly composed of olive wood; L.E. Stager, "An
    Odyssey Debate: Were Living Children Sacrificed to the Gods?", *ArchOd* Nov/Dec
    (2000), 28-31 (31).
91 Fedele, "Tharros", 641-643.
92 Brown, *Child Sacrifice*, 72.
93 Stager and Wolff, "Child sacrifice", 36-38; Brown, *Child Sacrifice*, 73-75. See also
    A.M. Bisi, *Le stele puniche* (Rome: University of Rome, 1967).
94 Stager and Wolff, "Child Sacrifice", 36.
95 Cf. Brown, *Child Sacrifice*, 172.

These material remains not only support Eissfeldt's proposal that Punic *mlk* is a sacrificial term, but also indicate that this term was employed predominantly within a cult of child sacrifice. It seems clear that a *mlk*-offering could be a child, a young animal, or perhaps even a stela, the latter two of which may have been offered in place of a child. The great similarities and the lack of variation exhibited by all the excavated sites at all periods demonstrate that this was a conservative practice which was relatively widespread throughout the Punic world.

Heider's primary objection to the direct association of this sacrificial practice with the biblical מֹלֶךְ texts is that a lack of physical evidence for the *mlk* rite in Phoenicia itself weakens the case for their identification.[96] This objection, however, appears to be silenced with the discovery of a sacred burial precinct in ancient Tyre. Some two hundred burial monuments and sixty urns containing human ashes and bone fragments have been recovered from a sacred area, set apart from the cemeteries of the settlement. Many characteristics familiar from other *mlk* sanctuaries were identified: amulets, beads and large stones and pebbles were found amongst the ashes within the urns; offering jugs and bowls were discovered within the precinct; the urns themselves were decorated with ceramic paints. The iconographic motifs attested upon the stelae include the sign of Tanit, the Crescent and Disc, the baetyl motif and a shrine-type symbol,[97] all of which are not only well-known from the other sacrificial sites, but actually compare best in style and presentation with those found upon the Punic sacrificial monuments.[98] Some of the stelae also bear brief inscriptions comprised essentially of theophoric personal names. These theophoric elements include the names Tanit,[99] *ḥmn* (an abbreviation of Baʿal Ḥammon, perhaps),[100] Ashtart and Melqart,

---

96 Heider, "Molech", 582; so too Albertz, *Israelite Religion*, vol. I, 190-195.
97 The iconography of the stelae is discussed in detail below.
98 See the discussions in H. Seeden, "A *tophet* in Tyre?", *Berytus* 39 (1991), 39-82; J. Conheeney and A. Pipe, "Note on some cremated bones from Tyrian cinerary urns", *Berytus* 39 (1991), 83-85; W.A. Ward, "The scarabs, scaraboid and amulet-plaque from Tyrian cinerary urns", *Berytus* 39 (1991), 89-99; H. Sader, "Phoenician stelae from Tyre", *Berytus* 39 (1991), 101-126; Sader, "Phoenician stelae from Tyre (continued)", *Studi Epigrafici e linguistici sul Vicino Oriente antico* 9 (1992), 53-79; H. Seeden, "Le premier cimetière d'enfants à Tyr", *OrEx* (1992), 10-12; S. Moscati, "Non è un Tofet a Tiro", *RSF* 21 (1993), 147-163.
99 The occurrence of the name Tanit provides important evidence for the worship of this goddess in Tyre, which had been questioned repeatedly; Sader, "Phoenician stelae", 122.
100 See Sader, "Phoenician stelae", 110-111; P. Xella, *Baal Hammon: Recherches sur l'identité et l'histoire d'un dieu phénicio-punique* (Studi fenici 32; Rome: Consiglio nazionale delle ricerche, 1991), 36.

although there is only one instance in which the divine recipient of the sacrifice may be named.[101] Though there is some dispute as to whether the human remains are those of infants or adults—primarily due to the poor nature of the samples examined—the characteristics of these finds are so very similar to those from the other Phoenician-Punic sacrificial precincts, that it is not unreasonable to identify this as evidence for the practice in Tyre itself.[102] Dating the precinct is problematic, for the artefacts were originally uncovered in a series of illicit digs, which resulted not only in the dislocation of these precious finds from their original contexts, but also entailed the emptying or destruction of many urns by unwitting local "excavators".[103] Consequently, dating the precinct relies essentially upon the palaeographic analysis of those monuments bearing inscriptions, all of which are dated sometime within the period between the early eighth and late seventh centuries BCE.[104] Given that many more monuments are uninscribed, and that many of the urns and a large jug seem to derive at least from the ninth century, it may be that activity at the precinct began well before the eighth century. Indeed, Sader is more comfortable in positing a period of activity at the site from at least the ninth to the sixth centuries BCE.

Further evidence for the existence of the *mlk* practice in mainland Phoenicia comes from Akhzib, nine miles north of Akko, on the Phoenician coast.[105] Like the Tyrian material, the site at Akhzib is best described as a sacrificial precinct, dating to the seventh-sixth centuries. Both decorated stelae and urns containing charred human remains have been recovered. Significantly, the stelae exhibit Tanit symbols and Crescent-Disc motifs, iconographic features identical to those found upon the Tyrian stelae and common to the symbol-systems of the Phoenician-Punic stelae, as will be seen. Similar archaeological remains have been found at other Palestinian sites. A sacred burial precinct at ʿAtlit, just north of Dor, has been uncovered and dated to the eighth and seventh centuries BCE. As well as containing stone stelae and buried urns filled with burned human remains, charred wood and fragments of burned human bones were also found scattered across the

---

101 Tanit appears to be addressed in one inscription, but because her name is inscribed with letters far bigger than those of the rest of the inscription, it is unclear whether this is intentional or whether it is best read separately. See the discussion in Sader, "Phoenician stelae", 112-113.
102 So too Cross, "Phoenician Inscription", 103.
103 Seeden, *"Tophet"*, 39-51.
104 Sader, "Phoenician Stelae", 122.
105 M. Prausnitz and E. Mazar, "Achzib", *NEAEHL*, vol. 1, 32-36; S.R. Wolff, "Archaeology in Israel", *AJA* 98 (1994), 481-519; Stern, *Archaeology*, 87.

site.[106] Additional precincts situated along the southern Palestinian coast have been associated with Phoenician settlements in the territory of Gaza. These sites, located at Tell el-ʾAjjul and Tell el-Farʿah (South) were both found to contain burial urns holding burned human remains. As yet, no stelae have been located.[107] The same is true for the largest southern Palestinian burial precinct yet to be found, that situated at Ruqeish, near the harbour established by the Assyrians serving as an important centre of trade with Egypt.[108] Many of these southern sites have been interpreted as burial grounds. However, though a sacrificial context for these burial precincts is difficult to establish, they nevertheless testify to the burning, interring and burying of human remains in southern Palestine. These Phoenician sacred precincts not only offer evidence that the practice known from the Mediterranean sites had parallels in Phoenicia, but also suggest that the colonial precincts may have been modelled upon mainland prototypes, as Mosca had already argued in 1975.[109] Moreover, as Dearman proposes, the Phoenician "tophets" may also provide a mediating cultural profile between the Mediterranean "tophets" and a theoretical "tophet" in Jerusalem.[110]

Intriguingly, a Phoenician inscription dated to the third/second century BCE and found on the Palestinian coast at Nebi Yunis, near Ashdod, appears to contain the term *mlk*.[111] This text could be the first *mlk* inscription to be found in Palestine, and as many scholars have argued, it offers strong evidence suggesting that *mlk*-sacrifices were offered in mainland Phoenicia, though at this late date, it may be that animals, rather than children, were offered.[112] Like many of the Punic inscriptions, this text begins with the words "stela of *mlk*", refers to a vow, and contains what would seem to be

---

106 C.N. Johns, "Excavations at Pilgrim's Castle, Atlit (1933)", *QDAP* 6 (1938), 121-152; Stern, *Archaeology*, 87-90.

107 Stern, *Archaeology*, 87-90; For a detailed archaeological discussion of Phoenician influence in the region, see G. Lehmann, "Phoenicians in Western Galilee: First Results of an Archaeological Survey in the Hinterland of Akko", in Mazar, *Studies*, 65-112.

108 W. Culican, "The Graves at Tell er-Ruqeish", *AJBA* 2/2 (1973), 66-105; A. Biran, "Tell er-Ruqeish", *IEJ* 24 (1974), 141-142, pl. 24:A.

109 Mosca, "Child Sacrifice", 97-98.

110 Dearman, "Tophet in Jerusalem", 64.

111 *RES* 367. The inscription was originally published by P. Lagrange, "Une inscription phénicienne", *RB* 1 (1892), 275-281.

112 B. Delavault and A. Lemaire, "Une stèle "Molk" de Palestine dédiée à Eshmoun? *RES* 367 reconsidéré", *RB* 83 (1976), 569-583; Delavault and Lemaire, "Les inscriptions phéniciennes de Palestine", *RSF* 7 (1979), 24-26; C. Picard, "Le monument de Nebi-Yunis", *RB* 83 (1976), 584-589; Smith, *Early History*, 133.

several personal names and/or genealogies.[113] Potentially, this evidence could set an important inscriptional precedent for the reconstruction of the *mlk* practice in Judah, for the inscription is dedicated to Eshmun, allowing for the possibility that the *mlk* ritual could be offered to deities other than Ba'al Hammon and Tanit.[114] Indeed, Eshmun is the protective deity of Sidon, about 120 miles north of Nebi Yunis. Though the site at Nebi Yunis is geographically closer to Tyre than to Sidon, the script itself has been identified as Sidonian, rather than Tyrian, which may indicate Sidonian control or influence in the region.[115] However, the text is considerably damaged, rendering many of the words illegible, including the crucial term following *mlk*. At best, this text supports the archaeological evidence suggesting that the *mlk* ritual was practised in mainland Phoenicia.[116] Yet given its fragmentary nature, it can contribute little more to the discussion.

Despite the wealth of material and inscriptional evidence, discerning the function of the *mlk* practice is not a straightforward task. This is primarily due to the ambiguous nature of the inscriptions, none of which, as has been seen, refer explicitly to child sacrifice, and are thus just as laconic as the biblical references. Classical and patristic texts accusing the Phoenicians of burning their children as sacrifices to the gods appear to support the archaeological evidence of Phoenician-Punic child sacrifice, although generally, these texts speak of a cult practised primarily in times of communal crisis.[117] But the archaeological evidence suggests that the *mlk*-offerings were not uncommon, and, between 400–200 BCE, were also frequent, as the sheer number of urns recovered from precincts attest. The inscriptions commonly describe the *mlk* offering being made in fulfilment of an individual's vow, rather than in times of crisis. This implies that the cult functioned as a public practice (the great number of sacrifices, the public nature of the inscriptions, the walled precinct) constructed upon the individual family's vow and *mlk* offering (the remains of the child or animal gathered and buried in an urn, the personal names upon inscribed stelae).

---

113 See the translation offered by A. Gianto, "Some Notes on the Mulk Inscription from Nebi Yunis (*RES* 367)", *Bib* 68 (1987), 397-400. Ba'al, Melqart, Isis and Amon appear as theophoric elements within these personal names. Gianto suggests these people are cultic functionaries of some sort ("Some Notes", 399, n. 12).

114 Cf. Delavault and Lemaire, "Une stèle", 569-583.

115 Gianto, "Some Notes", 399, n. 11.

116 Indeed, even Heider (*Molek*, 182-185) concedes that this text may demonstrate limited evidence of the use of the term *mlk* as a sacrificial term in Phoenicia.

117 For examples, see Mosca, "Child Sacrifice", 2-35, and the appendix in Day, *Molech*, 86-91.

In seeking to establish the function of the cult, the votive nature of the inscriptions suggests that each offering is likely to have been made with regard to a specific set of circumstances. The sacrifice of a human child or a young animal is heavily suggestive of a fertility rite. The *mlk*-offerings of the seventh and sixth centuries were predominantly newborn babies, each child's remains carefully collected from the pyre or altar where it was burned, interred in a jar, sealed with stones, a lid or a bowl, and buried.[118] This exacting process demonstrates the high value and importance of the offering, which in turn suggests the importance of the situation prompting the vow and sacrifice. The fact that newborn babies are the predominant human offering has led some scholars to suggest that the earlier history of the *mlk* offering may have been a cult of firstborn sacrifice, in which the deity's blessing of fertility is returned as a gift, in hope of continued blessing.[119] Müller[120] notes that most inscriptions refer to an answered prayer (eg. *kšm ʿ qlʾ*, "because he heard his voice")[121] or a blessing received (for example, *brkʾ*, "he blessed him"; *tbrkʾ*, "may she bless him").[122] An admittedly fragmentary text from Constantine suggests that the prayer was answered with the blessing of a pregnancy.[123] Ackerman proposes an evolution in the idea of the firstborn-sacrifice, suggesting that in a later period, this element of the cult was lost, and all children became potential dedications to the god, accounting for the decrease in animal substitutions in later periods.[124] Certainly, this proposal makes good sense of the Punic evidence. However, there is nothing in the archaeological evidence to suggest that these newborn babies were firstborns.

In attempting to discern more about the rituals and ideologies of this apparent cult of child sacrifice, scholarly attention has tended to concentrate upon the inscriptions rather than the iconography of the stelae. However, given the laconic nature of the inscriptions, it may be that greater attention to the iconography of the memorials sheds a little more light upon the practice. Previous studies have tended to focus only upon one iconographic monument associated with the *mlk* practice, the famous Punic relief from Pozo Moro in Spain, dated to about 500 BCE. It depicts a grotesque figure with human

---

118 Stager, "View from the Tophet", 159.
119 E. Lipiński, "Rites et sacrifices dans la tradition Phénico-Punique", in Quaegebeur, *Ritual and Sacrifice*, 257-281 (280); *idem.*, "Sacrifices d'enfants", 151-162; Ackerman, *Under Every Green Tree*, 138-139.
120 Müller, "*mōlek*", 382-383.
121 *KAI* 110, 4; *ANET*, 658.
122 *KAI* 107; 79, 6.
123 *KAI* 162.
124 Ackerman, *Under Every Green Tree*, 138-139.

features seated upon a throne at a banquet table. Behind or beside the throne stands another grotesque figure. Both figures are depicted with their mouths wide open, tongues protruding.[125] In the right hand of the enthroned figure is a bowl, over the rim of which can be seen the head and feet of a small person or child, who appears to be staring up the figure. In his left hand the figure holds the left hindleg of a pig, whose body lies on the banqueting table. Behind the table stands a third figure with an open mouth and lolling tongue, wearing a fringed robe and raising up a bowl. The right hand panel of the relief is damaged, but enough remains to see a fourth figure standing behind the table, holding a curved sword in his raised right hand. His head is shaped like a bull or a horse,[126] and with his left hand he touches the head of a second small person or child in a bowl on top of an altar next to the banqueting table.[127] Heider enthusiastically describes this relief as being "as close as we are ever apt to come to a photograph of the ancient cult in action".[128] However, though certainly intriguing, this monument is by no means the most useful iconographic material to be employed within the discussion, for it is apparently unrelated to a sacrificial precinct, but simply a cemetery. Rather, the iconography of the Phoenician-Punic sacrificial monuments may offer a more valuable insight into the *mlk* practice.

Though the interpretation of ancient symbol-systems can be problematic and misleading, Brown has devoted a monograph to the study of the late

---

125 Most scholars interpret this scene as depicting a double-headed monster, for the head of the second figure appears above that of the first. However, it is more likely that the second head belongs to a separate figure, for it appears to be separated quite distinctly from the head of the seated figure. So too A. Kempinski, "From Death to Resurrection: The Early Evidence", *BAR* 22/5 (1995), 57-65, 82.

126 Some scholars account for these figures' strange faces by interpreting them as cult masks, which are well-known from elsewhere in the Phoenician-Punic world. See S. Moscati, "New Light on Punic Art", in W.W. Ward (ed.), *The Role of the Phoenicians in the Interaction of Mediterranean Civilizations; Papers Presented to the Archaeological Symposium at the American University of Beirut, March 1967* (Beirut: American University of Beirut, 1968), 68-72; Smith, *Early History*, 134. S. O'Bryhim is explicit in connecting bull masks to an originally Phoenician cult of child sacrifice in ancient Cyprus ("The *Cerastae* and Phoenician Human Sacrifice on Cyprus", *RSF* 27 [1999]: 3-20). On Phoenician cult masks in general, see E. Stern, "Phoenician Masks and Pendants", *PEQ* 108 (1976), 109-118; W. Culican, "Some Phoenician Masks and other Terracottas", *Berytus* 24 (1975-76), 47-87; A. Ciasca, "Masks and Protomes", in Moscati, *Phoenicians*, 354-369.

127 See C.A. Kennedy, "The Mythological Reliefs from Pozo Moro, Spain", *SBLSP* (1981), 209-216; Kempinski, "From Death to Resurrection", 57-65, 82. See also S. O'Bryhim, "An Oracular Scene from the Pozo Moro Funerary Monument", *NEA* 64 (2001), 67-70.

128 Heider, *Molek*, 191.

Carthaginian stelae, in which she analyses the major iconographical themes of the monuments, and their developments and changes over hundreds of years.[129] Her cautious approach is indicative of the ambiguous nature of the iconographic material, but it may be that tentative conclusions can be drawn. As she comments:

> Given our current limited understanding of Phoenician religion, it seems unlikely that a "definitive" interpretation of a motif is possible. Religious symbols, especially those that survive for centuries, may take on many connotations and may be viewed differently even by believers ... Nevertheless, especially in the case of motifs considered ... to be the most important in sacrificial iconography ... it is possible to identify their probable sources and to suggest reasonable, if tentative, explanations for them.[130]

Analysing iconographic motifs upon Phoenician-Punic stelae in order to understand more about the *mlk* ritual is particularly justified given their relative lack of variation; a tendency to maintain traditional forms is observable within all Phoenician crafts.[131] Indeed, as Moscati asserts, Phoenician-Punic stelae undoubtedly have their roots in the Phoenician mainland, although stelae production in the West appears to have surpassed that of the East in both quantity and quality.[132] Among the many motifs found upon sacrificial stelae, the most dominant and long-lived found at both North African and Mediterranean sites include the Tanit, the Crescent-Disc, the Hand and the "Bottle".[133] Though these motifs are not exclusively sacrificial,

---

129 S. Brown, *Late Carthaginian Child Sacrifice and Sacrificial Monuments in their Mediterranean Context* (JSOT/ASORMS 3; Sheffield: JSOT Press, 1991). See also Moscati, "Stelae", in *idem.*, *Phoenicians*, 364-379; M. Hours-Miedan, "Les représentations sur les stèles de Carthage", *Cahiers de Byrsa* 1 (1950), 15-76; C. Picard, "Les représentations de sacrifice Molk sur les ex-voto de Carthage", *Karthago* 17 (1976), 67-138; *idem.*, "Les représentations de sacrifice Molk sur les ex-voto de Carthage", *Karthago* 18 (1978), 5-116.

130 Brown, *Child Sacrifice*, 119-120.

131 Moscati, *L'enigma dei Fenici* (Rome: Arnoldo Mondadori, 1982), 70; Brown, *Child Sacrifice*, 105.

132 Moscati, "Stelae", 364.

133 As has been seen, the image of a lamb is also an extremely popular motif, occurring frequently at nearly all sites. This motif has been almost universally interpreted as representing the substitution animal offered in place of a child, although a direct correlation of stelae bearing lamb motifs and urns containing the remains of lambs has not been established. Moreover, evidence from Tharros indicates that lambs may have been offered along with babies, rather than as substitution sacrifices, for the bones of both have been found within the same urns (Brown, *Child Sacrifice*, 137). It may be that

they are more frequently associated with the sacrificial precincts than any other iconographic motifs, and also occur more frequently in a sacrificial context than any other setting.[134] Thus they are probably best understood as the most important motifs within the symbol-system of Phoenician-Punic child sacrifice.[135] Given this strong association with the sacrificial precincts, each symbol will be described and interpreted briefly.

The most frequently attested of motifs within the sacrificial symbol-system of the Phoenician-Punic sanctuaries, the Tanit is composed of a triangle topped with a circle or semi-circle, with a crossbar between the two shapes. It has been named after the goddess because of its popularity and longevity within the Carthaginian precinct,[136] and because it is widely held to represent a schematized female figure in a flaring robe with outstretched arms (the circle and triangle forming the head and body, and the crossbar representing the arms).[137] The identification of this symbol with the goddess named within the inscriptions seems reasonable, though the origin and interpretation of the motif continues to be contested.[138] Despite its strong association with Carthage, the Tanit symbol may have a Semitic origin. Indeed, as observed above, the Tanit motif occurs upon the seventh-sixth century stelae found in Tyre in the Phoenician mainland, which also bear inscriptions of dedication to Tanit, and personal names including Tanit as a

---

the lamb motif represented sacrifice in general, rather than the specific offering of a sheep.

134 Brown, *Child Sacrifice*, 123; Moscati, "Stelae", 366.

135 As Sader comments, the Phoenician origin of many of these symbols, which is frequently questioned and denied, is supported by their appearance upon the Tyrian monuments. Sader, "Phoenician stelae", 122. For further discussion of these symbols, see Brown, *Child Sacrifice*, 116-117, 123; cf. Moscati, "Stelae", 366.

136 Indeed, it appears from an early period upon Carthaginian cippi; Brown, *Child Sacrifice*, 124.

137 Brown, *Child Sacrifice*, 97, 123-131; Moscati, "Stelae", 366. Linder argues that a cargo of female figurines bearing Tanit motifs discovered within the remains of a ship wrecked off the coast of Israel near Akko in the late fifth-early fourth century BCE almost certainly proves the association of this symbol with the goddess. E. Linder, "A Cargo of Phoenicio-Punic Figurines", *Arch* 26 (1973), 182-187; R.R. Stieglitz, "Die Göttin Tanit im Orient", *Antike Welt* 21 (1990), 106-109. See also G. Benigni, "Il 'segno di Tanit' in Oriente", *RSF* 3 (1975), 17-18.

138 Moscati "Stelae", 366. Brown, *Child Sacrifice*, 124, comments that the inability to prove the correlation of the Tanit symbol with dedications on the stelae need not weaken the argument that the symbol is intended to represent the goddess. Other interpretations of the symbol include an anchor, an Egyptian *ankh*, a palmette, or a Minoan female idol; see the literature cited Brown, *Child Sacrifice*, 183, n. 3.

theophoric element.[139] Brown suggests that the Tanit motif which appears on Phoenician-Punic sacrificial monuments represents the receptive presence of the goddess Tanit within the cult of child sacrifice, her hands raised in a ritual greeting.[140]

The Crescent-Disc motif is composed of an inverted crescent above a disc. Sometimes the points of the crescent curl around the disc. Though this motif is perhaps the earliest and most enduring of Phoenician-Punic sacrificial iconography, its components are widely held to be very ancient astral symbols, common throughout the ancient Near East, probably originating in the Middle or Late Bronze Age.[141] Consequently, their likely interpretation is difficult to ascertain. Most scholars interpret the crescent as the moon, and the disc as the sun, though others argue that the disc is better understood as the full moon.[142] In the specific context of the Phoenician-Punic sacrificial monuments, this iconographic motif is widely held to represent either Ba'al Ḥammon, or both Ba'al Ḥammon (the sun disc) and Tanit (the lunar crescent) as the divine couple.[143]

The Hand motif consists of a raised right hand with an open palm facing the viewer. Sometimes the hand is depicted with the wrist, or even with the forearm and elbow. Occasionally this dominant symbol is incorporated into the portrayal of a figure, the hand disproportionately enlarged to draw attention to it.[144] Indeed, scholars generally associate the disembodied hand with the common depiction of human figures with one hand or both hands raised. When only one palm is raised (because the other is occupied) it is always the right hand.[145] Identifying the likely symbolism of this motif within

---

139 As Sader states, "The Oriental origin of the Punic symbols, which has often been questioned and denied, appears to find substantial support in the Tyrian finds", Sader, "Phoenician Stelae", 122. Evidence for the worship of Tanit in mainland Phoenicia is also discussed by J.B. Pritchard, "The Tanit Inscription from Sarepta", in Niemeyer, *Phoenizier im Westen*, 83-92; M. Dothan, "A Sign of Tannit from Tell Akko", *IEJ* 24 (1974), 44-49; Wolff, "Archaeology", 489-536.

140 Brown, *Child Sacrifice*, 130.

141 Brown, *Child Sacrifice*, 136, 144-147.

142 See the discussions and comments in Hours-Miedan, "Les représentations figurées", 15-76; Picard, "Les représentations", 82; Moscati, "Stelae", 366.

143 Sader, "Phoenician stelae", 110-111; Y. Yadin, "Symbols of deities in Zinjirli, Carthage, and Hazor", in Sanders, *Near Eastern Archaeology*, 199-231 (216-219); Stager and Wolff, "Child Sacrifice", 46. Brown is reluctant to interpret this motif, preferring simply to state that it has astral and divine symbolism, without associating it with a particular deity; Brown, *Child Sacrifice*, 144.

144 See the photograph reproduced in Moscati, "Stelae", 369.

145 Brown, *Child Sacrifice*, 134-135.

the specific context of the sacrificial monuments is complicated given the ambiguous status of figures with raised hands depicted upon the stelae. Consequently, the Hand could be interpreted as a gesture of blessing or greeting by a deity, or as an action of prayer or supplication by a worshipper, given that both divine and human figures are depicted raising their hands like this throughout the ancient Near East.[146] Within Phoenician and Punic iconography, it would appear that the depiction of a human figure with a raised right hand gradually broadened in context, for it begins to appear homogeneously upon funerary stelae unassociated with human sacrifice in the third and second centuries BCE, and is commonly considered to represent the deceased.[147] This subsequent development may serve as a clue to the primary symbolism of this motif upon the sacrificial monuments. It is perhaps more likely that the Hand motif was a sacrificial symbol associated with the mortal worshipper which was later incorporated into the broader context of funerary iconography, rather than positing the Hand as a divine symbol subsequently "desacralized" and applied to human funerary figures. Moreover, as Brown comments, given that the Tanit is probably a symbol representing the deity, it is unlikely that the Hand too would function in this way upon the sacrificial stelae, particularly in view of the fact that when the Tanit and Hand appear together, the Tanit is always assigned the central position.[148] Despite its early ancient Near Eastern attestations and later transference to the funerary sphere, the Hand motif within the Phoenician-Punic sacrificial cult remained distinctively Phoenician, unaffected by the influences of foreign iconographies.[149] In this sense, it is, like the Tanit symbol, peculiarly characteristic of the Phoenician-Punic cult of child sacrifice. As Brown argues, the Hand motif is best understood as representing the raised right hand of the worshipper engaged in the sacrificial ritual.[150]

The "Bottle" motif varies in shape and size, but is usually composed of a short neck, rounded shoulders, and a flat or rounded bottom. It is usually accompanied by the Crescent-Disc motif, positioned above it. The simplicity of this shape allows a variety of interpretations, which include its identification as a geometric shape,[151] or a vase,[152] or even a burial urn.[153]

---

146 See further Hours-Miedan, "Les représentations", 32; Brown, *Child Sacrifice*, 134-136.
147 Cf. Moscati, "Stelae", 367; J.M. Turfa, "Evidence for Etruscan-Punic Relations", *AJA* 81 (1981), 368-374 (369).
148 Brown, *Child Sacrifice*, 136.
149 Brown, *Child Sacrifice*, 145.
150 Brown, *Child Sacrifice*, 145.
151 Moscati, "Stelae", 366-337.

However, this motif frequently takes on a more anthropomorphic form, for in many cases, the neck of the bottle is replaced or topped with a circular shape much like a head, which many commentators have argued simply represents the amalgamation of the accompanying crescent and disc motif with the Bottle itself.[154] But this motif is often further humanized by the addition of a face on the neck or "head" of the Bottle, usually depicted by means of eyes and a nose,[155] and the inclusion of what appear to be feet protruding from Bottle motifs known from Motya and Tharros.[156] This common anthropomorphic depiction of the Bottle suggests for many that the motif represents the sacrificed child. This appears to be supported by the representation of a swaddled baby, roughly "Bottle-shaped", upon a Carthaginian stela of the third century.[157] Etruscan terra cotta figurines of swaddled babies resembling the Bottle motif provide further support for this identification.[158] Indeed, if the Bottle motif is interpreted as symbolic of the swaddled, sacrificed baby central to the *mlk* rite, it would fill the peculiar void in the symbol-system of sacrificial iconography, in which the deities, worshippers and animal offerings are frequently represented, whilst the sacrificial children are not.[159] There are only three other known depictions of babies upon the stelae. The most unambiguous is the famous Carthaginian image of an adult, presumably a priest (given his headgear), carrying an infant in the crook of his left arm and raising his right hand in the stereotypical manner.[160] A stela from Monte Sirai portrays a woman holding a swaddled baby,[161] and a stela from Tharros seems to depict the head of a child and the head of an adult, each in profile, facing each other.[162] However, like the inscriptions themselves, the actual sacrifice of a baby is never explicitly attested within the iconography of the stelae, although objects associated with the ritual do appear to be depicted.

---

152 S. Gsell, *Histoire ancienne de l'Afrique du Nord*, vol. 4 : *La civilisation carthaginoise* (Paris: Librairie Hachette, 1920), 370-371.
153 *Contra* Hours-Miedan, "Les représentations", 25; G. Picard, *Les religions de l'Afrique antique* (Paris: Librairie Plon, 1954), 76.
154 Brown, *Child Sacrifice*, 102, 138.
155 See Brown, *Child Sacrifice*, fig. 15 no. 43; fig. 22 nos. 276, 27.
156 Moscati and Uberti, *Scavi al tofet di Tharros*, 44, 78.
157 Brown, *Child Sacrifice*, fig. 56d.
158 Brown, *Child Sacrifice*, 141, and the literature cited there.
159 Brown, *Child Sacrifice*, 141.
160 Moscati, "Stelae", 366; cf. 433; Brown, *Child Sacrifice*, fig. 64:c.
161 Brown, *Child Sacrifice*, fig. 61:c.
162 Moscati and Uberti , *Scavi al tofet di Tharros*, stela 142, fig. 23, pl. LVI.

The most common of these is the Baetyl (sacred standing stone) motif, which can be single, double, triple, or quintuple. This representation of sacred monuments—perhaps depicting the stelae of the precinct—predominantly occurs upon sacrificial stelae of the seventh-sixth centuries BCE, although it does continue to appear upon later monuments.[163] Equally intriguing is the frequent depiction of an altar, which Brown describes as resembling "a hamburger with only a top bun".[164] This symbol is often presented alongside a jug or pitcher motif, and occasionally, human figures, perhaps worshippers, are portrayed holding out their arms before the altar. Other objects depicted upon the stelae include a variety of vessels and implements, including bowls, jugs, ladles and incense burners, presumably the paraphernalia of ritual.[165] These motifs suggest that there were rituals performed to accompany the actual burning and burial of children and animals. However, the consistency with which these motifs occurs contrasts sharply with the fact that none of the sacrificial sanctuaries have yielded fixed altars, nor many vessels, despite evidence for intensive burning within the site. This contrast suggests that the preliminary rituals associated with the sacrifice took place away from the burial ground, perhaps in a nearby temple or sanctuary. The walls enclosing the precincts are certainly suggestive of a distinct desire to separate the burial precinct entirely from all other areas of activity, perhaps even including the local sanctuary at which rituals prefiguring the burning and burial of the offerings may have been performed.[166]

Analysis of the stelae certainly offers a greater insight into the Phoenician-Punic *mlk* sacrifice, despite a lack of any explicit reference to child sacrifice in the inscriptions and iconography. The very existence of the stelae themselves indicates that the sacrifice was pre-planned, complementing the inscriptional evidence suggesting that the sacrifice was offered in fulfilment of a past vow. Indeed, Brown argues that the stelae were probably custom-made before the sacrifice, with the quality, designs and motifs perhaps chosen by the parents according to taste or financial means: no two stelae are exactly the same, although some appear to be prefabricated, often

---

163 Moscati, "Stelae", 366.

164 Brown, *Child Sacrifice*, 102.

165 Although this is the most reasonable interpretation of these symbols, it should be noted that not every motif depicted upon the stelae is to be directly related to the practice. At Carthage, elephants, dolphins, horses, boats, fish, frogs and carpentry tools may represent the status or professions of the parents commissioning the stelae, or they may simply function as decorative motifs; Brown, *Child Sacrifice*, 100.

166 Cf. Brown, *Child Sacrifice*, 142-143, 171.

bearing an obvious space ready for an inscription which has not been filled; the dedications upon the stelae—particularly those naming the parents— would presumably have to be pre-arranged; two contemporaneous stelae may exhibit similar designs, but the craftsmanship of one may be far better, and hence more costly, than the other.[167] The iconography of the monuments is essentially conservative, with a handful of motifs occurring at all precincts and repeated with little variation over hundreds of years. This complements the style of the burials themselves, which remains basically unchanged at all sites; the types and shapes of the burial markers exhibit only gradual changes over time, from cairns of stones to cippi and then to stelae. The most long-lived and stylistically unchanged motifs common to nearly all sacrificial precincts are those depicting the crucial elements of the practice: the Tanit and Crescent and Disc probably represent the gods to whom the sacrifice was offered; the Hand probably symbolizes the worshipper, perhaps responding to the raised arms of Tanit; and the Bottle, representing the swaddled baby, and the Sheep[168] represent the victims of the sacrifice; the baetyl, altar and vessels likely depict the rituals associated with the practice.

In assessing the archaeological evidence, a picture thus emerges of a careful, preplanned, and important ritual of child sacrifice. The parents would presumably make their vow to the gods, a vow perhaps answered with a pregnancy. The preparations for the sacrifice of the coming child would then be made: the burial urn and perhaps marker would be made ready; from the sixth century, this would probably include the selection of a stela and its design and inscription. The birth of the promised child would probably be followed fairly swiftly by rituals in a temple or sanctuary, from where it would be taken to the walled precinct and burned, possibly upon a pyre of olive wood.[169] Scientific analysis of human remains from Tharros indicates that the flesh and bones were intact and motionless when cremated, suggesting that the child was rendered unconscious or killed before being burned.[170] The ashes of the child were then carefully collected and interred in an urn, into which could also be placed amulets and beads.[171] Large pebbles

---

167 Brown, *Child Sacrifice*, 104-105, 114-115, 171.
168 See above, n. 133.
169 Charred olive wood seems to predominate within ash layers recoverable in the precincts; cf. Stager, "*Odyssey* Debate", 31; Fedele, "Tharros", 641-643.
170 Fedele, "Tharros", 641-643.
171 The baby may have been wearing these items before its sacrifice, as beads and amulets found within urns are often perforated, suggesting they were strung together as a necklace or bracelet; cf. Stager and Wolff, "Child Sacrifice", 36, 44, 45; Seeden, "*Tophet* in Tyre?", 76.

or stones were usually deliberately placed on top of the ashes, possibly to weigh them down, or as a specific ritual,[172] before the urn was sealed with a stopper or bowl, and placed in a pit, often itself lined with stones.[173] The burial marker would then be placed over the urn, whether it was a cairn of stones, cippus or stela. An inscribed stela would also publicize the sacrifice, naming the family. In those instances in which the cremated remains of an older infant and a newborn of the same family were buried in one urn, it may be that the promised child was stillborn, and thus the life of its older sibling was offered instead, both children being cremated and buried together. Animal sacrifices may have functioned in a similar way: childless couples perhaps offered a lamb in the hope of a conceiving a child. Perhaps an animal could be offered in place of an older infant if the promised newborn was stillborn; or an animal may have been sacrificed if the promised baby was miscarried at an early stage of the pregnancy.

Though admittedly speculative in places, this reconstruction of the *mlk* sacrifice is perfectly plausible in light of the archaeological, inscriptional and iconographic material assessed here. Moreover, this evidence strongly supports Eissfeldt's assertion that Phoenician-Punic *mlk* is a sacrificial term which is to be directly related to the biblical term מֹלֶךְ. However, the most recent challenge to Eissfeldt's thesis is a small, but increasingly vocal, minority of scholars who argue that the archaeological material of the Phoenician-Punic precincts has been widely misinterpreted.[174] These scholars propose that classical and Patristic accounts of Phoenician and Punic child sacrifice have influenced too directly the interpretation of the archaeological data, as have the biblical allusions to the practice examined above. Though they do not dispute that these ancient texts may offer evidence of Phoenician child sacrifice, they contend that the weight of this evidence is nearly always applied unthinkingly to the material data, thereby distorting its interpretation.

---

172 Cf. Seeden, "*Tophet* in Tyre?", 79; Fedele, "Tharros", 643.

173 Stager and Wolff, "Child Sacrifice", 36.

174 The most notable publications of this group are : H. Benichou-Safar, "À propos des ossements humains du tophet de Carthage", *RSF* 9 (1981), 5-9; *Les tombes puniques de Carthage: Topographie, structures, inscriptions et rites funéraires* (Paris: Éditions du Centre national de la recherche scientifique, 1982); A. Simonetti, "Sacrifici umani e uccisioni rituali nel mondo fenicio-punico: Il contributo delle fonti letterarie", *RSF* 11 (1983), 91-111; S. Moscati, "Non è un Tofet a Tiro", *RSF* 21 (1993), 147-152; *idem.*, "Il sacrificio punico dei fanciulli: Realità o invenzione?", *Problemi attuali di scienza e di cultura. Accademia Nazionale dei Lincei* 261 (1987), 3-15 (*contra idem.*, "Il sacrificio dei fanciulli", 1-8); Fedele and Foster, "Tharros", 46; M. Gras, P. Rouillard, J. Teixodor, "The Phoenicians and Death", *Berytus* 39 (1991), 127-176.

Rather, they urge that a more considered, measured approach to both the literary and material evidence is crucial if the data are to be understood correctly. Consequently, their arguments place a heavy emphasis upon the shortcomings and inconsistencies inherent within the literary material: first, there are very few *direct* literary sources surviving from the Phoenician-Punic world, resulting in a near total lack of ritual and mythological texts.[175] Second, given this lack of Phoenician-Punic literary evidence, scholars tend to employ the surviving *indirect* literary material, which is dominated by Greek and Roman works, the polemical nature of which automatically undermines the reliability of the texts. Third, the reliability of the ancient sources is challenged further by the fact that other ancient historians, such as Herodotus, Thucydides, Polybius and Livy, appear not to refer child sacrifice at all.[176] Lastly, the classical sources are highly inconsistent in that they differ considerably in their descriptions of the rites, victims, and recipient deities associated with the practice.[177]

In challenging the credibility of the literary sources, the revisionists thereby seek to interpret the archaeological data independently. They therefore contend that babies whose burnt remains have been found buried in jars are not the victims of sacrifice, but the victims of the high infant mortality rates afflicting all ancient societies. Benichou-Safar thus argues that these precincts are best understood as children's cemeteries, deliberately set apart from the burial grounds of the adult populations.[178] Similarly, Ribichini suggests that infants who died naturally at such a young age were accorded a special status which was reflected in their separation from the "ordinary dead", for, "according to a specific religious conception, the children buried in the *tophet* were destined to a glorious (or at any rate special) afterlife".[179] However, these arguments do not account for the presence of incinerated animal bones and ashes, nor does it explain the votive nature of the inscriptions upon many of the stelae. This clearly demands a more careful

---

175 See particularly the discussions in Moscati, *Phoenicians*, by F. Mazza ("The Phoenicians as Seen by the Ancient World", 628-653); S. Moscati, ("A Civilization Rediscovered", 8-16); and S. Ribichini, ("Beliefs and Religious Life", 120-152).
176 Fantar in M.H. Fantar, L.E. Stager and J.E. Greene, "An *Odyssey* Debate: Were Living Children Sacrificed to the Gods?", *ArchOd* (Nov/Dec 2000), 28-31.
177 Ribichini, "Beliefs", 140-141.
178 H. Benichou-Safar, "À propos", 5-9.
179 Ribichini, "Beliefs", 141. Gras, Rouillard and Teixodor ("Phoenicians and Death", 172-173) argue that these babies were not fully-integrated members of society because of their tender age; thus they were "marginalised", and their cemeteries set apart from those of full-status members of society.

explanation for the archaeological evidence, a challenge adeptly taken on by Fantar in defending the Phoenicians against the charge of child sacrifice:

> Punic children who died young possessed a special status. They were accordingly incinerated and buried inside an enclosure reserved for the cult of lord Ba ʿal Hammon and lady Tanit. These children were not "dead" in the usual sense of the word; rather, they were retroceded. For mysterious reasons, Ba ʿal Hammon decided to recall them to himself. Submitting to the divine will, the parents returned the child, giving it back to the god according to a ritual that involved, among other things, incineration and burial. In return, the parents hoped that Ba ʿal Hammon and Tanit would provide a replacement for the retroceded child—and this request was inscribed upon a funeral stela. Thus the Tophet burials were not true offerings of children to the gods. Rather, they were restitutions of children or fetuses [*sic*] taken prematurely, by natural death.[180]

Fantar prefaces his suggestion by arguing that the archaeological evidence itself is far more ambiguous than is usually supposed. For him, the lack of any explicit reference to death, coupled with the very occasional Greek transliteration within the inscriptions, could just as easily suggest that these burial areas were simply public sanctuaries, enabling locals and visiting foreigners alike to make a vow or pay homage to the local deities.[181]

Though Fantar's interpretation is seemingly plausible, he is still unable to account convincingly for the presence of animal remains buried within the precincts. His only suggestion is that parents would sometimes sacrifice animals in order to solicit divine favour, perhaps in the form of a new pregnancy. These animal offerings were then commemorated with funerary stelae.[182] However, Fantar's entire argument is seriously weakened by his recourse to a sacrificial interpretation of the animal remains. In interpreting

---

180 Fantar, "*Odyssey* Debate", 30; see also Ribichini, "Beliefs", 141.

181 Fantar, "*Odyssey* Debate", 30. The lack of any explicit reference to death within the inscriptions is not in itself a compelling reason to doubt the sacrificial nature of the archaeological material. The likelihood that the language of the *mlk* inscriptions is deliberately euphemistic is generally accepted—this would then heighten the possibility that the non-*mlk* inscriptions are also euphemistic in character. Regardless, the lack of any mention of death within the inscriptions supports neither Fantar nor those arguing for a sacrificial interpretation.

182 Fantar, "*Odyssey* Debate", 30; cf. Gras, Rouillard, Teixodor, "Phoenicians and Death", 173. An alternative suggestion is that animals were burned and buried alongside the remains of children in order that they might accompany the dead babies upon their journey to the underworld. However, this does not account adequately for the instances in which animal remains are buried alone in individual urns, nor can the votive nature of the inscriptions be seen to support this argument.

the burned, buried, and commemorated animal remains as sacrifices, he is clearly—though perhaps unwittingly—allowing for the notion that the burned, buried, and commemorated remains of human babies could also be sacrifices. Indeed, the underlying motivation for Fantar's sacrificial interpretation of the animal burials is that it is simply unavoidable, because this makes the best sense of the archaeological evidence. Though the interpretation of the Phoenician-Punic precincts as special, sacred cemeteries for stillborn or young babies is more palatable than the usual identification of these sites as sacrificial arenas, the evidence is simply not persuasive enough. Given the separation of the precincts from other burial grounds, the identical, careful treatment of human and animal remains, and the votive nature of the inscriptions upon the stelae, the balance of probability clearly favours a sacrificial understanding of these remarkable sites.

Despite the essential weaknesses of the revisionists' case for the non-sacrificial interpretation of the Phoenician-Punic precincts, their arguments remain valuable, for they seriously challenge the conventional way in which the ancient literary material has been employed within this debate. Mazza's persuasive argument demonstrating the basic unreliability of the Greek and Roman accounts of Phoenician child sacrifice is illustrative of this important contribution. As he comments, "It is ... likely that in the few descriptions which have come down to us, echoes of legends and gossip, combined with negative propaganda aims, induced the writers to give such a dark picture of the cultural phenomena of a world that was felt to be completely foreign".[183] In emphasizing the tendentious nature of the classical and patristic works describing the Phoenician and Punic cultures, the revisionists urge a more cautious approach to the ancient literature, mirroring the increasingly careful way in which biblical texts are used to illuminate the cultural histories of Israel and Judah.[184]

---

183 Mazza, "Phoenicians", 650.

184 It is interesting to note that many scholars supporting a non-sacrificial interpretation of the Phoenician-Punic precincts are Tunisian or French. In seeking to defend the Phoenician-Punic people against the charge of child sacrifice, and the "moral" implications such a charge carries with it, are they echoing, in some way, the biblical authors, who similarly sought to defend their "ancestors" against the charge of child sacrifice?

5.3 *Mōlek* as a Sacrificial Term in the Hebrew Bible

Having thus established that Punic *mlk* is a term for a type of sacrifice
directly related to a cult in which children and substitution animals were
burned as sacrifices to Baʿal Ḥammon and Tanit, the discussion will now turn
to examining the extent to which the Punic *mlk* cult can shed light on the
biblical term מֹלֶךְ.

Eissfeldt's monograph has remained highly controversial, not as a
reflection of his interpretation of the Punic term *mlk*, which, in general terms
has now been widely adopted, but because of his related assertion that מֹלֶךְ
and Punic *mlk* are cognate sacrificial terms. The most threatening challenge
to Eissfeldt's theory was articulated by Heider, who argued that a lack of
archaeological evidence for the *mlk* practice in mainland Phoenicia suggested
that the practice, and its terminology, was an intra-Punic development
unrelated to the practice described in the Hebrew Bible.[185] Yet as has been
demonstrated in the preceding section, this challenge has been repelled by
increased archaeological evidence from Tyre itself. Other scholars have
found Eissfeldt's interpretation of מֹלֶךְ appealing yet problematic. Many
attempt to solve the problem by suggesting that *mlk* as "sacrificial offering"
is a Phoenician loanword lying behind the biblical references, but a loanword
which has been misunderstood by the Hebrew Bible.[186] This view is
appealing because it allows the understanding of *mlk* as a technical sacrificial
term to stand, thereby preventing the contextual parallel between Punic *mlk*
and biblical מֹלֶךְ from becoming a mere coincidence, whilst maintaining the
traditional rendering of מֹלֶךְ as a divine name. However, Day rejects this
view, arguing that it is inconceivable that *all* the biblical writers would have
mistaken a sacrificial term for the name of a god, for, "It is surely more
scientific to accept the testimony of these first-hand sources, whose authors
were well placed to know the facts, than to suppose that we are in a position
to overturn this evidence on the basis of Punic texts written in a different part
of the world".[187] Yet Day undermines his own argument in his understanding
of the biblical material as a reliable witness to the historical reality of
Judahite deity-worship. Though he is correct in stating that it is improbable
that all the biblical writers have misunderstood the sacrificial term *mlk*, is it
not possible that the Hebrew Bible has *deliberately* misrepresented the term?

---

185 Heider, *Molek*, 196-203, 401.
186 E.g., De Vaux, *Studies*, 87-90; Cazelles, "Molok", 1337-1346.
187 Day, *Molech*, 13.

Given the essential weakness of the non-biblical evidence for an ancient Near Eastern god of child sacrifice named "Molek" or "Melek", the strongest support for this position ultimately remains the evidence of the Hebrew Bible itself. As has been seen, the Masoretic text clearly *intends* to present the term vocalized מֹלֶךְ as the name or title of a deity distinct from YHWH. However, Eissfeldt's hypothesis that מֹלֶךְ is a common noun cognate with Punic *mlk* clearly challenges this interpretation of the biblical term. Defenders of a god "Molek" are thus heavily dependent upon the persuasiveness of their arguments in support of the MT, which would thereby invalidate the interpretation of מֹלֶךְ as a sacrificial term. The strongest arguments in favour of מֹלֶךְ as the proper name or title of a god may be summarized as follows:

First, verbs associated with the practice indicate that מֹלֶךְ is regarded as a god and not as a type of sacrifice: הֶעֱבִיר ("pass over", "offer up"), נתן ("give"), and שרף ("burn"), followed by the particle ל, function as a *nota dativi*, thereby indicating that the noun or pronominal suffix with ל is the recipient of the sacrifice, not the sacrifice itself.[188] Supporting this further is the phraseology of Lev. 20:5 which refers to idolatrous Israelites "whoring after" the "Molek" (לזנות אהרי המלך), a biblical phrase which consistently finds as its object a deity or supernatural object.[189]

Second, the occurrence of מֹלֶךְ with the definite article in Lev. 20:5 (הַמֹּלֶךְ) supports the Masoretic vocalization of the article with the preposition ל in all six other accepted occurrences of מֹלֶךְ,[190] thereby indicating at least that the term was understood as a title or epithet of a foreign god, which may indeed serve as a proper divine name, as perhaps in the case of Baʿal in the Hebrew Bible.[191] Finally, the Septuagint renders the term either as a common noun, ἄρχων, "ruler" (Lev. 18:21; 20:2-5), or βασιλευς, "king" (3 Kgdms 11:5)[192] or as a proper name, Μολοχ, "Moloch" (4 Kgdms 23:10; Jer. 39:35),[193] thereby suggesting that the Greek translator understood מלך in

---

188 Day, *Molech*, 12; Buber, *Kingship of God*, 173.
189 E.g., Exod. 34:15-16; Lev. 17:7; Deut. 31:16; Judg. 2:17; 8:33; 1 Chr. 5:25; 2 Chr. 21:11, 13; Ps. 106:39; Isa. 57:3; Jer. 3:1, 2, 6, 8-9; Ezek. 6:9; 16:15, 16, 17, 26, 28, 30, 31, 33, 34, 35, 41; 20:30; 23:3, 5, 19, 43, 44; Hos. 1:2; 2:7; 4:12 (ET 5); 5:3; Mic. 1:7; Heider, "Molech", 583; Day, *Molech*, 10-11.
190 Interestingly, מֹלֶךְ in 1 Kgs 11:7, which is usually emended to מַלְכֹּם, "Milkom", is the only example of MT מֹלֶךְ to occur without the definite article.
191 Day, *Molech*, 46; Heider, "Molech", 583.
192 MT 1 Kgs 11:7.
193 MT 2 Kgs 23:10; Jer. 32:35.

these texts not as a sacrificial term, but as the name or title of a deity.[194] Upon closer examination, however, these arguments are not compelling.

Eissfeldt, followed by Mosca, argues that within the biblical phrases העביר למלך and נתן למלך, the particle ל can introduce the result of a verb which describes the creation, appointment or transformation of something.[195] Thus the sacrificial victim itself may be introduced by the particle ל, rendering the phrases העביר למלך and נתן למלך as "pass over as a *mlk*-sacrifice" and "donate as a *mlk*-sacrifice", respectively. In support of this, Mosca offers for comparison Ezek. 43:19, "You shall give (נתתה) to the Levitical priests ... a bull for a sin-offering (לחטאת)", and 1 Chr. 21:23, in which Ornan tells David, "I give (נתתי) the oxen for the burnt offerings (לעלות), the threshing sledges for the wood (לעצים), and the wheat for the cereal offering (למנחה)".[196] Müller[197] offers further support in highlighting Ezek. 23:37 as an example in which the two functions of ל (as a dative particle and as ל-*essentiae*) are illustrated within the same verse: העבירו להם לאכלה.

Moreover, the use of the verb זנה, "whore (after)" in Lev. 20:5 need not demand the interpretation of מלך as the name or title of a deity. The conventional insistence that biblical Israelites cannot whore after a sacrifice is essentially based upon a misunderstanding of Eissfeldt's proposal, as several commentators have observed. Eissfeldt's critics argue that although Israelites may whore after gods, spirits and ghosts, to whore after a sacrifice would be "quite different and totally unparalleled".[198] However, with the support of the example of the אפוד (Judg. 8:27) Eissfeldt argues that the term מלך may be seen as the object after which Israelites whore.[199] In drawing this comparison, Eissfeldt is arguing that the term מלך in Lev. 20:5 refers to the physical object to be sacrificed, thereby proposing that מלך could refer to the *act* of sacrifice or to the sacrificial *victim* itself. Yet Eissfeldt's critics appear

---

194 Day, *Molech*, 12; Heider, "Molech", 581.

195 Eissfeldt, *Molk*, 38-40, Mosca, "Child Sacrifice", 157; *GKC* §119t.

196 Other examples include Gen. 17:20; 48:4; 2 Chr. 8:9. Mosca, "Child Sacrifice", 157-158.

197 Müller, "*mōlek*", 385; cf. Day, *Molech*, 12.

198 Day, *Molech*, 11; cf. E. Dhorme, Review of *Molk als Opferbegriff*, by O. Eissfeldt, *RHR* 113 (1936), 277; Buber, *Kingship of God*, 179; Weinfeld, "Worship of Molech", 136; W. Kornfeld, "Der Moloch: Eine Untersuchung zur Theorie O. Eissfeldts", *WZKM* 51 (1952), 287-313 (301); K. Dronkert, *De Molochdienst in het Oude Testament* (Leiden: Brill), 1953, 61-62; De Vaux, *Studies*, 89.

199 Eissfeldt, *Molk*, 39.

to view his מלך only in an abstract sense as a practice, rather than as referring to the sacrificial victim also.[200] But Mosca supports Eissfeldt's assertion by emphasizing the function of similar Hebrew terms such as זבח and עלה, terms which refer not simply to the ritual itself, but rather denote primarily "the concrete objects—cattle, sheep, and goats—which were sacrificed".[201] As such, Lev. 1:2-9 supports this distinction in the description of ritual slaughter in which the sacrificial animal itself is the עלה (vv. 4, 6). Thus as Mosca comments, "the same would be true of מלך, if we follow Eissfeldt in taking it as a sacrificial term; it must refer, strictly speaking, not to the 'practice', but to the all-too-concrete victim—an 'object'".[202] Consequently, the phraseology associated with the biblical מלך does not necessarily demand the interpretation of this term as the name or title of a deity. However, it remains that Lev. 20:5 would offer the only biblical example of the outlawing of whoring after a type of sacrificial object. The discussion will return to this problematic verse in due course.[203]

The Masoretic vocalization of the definite article in למלך has been cited in support of those continuing to interpret מלך as the name or epithet of a god. But Eissfeldt simultaneously strengthens the parallel between מלך and עלה, and weakens the case for מלך as a title of a foreign god by arguing that the definite article is secondary. Indeed, it is only in Lev. 20:5 that the term מלך appears with the definite article written consonantally (המלך). All six other occurrences of the word are preceded by the particle ל, so that the consonantal text is "neutral", and could be read למלך, "as a *mlk*-offering", just as לעלה reads "as a burnt offering" (Gen. 22:2) and לאשם reads "as a guilt offering" (Lev. 5:18).[204] Moreover, the absence of the definite article in the Greek rendering of Lev. 18:21; 20:2-4 supports further the possibility that in the Hebrew consonantal text the vocalization of ל in למלך reflected the indefinite.[205] It must be noted, however, that the Septuagint also offers

---

200 Mosca ("Child Sacrifice", 155) suggests that Eissfeldt's terminology has probably contributed unintentionally to this misunderstanding in his translation of Punic *mlk* and Hebrew מלך as "Gelübde, Versprechen" (Eissfeldt, *Molk*, 37).
201 Mosca, "Child Sacrifice", 155.
202 Mosca, "Child Sacrifice", 156 (for further examples, see 155-157).
203 For further discussion of Lev. 20:5, see below.
204 Eissfeldt, *Molk*, 36-38; Mosca, "Child Sacrifice", 153; Müller, "*mōlek*", 385.
205 Heider, following Mosca and Eissfeldt, concedes that the Greek translator of Leviticus is reasonably reliable in reflecting the presence or absence of the definite article in its Hebrew *Vorlage*; Heider, *Molek*, 235; Mosca, "Child Sacrifice, 153; Eissfeldt, *Molk*, 37, n.1.

evidence in favour of the traditionalists arguing for the retention of the definite article, for this grammatical feature does appear in the Greek rendering of מלך in 4 Kgdms 23:10 and Jer. 39:35.[206] However, these texts employ a different vocabulary than that utilized by the Greek translator of Leviticus, and will be treated separately below.

One final point about the presence or absence of the definite article remains: once again, the tricky text of Lev. 20:5 confuses matters further. Although המלך in Lev. 20:5 is rendered with the definite article in the Greek translation, it is actually found in the *plural* form τους ἄρχοντας, thereby undermining the witness of the Septuagint for both those arguing for the originality of the definite article, and hence the understanding of מלך as a divine title, and those contending that מלך is a sacrificial term, and thus that the definite article is secondary.[207] However, it should be noted that those defending מלך as the name or title of a deity readily point out that the presence or absence of the definite article in the original Hebrew has no real effect upon their case: a lack of the article renders the term מלך a proper name, whereas the presence of the article renders the term as a title, comparable to "the Ba'al" (הבעל) elsewhere in the Hebrew Bible.[208]

Eissfeldt was aware that the Greek translation of MT מֹלֶךְ as ἄρχων (Lev. 18:21; 20:2, 3, 4; plural ἄρχοντας in 20:5), Μολοχ (4 Kgdms 23:10) and the compounded Μολοχ βασιλει[209] (Jer. 39:35) implies that the translators did not interpret the Hebrew word as a sacrificial term.[210] However, the possibility that this was the original meaning of the term, lost or disguised by later scribes and translators, remains viable. For both Eissfeldt and Mosca, מֹלֶךְ is a sacrificial term cognate with Punic *m(o)lk*, thus the vocalization of מֹלֶךְ as original is essential to their arguments. The evidence of the Septuagint

---

206 MT 2 Kgs 23:10; Jer. 32:35.

207 It may be that this Greek plural is due simply to a reading of המלך with a dittography of מ in the following מקרב, as Eissfeldt himself suggested (*Molk*, 38, n. 1). For Mosca ("Child Sacrifice", 129-32, 249, n. 79.), this Greek plural form is support for his reconstruction of מֹלֶךְ as an original *qutl*-type noun cognate with Ugaritic, Phoenician and Punic *mulk*, "kingdom, kingship, royalty". He argues that this form has been exorcised from other texts of the Hebrew Bible, including Gen. 49:20 and Num. 23:21, both of which the Septuagint renders as the plural ἄρχοντες. If correct, this theory would eradicate the need to explain how a presumed Phoenician-Punic loanword might have entered biblical usage.

208 E.g. Heider, *Molek*, 235-236; see also Milgrom, *Leviticus 17–22*, 1557.

209 This conflate reading suggests an ambiguity in the Hebrew *Vorlage* of the Greek texts.

210 Eissfeldt, *Molk*, 40.

appears to support this: the fact that in 4 Kgdms 23:10 and Jer. 39:32 the Hebrew is transliterated Μολοχ is heavily suggestive that מלך in these texts was, if not originally, then from a very early point in transmission, vocalized מֹלֶךְ, rather than מֶלֶךְ or even as the divine names Malik[211] or Milkom.[212] Moreover, Eissfeldt argues that the Greek translation of מלך as ἄρχων "ruler", "official", instead of the expected βασιλευς, "king" also suggests an original מֹלֶךְ rather than מֶלֶךְ in the relevant Levitical texts.[213] These points thus cast sufficient doubt upon Geiger's theory,[214] adopted by Day,[215] that the vocalization of an original title מֶלֶךְ, "King" has been deliberately distorted and debased by the Masoretic substitution of the vowels of בֹּשֶׁת, "shame".[216] Indeed, in his thorough refutation of Geiger's hypothesis, Mosca[217] puts forward several detailed reasons to doubt further the originality of a reading מֶלֶךְ, not the least of which is the complexity of the dysphemism itself. Unlike other forms of dysphemism within the Hebrew Bible, Geiger's dysphemism is not easily categorized: it is neither "free", whereby an originally neutral term is replaced by a completely unrelated pejorative (for example, the substitution of אֹהֶל[ים] with שׁקץ in 1 Kgs 11:5 and תועבת in 2 Kgs 23:13), nor is it "associational", whereby the pejorative term is determined by the principle of paranomasia, whereby a similarity in sound has governed the selection of the pejorative term (such as the frequent

---

211 *Contra* G. del Olmo Lete, who argues that מֹלֶךְ was originally a reference to the god Malik; "Per vivencias cananeas (ugaríticas) en el culto fenicio—Il El culto '*mlk*'", *Semitica* 39 (1990), 67-76.

212 *Contra* J. Trebolle Barrera, "La transcripción *mlk* = *moloch*: Historia del texto e historia de la lengua", *Aula Orientalis* 5 (1987), 125-128; cf. J. Lust, "The Cult of Molek/Milchom: Some remarks on G.C. Heider's Monograph", *ETL* 63 (1987), 361-366.

213 Eissfeldt, *Molk*, 33-36; see also Mosca, "Child Sacrifice", 122-134.

214 Geiger, *Urschrift und Übersetzungen*, 299-308. Geiger suggests a further twenty-five instances of MT מֶלֶךְ are to be regarded as references to the idolatrous king-god, but were missed by the scribal correctors. Only one, Isa. 30:33, has been widely accepted. A second possible reference in Isa. 57:9 has also received considerable attention. These texts will be examined below. For discussions of other possible occurrences of מֹלֶךְ, see, for example, Heider, *Molek*, 278-282, 301-316, 332-336, 364-365; Day, *Molech*, 72-81; Berlin, *Zephaniah*, 75-77; H.G.M. Williamson, "Isaiah 8:21 and a new Inscription from Ekron", *BAIAS* 18 (2000), 51-55.

215 Day, *Molech*, 46.

216 Geiger's dysphemism theory has been seriously questioned by Tsevat, "Ishbosheth", 71-87; Eissfeldt, *Molk*, 33-36; Dronkert, *De Molochdienst*, 12-24; Mosca, "Child Sacrifice", 122-126; Heider, *Molek*, 224.

217 Mosca, "Child Sacrifice", 125-128.

replacement of בעל with בשת,[218] or the wordplay of אלוהים and אלילים in Lev. 19:4). Rather, Geiger's construction is a complicated combination of the consonants of an original מֶלֶךְ and the vowels of the pejorative בֹּשֶׁת. As the need for this discussion itself demonstrates, this complex construction is far too oblique to be effective in its presumed polemical purpose, for as Mosca comments:

> Since the primary function of dysphemism was to concretize a redactor's (or even an author's) loathing for idolatry, the ambiguity necessarily inherent in Geiger's hybrid would be self-defeating ... The theory that a form of מֹלֶךְ would immediately suggest to the reader or hearer the word בֹּשֶׁת rather than קֹדֶשׁ or even (אֹהֶל) is the product of a nineteenth century ingenuity, not of Massoretic or pre-Massoretic tendentiousness.[219]

Thus arguments for an original מֶלֶךְ fall flat, leaving only two possibilities remaining: that מֹלֶךְ is either the original vocalization of the name or epithet of a god of child sacrifice, or it is a sacrificial label which has gone unrecognized, albeit intentionally or unintentionally, by later redactors, scribes and translators of the consonantal Hebrew text.

Persuaded by Mosca's cogent arguments rejecting Geiger's dysphemism theory, Heider is clearly aware of the tight corner in which he finds himself.[220] Seeking to reconcile the use of ἀρχων in the Levitical texts with his exhaustive—but essentially unpersuasive—examination of ancient Near Eastern *m-l-k* titles and epithets, Heider argues that the Greek translators simply rendered one active participle meaning "Ruler" for another.[221] Though it is perhaps plausible that the Greek translators of Lev. 18:21; 20:2-4 may have read מֹלֵךְ,[222] Heider instead seeks to defend the Masoretic vocalization מֹלֶךְ and is thus forced to argue that מֹלֶךְ is a peculiar, frozen form of the *qal* active participle with *seghol* rather than *ṣere*, meaning "the Reigning One", a form which lost its case ending when the word was used as a proper name.[223] However, there are severe limitations to this hypothesis, not least of which is the unusual stress on the penultimate, rather than last, syllable of מֹלֶךְ, a problem Heider recognizes but leaves unsolved.[224]

---

218 E.g., Jer. 3:24 cf. 11:13; 2 Sam. 2:8; cf. 1 Chr. 8:33.
219 Mosca, "Child Sacrifice", 127.
220 Heider, *Molek*, 224.
221 Heider, *Molek*, 236.
222 Also noted by Milgrom, *Leviticus 17–22*, 1555; Day, *Molech*, 58.
223 Heider, *Molek*, 223-228; cf. G. O'Ceallaigh, "And *So* David did to *All the Cities*", 186.
224 Heider comments, "it is the better part of wisdom to admit our limitations here: we simply do not understand the principles of stress in Hebrew well enough to propose

Furthermore, Edelman has pointed out that Heider's philological reconstruction is not easily reconciled with the variant vocalizations of the divine titles he posits for Mari, Ugarit and Phoenicia.[225]

The case for מֹלֶךְ as a divine name or title is thus weakened, but the evidence of the Septuagint nevertheless suggests that the Hebrew term was *understood* to be the name or title of a deity. However, as has been seen, this Greek evidence is itself inconsistent, rendering MT מֹלֶךְ in four different ways: ἄρχων (Lev. 18:21; 20:2, 3, 4), ἄρχοντας (Lev. 20:5), βασιλεῖ (3 Kgdms 11:7[33]), Μολοχ (4 Kgdms 23:10) and the compound Μολοχ βασιλεῖ (Jer. 39:35). Moreover, the Greek texts find reference to Μολοχ where the MT does not: in Amos 5:26 (the Greek manuscripts are unanimous in this reading; cf. MT מלככם, "your king"); and in Zeph. 1:5 (the main Greek manuscripts read βασιλευς but others have Μολοχ or Μελχομ; cf. MT מלכם, "their king").[226] Indeed, among the Greek manuscripts, Μολοχ often appears as one of many variants for Μελχομ, thereby indicating that the Greek translators themselves are clearly confused as to who or what מֹלֶךְ is.[227]

As has been seen, this confusion is also present within the MT. 1 Kgs 11:7 describes מֹלֶךְ as "the abomination of the Ammonites", but is most probably to be emended as a reference to Milkom. Jer. 32:35 claims that the ritual is performed at the cult places of Baʿal, yet the offerings are made to "Molek". This contradicts 19:5, in which the sacrifices are made at the cult places of Baʿal for Baʿal, which in its turn conflicts with the account in 7:31, which labels the cult place תפה, but does not name the recipient deity. Furthermore, in Leviticus, the מֹלֶךְ ritual appears to be located in YHWH's sanctuary (Lev. 20:3). Only one biblical מֹלֶךְ text contains all of those elements essential for

---

reliable reconstructions of pre-Masoretic developments" (*Molek*, 227). Yet it remains that Heider's frozen participial form is problematic, as others have also commented (Day, *Molech*, 58; Edelman, "Biblical *Molek*", 729; Olyan and Smith, Review, 274).

225 Edelman, "Biblical *Molek*", 728-729; see also Ackerman, *Under Every Green Tree,* 131-132.

226 The vocalization Μολοχ may support Eissfeldt's argument that MT מֹלֶךְ is cognate with Punic *m(o)lk*, but further undermines Geiger's thesis that the term was originally vocalized מֶלֶךְ. Moreover, as Smelik ("Moloch, Molekh", 133 n. 3) suggests, the occurrence of Μολοχ also precludes the equation of מֹלֶךְ with the Akkadian god Malik(u), and testifies against Edelman's suggestion that the term is related to a supposed cult of Baʿal-Melek (see also Berlin, *Zephaniah*, 75-77).

227 Cf. J. Lust, "Molek and ΑΡΧΩΝ", in E. Lipiński (ed.), *Phoenicia and the Bible: Proceedings of the Conference held at the University of Leuven on the 15th and 16th of March 1990* (Studia Phoenicia 11; Leuven: Peeters, 1991), 193-208; Trebolle Barrera, "La transcripción *mlk*", 125-128.

some sense of coherence: 2 Kgs 23:10 refers to מֹלֶךְ, locates the ritual at the תֹּפֶת, in the Valley of Ben Hinnom, and speaks of male and female children being passed over in fire (הַעֲבִיר בָּאֵשׁ).

It is thus clear that both the Masoretic and Septuagint texts are comparably confused in their understanding of מֹלֶךְ. On reflection, this is hardly surprising given that there are only seven widely accepted occurrences of מֹלֶךְ in the MT, occurrences which are not only far outweighed by texts which clearly speak of the practice without reference to מֹלֶךְ at all, but are also heavily concentrated in Leviticus. Although the Masoretic and Septuagint texts portray מֹלֶךְ as the name or title of a deity, the confusion surrounding this term is sufficiently pervasive to merit the suggestion that the original meaning of מֹלֶךְ is either unknown, or was purposefully forgotten, by later Hebrew scribes and the Greek translators.

Yet when this confusion is viewed in the light of the preceding discussion, it seems reasonable to suggest that מלך in Lev. 18:21; 20:2-5; 2 Kgs 23:10 and Jer. 32:35 may indeed originally have been a sacrificial term, as Eissfeldt suggested in 1935. The sheer peculiarity of the references in Leviticus themselves further supports this suggestion: not only are five of the seven occurrences of מֹלֶךְ found clustered in Lev. 18 and 20, but if מֹלֶךְ is interpreted as the name of a deity, these concentrated references would be the only instances in which a specific god is named and outlawed within the legal collections of the Hebrew Bible.[228] Moreover, this god would be restricted in his biblical appearances to sacrificial contexts alone.[229] Furthermore, the similarity between the Punic term *mlk* and Hebrew מֹלֶךְ, combined with their shared context of child sacrifice by fire is, as Smelik comments, "too striking to be thought merely coincidental".[230]

In view of the evidence evaluated here, it is therefore far more plausible to interpret מֹלֶךְ as a sacrificial term, subsequently misunderstood within later textual traditions. This misunderstanding is probably best regarded as resulting from the deliberate distortion of the sacrificial label מֹלֶךְ into the name of a supposedly foreign god, "Molek". Smelik, followed by Römer, argues that this transformation was effected by scribes concerned with the sanctity of YHWH, who inserted the definite article into the sacrificial

---

228 See also Edelman ("Biblical *Molek*", 730), who additionally notes that even Deuteronomy, which contains two condemnations of the practice elsewhere associated with מֹלֶךְ (12:31; 18:10), does not name the recipient deity (nor any foreign god at all).
229 See also Müller, "*mōlek*", 385.
230 Smelik, "Moloch, Molekh", 138.

expression (thus לַמֹּלֶךְ).[231] This suggestion certainly seems plausible in view of the preceding discussions of both the ideological dynamics of the biblical presentation of child sacrifice and the persuasive arguments for the correlation of מֹלֶךְ and Punic *mlk* offered by Eissfeldt and Mosca. Yet the occurrence of מֹלֶךְ in Lev. 20:5 remains problematic, for, as has been seen, the term has the definite article written consonantally, which challenges the reinterpretation of למלך elsewhere as "as a *mlk*-offering". Moreover, the expression לזנות אחרי המלך continues to be highlighted by defenders of a god "Molek", who in accepting Eissfeldt's compelling example of the אפוד (Judg. 8:27), continue to argue that this phrase is associated with worshipping foreign deities, and, by extension, seeking oracles (Day)[232] or employing supernatural objects (Heider),[233] categories into which an assumed "*mlk*-offering" could not be placed.[234] Thus Lev. 20:5 offers a serious challenge to the interpretation of מלך as a term for a type of sacrifice. This may be addressed in one or more of the following ways:

The first possibility is to dismiss Lev. 20:5 altogether. Smelik argues that the phrase לזנות אחרי המלך is a deliberate and later insertion by recalling Noth's suggestion that these words are a secondary addition to an already composite passage,[235] and citing the opinion of Lipiński, who similarly argues that this phrase is a later gloss.[236] However, there is a certain weakness in arguing for an ideological distortion of a sacrificial term into the

---

231 Smelik, "Moloch, Molekh", 140 n. 40; Römer, "Le sacrifice humain", 17-26; see also Gerstenberger, *Leviticus*, 253-254, 292-294.

232 In order to accommodate Eissfeldt's example of the ephod, whilst at the same time maintaining that Israelites could not "whore after" a *mlk* offering, Day (*Molech*, 10-11) argues that it is the ephod's function as an *oracular* object which enables it to be directly associated with the expression לזנות אחרי.

233 Heider, *Molek*, 243-245.

234 However, note that Num. 15:39 appears to offer an example of a biblical text in which it is neither gods and spirits, nor oracular and supernatural objects, that are associated with the metaphorical language of "whoring"; rather, it is either one's "eyes" and "hearts", or a "tassel" which seems to be the object after which Israelites are not to whore; cf. Mosca, "Child Sacrifice", 156-157.

235 M. Noth, *Leviticus: A Commentary* (trans. J.E. Anderson; OTL; London: SCM Press, 1965), 148-149; see also N.H. Snaith, *Leviticus and Numbers* (CB; London: Thomas Nelson, 1967), 137.

236 Lipiński, "*nātan*", 130; "Sacrifices d'enfants", 153 n. 10; see also K. Elliger, *Leviticus* (HAT 4; Tübingen: J.C.B. Mohr, 1966), 269.

name of a deity by simply rubbishing the textual integrity of the challenging verse.[237]

Second, the phrase לזנות אחרי המלך in this verse can be identified as the "first misunderstanding of the sacrificial term as the designation of a deity",[238] whether unintentionally (perhaps encouraged by the use of זנה in the following verse),[239] or intentionally (whereby the *mlk* practice is subject to a deliberate, polemical reinterpretation in the presentation of idolatrous Israelites "whoring after the Molek").[240] Indeed, though admittedly speculative, it is possible that the presentation of the term מלך in Lev. 20:5 as the name or title of a god reflects in part a potential misinterpretation of 18:21. The expression להעביר למלך in this latter verse contains the only example of the term העביר used to describe the *mlk* practice in Leviticus. With the exception of 20:5, all other references to the *mlk* ritual (20:2-4) employ only the verb נתן. Some of the Versions seem not to have understood this usage of להעביר, for the Samaritan Pentateuch has instead להעביד, "to serve", a reading supported by the Septuagint's λατρευειν, "to worship". These interesting variants thus suggest that מלך in 18:21 may have been misunderstood by later scribes and translators not as a type of offering which is "passed over", but as the name or title of a deity who is "served" or "worshipped" by idolatrous Israelites. It is not beyond the bounds of reason to suppose therefore that the expression להעביר למלך in 18:21 may have been similarly misunderstood by the writer of 20:5, who assumed that מלך was the name or title of a deity (after whom Israelites could whore), and not a type of sacrifice. All of these ideas certainly seem plausible, though it must be conceded that they are potentially undermined by those who would argue

---

237 Interestingly, however, the location of Lev. 20:2-5 within a chapter dealing with illicit sexual practices may cast into doubt the reliability of the context of this passage. The formulaic phrase introducing verses 2-5 ("Any man, be he Israelite or an alien residing in Israel, who ...") is not found anywhere else in the chapter, yet similar formulae do occur in chapter 17, a chapter concerned not with sexual behaviour, but sacrifice. It is possible that the laws concerning מֹלֶךְ have been displaced from their original setting as sacrificial regulations, in ch. 17. See further below, 6.1, plus Mosca, "Child Sacrifice", 248, n. 71; *contra* J.E. Hartley and T. Dwyer, "An Investigation into the Location of the Laws on Offerings to Molek in the Book of Leviticus", in J.E. Coleson and V.H. Matthews (eds.), *"Go to the Land I will Show You": Studies in Honor of Dwight W. Young* (Winona Lake: Eisenbrauns, 1996), 81-93.

238 Müller, "*mōlek*", 385; "Malik", 539; Gerstenberger, *Leviticus*, 253-254, 292-294.

239 Müller, "*mōlek*", 385;

240 Olyan and Smith, Review, 274; Gerstenberger, *Leviticus*, 292.

for the integrity of Lev. 18 and 20 and the coherence of the מֹלֶךְ laws in these chapters.[241]

Third, the occurrence of מלך with the definite article written consonantally in 20:5 need not weaken the case for למלך elsewhere as originally meaning "as a *mlk*-offering". Rather, given that the term מלך is attested in the preceding verses (vv. 2-4), and that it is understood as referring to the sacrificial victim itself, the form המלך may be understood as a collective in the singular,[242] particularly as it follows the attestations of מלך three times in the preceding verses (vv. 2-4). Thus the phrase לזנות אחרי המלך could be understood to refer to whoring after "*mlk*-offerings".

Finally, as Eissfeldt and others have noted,[243] the language of whoring in 20:5 appears to parallel that employed in the following verse, in which whoring after "ancestral ghosts" (אבת) and "Knowers" (ידענים) is prohibited (v. 6).[244] Though in itself this correlation of vocabulary in the two verses can offer only a limited explanation for the expression לזנות אחרי המלך in verse 5, closer consideration reveals a more significant reason as to why the *mlk*-offering has come to be regarded as something after which idolatrous Israelites may whore. Three texts alluding to the *mlk* sacrifice associate the ritual with various divinatory practices: Deut. 18:10-11; 2 Kgs 17:17; and 21:6 (cf. 2 Chr. 33:6).[245] Furthermore, two of these texts employ the same terminology in referring to these divinatory practices as that found in Lev. 20:6: אוב and ידעני. Thus it may be that the strong association of the *mlk* ritual with divinatory practices in Lev. 20:5-6; Deut. 18:10-11; 2 Kgs 17:17; 21:6 (2 Chr. 33:6) has influenced the presentation of the *mlk* sacrifice in Lev. 20:5—because idolatrous Israelites are forbidden from whoring after "ancestral ghosts" and "Knowers" (v. 6), so too they are forbidden from whoring after the *mlk*-offering with which these and other divinatory practices are so closely associated. Moreover, the prevous chapter has demonstrated the way in which references and allusions to child sacrifice are often accompanied by the language of metaphorical whoring.[246] It is not unreasonable to propose that the biblical association of child sacrifice with

---

241 Cf. Hartley and Dwyer, "Investigation", 81-93.
242 *GKC* §126m; see also §126d, i, l; Mosca, "Child Sacrifice", 154; Heider, *Molek*, 242.
243 Eissfeldt, *Molk*, 38-39; Müller, "*mōlek̲*", 385; cf. Hartley and Dwyer, "Investigation", 89-90.
244 On these labels, see above, 23-24, nn. 35, 36.
245 Cf. Heider, *Molek*, 383-400; Hartley and Dwyer, "Investigation", 90.
246 See especially 4.1.2.

metaphorical whoring may have encouraged the correlation of this language specifically with the term מֹלֶךְ in this verse.

In the light of these possibilities, it would appear that Lev. 20:5 need not preclude the interpretation of מֹלֶךְ as a sacrificial term, as Eissfeldt proposed. Thus in the Hebrew Bible, מֹלֶךְ probably referred originally to the sacrificial victim itself, the "*mlk*-offering", and not to a deity. However, מֹלֶךְ appears to have been secondarily distorted into the name of a foreign god. Given the evidence of the Greek texts, which variously render MT מֹלֶךְ as ἄρχων, ἄρχοντας, βασιλει, Μολοχ, and Μολοχ βασιλει, this transformation probably occurred in the late Persian period.[247] In this way, early scribes sought to distance their god from what had come to be regarded as an abominable practice by distorting the biblical term מֹלֶךְ into the proper name of a foreign god.[248] This distortion serves a very specific purpose: it disguises the fact that the biblical texts describing or alluding to the fiery sacrifice consistently associate YHWH with the practice.

Indeed, in returning to the biblical texts in the light of this discussion, it would appear that some of those seven verses referring מֹלֶךְ actually do associate YHWH with the ritual: in rejecting the practice, Lev. 18:21 describes it as a profanation of YHWH's name; similarly, 20:3 refers to the sacrifice as defilement of YHWH's sanctuary, as well as a profanantion of his name. More problematic, however, are the occurrences of מֹלֶךְ in Jeremiah. Yet a closer examination of the texts may suggest otherwise. The term מֹלֶךְ occurs only once in Jeremiah (32:35), although there are two other passages in this book referring to child sacrifice which employ exactly the same language as that associated with the מֹלֶךְ ritual, 7:31 and 19:5. As has been seen, a peculiar feature of all three texts is the insistence that YHWH did not command the sacrifices. This appears to reflect and to reject a perception that the children were sacrificed to YHWH, as opposed to any other deity.[249] Certainly, this

---

247 Smelik, "Moloch, Molekh", 141; Römer, "Le sacrifice humain", 23.

248 In support of the thesis that scribes would intentionally alter the texts in order to protect YHWH's reputation, Smelik cites the example of 1 Chr. 21, in which the account of the census known from 2 Sam. 24 is adapted by the Chronicler, who replaces the name of YHWH with the name Satan. Smelik, "Moloch, Molekh", 140, n. 38. Some modern scholars also appear to be concerned with distancing "pure" *Yhwh*-worship from such an unpleasant ritual, as discussed in 6.2.

249 So Smelik, "Moloch, Molekh", 139; Levenson, *Beloved Son*, 4-5; Day, *Molech*, 68; Olyan, *Asherah*, 13. In contrast, Edelman ("Biblical *Molek*", 730-731) proposes that Jer. 2:32; 3:24; 19:5; 32:35 indicate that the divine recipient of the sacrifices was a form of Baʿal ("Baʿal Melek" or "Baʿal Molek"). See above, 160, n. 82.

resonates with the explicit claim in Ezek. 20:25-26 that YHWH commanded that the firstborn be sacrificed to him, and recalls the association of child sacrifice with YHWH's sanctuary in Lev. 20:3. Yet this insistence that YHWH did not command the sacrifices is particularly curious in view of the fact that in 32:35, the divine recipient is named as "Molek" and in 19:5, the recipient is Ba'al. This would suggest that the strong disassociation of YHWH from child sacrifice is unwarranted. And yet it is a characteristic feature of all three texts. The material in the book of Jeremiah thus indicates a degree of confusion, yet closer examination reveals that this confusion may be a secondary feature. As has been seen, in 19:5 it is stated that the children are sacrificed to Ba'al, rather than "Molek", claiming that the people of Judah have "gone on building the high places of Ba'al to burn their sons in the fire as burnt offerings to Ba'al, which I did not command or decree, nor did it enter my mind" (19:5). Significantly, the Septuagint does not reflect this reference to Ba'al as the recipient of the offerings. Moreover, in 7:31, which is almost a word-for-word parallel to both 19:5 and 32:35, the reference to Ba'al is similarly absent. Therefore it may be that the designation of Ba'al as the recipient of the sacrifices in 19:5 is a later scribal gloss, encouraged both by the immediately preceding reference to the *bamoth* of Ba'al, and by a theological desire to distance YHWH from the practice. If this is the case, 19:5 would originally have been even more closely aligned with 7:31, in which the divine recipient of the sacrificed children is not named, associating YHWH alone with the practice, prompting the insistence that he did not command such sacrifices. This in turn throws a different light upon the claim in 32:35 that the sacrifices are offered to "Molek". In view of the preceding discussion, the term מֹלֶךְ in this text must not be taken as a divine name, but rather as a type of sacrifice. As such, 32:35 similarly speaks of child sacrifice, but associates only YHWH with the ritual in the denial that YHWH ever demanded the offerings.

Though MT Isa. 57:9 does not include the term מֹלֶךְ, it is nevertheless regarded as an important text, for as has been seen, מֶלֶךְ occurs here, and it is thus widely cited as offering decisive evidence on all sides within the so-called "Molek" debate. As such, this verse, and the poem in which it occurs, merits further attention here. In the previous chapter, it was argued that Isa. 57:3-13 portrays child sacrifice not as a ritual dedicated to a foreign god, but as a practice carried out by YHWH-worshippers. Indeed, the preceding examination of the *mlk* ritual of the Phoenician and Punic worlds throws new light onto this biblical poem, for it appears to exhibit imagery reminiscent of that identified as consistently characteristic of the Phoenician-Punic cult of child sacrifice. The poem reads:

3   But you, come here,
           sons of a sorceress,
           seed of an adulterer and a whore![250]
4   At whom do you jeer?
           At whom do you widen the mouth,
           lengthen the tongue?
           Is it not you[251]—offspring of transgression, seed of deceit?
5   You who warm yourselves among the (great) trees[252]
           under every green tree;
           slaughtering children in the wadis,
           under the clefts of the rocks.
6   With the dead[253] of the wadi is your portion,
           they, indeed they are your lot;
           even to them you have poured out a drink offering,
           you have offered up a grain offering.
           Should I be comforted by these things?[254]
7   Upon a high and lofty mountain
           you have made your grave;[255]
           there you have gone up to offer sacrifice.
8   Behind the door and doorpost
           you have set your memorial monument;[256]

---

250 On this problematic verse, see above, 172-174.
251 הלוא־אתם seeks to answer the rhetorical question posed by the verse (so Oswalt, *Isaiah*,
    472, n. 4; *GKC* §150e).
252 See above, 175, n. 139.
253 See above, 170, n. 120.
254 העל אלה אנחם is possibly transposed, perhaps from the end of v. 5 (so, for example,
    Blenkinsopp, *Isaiah 56–66*, 152), or perhaps from the end of verse 7 (so, for example,
    BHS).
255 Though משכב is usually translated "bed", its alternative rendering "grave", "tomb", is
    preferable here, as it is in 57:1-2; Ezek. 32:25; 2 Chr. 16:14; cf. *DCH*, vol. 5, 526; *BDB*,
    1012; Lewis, *Cult of the Dead*, 149-150). משכב, "grave", is well-attested in North-West
    Semitic inscriptions (*DNWSI*, vol. 2, 701), most intriguing of which is its occurrence in
    the Deir ʿAllā texts, which have a special bearing upon this discussion (see below, 5.4).
    Ackerman ("Sacred Sex", 39, 42) follows Hanson (*Dawn of Apocalyptic*, 199-200) in
    highlighting the deliberate wordplay on משכב (which Hanson renders "bed") and משכן,
    "shrine", emphasizing the expressly cultic nature of the practice described. For
    Ackerman, the meaning of משכב as both "bed" and "grave" serves well her argument
    for the interrelationship of fertility and death cults. However, the poem is entirely
    concerned with child sacrifice—not the variety of cults that Ackerman reads into the
    text.
256 זכרון, "memorial monument", is widely held to derive from זכר, "remember" (cf.
    LXX's μνηοσυνα); see also Num. 31:54; Josh. 4:7; Zech. 6:14. Many commentators
    render this word "phallic symbol" or "phallus" as a supposedly further reference to a
    fertility cult, or even temple prostitution, arguing for the deliberate pun on זכר, "male",

for a hundred times (?)[257] you displayed, went up to,
and enlarged your grave;
you cut (a pact?)[258] for yourself with them;
you loved their grave,
the Hand[259] you gazed (upon).

9   You lavished[260] (the) *mlk*-victim with oil,
you multiplied your perfumes,
you sent your envoys to a remote place,
you made them go down (even?) to Sheol.

10   On your many paths you grew weary,
(but) you did not say "It is hopeless";
you secured the life of your Hand
so therefore you did not grow weak.

11   Whom did you dread and fear,
that you lied to me?

---

so K. Koenen, "Sexuelle Zweideutigkeiten und Euphemismen in Jes 57,8", *BN* 44 (1988), 46-53; Ackerman, "Sacred Sex", 39; Westermann, *Isaiah 40–66*, 324; B. Schramm, *Opponents*, 132, n.1. However, "memorial monument" makes better sense of both the text and context.

257 MT מֵאֹתִי is extremely uncertain. Dahood ("Hebrew-Ugaritic Lexicography IV", *Bib* 47 [1966]: 403-419 [413]) suggests this is a denominative verb derived from מֵאָה, "do a hundred times". He is followed by Scullion, "Difficult Texts", 111; Ackerman, *Under Every Green Tree*, 104 (*contra* McKenzie, *Second Isaiah*, 156). Others render the MT, "away from me" (e.g., Oswalt, *Isaiah*, 473; Westermann, *Isaiah 40–66*, 323, n. a).

258 MT וַתִּכְרָת is either a third feminine singular or a second masculine singular of כרת, "cut (a pact)". But following Scullion ("Difficult Texts", 111-112) and Schramm (*Opponents*, 131 n. 2), one can read with 1QIsaᵃ the second feminine singular form וַתִּכְרוֹתִי. See further the discussion in Ackerman, *Under Every Green Tree*, 105 n. 12.

259 See further below, 257-259.

260 וַתָּשֻׁרִי is often translated "you journeyed" on the basis of שָׁרוֹתַיִךְ in Ezek. 27:25 and the supposed root שׁוּר (cf. Song 4:8). However, the meaning in both verses is equally uncertain (Scullion, "Difficult Texts", 113) and the only evidence that שׁוּר means "journey" or "travel" is Arab. *sāra*, "journey", "travel". Instead, G.R. Driver ("Difficult Words in the Hebrew Prophets", in H.H. Rowley [ed.], *Studies in Old Testament Prophecy* [Edinburgh: T&T Clark, 1950], 52-72) has highlighted an alleged Akkaddian term *šarāru*, "gleam", "shine", and Arab. *sarra* "rejoiced". Given that the LXX renders both וַתָּשֻׁרִי in Isa 57:8 and שָׁרוֹתַיִךְ in Ezek. 27:25 by a word derived from the root πληθ-, P. Wernberg-Møller ("Two Notes", *VT* 8 [1958], 305-308) argues for the Hebrew root שׁרה meaning "lavish", "multiply", related to Ug. *trt*, "abundance", "fertility" and Arab. *tarā* "be considerable", "multiply", which makes good sense of both Isa. 57:8 and Ezek. 25:27 (cited in Scullion, "Difficult Texts", 113). Thus far no consensus has been reached. Those defending the concept of a deity called "Molek" tend to adhere to the traditional rendering "you journeyed". Illustrative of this view is Day (*Molech*, 50-52), who argues that "you journeyed" is supported by דרך in v. 10 and the reference to descending to Sheol. Those reading מֹלֶךְ as a sacrificial term, "*mlk*-sacrifice", tend to follow Wernberg-Møller and supporters, as here.

You did not remember,
you did not fix it in your heart.
Did I not remain silent and avert my gaze[261]
and yet you did not fear me?
12   I, I will tell of your righteousness,
but your works will not benefit you.
13   When you cry out, let your gathered ones[262] deliver you;
the wind will carry them all off,
a breath will take them away.
But whoever seeks refuge in me will possess the land,
and will inherit my holy mountain.

It has already been established that the interpretation of this poem as an invective against outlawed fertility cults is mistaken, for the poem deals in its entirety with child sacrifice. But what is particularly striking about this poem is that it appears to refer to the *mlk* practice without recourse to the stereotypical language employed of the practice elsewhere in the Hebrew Bible. Instead, it uses language which may be taken as an allusion to the physical reality of the ritual, details reminiscent of the archaeological findings in both the Mediterranean and in Palestine. It must be emphasized that the poem's provenance and language is far too uncertain to allow any firm correlation with the Phoenician-Punic cult of child sacrifice; however, reading this poem within the context of the archaeology and iconography of the Phoenician-Punic *mlk* cult is certainly very striking.

Clearly, the most obvious allusion to the *mlk* practice occurs in verse 9, which portrays the *mlk*-victim (MT מֶלֶךְ) as one of many envoys, presumably other children, sent to the underworld. As has been seen, this verse is assigned a central position within all sides of the "Molek" debate: the traditionalists choose to emend MT מֶלֶךְ to מֹלֶךְ (as in Isa. 30:33), clearly interpreting the reference to Sheol as the habitat of a god "Molek".[263] Those following Eissfeldt's hypothesis, as here, tend to render מלך as "*mlk*-

---

261 Reading מַעְלָם for MT מֵעֹלָם.

262 קבוצים is a *hapax legomenon*, probably equivalent to Ugaritic *qbṣm*, which itself occurs in parallel with *rpm*, "shades of the dead" (Lewis, *Cults of the Dead*, 151-152; Ackerman, "Sacred Sex", 41; Blenkinsopp, *Isaiah 56–66*, 155). Heider (*Molek*, 124, 381) agrees that it is a reference to dead ancestors.

263 For Day (*Molech*, 50-52), the reference to מֶלֶךְ is an example of a reference to the Canaanite god that has not been subject to later dysphemism. Indeed, given the emphasis Day places upon this verse, it is easy to understand why he adheres so strongly to Geiger's problematic dysphemism hypothesis.

victim",[264] with the notable exception of Eissfeldt himself, who understands מֶלֶךְ here as a reference to the human, Babylonian king.[265] That מלך is best rendered *"mlk*-victim" suits the context admirably, for the verse appears to describe the anointing of the victim in readiness for burning. As Ackerman proposes, this verse may describe "the preparation of the sacrificed child's body for immolation and/or burial. To anoint and perfume corpses is, of course, standard burial practice in the ancient Near East ... Alternatively, it may be that the corpse is drenched in oil to make it burn better".[266] The preceding verse (8) also exhibits allusions to the *mlk* practice; this time the focus appears to be the burial precinct. The explicit reference to a memorial monument (זכרון) recalls the burial markers and stelae of the *mlk* rite. This recollection is heightened further by the monument's apparent location in a משכב, "grave",[267] a grave which is repeatedly visited and enlarged, details reminiscent of the archaeological evidence indicating that sacrificial precincts were often expanded to make room for new burials. The allusion to the *mlk* sacrifice continues through the verse, referring perhaps to a pact between worshipper and the gods recalling the vows recorded upon the inscribed Phoenician-Punic stelae.[268]

More certain is the explicit reference to the Hand (יד) in this verse and again in verse 10, which is here understood to refer directly to the common iconographical motif of the Phoenician-Punic *mlk* sacrifice, and extends the image of the memorial monument described in the first part of the verse. This new interpretation makes far more sense of the text. The majority of commentators understand this occurrence of יד as a euphemism or *double-entendre*, usually rendering the term as "phallus" or "phallic symbol" and the like, and thereby perpetuating the misinterpretation of the poem as an

---

264 Mosca, "Child Sacrifice", 234; Ackerman, "Sacred Sex", 40.

265 Eissfeldt, *Molk*, 45 n.1.

266 Ackerman, *Under Every Green Tree*, 108, n. 17; cf. L.E. Stager and S.R. Wolff, "Production and Commerce in Temple Courtyards: An Olive Press in the Sacred Precinct at Tel Dan", *BASOR* 243 (1981), 95-102 (97, 100, n. 3).

267 See also v. 7.

268 C.A. Kennedy seeks to render נחל in Isa. 57:5-6 as "(rock-cut) tomb" on the basis of archaeological evidence for post-exilic tombs in valleys surrounding Palestinian towns ("Isaiah 57:5-6: Tombs in the Rocks", *BASOR* 275 [1989]: 47-52). Though Kennedy's translation may cohere with the death imagery of the poem, it is ultimately unsuitable given that the overarching subject of the poem is not simply burial practices, but child sacrifice. A direct link with rock-cut tombs in the valleys with this practice is too tendentious for this study. Thus the translation of נחל as "wadi" is maintained.

extended "whore metaphor" or an attack upon a fertility cult.[269] However, given the context of child sacrifice, the centrality of the Hand motif within the iconography of the Phoenician-Punic *mlk* rite, and the fact that רגל is the more common biblical euphemism for phallus, it is far more suitable to understand יד here as a possible reference to the Hand symbol upon the aforementioned memorial monument. Indeed, יד meaning "phallus" is unparalleled within the Hebrew Bible.[270] Moreover, the use of יד for "memorial monument" is attested elsewhere in the Hebrew Bible, not least in the preceding oracle, in which יד in 56:5 is commonly rendered "monument" in the light of 1 Sam. 15:12; 2 Sam. 18:18 and 1 Chr. 18:3.[271] The discovery of a thirteenth century BCE stela with two upstretched hands depicted upon it in the so-called "Stele Temple" at Hazor is frequently cited as confirmation of יד as a designation for a funerary or memorial monument.[272] It is significant that upon this stela, the Crescent-Disc motif also occurs, presenting a striking parallel with the Phoenician-Punic burial stelae. Indeed, Yadin has noted the similarities between this monument and the Phoenician-Punic monuments in relation to the symbol-systems associated with Ba῾al Hammon,[273] whilst Mittmann and Brown have both drawn particular attention to the shared Hand and Crescent-Disc iconography exhibited by the stelae at Hazor and Phoenician-Punic sites.[274] The Hazor material also

---

269 E.g. Schramm, *Opponents*, 132 n. 1; Westermann, *Isaiah 40-66*, 323, n. c; Ackerman, "Sacred Sex", 39; *idem.*, *Under Every Green Tree*, 106 n. 14; M. Delcor, "Two Special Meanings of the Word *yd* in Biblical Hebrew", *JSS* 12 (1967), 230-240.

270 Isa. 57:8, 10 are the only biblical verses cited in *HALOT* (vol. 2, 387) in which יד may mean "phallus"; On Song 5:4 see M.H. Pope, *Song of Songs* (AB 7C; Garden City: Doubleday, 1977), 517-518.

271 *HALOT*, vol. 2, 388; *BDB*, 390. Bloch-Smith (*Burial Practices*, 113-114) accepts unquestioningly the supposed double-meaning of biblical יד as "hand" and "phallus", suggesting that it reflects the association of burial markers with fertility rites within ancestral death cults, for within the Hebrew Bible, burial markers are used for childless men and righteous individuals. If so, this would be reminiscent of the fertility functions of the *mlk* sacrifice in which burial markers came to be so prominent.

272 Y. Yadin, (ed.), *Hazor I* (Jerusalem: Magnes, 1958), 89, pl. xxviii-xxix; cf. K. Galling, "Erwägungen zum Stelenheiligtum von Hazor", *ZDPV* 75 (1959), 1-13; note also Scullion ("Difficult Texts", 106-107), who renders "inscribed stele".

273 Yadin, "Symbols", pl. 26; *idem.*, *Hazor: The Rediscovery of a Great Citadel of the Bible* (New York: Random House, 1975), 43-47.

274 S. Mittmann, "Die Grabinscrift des Sängers Uriahu", *ZDPV* 97 (1981), 139-152; *idem.*, "Das Symbol der Hand in der altorientalischen Ikonographie", R. Kieffer and J. Bergman (eds.), *La Main de Dieu/Die Hand Gottes* (Tübingen: Mohr, 1997), 19-47; Brown, *Child Sacrifice*, 134-137, 306, fig. 64:e; cf. Bisi, *Le stele puniche*, 27.

provides archaeological evidence for the existence of this iconography in Palestine (though admittedly it dates from the Late Bronze Age); evidence supported by the discovery in Phoenicia of several amulets in the form of ivory hands,[275] and the use of similar hand motifs within the symbol-systems of stamp and cylinder seals throughout the ancient Near East.[276] When the understanding of יד as memorial monument, and its more literal meaning "hand", is set alongside the allusion to the *mlk* ritual in verse 9 and the repeated grave imagery (vv. 7, 8; cf. v. 2) throughout a poem concerned with child sacrifice (vv. 5, 9), it is reasonable to suggest that this important term intentionally functions on two levels, referring to both a burial monument and the Hand motif depicted upon it. The phrase יד חזית, "the Hand you gazed (upon)", may thus be understood as a reference to the iconographical motif depicted upon sacrificial monuments.

The allusion to the *mlk* sacrifice may also be in view in verse 5. The poet addresses the practitioners of child sacrifice as "You who warm yourselves (הנחמים) among the (great) trees".[277] As observed in the previous chapter, most commentators are mistaken in reading any sexual connotation into הנחמים. Rather, the term refers to being or becoming warm or hot by means of fire, natural heat, or clothing.[278] It may be, therefore, that the poet is describing a scene in which worshippers are gathered around or near a fire. That this fire may be a sacrificial pyre is suggested by the second half of the verse, which accuses the people of slaughtering the children in the wadis, under the clefts of the rocks, and the allusions to the *mlk* practice discussed

---

275 Several small amulets in the form of bone hands were amongst the ashes found inside the burial urns at the Tyrian precinct, but these hands are in the form of a fist, with the thumb squeezed between the first and second fingers, perhaps symbolizing protection, good luck, or fertility; Seeden, "*Tophet* in Tyre?", 76.

276 See Mittmann, "Das Symbol der Hand", 34, fig.1, a-k. Mittmann has sought to relate the Hand motif known from Hazor and the Phoenician-Punic monuments with the large hand accompanying the Khirbet el-Qôm tomb inscription referring to *Yhwh* and Asherah from eighth century Judah ("Die Grabinschrift", 139-152; see also Wyatt, "Asherah", 103-104). However, this hand points downwards, not upwards. See the criticisms of Schroer, who argues that the hand at Khirbet el-Qôm does not represent the worshipper, but has an apotropaic function, serving to ward off evil (S. Schroer, "Zur Deutung unter der Grabinschrift von Chirbet el-Qôm", *UF* 15 (1984), 191-199; cf. Keel and Uehlinger, *Gods,* 237-240). Schroer is probably correct, but the hand's location within a context of death is certainly striking. See Smelik, *Writings*, 154-155.

277 On the term אלים see 175, n. 139.

278 See above, 174-175.

above.[279] If this interpretation is correct, this poem may thus describe the *mlk* sacrifice without employing the seemingly stereotypical language and terminology favoured by other biblical texts, such as באש העביר, נתן and חפה.

Having examined these biblical texts in the light of inscriptional, archaeological, and iconographic evidence, it is highly probable that memories of the *mlk* practice exist within the Hebrew Bible. The biblical texts themselves claim that children were sacrificed in Israel and Judah, but material evidence supporting this claim has yet to be found. However, sacrificial precincts dating from the ninth/eighth to the sixth/fifth centuries BCE have been discovered in Phoenicia and all along the Levantine coast, as far south as Tell el-Farʿah, near Beer-Sheba. This provides indirect archaeological evidence for the existence of the practice in Palestine, essentially locating it in the right place, at the right time. This undoubtedly strengthens Eissfeldt's argument that the biblical word מֹלֶךְ is a sacrificial term related to the Phoenician-Punic *mlk* sacrifice. The popular concept of "Molek" as a god of child sacrifice, a god distinct from YHWH, must be finally abandoned. The biblical texts describing or alluding to the *mlk* practice consistently associate YHWH with the sacrifice, though attempts have been made to disguise, distort or conceal this association on many different levels. The texts generally locate this practice in or near YHWH's sanctuary in Jerusalem, though archaeological evidence for a sacrificial precinct in this area has not yet come to light. In a realistic sense, this is not altogether surprising, for excavations in Jerusalem are relatively restricted for practical, political and religious reasons. It is essential to consider the probability that searching for a "tophet" in Jerusalem and other Israeli and Palestinian sites would not necessarily be a welcome exercise. Indeed, the difficult nature of

---

279 It is interesting to note the description of the worshipper who widens the mouth and lengthens the tongue in v. 4. Though a clear allusion to the *mlk* practice is difficult to ascertain, this description is reminiscent of Phoenician-Punic cult masks with wide, grinning mouths and protruding tongues, dated to the seventh and sixth centuries (see, for example, Ciasca, "Masks and Protomes", 410, 412). Interestingly, female cult masks bearing the crescent-disc motif associated with Baʿal Ḥammon have been found at the same site as the Hand stela from Hazor. Yadin identifies these masks as representations of the Punic title of Tanit as "the face of Baʿal", known from the *mlk* inscriptions at Carthage, and two small ivory cult masks found in the temple of Tanit in Carthage (Yadin, "Symbols", 221-224). The description of the worshipper widening the mouth and lengthening the tongue also recalls the iconography of the Pozo Moro monument, in which the practitioners are depicted with open mouths and lolling tongues, which some scholars have identified as cult masks.

such an archaeological project has already been experienced by Seeden, whom in describing the salvaging of the sacred precinct in Tyre (modern-day Beirut), comments:

> Witnessing some of the negative reactions from here and abroad during our small rescue operation of 1991, we stopped to wonder at times whether the first Tyrian *tophet* was really an unwanted child of science which might much rather have remained unborn and hidden from the eyes of this world.[280]

The biblical portrayal of a god called "Molek" or "Melek" must therefore be dismissed as fictitious. "Molek" or "Melek" is better understood as a biblical character, a character masking the probability that in reality, children were sacrificed to *Yhwh*. The probability that child sacrifice existed within Judahite deity-worship is heightened further in view of independent epigraphic evidence suggesting that a tradition of child sacrificed existed within a cult of *Šadday*, a deity explicitly and repeatedly identified with YHWH in the Hebrew Bible. It is to this evidence that the discussion will now turn.

5.4 Child Sacrifice in the Deir ʿAlla Texts

In attempting to recover the historical reality of child sacrifice, it may be that the Deir ʿAlla plaster texts can provide a further historical link between religious traditions underlying certain traditions of the Hebrew Bible and a form of child sacrifice. These important texts, generally dated to the eighth century BCE, have been the subject of intense academic attention since their discovery in the Transjordan some thirty-five years ago.[281] Dominating scholarship is the figure of Balaam ben Beor, who appears within both the Deir ʿAlla texts and the Hebrew Bible as a visionary prophet. However, despite this shared feature, and due to the burned and fragmentary nature of

---

280 Seeden, "A *tophet* in Tyre?", 52.

281 Though initially—and partially—published in the year of discovery by their excavator (H.J. Franken, "Texts from the Persian Period from Deir ʿAllā", *VT* 17 [1967], 480-481) the inscriptions were published in full by J. Hoftijzer and G. van der Kooij, *Aramaic Texts from Deir ʿAllā* (Documenta et Monumenta Orientis Antiqui 19; Leiden: Brill, 1976). See also J. Hoftijzer, "The Prophet Balaam in a Sixth Century Aramaic Inscription", *BA* 39 (1976), 11-17.

the Deir ʿAlla texts,[282] philological[283] and epigraphic[284] difficulties continue to prohibit their comprehensive understanding. Consequently, interpretations of the texts vary considerably. Of primary significance to this discussion is the interpretation offered by Hackett, who argues that the Deir ʿAlla texts contain a description of the sacrifice of a child to a group of gods called the *šdyn* which functions as a means of averting the impending infertility of the

---

282 119 fragments of plaster texts were discovered in two roughly disparate groups, commonly known as "Combination I" and "Combination II", although several scattered fragments were found lying between the combinations, suggesting that all the fragments were scattered when the wall upon which they were written collapsed in an earthquake and subsequent fire. See Hoftijzer and Van der Kooij, *Aramaic Texts from Deir ʿAllā*, 12-15; G. van der Kooij and M.M. Ibrahim, *Picking Up the Threads: A Continuing Review of Excavations at Deir ʿAllā*, National Museum of Antiquities, Leiden, 1989, 63-69; M.M. Ibrahim and G. van der Kooij, "The Archaeology of Deir ʿAlla Phase IX", in J. Hoftijzer and G. van der Kooij (eds.), *The Balaam Text from Deir ʿAllā Re-Evaluated: Proceedings of the International Symposium held at Leiden 21–24 August 1989* (Leiden: Brill, 1991), 16-29.

283 As P.K. McCarter comments, the language of the texts seems to fall somewhere between Aramaic and Canaanite ("The dialect of the Deir ʿAlla texts", in Hoftijzer and Van der Kooij, *Balaam Text*, 87-99). See also J.-A. Hackett, "Deir ʿAlla: texts", *ABD*, vol. 2, 129; Hoftijzer and van der Kooij, *Aramaic Texts*, 300; D. Pardee, "Response: The Linguistic Classification of the Deir ʿAlla Text written on Plaster", in Hoftijzer and van der Kooij, *Balaam Text*, 100-105; E. Lipiński, "Plaster Inscription", in *idem.*, *Studies in Aramaic Inscriptions and Onomastics, II* (OLA 57; Leuven: Peeters, 1994), 168-170. G. Garbini ("L'iscizioni di Balaam Bar-Beor", *Henoch* 1 [1979], 166-188) and J. Huehnergard ("Remarks on the Classification of the Northwest Semitic Languages", in Hoftijzer and Van der Kooij, *Balaam Text*, 282-293, esp. 293) independently offer an intriguing solution, suggesting that the Deir ʿAlla texts represent a new, previously unknown Northwest Semitic language. Given the relatively isolated location of the settlement, this interpretation is particularly attractive, for it may be that the language is best understood as indigenous to the general area of Deir ʿAlla; see also B.A. Levine, *Numbers 21–36* (AB 4A; Garden City: Doubleday, 2000), 266-267; *idem.*, "The Deir ʿAlla Plaster Inscriptions", *COS*, vol. 2, 140-145.

284 The script of the texts continues to be contested: some argue it is Aramaic (e.g. J. Naveh "The Date of the Deir ʿAlla Inscription in Aramaic Script", *IEJ* 17 [1973], 256-258; Van der Kooij, *Aramaic Texts from Deir ʿAlla*, 12), whilst others classify it as an Ammonite or "Gileadite" offshoot of Aramaic (e.g. P.K. McCarter, "The Balaam Texts from Deir ʿAlla: The First Combination", *BASOR* 239 [1980], 49-60 [50]; F.M. Cross, "Epigraphic Notes on the Amman Citadel Inscription", *BASOR* 193 [1969], 13-19; Hackett, *Balaam Text*, 9-19). J.W. Wesselius' argument that the texts are written in Hebrew is unpersuasive ("Thoughts about the Balaam: The Historical Background of the Deir Alla Inscription on Plaster", *BO* 44 [1987]: 589-599).

earth.[285] Though Hackett's interpretation has not been widely adopted, her evidence is persuasive in view of the present discussion, and demands re-evaluation here.

Despite their variations in interpretation, the majority of scholars are widely agreed that Combination I describes a meeting of El's divine assembly, which is witnessed by the seer Balaam. The divine council appears to be composed of a group of gods called *šdyn* and *ʾlhn*; it is initially unclear whether these labels refer to the same group of gods or to two divine groups within the council.[286] The terms are commonly vocalised *šaddāyîn*[287] and *ʾelāhîn* (the latter is usually translated "gods"). Alongside El and his council is a goddess to whom the council speaks. The identity of the goddess is uncertain, for only the first letter of her name, *š*, is legible.[288] Given that the divine name(s) *šgr wʿštr* (Šagar-and-Ištar) appears further in this combination, most scholars reconstruct the name *šgr* here.[289] However, some

---

285 J.-A. Hackett, *The Balaam Text from Deir ʿAllā* (HSM 31; Chico: Scholars Press, 1984); see also Hackett, "Religious Traditions in Israelite Transjordan", in Miller, Hanson and McBride, *Ancient Israelite Religion*, 125-136.

286 For example, Levine understands that two groups are implied (Levine, "The Plaster Inscriptions from Deir ʿAlla: General Interpretation", in Hoftijzer and Van der Kooij, *Balaam Text*, 58-72 [60]) yet Hackett (*Balaam Text*, 85-87) and M. Weippert ("The Balaam Text from Deir ʿAllā and the Study of the Old Testament", in Hoftijzer and van der Kooij, *Balaam Text*, 151-184 [170]) argue that two labels are employed of the same group of gods.

287 The notable exception is Weinfeld, who vocalises *šdym* as Hebrew *šēdîm*, cited in Weippert, "The Balaam Text", 170 n. 69. See further 5.5 below. The designation *šdyn* may be rendered "*šadday*-gods" (eg. Weippert, "The Balaam Text", 156; Levine, *Numbers 21–36*, 245, 249; idem., *COS*, vol. 2, 142, n. 8), "*šadday*-beings", (Levine, "The Plaster Inscriptions from Deir ʿAllā: General Interpretation", in Hoftijzer and van der Kooij, *Balaam Text*, 58-72), or left untranslated.

288 But note the reconstructions of Wesselius ("Thoughts about Balaam", 593-594), who suggests that the city Samaria is addressed, not a goddess; McCarter, who argues that Sheol is in view here ("Balaam Text", 53), and H. Lutzky ("Shadday as a Goddess Epithet", *VT* 48 [1998], 15-36), who argues that the goddess is called *šadday*.

289 E.g., Hoftijzer and Van der Kooij, *Balaam Text*, 272-275; M. Dijkstra, "Is Balaam Also Among the Prophets?", *JBL* 114 (1995), 43-64; H-P. Müller, "Einige alttestamentliche Probleme zur aramäischen Inschrift von Dēr ʿAllā", *ZDPV* 94 (1978), 56-67 (64 n. 49); idem., "Die aramäische Inschrift von Deir ʿAllā und die älteren Bileamsprüche", *ZAW* 94 (1982), 214-244 (217-218, 223); Milgrom, *Numbers* (JPS Torah Commentary; Philadelphia: JPS, 1990), 474; Smelik, *Writings*, 87-88. Levine reconstructs *š[gr wʿštr]* ("The Deir ʿAlla Plaster Inscriptions", *JAOS* 101 [1981], 195-205), but in his recent detailed commentary on the texts, employs the shortened designation "Shagar" (*Numbers 21–36*, 243, 249-250). Note however that the combination *šgr wʿštr* may also be translated "procreation and fertility" or such like, rather than as a (pair of) divine

contend that *šgr* is a masculine (moon) deity, [290] whilst others take as their cue the apparent darkness which is described in the oracle, and argue that the divine name here is *šmš*, the sun deity, attested as a female deity at Ugarit.[291] Given the uncertainty, the name of the goddess is best left unreconstructed. The apparent purpose of the divine assembly's meeting is revealed to Balaam as a vision of a threatened crisis, of which Balaam warns the people the following day, as related in Combination I, 4-7a:

> And his people came up to him [*and said to*] him, "Balaam, son of Beor, why are you fasting and crying?" And he said to them, "Sit down! I will tell you what the Šadda[yyin *have done.*] Now, come, see the works of the gods! The g[o]ds gathered together; the Šaddayyin took their places as the assembly. And they said to Š[   ]: "Sew up, bolt up the heavens in your cloud, ordaining darkness instead of eternal light! And put the dark [se]al on your bolt, and do not remove it forever![292]

Following Hackett's reconstruction and interpretation of the text, it would appear that the description of disaster is expressed in terms of the failure of fertility and universal darkness. For Hackett and others, this disaster is decreed by the *šdyn*,[293] who instruct the goddess to produce celestial darkness

---

name(s). See further Weippert, "Balaam Text", 158, n. 27; Hackett, *Balaam Text*, 41-42; Dijkstra, "Is Balaam Also Among the Prophets?", 53 n. 30. Interestingly, this pair occurs within the Hebrew Bible as a formulaic expression for the fertility and young of cattle and sheep (Deut. 7:13; 28:4, 18, 51 cf. Exod. 13:12), see *BDB*, 800, 993; M. Delcor, "Astarté et la fécondité des troupeaux en Deut. 7:13 et parallèles", *UF* 6 (1974), 7-14; J.M. Hadley, "The fecundity of the flock? The De-Personalization of Astarte in the Old Testament", in B. Becking and M. Dijkstra (eds.), *On Reading Prophetic Texts: Gender-Specific and Related Studies in Memory of Fokkelien van Dijk-Hemmes* (Leiden: Brill, 1996), 115-133.

290 E.g., Lipiński, "Plaster Inscription", 126; S. Dalley and B. Teissier, "Tablets from the Vicinity of Emar and Elsewhere", *Iraq* 54 (1992), 83-111.

291 Weippert, "Balaam Text", 170, Lipiński, "Plaster Inscription", 116, 127-128; *idem.*, "Shemesh", *DDD*, 764-768 (764). See also Müller, "Einige alttestamentliche Probleme", 64-65; *idem.*, "Die aramäische Inschrift", 230; M. Delcor, "Le Texte de Deir ʿAlla et le Oracles Bibliques de Balaʿam", in J.A. Emerton (ed.), *Congress Volume Vienna, 1980* (VTSup 32; Leiden: Brill, 1981), 52-73.

292 Unless otherwise stated, all reconstructions and translations are those of Hackett, *Balaam Text*, whose working text is primarily based upon the work of Van der Kooij, *Aramaic Texts from Deir ʿAlla*, 99-167.

293 Hackett vocalizes *šdyn* according to the vocalization of biblical שֵׁדִי (Hackett, *Balaam Text*, 40). However, although the two terms are to be related (as argued below), it is preferable to render the Deir ʿAlla term simply as *šdyn* wherever possible in order to maintain clarity and so avoid circularity of argument.

by covering the heavens with dense cloud.[294] The remainder of Combination I speaks of the coming disaster as the result of the chaotic reversal of the order of the earth, in which large birds are attacked by small birds (I, 8-9b), the staff which leads ewes is itself led (I, 9b), the poor woman prepares myrrh instead of the priestess (I, 11) and the deaf hear from afar (I, 13).[295] The last lines of Combination I are illegible or broken.

Though the fragments of Combination II are larger and better preserved than those of Combination I, scholars are frequently more hesitant in their interpretations. Primarily, this may be due to the fact that the last halves of most lines of text are broken or illegible. This not only hinders a comprehensive transliteration, but also facilitates a variety of interpretations. It is widely agreed, however, that Combination II deals entirely with death and the grave or the underworld. As is the case in the first Combination, El appears to be the main deity in view here, yet, following Hackett's stimulating thesis, this time El is at the centre of a ritual of child sacrifice. Within Combination II occurs the key word *nqr*, a term cognate with biblical נֵצֶר, "sprout" or "scion",[296] and comparable to Phoenician and Punic *ṣmh*, "scion" (cf. biblical צֶמַח), which occurs repeatedly in inscriptions upon burial monuments within sacrificial precincts.[297] Lines 4-8 thus appear to describe the fate of the "sprout" or "scion":

---

294 Hackett, *Balaam Text*, 29, 75; *idem.*, "Religious traditions", 125; Levine, "Plaster Inscriptions", 60. However, some scholars argue that the gods are attempting to dissuade the goddess from unleashing disaster, for example Dijkstra, "Is Balaam Also Among the Prophets?", 53, plus n. 24 and the literature cited there.

295 Hackett, *Balaam Text*, 46-48, 75-76; *idem.*, "Response to Baruch Levine and Andre Lemaire", in Hoftijzer and Van der Kooij, *Balaam Text*, 73-84 (77); McCarter, "Balaam Texts", 58-59; Müller, "Die aramäische Inschrift", 225-227; Dijkstra, "Is Balaam Also Among the Prophets?", 53-54.

296 Postulating that *q* in the Deir ʿAlla text represents *δ>ṣ in Hebrew (Hackett, *Balaam Text*, 77-85; *idem.*, "Religious Traditions", 126; *idem.*, "Response", 77-79; see also Cross, "Phoenician Inscription", 98). Hackett follows Caquot and Lemaire, "Les textes araméens", 202, 205; so too McCarter, "Balaam Texts", 51; Lipiński, "Plaster Inscription", 144-145. However, the term *nqr* is disputed by some: Dijkstra ("Is Balaam Also Among the Prophets?", 62-63) follows Hoftijzer (*Aramaic Texts*, 237, 306) in rendering *nqr*, "the blinded one"; H. Ringgren suggests it is best rendered "crowned prince" ("Balaam and the Deir ʿAlla Inscription", in A. Rofé and Y. Zakovitch [eds.], *Isaac Leo Seeligmann Volume: Essays on the Bible and the Ancient World*, vol. 3 [Jerusalem: Rubenstein, 1983], 93-98 [97]), whilst Levine ("The Deir ʿAlla Plaster Inscriptions", 201; *idem.*, "Plaster Inscriptions: General Interpretation", 68-70; *Numbers 21–36*, 260-262; 267-268) renders *nqr* here as "corpse", "carrion" (cf. Isa. 14:19); however, note the persuasive criticisms of Hackett, "Response", 73-84 (esp. 77-79).

297 E.g., *KAI* 43.11, 162.2, 163.3; cf. Jer. 23:5; 33:15; Zech. 3:8; 6:12.

4   his boy, full of love [   ]
5   (?) "Why are/do the scion and the firepit containing foliage [... "   "... *so that*]
6   El will be satisfied. Let him go (lit.: 'cross over' [*yʿbr*])[298] to
     the House of Eternity, the hou[se   ]
7   the house where the traveller does not rise, and the bridegroom does not
     rise, the house [. . ."   ". . .   ]
8   and the worm from the tomb, from those who have arisen
     among human beings, and from the graves of [. . . "   ]

It is striking that the language used in association with the sacrifice of the child (*yʿbr*) parallels that frequently employed within the biblical descriptions of the firstborn sacrifice and the *mlk* sacrifice, namely the verb עבר, a point overlooked by Hackett, but supporting her interpretation. A further parallel is suggested by the word *mdr*, "firepit", in line 5, reminiscent as it is of biblical מדרה, the firepit of the תפה in Isa. 30:33 (MT תָּפְתֶּה).[299] Hackett interprets the reference to the *ḥtn*, "bridegroom", as a title or metaphor for the sun, describing the underworld as a place where the sun does not rise and, therefore, never shines.[300] However, in view of the common language associated with biblical circumcision and child sacrifice discussed above, it is attractive to interpret the reference to the *ḥtn* (cf. biblical חתן) in relation to the preceding discussion of the firstborn sacrifice, in which the term appears to play an associated role in biblical traditions.[301] A further point of interest is that the root *mlk*, well known from non-biblical and biblical child sacrifice texts, occurs several times in Combination II, two occurrences of which follow the description of the grave:

9   [   ] "As for counsel, is it not you with whom he will take counsel;
     or for advice (*mlkh*), will he not ask advice (*ytmlk*) from one residing [... ?   ]
10   [   ] you will cover him with one garment. If you are unkind to
     him (lit.: 'hate him') he will falter. If you [... "   ]
11   "I will put [   ] under your head. You will lie
     down on your eternal bed to perish [... "   ]

Though Hackett is aware that the use of *mlk* may suggest a further association with the *mlk* sacrifice, she concedes that, "it is difficult to avoid

---

298 For the purposes of specific emphasis within this study, the transliteration of key terms within the cited text has been inserted where necessary.
299 Hackett, *Balaam Text*, 82-83. Note, however, as Hackett also obersves, that the Deir ʿAlla term *mdr* is masculine, whereas biblical מדרה is feminine.
300 Cf. Ps.19:5b-6 (Hackett, *Balaam Text*, 61).
301 See above, 197-201.

the more common meaning of advising that *mlk* has in the reflexive in Aramaic and later Hebrew".[302] Indeed, this interpretation is supported by its apparent parallelism with "counsel" (ʿ*sh*) in the same line.[303] However, in a later publication, she does place more of an emphasis upon the potential sacrificial connotations of *mlk* in lines 15 and 18 of her reconstruction of Combination II.[304] A particularly striking feature of this section is the use of the word *mškb* in line 11, which Hackett renders "bed".[305] However, as has been seen, this word can also mean "grave",[306] which is probably the intended implication of the phrase "eternal bed" in this text, though Hackett does not refer to this double-meaning. It is especially noteworthy that the word משכב recurs throughout Isa. 57:3-13, a biblical child sacrifice text examined above.[307] Moreover, in line 11 of Combination II, the term *lḥlq*, "to pass way", "to disappear", features within this context of death, which is striking in view of the occurrence of חלק in Isa. 57:6, which is similarly taken as a reference to death.[308] In general terms, Hackett interprets this section as a conversation, presumably between the child's parents and the person or god recommending the sacrifice, concerning the manner in which the child's fears should be calmed. If Hackett's interpretation is correct, the reference to taking advice from someone other than the presumed parents or listeners may reflect a consultative function of the sacrifice, in which the sacrificer requests advice or information from the deity. This is also suggested within Isa. 57:3-13, in which the children as *mlk*-victims are described as "envoys" or "messengers" (צירים), travelling to the underworld on behalf of the sacrificers (57:9). The experience of the child during the sacrifice appears to be alluded to in lines 12b-15:

---

302 Hackett, *Balaam Text*, 83-84. Interestingly, Lipiński's interpretation of these lines ("Plaster Inscription", 146-147) does allow for the understanding of *mlk* as "reign", "be king". He thus translates accordingly, though within his interpretation, *mlk* refers to kingship, not a type of sacrifice.

303 Cf. Levine in *COS*, vol. 2, 144, n. 4.

304 Hackett, "Religious Traditions", 126.

305 Hackett, *Balaam Text*, 30, 67-68.

306 See above, 254, n. 255.

307 Isa. 57:7, 8, (2). See the discussion of Isa. 57:3-13 in 5.3 above. Given the double-meaning of the word *mškb*, many translations of Combination II apply a sexual tone to its language, an interpretation which is not necessarily present within the text and its context. This is reminiscent of the tendency within biblical scholarship to read sexual innuendo into the language of Isa. 57:3-13.

308 See above, 170, n. 120.

12   [   ] to themselves (lit.: "in their heart").
     The scion sighs to himself (lit.: "in his heart"). [*The scion* (?)] sighs [   ]
13   [   ] Death will take the newborn
     child, the suckling [   ]
14   [   ] (?) [   ] (?) The heart of the scion is
     weak for he goes to [   ]
15   to his end [   ] (?) [   ]

Though Combination II is obviously fragmentary, the reference to the scion (*nqr*) and the ritual language of death and the grave is reasonably secure, enabling Hackett to maintain that these elements of the text are "too concrete to allow for a 'metaphorical' interpretation", and are thus best interpreted as a description of the sacrifice of a child.[309] But one important issue remains: is the ritual described in Combination II related to the assembly of gods and the threatened infertility depicted in Combination I?

Given that both Combinations of plaster text fragments appear to have been written by the same scribe at the same time, their interrelation is presumably possible. It is generally considered that Combination II was situated below Combination I within the same column when the plaster text was intact upon the wall.[310] Several scholars have thus sought to connect Combinations I and II in their reconstructions of the plaster fragments. Garbini suggests that the last four lines of Combination I originally ran into the first four lines of Combination II, but this has been sharply criticised.[311] In a similar vein, however, Dijkstra argues that the two Combinations are unlikely to have been located too far from each other if they were situated one below the other within the same column. He thus proposes that fragments IX–XI could have been situated between the Combinations, presumably like pieces of a jigsaw puzzle, thereby providing continuity between the end of

---

309 Hackett, *Balaam Text*, 85. Indeed, despite Levine's criticism of Hackett's sacrificial interpretation of Combination II, he is unable to avoid the clear description of death in his own translation of this text ("Plaster Inscriptions: General Interpretation", 68-71; *idem.*, *Numbers 21–36*, 254-263).

310 E.g. E. Puech, Review of *Aramaic Texts from Deir 'Alla*, edited by J. Hoftijzer and G. van der Kooij, *RB* 85 (1978), 114-117 (116); McCarter, "Balaam Texts", 49; Garbini, "L'iscrizioni di Balaam", 166-168; Delcor, "Le texte de Deir 'Alla", 52-73; Ibrahim and Van der Kooij, *Picking Up the Threads*, 64, fig. 81; Dijkstra, "Is Balaam Also Among the Prophets?", 43-64. Those arguing that the texts were written in two or more unrelated columns include A. Lemaire, "Les inscriptions sur plâtre de Deir 'Alla et leur signification historique et culturelle", in Hoftijzer and van der Kooij, *Balaam Text*, 33-57.

311 Garbini, "L'iscrizioni di Balaam", 171-172, 182; criticised by Müller, "Die arämaische Inschrift", 231.

Combination I and the beginning of Combination II. This coheres with his interpretation of the first part of Combination II, which he understands to be a continuation of Balaam's message.[312] However, fragments IX–XI are difficult to read.

Linguistic considerations would appear to strengthen the possibility that the Combinations are interrelated. The occurrence of *spr*, "account" or "book", in II, 17 may refer back to the use of *spr* in I, 1.[313] Similarly, the designation *ʿmh*, "his people", which occurs in I, 4 to refer to Balaam's group, is also used in II, 17, suggesting that Balaam's people may be in view in the child sacrifice text (though admittedly, Balaam's name does not appear in this Combination).[314] Moreover, the god El is clearly present within both Combinations: in the first, Balaam sees "a vision like an oracle of El" (I, line 1); in the second, "El will be satisfied" (II, 6), presumably as a result of the sacrifice.[315] Indeed, Levine argues that the fundamental link between the two Combinations is expressed by the presence of El and the descriptions of his acts. He thus describes Combinations I and II as belonging to the "El *repertoire*" of Deir ʿAlla.[316] But it is Hackett's interpretation of Combination II which specifically suits the context of Combination I. Two readable phrases at the end of Combination II (lines 35-36) read "they (fem. pl.) will drip with heavy rain" and "they will drip with dew". Hackett suggests that these phrases indicate that the earthly infertility commanded by the divine assembly in Combination I is reversed at the end of Combination II; perhaps "they" are the clouds of the heavens.[317] Consequently, Hackett proposes that the likely break between the two Combinations may have contained an account of the decision to sacrifice a child to appease the gods and return fertility to the earth.[318] If Hackett's interpretation of the plaster text is correct,

---

312 Dijkstra, "Is Balaam Also Among the Prophets?", 43-47, 56.

313 Line numbers are according to Hackett's reconstruction of the fragments.

314 Hackett, *Balaam Text*, 77.

315 Hackett, *Balaam Text*, 29.

316 But note that Levine interprets the second Combination as an account of El's construction of Sheol for the people. Levine, "Plaster inscriptions", 71-72; *Numbers 21–36*, 275. See 276-277 for further discussion of Levine's "El *repertoire*".

317 Milgrom (*Numbers*, 475-476) suggests that as (a) fertility god(s) Šagar-and-Ištar may be responsible for ending the disaster by causing the rain and dew to return to the land.

318 Hackett, *Balaam Text*, 80. Similarly, Milgrom (*Numbers*, 476) suggests that a missing section of text connecting Combinations I and II may have contained an account of Balaam's appeal to the gods by means of a sacrifice, much like the biblical Balaam (Num. 23:1-2, 14, 29-30). Ahlström (*History of Ancient Palestine*, 649, n. 3) also suggests that a ritual was performed by Balaam and the people in response to the

Combination I may thus provide a broader religious context for the child sacrifice text of Combination II. In this case, the divine assembly of Combination I demands closer examination.

Both Combinations portray El as the chief deity (I, 2; II, 6). In the first Combination, the divine assembly is composed of El, one (or more) goddess, and a group of gods called the *šdyn* and/or the *'lhn*. It is unclear whether the *šdyn* are identical to the *'lhn*, for, although it is the *'lhn* who come to Balaam in the night and show him the vision of the divine assembly (I, 1-2), as he describes his vision to his people, Balaam appears to refer to the *'lhn* and the *šdyn* interchangeably. The likelihood that the *'lhn* and the *šdyn* are alternative but parallel designations for the same group of gods is strengthened in light of the apparent parallelism of I, 5-6a:

> "Sit down! I will tell you what the Šadda[yyin *have done*.] Now, come, see the works of the gods (*'lhn*)! The g[o]ds (*'lhn*) gathered together; the Šaddayyin took their places as the assembly.

This perceived parallelism is recognised by the majority of scholars, who generally agree that the *'lhn* and the *šdyn* are the same group of gods within the divine assembly; the label *šdyn* is a specific name, and the designation *'lhn* functions as a generic term.[319] Indeed, as both Weippert and Lipiński have commented, a chiasmus is created by the reversal of the sequence of these designations.[320]

But perhaps most significant is the striking similarity between the name of the *šdyn* gods and that of the biblical god "El Šadday". Indeed, it is widely accepted that these divine titles are to be directly related.[321] It is reasonable to suppose that an individual among the *šdyn* gods could be known as *šdy*

---

message warning of the coming disaster, though he is skeptical about it being the sacrifice of a child.

319 E.g., Hackett, *Balaam Text*, 85-87; *idem*., "Response", 76; Weippert, "Balaam Text", 156, n. 20; McCarter, "Balaam Texts", 57; Lipiński, "Plaster Inscription", 123; Dijkstra, "Is Balaam Also Among the Prophets?", 61. Levine ("Plaster Inscriptions", 60) implies a distinction between the gods by describing the divine assembly as "some gods and Shadday-beings".

320 *šdyn* followed by *'lhn* (name, followed by general term), *'lhn* followed by *šdyn* (general term, followed by name); Weippert, "Balaam Text", 156, n. 20; Lipiński, "Plaster Inscription", 123; *contra* Lutzky, "Shadday", 31.

321 Hoftijzer, *Aramaic Texts*, 275-276; Müller, "Einige Probleme", 65-67; Weippert, "Die Balaam Inschrift", 88-90; H. Weippert and M. Weippert, "Die 'Bileam' Inschrift von Tell Deir ʿAlla", *ZDPV* 98 (1982), 77-103 (88-92); Hackett, *Balaam Text*, 85-89; Dijkstra, "Is Balaam Also Among the Prophets?", 61; E.A. Knauf, "Shadday", *DDD*, 750; Smelik, *Writings*, 86-87.

(*šadday*).[322] But Hackett goes further and suggests that the interchangeable designations *ʾlhn* and *šdyn* within the Deir ʿAlla text may go some way to explain the biblical divine name El Šadday (אֵל שַׁדַּי). She argues that because the gods in the Deir ʿAlla sanctuary are referred to as the *šdyn*, it is reasonable to suspect that *šdy* is applied as an epithet to El (*ʾl*) in his position as chief god over the council.[323] Hackett offers similar examples: within the Hebrew Bible, אֵל is the head of the divine assembly in many texts, whilst the other gods of the heavenly council are called the אֱלֹהִים.[324] So too at Ugarit, where the assembly of the gods is described as the *pḫr ilm*, though there exists another group of gods entitled *ilnym*. It is thus reasonable to posit *šdy* as an epithet of El (*ʾl*) at Deir ʿAlla, given that his council appears to have been called the *šdyn*.[325] However, Hackett does not spell out the full implication of her argument, which, if correct and followed to its logical conclusion, would thus suggest that the deity called *ʾl* who will be satisfied by the sacrifice of a child in Combination II, could also be called *ʾl šdy*.

The Deir ʿAlla texts thus appear to provide evidence for the historical reality of child sacrifice in Iron Age Transjordan. Though excavations at Tel Deir ʿAlla have not revealed physical evidence for this practice,[326] these important plaster texts would appear to preserve a tradition associating Balaam, *ʾl* (*šdy*), and the *šdyn* with child sacrifice. The use of language reminiscent of biblical child sacrifice texts, combined with the prominence of

---

322 J. Hoftijzer, "Interpretation and Grammar", in Hoftijzer and Van der Kooij, *Aramaic Texts from Deir ʿAlla*, 173-224, 275-276; Delcor, "Deir ʿAlla", 39-40; Smith, *Early History*, 23; Caquot, "Préhistoire", 8; R. de Hoop, *Genesis 49 in Its Literary and Historical Context* (OTS 29; Leiden: Brill, 1999), 209.

323 Hackett, *Balaam Text*, 87; followed by Day, *Yahweh*, 33.

324 E.g., Ps. 82:1-2; cf. 89:7-8.

325 Hackett, *Balaam Text*, 87; so too Ahlström, *History of Ancient Palestine*, 649.

326 Evidence for the ritual burning of human remains has been found at the airport site in Amman, Jordan. Excavations have revealed a Late Bronze Age cult place filled with burned human bones (and unburned animal bones), thick ash layers from several isolated fires, and a charred stone altar. However, osteological analysis suggests that the bones are those of adults, not children. Despite this, the finds at this site do allow for the possibility that the ritual burning of humans was known in the Transjordan. See G. Lankester Harding, "Recent Discoveries in Jordan", *PEQ* 90 (1958), 10-12; J.B. Hennessy, "Excavation of a Bronze Age Temple at Amman", *PEQ* 98 (1966), 155-162; *idem.*, "A Temple of Human Sacrifice at Amman", *Sydney University Gazette* 2/20 (1970), 307-309; *idem.*, "Thirteenth Century BC Temple of Human Sacrifice at Amman", in E. Gubel and E. Lipiński (eds.), *Studia Phoenicia 3: Phoenicia and Its Neighbours* (Leuven: Peeters, 1985), 85-104; L.G. Herr (ed.), *The Amman Airport Excavations, 1976* (AASOR 48; Winona Lake: Eisenbrauns, 1983); *idem.*, "The Amman Airport Structure and the Geopolitics of Ancient Transjordan", *BA* 46 (1983), 223-229.

El Šadday and Balaam within the Hebrew Bible, thus demands a closer examination of the biblical texts.

5.5 *Šadday* as a God of Child Sacrifice

Before turning to examine the biblical El Šadday, it is more prudent to first assess what appear to be traces of the *šdyn* in the Hebrew Bible. The term שדין occurs in the same form as that of Deir ʿAlla as a *hapax legomenon* in Job 19:28-29, a difficult text in which the protagonist laments his sudden misfortune, warning his audience that they too may be similarly and suddenly afflicted:

> 28   If you say, "How we will persecute him!"
>   and, "The root of the problem is in him",[327]
> 29   then be afraid of the sword,
>   for wrath's punishment is the sword,
>   so that you (too) might come to know שדין!

Though the term שדין here has been interpreted in a variety of ways,[328] it is best left untranslated, particularly given its probable relation to the term שדי, the divine name which litters the book of Job. As Moore comments, "the single appearance of *šdyn*, as well as the multiple appearances of *šdy* in the Joban dialogues, seems neither arbitrary nor accidental".[329] The implication of 19:29 seems to be that the שדין are responsible for Job's misfortune. Though notionally reminiscent of the function of the Deir ʿAlla *šdyn*, who command disaster upon the mortal world, the biblical text is too difficult to allow any further parallels to be drawn initially.

More telling, however, is another biblical text which may allude to the *šdyn* deities. Deut. 32:16-18 refers to sacrifices being offered to a group called the שֵׁדִים:

---

327 Reading בו with many mss and Versional support, for MT בי.
328 See the summary provided by M.S. Moore, "Job's Texts of Terror", *CBQ* 55 (1993), 662-675.
329 Moore, "Texts of Terror", 667.

16 They made him jealous with strange (gods),
   with abominations they provoked him;
17 they sacrificed to the שֵׁדִים, not Eloah,
   to gods (אֱלֹהִים) they did not know,
   to new ones recently arrived,
   whom your ancestors did not dread.
18 You forgot the Rock who begot you,
   you ignored אֵל who gave you birth.

In this text, MT שֵׁדִים is commonly rendered "demons" in light of Akkadian *šēdu*. Defining the precise nature of ancient Mesopotamian *šēdu* beings is problematic, for this term can occur with or without the determinative for deity, and is employed of both protective daimons and devouring demons in several exorcist texts.[330] However, it is widely held that the *šēdu* was not regarded as a deity, but simply as a lesser divine being.[331] Indeed, there is no evidence that sacrifices were offered to the Akkadian *šēdu*, yet in this biblical poem, the paralleling of the שֵׁדִים with gods (אֱלֹהִים) here suggests that the שֵׁדִים are deities, not demons or spirits, who receive sacrifices, thus rendering this identification problematic.[332] However, this complication is eradicated in light of the parallelism of the *šdyn* and the *ʾlhn* in the Deir ʿAlla text, which is strikingly reminiscent of the paralleling of the שדים with the gods in this biblical poem. In view of this, it is increasingly agreed that MT שֵׁדִים may be revocalised as שַׁדַּיִם and identified with the *šdyn* of Deir ʿAlla, so that the י, which was probably understood by the Masoretes as the *mater* in the plural ending of שֵׁדִים, would have been consonantal in an older orthography.[333] As de Hoop comments, it is possible that the term שֵׁדִים had a vocalization similar to that of שַׁדַּי, but was deliberately "reinterpreted" in line with

330 Moore, "Texts of Terror", 663; *contra* Hackett (*Balaam Text*, 88), who suggests that Akkadian *šēdu* is usually a protective spirit, and means "demon" only when compounded with *lemnu*. See also P. Sanders, *The Provenance of Deuteronomy 32* (OTS 37; Leiden: Brill, 1996), 182, n. 453.
331 P.V. Mankowski, *Akkadian Loanwords in Biblical Hebrew* (HSS 47; Winona Lake: Eisenbrauns, 2000), 139; *contra* Moore, ("Texts of Terror", 662-663), who argues that the occasional use of the broader descriptive term *ʾēl* with Akkadian *šēdu* may suggest that this being could be regarded as a deity.
332 H. Vorländer, *Mein Gott: Die Vorstellungen vom persönlichen Gott im Alten Orient und im Alten Testament* (AOAT 23; Neukirchen-Vluyn: Kevelaer, 1975), 218; De Hoop, *Genesis 49*, 208-209. See further Sanders (*Deuteronomy 32*, 184), who also argues that אֱלוֹהַ in v. 16 (rendered here as "Eloah") was originally a broken plural of אֵל.
333 Hackett, *Balaam Text*, 88; *idem.*, "Some observations", 220; *idem.*, "Religious traditions", 213; followed by Mankowski, *Akkadian Loanwords*, 139-140.

274   The Historical Reality of Child Sacrifice

Akkadian *šēdu* to differentiate and disassociate these divine beings from the biblical אל שדי.[334] Mankowski observes:

> On the assumption that the *šaddayîm* were no longer known by the third century BC, it is possible that the more familiar word [*šēdîm*] suggested itself to the early translators by the consonantal spelling and by the malice associated with what had by then become a diabolical entity. This leads to the highly paradoxical conclusion that a Hebrew borrowing of Akkadian *šēdu* is attested in the Masoretic text but not in the Bible itself.[335]

It is therefore reasonable to revocalize MT שֵׁדִים as שַׁדַּיִם and to identify the שַׁדַּיִם of this poem with the *šdyn* of Deir ʿAlla. In the light of a second occurrence of MT שֵׁדִים in Ps. 106:34-39 (a text initially examined in the previous chapter), the precise motivations for this apparent Masoretic distortion become apparent, for this text describes claims that rebellious Israelites "sacrificed their sons and their daughters to the שַׁדַּיִם (MT שֵׁדִים)" (v. 37). The distortion of the term orginally vocalized שַׁדַּיִם into שֵׁדִים can thus be understood as an attempt to distance YHWH's biblical alias אל שדי from the charge of child sacrifice, a distortion not entirely dissimilar to the distortion of the sacrificial term מלך into the name of a god, "Molek". The identification of the שדים with the *šdyn* of Deir ʿAlla is further suggested by the portrayal of the שדים as the recipients of sacrificed children in this psalm. This is striking in view of the possible affiliation of the *šdyn* gods with child sacrifice in the Deir ʿAlla text. Moreover, this identification is strengthened further by an earlier section of the psalm, which refers to the worship of Baʿal-Peor, a cult crime explicitly associated with Balaam elsewhere in the Hebrew Bible.[336] Ps. 106:28-29 reads:

---

334 De Hoop, *Genesis 49*, 215; so too Mankowski, *Akkadian Loanwords*, 139-140; Vorländer, *Mein Gott*, 216; Hackett, *Balaam Text*, 88; *contra* Weippert, who supports instead the conventional rendering of שֵׁדִים in Deut. 32:17; Ps. 106:37 as "demons", ("Balaam Text", 170). Note however the general agreement that all these forms (biblical שדי, שדים, שדין and Deir ʿAlla *šdyn*) are to be related: M. Delcor, "Des inscriptions de Deir ʿAlla aux traditions bibliques, à propos des *šdyn*, des *šēdîm* et de *šadday*", in A. Müller and M. Görg (eds.), *Die Väter Israels: Beiträge zur Theologie der Patriarchüberlieferungen im Alten Testament* (Stuttgart: Katholisches Bibelwork, 1989), 33-40; Moore, "Texts of Terror", 663; Sanders, *Deuteronomy 32*, 182-183; De Hoop, *Genesis 49*, 208-215.
335 Mankowski, *Akkadian Loanwords*, 140.
336 Hackett, *Balaam Text*, 88.

> Then they attached themselves to Baʿal-Peor,
> and ate sacrifices offered to the dead.
> They provoked YHWH to anger with their deeds
> And a plague broke out among them.

In describing the crime of Baʿal-Peor as the eating of sacrifices offered to the dead, Ps. 106:28-29 fills in the details strangely absent from the vague account of Num. 25, in which it is claimed merely that the Israelites yoked themselves to Baʿal-Peor when they had sexual relations with the Moabite women, and that they "ate and bowed down to their gods" (25:1-3). This seems to suggest some sort of fertility and death-cult context for the worship of Baʿal-Peor. In the reiteration of the story in Num. 31, the link with the Deir ʿAlla material is provided in the figure of the visionary Balaam ben Beor, who appears to be held responsible for the cult crime of Baʿal-Peor, as verses 15-17 demonstrate:

> Moses said to them, "Have you allowed all the women to live? These women here, on Balaam's advice, made the Israelites act treacherously against YHWH in the affair of Peor, so that the plague came among the congregation of YHWH. Now therefore, kill every male among the little ones, and kill every woman who has known a man by sleeping with him. But you may spare for yourselves all the children among the females [and] who have not known a man by sleeping with him."

This version of the tradition is especially noteworthy, for it associates the killing of male and unborn children with the worship of Baʿal-Peor, an association which may be implied within Ps. 106:28, 34-39.[337] This association is also evident within Hos. 9:10-14, 16, in which the ancestors' crime of Baʿal-Peor is punished with the divine threat of human infertility and the slaughtering of children.

The merging of Balaam, the cult of the dead, child sacrifice, infant slaughter and the שדים within this biblical material heightens further the parallels between the Deir ʿAlla texts and the biblical traditions. Moreover, the characterization of Balaam in Numbers 22–24 as a whole compounds further the probability that the *šdyn* of Deir ʿAlla are to be related to the biblical שדים and אל שדי. Though the biblical Balaam is generally depicted as a foreign prophet of YHWH, he is also explicitly—and more frequently— associated with אל and שדי, as his biblical titulary in 24:3b-4 indicates:

---

337 In the present form of the text, Moses is depicted as acting according to the Deuteronomic legislation of war with foreign towns and cities; see Deut. 20:13-14; cf. Judg. 21:11-12. See the comments of Levine, *Numbers 21–36*, 456-457, 466-470.

> The oracle of Balaam ben Beor,
> the oracle of the man whose eye is open,
> the oracle of one who hears the words of אל,
> who sees the vision of שדי ...[338]

Furthermore, within the biblical texts, the sacrifice of children to the שדים, the worship of Ba'al-Peor and Balaam are all located within the Transjordanian wilderness, providing a geographical context mirroring that of Deir 'Alla. Lipiński argues that the biblical tradition itself alludes to Deir 'Alla as the residence of Balaam. Whilst the MT locates Balaam in Num. 22:5 "at Pethor, which is on the river, in the land of the sons of 'Ammô/his people (בני עמו), the Samaritan Pentateuch renders it differently. Here it is stated that Balaam ben Beor dwelt "on the river, in the country of the sons of Ammon ('mwn)", a reference Lipiński assumes to indicate the site of Deir 'Alla on the Jordan river, at the traditional border of the Ammonite territory. The reference to Ammon in the Samaritan Pentateuch is supported by several Masoretic manuscripts, the Peshitta, and the Vulgate. Lipiński reasons that the final n of 'mwn has been deliberately omitted from the main codices in order to bring Num. 22:5 into line with Deut. 23:5, which locates Balaam in Aram-Naharaim not Ammon, thereby rendering the text "the country of the sons of 'Ammô/his people", instead of, "the country of the sons of Ammon".[339]

Levine also sees a direct, historical relationship between the biblical Balaam traditions and the Deir 'Alla material. Basing his argument upon the literary independence and priority of the poems[340] within the Balaam Pericope (Num. 22–24), and their multiple affinities with the Deir 'Alla material, Levine proposes that the biblical Balaam poems were composed in the same Transjordanian location as the Deir 'Alla material.[341] This builds

---

338 Cf. Num. 24:16. The title of the biblical Balaam as the one who "sees the vision of Šadday" (מחזה שדי) recalls the language of the Deir 'Alla text, which describes Balaam as seeing a vision (mḥzh) according to the utterance of El (so Levine, *Numbers 21–36*, 194.

339 Lipiński, "Plaster Inscription", 111; see also Levine, *Numbers 21–36*, 145-149; S. Mowinckel, "Die Ursprung der Bileamsage", *ZAW* 48 (1930), 233-271.

340 *Contra* Milgrom (*Numbers*, 467), who argues that the poems of Num. 22–24 were composed in light of the prose.

341 Levine, *Numbers 21–36*, 208, 230-234. Levine also suggests that the Sheol oracle of Isa. 14 (which he examines in light of Combination II of the Deir 'Alla text) may also have originated in the Transjordan as a part of this *repertoire* (209, 267-271).

upon his earlier suggestion that an "El *repertoire*" of mythical or ritualistic material was originally composed at various centres of El-worship located on both sides of the Jordan.[342] Examples of this literary corpus would thus include the Deir ʿAlla texts and those biblical texts which synthesize El and YHWH, including the Balaam poetry in Num. 22–24.[343] He says:

> The use of divine referents [שדי, אל, אל ין] in the Balaam poems reflects their *Sitz-im-Leben* as Transjordanian, biblical literature; as part of an El repertoire upon which biblical writers drew. The Balaam inscriptions from Deir ʿAlla derive from the same cultural context, although they speak for different circles of worshippers...instead of reflecting the synthesis of El and YHWH, or operating with divine epithets, the biblical poets who gave us the Balaam orations conceived of a compatible, West Semitic pantheon, consisting of El, Shaddai and Elyon, along with the national God of Israel, YHWH.[344]

Moore adopts Levine's thesis in suggesting that some of the mythical material underlying the Joban dialogues—including the enigmatic reference to the שדין in 19:29—may indeed derive from an El *repertoire* located around the Jordan.[345] Indeed, perhaps the שדים traditions of Deut. 32:16-18 and Ps. 106:34-39 are best explained by means of Levine's concept of a Transjordanian *repertoire*. Though impossible to prove, Levine's thesis is attractive in its accounting for the striking similarities between many of the Balaam and *šadday*-god(s) traditions of the Hebrew Bible and the Deir ʿAlla material. Interestingly, Hackett has also emphasized the Transjordanian location of Balaam, the *šadday*-god(s) and child sacrifice shared by both the Deir ʿAlla material and the Hebrew Bible.[346] In this context, it is striking to recall that two other biblical stories of child sacrifice are given a Transjordanian setting: Jephthah's sacrifice of his daughter (Judg. 11:29-40) and King Mesha of Moab's sacrifice of his firstborn son (2 Kgs 3:26-27). In the light of this complex of biblical and non-biblical material, it remains to attempt to characterize or define the *šadday*-god(s) more precisely.

"El Šadday" is an important deity in the Hebrew Bible. Despite the common, scholarly description of biblical שדי as an epithet of אל (and hence

342 Levine, *Numbers 21–36*, 208.
343 Levine, "Plaster Inscriptions", 58-72; *idem*, "The Balaam Inscription", 326-339.
344 Levine, *Numbers 21–36*, 196.
345 Moore, "Texts of Terror", 665.
346 Hackett, "Religious Traditions", 134.

a shortened version of אל שדי),[347] the longer designation אל שדי occurs only seven times in the Hebrew Bible,[348] whereas שדי occurs 41 times,[349] though many of these occurrences seem to parallel שדי with אל.[350] The biblical material may indicate that within the historical reality of ancient deity-worship, the divine name *šdy* existed independently as the proper name or title of a deity before becoming equated and/or compounded with *ʾl* as an epithet (and subsequently as an epithet of YHWH within biblical tradition).[351] Complementing this idea is the evidence of the Deir ʿAlla texts, which allow the supposition that an individual member of the *šdyn* group could be designated *šdy*.

The etymology of biblical שדי has not been satisfactorily explained.[352] It is widely-accepted that biblical שדי is to be equated with Akkadian *šadû*, "mountain", and more specifically the Akkadian noun *šaddûʾa/ šaddāʾu*, "mountain-dweller", thereby rendering biblical שדי as "He of the mountain".[353] This would presuppose a Proto-Semitic form *ṯdw/y*, primitively meaning "breast", a form Cross defends in detail.[354] The location of El's divine council upon a mountain within Ugaritic and biblical literature might

---

347 E.g., Knauf, "Shadday", 749; Hackett, *Balaam Text*, 87; Cross, *Canaanite Myth*, 46-60; Day, *Yahweh*, 33-34.

348 The compound form occurs almost exclusively in material commonly associated with the Priestly writer: Gen. 17:1; 28:3; 35:11; 43:14; 48:3; Exod. 6:3. It also occurs in Gen. 49:25, part of a complex poem which will be considered further below.

349 Num. 24:4, 16; Ruth 1:20, 21; Pss. 68:15; 91:1; Isa. 13:6; Ezek. 1:24; Joel 1:15; plus 31 times in Job (5:17; 6:4, 14; 8:3; 11:7; 13:3; 15:25; 21:15, 20; 22:3, 17, 23-26; 23:16; 24:1; 27:2, 10-11, 13; 29:5; 31:2, 35; 32:8; 33:4; 34:10, 12; 35:13; 37:23; 40:2).

350 Num. 24:4, 16; Job 5:17; 6:4; 8:3, 5; 13:3; 15:25; 22:17, 26; 23:16; 27:2, 10, 13; 31:2, 35; 33:4; 34:10, 12; 35:13.

351 This idea may be supported by the occurrence of *šdy* as a theophoric element in three personal names in the Hebrew Bible: Surishaddy (Num. 1:6; 2:12; 7:36; 7:41; 10:19) Ammishaddy (Num. 1:12; 2:25; 7:66, 71; 10:25) and Shedeur (Num. 1:5). D. Launderville ("Zurishaddai", *ABD*, vol. 4, 1176) suggests that the name Sarasaday in Judith 8:1 may be a variant of Surishadday.

352 So Levine, *Numbers 21–36*, 195; De Hoop, *Genesis 49*, 211; Knauf, "Shadday", 749.

353 See W.F. Albright, "The Names Shaddai and Abram", *JBL* 54 (1935), 180-187; Albright, *Yahweh*, 94; F.M. Cross, "Yahweh and the Gods of the Patriarchs", *HTR* 55 (1962), 244-250; *idem.*, *Canaanite Myth*, 52-60; T.N.D. Mettinger, *In Search of God: The Meaning and Message of the Everlasting Names* (trans. F.H. Cryer; Philadelphia: Fortress Press, 1988), 69-72; Day, *Yahweh*, 32-34. Compare also the title *bēl šadê*, commonly rendered "Lord of the mountain", discussed by J. Ouellette, "More on ʾĒl Šadday and Bêl Šadê", *JBL* 88 (1969), 470-471; L.R. Bailey, "Israelite ʾĒl Šadday and Amorite Bêl Šadê", *JBL* 87 (1968), 434-438; Mettinger, *In Search*, 71.

354 Cross, *Canaanite Myth*, 52-55, followed most recently by Day, *Yahweh*, 33.

support the translation of the compound שַׁדַּי אֵל as "El, the mountain one".[355]
Alternatively, שַׁדַּי has been related to Ugaritic *šd* and Hebrew שָׂדֶה, meaning
"field", rendering שַׁדַּי אֵל as "El of the field".[356]   This proposal, most
comprehensively defended by Weippert, benefits from its freedom from
theories of cultural borrowing, given that linguistically it may be related
directly to Palestine.[357] However, the apparent incongruity of the initial שׂ (*ś*)
of שָׂדֶה and the שׁ (*š*) of biblical שַׁדַּי remains a stumbling block for many
commentators. A further alternative, striking a conceptual balance between
"He of the mountain" and "He of the field", is offered by Knauf, who
suggests that שַׁדַּי derives from Akkadian *šadû*, "the mountain wilderness".
Knauf argues that the theophoric element in the Thamudic personal name
ʾlšdy presupposes an original *saday, the first consonant rendered *š* in
Ugaritic, Phoenician and "Israelite".[358] Therefore Akkadian *šadû*, "the
mountain wilderness" and biblical שָׂדֶה, "the (uncultivated) field", "the
hunting ground", are both derived from the root *šdy*.[359] Thus any type of *ʾl*
šdy is a "god of the wilderness", a concept Knauf directly relates to the
widely-attested ancient Near Eastern iconographic motif of the "lord of the
animals", which appears to have been particularly popular within Late
Bronze and Early Iron Age Syro-Palestine.[360] On balance, Knauf's thesis
suits the Transjordanian wilderness context of the *šdyn* of Deir ʿAlla and the
שֵׁדִים of Deut. 32 and Ps. 106 quite well.[361]

The fact that a satisfactory etymology remains to be established within
modern scholarship testifies to the continued uncertainty surrounding the
meaning of the biblical term שַׁדַּי, and the Deir ʿAlla designation *šdyn*. This
uncertainty is long-lived, for it is also apparent within the Hebrew Bible, in
which the term שַׁדַּי appears to have been re-etymologized within several

355 Hackett, *Balaam Text*, 87; Day, *Yahweh*, 32.
356 M. Weippert, "Erwägungen zur Etymologie des Gottesnames ʾĒl šaddaj", *ZDMG* 111
    (1961), 42-62; O. Loretz, "Der kanaanäische Ursprung des biblischen Gottesnamens El
    šaddaj", *UF* 12 (1980), 420-421; W. Wifall, "El Shaddai or El of the Fields", *ZAW* 92
    (1980), 24-34.
357 Wifall, "El Shaddai", 26.
358 E.A. Knauf, "Shadday", 750. Knauf intentionally differentiates "Israelite" from
    "Judaean" (and hence biblical) Hebrew, arguing that biblical *ʾēl šadday* is a loanword
    from Israelite.
359 Knauf, "Shadday", 750.
360 Keel and Uehlinger, *Gods, Goddesses,* 182-191, 277, 290, 313.
361 Lipiński ("Plaster Inscription", 123) offers an alternative etymology for the *šdyn* of Deir
    ʿAlla, suggesting that their name derives from the Aramaic root *šdy*, "sprinkle", "pour
    out", reflecting their function as water suppliers and fertility gods.

texts. Gen. 49:25, perhaps one of the oldest biblical attestations of שַׁדַּי, also contains a reference to "breasts" (שָׁדַיִם) which may be an intentional play upon the term שַׁדַּי.[362] Another example of the re-etymologization of שַׁדַּי within biblical literature is Isa. 13:6 and Joel 1:15, which warn that "the Day of YHWH" will come "like destruction from שַׁדַּי", clearly interpreting the divine name as a derivation of שָׁדַד ("destroy"). Knauf suggests that this understanding of the name may lie behind the portrayal of שַׁדַּי as the violent and powerful god in Ruth 1:20-21 and Ps. 91:1.[363] Within early Judaism, שַׁדַּי was derived from שֶׁ plus דַּי, and rendered "he who is sufficient".[364]

Whilst a widely-accepted etymology is unlikely to reveal much about the characteristics and functions of the šadday-god(s), it may be that further non-biblical material will prove more illuminating. Moore seeks to relate epigraphic šdyn with the biblical terms שַׁדַּי, שֵׁדִין and Masoretic שֵׁדִים; these terms, he argues, are all to be related to Akkadian šēdu.[365] Moore suggests that the šdyn were demonic beings well-known from the incantation literature of the ancient Near East, particularly within exorcism texts. Incantation rituals, he believes, form the backdrop to many of the שַׁדַּי texts in Job.[366] This thesis may go some way to account for some of the characteristics of the šdyn and the שֵׁדִים in the Deir ʿAlla text and the Hebrew Bible, respectively. But there may also be parallels within the Ugaritic literature. Some scholars have tentatively located a deity šd within a handful of Ugaritic texts.[367] Interestingly, one of these texts is an incantation invoking deities and beings associated with the dead (KTU 1.108) including rpu (probably one of the

362 Contra H. Lutzky, "Shadday as a Goddess Epithet", VT 48 (1998), 15-36; D. Biale, "The God with Breasts: El Shaddai in the Bible", HR 21 (1981-1982), 240-256; M. Canney, "Shaddai", ET 34 (1922-1923), 332.
363 Knauf, "Shadday", 751.
364 Mettinger, In Search, 70.
365 Moore ("Texts of Terror", 662-663, 667), also includes within this group of forms the emphatic plural šdyʾ, which occurs in a Late Aramaic inscription from Palmyra (cf. Weippert, "Bileam-Inschrift", 88-90) and the plural form šydyn, which appears upon several incantation bowls (C.D. Isbell, Corpus of the Aramaic Incantation Bowls [SBLDS 17; Atlanta: Scholars Press, 1975], 3.14; 7.17; 47.2; 48.1).
366 Moore, "Texts of Terror", 662-674; idem., The Balaam Traditions: Their Character and Development (SBLDS 113; Atlanta: Scholars Press, 1990), 66-96.
367 KTU 9.432; 1.108.12; 1.166.12. See O. Loretz, "Der kanaanäische Ursprung des biblischen Gottesnamens El Šaddaj", UF 12 (1980), 420-421; A. Caquot, "Une contribution ougaritique à la préhistoire du titre divin Shadday", in J.A. Emerton (ed.), Congress Volume Paris, 1992 (VTSup 61; Leiden: Brill, 1995), 1-12; Sanders, Provenance of Deuteronomy 32, 182-183; De Hoop, Genesis 49, 208-211.

Rephaim),[368] with whom *šd* may be connected.[369] De Hoop suggests that the association of *šd* with the ancestral cult at Ugarit is also indicated by the use of *kbkb*, "star", as an apparent determinative applied to *šd*, recalling the widespread ancient Near Eastern belief that dead kings and heroes became stars.[370] It may be, then, that the Ugaritic *šd* was a deified ancestor of some sort.[371] This is not only reminiscent of the association of the biblical שׁדים with the cult of the dead in Ps. 106, but also recalls the biblical personal name Ammishadday, "*šadday* is my ancestor" (Num. 1:12; 2:25; 7:66, 71; 10:25).[372] Further complementing this notion is the portrayal of שׁדי as a protective, personal deity within the blessings of Gen. 49:24-25, in which שׁדי is parallelled with אל אביך "El your father", a title frequently connected with Ugaritic *il abk*, "Ilu your father", and *ilib*, "deified father", titles associated with the protection and blessing of the family.[373] In view of this material, the portrayal of "El Šadday" in the Hebrew Bible is all the more striking. This god is inextricably bound up with the ancestors of Israel, and is explicitly identified with YHWH in Exod. 6:2-3: "I am YHWH. I appeared to Abraham, Isaac and Jacob as אל שׁדי, but by my name YHWH I did not make myself known to them." Significantly, it is "El Šadday" who establishes the covenant with the great ancestor Abram in Gen. 17. As has been seen, this important narrative is one of the ideological foundations upon which the story of the biblical Israel is constructed. Moreover, at the very heart of this

---

368 For useful overviews of the Rephaim as the royal dead, see further H. Rouillard, "Rephaim", *DDD*, 692-700; M.S. Smith, "Rephaim", *ABD*, vol. 5, 674-676; cf. Schmidt, *Beneficent Dead*, 71-100; *contra* P. Johnston, Review of *Israel's Beneficent Dead*, by B.B. Schmidt, *JTS* 47 (1996), 169-172.

369 De Hoop, *Genesis 49*, 211.

370 De Hoop, *Genesis 49*, 211; see also J.C. de Moor, "Standing Stones and Ancestor Worship", *UF* 27 (1995), 1-20 (11); F. Lelli, "Stars", *DDD*, 809-815; I. Zatelli, "Astrology and the Worship of the Stars in the Bible", *ZAW* 103 (1991), 86-99.

371 De Hoop, *Genesis 49*, 211, n. 842; K. van der Toorn, "Ancestors and Anthroponyms: Kinship Terms as Theophoric Elements in Hebrew Names", *ZAW* 108 (1996), 1-11.

372 This recalls the name *ša-di-'-m-i/ šadê-'ammî/* written upon an Egyptian statuette of the late fourteenth century BCE, discussed by Cross, *Canaanite Myth*, 53-54.

373 N. Wyatt, "The Problem of the 'God of the Fathers'", *ZAW* 90 (1978), 101-104; D.N. Freedman, "Divine Names and Titles in Early Hebrew Poetry", in F.M. Cross, W.E. Lemke and P.D. Miller (eds.), *Magnalia Dei: The Mighty Acts of God* (Garden City: Doubleday, 1976), 55-108; Smith, *Early History*, 16-17; M.C.A. Korpel, *A Rift in the Clouds: Ugaritic and Hebrew Descriptions of the Divine* (UBL 8; Münster: Ugarit-Verlag, 1990), 533. For *ilib*, see particularly J.F. Healey, "Ilib", *DDD*, 447-448; K. van der Toorn, "Ilib and the 'God of the Father'", *UF* 25 (1993), 379-387 (382); De Moor, "Standing Stones", 7-8, 12.

narrative is the covenant of circumcision between "El Šadday" and the newly-named Abraham, which results in the blessing of perpetual fertility for Abraham and his descendants. The close affiliation of child sacrifice and circumcision in the Hebrew Bible, described in the previous chapter, is in view in Gen. 17, as the blessing within this circumcision narrative foreshadows the divine blessing prompted by Abraham's willingness to sacrifice his son in Gen. 22. Furthermore, the location of "El Šadday" at the centre of this covenant of circumcision implicitly associates this god with both child sacrifice, an association attested of the שדים in Ps. 106 and the *šdyn* of the Deir ʿAlla text. Significant too is the fact that, in focusing these religious nuances upon the figure of Abraham, the great ancestor (or "father") of the biblical "Israel", the stories of Gen. 17 and 22 are suggestive of the important role of the ancestors within child sacrifice, a role which may be partially reflected in those biblical and non-biblical texts explored here.[374]

In summary, it is highly probable that the Deir ʿAlla texts describe the sacrifice of a child, in an attempt to avert the earthly darkness decreed by the *šdyn*. It is increasingly agreed that the biblical terms שדי, שדין and שדים are to be identified with the *šdyn* of Deir ʿAlla. The repeated biblical attestations linking שדי (אל), the שדים and Balaam with child sacrifice and related practices (circumcision, sacrificing to the dead) cannot be dismissed as a coincidence in view of the Deir ʿAlla texts, which also appear to associate Balaam and the *šdyn* with child sacrifice. This is strengthened further by the use of terminology associated with child sacrifice shared by the Deir ʿAlla texts and the Hebrew Bible, including *yʿbr* ("pass over"), *mdr* ("firepit"), *mškb* ("grave") and possibly even *mlk*. The possible Ugaritic association of *šd* with the cult of the deified ancestors may go some way to account for the biblical location of שדי and the שדים at the epicentre of a complex of traditions dealing with human fertility, circumcision, child sacrifice and the cult of the dead. This discussion has thus tentatively located a further tradition of child sacrifice that the biblical ideology has been unable to disguise fully: the sacrifice of children to the "*šadday*-god(s)".

---

374 The intriguing suggestion that Abraham may have been revered as a deified ancestor and "begetter" is summarized in M. Dijkstra, "Abraham", *DDD*, 3-6.

5.6 Child Sacrifice in Judah

Given the archaeological, epigraphic and textual evidence for child sacrifice assessed above, the discussion can now turn to reconstructing a plausible picture of child sacrifice in Judah. The lack of direct archaeological evidence for the practice in Judah renders the investigation dependent upon a careful, critical reading of the biblical texts in light of the non-biblical evidence. This task is facilitated further by the observations of chapter 4, in which the ideological and polemical functions of child sacrifice within the Hebrew Bible were assessed, making possible a more plausible and self-critical interpretation of the biblical material.

Though the Hebrew Bible portrays child sacrifice as a foreign practice, several texts indicate that it was a native element of Judahite deity-worship. As many as three possible cults of child sacrifice may be located within the Hebrew Bible: the sacrifice of the firstborn to YHWH; the fiery *mlk* sacrifice of children to YHWH in Jerusalem; and the sacrifice of children to the שדים. Each of these possibilities will be dealt with in turn.

In chapter 4 it was argued that the Hebrew Bible evidences a cluster of laws allowing for the sacrifice of the human firstborn to YHWH. Although many of these texts are subsequently qualified with clauses permitting the redemption of the human firstborn, Exod. 22:28-29 and 13:1-2 represent an unqualified rule, whereby a parent could sacrifice the firstborn child to YHWH. Elsewhere in the Hebrew Bible this appears to be confirmed in the explicit statement that YHWH demanded the sacrifice of firstborn (Ezek. 20:25-26) and the inclusion of the firstborn within a list of sacrificial offerings (Mic. 6:7).

Of the three possible cults of child sacrifice tentatively identified within this discussion, the firstborn-sacrifice is the most difficult to divorce from the biblical texts, given that it is difficult to locate within the archaeological record. But in view of the very existence of the biblical claims that YHWH demanded this type of sacrifice, the majority of commentators agree that, historically, it is perfectly plausible that some *Yhwh*-worshippers[375] did indeed sacrifice their firstborn children. Given the tendentious and created nature of the biblical story of Israel and Judah, it is highly unlikely that such a provocative and theologically-difficult premise would have been invented.

---

375 The reader is reminded of the distinction drawn in this study between YHWH, the central character and god of the Hebrew Bible, and *Yhwh*, a deity worshipped in and around ancient Palestine (see above, 8).

In seeking to discern a more precise historical context for these biblical texts relating to the sacrifice of the firstborn, many scholars maintain the more conventional view that the sacrifice of the human firstborn was an ancient practice gradually usurped by the sacrifice of an animal as a substitute. Those supporting this interpretation tend to assign Exod. 22:28-29 to a very early period within the religious history of *Yhwh*-worship, describing it as an archaic precept preserved at an early stage within the so-called Covenant Code, which itself tends to be given a correspondingly ancient provenance.[376]

However, as many other commentators have pointed out, it is far from certain whether Exod. 22:28-29 and the other biblical laws relating to the firstborn-sacrifice may be convincingly assigned to an early period.[377] Indeed, as has been seen, there are some biblical texts conventionally dated to the monarchic and post-monarchic periods that refer to the sacrifice of the human firstborn, such as Mic. 6:7; Ezek. 20:25-26 (cf. Josh. 6:26; 1 Kgs 16:34). Thus as Römer points out, it may be that the sacrifice of the firstborn animal did not replace the sacrifice of the human victim, but rather coexisted alongside the sacrifice of the human firstborn,[378] just as appears to have been the case in the Phoenician and Punic worlds.[379] Thus two possibilities are set out within the biblical laws: the YHWH-worshipper could sacrifice the human firstborn, or sacrifice an animal in place of the firstborn. This interpretation of the laws of the firstborn counters the conventional criticism of those unable to comprehend the possibility that the firstborn-sacrifice could be

---

376 E.g., Erling, "First-Born and Firstlings", 472-473; cf. H.J. Boecker, *Law and the Administration of Justice in the Old Testament and Ancient East* (Minneapolis: Augsburg, 1980), 135.

377 See especially Van Seters, "The Law on Child Sacrifice", 367-371; Kaiser, "Den Erstgeborenen", 24-48; Römer, "Le sacrifice humain", 20-22; Heider, *Molek*, 253.

378 Römer, "Le sacrifice humain", 21; cf. Kaiser, "Die Bindung Isaaks" 199-223. This is supported further by Van Seters ("Law on Child Sacrifice", 370-371), who argues that the unqualified law of the firstborn sacrifice is not necessarily the earliest of the firstborn regulations. Kaiser regards the inclusion of the human firstborn in the firstlings laws as a secondary expansion of the older custom of offering the animal firstborn; Kaiser, "Den Erstgeborenen", 164. Eissfeldt moderated his original position and suggested that the redemption of the firstborn had always been permitted; Eissfeldt, "Menschenopfer", *RGG3* 4 (1960), 868; cf. Eissfeldt, *Molk*, 51-55. Note also Heider ("A Further Turn on Ezekiel's Baroque Twist in Ezek. 20:25-26", *JBL* 107 [1988], 721-724), who writes, "it is ... easy to suppose that the cult's practitioners saw themselves as supremely devoted, by going 'above and beyond' the strict demands of the law" (723 n. 11).

379 Though the Phoenician-Punic practice may have begun as a cult of the sacrifice of the firstborn, it appears to have developed into a practice in which all young children were potential offerings.

carried out during the monarchic and early post-monarchic period of *Yhwh*-worship, a point of view exemplified by de Vaux, who asserts, "It would indeed be absurd to suppose that there could have been in Israel or among any other people, at any moment of their history, a constant general law, compelling the suppression of the first-born, who are the hope of the race".[380] De Vaux's comment not only betrays his misguided presupposition that the biblical texts accurately reflect a coherent legal system enforceable upon the whole population, but also demonstrates that he misunderstands both the optional sense which the firstborn regulations of the Hebrew Bible carry and the high value of the firstborn sacrifice. Certainly, de Vaux is correct in suggesting that the common and widespread sacrifice of the firstborn would be clearly damaging to the continued existence of communities. Moreover, it would also result in the depreciation of the value of the firstborn as a sacrifice.[381] But the co-existence of the sacrifice of the human or animal firstborn would give families the option of sacrificing either a firstborn child or an animal, presumably depending upon the circumstances of the (extended) family. Indeed, in considering the likely function of the firstborn sacrifice, the possible circumstances under which a family might choose to sacrifice a firstborn child come into view.

As has been seen, the biblical presentation of the firstborn-sacrifice is closely tied to issues of potential or divinely-promised fertility. Most of the biblical laws of the firstborn-sacrifice identify both the human and animal firstborn as the "the one who opens the womb" (פטר רחם),[382] thus defining the firstborn in terms of the mother's fertility.[383] This appears to be reflected in the example of Isaac, who is not Abraham's firstborn, but is explicitly and consistently portrayed as the first child of Sarah (Gen. 16:1; 17:19; 21:1-12). Though Isaac is not designated פטר רחם nor בכור, he is repeatedly labelled יחיד, "only-begotten" (Gen. 22:2, 12, 16), a special label that appears to be equated in status and value with the firstborn, as Zech. 12:10 suggests. The same title is also applied to Jephthah's daughter (Judg. 11:34). The fertility

---

380 De Vaux, *Studies*, 71. See also W.O.E. Oesterley, *Sacrifices in Ancient Israel: Their Origin, Purposes and Development* (London: Hodder & Stoughton, 1937), 118-119; Buber, *Kingship of God*, 219.

381 See also Kaiser, "Den Erstgeborenen", 163.

382 Exod. 13:2, 12, 15; 34:19; Num. 3:11-13; 8:13-18; 18:15; cf. Ezek. 20:25-26. The notable exception is Exod. 22:29, although note that 13:2 employs both בכור and פטר רחם.

383 This stands in contrast to the definition of the firstborn (בכור) in relation to the father within non-sacrificial Deuteronomic law (Deut. 21:15-17).

function of the sacrifice of the firstborn or only-begotten is centred within the biblical texts upon the figure of the sacrificial victim: because Abraham is willing to sacrifice his son Isaac, YHWH will bless him with a multitude of descendants (Gen. 21:12; 22:15-18). As the sacrificial victim Isaac is thus a symbol of potential fertility. So too is Jephthah's daughter, who is called בתולה: a girl who has reached puberty but has not yet given birth to her first child.[384] Similarly, the description of the sacrificed firstborn as the "fruit" of the "belly" or "womb" (פרי בטן) in Mic. 6:7 carries with it connotations of fertility. The close biblical association of circumcision and the firstborn-sacrifice is also suggestive of a fertility context for the sacrifice, as argued above. Thus although the biblical texts cannot offer historically accurate information about the purpose of the firstborn-sacrifice, it is possible that it was bound up with the hope of continued fertility. Indeed, as Ackerman has shown, the Hebrew Bible resonates with stories attributing human fertility and infertility to YHWH.[385] She argues that "the idea [is] that if Yahweh fills the womb, then Yahweh has a particular claim on what comes forth".[386] Though admittedly speculative, it is possible that some parents sacrificed their firstborn child to *Yhwh* in the hope that the deity would accept their most precious offering and bless them with further children.[387] In socio-economic terms, a large family was essential for the individual's subsistence. In religious terms, a large family was essential for a peaceful afterlife: within

---

384 Judg. 11:37, 38.

385 S. Ackerman, "Child Sacrifice: Returning God's Gift", *BR* 9/3 (1993), 20-29, 56.

386 Ackerman, "Child Sacrifice", 27. In a different publication, Ackerman explains *Yhwh*'s sacrificial claim upon children by emphasizing the well-known idea that *Yhwh* was originally an El figure, and that child sacrifice is integral to El's nature (*Under Every Green Tree*, 155-159).

387 This has also been generally suggested by J. Morgenstern, *Rites of Birth, Marriage, Death and Kindred Occasions among the Semites* (Cincinnati: Hebrew Union College Press, 1966), 63-64; M.H. Pope, "Fertility Cults", *IDB*, vol. 2, 265; H. Gese, "Ezechiel 20.25f und die Erstgeburtsopfer", in H. Donner, R. Hanhaert and R. Smend (eds.), *Beiträge zur alttestamentlichen Theologie: Festschrift für Walther Zimmerli zum 70. Geburtstag* (Göttingen: Vandenhoeck & Ruprecht, 1977), 140-151 (147); Ackerman, "Child Sacrifice", 20-29, 56; *contra* Green, *The Role of Human Sacrifice*, 202-203. A modified interpretation is represented by R. Girard (*Violence and the Sacred* [Baltimore: Johns Hopkins, 1977]) and W. Burkert (*Homo Necans: The Anthropology of Ancient Greek Sacrificial Ritual and Myth* [trans. P. Bing; London: University of California Press, 1983]) who describe human and animal sacrifice as the ritualised encounter with death, encompassing both the need to perpetuate fertility and to express the inescapable violence inherent within human nature. See further R.G. Hamerton-Kelly (ed.), *Violent Origins. Walter Burket, René Girard, and Jonathan Z. Smith on Ritual Killing and Cultural Formation* (Stanford: Stanford University Press, 1987), esp. 149-176.

the perpetual cycle of life and death, the living administered cultically to their dead ancestors to secure their blessings upon the family and to pave the way for their own inevitable role as one of the ancestors. However, as this understanding of the function of the firstborn-sacrifice is not grounded within reliable historical evidence, it can only remain a possibility.[388]

The threat of domestic crisis or military emergency is frequently offered as an alternative and more reliable interpretation accounting for the sacrifice of the firstborn.[389] Certainly, the biblical story of King Mesha's sacrifice of his firstborn son and heir to stave off military defeat (2 Kgs 3:26-27) complies with this interpretation. Yet the historical reliability of this story is to be seriously doubted, given its very nature as a biblical text. However, an Egyptian relief probably dating to the reign of Merneptah[390] may depict the

---

388 Some scholars have sought to associate the numerous examples of infant jar-burials at Palestinian sites with the firstborn sacrifice, e.g., R.A.S. Macalister, *Excavations at Gezer, Vol. II (1907-1909)* (London: John Murray, 1912), 401-406, 431-435; S.H. Hooke, *The Origins of Early Semitic Ritual* (Oxford: Oxford University Press, 1938), 48-50; W.C. Graham and H.G. May, *Culture and Conscience: An Archaeological Study of the New Religious Past in Ancient Palestine* (Chicago: Chicago of University Press, 1940), 74-79; J. Finegan, *Light from the Ancient Past* (Princeton: Princeton University Press, 1959), 147-149; N.M. Sarna, *Understanding Genesis* (New York: Schocken, 1966), 158-159; E. Anati, *Palestine Before the Hebrews: A History, from the Earliest Arrival of Man to the Conquest of Canaan* (New York: Knopf, 1963), 427, cited in Green, *Human Sacrifice*, 153, 328, n. 7. However, there is very little within the archaeological context to argue against the probability that these children died of natural causes. But the finds have continued to receive a cultic interpretation (Dever, "Gezer", *EAEHL*, vol. 2, 438). Indeed, the site itself has been identified as a cult place for the veneration of dead ancestors (Albright, "The High Place in Ancient Palestine", 242-258). Infants buried beneath or near walls have been identified as foundation sacrifices and associated with Hiel's sacrifice of his sons in 1 Kgs 16:34 (cf. Josh. 6:26). However, the available evidence is scarce and open to a variety of interpretations. See the discussion in Green, *Human Sacrifice*, 153-156.

389 E.g., B. Margalit, "Why King Mesha of Moab Sacrificed his Oldest Son", *BAR* 12/6 (1986), 62-63, 76; J.K. Hoffmeier, "Further Evidence for Infant Sacrifice in the Ancient Near East", *BAR* 13/2 (1987), 60-61; Smith, *Early History*, 135-136; Ackerman, *Under Every Green Tree*, 120-121; Green, *Human Sacrifice*, 202.

390 P. Derchain attributes the relief to the reign of Ramses II ("Les plus anciens témoignages de sacrifice d'enfants chez les sémites occidentaux", *VT* 20 [1970]: 351-355 [351, n. 2]) but it has been redated to the reign of Merneptah; see F. Yurco, "Merneptah's Palestinian Campaign", *The Society for the Study of Egyptian Antiquities Journal* 8/3 (1978), 70; L.E. Stager, "Merneptah, Israel and Sea Peoples: New Light on an Old Relief", *EI* 18 (1985), 56-64.

sacrifice of children during a siege of Ashkelon.[391] The relief depicts the besieged inhabitants of the town holding their arms aloft to the sky. A bearded figure raises with his left hand an incense burner, his open-palmed right hand held up in a pose intriguingly reminiscent of the Hand motif associated with child sacrifice in the Phoenician and Punic worlds. Two further bearded figures are each portrayed dangling the limp body of a small child over the fortified city walls, suggesting to both Derchain and Spalinger that these children have been sacrificed to avert the attack. Though an attractive possibility, this scene can also be interpreted more innocuously as depicting the movement of the children from one level of the city to another.[392] Thus of the many possible functions of the firstborn-sacrifice, the weight of probability rests with that of a fertility ritual, though it must be re-emphasized that this suggestion can only remain speculative. However, given the pervading presence of the motif of the firstborn-sacrifice throughout the Hebrew Bible, it seems likely that a *Yhwh*-cult of the sacrifice of the firstborn was known and practised in Judah.

A further cult of child sacrifice which was probably known in Judah is that of the *mlk* sacrifice. As argued above, this cult is to be related to the *mlk* cult known from the Phoenician and Punic worlds. A wealth of archaeological, inscriptional and iconographic data combines to reveal a fairly detailed picture of this practice: young children, usually babies, were burned in fire as a sacrifice to the primary deities of the community; their remains were collected in an urn and buried in a sacred precinct, the burial place often marked with a stela, inscribed with iconographic motifs or a public declaration. This detailed picture supports the identification of similar burial sites in Phoenicia and along the Palestinian coast, allowing for the probability that Judahite people of the monarchic and post-monarchic periods at least knew something of the practice. Indeed, several biblical texts appear to indicate that the practice was known in Judah.

The biblical texts tend to employ stereotypical phraseology to describe the *mlk* sacrifice: it is a practice in which children are either "made to pass over" (העביר) and/or are "given" (נתן) or "burned" (שרף) "in the fire" (באש)

---

391 Derchain, "Les plus anciens témoignages", 351-355; A.J. Spalinger, "A Canaanite Ritual Found in Egyptian Reliefs", *The Society for the Study of Egyptian Antiquities Journal* 8/2 (1978), 47-60; M. Artzy, "Pomegranate Scepters and Incense Stand with Pomegranates found in Priest's Grave", *BAR* 16/1 (1990), 48-51.

392 Ackerman, *Under Every Green Tree*, 121.

as a *mlk*-offering (למלך) to YHWH.[393]   2 Kgs 23:10 and Isa. 30:33 label the place of burning as תפה, probably a firepit of sorts, which Kings and Jeremiah locate in the Valley of Ben Hinnom (2 Kgs 23:10; Jer. 7:31-32; 19:6). This may cohere with Phoenician and Punic evidence that the sacred precincts were probably separated from urban areas. However, several other biblical texts appear to associate the practice with the temple or Zion: Isa. 31:9 locates YHWH's "fire" and "furnace" in Zion, seemingly contradicting the location of the תפה away from YHWH's temple in Kings and Jeremiah. This recalls references to YHWH-worshippers sacrificing their children and worshipping in YHWH's sanctuary (Ezek. 23:37-39). A similar assertion is made in Lev. 20:3, which explicitly prohibits the sacrificing of children as "*mlk*-offerings" in YHWH's sanctuary. Yet this seeming contradiction may be remedied with reference again to the Phoenician and Punic iconographic evidence suggesting that accompanying rituals were performed in a separate temple or sanctuary.[394] Thus it is reasonable to envisage a practice in which rituals (perhaps even including the death of the child) occurred in *Yhwh*'s temple before the burning and interring of the sacrificed child at the תפה, which may well have been located in one of the valleys around Jerusalem. The pervading association of the Ben Hinnom Valley with fires and death within post-biblical traditions suggests that this may indeed have been the location of the sacrificial precinct.

In attempting to determine the function of the *mlk* sacrifice in Judah, the only evidence is that offered by the biblical texts and the Phoenician and Punic material. There is a tendency among scholars to suggest that this type of sacrifice was offered as a response to a military crisis. This view is clearly influenced by classical and patristic accounts of the Phoenician practice as an emergency cult, and further encouraged by the biblical association of this sacrifice with Ahaz (2 Kgs 16:3) and Manasseh (21:6), leading to the speculative conclusion that the threat of military destruction during their reigns, in the form of the so-called Syro-Ephraimite war (Ahaz) and in the aftermath of the Assyrian subjugation of Judah (Manasseh), prompted the kings to sacrifice their sons. However, there is no textual evidence to support the notion that the Judahite *mlk* sacrifice was an emergency cult practised in times of military threat or national crisis. Rather, the biblical texts do not offer any explanation as to the purpose of the sacrifice. Consequently,

---

393 The shared terminology exhibited in references to both the *mlk* sacrifice and the firstborn sacrifice (נתן, העביר) is an important feature, the implications of which will be discussed below.
394 See 5.2 above.

evidence from the Phoenician and Punic worlds may shed light upon a possible function of the *mlk* sacrifice. The possibility that the *mlk* sacrifice was bound up with human fertility is suggested by the sheer predominance of individual newborns (human and animal) burned and buried within the Phoenician and Punic precincts. The epigraphic evidence from these sites indicates that the sacrifices were made in fulfilment of a personal vow, a vow made in explicit anticipation of a divine blessing. Thus the child was probably sacrificed only after the deity was perceived to have accepted and granted the dedicant's request. In light of the fact that most of the remains recovered from the precincts are those of newborns, it is thus more than likely that the initial vow was made before or during the pregnancy. The fertility context of the sacrifice is also implied by the Constantine inscription (*KAI* 162), a text suggesting that a pregnancy was interpreted as the divine fulfilment of the dedicant's request. Additionally, the inscriptions upon the sacrificial monuments frequently include lengthy genealogies, perhaps locating the request for human fertility within the context of a prolific ancestry.

In light of this evidence, it is even possible to speculate that the *mlk* sacrifice may have had associations with a firstborn cult. In partial support of this suggestion is the euphemistic use of the term *ytn*, "to give", within Punic inscriptions describing the sacrifice of a child or an animal; this term is clearly reminiscent of the sacrificial meaning of the biblical term נתן, frequently employed throughout the texts relating to child sacrifice, including those associated with the offering of the firstborn. Further evidence may be found in the supposed foundation myth of the Phoenician cult of child sacrifice, ascribed to the Phoenician historian Sakkunyaton within the *Phoenician History* of Philo of Byblos, which is itself cited in Eusebius' *Praeparatio evangelica*. Sakkunyaton reportedly accounts for Phoenician child sacrifice by twice describing the myth associated with the practice:[395]

Kronos then, whom the Phoenicians call Elus, who was king of the country and subsequently, after his decease, was deified as the star of Saturn, had by a nymph of the country named Anobret an only-begotten son, whom they on this account called Iedoud, the only-begotten being still so called among the Phoenicians; and when very great dangers from war had beset the country, he arrayed his son in royal apparel, and prepared an altar, and sacrificed him.[396]

---

395 Euseb. *Praep. ev.* 1.10.33, 44.
396 Translation from E.H. Gifford (ed.), *Eusebii Pamphili evangelicae praeparationis*, vol. 3, part 1 (Oxford: Oxford University Press, 1903), 171.

Within this version the son is repeatedly described as the "only-begotten" of El/Kronos, supporting the possibility that the cult was understood within some circles as a firstborn-sacrifice. Indeed, though the name of the son is here rendered "Iedoud", probably to be related to Hebrew יָדִיד, "beloved", "precious" (cf. Deut. 33:12), in another manuscript he is sacrificed as a whole burnt offering (ὁλοκαρποι) and named "Ieoud", which is widely-held to be related to biblical יָחִיד, "only-begotten", and other Semitic cognates.[397] This alternative name thus complements the description of the sacrificed son as "only-begotten" (μονογενης), a designation of which the biblical equivalent, יָחִיד, is also particularly prominent within texts relating to the firstborn-sacrifice (Gen. 22:2, 12, 16; Judg. 11:34). However, there is evidence to suggest that the confusion of "Iedoud" and "Ieoud" is more than coincidental. Levenson argues that the Hebrew epithet יָדִיד, "beloved", is applied to Benjamin because he is the precious young son of his father's old age, just as Isaac (Gen. 21:2) and Joseph (Gen. 37:3; 44:20) are the favourites because they are the sons of their fathers' old age.[398] In this sense then, the high socio-religious value of the beloved son is not necessarily strictly dependent upon his status as a firstborn of either his mother or father.

However, Levenson also demonstrates that the "only-begotten" and "beloved" could be equated. The translators responsible for the Septuagint appear to have associated, or in some places even replaced the word יָחִיד, "only-begotten", with language describing love.[399] Significantly, this apparent confusion occurs in the stories of both the Aqedah and Jephthah's daughter. In the MT, Abraham's son is described as בִּנְךָ אֶת־יְחִידְךָ אֲשֶׁר אָהַבְתָּ, "your son, your only-begotten son whom you love" (Gen. 22:2), yet this is rendered in the Septuagint as τον υιον σου τον αγαπητον ὁν ηγαπησας, "your beloved son, whom you love". Another Septuagint text describes Jephthah's daughter not simply as μονογενης, "only-begotten", as in MT Judg. 11:34, but as μονογενης αὐτω αγαπητη, "his only-begotten and beloved".[400] In the MT, mourning for an only-begotten child (יָחִיד) in Amos 8:10 and Jer. 6:26 is rendered in the Septuagint as πενθος αγαπητου, "mourning for the beloved one". Levenson draws attention to the function of the labels יָחִיד and יָדִיד as

---

397 Eg. H.W. Attridge and R.A. Oden, *Philo of Byblos, The Phoenician History* (CBQMS 9; Washington: Catholic Biblical Association of America, 1981), 94, n. 150; Albright, *Yahweh*, 203; Levenson, *Beloved Son*, 27; Ackerman, *Under Every Green Tree*, 138; Smith, *Early History*, 135.

398 Levenson, *Beloved Son*, 29.

399 Levenson, *Beloved Son*, 26-31.

400 LXX[A].

important motifs within the biblical portrayal of child sacrifice. As such, their apparent confusion within the Septuagint and Eusebius' rendering of Philo of Byblos may not be a simple coincidence, but rather could reflect the emphasis placed upon the high socio-religious value of the sacrificed child within these ancient texts and within the Hebrew Bible.

Interestingly, a further connection between this Phoenician foundation myth and the biblical portrayal of child sacrifice is Sakkunyaton's assertion that the practice of circumcision was introduced to commemorate the sacrifice of Iedoud/Ieoud.[401] This is particularly striking in light of the prominent association of the firstborn-sacrifice with circumcision within the Hebrew Bible.

Despite this admittedly circumstantial evidence, there exists archaeological data which could contest the suggestion that the *mlk* sacrifice had some association with a firstborn cult. Material remains recovered from the fourth century stratum of the Carthaginian precinct would seem to indicate that all young children could be sacrificed, not simply the firstborn: some urns have been found to contain the remains of a newborn baby along with one or sometimes even two older children from the same family. In answer to this challenge, it has been suggested that this evidence reflects an evolution of the firstborn-sacrifice in Carthage, whereby all children eventually became potential offerings within the cult. Thus if a pregnancy promised for sacrifice resulted in a stillbirth, older children from the same family were offered instead to fulfil the vow. However, whether these older children shared the same mother as the newborn, or were half-siblings (perhaps the children of another wife), or even cousins is currently unknown. In light of the limitations of the archaeological, epigraphic and textual evidence, it is impossible to ascertain whether the Phoenician and Punic *mlk* practice was ever a firstborn cult. What is more certain, however, is the suggestion that the *mlk* sacrifice in general was bound up with human fertility.

Having exhausted the non-biblical evidence, the discussion is subsequently dependent upon the biblical texts in seeking to establish the likely character and function of the *mlk* sacrifice in Judah. Recognizing the severe limitations of the biblical material as an historically reliable witness to the practice, it is nevertheless possible to draw a few, very tentative, conclusions which, though speculative, are plausible in light of the preceding discussion.

---

401 Euseb. *Praep. ev.* 1.10.33, 44; Attridge and Oden, *Philo of Byblos*, 57.

The overwhelming association of the *mlk* practice with the Jerusalem cult of YHWH throughout the Hebrew Bible, in spite of biblical attempts to distance YHWH from all forms of child sacrifice, is highly suggestive of the cult's historical existence within the royal cult in monarchic Judah. Alongside the more obvious royal associations of the sacrifice within the accounts of the reigns of Ahaz (2 Kgs 16:3) and Manasseh (21:6), the account of the destruction of the תפת in the story of Josiah's reform (23:10) also implies that the practice was understood to be a part of the royal cult. Interestingly, the following verse refers to a cult functionary located at the entrance to YHWH's temple called "Nathan-Melek" (נתן מלך), who is associated with the supposedly illicit practices of the state cult. Though this character is not explicitly connected with the תפת, it is interesting to note that his name is comprised of two of the terms associated with the *mlk* sacrifice.[402]

The Jerusalem-centred, royal character of the sacrificial practice in which children are "made to pass over in the fire" is far more pervasive throughout the Hebrew Bible than is the term מלך, yet it is this term which has dominated the perspective of academic enquiry. In light of this contrast and the evidence surveyed here, it is thus reasonable to refer again to the arguments of Albright and Mosca that both Hebrew מלך and Punic *mlk* are derived from the stem *mlk*, "royal".[403] As such, these terms reflect the overtly royal cultic setting of this sacrifice.[404] Indeed, following Pope, Smith comments that a royal origin of the Punic term may well be reflected in the myth of El/Kronos arraying his (only-begotten) son in royal apparel and

---

402 Also noted by Heider, *Molek*, 230-231. Day (*Molech*, 58-64) argues that the "covenant with death" in Isa. 28:15, 18 is an allusion to this sacrifice. If so, the poet's accusation that the rulers of Jerusalem have made this covenant may offer further support for the royal character of the sacrifice. However, Day's interpretation is contested. See most recently, J. Blenkinsopp, "Judah's covenant with Death (Isaiah XXVIII 14-22)", *VT* 50 (2000), 14-22. See also Schmidt, *Beneficent Dead*, 158-162; B. Halpern, "'The Excremental Vision': The Doomed Priests of Doom in Isaiah 28", *HAR* 10 (1986), 109-121.

403 See 5.3 above.

404 This possibility is suggested further by an Ugaritic text distinguishing a *dbh mlk*, "royal sacrifice" (RS 19.15.2). Though this does *not* imply any relation to child sacrifice, it may support the suggestion that certain sacrifices were specifically connected to the royal cult. See C.F.A. Schaeffer, "Sacrifice à M-l-k, Moloch ou Melek", in C.F.A. Schaeffer and J.C. Courtois (eds.), *Ugaritica IV: Découvertes des XVIIIe et XIXe campagnes, 1951–1955* (Mission de Ras Shamra 15/Bibliothèque archéologique et historique 74; Paris: Imprimerie Nationale, 1962), 77-83.

sacrificing him.[405] As Smith states, "If one were to follow the etymology of *mlk*, it might be supposed that the *mlk* perhaps originated either as a Canaanite royal child sacrifice devoted to the main god of the locality or a sacrifice devoted to the deity considered in the locality as the king of the pantheon".[406] Though Mosca accredits the classical and biblical texts with more historical reliability than this discussion would allow, his comments are nevertheless instructive:

> The *mulk*-sacrifice does ... seem to have been *the* "royal sacrifice" *par excellence*. Not only was the offering consistently made to the appropriate divine "king": El, Baal Hamon, Yahweh, and possibly also Adrammelech and Anammelech. In many cases, also, the offerer was himself a king: Ahaz, Manasseh, and probably Mesha. And this, in turn, would mean that the victims themselves were children of royal blood. Thus, the *mulk*-sacrifice may have been originally the offering of royalty, by royalty, to royalty.[407]

In seeking to discern the likely function of the *mlk* sacrifice in Judah, it is thus plausible to describe that practice as a royal sacrifice offered by the king within the royal *Yhwh* cult of Jerusalem. Its fundamental function as a fertility ritual and an apotropaic rite would probably have held an important place within the royal ideology. As such, the *mlk* sacrifice should probably be directly related to the desire for the perpetuation of the royal dynasty, of which *Yhwh* of Zion was patron-deity.[408] It is thus notable that the term צמח, "scion", is often employed to describe a legitimate heir of the Davidic monarchy within the Hebrew Bible (e.g., Jer. 23:5; 33:15; Zech. 3:8; 6:12). This term is cognate with Phoenician and Punic *ṣmḥ*, "scion, sprout", which often occurs within the Punic inscriptions attesting to child sacrifice.[409] Cross

---

405 Smith, *Early History*, 135; Levenson, *Beloved Son*, 27.

406 Smith, *Early History*, 136.

407 Mosca, "Child Sacrifice", 273. As Mosca states, the characteristics peculiar to the Carthaginian sacred precinct would seem to indicate that by the fourth century, the *mlk* sacrifice at Carthage had broken its royal bonds and become "democratized", enabling a wider range of Carthaginians to participate within the cult.

408 Echoes of this royal, Zion ideology of dynasty pervade the Hebrew Bible, for example, 2 Sam. 7:11-29; Pss. 2; 45; 72; 89:1-3, 26-37; 132; Isa. 9:6-7. See further A. Laato, "Second Samuel 7 and Ancient Near Eastern Royal Ideology", *CBQ* 59 (1997), 244-269; T. Ishida, *The Royal Dynasties in Ancient Israel: A Study on the Formation and Development of Royal-Dynastic Ideology* (BZAW 142; Berlin: de Gruyter, 1977); J.J.M. Roberts, "In Defense of the Monarchy: The Contribution of Israelite Kingship to Biblical Theology", in Hanson, Miller, McBride, *Ancient Israelite Religion*, 337-396.

409 E.g., *KAI* 162, 163.

argues that within Hebrew, Phoenician and Punic, the word is a *terminus technicus*, used to describe a (possibly royal) legitimate heir.[410]

It is possible that the Judahite *mlk* sacrifice was bound up with the royal cult of the dead, in which the royal dead ancestors were not necessarily worshipped, but provided for by means of offerings and libations, in hope, acknowledgement, or appeasement of their continuing influence within the earthly, royal realm.[411] Indeed, the biblical description of the royal temple in Jerusalem in 1 Kgs 6–7 refers to two pillars set up in the temple entrance (7:21) called יָכִין (Jachin) and בֹּעַז (Boaz). The former name is that of the biblical David's ancestor (Ruth 2:1–4:22; 1 Chr. 2:11-12) and the latter not only appears frequently among the names of deified ancestors in the ancient Near East, but also occurs within the name of the later Davidic king Jehoiachin (יְהוֹיָכִין).[412] In this context, Heider's association of the fiery sacrifice with a (possibly royal) cult of the dead in which the ancestors became an indirect object of the cult's attentions is useful in places.[413] However, given the admittedly oblique nature of this association, little more can be claimed before plausible speculation becomes unpersuasive imagination.

Given the possible points of contact between the *mlk* sacrifice and the firstborn offering noted above, it may be that the two were related at some point in their histories. Certainly, the possibility that the Judahite *mlk* sacrifice was related in some way to the firstborn offering finds some support within the biblical texts, not least in their shared terminology (נתן, עבר). Moreover, though ostensibly firstborn offerings, the nature of the near-sacrifice of Isaac and the sacrifice of Mesha's son as burnt offerings (cf. Mic. 6:6-7) suggests the possibility of a conceptual link between the two. Indeed, the royal context of Mesha's sacrifice of his firstborn son and heir may also support a biblical connection between the firstborn-sacrifice and the *mlk* sacrifice.[414] However, as with so much else within this discussion, a consensus opinion is yet to be reached. The majority of scholars argue that the *mlk* sacrifice and the offering of the firstborn are unrelated because the

---

410 Cross, "Phoenician Inscription", 98.

411 Controversy continues to surround the debate concerning the cult of the dead in Judah. For a useful summary, see Smith, *Early History*, 126-132. For more detailed discussions, see the literature cited in chapter 1 (23, n. 35).

412 2 Kgs 24:8–25:30. See De Moor, "Standing Stones", 16-17.

413 Heider, *Molek*, 383-400.

414 The term *'lh*, cognate with the biblical term עֹלָה, is also used within Punic inscriptions attesting to the *mlk* sacrifice.

biblical laws concerning the firstborn-sacrifice appear to apply only to the male firstborn (Exod. 13:12-15; 22:28-29; 34:19)[415] whereas some of the texts referring or alluding to the *mlk* sacrifice speak of both sons and daughters being sacrificed (Deut. 12:31; 18:10; 2 Kgs 17:17; 23:10; Jer. 7:31; 32:35).[416] Weakening this position, however, is Num. 27:1-8, which appears to allow a daughter to substitute for the firstborn son and heir. Other scholars, most notably Ackerman, identify the two sacrifices with little or no explanation.[417] Confusing the issue further is Mosca, who argues for the separation of the *mlk* sacrifice and the firstborn offering, yet unintentionally connects the two by concluding that the human firstborn would probably have been redeemed, so that if the firstborn child was sacrificed, it would have been as a *mlk*-sacrifice, not as a firstborn offering.[418]

This variety of opinions within scholarship testifies to the ambiguous nature of the relationship between the Judahite *mlk* sacrifice and the firstborn offering.[419] Given the evidence surveyed here, a preferable understanding of the relationship of these two *Yhwh*-sacrifices springs from interpreting the Jerusalem *mlk* cult as a royal specialization of the fertility rite of the firstborn sacrifice, in which a royal pregnancy was promised as a gift to *Yhwh*, the patron-deity of the Judahite royal family, and sacrificed in fire shortly after the birth as a means of encouraging the divine perpetuation of the royal dynasty. A faint but intriguing echo of the relationship of the Jerusalem royal dynastic ideology and the *mlk* sacrifice may also be heard in the nomenclature of the Hebrew Bible, which employs designations prominently associated with child sacrifice: the name of the legendary founder of the royal dynasty in Jerusalem is David (דוד), which could be rendered "Beloved One";[420] his son Solomon, who replaces David and Bathsheba's dead

---

415 Reading in Exod. 34:19, with the support of the Versions, הזכר instead of MT תזכר.
416 E.g., Day, *Molech*, 67; Heider, *Molek*, 254. Those maintaining that מֹלֶךְ is the proper name of a god necessarily hold the biblical firstborn sacrifice and the presumed sacrifice to "Molek" as unrelated offerings in order to maintain their separation of YHWH and "Molek".
417 Ackerman, *Under Every Green Tree*, 137.
418 Mosca, "Child Sacrifice", 236-238.
419 Interestingly, the practices of modern Samaritans may harbour a memory of a relationship between the firstborn offering and the *mlk* sacrifice: at Passover— biblically connected with the firstborn sacrifice—the Samaritans sacrifice lambs as burnt offerings within a deep firepit, reminiscent of the burning pit at Sousse (see above, 5.2) and the biblical חפה. For illustrations and a description of the firepit, see R. Pummer, *The Samaritans* (Leiden: Brill, 1987), 21-22, pls. XXXIIIa.
420 *BDB*, 187; see also Halpern, *David's Secret Demons*, 266, 269.

firstborn, is said to be loved by YHWH and is thus renamed Jedidiah (ידידיה),
"Beloved of *Yah*".[421] This all casts a different light upon the presumed
background of Zech. 12:10-12, in which YHWH announces:

> I will pour out a spirit of compassion and supplication upon the House of David and
> upon the inhabitants of Jerusalem, so that when they look upon the one whom they
> have pierced, they shall mourn for him, as one mourns for an only-begotten child
> (יחיד), and weep bitterly over him, as one weeps over a firstborn (בכור). On that day
> the mourning will be as great as the mourning for Hadad-rimmon in the plain of
> Megiddo. The land shall mourn, each family by itself; the family of the house of
> David by itself, and their wives by themselves; the house of Nathan (נתן) by itself,
> and their wives by themselves.

A further cult of child sacrifice which was probably known in Judah is that of
the sacrifice to the *šadday*-god(s). The Deir ʿAlla texts suggest that child
sacrifice existed within the worship of the *šdyn* in the Transjordan. The
description of the sacrifice of a newborn child exhibits many striking
similarities with the biblical phraseology of the firstborn-sacrifice and the *mlk*
sacrifice. The term *yʿbr*, "pass over", may describe the journey of the child
from life to death, just as the biblical term העביר is used repeatedly to refer
to the sacrifice of a child within the firstborn-sacrifice and the *mlk* cult. This
non-biblical attestation of the term within a context of child sacrifice may
thus confirm that the euphemistic language of child sacrifice within the
Hebrew Bible is not simply the result of theological sensitivities, but was
originally a stock component of the vocabulary of child sacrifice in this
region. Indeed, the Punic inscriptions upon sacrificial stelae similarly do not
employ the explicit language of killing, but rather use euphemistic
terminology (including *ytn*, "give") to speak of child sacrifice.[422]

A further parallel with the firstborn-sacrifice is evident in the use of the
term *htn*, "bridegroom", cognate with Hebrew חתן and related to the Arabic
verb *ḥatana*, "circumcise", a term and concept closely bound up with the
firstborn-sacrifice within the biblical texts. Striking parallels between the
biblical portrayal of the *mlk* sacrifice and the ritual partially described in the
Deir ʿAlla texts are also apparent: not only does the root *mlk* occur

---

421 2 Sam. 12:24-25. On this text see further Levenson, *Beloved Son*, 29-30.
422 Mosca ("Child Sacrifice", 172-174) highlights the biblical distinction in terminology
    between "Israelites", whose behaviour is described with the expression העביר באש and
    who treat YHWH as if he were an idol, and the outright and "non-Israelite" idolatrous,
    whose behaviour is described with the expression שרף באש; see Deut. 12:31; 2 Kgs
    17:31; cf. Deut. 18:10; 2 Kgs 16:3; 17:17; 21:6.

throughout the plaster text, but the term *mdr*, "firepit", instantly recalls the description in Isa. 30:27-33 of the תפת (MT תפתה), in which the firepit is termed מדרה (v. 33). Similarly, the use of *mškb*, "grave", within the Deir ʿAlla text parallels the repeated use of its cognate משכב throughout Isa. 57:3-13, a biblical poem describing the *mlk* sacrifice. More significant, perhaps, is the description of the sacrificed child as the *nqr*, "scion", "sprout", a term connected with the *mlk* sacrifice, as argued earlier in the discusssion.

As has been seen, the context of child sacrifice shared by the *šdyn* of Deir ʿAlla and the שדים of the Hebrew Bible strongly suggests that traditions underlying the portrayal of the biblical god אל שדי at some point associated this deity with child sacrifice. This suggestion is strengthened further by the role of the biblical אל שדי as the divine bestower of fertility upon the great ancestor Abram/Abraham and his descendants by means of circumcision, a practice directly related to child sacrifice. Indeed, the prominent association of Abraham with אל שדי, child sacrifice and circumcision is probably directly related to his role as the great ancestor of the biblical Israel. The possible fertility function of the sacrifice to the *šadday*-god(s) is also suggested within the Deir ʿAlla text. In this text, it may be that the child is sacrificed to stave off the impending infertility of the earthly realm: the darkness and chaos of the first combination appears to be reversed after the sacrifice at the end of Combination II, which describes the dripping of heavy rain and dew. The fertility context of the sacrifice is also suggested by the divine name(s) *šgr* *wʿštr*, which can be rendered "procreation and fertility", and also occurs within the Hebrew Bible as a formulaic expression for fertility (Deut. 7:13; 28:4, 18, 51; cf. Exod. 13:12).[423]

In light of the preceding discussion, it is thus plausible to reconstruct the existence or memory of a cult of the *šadday*-god(s) in Judah, in which child sacrifice, fertility and a cult of dead ancestors were closely bound. Indeed, the possibility that both *Yhwh* and *Šadday* may have functioned as gods of child sacrifice within Syro-Palestine may even suggest that this shared practice played a formative role in their eventual equation in the Hebrew Bible, demonstrated not only in their explicit identification in Exod. 6:2-3, but also in the stories of the divine blessing of the great ancestor Abraham in Genesis. The stories of the Aqedah (Gen. 22:1-19) and the covenant of circumcision

---

423 An alternative interpretation could be the consultative function of the sacrifice, possibly suggested by line 9 of Combination II and comparable to Isa. 57:9. However, though possible, this interpretation is too uncertain to eclipse the clearer fertility context of the sacrifice.

(Gen. 17:1-27) are very similar. In the Aqedah, Abraham receives YHWH's fertility blessing of a multitude of descendants because he will sacrifice his son. In Gen. 17:1-27, it is "El Šadday" who blesses Abraham with a multitude of descendants by means of the covenant of circumcision, a practice inextricably bound to child sacrifice.

Thus it would appear that three possible cults of child sacrifice may plausibly have existed within Judah: the firstborn sacrifice, the *mlk* sacrifice, and the sacrifice to the *šadday* gods. Though there are fundamental differences among these three cults which disallow their identification, they do exhibit striking parallels, which are suggestive of their possible interrelation at some point during the history of Judahite deity-worship or during the period of the formation of the biblical material. Perhaps one of the central facets of these forms of child sacrifice was the association of the practice with fertility; though seemingly paradoxical, the sacrificed child appears to have functioned as a religious symbol of, and stimulus for, fertility and the perpetuation of the family. A final point remains. The range of material pertaining to child sacrifice examined here throws into sharp relief the scholarly preoccupation with the term מֹלֶךְ. Though the term is naturally assigned an important place within this study, the proposals detailed here suggest that the parameters of scholarly discussions of child sacrifice extend well beyond the bounds of the מֹלֶךְ debate. Indeed, child sacrifice in Judah is likely to have existed in various forms, as a normative though infrequent element of indigenous, Judahite religious practice.

The Distortion of Child Sacrifice

The discussions of the preceding chapters suggest that the historical reality of Judahite child sacrifice was very different from its biblical portrayal. This may find partial explanation in the suggestion that during the post-monarchic period, when many biblical traditions were subject to intense literary attention, monarchic forms of Judahite child sacrifice had been marginalized, abandoned, or forgotten. Consequently, this may have resulted in the unintentional misrepresentation of child sacrifice within the Hebrew Bible. However, it is not unreasonable to suggest that, in many places, the biblical writers deliberately sought to distort their presentation of child sacrifice in an attempt to distance YHWH from a practice which came to be rejected within certain post-monarchic circles. Some of the possible processes of this distortion of child sacrifice will be explored briefly below. However, before turning to that discussion, it is important to acknowledge that, in spite of biblical attempts to distort the historical reality of Judahite child sacrifice, it survives in several forms as a powerful motif within several biblical and post-biblical texts. These "afterlives" of child sacrifice are perhaps further, albeit indirect, evidence of the deep-rooted place of child sacrifice within the deity-worship of Judah. Accordingly, it is to this matter that the discussion shall turn first.

6.1 Afterlives of Child Sacrifice

The biblical transformation of the *mlk* sacrifice into the fictitious, foreign god "Molek" is perhaps the most obvious illustration of the way in which this Judahite sacrifice continued to exist in an altered form after its presumed historical demise. Close textual examination suggests that the biblical "afterlife" of the *mlk* rite as "Molek" probably came into being at a point during the late Persian period, before the rendering of the Hebrew texts into

Greek.[1] However, the metamorphosis of the *mlk* sacrifice did not end there. Within rabbinic traditions,[2] the further transformation of the sacrifice is evident. A handful of texts speak of burning children in fire.[3] However, most interpret "Molek" worship as the handing over of children to idolatrous priests, who passed the children (alive)[4] through fire.[5] Similarly, the biblical phrase העביר למלך באש was taken by Rabbi Judah to refer to a ritual in which children were "passed over" into a covenant of idolatry, perhaps in an illicit version of the covenantal ritual of Gen. 15 and Jer. 34.[6] A further rabbinic interpretation of "Molek" worship is ascribed to Rabbi Ishmael, who interprets Lev. 18:21 as prohibiting the begetting of children with an "Aramaean" (i.e. gentile) woman.[7] The Peshitta is in agreement, interpreting Lev. 18:21 and 20:2-4 as the prohibition of sexual intercourse with a gentile woman or rendering a gentile woman pregnant. Targum Pseudo-Jonathan (Lev. 18:21) appears to combine these traditions in its outlawing of sexual intercourse with a gentile woman for fear of conceiving a child destined for idolatry.[8] Despite their variations, all these post-biblical traditions share not only the view that this idolatrous practice is non-sacrificial, but also the understanding that the biblical "Molek" texts prohibit the transference of "Israelite" children or semen to foreign gods or foreign women.

Interestingly, a version of this "afterlife" of the *mlk* sacrifice also exists within the book of Jubilees, in which the Israelite man who gives his daughter or sister to a Gentile, or who accepts for his son the daughter of a Gentile, shall be stoned to death:

> And if there is any man in Israel who wishes to give his daughter or his sister to any man who is from the seed of the gentiles, let him surely die, and let him be stoned because he has caused shame in Israel. And also the woman will be burned with fire because she has defiled the name of her father's house and so she will be uprooted from Israel. And do not let an adultress or defilement be found in Israel in all of the

---

1   See the detailed discussion in 5.3.
2   Some of these traditions are usefully collated in Mosca, "Child Sacrifice", 141-143, 147-150; Weinfeld, "Worship of Molech", 142-144.
3   E.g., *Yalqut* on Jer. 7:31, citing the *Midr. Yelammedenu*; *Lam. Rab.* 1, 9; *Midr. ha-Gadol*, cited in Weinfeld, "Worship of Molech", 142, n. 74.
4   *b. Sanh.* 64b.
5   See the range of rabbinic literature cited in Weinfeld, "Worship of Molech", 142-143.
6   *Sifrei*, Deut. 171; cf. Weinfeld, "Worship of Molech", 143, n. 77.
7   *Sifrei*, Deut. 171; cf. *b. Meg.* 25a; *y. Meg.* 4.10, 75c; *y. Sanh.* 9.11, 27a.
8   See further G. Vermes, "Leviticus 18:21 in ancient Jewish Bible Exegesis", in J.J. Petuchowski and E. Fleischer (eds.), *Studies in Aggadah, Targum and Jewish Liturgy in Memory of Joseph Heinemann* (Jerusalem: Magnes Press, 1981), 108-124.

days of the generations of the earth because Israel is holy to the LORD. And let any man who causes defilement surely die, let him be stoned because thus it is decreed and written in the heavenly tablets concerning all of the seed of Israel: "Let anyone who causes defilement surely die. And let him be stoned." And there is no limit of days for this law. And there is no remission or forgiveness except that the man who caused defilement of his daughter will be rooted out from the midst of all Israel because he has given some of his seed to Moloch and sinned so as to defile it. And you, Moses, command the children of Israel and exhort them not to give any of their daughters to the gentiles, and not to take for their sons any of the daughters of the gentiles because that is contemptible before the LORD.[9]

Though all these post-biblical traditions are probably anchored within the biblical portrayal of the "Molek" offering as a foreign practice,[10] they nevertheless attest to the transformation of the *mlk* rite.[11]

In attempting to understand how this transformation may have arisen, it is possible that the location of the *mlk* prohibitions in Leviticus can offer a partial explanation. Both Lev. 18:21 and 20:2-5 occur within a series of laws regulating sexual, rather than sacrificial, behaviour. This may suggest that the biblical writer or redactor equated child sacrifice with various illicit sexual practices because all were seen to threaten family solidarity.[12] More specifically, these laws may seek to curb practices defiling the essential procreative function of sexual intercourse: procreation is either impossible (homosexuality, bestiality), possible but illicit (incest), or successful but followed by the deliberate destruction of the child (sacrifice "as a *mlk*-offering" or "to Molek"). In this sense then, the biblical writer asserts that procreation belongs within YHWH's realm, and that any human practice wasting Israelite "seed" trespasses upon this divine territory, and is thus a crime against YHWH.[13]

However, despite these observations, it may be that the prohibitions of the so-called "Molek" practice in Lev. 18 and 20 have been dislocated from a different setting and relocated within material dealing with outlawed sexual behaviour. In an earlier chapter, it was noted that the formulaic language of

---

9   Jub. 30:7-11, following the translation of O.S. Wintermute, *OTP*, vol. 2, 35-142.

10   So 4.1.1. Notice also the imagery of defilement and adultery in these verses, associated
     in many biblical texts with child sacrifice.

11   Note that not all of these post-biblical traditions refer explicitly to "Molek".

12   J.E. Hartley, *Leviticus* (WBC 4; Dallas: Word, 1992), 289-290.

13   See also Milgrom, *Leviticus 17–22*, 1558-1559, 1729-1730. A modification of this view
     is offered by J.E. Miller ("Notes on Leviticus 18", *ZAW* 112 [2000], 401-403), who
     suggests that the laws of Lev. 18 and 20 are more concerned with *where* the semen is
     deposited rather than if it is wasted.

20:2-5 is strikingly akin to that of chapter 17, which deals not with illicit sexual practices, but sacrifice.[14] Thus following Mosca, it may be that the laws of 20:2-5 belonged originally to chapter 17, and have been subsequently displaced or relocated in chapter 20, which deals with sexual behaviour.[15] Similarly, 18:21 may be out of place. It occurs within a series of laws prohibiting general sexual practices (vv. 19-23), supplementing a kernel of laws dealing with incest (vv. 6-18). However, 18:21 stands out amongst these supplementary regulations in terms of its phraseology (אני יהוה and ולא תחלל את שם אלהיך), which is not attached to any other specific prohibition within the chapter, and is much closer to the style and phraseology of chapter 19.[16] If this is the case, it may be that both 18:21 and 20:2-5 have been displaced as a result of their later reinterpretation as prohibitions of a sexual practice; this was probably prompted by a literal understanding of זרע as "semen", and the similarity between Hebrew העביר and Aramaic עבר, "impregnate".[17]

---

14 See above, 250, n. 237.

15 Mosca, "Child Sacrifice", 248, n. 71.

16 Mosca, "Child Sacrifice", 151. The possible original location of 18:21 has been discussed by many commentators. For a sampling of views, see the summary in Hartley and Dwyer, "Investigation", 90, n. 29. It may be that the law concerning marriage to two sisters in Lev. 18:18 has attracted the displaced prohibition of the מלך ritual on the basis of the prominent role of child sacrifice in the story of Oholah and Oholibah in Ezek. 23. Note, however, that some scholars defend the location of 18:21 as original on the basis of the use of the terms נתן and/or זרע in vv. 20, 22, 23. See further Milgrom (*Leviticus 17–22*, 1551-1552, 1558-1559, 1766), who argues that the "Molek" prohibition is included within sexual regulations because both were deemed to be "Canaanite" practices leading to exile (18:24-30; 20:22). But this does not explain why other supposedly "Canaanite", non-sexual practices are not also included in ch. 18 (though in ch. 20, necromancy occurs alongside the "Molek" practice), nor why "Molek", if mistaken as a divine name, is the only foreign god to be named in the legal texts of the Hebrew Bible. Note also C.M. Carmichael (*Law, Legend, and Incest in the Bible: Leviticus 18–20* [Ithaca: Cornell University Press, 1997], 52-53) who suggests that the prohibition of child sacrifice in Lev. 18:21 intentionally follows that of adultery on the structural basis of Abimelech's attempted adultery with Sarah in Gen. 20, which is followed by Isaac's birth (Gen. 21) and near-sacrifice (Gen. 22). Miller ("Notes", 402-403) tentatively defends the sexual context of the anti-"Molek" laws in Lev. 18 and 20 by suggesting that they refer to a fertility vow whereby as yet unconceived children were promised for sacrifice to "Molek".

17 Mosca, "Child Sacrifice", 151. Milgrom (*Leviticus 17–22*, 1553) suggests that the rabbis deliberately misread the plain meaning of both 18:21 and 20:2-5 in an attempt to include sexual intercourse with a gentile among the sexual prohibitions of chapters 18 and 20, which do not forbid intermarriage. It is important to note that Milgrom is forced both to

Mosca's perceptive observations may go some way to explain the later distortion of the "Molek" practice into illicit sexual behaviour involving the transference of children or semen to the "foreign" realm, whether represented by a foreign god, a foreign man, or a foreign woman. Indeed, the roots of this particular afterlife of the *mlk* sacrifice may be located within the biblical portrayal of child sacrifice as a ritual dedicated to a foreign god or gods, a crime which is frequently couched in the sexual, metaphorical language of whoring and adultery. This biblical polemic may be seen in Isa. 57:3, in which the poem condemning the practice is awkwardly addressed to the "seed of an adulterer and a whore"; in Ezek. 16 and 23, in which child sacrifice is portrayed as one of the "whoring" practices of an adulteress unfaithful to YHWH;[18] and in Lev. 20:5, in which the metaphorical language of whoring is explicitly applied to the *mlk* sacrifice. Indeed, it would appear that this metaphorical language was taken literally by the tradents of the traditions underlying certain Levitical legislation, thereby accounting for the inclusion of the prohibitions of the *mlk* sacrifice among laws regulating sexual behaviour in Lev. 18 and 20.

The distortion of other forms of *Yhwh* child sacrifice is also evident elsewhere within both biblical and post-biblical traditions. One of the most prominent afterlives of child sacrifice is probably its transformation into a circumcision rite. The biblical and non-biblical texts examined here suggest that circumcision was associated with child sacrifice at an early stage, probably on the basis of their shared fertility function. Indeed, some biblical texts suggest that the purpose of circumcision was to enable the phallus to attain its full potential in its fertility function: just as "circumcised" fruit trees produce an increased yield (Lev. 19:23-25) so Gen. 17 suggests that the blessing of multiple descendants is bestowed by means of circumcision, for it is only after Abraham is circumcised that Sarah is able to conceive. As Eilberg-Schwartz comments, "Cutting away the foreskin is like pruning a fruit tree. Both acts of cutting remove unwanted excess and both increase the desired yield. One might say that when Israelites circumcise their male children, they are pruning the fruit trees of God".[19] This also elucidates the

---

accuse the rabbis of intentional textual misinterpretation and to defend the problematic locations of 18:21 and 20:2-5 as original because of his view that these chapters are monarchic in date (*Leviticus 17–22*, 1361-1364, 1553).

18 Ezek. 16:15-22.

19 H. Eilberg-Schwartz, *The Savage in Judaism: An Anthropology of Israelite Religion and Ancient Judaism* (Bloomington: Indiana University Press, 1990), 152 (*contra* Milgrom, *Leviticus 17–22*, 1679); see also C. Delaney, *Abraham on Trial: The Social Legacy of Biblical Myth* (Princeton: Princeton University Press, 1998), 96-101.

use of the metaphor of "uncircumcision" elsewhere in the Hebrew Bible, in which uncircumcised lips (Exod. 6:12, 30), ears (Jer. 6:10) and hearts (Lev. 26:41; Deut. 10:16; 30:6; Jer. 4:4; 9:25-26; Ezek. 44:7, 9) are organs which are unable to perform as divinely-intended. Theologically, this prevents the metaphorically uncircumcised from participating in YHWH's activity, just as the literally uncircumcised are prohibited from eating Passover (Exod. 12:43-51), are unable to dwell in the land (Josh. 5:2-9) and are cut off from the community (Gen. 17:14). As the context of the example of the fruit trees in Lev. 19 illustrates, circumcision renders the Israelite male "holy" or "set apart" (קדשׁ), allowing his inclusion among YHWH's people and land.[20] This recalls the language of the firstborn law in Exod. 13:2, in which it is commanded that the firstborn of human and animals is to be "set apart" (קדשׁ) for YHWH, and the law of Exod. 22:28-30, which juxtaposes the command to sacrifice the firstborn with YHWH's statement that the people shall be set aside (קדשׁ) for him. This may suggest that circumcision functions as a suitable replacement for the firstborn offering, for it renders the Israelite male "holy" and thereby acceptable to YHWH.[21] It is thus reasonable to speculate that within certain biblical circles, a circumcision ritual eventually eclipsed the firstborn sacrifice, as Exod. 4:25-26 and Gen. 17 may indicate, particularly in view of the קדשׁ context of both the firstborn sacrifice and circumcision, and the eighth-day law shared by Gen. 17:12 and Exod. 22:29 (cf. Gen. 21:4; Lev. 12:3).[22] Certainly, the connection between circumcision and sacrifice is recognized within rabbinic literature:

> Rabbi Isaac said: "Man and beast You deliver, O YHWH". The ordinance relating to man and the ordinance relating to beasts are on a par. The ordinance relating to man: "On the eighth day the flesh of his foreskin shall be circumcised". The ordinance relating to beasts: "and from the eighth day on it shall be acceptable as an offering by fire to YHWH".[23]

---

20 For the theme of holiness in Lev. 19 see Milgrom, *Leviticus 17–22*, 1711-1726.

21 This may be reflected in the present form of the biblical story of Isaac: does the circumcision of Isaac eight days after his birth (Gen. 21:4) render him an acceptable sacrificial offering in the next chapter?

22 Though note Eilberg-Schwartz, *Savage in Judaism*, 174-175, who suggests that the eighth-day law is rooted in issues of impurity, birth and blood: the mother (and by extension her newborn son) are considered to be impure for seven days after the birth.

23 *Lev. Rab.* 27:1. Note also *Pirque R. El.* 29, which claims that on the night of the first Passover, the Israelites applied both the blood of circumcision and the blood of the lamb to the lintel of their houses.

However, it is important to note that within the Hebrew Bible, circumcision is not explicitly restricted to the firstborn son. This perhaps reflects the symbolic imaging of a valued child as a firstborn (as the close interrelation of the concepts of the "only-begotten" child and the "beloved" child may suggest),[24] or the later ideological elevation of all Israelite men as holy to YHWH, and thus circumcised. Within the Hebrew Bible, circumcision is one of the most outstanding ideological symbols, both defining "Israel" as the people of YHWH and distinguishing "Israel" from foreigners. As such, the continuing practice of circumcision may be one of the longest-lasting "afterlives" of child sacrifice.

A further biblical afterlife of child sacrifice may be seen in the designation of the Levites, an apparently distinct group of cultic functionaries, as the substitutes for the firstborn. Num. 3:11-13 is explicit in defining this substitution in terms of the firstborn sacrifice of the Passover myth and clear allusions to the sacrificial firstborn laws of Exodus:

> YHWH spoke to Moses, saying, "I hereby accept the Levites from among the children of Israel as substitutes for all the firstborn (בכור) that open the womb (פטר רחם) among the children of Israel. The Levites shall be mine; when I killed all the firstborn in the land of Egypt, I set apart (קדש) for my own all the firstborn in Israel, both human and animal; they shall be mine. I am YHWH".[25]

The setting apart (קדש) of the Levites also complements the portrayal of their dedication to YHWH as a sacrifice, specifically an elevation offering (תנופה) in Num. 8:11, 13, 15, 21,[26] although a series of sacrificial and cultic terms are employed elsewhere in the book.[27] Indeed, Miller suggests that the implicit, biblical sense of the holiness of the Levites is probably derived from the notion that they were substitutes for the firstborn.[28] It is interesting to recall that it is this portrayal of the Levites that lies behind Weinfeld's suggestion

---

24 Cf. Zech. 12:10, and the discussion in 5.6.
25 Cf. Num. 8:14-19.
26 Levenson, *Beloved Son*, 46-47.
27 For example, נתן, "give" (Num. 8:19), הפקד, "appoint" (1:50), הקרב, "advance" (3:6), הבדיל, "separate" (8:14), לקח, "take" (3:41; cf. 3:12, 45; 8:16, 18), though notably, not העביר. Milgrom (*Leviticus 17–22*, 1555) notes that the term הקדיש, "sacrifice", is also avoided so as not to cast the Levites in a priestly role.
28 Miller, *Religion of Ancient Israel*, 139. Interestingly, a reversal of the Levitical substitution is evident within modern Jewish practice. According to Levenson (*Beloved Son*, 47), if there is no Levite available to pour water over the hands of the priest before the pronunciation of the Aaronic blessing, a man who is his mother's firstborn substitutes for the Levite.

that the firstborn were not sacrificed, but donated to the sanctuary as cultic officiants.[29]

The monetary rescue or redemption (פדה) of the firstborn is a closely-related tradition, which may also be seen as an afterlife of the firstborn sacrifice within the Hebrew Bible. In assigning the priestly portions of the firstfruits and firstborn, the monetary redemption of the firstborn is permitted, as Num. 18:15-16 illustrates:

> Every first issue of the womb (כל פטר רחם) of all flesh, human and animal, which is offered to YHWH, shall be yours; but the firstborn (בכור) of humans you shall redeem (פדה), and the firstborn of unclean animals you shall redeem. Their redemption price, reckoned from one month of age, you shall fix at five shekels of silver, according to the shekel of the sanctuary (that is, twenty *gerahs*).[30]

Financial payment to the sanctuary thus appears to protect the child from sacrifice. This form of "rescue" is given a specific foundation within the biblical schema of the substitution of the Levites. Num. 3:39-43[31] combines the monetary redemption of the firstborn with their Levitical substitutes in claiming that there were not enough Levites to match the number of firstborn males, thereby necessitating a financial payment to the sanctuary to rescue the excess firstborn (from sacrifice).

Some scholars associate the Nazirites with child sacrifice, suggesting that their dedication or consecration (נזר) to the cult substituted for their sacrifice (Num. 6:1-21; 8:16; 1 Sam. 1:11; cf. Judg. 13:2-7).[32] The Nazirites are frequently described as being vowed (נדר) to the sanctuary, and are thus "holy" or "set apart" (קדש). As has been seen, these key terms are well-known from other biblical and non-biblical texts relating to child sacrifice, and thus support the possibility that within the Hebrew Bible, the Nazirites, like the Levites, may function as substitutes for child sacrifice. Interestingly, of the three characters named or titled נזיר in the Hebrew Bible, all are the

---

29 Weinfeld, "Worship of Molech", 141; *idem.*, "Burning Babies", 412.
30 Cf. Exod. 13:12-13, 15; 34:19-20, which do not specify how the human firstborn is to be rescued.
31 Cf. 3:46-48; 18:15-18.
32 Février, "Le rite substitution", 8; Levenson, *Beloved Son*, 47-48; S. Ackerman, "Child Sacrifice: Returning God's Gift", *BR* 9/3 (1993), 20-28, 56.

firstborn sons of previously barren mothers.[33] Thus a further biblical afterlife of the firstborn sacrifice may be the consecration of the Nazirites to YHWH.[34]

The New Testament story of Jesus is an extensive illustration of a further afterlife of child sacrifice, as has been well demonstrated by Levenson.[35] Examples of biblical motifs of child sacrifice, which are employed as powerful imagery in the New Testament, include the repeated labelling of Jesus as the "only-begotten",[36] "beloved",[37] or firstborn son;[38] the portrayal of Jesus as a sacrificial lamb and his death as a Passover sacrifice;[39] the royal descent of Jesus and his claim to the Davidic throne;[40] his association with Abraham;[41] and his miraculous birth to a previously childless woman.[42] To this may also be added the story of Herod's killing of infants whilst the newborn Jesus is taken to Egypt for safety, which may almost be seen as a reversal of the biblical foundation myth of the firstborn sacrifice at the Passover.[43]

This wealth of material pertaining to the afterlives of child sacrifice would appear to indicate that child sacrifice survived as a religious motif long after its demise as an acceptable practice. As Levenson comments, "the impulse to sacrifice the firstborn son remained potent long after the literal practice had become odious and fallen into desuetude".[44] Levenson's remark has relevance not only for the firstborn sacrifice, but for other forms of Judahite child sacrifice also. Whether positively or negatively construed, the

---

33 Samson (Judg. 13:2-7), Samuel (1 Sam. 1:2, 11) and Joseph (נזיר אחיו; Gen. 49:26; cf. 30:2, 22-24); note also the portrayal of John the Baptist in Luke 1:7, 15. See too Ackerman, "Child Sacrifice", 27; Levenson, *Beloved Son*, 48.

34 It is notable that in Hos. 9:10 the verb נזר is used to describe the participation of the Israelites within the cult of Baal-Peor, a practice associated with the sacrifice of children to the שדים in Ps. 106:28-31, 34-39.

35 Levenson, *Beloved Son*, chs. 15–16; see also Delaney, *Abraham on Trial*, chs. 5–7, who examines Jewish, Christian and Muslim interpretations of the Aqedah.

36 John 3:16. The language employed in this verse is also reminiscent of that of child sacrifice in the Hebrew Bible: τον υιον τον μονογενη εδωκεν, "he gave (cf. נתן) his only-begotten (cf. יחיד) son".

37 Matt. 3:17; 17:5; Mark 1:11; 9:7; Luke 3:22; 9:35; 2 Pet. 1:17.

38 Rom. 8:29.

39 Matt. 26:17-20; Mark 14:12-17; Luke 22:7-15; John 1:29-34; 13:1; 18:28; 19:31-37; 1 Cor. 5:6-8.

40 Matt. 1:1-17; 22:41-45; Luke 1:32-33; 3:23-38; Rom. 1:3.

41 Matt. 1:1; Gal. 3:16.

42 Matt. 1:18-25; Luke 1:26-38 (compare also 1:46-55 with 1 Sam. 2:1-10).

43 Matt. 2:1-18; cf. Exod. 4:22-23.

44 Levenson, *Beloved Son*, 52.

sheer variety of the "afterlives" of child sacrifice within biblical and post-biblical traditions suggest that the practice was impossible to eradicate from the cultural and religious matrix of the inheritors of Judahite deity-worship. Indeed, the prominent role of child sacrifice within Judahite deity-worship appears to be reflected in the very persistence of its "afterlives" which permeate biblical and post-biblical traditions.

6.2 Distorting Child Sacrifice

This discussion has argued that the biblical portrayal of child sacrifice as a foreign practice is historically unreliable. It has been suggested that child sacrifice is instead better understood as a native and normative element of Judahite religious practice, including *Yhwh*-worship. Closer examination of the biblical texts suggests that child sacrifice is intentionally presented as a foreign practice in order to distance the ancestors of the biblical writers and their god YHWH from this type of sacrifice. The means and processes of this deliberate distortion may be identifiable within the biblical texts.

Though the term מֹלֶךְ occurs within the Masoretic text as the name of a god, closer textual examination suggests that originally this word was a technical term for a royal sacrifice in which a (possibly royal) infant was burned in fire as an offering to *Yhwh* in his role as the patron deity of the Judahite royal dynasty. This sacrifice may have functioned as a means of perpetuating the fertility of the royal dynasty. As such, it may be understood as a specialization of the firstborn sacrifice. However, many biblical texts seek to disassociate this practice from YHWH by portraying it as an idolatrous sacrifice offered to a foreign god. As has been seen, this is effected by distorting the term מֹלֶךְ into the divine name "Molek" by reading the consonantal text למלך which was originally rendered "as a *mlk*-sacrifice", as "to/for the Molek". Another form of the distortion of the *mlk* ritual may also be evident. As has been seen, Jer. 19:5 seeks to associate Baʿal, rather than Molek, with the fiery sacrifices. But as has been argued, not only is this association unlikely,[45] but comparative textual evidence suggests that the character of Baʿal has been deliberately grafted into the text in a further effort to distance YHWH from child sacrifice.

---

45 *Pace* Edelman, "Biblical *Molek*", 730-731.

The distortion of מֹלֶךְ into Molek is reminiscent of the apparent distortion of the biblical term שׁדים, originally vocalized as שַׁדַּים, into the Masoretic שֵׁדִים. As has been argued, the Deir ʿAlla material suggests that the association of the *šadday*-god(s) with child sacrifice was not only known to the biblical writers, but was subsequently and perhaps deliberately disguised by rendering the biblical שׁדים as שֵׁדִים, "demons". In this way, the biblical god "El Šadday", whose name is probably related to the ancient Near Eastern *šadday*-god(s), and with whom YHWH is explicitly identified in the Hebrew Bible, is distanced from child sacrifice. However, a memory of this relationship persists within the important biblical tradition of the blessing of multiple descendants bestowed upon Abraham by "El Šadday", and effected by means of the covenant of circumcision, itself an "afterlife" of child sacrifice.

However, for some biblical writers the association of the god of the Hebrew Bible with child sacrifice is more difficult to disguise or to ignore. Accordingly, though YHWH commands the sacrifice of Isaac, his theological reputation is ultimately defended by the substitution of a ram for Isaac in the final moments. Other biblical texts seek to present child sacrifice as a divine punishment devised deliberately by YHWH to bring about a specific theological end. Thus in rebuilding Jericho, Hiel of Bethel brings YHWH's curse upon himself and sacrifices his firstborn and lastborn as foundation sacrifices (Josh. 6:26; 1 Kgs 16:34). Similarly, the startling claim in the book of Ezekiel, that YHWH commanded the sacrifice of the firstborn in order to devastate his people, is also presented as an intentional divine punishment (20:25-26). This is also reminiscent of the "exodus" context of the biblical myth of the first Passover, behind which, as has been argued, lurks the spectre of the firstborn sacrifice. YHWH's punishment of the Egyptians is the killing of all the firstborn, from which the Israelites can protect themselves by means of the blood of a sacrificed lamb. In this way, the killing of the firstborn functions both as a slaying act and as a saving act. This is all a far cry from the reconstructed historical reality of child sacrifice, which may have included three co-existing and closely-related cults: the firstborn sacrifice, the *mlk* sacrifice, and sacrifice to the *šadday*-god(s).

Having suggested how the biblical texts have distorted the probable historical reality of child sacrifice, the remaining question to be addressed is *why*? An abbreviated answer is that YHWH's association with child sacrifice became theologically-problematic for biblical writers of the post-monarchic era, who thus sought to distance their god from the practice and to preserve the sanctity of YHWH's name and reputation. The transformation of the language of the royal cult of child sacrifice into a biblical character called

"Molek" may thus be seen as an attempt to disguise the historical reality of *Yhwh*'s appetite for children.

However, the creation of "Molek" as a biblical character is not simply symptomatic of a scribal desire to maintain the sanctity of YHWH. It is at the same time a characteristic of the YHWH-ideology of separateness that shapes the biblical portrayal of Israel. This is illustrated in the language of the Kings Writer. In causing their sons to "pass over in the fire" (העביר באש) both Ahaz and Manasseh are described as behaving "according to the abominable practices of the nations whom YHWH drove out before the people of Israel", (2 Kgs 16:3; 21:2-6). As discussed in chapter 1, it seems likely that the Kings Writer based his presentation of both kings upon an ideologically-motivated concern to distinguish "Israel" from the surrounding nations; this is well-illustrated in the legislation set out in Deut. 18:9-12. This text, among others, makes it clear that because of their abominable religious practices, YHWH cast out the nations and gave the land to "Israel". The implication is plain: if YHWH's people imitate the practices of the nations, they too will be cast out of the land. Child sacrifice is therefore deemed to be an abominable practice of the foreign nations, along with other religious rites with which it is associated.

In the light of the loss of the Judahite king, Zion, and the destruction of the temple, some groups of exiled Judahite elites probably perceived the royal ideology to have failed. Given the role of child sacrifice within the royal Jerusalem cult, with its patronage from *Yhwh*, and probably from the dead kings also, the royal cult of child sacrifice may also have been perceived as having failed. Without a royal arena, the practice appears to have become displaced in the post-monarchic period. Thus YHWH became the only king of "Israel" in a redefinition of a monarchic role which, given its inextricable association with Zion, could not be totally abandoned. However, the newly-returned elites—the new "Israel"—determined that they would differentiate the god of "Israel" from the other god-kings surrounding her. Accordingly, previously normative practices specifically related to the royal ideology and thus associated with the royal cult, were now deemed ineffective, inappropriate or simply redundant, and consequently held responsible for the loss of the land and the king. This would account for the apparent rejection of the *mlk* sacrifice among some groups within the post-monarchic period (as the polemical tone of Isa. 57:3-13 might suggest) and the transformation of the cult of the firstborn into a redemptive or non-sacrificial ritual.

Consequently, the Kings Writer's schema, evaluating who is and who is not to be considered a part of "Israel", regards the monarchic *mlk* sacrifice as one of the practices associated with loss of the land, and a defining characteristic of those located outside the ideological boundaries of the biblical "Israel": it is no longer the ultimate life-giving rite, but a practice bringing loss. Thus along with Ahaz and Manasseh (2 Kgs 16:3; 21:2-6), the "Canaanites" (Deut. 12:31), the Northern Kingdom (2 Kgs 17:17), the former Judahites (2 Kgs 23:10; Jer. 7:31; 19:5; 32:35) and the new inhabitants of the former Northern Kingdom (2 Kgs 17:31-34) are defined as outside of the biblical Israel—and thus dispossessed of their land—on the basis of their sacrifice of children. Accordingly, the biblical Israel is differentiated from those peoples who sacrifice their children, and the biblical YHWH is differentiated from the *Yhwh* who demands these sacrifices.

However, the biblical ideology of "Israel" is unable to eliminate the central role of the firstborn altogether. Though the potential sacrifice of the firstborn is marginalized within biblical YHWH-worship, the deity's special claim upon the precious firstborn persists within the self-definition of the biblical Israel:

> With weeping they shall come,
> and with consolations I will lead them back,
> I will let them walk by brooks of water,
> in a straight path in which they shall not stumble;
> for I have become a father to Israel,
> and Ephraim is my firstborn.[46]

In this way then, the cessation of the Judahite monarchy resulted in the transference of the king's role as YHWH's "beloved" son to the new "Israel". This may be reflected in the post-monarchic prominence given to the Passover traditions as a foundation myth of the biblical Israel, in some versions of which the imaging of YHWH as the simultaneous slayer and saviour of the firstborn is central.[47]

The historical reality of child sacrifice is thus distorted in a variety of ways within the Hebrew Bible. Though some of these distortions may be unintentional, this discussion has argued that others are likely to be deliberate

---

46 Jer. 31:9; cf. Exod. 4:22-23; Hos. 11:1.

47 Indeed, the biblical paralleling of exodus traditions with reference to exile-and-return suggests that for some biblical writers, the return to the land was understood as a second Exodus (eg. Isa. 51:11, 14; Ezek. 20:34-38, 41-42). However, the absence of the firstborn sacrifice within Deuteronomy's Passover and exodus stories is so noticeable as to be significant. Though as in Exodus, the firstborn offerings and the Passover are juxtaposed (Deut. 15:19–16:8), the Deuteronomic author makes no mention of the human firstborn, and appears at pains to distance the animal sacrifice from any presumed notion of its function as a substitution offering by allowing the animal to be boiled, rather than burned as a עלה (16:7).

attempts to disguise the probability that within the deity-worship of
monarchic Judah, children were sacrificed to *Yhwh*. Yet the distortion of the
historical reality of child sacrifice is also perpetuated within scholarship,
particularly with regard to the *mlk* practice. As has been seen, the majority of
scholars defend the notion that מֹלֶךְ refers to a foreign god, distinct from that
of Israel. Recent historical reconstructions of Israelite and Judahite religions
are increasingly emphasizing the polytheistic character of the royal religions
as both native and original.[48] Yet despite this recent shift within the
conceptualization of the religious climate of these kingdoms, many scholars
remain unable to accept that the fiery cult of child sacrifice was probably an
indigenous and normative element within royal Judahite religious practice.
Accordingly, the majority of scholars who maintain that מֹלֶךְ refers to a god
do not consider the possibility that if such a god were worshipped in Judah,
that this deity could be a legitimate member of the native Judahite pantheon.
Rather, the assumption is that the worship of any such theoretical deity
necessarily would have been a syncretistic element within religious practice,
as Miller's comment illustrates:

> If it could be demonstrated conclusively that the *molek* to whom children were
> sometimes dedicated in sacrifice was a deity and not a technical term for a type of
> sacrifice, the syncretistic character of child sacrifice in ancient Israel would be quite
> clear. But that is surely the case in any event.[49]

Distorting this misconception further is the view that "Molek" is a Canaanite
god, thereby emphasizing the supposedly syncretistic character of Judahite
deity-worship even more. Despite the increasing acceptance of evidence
suggesting that historically, Israel and Judah emerged from within the land of
Canaan from Canaanite stock, many scholars continue to place a heavy
emphasis upon the presumed distinction between "Israelite" and "Canaanite"
cultural and religious practices. This dichotomy between "Israelite" and
"Canaanite" is essentially based upon an uncritical acceptance of the biblical
version of the story of "Israel", which is itself constructed upon the
ideological self-definition of "Israel" as a distinct ethnic group originally
separate from the surrounding "foreign" peoples. Consequently, the biblical
portrayal of Canaanites and other "foreign" peoples is tendentious, polemical
and historically unreliable. In reconstructing the historical reality of ancient
Israelite and Judahite religious practices, the dichotomy between "Israelite"

---

48   See the discussion above, 6-8, and the literature cited there.
49   Miller, *Religion of Ancient Israel*, 59.

and "Canaanite" is thus as unhelpful as it is unlikely. However, many scholars continue to assume this false Israelite/Canaanite dichotomy, offering as support the biblical texts themselves, as Heider appears to do:

> ... we must take note of the unanimous view of Biblical passages which comment on the subject that the practice was a Canaanite institution. While one cannot exclude the possibility that Israel always had the cult, both the Biblical testimony and the apparently Syro-Palestinian origins of the god suggest that to hold the Biblical view as a polemic directed at the Canaanites has no support in historical data.[50]

However, as has been seen, this argument is undermined by its circularity: in pointing to the Canaanite character of the biblical god "Molek", support is garnered for the argument that such a god may be detected within the Ugaritic texts, which is in turn used to historicize the Canaanite character of the biblical god "Molek". Within this context, and on the basis of the distorted Israelite/Canaanite dichotomy, Day assumes that his reconstructed deity must be a foreign infiltrator within Judah's heavenly realm *because* of his Canaanite character, because "the fact that the cult is clearly Canaanite indicates it may have been appropriated from the local Canaanite inhabitants of Jerusalem, the Jebusites".[51] Alternative attempts to identify the supposedly "foreign" origins of the biblical god "Molek" include the suggestion that worship of this god was imported into Judah from Phoenicia by the syncretistic Solomon,[52] or that the Sepharvites introduced the practice when they were resettled in the former Northern Kingdom by the Assyrians.[53] Those defending the view that מֹלֶךְ refers to a deity distinct from *Yhwh* rather than a type of sacrifice presumably seek to bolster their arguments in identifying the supposedly "foreign" origin of the cult. Yet in distancing *Yhwh* and his worshippers from direct responsibility for this practice, this position is curiously similar to that of earlier scholars supporting Eissfeldt's thesis, who in seeking to ease their apparent discomfort in arguing that children were sacrificed to *Yhwh* as *mlk*-offerings, blamed the introduction of the *mlk* practice upon the Phoenicians.[54] Interestingly, this scholarly reluctance to identify child sacrifice as a native and original element of *Yhwh*-worship is also evident within discussions of the firstborn sacrifice.

---

50 Heider, *Molek*, 404. See also Day, *Molech*, 31, 47; *idem.*, *Yahweh*, 211-212.
51 Day, *Molech*, 55; followed by Milgrom, *Leviticus 17–22*, 1557-1558; Doyle, "Molek of Jerusalem?", 182, 205.
52 Heider, *Molek*, 404-405.
53 Milgrom, *Leviticus 17–22*, 1557.
54 For example, De Vaux, *Studies*, 59, 89-90; Cazelles, "Molok", cols. 1337-1346.

Many commentators argue that the supposedly early provenance of the
firstborn laws in the so-called Covenant Code demonstrate that this form of
child sacrifice was a "Canaanite", rather than a native "Israelite", practice.[55]

In arguing for the originally foreign and thus syncretistic nature of child
sacrifice, many scholars consequently perpetuate the distortion of its
historical reality further. With specific regard to biblical מֹלֶךְ, the majority of
scholars continue to assume that this was a syncretistic element of Judahite
deity-worship by adopting the distorted view of the biblical texts, which
necessarily insist that the fiery sacrifice of children was a foreign practice,
alien to correct YHWH-worship.

Given the preceding discussion, it is therefore reasonable to suggest that
despite biblical attempts to disguise and distort the historical reality of
Judahite child sacrifice, it survives as a religious motif within several biblical
and post-biblical texts. Though the sacrificial nature of the motif has been
lost, disguised or distorted within some of these texts, the continued presence
and variety of the "afterlives" of child sacrifice within these traditions
suggests that the practice was impossible to eradicate from the collective
memory of the religious descendants of Judahite deity-worship. Indeed, the
enduring impact of child sacrifice as a ritual, and subsequently as a religious
motif, testifies to the integral role child sacrifice played within the deity-
worship of Judah. Yet one final point remains: in tracing the distortions of
child sacrifice pervading the Hebrew Bible, post-biblical literature and
modern scholarship, it must be observed that the misrepresentation of this
practice within both the ancient texts and modern scholarship, whether
conscious or not, may derive in part from the discomfort in acknowledging
that one's ethnic, religious or cultural ancestors willingly participated within
such a ritual. But the distortions and residual afterlives must not be permitted
to prevent the recognition that the historical reality was one in which child
sacrifice played an integral role within Judahite deity-worship, including the
worship of *Yhwh*.

---

55 Despite acknowledging the tendentiousness of the biblical portrayal of the "Canaanites",
    Erling ("First-born and Firstlings", 470, 472) nevertheless suggests that the firstborn
    laws of Exodus refer to a Canaanite practice; see also De Vaux, *Studies*, 55; *idem.,
    Ancient Israel*, 444; Childs, *Exodus*, 479-480.

Conclusions

In recognizing the ideological nature of the Hebrew Bible, this study has sought to examine the presentation of King Manasseh as the most reprehensible person in the biblical story of "Israel", and the portrayal of child sacrifice as the most objectionable practice. Within the Hebrew Bible, both Manasseh and child sacrifice play an important role: they appear to function as ideological boundary markers, qualifying and defining the behaviour that allows or prohibits access to "Israel". This study has had two related aims: to reconstruct the likely historical realities of Manasseh and child sacrifice so as to ascertain whether their biblical reputations are justified, and to discern precisely how and why Manasseh and child sacrifice have been distorted into the most deviant person and the most reprehensible practice within the Hebrew Bible.

Though the main conclusions of this study have been summarized in the preceding chapters, their review is appropriate here. In chapters 1 and 4 it was argued that Manasseh and child sacrifice are intended to function as ideological boundary markers in their portrayal as "foreign" within the biblical texts. The biblical distinction between what is native to correct YHWH-worship and what is foreign may be designated an "ideology of separation". This ideology is constructed upon the biblical notion that what is foreign is forbidden. Accordingly, foreign cult practices inevitably lead to expulsion from YHWH's land. Thus in seeking to account for the destruction and exile of Judah, the Kings Writer construes the Babylonian conquest as a divine punishment provoked by the foreign cult practices of Manasseh (2 Kgs 21:1-18; 23:26-27; 24:3-4). His cult crimes are the practices of the foreign nations whom YHWH expelled from the land, and they are the practices adopted by the disobedient Northern Kingdom of Israel which YHWH exiled at the hands of Assyria. Manasseh's foreign cult practices therefore lead to the exile of Judah. Of all his foreign cult practices, child sacrifice is portrayed as the most reprehensible. Thus within the Hebrew Bible, participation in this practice appears to be limited to the idolatrous—foreigners and disobedient YHWH-worshippers, who, alongside Manasseh, include King Mesha of Moab (2 Kgs 3:26-27), the Sepharvites (17:31), Ahaz (16:3); the Northern Kingdom

(17:17), and apostate Judahites (e.g., Isa. 57:3-13; Jer. 7:30-32; 19:5; 32:35; Ezek. 16:20-21; 20:30-31).

However, this ideological schema is not as coherent as it initially appears. Despite the biblical exhortation that child sacrifice is alien to YHWH-worship, practised by the foreign and the idolatrous, and consistently outlawed by YHWH, closer inspection of this biblical portrayal instead locates child sacrifice within the mainstream of its presentation of YHWH. Again, despite the Kings Writer's repeated insistence that Manasseh's foreign practices provoked the expulsion of Judah from the land, it is not Manasseh and his generation who are exiled, but the Judahites of later generations. This may have been a factor motivating the Chronicler's account of Manasseh's brief exile.

Moreover, the reconstructions of the probable historical realities of Manasseh and child sacrifice in chapters 2 and 5 argue that contrary to their biblical portrayals, Manasseh and child sacrifice were neither deviant nor "foreign". Child sacrifice appears to have been a native and normative element of Judahite religious practice, three cults of which may plausibly have existed within Judah: the sacrifice of the firstborn to *Yhwh*; the royal *mlk* sacrifice to *Yhwh* in Jerusalem; and the sacrifice to the *šadday*-gods. The functions of these cults of child sacrifice are far from certain; however, their location within fertility contexts and an association with cults of the dead ancestors seems likely. Though these cults of child sacrifice were probably distinct from one another, their shared terminology may suggest that they were interrelated at some point, either during the history of Judahite deity-worship or during the period of the formation of the biblical material.

Though the crime of child sacrifice functions polemically upon Manasseh's biblical charge sheet (2 Kgs 21:6; 2 Chr. 33:6), it may in fact be broadly representative of the religious milieu of monarchic Judah, in which child sacrifice was not a foreign, non-*Yhwh*istic ritual, but a powerful aspect of the indigenous, normative religion of Judah. Indeed, the historical reconstruction of Manasseh offered by this study stands in sharp contrast to the Kings Writer's portrayal of Manasseh as the murderous monarch whose apostasy provoked the destruction of the kingdom. Rather, the historical Manasseh master-minded the expansion of his floundering city-state into an enlarged and prospering kingdom by remaining obedient to his imperial overlords and taking full advantage of the increased trading opportunities offered by Assyrian hegemony within the region. Thus rather like the northern territory of the same name, Manasseh is perhaps best understood as the powerful lifeblood of his kingdom, facilitating its increased strength and prosperity.

The historical reconstructions of Manasseh and child sacrifice therefore suggest that their distortion into the most deviant person and the most deviant practice within the biblical story of "Israel" is not only misrepresentative, but even deliberate. As has been seen, this distortion is effected by their portrayal as "foreign". Thus within the Hebrew Bible, one of Judah's most successful monarchs becomes the destroyer of his kingdom; the firstborn sacrifice becomes a substitution ritual; the *mlk* sacrifice becomes an offering to a foreign god named "Molek"; and the sacrifice to the *šadday*-gods becomes an idolatrous offering to the "demons". The reason for the distortion of Manasseh into the "foreign" one is the Kings Writer's need for a scapegoat to carry the blame for the Babylonian exile. In scapegoating Manasseh, the Kings Writer seeks to distance both Judah and his intended audience from direct responsibility for YHWH's punishment of the kingdom. It is usually assumed that the portrayal of Manasseh as the most reprehensible of Judah's kings reflects to some degree an historical memory of Manasseh as a particularly idolatrous and wicked king. However, this study has argued instead that the scapegoating of Manasseh within Kings is facilitated by his name. Sharing his name with the dominant Manasseh territory of the neighbouring Kingdom of Israel singled the Judahite king out as a "foreigner" and hence as a deviant in the eyes of the Kings Writer. King Manasseh thus falls victim to the anti-Northern polemic pervading Kings, and is portrayed as the villainous "foreign" king who causes the destruction of Judah and the exile of her people. The distortion of Manasseh also functions ideologically for the Chronicler, though the king functions not as a scapegoat, but as a paradigm for the Chronicler's audience. In the exiling of Manasseh to Babylon and his subsequent repentance and restoration in Jerusalem, the Chronicler casts Manasseh as a paradigm for the restored post-exilic "Israel", demonstrating to his audience that despite their sinful cult crimes of the past, their humbling and repentance can lead to divine forgiveness and restoration. However, the Chronicler's rehabilitation of Manasseh is wholly dependent upon his portrayal as the most reprehensible of Judah's monarchs in Kings, a reputation the Chronicler worsens further by the proliferation of Manasseh's foreign cult practices.

The distortion of child sacrifice into a "foreign" practice within the Hebrew Bible may find partial explanation in the suggestion that during the post-monarchic period, when many biblical traditions were subject to intense literary attention, monarchic forms of Judahite child sacrifice had been marginalized, abandoned, or forgotten, resulting in the unintentional misrepresentation of the practice. However, this study has argued that in many places, it would appear that the biblical writers have intentionally distorted their presentation of child sacrifice in an attempt to distance their ancestors and their god YHWH from a practice which came to be rejected within certain post-monarchic circles. The apparent rejection of child sacrifice within the Hebrew Bible probably reflects in part a cultural shift within the ethical framework of the biblical writers, illustrated perhaps by the assertion in the book of Ezekiel that the firstborn sacrifice was intended to defile and to devastate the people (20:25-26). However, in the case of the *mlk* sacrifice, a further explanation for its post-monarchic rejection may be its perceived failure. In view of the loss of the Judahite king, Zion, and the destruction of the Temple, some groups of exiled Judahites probably reasoned that the royal ideology had failed. Given the role of the *mlk* sacrifice within the Jerusalem cult, with its patronage from *Yhwh*, and probably from the dead kings also, this royal cult of child sacrifice may also have been seen to have failed, resulting in its displacement and rejection during the post-monarchic period.

This study has proposed that despite their biblical distortion into the foreign and the deviant, both Manasseh and child sacrifice remained potent within biblical and post-biblical traditions. In chapter 3 this was illustrated in both the villainous and penitent characterizations of Manasseh within Chronicles, rabbinic traditions, the writings of Josephus, and the Prayer of Manasseh. Yet in spite of the apparent rehabilitation of Manasseh within some of these traditions, all of the "afterlives" of Manasseh highlighted in this study necessarily depend upon the Kings Writer's portrayal of Manasseh as archvillain and the ultimate idolater. Moreover, the polemical connotations of Manasseh's name appear to inform several traditions, including the reversal of status of Ephraim and Manasseh in Gen. 48 and related texts; the distortion of the name of Moses into that of Manasseh in Judg. 18:30; the prayer of the ultimate penitent in the Prayer of Manasseh; and the Jewish tradition denigrating the Samaritan temple in the claim that its first high priest was named Manasseh. This study has argued that this is all suggestive of an anti-Manasseh polemic pervading biblical and post-biblical traditions. This anti-Manasseh polemic is probably to be related to the curious lack of references to King Manasseh and the period of his reign outside of 2 Kgs 21:1-18; 2 Chr. 33:1-20 and Jer. 15:3-4, suggesting perhaps that Manasseh has been deliberately censored or excluded from other biblical texts.

Despite biblical attempts to distort the historical reality of child sacrifice, it survives in several forms as a powerful motif within many biblical and post-biblical texts. Some of these "afterlives" of child sacrifice were detailed in chapter 6. It was argued that the biblical distortion of the *mlk* sacrifice into the name of a foreign god of child sacrifice was itself transformed into a conceptual abbreviation for illicit sexual behaviour involving the transference of children or semen to the "foreign" realm, whether represented by a foreign deity, a foreign man, or a foreign woman. It was also suggested that circumcision, the dedication of the Levites, and the consecration of the Nazirites, functioned as "afterlives" of child sacrifice within the Hebrew Bible. Of these, the most prominent is the transformation of child sacrifice into a circumcision rite. Though historically it is likely that the two were associated at an early stage, it would appear that within the biblical texts, circumcision is perceived to function as a suitable replacement for the firstborn sacrifice. Moreover, this substitution rite appears to have taken on its own ideology of separation: within the Hebrew Bible, circumcision is one of the most prominent ideological symbols both defining "Israel" as the people of YHWH, and distinguishing "Israel" from foreigners. The continuing practice of circumcision may be one of the longest-lasting "afterlives" of child sacrifice. Another long-lasting "afterlife" of child sacrifice may also be perceived in the continuing Christian designation of Jesus as the "only-begotten", "beloved" and "firstborn" son of God, sacrificed as a Passover lamb. Indeed, the New Testament story of Jesus is an extensive illustration of a further "afterlife" of child sacrifice. The variety of the "afterlives" of child sacrifice within biblical and post-biblical traditions suggests that the practice was impossible to erase from the cultural and religious memory of the inheritors of Judahite deity-worship.

The distortion of Manasseh and child sacrifice is also perpetuated within modern scholarship, as illustrated in chapters 3 and 6. Having been scapegoated by the Kings Writer, it may be that the historical Manasseh remains an easy target for some scholars seeking to account for supposedly alien elements of Judahite religious practice in the seventh century BCE. Whether construed as a hapless vassal susceptible to the imperial influences invading Judahite culture and religion, or as tyrannical villain intent on corrupting the spiritual heritage of his people, Manasseh continues to function as a scapegoat for many modern scholars. Of all the accusations leveled at the historical Manasseh within scholarship, child sacrifice is the most prevalent. The majority of scholars continue to regard Judahite child sacrifice either as a foreign practice dedicated to a deity other than *Yhwh*, or as an originally foreign cult imported as a syncretistic element within Judahite *Yhwh*-worship. Accordingly, many ascribe its introduction or promotion to Manasseh. However, this study has argued that the scholarly misconception of child sacrifice and the imaging of Manasseh as an idolater is rooted in an uncritical acceptance of the biblical version of the story of "Israel", in which "Israel" is a distinct ethnic group originally separate from the surrounding "foreign" peoples. This ideological construct of "Israel" and her religious beliefs and practices must be distinguished from the likely historical reality of Judahite society and its deity-worship, which, as this study's examination of Manasseh and child sacrifice indicates, were probably very different.

In the light of these conclusions, several questions arise, the potential answers to which regrettably lie beyond the scope of this study. The proposed anti-Manasseh polemic of the Hebrew Bible demands further attention, particularly in view of the biblical claim that the tribe of Manasseh did not drive out the "Canaanites" from their territory (Judg. 1), and the association of the half-tribe of Manasseh with the building of a rival altar in the Transjordan (Josh. 22). Another potentially fertile area of enquiry lies in the closer examination of the designation צוּר, "Rock", and its synonyms, and a possible relation to cults of child sacrifice, as tentatively noted in chapter 4.

Perhaps a further issue arising from this study is the recognition that this discussion has touched on sensitive ground in a number of ways. One relates to the presentations of Judaism throughout history: an ugly feature of Christian Europe—and particularly medieval England—through the ages has been the caricature of the Jew as child-killer. To challenge the biblical portrayal of child sacrifice as an alien and outlawed practice, as this study has done, may invite misdirected charges of antisemitism from some circles. However, this should not deflect from a clear-sighted and self-critical attempt to reconstruct the probable historical reality of ancient Judahite child sacrifice.

Another way in which this study has touched on sensitive ground is in raising the basic human question of how human beings could engage in the sacrifice of children. Though it is possible to offer partial answers to this question, couched in terms of the perceived functions of this form of sacrifice—as indeed this study has done—or perhaps with recourse to the insights offered by social anthropology and psychology, modern appraisals of child sacrifice should beware of assuming a self-righteous stance of criticism. This is not to presume that modern scholarship must maintain a skeptical position of detached observation, and remain unmoved; this is naturally impossible. However, it is no part of the present task to attempt to arbitrate between the ethical values of different cultures, be they ancient or modern.

It is hoped that, in highlighting some of the the biblically-based biases undergirding many modern reconstructions of Judahite history and religion, this study has gone some way to redress the imbalance of many modern presentations of Manasseh and child sacrifice. In blaming the Manasseh of history for the promotion of child sacrifice, too many modern scholars continue to scapegoat Manasseh for what amounts to an uncomfortable reality within the history of ancient Judahite deity-worship.

Bibliography

Ackerman, S., "Sacred Sex, Sacrifice and Death: Understanding a Prophetic Poem", *BR* 6 (1990), 38-44.

—*Under Every Green Tree: Popular Religion in Sixth-Century Judah* (HSM 46; Atlanta: Scholars Press, 1992).

—"Child Sacrifice: Returning God's Gift", *BR* 9/3 (1993), 20-28, 56.

Ackroyd, P.R., "The Biblical Interpretation of the Reigns of Ahaz and Hezekiah", in W.B. Barrick and J.R. Spencer (eds.), *In the Shelter of Elyon: Essays on Ancient Palestinian Life and Literature* (JSOTSup 31; Sheffield: JSOT Press, 1984), 247-259.

—"The Theology of the Chronicler", in *idem*., *The Chronicler in His Age* (JSOTSup 101; Sheffield: JSOT Press, 1991), 273-289.

Acquaro, E., "Sardinia", in S. Moscati (ed.), *The Phoenicians* (second edn; New York: Rizzoli, 1997), 259-278.

—"Scarabs and Amulets", in S. Moscati (ed.), *The Phoenicians* (second edn; New York: Rizzoli, 1997), 445-455.

Aharoni, Y., "Excavations at Tel Beer-Sheba", *BA* 35 (1972), 111-127.

Ahlström, G.W., *Royal Administration and National Religion in Ancient Palestine* (SHANE 1; Leiden: Brill 1982).

—*Who Were the Israelites?* (Winona Lake: Eisenbrauns, 1986).

—"The Role of Archaeological and Literary Remains in Reconstructing Israel's History", in D.V. Edelman (ed.), *The Fabric of History: Text, Artifact and Israel's Past* (JSOTSup 127; Sheffield: JSOT Press, 1991), 116-141.

— *The History of Ancient Palestine* (Minneapolis: Fortress Press, 1993).

Albertz, R., *Persönliche Frömmigkeit und offizielle Religion* (Stuttgart: Calwer Verlag, 1978).

—*A History of Israelite Religion in the Old Testament Period* (2 vols; trans. J. Bowden; Louisville: Westminster/John Knox, 1994).

Albright, W.F., "The Site of Tirzah and the topography of Western Manasseh", *JPOS* 11 (1931), 241-251.

—"The Names Shaddai and Abram", *JBL* 54 (1935), 108-187.

—"A Case of Lèse Majesté in Pre-Israelite Lachish, with Some Remarks on the Israelite Conquest", *BASOR* 87 (1942), 32-38.

—*The Biblical Period* (Oxford: Blackwell, 1952).

—*Yahweh and the Gods of Canaan* (London: Athlone, 1968).

—*Archaeology and the Religion of Israel* (third edn; Baltimore: Johns Hopkins, 1969).

Allen, L.C., *Psalms 101–150* (WBC 21; Waco: Word, 1983).

— *Ezekiel 20–48* (WBC 29; Dallas: Word, 1990).

Alquier, J. and P., "Stèles votives à Saturne découvertes près de N'gaous (Algérie)", *CRAIBL* (1931), 21-26.

Alt, A., "Israels Gaue unter Salomo", *BWAT* 13 (1913), 1-39.

Amaru, B.H., "The Killing of the Prophets: Unravelling a Midrash", *HUCA* 54 (1983), 170-173.

Amiran, R., *Ancient Pottery of the Holy Land* (Jerusalem: Masada, 1969).

Amit, Y., *History and Ideology: An Introduction to Historiography in the Hebrew Bible* (trans. Y. Lotan; BS 60; Sheffield: Sheffield Academic Press, 1999).

Anati, E., *Palestine Before the Hebrews: A History, from the Earliest Arrival of Man to the Conquest of Canaan* (New York: Knopf, 1963).

Anderson, F.I., and D.N. Freedman, *Micah: A New Translation with Introduction and Commentary* (AB 24E; Garden City: Doubleday, 2000).

Artzy, M., "Pomegranate Scepters and Incense Stand with Pomegranates found in Priest's Grave", *BAR* 16/1 (1990), 48-51.

Ash, P. S., "Jeroboam I and the Deuteronomistic Historian's Ideology of the Founder", *CBQ* 60 (1998), 16-24.

Astour, M.C., "Two Ugaritic Serpent Charms", *JNES* 27 (1968), 13-36

Attridge, H.W., and R.A. Oden, *Philo of Byblos, The Phoenician History* (CBQMS 9; Washington: Catholic Biblical Association of America, 1981).

Aubet, M.E., *The Phoenicians and the West: Politics, Colonies, and Trade* (trans. M. Turton; second edn; Cambridge: Cambridge University Press, 2001).

Auld, A.G., *Kings Without Privilege: David and Moses in the Story of the Bible's Kings* (Edinburgh: T&T Clark, 1994).

—"The Deuteronomists and the Former Prophets, or What Makes the Former Prophets Deuteronomistic?", in L.S. Schearing and S. L. McKenzie (eds.), *Those Elusive Deuteronomists: The Phenomenon of Pan-Deuteronomism*, (JSOTSup 268; Sheffield: Sheffield Academic Press, 1999), 116-126.

—"What if the Chronicler did use the Deuteronomistic History?", *BibInt* 8 (2000), 137-150.

Avigad, N., "A Seal of "Manasseh Son of the King"", *IEJ* 13 (1963), 133-136.

—*Discovering Jerusalem* (Nashville: Thomas Nelson, 1983).

—*Hebrew Bullae from the Time of Jeremiah* (Jerusalem: Israel Exploration Society, 1986).

—"The Contribution of Hebrew Seals to an Understanding of Israelite Religion and Society", in P.D. Miller, P.D. Hanson and S.B. McBride (eds.), *Ancient Israelite Religion: Essays in Honor of Frank Moore Cross* (Philadelphia: Fortress Press, 1987), 195-208.

—and B. Sass, *Corpus of West Semitic Stamp Seals* (Jerusalem: Israel Exploration Society, 1997).

Bahat, D., "The Wall of Manasseh in Jerusalem", *IEJ* 28 (1978), 235-236.

Bailey, L.R., "Israelite *ʾĒl Šadday* and Amorite *Bêl Šadê*", *JBL* 87 (1968), 434-438.

Barnes, W.H., *Studies in the Chronology of the Divided Monarchy of Israel* (HSM 48; Atlanta: Scholars Press, 1991).

Barr, J., *History and Ideology in the Old Testament: Biblical Studies at the End of a Millennium* (Oxford: Oxford University Press, 2000).

Barrick, W.B., "On the Removal of the High Places in 1–2 Kings", *Bib* 55 (1974), 257-259.

—"Dynastic Politics, Priestly Succession, and Josiah's Eighth Year", *ZAW* 112 (2000), 564-582.

—"Genealogical Notes on the 'House of David' and the 'House of Zadok'", *JSOT* 96 (2001), 29-58.

— *The King and the Cemeteries: Toward a New Understanding of Josiah's Reform* (VTSup 88; Leiden: Brill, 2002).

Bartlett, J. R., "The 'United' Campaign against Moab in 2 Kings 3:4-27", in J.F.A. Sawyer and D.J.A. Clines (eds.), *Midian, Moab and Edom: The History and Archaeology of Late Bronze and Iron Age Jordan and North-West Arabia* (JSOTSup 24; Sheffield: JSOT Press, 1983), 135-145.

Baumann, G., *Love and Violence: Marraige as Metaphor for the relationship between YHWH and Israel in the Prophetic Books* (trans. L.M. Maloney; Collegeville: Liturgical Press, 2003).

Becking, B., *The Fall of Samaria: An Historical and Archaeological Study* (SHANE 2; Leiden: Brill, 1992).

—"From Apostasy to Destruction: A Josianic View on the Fall of Samaria (2 Kings 17, 21-23)", in M. Vervenne and J. Lust (eds.), *Deuteronomy and Deuteronomic Literature: Festschrift C. H. W. Brekelmans* (BETL 133; Leuven: Peeters, 1997), 279-297.

—"Inscribed Seals as Evidence for Biblical Israel? Jeremiah 40.7-41.15 par example", in L.L. Grabbe (ed.), *Can a "History of Israel" be Written?* (JSOTSup 245/ESHM 1; Sheffield: JSOT Press, 1997), 65-83.

—"From Exodus to Exile: 2 Kgs 17, 7-20 in the Context of Its Co-Text", in G. Galil and M. Weinfeld (eds.), *Studies in Historical Geography and Biblical Historiography Presented to Zecharia Kallai* (VTSup 81; Leiden: Brill, 2000), 215-231.

—"The Gods, In Whom They Trusted ... Assyrian Evidence for Iconic Polytheism in Ancient Israel", in B. Becking, M. Dijkstra, M.C.A. Korpel and K.J.H. Vriezen, *Only One God? Monotheism in Ancient Israel and the Veneration of the Goddess Asherah* (BS 77, London: Continuum, 2001), 151-163.

Beit-Arieh, I., "Tel ʿIra—A Fortified City of the Kingdom of Judah", *Qadmoniot* 18 (1985), 17-28 (Hebrew).

Beit-Arieh, I., and B.C. Cresson, "Ḥorvat ʿUza: A Fortified Outpost on the Eastern Negev Border", *BA* 54 (1991), 126-135.

Ben-Barak, Z., "The Status and Right of the Gebira", *JBL* 110 (1991), 23-34.

Benichou-Safar, H., "À propos des ossements humains du tophet de Carthage", *RSF* 9 (1981), 5-9.

—*Les tombes puniques de Carthage: Topographie, structures, inscriptions et rites funéraires* (Paris: Éditions du Centre national de la recherche scientifique, 1982).

Benigni, G., "Il 'segno di Tanit' in Oriente", *RSF* 3 (1975), 17-18.

Ben Zvi, E., "The Account of the Reign of Manasseh in II Reg 21, 1–18 and the Redactional History of the Book of Kings", *ZAW* 103 (1991), 355-374.

—"On the Reading '*bytdwd*' in the Ramaic Stele from Tel Dan", *JSOT* 64 (1994), 29-32.

—"Prelude to a Reconstruction of the *Historical* Manassic Judah", *BN* 81 (1996), 31-44.

—"The Chronicler as Historian: Building Texts", in M.P. Graham, K.G. Hoglund and S.L. McKenzie (eds.), *The Chronicler as Historian* (JSOTS 238, Sheffield: Sheffield Academic Press, 1997), 32-149.

Bergmann, M.S., *In the Shadow of Moloch: The Sacrifice of Children and Its Impact on Western Religions* (New York: Columbia University Press, 1992).

Berlin, A., *Zephaniah: A New Translation with Introduction and Commentary* (AB 25A; Garden City: Doubleday, 1994).

Berlinerblau, J., "The "Popular Religion" Paradigm in Old Testament Research: A Sociological Critique", *JSOT* 60 (1993), 3-26.

—*The Vow and the "Popular Religious Groups" of Ancient Israel: A Philological and Sociological Inquiry* (JSOTSup 210; Sheffield: Sheffield Academic Press, 1996).

Berthier, A., and R. Charlier, *Le sanctuaire punique d'El Hofra à Constantine* (2 vols. Paris: Arts et métiers graphiques, 1955).

Biale, D., "The God with Breasts: El Shaddai in the Bible", *HR* 21 (1982), 240-256.

Bible and Culture Collective, *The Postmodern Bible* (New Haven: Yale University Press, 1995), 272-308.

Bin-Nun, S., "Formulas from Royal Records of Israel and Judah", *VT* 18 (1968), 414-432.

Biran, A., "Tell er-Ruqeish", *IEJ* 24 (1974), 141-142, pl. 24:A.

—and J. Naveh, "An Aramaic Fragment from Tel Dan", *IEJ* 43 (1993), 81-98.

—and J. Naveh "The Tel Dan Inscription: A New Fragment", *IEJ* 45 (1995), 1-18.

Bird, P.A., "'To Play the Harlot': An Inquiry into an Old Testament Metaphor", in P.L. Day (ed.), *Gender and Difference in Ancient Israel* (Minneapolis: Fortress Press, 1989), 75-94

—"The End of the Male Cult Prostitute: A Literary-Historical and Sociological Analysis of Hebrew *Qādēš-Qĕdēšîm*", in J.A. Emerton (ed.), *Congress Volume Cambridge, 1995* (VTSup 66; Leiden: Brill, 1997), 37-80

Bisi, A.M., *Le stele puniche* (Rome: University of Rome, 1967).

Blenkinsopp, J., *Ezra-Nehemiah: A Commentary* (OTL; London: SCM Press, 1988).

—"Judah's covenant with Death (Isaiah XXVIII 14-22)", *VT* 50 (2000), 14-22.

—*Isaiah 1–39: A New Translation with Introduction and Commentary* (AB19; New York: Doubleday, 2000).

—*Isaiah 56–66: A New Translation with Introduction and Commentary* (AB19B; New York: Doubleday, 2003).

Bloch-Smith, E., *Judahite Burial Practices and Beliefs about the Dead* (JSOTSup 123; Sheffield: JSOT Press, 1992).

Block, D.I., *The Gods of the Nations. Studies in Ancient Near Eastern National Theology* (second edn; Grand Rapids: Baker Academic, 1988).

—*The Book of Ezekiel* (2 vols. NICOT; Grand Rapids: Eerdmans, 1997, 1998).

Bodi, D., "Les *gillûlîm* chez Ezéchiel et dans l'Ancien Testament, et les différentes practiques cultuelles associées à ce terme", *RB* 100 (1993), 481-510.

Boecker, H.J., *Law and the Administration of Justice in the Old Testament and Ancient East* (Minneapolis: Augsburg, 1980).

Boehm, O., "The Binding of Isaac: An Inner-Biblical Polemic on the Question of 'Disobeying' a Manifestly Illegal Order", *VT* 52 (2002), 1-12.

Borrowski, O., "Hezekiah's Reforms and the Revolt against Assyria", *BA* 58 (1995), 148-155.

Bosman, H.L., "Redefined Prophecy as Deuteronomic Alternative to Divination in Deut.18:9-22", *Acta Theologia* 16 (1996), 1-23.

Bottéro, J., "Les morts et l'au-delà dans le rituels en accadien contre l'action des 'revenants'", *ZA* 73 (1983), 153-203.

Braun, R.L., "A Reconsideration of the Chronicler's Attitude toward the North", *JBL* 96 (1977), 59-62.

Brett, M.G., "Interpreting Ethnicity: Method, Hermeneutics, Ethics", in M.G. Brett (ed.), *Ethnicity and the Bible* (Leiden: Brill, 2002), 3-22.

Brettler, M.Z, "Ideology, History and Theology in 2 Kings XVII 7-23", *VT* 39 (1989), 268-282.

—*The Creation of History in Ancient Israel* (London: Routledge, 1995).

Bright, J., *A History of Israel* (third edn; Philadelphia: Westminster, 1981).

Brin, G., *Studies in Biblical Law* (JSOTSup 176; Sheffield: JSOT Press, 1994).

Brockington, L.H., *A Critical Introduction to the Apocrypha* (London: SCM Press, 1961).

Broshi, M., "The Expansion of Jerusalem in the Reigns of Hezekiah and Manasseh", *IEJ* 24 (1974), 21-26.

—and I. Finkelstein, "The Population of Palestine in Iron Age II", *BASOR* 287 (1992), 47-60.

Brown, S., *Late Carthaginian Child Sacrifice and Sacrificial Monuments in their Mediterranean Context* (JSOT/ASORMS 3; Sheffield: JSOT Press, 1991).

Buber, M., *Kingship of God* (trans. R. Scheimann; third edn; London: George Allen & Unwin, 1967).

Burkert, W., *Homo Necans: The Anthropology of Ancient Greek Sacrificial Ritual and Myth* (trans. P. Bing; London: University of California Press, 1983).

Burns, J.B., "Why did the Besieging Army Withdraw (2 Reg. 3:27)?", *ZAW* 102 (1990), 187-194.

Cahill, J.M., and D. Tarler, "Excavations Directed by Yigal Shiloh at the City of David, 1978-1985", in H. Geva (ed.), *Ancient Jerusalem Revealed* (Jerusalem: Israel Exploration Society, 1994), 30-45.

—"Respondents", in A. Biran and J. Aviram (eds.), *Biblical Archaeology Today* (Jerusalem: Israel Exploration Society, 1993), 625-626.

Campbell, E.F., "A Land Divided: Judah and Israel from the Death of Solomon to the Fall of Samaria", in M.D. Coogan (ed.), *The Oxford History of the Biblical World* (Oxford: Oxford University Press, 1998), 206-241.

Canney, M., "Shaddai", *ET* 34 (1922–1923), 332.

Caquot, A., "Une contribution ougaritique a la prehistoire du titre divin Shadday", in J. A. Emerton (ed.), *Congress Volume Paris, 1992* (VTSup 61; Leiden: Brill, 1995), 1-12.

Carcopino, J., "Survivances par substitution des sacrifices d'enfants dans l'Africa romaine", *RHR* 106 (1932), 592-599.

Carmichael, C.M., *Law, Legend, and Incest in the Bible: Leviticus 18–20* (Ithaca: Cornell University Press, 1997).

Carroll R., M. Daniel, "Re-Examining 'Popular Religion': Issues of Definition and Sources. Insights from Interpretative Anthropology", in M. Daniel Carroll R. (ed.), *Rethinking Contexts, Rereading Texts: Contributions from the Social Sciences to Biblical Interpretation* (JSOTSup 299; Sheffield: Sheffield Academic Press, 2000), 146-167.

Carroll, R.P., *From Chaos to Covenant: Uses of Prophecy in the Book of Jeremiah* (London: SCM Press, 1981).

— *Jeremiah: A Commentary* (OTL; London: SCM Press, 1986).

— *Wolf in the Sheepfold: The Bible as a Problem for Christianity* (second edn; London: SCM Press, 1997).

—"Poststructuralist Approaches; New Historicism and postmodernism", in J. Barton (ed.), *The Cambridge Companion to Biblical Interpretation* (Cambridge: Cambridge University Press, 1998), 50-66.

Cathcart, K.J., "The 'Demons' in Judg. 5:8a", *BZ* 21 (1977), 111-112.

Cazelles, H., "Molok", *DBS*, vol. 5, cols. 1337-1346.

—"The History of Israel in Pre-Exilic Times", in G.E. Anderson (ed.), *Tradition and Interpretation* (Oxford: Clarendon Press, 1979), 274-319.

Chabot, J.-B., "Note complémentaire de M. J.-B. Chabot", *CRAIBL* (1931), 27.

Charlesworth, J.H., "The Prayer of Manasseh", in J.H. Charlesworth (ed.), *The Old Testament Pseudepigrapha* (2 vols. London: Darton, Longman & Todd, 1985), vol 2, 625-637.

—"Manasseh, Prayer of", *ABD*, vol. 4, 499-500.

Charlier, R., "La nouvelle série de stèles puniques de Constantine et la question des sacrifices dits "molchomor", en relation avec l'expression 'BŠRM BTM'", *Karthago* 4 (1953), 1-48.

Childs, B.S., *The Book of Exodus: A Critical, Theological Commentary* (OTL; Louisville: Westminster Press, 1974).

Ciasca, A., "Masks and Protomes", in S. Moscati (ed.), *The Phoenicians*, (second edn; New York: Rizzoli, 1997), 354-369.

Ciasca, A. (ed.) *Mozia I* (SS 12; Rome: University of Rome, 1964).

—*Mozia II* (SS 19; Rome: University of Rome, 1966).

—*Mozia VI* (SS 37; Rome: Consiglio nazionale delle ricerche, 1970).

—*Mozia VIII* (SS 45; Rome: Consiglio nazionale delle ricerche, 1973).

Cintas, P., "Le sanctuaire punique de Sousse", *Revue africaine* 91 (1947), 1-80.

Clements, R.E., *Isaiah and the Deliverance of Jerusalem: A Study of the Interpretation of Prophecy in the Old Testament* (JSOTSup 13; Sheffield: JSOT Press, 1980).

Clines, D.J.A., *Interested Parties: The Ideology of Writers and Readers of the Hebrew Bible* (JSOTSup 205/GCT 1; Sheffield: Sheffield Academic Press, 1995).

Cogan, M., *Imperialism and Religion: Assyria, Judah and Israel in the Eighth and Seventh Centuries BCE* (SBLMS 19; Missoula: Scholars Press, 1974).

—"Israel in Exile—The View of a Josianic Historian", *JBL* 97 (1978), 40-44.

—"The Chronicler's Use of Chronology as Illuminated by Neo-Assyrian Royal Inscriptions", in J.H. Tigay (ed.), *Empirical Models for Biblical Criticism* (Philadelphia: University of Pennsylvania Press, 1985), 197-209.

—"Into Exile: From the Assyrian Conquest of Israel to the Fall of Babylon", in M. D. Coogan (ed.), *The Oxford History of the Biblical World* (Oxford: Oxford University Press, 1998), 242-275.

—*I Kings: A New Translation with Introduction and Commentary* (AB 10; Garden City: Doubleday, 2000).

—"Sennacherib's Siege of Jerusalem—Once or Twice?", *BAR* 27/1 (2001), 40-45, 69.

—and H. Tadmor, *II Kings: A New Translation with Introduction and Commentary* (AB 11; Garden City: Doubleday, 1988).

Coggins, R.J., "The Old Testament and Samaritan Origins", *ASTI* 6 (1967–1968), 35-42.

—*Samaritans and Jews* (Oxford: Blackwell, 1975).

—"What Does 'Deuteronomistic' Mean?", in L.S. Schearing and S.L. McKenzie (eds.), *Those Elusive Deuteronomists: The Phenomenon of Pan-Deuteronomism* (JSOTSup 268; Sheffield: Sheffield Academic Press, 1999), 22-35.

Conheeney, J., and A. Pipe, "Note on some cremated bones from Tyrian cinerary urns", *Berytus* 39 (1991), 83-85.

Cooper, A., "Divine Names and Epithets in the Ugaritic Texts", in S. Rummel (ed.), *Ras Shamra Parallels*, vol. 3 (Rome: Pontifical Biblical Institute, 1981), 333-469.

Cross, F.M., "Yahweh and the Gods of the Patriarchs", *HTR* 55 (1962), 244-250.

—"The Discovery of the Samaria Papyri", *BA* 26 (1963), 110-121.

—"Aspects of Samaritan and Jewish History in Late Persian and Hellenistic Times", *HTR* 59 (1966), 201- 211.

—"Epigraphic Notes on the Ammān Citadel Inscription", *BASOR* 193 (1969), 13-19.

—"Papyri of the Fourth Century BC from Dâliyeh: A Preliminary Report on their Discovery and Significance", in D.N. Freedman and J.C. Greenfield (eds.), *New Directions in Biblical Archaeology* (Garden City: Doubleday, 1969), 41-62.

—"The Cave Inscriptions from Khirbet Beit Lei", in J.A. Sanders (ed.), *Near Eastern Archaeology in the Twentieth Century: Essays in Honor of Nelson Glueck* (Garden City: Doubleday, 1970), 299-306.

—*Canaanite Myth and Hebrew Epic: Essays in the History of the Religion of Israel* (Cambridge: Harvard University Press, 1973).

—"A Reconstruction of the Judean Restoration", *JBL* 94 (1975), 4-18.

—"A Phoenician Inscription from Idalion: Some Old and New Texts Relating to Child Sacrifice", in M.D. Coogan, J.C. Exum and L.E. Stager (eds.), *Scripture and Other Artifacts: Essays on the Bible and Archaeology in Honor of Philip J. King* (Louisville: Westminster John Knox, 1994), 93-107.

—"King Hezekiah's Seal bears Phoenician Imagery", *BAR* 25/2 (1999) 42-45, 60.

— "The Prayer of Manasseh", *ECB*, 859-861.

—and D.N. Freedman, "Josiah's Revolt against Assyria", *JNES* 12 (1953), 56-58.

Cryer, F.H., *Divination in Ancient Israel and Its Near Eastern Environment: A Socio-Historical Investigation* (JSOTSup 142; Sheffield: JSOT Press, 1994).

—"On the Recently Discovered 'House of David' Inscription", *SJOT* 8 (1994), 3-19.

—"A '*betdawd*' Miscellany: *dwd, dwd*' or *dwdh*?", *SJOT* 9 (1995), 52-58.

Culican, W., "The Graves at Tell er-Ruqeish", *AJBA* 2 (1973), 66-105.

—"Some Phoenician Masks and other Terracottas", *Berytus* 24 (1975-76), 47-87.

Curtis, E.L., and A.A. Madsen, *A Critical and Exegetical Commentary on the Books of Chronicles* (ICC; Edinburgh: T&T Clark, 1910).

Dahood, M., "Hebrew-Ugaritic Lexicography II", *Bib* 45 (1964), 393-412.

—"Hebrew-Ugaritic Lexicography IV", *Bib* 47 (1966), 403-419.

—*Psalms 101–150* (AB 17; Garden City: Doubleday, 1970).

Dalley, S., "Foreign Chariotry and Cavalry in the Armies of Tiglath-pileser III and Sargon II", *Iraq* 47 (1985), 31-38.

—"Yabâ, Atalyā and the Foreign Policy of Late Assyrian Kings", *SAAB* 12 (1998), 83-98.

—and B. Teissier, "Tablets from the Vicinity of Emar and Elsewhere", *Iraq* 54 (1992), 83-111.

Davies, P.R., *In Search of "Ancient Israel"* (JSOTSup 148; Sheffield: JSOT Press, 1992).

—"*Bytdwd* and *Swkt Dwyd*: A Comparison", *JSOT* 64 (1994), 23-24.

—"'House of David' built on Sand", *BAR* 20/4 (1994), 54-55.

— "Method and Madness: Some Remarks on Doing History with the Bible", *JBL* 114 (1995), 699-705

—and J. Rogerson, "Was the Siloam Tunnel Built by Hezekiah?", *BA* 59 (1996), 138-149.

Day, J., *Molech: A god of human sacrifice in the Old Testament* (UCOP 41; Cambridge: Cambridge University Press, 1989).

—*Yahweh and the Gods and Goddesses of Canaan* (JSOTSup 265; Sheffield, Sheffield Academic Press, 2000).

—"The Religion of Israel", in A. D. H. Mayes (ed.), *Text in Context* (Oxford: Oxford University Press, 2000), 428-453.

Day, P.L., "From the Child is Born the Woman: The Story of Jephthah's Daughter", in P.L. Day (ed.), *Gender and Difference in Ancient Israel* (Minneapolis: Fortress Press, 1989), 58-74.

Dearman, J.A., "The Tophet in Jerusalem: Archaeology and Cultural Profile", *JNSL* 22 (1996), 59-71.

Delamarter, S., "The Vilification of Jehoiakim (a.k.a. Eliakim and Joiakim) in Early Judaism", in C.A. Evans and J.A. Sanders (eds.), *The Function of Scripture in Early Jewish and Christian Tradition* (JSNTSup 154/SSEJC 6; Sheffield: Sheffield Academic Press, 1998),190-204.

Delaney, C., *Abraham on Trial: The Social Legacy of Biblical Myth* (Princeton: Princeton University Press, 1998).

Delavault, B., and A. Lemaire, "Une stèle 'Molk' de Palestine dédiée à Eshmoun? *RES* 367 reconsidéré", *RB* 83 (1976), 569-583.

—"Les inscriptions phéniciennes de Palestine", *RSF* 7 (1979), 24-26.

Delcor, M., "Two Special Meanings of the Word *yd* in Biblical Hebrew", *JSS* 12 (1967) 230-240.

—"Astarté et la fécondité des troupeaux en Deut. 7:13 et parallèles", *UF* 6 (1974), 7-14.

—"Le Texte de Deir ʿAlla et le Oracles Bibliques de Balaʾam", in J.A. Emerton (ed.), *Congress Volume Vienna, 1980* (VTSup 32; Leiden: Brill, 1981), 52-73.

—"Des inscriptions de Deir Alla aux traditions bibliques, à propos des *šdyn*, des *šēdîm* et de *šadday*", in A. Müller and M. Görg (eds.), *Die Väter Israels: Beiträge zur Theologie der Patriarchüberlieferungen im Alten Testament* (Stuttgart: Katholisches Bibelwork, 1989), 33-40.

Deller, K., Review of *Les sacrifices de l'Ancien Testament*, by R. de Vaux, *Or* 34 (1965), 182-186.

Derchain, P., "Les plus anciens témoignages de sacrifice d'enfants chez les sémites occidentaux", *VT* 20 (1970), 351-355.

Deutsch, R., *Messages from the Past: Hebrew Bullae from the Time of Isaiah through the Destruction of the First Temple—Shlomo Moussaieff Collection and an Updated Corpus* (Tel Aviv: Archaeological Center Publications, 1999).

Dever, W.G., "Monumental Architecture in Ancient Israel in the Period of the United Monarchy", in T. Ishida (ed.), *Studies in the Period of David and Solomon and Other Essays* (Winona Lake: Eisenbrauns, 1982), 269-306.

—"Solomon and the Assyrian 'Palaces' at Gezer", *IEJ* 35 (1985), 217-230.

—"How to Tell a Canaanite from an Israelite", in H. Shanks (ed.), *The Rise of Ancient Israel* (Washington: Biblical Archaeology Society, 1992), 27-56.

—"'Will the Real Israel Please Stand Up?' Archaeology and Israelite Historiography: Part I", *BASOR* 297 (1995), 61-80.

—"Archaeology, Ideology, and the Quest for an 'Ancient' or 'Biblical' Israel", *NEA* 61 (1998), 39-52.

—"Histories and Nonhistories of 'Ancient Israel'" *BASOR* 316 (1999), 89-105.

—*What Did the Biblical Writers Know and When Did they Know It? What Archaeology Can Tell Us about the Reality of Ancient Israel* (Grand Rapids: Eerdmans, 2001).

—"Gezer", *EAEHL*, vol. 2, 438.

—*Who Were the Early Israelites and Where Did They Come From?* (Grand Rapids: Eerdmans, 2003).

Dhorme, E., Review of *Molk als Opferbegriff*, by O. Eissfeldt, *RHR* 113 (1936), 277.

—"Le Dieu Baal et le Dieu Moloch dans la tradition biblique", *Anatolian Studies* 4 (1956), 59-60.

Dietrich, M., O. Loretz, and J. Sanmartín, "Einzelbemerkungen zu RS 24, 251", *UF* 7 (1975), 127-131.

Dietrich, W., *Prophetie und Geschichte: Eine redaktionsgeschichtliche Untersuchung zum deuteronomistischen Geschichtswerk* (FRLANT 108; Göttingen: Vandenhoeck & Ruprecht, 1972).

—"Der Eine Gott als Symbol politischen Widerstands: Religion und Politik im Juda des 7. Jahr-hunderts", in W. Dietrich and M.A. Klopfenstein, *Ein Gott allein? JHWH-Verehrung und biblischer Monotheismus im Kontext der israelitischen und altorientalischen Religionsgeschichte* (OBO 139; Göttingen: Vandenhoeck and Ruprecht, 1994), 463-490.

—"1 and 2 Kings", *OBC*, 232-266.

Dijkstra, M., "Is Balaam also among the Prophets?" *JBL* 114 (1995), 43-64.

—"Abraham", *DDD*, 3-5.

—"I have Blessed you by YHWH of Samaria and his Asherah: Texts with Religious Elements from the Soil Archive of Ancient Israel", in B. Becking, M. Dijkstra, M.C.A. Korpel, and K.J.H. Vriezen, *Only One God? Monotheism in Ancient Israel and The Veneration of the Goddess Asherah*, (BS 77; London: Continuum, 2001), 17-39.

Donner, H., "The Separate States of Israel and Judah", in J.H. Hayes and J.M. Miller (eds.), *Israelite and Judaean History* (London: SCM Press, 1977), 381-434.

—*Geschichte des Volkes Israel und seiner Nachbarn in Grundzügen. Teil 2, Von der Königszeit bis zu Alexander dem Gro en mit einem Ausblick auf die Geschichte des Judentums bis Bar Kochba* (Göttingen: Vandenhoeck & Ruprecht, 1986).

Dothan, M., "A Sign of Tannit from Tell Akko", *IEJ* 24 (1974), 44-49.

Doyle, R., "Molek of Jerusalem?", in R.S. Hess and G.J. Wenham (eds.), *Zion, City of Our God* (Cambridge: Eerdmans, 1999), 171-206.

Driver, G.R., "Difficult Words in the Hebrew Prophets", in H.H. Rowley (ed.), *Studies in Old Testament Prophecy* (Edinburgh: T&T Clark, 1950), 52-72.

Dronkert, K., *De Molochdienst in het Oude Testament* (Leiden: Brill, 1953).

Dyck, J.E., "A Map of Ideology for Biblical Critics", in M. Daniel Carroll R. (ed.), *Rethinking Contexts, Rereading Texts: Contributions from the Social Sciences to Biblical Interpretation* (JSOTSup 299; Sheffield: Sheffield Academic Press, 2000), 108-128.

Eagleton, T., *Criticism and Ideology: A Study in Marxist Theory* (London: Verso, 1976.

—*Ideology: An Introduction* (London: Verso, 1991).

Edelman, D.V., "The Meaning of *qiṭṭēr*", *VT* 35 (1985), 395-404.

—"Biblical *Molek* Reassessed", *JAOS* 107 (1987), 727-731.

—"Solomon's Adversaries Hadad, Rezon and Jeroboam: A Trio of 'Bad Guy' Characters Illustrating the Theology of Immediate Retribution", in S.H. Holloway and L.K. Handy (eds.), *The Pitcher Is Broken: Memorial Essays for Gösta Ahlström* (JSOTSup 190; Sheffield: Sheffield Academic Press, 1995), 166-191.

—(ed.), *The Triumph of Elohim: From Yahwisms to Judaisms* (CBET 13; Kampen: Kok Pharos, 1995).

—Review of *Yahweh and the God and Goddesses of Canaan*, by J. Day, *BibInt* 10 (2002), 79-81.

Ehrlich, E.L., "Der Aufenthalt des Königs Manasse in Babylon", *ThZ* 21 (1965), 281-286.

Eichrodt, W., *Ezekiel* (trans. C. Quin; OTL; Philadelphia: Westminster, 1970).

Eilberg-Schwartz, H., *The Savage in Judaism: An Anthropology of Israelite Religion and Ancient Judaism* (Bloomington: Indiana University Press, 1990).

Eissfeldt, O., *Molk als Opferbegriff im Punischen und Hebräischen und das Ende des Gottes Moloch* (Halle: Niemeyer, 1935).

—"The beginnings of Phoenician epigraphy according to a letter written by Wilhelm Gesenius in 1835", *PEQ* 79 (1947), 68-86.

Eitam, D., "Olive-Oil Production during the Biblical Period", in M. Heltzer and D. Eitam (eds.), *Olive Oil in Antiquity* (Haifa: University of Haifa, 1987).

Erling, B., "First-Born and Firstlings in the Covenant Code", *SBLSP* 25 (1986), 470-478.

Evans, C.D., "Judah's Foreign Policy from Hezekiah to Josiah", in C.D. Evans, W.W. Hallo and J.B. White (eds.), *Scripture in Context: Essays on the Comparative Method* (PTMS 34; Pittsburgh: Pickwick Press, 1980), 157-178.

—"Naram-Sin and Jeroboam: The Archetypal *Unheilsherrscher* in Mesopotamian and Biblical Historiography", in W.W. Hallo, J.C. Moyer and L.G. Perdue (eds.), *Scripture in Context, II: More Essays on the Comparative Method* (Winona Lake: Eisenbrauns, 1983), 114-124.

—"Manasseh, King of Judah", *ABD*, vol. 4, 496-499.

Eynikel, E., *The Reform of King Josiah and the Composition of the Deuteronomistic History* (OTS 33; Leiden: Brill 1996).

—"The Portrait of Manasseh and the Deuteronomistic History", in M. Vervenne and J. Lust (eds.), *Deuteronomy and Deuteronomic Literature. Festschrift C.H.W. Brekelmans* (BETL 133; Leuven: Peeters, 1997), 233-261.

Fabry, H.-J., "*nātan*", *TDOT*, vol. 10, 90-109.

Fantar, M.H., "Formules propitiatoires sur des stèles puniques et néo-puniques", in J. Quaegebeur (ed.), *Ritual and Sacrifice in the Ancient Near East* (Leuven: Peeters, 1993), 125-133.

—"An *Odyssey* Debate: Were Living Children Sacrificed to the Gods?", *ArchOd* (Nov/Dec 2000), 28-31.

Fedele, F.G., "Tharros: Anthropology of the Tophet and Paleoecology of a Punic Town", in P. Bartoloni (ed.), *Atti del I Congresso internaionale di studi fenicie punici: Roma, 5-10 novembre 1979* (CSF 16; Rome: Consiglio nazionale delle ricerche, 1983), 637-650.

—and G.V. Foster, "Tharros: Ovicaprini sacrificali e rituale del Tofet", *RSF* 16 (1988), 46.

Feldman, L.H., "Use, Authority and Exegesis of Mikra in the Writings of Josephus", in M. J. Mulder and H. Sysling (eds.), *Mikra: Text, Translation, Reading and Interpretation of the Hebrew Bible in Ancient Judaism and Early Christianity* (CRINT 2.1; Assen: Van Gorcum, 1988), 466-470.

—"Josephus' Portrait of Manasseh", *JSP* 9 (1991), 3-20.

Ferrara, A.J., and S.B. Parker, "Seating Arrangements at Divine Banquets", *UF* 4 (1972), 37-39.

Ferron, J., *Mort-dieu de Carthage: ou les stèles funéraires de Carthage* (Paris: Librairie orientaliste Paul Geuthner, 1975).

Février, J.G., "Molchomor", *RHR* 143 (1953), 8-18.

—"Le vocabulaire sacrificiel punique", *JA* 243 (1955), 49-63.

—"Essai de reconstruction du sacrifice Molek", *JA* 248 (1960), 167-18.

—"Le rite de substitution dans les textes de N'gaous", *JA* 250 (1962), 1-10.

Finegan, J., *Light from the Ancient Past* (Princeton: Princeton University Press, 1959).

Finkelstein, I., *The Archaeology of the Israelite Settlement* (Jerusalem: Israel Exploration Society, 1988).

—"The Emergence of the Monarchy in Israel and the Environmental and Socio-Economic Aspects", *JSOT* 44 (1989), 43-74.

—"The Archaeology of the Days of Manasseh", in M.D. Coogan, J.C. Exum and L.E. Stager (eds.), *Scripture and Other Artifacts: Essays on the Bible and Archaeology in Honor of Philip J. King* (Louisville: Westminster John Knox, 1994), 169-187.

—"The Date of the Settlement of the Philistines in Canaan", *TA* 22 (1995), 213-139.

—"The Emergence of Israel: A Phase in the Cyclic History of Canaan in the Third and Second Millennia BCE", in I. Finkelstein and N. Na'aman (eds.), *From Nomadism to Monarchy: Archaeological and Historical Aspects of Early Israel* (Jerusalem: Israel Exploration Society, 1994), 150-178.

—"The Great Transformation: The 'Conquest' of the Highlands Frontiers and the Rise of the Territorial States", in T.E. Levy (ed.), *The Archaeology of Society in the Holy Land* (London: Leicester University Press, 1995), 349-363.

—"The Archaeology of the United Monarchy: An Alternative View", *Levant* 28 (1996), 177-187.

—"The Stratigraphy and Chronology of Megiddo and Beth-Shan in the 12th–11th Centuries BCE", *TA* 23 (1996), 170-184.

—"Bible Archaeology or Archaeology of Palestine in the Iron Age? A Rejoinder", *Levant* 30 (1998), 167- 174.

—"Hazor and the North in the Iron Age: A Low Chronology Perspective", *BASOR* 314 (1999), 55-70.

—"State Formation in Israel and Judah: A Contrast in Context, A Contrast in Trajectory", *NEA* 62 (1999), 35-52.

—"Hazor XII–XI with an Addendum on Ben-Tor's Dating of Hazor X–VII", *TA* 27 (2000), 231-247.

—and N.A. Silberman, *The Bible Unearthed: Archaeology's New Vision of Ancient Israel and the Origin of Its Sacred Texts* (New York: Free Press, 2001).

Fishbane, M., *Biblical Interpretation in Ancient Israel* (Oxford: Clarendon Press, 1985).

Foucher, L., *Hadrumetum* (Paris: Presses Universitaires de France, 1964).

Fowl, S., "Texts Don't Have Ideologies", *BibInt* 3 (1995), 15-34.

Fox, E., "Stalking the Younger Brother: Some Models for Understanding a Biblical Motif", *JSOT* 60 (1996), 45-68.

Fox, M.V., "The Sign of the Covenant", *RB* 81 (1974), 557-596.

Frankel, R., *Wine and Olive Oil Production in Antiquity in Israel and Other Mediterranean Countries* (ASORM 10; Sheffield: Sheffield Academic Press, 1999).

Franken, H.J., "Texts from the Persian Period from Deir ʿAllā", *VT* 17 (1967), 480-481.

—and M.L. Steiner, "Urusalim and Jebus", *ZAW* 104 (1992), 110-111.

Franklin, N., "A Room with a View: Images from Room V at Khorsabad, Samaria, Nubians, the Brook of Egypt and Ashdod", in A. Mazar (ed.), *Studies in the Archaeology of the Iron Age in Israel and Jordan* (JSOTSup 331; Sheffield: Sheffield Academic Press, 2001), 257-277.

Freedman, D.N., "Josiah's Revolt against Assyria", *JNES* 12 (1953), 56-58.

—"The Chronicler's Purpose", *CBQ* 23 (1961), 436-442.

—"Divine Names and Titles in Early Hebrew Poetry", in F.M. Cross, W.E. Lemke and P.D. Miller (eds.), *Magnalia Dei: The Mighty Acts of God* (Garden City: Doubleday, 1976), 55-108.

Frick, F.S., and P.R. Davies, *The Origin of the Ancient Israelites States* (JSOTSup 228; Sheffield: Sheffield Academic Press, 1996).

Friedman, R.E., *The Exile and Biblical Narrative: The Formation of the Deuteronomistic and Priestly Codes* (HSM 22; Atlanta: Scholars Press, 1981).

—"From Egypt to Egypt: Dtr[1] and Dtr[2]", in B. Halpern and J.D. Levenson (eds.), *Traditions in Transformation: Turning Points in Biblical Faith* (Winona Lake: Eisenbrauns, 1981), 167-192.

Fritz, V., "Israelites and Canaanites: You Can Tell Them Apart", *BAR* 28 (2002), 28-31.

—*1 & 2 Kings* (trans. A. Hagedorn; Continental; Minneapolis: Fortress Press, 2003).

Frost, S.B., "The Death of Josiah: A Conspiracy of Silence", *JBL* 87 (1968), 369-382.

Fuhs, H.F., "ʿābar", *TDOT*, vol. 10, 408-425.

Galambush, J., *Jerusalem in the Book of Ezekiel: The City as Yahweh's Wife* (SBLDS 130; Atlanta: Scholars Press, 1992).

Galil, G., *The Chronology of the Kings of Israel and Judah* (SHANE 9; Leiden: Brill 1996).

Gallagher, W.R., *Sennacherib's Campaign to Judah: New Studies* (SHANE 18; Leiden: Brill, 1999).

Galling, K., "Erwägungen zum Stelenheiligtum von Hazor", *ZDPV* 75 (1959), 1-13.

Gane, R., "The Role of Assyria in the Ancient Near East during the Reign of Manasseh", *AUSS* 35 (1997), 21-32.

Garbini, G., "L'iscizioni di Balaam Bar-Beor", *Henoch* 1 (1979), 166-188.

—*History and Ideology in Ancient Israel* (trans. J. Bowden; London, SCM Press, 1988).

—"L'iscrizione aramaica di Tel Dan", *Atti della Accademia Nazionale dei Lincei* 391 (1994), 461-471.

Gaster, T.H., *Myth, Legend, and Custom in the Old Testament* (London: Duckworth, 1969).

Geiger, A., *Urschrift und Übersetzungen der Bibel in ihrer Abhängigkeit von der innern Entwickelung des Judenthums* (Breslau: Verlag von Julius Hainauer, 1857).

Gelinas, M. M., "United Monarchy—Divided Monarchy: Fact or Fiction?", in E.W. Holloway and L.K. Handy (eds.), *The Pitcher is Broken: Memorial Essays for Gösta W. Ahlström* (JSOTSup 190; Sheffield: Sheffield Academic Press, 1995), 27-237.

Gerstenberger, E.S., *Leviticus: A Commentary* (trans. D.W. Stott; OTL; Louisville: Westminster John Knox, 1996).

—*Theologies in the Old Testament* (trans. J. Bowden; Edinburgh: T&T Clark, 2002).

Gese, H., "Ezechiel 20.25f und die Erstgeburtsopfer", in H. Donner, R. Hanhaert and R. Smend (eds.), *Beiträge zur alttestamentlichen Theologie: Festschrift für Walther Zimmerli zum 70. Geburtstag* (Göttingen: Vandenhoeck & Ruprecht, 1977), 140-151.

Geus, C.H.J. de, *The Tribes of Israel: An Investigation into Some of the presuppositions of Martin Noth's Amphictyony Hypothesis* (Assen and Amsterdam: Van Gorcum, 1976).

—"Manasseh (Place)", *ABD*, vol. 4, 494-496.

Gianto, A., "Some Notes on the Mulk Inscription from Nebi Yunis (*RES* 367)", *Bib* 68 (1987), 397-400.

Gifford, E.H. (ed.), *Eusebii Pamphili evangelicae praeparationis* (Oxford: Oxford University Press, 1903).

Girard, R., *Violence and the Sacred* (trans. P. Gregory; Baltimore: Johns Hopkins University Press, 1977).

Gitin, S., "Tel Miqne-Ekron: A Type Site for the Inner Coastal Plain in the Iron Age II Period", in S. Gitin and W.G. Dever (eds.), *Recent Excavations in Israel: Studies in Iron Age Archaeology* (AASOR 49; Winona Lake: Eisenbrauns, 1989), 23-58.

—"Ekron of the Philistines, Part II: Olive Oil Suppliers to the World", *BAR* 16/2 (1990), 32-42, 59.

Goldberg, J., "Two Assyrian Campaigns against Hezekiah and Later Eighth Century Biblical Chronology", *Bib* 80 (1999), 360-390.

Gomes, J., "Popular Religion in Old Testament Research: Past, Present and Future", *TynBul* 54 (2003), 31-50.

Gottwald, N.K., *The Hebrew Bible: A Socio-Literary Introduction* (Philadelphia: Fortress Press, 1986).

—"Triumphalist versus Anti-Triumphalist Versions of Early Israel", *CR:BS* 5 (1997), 15-42.

Grabbe, L.L., "Josephus and the Reconstruction of the Judean Restoration", *JBL* 106 (1987), 231-246.

—*Judaism from Cyrus to Hadrian* (London: SCM Press, 1992).

—(ed.), *Can a "History of Israel" Be Written?* (JSOTSup 245/ESHM 1; Sheffield: Sheffield Academic Press, 1997).

Graham, W.C., and H.G. May, *Culture and Conscience: An Archaeological Study of the New Religious Past in Ancient Palestine* (Chicago: Chicago University Press, 1940).

Gras, M., and P. Rouillard, J. Teixodor, "The Phoenicians and Death", *Berytus* 39 (1991), 127-176.

Gray, G.B., *Sacrifice in the Old Testament* (Oxford: Clarendon Press, 1925).

Gray, J., *I & II Kings: A Commentary* (OTL; third edn.; London: SCM Press, 1977).

Green, A.R.W., *The Role of Human Sacrifice in the Ancient Near East* (ASORDS 1; Missoula: Scholars Press, 1975).

Greenberg, M., *Ezekiel 1–20: A New Translation with Introduction and Commentary* (AB 22; Garden City: Doubleday, 1983).

—*Ezekiel 21–37: A New Translation with Introduction and Commentary* (AB 22A; Garden City: Doubleday, 1997).

Greene, J.E., "An *Odyssey* Debate: Were Living Children Sacrificed to the Gods?", *ArchOd* (Nov/Dec 2000), 28-31.

Greenwood, D.C., "On the Jewish Hope for a Restored Northern Kingdom", *ZAW* 88 (1976), 376-385.

Gruber, M.I., "Gillulim", *DDD*, 346-347.

Gruenwald, I., "God the "Stone/Rock": Myth, Idolatry, and Cultic Fetishism in Ancient Israel", *JR* 76 (1996), 428-449.

Gsell, S., *Histoire ancienne de l'Afrique du Nord*, vol. 4: *La civilisation carthaginoise* (Paris: Librairie Hachette, 1920).

Gwaltney, W.C., "Assyrians", in A.J. Hoerth, G.L. Mattingly and E.M. Yamauchi (eds.), *Peoples of the Old Testament World* (Grand Rapids: Baker Books, 1994), 77-106.

Hackett, J.A., *The Balaam Text from Deir ʿAllā* (HSM 31; Chico: Scholars Press, 1984).

—"Religious Traditions in Israelite Transjordan", in P.D. Miller, P.D. Hanson and S.B. McBride (eds.), *Ancient Israelite Religion: Essays in Honor of Frank Moore Cross* (Philadelphia: Fortress Press,1987), 125-136.

—"Response to Baruch Levine and Andre Lemaire", in J. Hoftijzer and G. van der Kooij (eds.), *The Balaam Text from Deir ʿAllā Re-evaluated: Proceedings of the International Symposium held at Leiden 21–24 August 1989* (Leiden: Brill, 1991), 73-84.

—"Deir ʿAlla: texts", *ABD*, vol. 2, 129.

— "Defusing Pseudo-Scholarship: The Siloam Inscription Ain't Hasmonean", *BAR* 23 (1997), 41-50, 68.

Hadley, J.M., "The fecundity of the flock? The De-Personalization of Astarte in the Old Testament", in B. Becking and M. Dijkstra (eds.), *On Reading Prophetic Texts: Gender-Specific and Related Studies in Memory of Fokkelien van Dijk-Hemmes* (Leiden: Brill, 1996), 115-133.

—*The Cult of Asherah in Ancient Israel and Judah: Evidence for a Hebrew Goddess* (UCOP 57; Cambridge: Cambridge University Press, 2000).

Hall, R.G., "Circumcision", *ABD*, vol. 1, 1025-1031.

Halpern, B., "'The Excremental Vision': The Doomed Priests of Doom in Isaiah 28", *HAR* 10 (1986), 109-121.

—"Jerusalem and the Lineages in the Seventh Century BCE: Kingship and the Rise of Individual Moral Liability", in B. Halpern, D.B. Hobson (eds.), *Law and Ideology in Monarchic Israel* (JSOTSup 124; Sheffield: JSOT Press, 1991), 11-107.

—"Erasing History: The Minimalist Assault on Ancient Israel", *BR* 11/6 (1995), 26-35, 47.

—"The Stela from Dan: Epigraphic and Historical Considerations", *BASOR* 296 (1995), 67-68.

—"Sybil, or the Two Nations? Archaism, Kinship, Alienation, and the Elite Redefinition of Traditional Culture in Judah in the 8th–7th Centuries BCE", in J. S. Cooper and G. M. Schwartz (eds.), *The Study of the Ancient Near East in the 21st Century: The William Foxwell Albright Centennial Conference* (Winona Lake: Eisenbrauns, 1996), 291-338.

—"The New Names of Isaiah 62:4: Jeremiah's Reception in the Restoration and the Politics of 'Third Isaiah'", *JBL* 117 (1998), 623-643.

—"Why Manasseh is Blamed for the Babylonian Exile: The Evolution of a Biblical Tradition", *VT* 48 (1998), 473-514.

—"The Gate of Megiddo and the Debate on the 10th Century", in A. Lemaire and M. Saebø (eds.), *Congress Volume Oslo, 1998* (VTSup 80; Leiden: Brill, 2000), 79-121.

—*David's Secret Demons: Messiah, Murderer, Traitor, King* (Grand Rapids: Eerdmans, 2001).

—and D.S. Vanderhooft, "The Editions of Kings in the 7th–6th Centuries BCE", *HUCA* 62 (1991), 179-244.

Hamerton-Kelly, R.G. (ed.), *Violent Origins: Walter Burket, René Girard and Jonathan Z. Smith on Ritual Killing and Cultural Formation* (Stanford: Stanford University Press, 1987).

Hampton, C., *The Ideology of the Text* (Milton Keynes: Open University Press, 1990).

Handy, L.K., "The Appearance of Pantheon in Judah", in D.V. Edelman (ed.), *The Triumph of Elohim: From Yahwisms to Judaisms* (CBET 13; Kampen: Kok Pharos, 1995), 27-43.

Hanson, P. D., *The Dawn of Apocalyptic* (rev. edn; Philadelphia: Fortress Press, 1979).

Haran, M., "The Disappearance of the Ark", *IEJ* 13 (1963), 46-58.

—*Temples and Temple-Service in Ancient Israel* (Oxford: Clarendon Press, 1978).

Hartley, J.E., *Leviticus* (WBC 4; Dallas: Word, 1992).

—and T. Dwyer, "An Investigation into the Location of the Laws on Offerings to Molek in the Book of Leviticus", in J.E. Coleson and V.H. Matthews (eds.), *"Go to the Land I will Show You": Studies in Honor of Dwight W. Young* (Winona Lake: Eisenbrauns, 1996), 81-93.

Hayes, J.H., "The Tradition of Zion's Inviolability", *JBL* 82 (1963), 419-426.

—and P.K. Hooker, *A New Chronology for the Kings of Israel and Judah and Its Implications for Biblical History and Literature* (Atlanta: John Knox Press, 1988).

—and J.K. Kuan, "The Final Years of Samaria (730-720 BC)", *Bib* 72 (1991), 153-181.

Healey, J.F., Review of *Molech: A god of human sacrifice in the Old Testament*, by J. Day, *ExpTim* 102 (1990), 54.

—"Ilib", *DDD*, 447-448.

—"Mot", *DDD*, 598-603.

Heider, G.C., *The Cult of Molek: A Reassessment* (JSOTSup 43; Sheffield: JSOT Press, 1985).

—"A Further Turn on Ezekiel's Baroque Twist in Ezek. 20:25-26", *JBL* 107 (1988), 721-724.

—"Molech", *ABD*, vol. 4, 895-898.

—"Molech", *DDD*, 581-585.

Hendel, R.S., "The Date of the Siloam Inscription: A Rejoinder to Rogerson and Davies", *BA* 59 (1996), 233-237.

Hennessy, J.B., "Excavation of a Bronze Age Temple at Amman", *PEQ* 98 (1966), 155-162.

—"A Temple of Human Sacrifice at Amman", *Sydney University Gazette* 2/20 (1970), 307-309.

—"Thirteenth Century BC Temple of Human Sacrifice at Amman", in E. Gubel and E. Lipiński (eds.), *Studia Phoenicia 3: Phoenicia and Its Neighbours* (Leuven: Peeters, 1985), 85-104.

Herr, L.G., "The Amman Airport Structure and the Geopolitics of Ancient Transjordan", *BA* 46 (1983), 223-229.

—(ed.), *The Amman Airport Excavations, 1976* (AASOR 48; Winona Lake: Eisenbrauns, 1983).

Herzog, Z., *Das Stadtor in Israel und in den Nachbarländen* (Mainz-am-Rhein: Phillip von Zabern, 1989).

—"The Beer-Sheba Valley: From Nomadism to Monarchy", in I. Finkelstein and N. Na'aman, *From Nomadism to Monarchy: Archaeological and Historical Aspects of Early Israel* (Jerusalem: Israel Exploration Society, 1994), 122-149.

Hestrin, R., and M. Dayagi, "A Seal Impression of a Servant of King Hezekiah", *IEJ* 24 (1974), 27-29.

Hill, A.E., *Malachi* (AB 25D; Garden City: Doubleday, 1998).

Hobbs, T.R., *2 Kings* (WBC 13; Waco: Word, 1985).

Hoffmann, H.-D., *Reform und Reformen: Untersuchungen zu einem Grundthema der deuteronomistischen Geschichtsschreibung* (ATANT 66; Zurich: Theologische, 1980).

Hoffmeier, J.K., "Further Evidence for Infant Sacrifice in the Ancient Near East", *BAR* 13/2 (1987), 60-61.

Hoffner, H.A., "Second Millennium Antecedents to the Hebrew *ʾôb*", *JBL* 86 (1967), 385-401.

Hoftijzer, J., "The Prophet Balaam in a Sixth Century Aramaic Inscription", *BA* 39 (1976), 11-17.

—"Eine Notiz zum punischen Kinderopfer", *VT* 8 (1958), 288-292.

—and G. van der Kooij, *Aramaic Texts from Deir ʿAllā* (Documenta et Monumenta Orientis Antiqui 19; Leiden: Brill, 1976).

Hoglund, K.G., "The Chronicler as Historian: A Comparativist Perspective", in M.P. Graham, K.G. Hoglund and S.L. McKenzie (eds.), *The Chronicler as Historian* (JSOTSup 238; Sheffield: Sheffield Academic Press, 1997), 19-29.

Holladay, J.S., "The Kingdoms of Israel and Judah: Political and Economic Centralization in the Iron IIA-B", in T.E. Levy (ed.), *The Archaeology of Society in the Holy Land* (London: Leicester University Press, 1995), 368-398.

Holladay, W.L., "On Every High Hill and Under Every Green Tree", *VT* 11 (1961), 170-176.

—*Jeremiah 1: A Commentary on the Book of the Prophet Jeremiah, Chapters 1–25* (Hermeneia; Philadelphia: Fortress, 1986).

—*Jeremiah 2: A Commentary on the Book of the Prophet Jeremiah, Chapters 26–52* (Hermeneia; Minneapolis: Fortress Augsburg, 1989).

Hölscher, G., "Komposition und Ursprung des Deuteronomiums", *ZAW* 40 (1922), 161-255.

Honeyman, A.M., "The Evidence for Regnal Names among the Hebrews", *JBL* 67 (1948), 13-25.

Hooke, S.H., *The Origins of Early Semitic Ritual* (Oxford: Oxford University Press, 1938).

Hoop, R. de, *Genesis 49 in Its Literary and Historical Context* (OTS 29; Leiden: Brill, 1999).

Horn, S.H., "The Chronology of King Hezekiah's Reign", *AUSS* 2 (1964), 40-52.

—"Did Sennacherib Campaign Once or Twice Against Hezekiah?", *AUSS* 4 (1966), 1-28.

Horst, van der, P.W., "'Laws that were not Good': Ezekiel 20:25 in Ancient Judaism and Early Christianity", in J.N. Bremmer and F. Garcia Martinez (eds.), *Sacred History and Sacred texts in Early Judaism: A Symposium in Honour of A. S. van der Woude* (Kampen: Kok Pharos, 1992), 94-118.

Hours-Miedan, M., "Les représentations sur les stèles de Carthage", *Cahiers de Byrsa* 1 (1950), 15-76.

Huehnergard, J., "Remarks on the Classification of the Northwest Semitic Languages", in J. Hoftijzer and G. van der Kooij (eds.), *The Balaam Text from Deir ʿAllā Re-Evaluated: Proceedings of the International Symposium held at Leiden 21–24 August 1989* (Leiden: Brill, 1991), 282-293.

Hughes, J., *Secrets of the Times: Myth and History in Biblical Chronology* (JSOTSup 66; Sheffield: JSOT Press, 1990).

Ibrahim, M.M., and G. van der Kooij, "The Archaeology of Deir ʿAllā Phase IX", in J. Hoftijzer and G. van der Kooij (eds.), *The Balaam Text from Deir ʿAllā Re-Evaluated: Proceedings of the International Symposium held at Leiden 21–24 August 1989* (Leiden: Brill, 1991), 16-29.

Irvine, S.A., *Isaiah, Ahaz, and the Syro-Ephraimitic Crisis* (SBLDS 123; Atlanta: Scholars Press, 1990).

Irwin, B.P., "Molek Imagery and the Slaughter of Gog in Ezekiel 38 and 39", *JSOT* 65 (1995), 93-112.

Irwin, W.H., "The Smooth Stones of the Wady? Isaiah 57:6", *CBQ* 29 (1967), 31-40.

Isbell, C.D., *Corpus of the Aramaic Incantation Bowls* (SBLDS 17; Atlanta: Scholars Press, 1975).

Ishida, T., "The House of Ahab", *IEJ* 25 (1975), 135-137.

—*The Royal Dynasties in Ancient Israel: A Study on the Formation and Development of Royal Dynastic Ideology* (BZAW 142; Berlin: de Gruyter, 1977).

Jacobsen, T., "The Graven Image", in P.D. Miller, P.D. Hanson, S.B. McBride (eds.), *Ancient Israelite Religion: Essays in Honor of Frank Moore Cross* (Philadelphia: Fortress Press, 1987), 15-32.

Jagersma, H., *A History of Israel in the Old Testament Period* (London: SCM Press, 1982).

Jameson, F., *The Political Unconscious: Narrative as a Socially Symbolic Act* (Ithaca: Cornell University Press, 1981).

Jamieson-Drake, D.W., *Scribes and Schools in Monarchic Judah: A Socio-Archaeological Approach* (SWBAS 9/JSOTSup 109; Sheffield: JSOT Press, 1991).

Japhet, S., *I & II Chronicles: A Commentary* (London: SCM Press, 1993).

—*The Ideology of the Book of Chronicles and Its Place in Biblical Thought* (trans. A. Barber; BEATAJ 9; Frankfurt am Main: Peter Lang, 1997).

Jarick, J., *1 Chronicles* (Sheffield: Sheffield Academic Press, 2002).

Jeffers, A., *Divination in Ancient Palestine and Syria* (SHCANE 8; Leiden: Brill, 1996).

Jensen, P., "Die Götter כמוש und מלך und die Erscheinungsformen *Kamush* und *Malik* des assyrischbablonischen Gottes *Nergal*", *ZA* 42 (1934), 235-237.

Jobling, D., and T. Pippin (eds.), *Ideological Criticism of Biblical Texts* (*Semeia* 59; Atlanta: Society of Biblical Literature, 1992).

Johns, C.N., "Excavations at Pilgrim's Castle, Atlit (1933)", *QDAP* 6 (1938), 121-152.

Johnston, P., Review of *Israel's Beneficent Dead*, by B.B. Schmidt, *JTS* 47 (1996), 169-172.

—*Shades of Sheol: Death and Afterlife in the Old Testament* (Leicester: Apollos, 2002).

Johnstone, W., "Guilt and Atonement: The Theme of 1 and 2 Chronicles", in J.D. Martin and P.R. Davies (eds.), *A Word in Season: Essays in Honour of William McKane* (JSOTSup 42; Sheffield: JSOT Press, 1986), 113- 138.

—*1 and 2 Chronicles* (2 vols. JSOTSup 253, 254; Sheffield: Sheffield Academic Press, 1997).

Jones, G.H., *1–2 Kings* (NCB; London: Marshall, Morgan & Scott, 1984).

—*1 & 2 Chronicles* (OTG; Sheffield: JSOT Press, Sheffield, 1993).

Joyce, P.M., *Divine Initiative and Human Response in Ezekiel* (JSOTSup 51; Sheffield: JSOT Press, 1989).

—"Israelites and Canaanites, Christians and Jews: Studies in Self-Definition", in J.M. Soskice, *et al.*, *Knowing the Other: Proceedings of the Catholic Theological Association of Great Britain, Leeds, 1993* (New Blackfriars, Vol. 75, No. 878, January 1994), 31-38.

Kaiser, O., *Introduction to the Old Testament: A Presentation of Its Results and Problems* (Oxford: Blackwell, 1975).

—"Den Erstgeborenen deiner Söhne sollst du mir geben. Erwägungen zum Kinderopfer im Alten Testament", in *idem.* (ed.), *Denkender Glaube: Festschrift Carl Heinz Ratschow* (Berlin: de Gruyter, 1976), 24-48; repr. in O. Kaiser (ed.), *Von der Gegenwartsbedeutung des Alten Testaments: gesammelte Studien zur Hermeneutik und zur Redaktionsgeschichte* (Göttingen: Vandenhoeck & Ruprecht, 1984), 142-166.

—"Die Bindung Isaaks. Untersuchungen zu Eigenart und Bedeutung von Genesis 22", in *idem.*, *Zwischen Athen und Jerusalem: Studien zur griechischen und biblischen Theologie, ihrer Eigenart und ihrem Verhältnis* (BZAW 320; Berlin/New York: de Gruyter, 2003), 199-223.

Kalimi, I., "Was the Chronicler a Historian?", in M.P. Graham, K.G. Hogland, S.L. McKenzie (eds.), *The Chronicler as Historian* (JSOTSup 238; Sheffield: Sheffield Academic Press, 1997), 73-89.

Kallai, Z., "Judah and Israel—A Study in Israelite Historiography", *IEJ* 28 (1978), 251-261.

— "The Twelve-Tribe System of Israel", *VT* 47 (1997), 53-90.

Kapelrud, A.S., *The Message of the Prophet Zephaniah: Morphology and Ideas* (Oslo: Universitets, 1975).

Kaplan, L., "'And the Lord Sought to Kill Him': (Exod. 4:24) Yet Once Again", *HAR* 5 (1981), 65-74.

Karageorghis, V., "A Tophet at Amathus in Cyprus", *OrExp* (1991), 11.

Kaufmann, Y., *The Religion of Israel. From Its Beginnings to the Babylonian Exile* (trans. M. Greenberg; Chicago: University of Chicago, 1960).

Keel, O., and C. Uehlinger, *Gods, Goddesses, and Images of God in Ancient Israel* (trans. T.H. Trapp; Edinburgh: T&T Clark, 1998).

Kelly, B., "Manasseh in the Books of Kings and Chronicles (2 Kings 21:1-18; 2 Chron 33:1-20)", V.Philips Long, D.W. Baker and G.J. Wenham (eds.), *Windows into Old Testament History: Evidence, Argument, and the Crisis of "Biblical Israel"* (Grand Rapids: Eerdmans, 2002), 131-146.

Kelly, B.E., *Retribution and Eschatology in Chronicles* (JSOTSup 211; Sheffield: Sheffield Academic Press, 1996).

Kempinski, A., "From Death to Resurrection: The Early Evidence", *BAR* 22/5 (1995), 57-65, 82.

Kennedy, C.A., "The Mythological Reliefs from Pozo Moro, Spain", *SBLSP* (1981), 209-216.

—"Isaiah 57:5-6: Tombs in the Rocks", *BASOR* 275 (1989), 47-52.

Keulen, P.S.F. van, *Manasseh Through the Eyes of the Deuteronomists: The Manasseh Account (2 Kings 21:1-18) and the Final Chapters of the Deuteronomistic History* (OTS 38; Leiden: Brill, 1996).

King, P.J., and L.E. Stager, *Life in Biblical Israel* (Louisville: Westminster John Knox, 2001).

Kingsbury, E.C., "He Set Ephraim before Manasseh", *HUCA* 38 (1967), 129-136.

Kletter, R., "Pots and Polities: Material Remains of Late Iron Age Judah in Relation to Its Borders", *BASOR* 314 (1999), 19-54.

Knauf, E.A., "El Saddai", *BN* 16 (1981), 20-26.

—"El Saddai—der Gott Abrahams", *BZ* 92 (1985), 97-103.

—"The Migration of the Script, and the Formation of the State in South Arabia", *PSAS* 19 (1989), 79-91.

—"From History to Interpretation", in D.V. Edelman (ed.), *The Fabric of History: Text, Artifact and Israel's Past* (JSOTSup 127; Sheffield: JSOT Press, 1991), 26-64.

—"Shadday" *DDD*, 749-753.

—"Does 'Deuteronomistic Historiography (DH)' Exist?", in A. de Pury, T. Römer and J.-D. Macchi (eds.), *Israel Constructs Its History: Deuteronomistic Historiography in Recent Research* (JSOTSup 306; Sheffield: Sheffield Academic Press, 2000), 388-398.

—"Jerusalem in the Late Bronze and Early Iron Ages: A Proposal", *TA* 27 (2000), 75-90.

—and A.de Pury, T. Römer, "*BaytDawīd* ou *BaytDōd*? Une relecture de la nouvelle inscription de Tel Dan", *BN* 72 (1994), 60-69.

Knibb, M.A., "Martyrdom and Ascension of Isaiah", *OTP*, vol. 2, 143-176.

Knohl, I., *The Sanctuary of Silence: The Priestly Torah and the Holiness School* (Philadelphia: Fortress Press, 1995).

Knoppers, G.N., "Solomon's Fall and Deuteronomy", in L.K. Handy (ed.), *The Age of Solomon: Scholarship at the Turn of the Millennium* (SHCANE 11; Leiden: Brill 1997), 392-410.

—"The Vanishing Solomon: The Disappearance of the United Monarchy from Recent Histories of Ancient Israel", *JBL* 116 (1997), 19-44.

—"Is There a Future for the Deuteronomistic History?", in T. Römer (ed.), *The Future of the Deuteronomistic History* (BETL 147; Leuven: Peeters, 2000), 119-134.

—"The Preferential Status of the Eldest Son revoked?", in S.L. McKenzie an T. Römer (eds.), *Rethinking the Foundations: Historiography in the Ancient World and in the Bible* (BZAW 294; Berlin/New York: de Gruyter, 2000), 117-126.

—"Rethinking the Relationship between Deuteronomy and the Deuteronomistic History: The Case of Kings", *CBQ* 63 (2001), 393-415.

Knowles, M. P., "'The Rock, His Work is Perfect': Unusual Imagery for God in Deuteronomy XXXII", *VT* 39 (1989), 307-322.

Koenen, K., "Sexuelle Zweideutigkeiten und Euphemismen in Jes 57,8", *BN* 44 (1988), 46-53.

Kooij, G. van der, and M.M. Ibrahim, *Picking Up the Threads: A Continuing Review of Excavations at Deir ʿAllā* (Leiden: University of Leiden, 1989).

Kornfeld, W., "Der Moloch: Eine Untersuchung zur Theorie O. Eissfeldts", *WZKM* 51 (1952), 287-313.

Korpel, M.C.A., *A Rift in the Clouds: Ugaritic and Hebrew Descriptions of the Divine* (UBL 8; Münster: Ugarit-Verlag, 1990).

—"Rock", *DDD*, 709-710.

—"Stone", *DDD*, 818-820.

Kosmala, H., "The 'Bloody Husband'", *VT* 12 (1962), 14-28.

Krahmalkov, C.R., *Phoenician-Punic Dictionary* (Studia Phoenicia 15; Leuven: Peeters, 2000).

Kraus, H.-J., *Psalms 60–150: A Commentary* (trans. H.C. Oswald; Continental; Minneapolis: Augsburg Fortress, 1989).

Krüger, T., *Geschichtskonzepte im Ezechielbuch* (BZAW 108; Berlin: de Gruyter, 1989).

Kuan, J.K., *Neo-Assyrian Historical Inscriptions and Syria-Palestine: Israelite/Judean-Tyrian-Damascene Political and Commercial Relations in the Ninth-Eighth Centuries BCE* (Hong Kong: Alliance Bible Seminary, 1995).

Laato, A., *Josiah and David Redivivus: The Historical Josiah and the Messianic Expectations of Exilic and Postexilic Times* (CB OTS 33; Stockholm: Almqvist & Wiskell, 1992).

—"Second Samuel 7 and Ancient Near Eastern Royal Ideology", *CBQ* 59 (1997), 244-269.

Lagrange, P., "Une inscription phénicienne", *RB* 1 (1892), 275-281.

Lankester Harding, G., "Recent Discoveries in Jordan", *PEQ* 90 (1958), 10-12.

Larsson, G., "The Chronology of the Kings of Israel and Judah as a System", *ZAW* 114 (2002), 224-235.

Lasine, S., "Manasseh as Villain and Scapegoat", in J.C. Exum, D.J.A. Clines (eds.), *The New Literary Criticism and the Hebrew Bible* (JSOTSup 143; Sheffield: JSOT Press, 1993), 163-183.

Launderville, D., "Zurishaddai", *ABD*, vol. 6, 1176.

Lehmann, G., "Phoenicians in Western Galilee: First Results of an Archaeological Survey in the Hinterland of Akko", in A. Mazar (ed.), *Studies in the Archaeology of the Iron Age in Israel and Jordan* (JSOTSup 331; Sheffield: Sheffield Academic Press, 2001), 65-112.

Lehmann, R.G., and M. Reichel, "Dod und Ashima in Tell Dan", *BN* 77 (1995), 29-31.

Lelli, F., "Stars", *DDD*, 809-815.

Lemaire, A., "Prières en temps de crise: Les inscriptions de Khirbet Beit Lei", *RB* 83 (1976), 558-568.

—"Les Bene Jacob", *RB* 85 (1978), 321-337.

—"Note sur le titre *bn hmlk* dans l'ancien Israël", *Semitica* 29 (1979), 59-65.

—"Galaad et Makîr: Rémarques sur la tribu de Manassé à L'est du Jourdain", *VT* 31 (1981), 39-61.

—"La haute Mesopotamie et l'origene de Bene Jacob", *VT* 34 (1985), 95-101.

—"Aux origines d'Israël: La montagne d'Éphraïm et le territoire de Manassé (XIII-XIC av. J.-C.)", in J. Briend, A. Caquot, H. Cazelles, A. Kempinski, E.-M. Laperrousaz, A. Lemaire, D. Valbelle, J. Yoyotte, *La Protohistoire d'Israël: De l'exode à la monarchie* (Paris: Les Éditions du Cerf, 1990), 183- 292.

—"The Tel Dan Stela as a Piece of Royal Historiography", *JSOT* 81 (1998), 3-14.

Lemche, N.P., *Early Israel: Anthroplogical and Historical Studies on the Israelite Society Before the Monarchy* (VTSup 37; Leiden: Brill, 1985).

—*The Canaanites and Their Land: The Tradition of the Canaanites* (JSOTSup 110; Sheffield: JSOT Press, 1991).

—"Early Israel Revisited", *CR:BS* 4 (1996), 9-34.

—*The Israelites in History and Tradition* (Louisville: Westminster John Knox Press, 1998).

—"'House of David': The Tel Dan Inscription(s)", in T.L. Thompson (ed.), *Jerusalem in Ancient History and Tradition* (JSOTSup 381/CIS 13; London: T&T Clark International, 2003), 46-67.

—and T.L. Thompson, "Did Biran Kill David? The Bible in Light of Archaeology", *JSOT* 64 (1994), 3-22.

Levenson, J.D., "Who Inserted the Book of the Torah?", *HTR* 68 (1975), 203-233.

—*Sinai and Zion: An Entry into the Jewish Bible* (Minneapolis: Winston, 1985).

—"Zion Traditions", *ABD*, vol. 6, 1098-1102.

—*The Death and Resurrection of the Beloved Son: The Transformation of Child Sacrifice in Judaism and Christianity* (New Haven: Yale University Press, 1993).

Levine, B.A., *Leviticus* (JPSTC; Philadelphia: Jewish Publication Society, 1989).

—"The Deir 'Alla Plaster Inscriptions", *JAOS* 101 (1981), 195-205.

—"The Plaster Inscriptions from Deir ʿAllā : General Interpretation", in J. Hoftijzer and G. van der Kooij (eds.), *The Balaam Text from Deir ʿAllā Re-Evaluated: Proceedings of the International Symposium held at Leiden 21–24 August 1989* (Leiden: Brill, 1991), 58-72.

—*Numbers 21–36* (AB 4A; Garden City: Doubleday, 2000).

—"The Deir ʿAlla Plaster Inscriptions", *COS*, vol. 2, 140-145.

Levinson, B.M., *Deuteronomy and the Hermeneutics of Legal Innovation* (Oxford: Oxford University Press, 1998).

Lewis, T.J., "Death Cult Imagery in Isaiah 57", *HAR* 11 (1987), 267-284.

—*The Cult of the Dead in Ancient Israel and Ugarit* (HSM 39; Atlanta: Scholars Press, 1989).

—"How Far Can Texts Take Us? Evaluating Textual Sources for Reconstructing Ancient Israelite Beliefs about the Dead", in B.M. Gittlen (ed.), *Sacred Time, Sacred Place: Archaeology and the Religion of Israel* (Winona Lake: Eisenbrauns, 2002), 169-217.

Linder, E., "A Cargo of Phoenicio-Punic Figurines", *Arch* 26 (1973), 182-187.

Linville, J.R., "Rethinking the 'Exilic' Book of Kings", *JSOT* 75 (1997), 21-42.

—*Israel in the Book of Kings: The Past as a Project of Social Identity* (JSOTSup 272; Sheffield: Sheffield Academic Press, 1998).

Lipiński, E., "North Semitic Texts from the first millennium BC", in W. Beyerlin (ed.), *Near Eastern Religious Texts Relating to the Old Testament* (Philadelphia: Westminster, 1978), 227-268.

—"Juda et 'tout Israël'. Analogies et contrastes", in *idem.*, (ed.), *The Land of Israel—Cross-Road of Civilisation* (OLA 19; Leuven: Peeters, 1985), 93-112.

—"Sacrifices d'enfants à Carthage et dans le monde sémitique oriental", in *idem.* (ed.), *Studia Phoenicia VI Carthago: Acta Colloquii Bruxellenis habiti diebus 2 et 3 mensis Maii anni 1986* (OLA 26; Leuven: Peeters, 1988), 151-185.

—"Rites et sacrifices dans la tradition Phénico-Punique", in J. Quaegebeur (ed.), *Ritual and Sacrifice in the Ancient Near East* (Leuven: Peeters, 1993), 257-281.

—"Plaster Inscription", in *idem.*, *Studies in Aramaic Inscriptions and Onomastics, II* (OLA 57; Leuven: Peeters, 1994), 168-170.

—"Shemesh", *DDD*, 764-768.

Livingstone, A., "Nergal", *DDD*, 621-622.

Lohfink, N., Review of *Von der politischen Gemeinschaft zur Gemeinde*, by U. Rüterwörden, *TLZ* 113 (1988), 425-430.

—"The Cult Reform of Josiah of Judah: 2 Kings 22–23 as a Source for the History of Israelite Religion", in P.D. Miller, P.D. Hanson and S.B. McBride (eds), *Ancient Israelite Religion: Essays in Honor of Frank Moore Cross* (Philadelphia: Fortress Press, 1987), 459-476.

—*Studien zur Deuteronomium und zur deuteronomistischen Literatur* (SBAB 8, 12, 20; Stuttgart: Katholisches Bibelwerk, 1990, 1991, 1995).

Long, B.O., *2 Kings* (FOTL 10; Grand Rapids: Eerdmans, 1991).

Long, V.P., "How Reliable are Biblical Reports? Repeating Lester Grabbe's Comparative Experiment", *VT* 52 (2002), 367-384.

Loretz, O., "Der kanaanäische Ursprung des biblischen Gottesnamens *El šaddaj*", *UF* 12 (1980), 420-421.

Lowery, R.H., *The Reforming Kings: Cults and Society in First Temple Judah* (JSOTSup 120; Sheffield: JSOT Press, 1991).

Lubetski, M., "King Hezekiah's Seal Revisited", *BAR* 27/4 (2001), 44-51, 59.

Lust, J., "On Wizards and Prophets", in D. Lys, *et al.*, *Studies on Prophecy* (VTSup 26; Leiden: Brill, 1974), 133-142.

—"The Cult of Molek/Milchom: Some remarks on G.C. Heider's Monograph", *ETL* 63 (1987), 361- 366.

—"Molek and ΑΡΧΩΝ", in E. Lipiński (ed.), *Phoenicia and the Bible: Proceedings of the Conference held at the University of Leuven on the 15th and 16th of March 1990* (Studia Phoenicia 11; Leuven: Peeters, 1991), 193-208.

Lutzky, H., "Shadday as Goddess Epithet", *VT* 48 (1998), 15-36.

Macalister, R.A.S., *Excavations at Gezer, Vol. II (1907-1909)* (London: John Murray, 1912).

Maccoby, H., *The Sacred Executioner: Human Sacrifice and the Legacy of Guilt* (London: Thames and Hudson, 1982).

Malamat, A., "Longevity: Biblical Concepts and some Ancient Near Eastern Parallels", in H. Hirsch and H.Hunger (eds.), *Vorträge gehalten auf der 28. Recontre Assyriologique Internationale am Wein, 6–10 Juli 1981* (CRRAI 28/*AfO* 19; Horn: F. Berger & Söhne, 1982), 215-224.

Mankowski, P.V., *Akkadian Loanwords in Biblical Hebrew* (HSS 47; Winona Lake: Eisenbrauns, 2000).

Marcus, D., *Jephthah and his Vow* (Lubbock: Texas Technical Press, 1986).

Margalit, B., "Why King Mesha of Moab Sacrificed his Oldest Son", *BAR* 12/6 (1986), 62-63, 76.

Martin, J.D., "Israel as a tribal society" in R.E. Clements (ed.), *The World of Ancient Israel: Sociological, Anthropological and Political Perspectives* (Cambridge: Cambridge University Press, 1989), 95-117.

Mathys, H.P., "1 and 2 Chronicles", *OBC*, 267-308.

Mayes, A.D.H., "The Period of the Judges and the Rise of the Monarchy", in J.H. Hayes and J. M. Miller (eds.), *Israelite and Judaean History* (London: SCM Press, 1977), 285-322.

—*The Story of Israel between Settlement and Exile: A Redactional Study of the Deuteronomistic History* (London: SCM Press, 1983).

—"Deuteronomistic Ideology and the Theology of the Old Testament", *JSOT* 82 (1999), 57-82.

Mazar, A., *Archaeology of the Land of the Bible, 10,000–586 BCE* (New York: Doubleday, 1990).

—"The Northern Shephelah in the Iron Age: Some Issues in Biblical History and Archaeology", in M.D. Coogan, J.C. Exum and L.E. Stager (eds.), *Scripture and Other Artifacts: Essays on the Bible and Archaeology in Honor of Philip J. King* (Louisville: Westminster John Knox, 1994), 247-267.

—"Iron Age Chronology: A Reply to I. Finkelstein", *Levant* 29 (1997), 157-167.

Mazar, B., "Die westliche Linie des Meerweges", *ZDPV* 58 (1935), 79-84.

Mazza, F., "The Phoenicians as Seen by the Ancient World", in S. Moscati (ed.), *The Phoenicians* (second edn; New York: Rizzoli, 1997), 628-653.

Mazor, L., "The Origin and Evolution of the Curse upon the Rebuilder of Jericho: A Contribution of Textual Criticism to Biblical Historiography", *Textus* 14 (1988), 1-26.

Mazza, F., "The Phoenicinas as Seen by the Ancient World", in S. Moscati (ed.), *The Phoenicians* (second edn; New York: Rizzoli, 1997), 628-653.

McCarter, P.K., "The Balaam Texts from Deir ʿAlla: The First Combination", *BASOR* 239 (1980), 49-60.

—"The Dialect of the Deir ʿAllā Texts", in J. Hoftijzer and G. van der Kooij (eds.), *TheBalaam Text from Deir ʿAllā Re-evaluated: Proceedings of the International Symposium held at Leiden 21–24 August 1989* (Leiden: Brill, 1991), 87-99.

—"Zion", *DDD*, 940-941.

McConville, J.G., "Narrative and Meaning in the Books of Kings", *Bib* 70 (1989), 50-73.

McKane, W., "Jeremiah II 23-25: Observations on the Versions and History of Exegesis", *OTS* 17 (1972), 73-88.

—*Jeremiah I–XXV* (ICC; Edinburgh: T&T Clark, 1986).

—*Jeremiah XXVI–LII* (ICC; Edinburgh: T&T Clark, 1996).

McKay, J.W., *Religion in Judah under the Assyrians, 732–609 BC* (SBT 26; London: SCM Press, 1973).

McKenzie, J.L., *Second Isaiah: Introduction, Translation and Notes* (AB 20; Garden City: Doubleday, 1968).

McKenzie, S.L., *The Chronicler's Use of the Deuteronomistic History* (HSM 33; Atlanta: Scholars Press, 1984).

—*The Trouble with Kings: The Composition of the Book of Kings in the Deuteronomistic History* (VTSup 42; Leiden: Brill, 1991).

—"Deuteronomistic History", *ABD*, vol. 2, 160-168.

—"The Book of Kings in the Deuteronomistic History", in S.L. McKenzie and M.P. Graham (eds.), *History of Israel's Traditions: The Heritage of Martin Noth* (JSOTSup 182; Sheffield: Sheffield Academic Press, 1994), 281-307.

Mein, A., *Ezekiel and the Ethics of Exile* (Oxford: Oxford University Press, 2001).

Mettinger, T.N.D., *In Search of God: The Meaning and Message of the Everlasting Names* (Philadelphia: Fortress Press, 1987).

Meyers, C., "David as Temple Builder", in P.D. Miller, P.D. Hanson and S.B. McBride (eds.), *Ancient IsraeliteReligion: Essays in Honor of Frank Moore Cross* (Philadelphia: Fortress Press, 1987), 357-376.

—"Kinship and Kingship: The Early Monarchy", in M.D. Coogan, (ed.), *The Oxford History of the Biblical World* (Oxford: Oxford University Press, 1998), 165-205.

Michel, A., *Gott und Gewalt gegen Kinder im Alten Testament* (FAT 37; Tübingen: Mohr Siebeck: 2003).

Milgrom, J., *Numbers* (JPSTC; Philadelphia: Jewish Publication Society, 1990).

—*Leviticus 17–22: A New Translation with Introduction and Commentary* (AB 3A; New York: Doubleday, 2000).

Millard, A.R., "Large numbers in the Assyrian Royal Inscriptions", in M. Cogan and I. Eph'al (eds.), *Ah, Assyria ... Studies in Assyrian History and Ancient Near Eastern Historiography presented to Hayim Tadmor* (Scripta Hierosolymitana 33; Jerusalem: Magnes Press, 1991), 213-222.

—"Adrammelech", *DDD*, 10-11.

Miller, J.E., "Notes on Leviticus 18", *ZAW* 112 (2000), 401-403.

Miller, J.M., and J.H. Hayes, *A History of Ancient Israel and Judah* (London: SCM Press, 1986), 363;

Miller, P.D., "Psalms and Inscriptions", in J. A. Emerton (ed.), *Congress Volume Vienna, 1980* (VTSup 32; Leiden: Brill, 1981), 311-332.

—*The Religion of Ancient Israel* (Louisville: Westminster John Knox, 2000).

Milson, D., "The Designs of the Royal Gates at Megiddo, Hazor, and Gezer", *ZDPV* 102 (1986), 87-92.

Minette de Tillesse, G., "Martin Noth et la 'Redaktiongeschichte' des Livres Historiques", in C.H. Hauret (ed.), *Aux grands carrefours de la révélation et de l'exegese de l'Ancien Testament* (Recherches Bibliques 8; Paris: Doornik, 1967), 51-75.

Mittmann, S., "Die Grabinscrift des Sängers Uriahu", *ZDPV* 97 (1981), 139-152.

—"A Confessional Inscription from the Year 701 BC Praising the Reign of Yahweh", *Acta Academica* 21 (1989), 15-38.

—"Das Symbol der Hand in der altorientalischen Ikonographie", in R. Kieffer and J. Bergman (eds.), *La Main de Dieu/Die Hand Gottes* (Tübingen: Mohr [Paul Siebeck], 1997), 19-47.

Moltz, H., "God and Abraham in the Binding of Isaac", *JSOT* 96 (2001), 59-69.

Montgomery, J.A., "The Holy City and Gehenna", *JBL* 27 (1908), 24-47.

—"Archival Data in the Book of Kings", *JBL* 53 (1934), 46-52.

—and H.S. Gehman, *A Critical and Exegetical Commentary on the Books of Kings* (ICC; New York: Scribners, 1951).

Moor, J.C. de, "Standing Stones and Ancestor Worship", *UF* 27 (1995), 1-20.

—and H.F. van Rooy (eds.), *Past, Present, Future: The Deuteronomistic History and the Prophets* (OTS 44; Leiden: Brill, 2000).

Moore, G.F., "Biblical Notes. 3: The image of Molech", *JBL* 16 (1897), 161-165.

—*A Critical and Exegetical Commentary on Judges* (ICC; second edn; Edinburgh: T&T Clark, 1898).

Moore, M.S., *The Balaam Traditions: Their Character and Development* (SBLDS 113; Atlanta: Scholars Press, 1990).

—"Job's Texts of Terror", *CBQ* 55 (1993), 662-675.

Morgenstern, J., *Rites of Birth, Marriage, Death and Kindred Occasions among the Semites* (Cincinnati: Hebrew Union College Press, 1966).

Mosca, P.G., "Child Sacrifice in Canaanite and Israelite Religion: A Study in *Mulk* and מלך"(Unpublished Ph.D. dissertation; Harvard University, 1975).

—"The Punic Inscriptions", Appendix to L.E. Stager, "Excavations at Carthage 1975. Punic Project: First Interim Report", *AASOR* 43 (1978), 186-190.

Moscati, S., "Il sacrificio dei fanciulli: Nuove scoperte su un celebre rito cartaginese", *Rendiconti della Pontificia Accademia Romana di Archeologia* 38 (1965–1966), 61-68.

—"New Light on Punic Art", in W.W. Ward (ed.), *The Role of the Phoenicians in the Interaction of Mediterranean Civilizations: Papers Presented to the Archaeological Symposium at the American University of Beirut, March 1967* (Beirut: American University of Beirut, 1968), 68-72.

—*L'enigma dei Fenici* (Rome: Arnoldo Mondadori, 1982).

—"Il sacrificio punico dei fanciulli: Realità o invenzione?", *Problemi attuali di scienza e di cultura: Accademia Nazionale dei Lincei* 261 (1987), 3-15.

—"Non è un Tofet a Tiro", *RSF* 21 (1993), 147-163.

—"A Civilization Rediscovered", in S. Moscati (ed.), *The Phoenicians* (second edn; New York: Rizzoli, 1997), 8-16.

—"Stelae", in S. Moscati (ed.), *The Phoenicians* (second edn; New York: Rizzoli, 1997), 364-379.

Moscati, S., and M.L. Uberti, *Scavi al tofet di Tharros* (CSF 21; Rome: Consiglio nazionale delle ricerche, 1985).

Mosis, R., *Untersuchungen zur Theologie des chronistischen Geschichtswerkes* (Freiburg: Herder, 1973).

Moughtin, S., "Death of a Metaphor; Birth of New Meaning: An Exploration of Sexual and Marital Metaphorical Language in the Prophetic Books of the

the Hebrew Bible" (Unpublished D.Phil. dissertation; University of Oxford, 2004).

Mowinckel, S., "Die Ursprung der Bileamsage", *ZAW* 48 (1930), 233-271.

Mullen, T.E., "The Sins of Jeroboam: A Redactional Assessment", *CBQ* 49 (1987), 212-232.

Müller, H.-P., "*mōlek*", *TDOT*, vol. 8, 375-388.

—"Einige alttestamentliche Probleme zur aramäischen Inschrift von Dēr ʿAllā", *ZDPV* 94 (1978), 56-67.

—"Die aramäische Inschrift von Deir ʿAllā und die älteren Bileamsprüche", *ZAW* 94 (1982), 214-244.

—"Malik", *DDD*, 538-542.

Murray, D.F., "Dynasty, People, and the Future: The Message of Chronicles", *JSOT* 58 (1993), 71-92.

Na'aman, N., "Sennacherib's 'Letter to God' on His Campaign to Judah", *BASOR* 214 (1974), 25-38.

—"Historical and Chronological Notes on the Kingdoms of Israel and Judah in the Eighth Century BC", *VT* 36 (1986), 71-92.

—"The Historical Background to the Conquest of Samaria (720 BC)", *Bib* 71 (1990), 206-225.

—"Hezekiah and the Kings of Assyria", *TA* 21 (1994), 235-254.

—"Beth-David in the Aramaic Stela from Tel Dan", *BN* 79 (1995), 20-21.

—"The Debated Historicity of Hezekiah's Reform in Light of Historical and Archaeological Research", *ZAW* 107 (1995), 179-195.

—"The Contribution of the Amarna Letters to the Debate on Jerusalem's Political Position in the Tenth Century BCE", *BASOR* 304 (1996), 17-27.

—"Cow Town or Royal Capital? Evidence for Iron Age Jerusalem", *BAR* 23/4 (1997), 43-47, 67.

—and R. Zadok, "Population Changes in Palestine Following Assyrian Deportations", *TA* 20 (1993), 104-124.

Naveh, J., "Old Hebrew Inscriptions in a Burial Cave", *IEJ* 13 (1963), 235-256.

—"The Scripts of Two Ostraca from Elath", *BASOR* 183 (1966), 27-30.

—"The Date of the Deir ʿAlla Inscription in Aramaic Script", *IEJ* 17 (1973), 256-258.

—*Early History of the Alphabet* (Jerusalem: Magnes Press, 1982).

Nelson, R.D., *The Double-Redaction of the Deuteronomistic History* (JSOTSup 18; Sheffield: JSOT Press, 1981).

—"Realpolitik in Judah (687–609 BCE)", in W.W. Hallo, J.C. Moyer and L.G. Perdue (eds.), *Scripture in Context, II: More Essays on the Comparative Method* (Winona Lake: Eisenbrauns, 1983), 177-189.

—*First and Second Kings* (Interpretation; Louisville: John Knox, 1987).

—*Deuteronomy* (OTL; Louisville/London: Westminster John Knox, 2002).

Nickelsburg, G.W.E., "Prayer of Manasseh", *OBC*, 770-773.

Niehr, H., "The Rise of YHWH in Judahite and Israelite Religion: Methodological and Religio-Historical Aspects", in D.V. Edelman (ed.), *The Triumph of Elohim: From Yahwisms to Judaisms* (CBET 13; Kampen: Kok Pharos, 1995), 45-72.

—"In Search of YHWH's Cult Statue in the First Temple", in K. van der Toorn (ed.), *The Image and the Book: Iconic Cults, Aniconism, and the Rise of Book Religion in Israel and the Ancient Near East* (CBET 21; Leuven: Peeters, 1997), 73-95.

—"Zaphon", *DDD*, 927-929.

Nielsen, E., "Political Conditions and Cultural Developments in Israel and Judah during the Reign of Manasseh", in *Fourth World Congress of Jewish Studies, Papers*, vol. 1 (Jerusalem: Union of Jewish Studies, 1967), 103-106.

Niemann, H.M., "Megiddo and Solomon: A Biblical Investigation in Relation to Archaeology", *TA* 27 (2000), 61-74.

Niemeyer, H.G., "Expansion et colonisation", in V. Krings (ed.), *La civilisation phénicienne et punique: Manuel de recherche* (Leiden: Brill, 1995), 247-267

Noth, M., *Überlieferungsgeschichtliche Studien: Die sammelnden und bearbeitenden Geschichtswerke im Alten Testament* (Darmstadt: Wissenschaftliche Buchgesellschaft, 1943); ET *The Deuteronomistic History* (JSOTSup 15; Sheffield: JSOT Press, 1981) and *The Chronicler's History* (trans. H.G.M. Williamson; JSOTSup 50; Sheffield: JSOT Press, 1987).

—*Leviticus: A Commentary* (trans. J.E. Anderson; OTL; London: SCM Press, 1965).

O'Bryhim, S., "The *Cerastae* and Phoenician Human Sacrifice on Cyprus", *RSF* 27 (1999), 3-20.

—"An Oracular Scene from the Pozo Moro Funerary Monument", *NEA* 64 (2001), 67-70.

O'Ceallaigh, G.C., "And *so* David did to *all the cities* of Ammon", *VT* 12 (1962), 185-189.

Ockinga, B.G., "The Inviolability of Zion: A Pre-Israelite Tradition?", *BN* 44 (1988), 54-60.

O'Connor, K.M., "Jeremiah", *OBC*, 487-528.

Oded, B., "Judah and the Exile", in J.H. Hayes and J.M. Miller (eds.), *Israelite and Judaean History* (London: SCM Press, 1977), 435-488.

—*Mass Deportations and Deportees in the Neo-Assyrian Empire* (Wiesbaden: Reichert, 1979).

—"2 Kings 17: Between History and Polemic", *Jewish History* 2 (1987), 37-50.

Oesterley, W.O.E., *An Introduction to the Books of the Apocrypha* (London: SPCK, 1935).

—*Sacrifices in Ancient Israel: Their Origin, Purposes and Development* (London: Hodder & Stoughton, 1937).

Ofer, A., "'All the Hill Country of Judah': From a Settlement Fringe to a Prosperous Monarchy", in I. Finkelstein and N. Na'aman (eds.), *From Nomadism to Monarchy: Archaeological and Historical Aspects of Early Israel* (Jerusalem: Israel Exploration Society, 1994), 92-121.

—"The Monarchic Period in the Judaean Highland: A Spatial Overview", in A. Mazar (ed.), *Studies in the Archaeology of the Iron Age in Israel and Jordan* (JSOTSup 331; Sheffield: Sheffield Academic Press, 2001), 14-37.

Ollenburger, B.C., *Zion the City of the Great King: A Theological Symbol of the Jerusalem Cult* (JSOTSup 41; Sheffield: JSOT Press, 1987).

Olmo Lete, G. del, "Per vivencias cananeas (ugaríticas) en el culto fenicio— Il El culto 'mlk'", *Semitica* 39 (1990), 67-76.

Olyan, S.M., *Asherah and the Cult of Yahweh in Israel* (SBLMS 34; Atlanta: Scholars Press, 1988).

—and M.S. Smith, Review of *The Cult of Molek: A Reassessment*, by G.C. Heider, *RB* 94 (1987), 273-275.

Oswalt, J.N., *The Book of Isaiah Chapters 40–66* (Grand Rapids: Eerdmans, 1998).

Ouellette, J., "More on ʾĒl Šadday and Amorite Bêl Šadê" *JBL* 88 (1969), 470-471.

Page, S., "A Stela of Adad-nirari III and Nergal-ereš from Tell al Rimah", *Iraq* 30 (1968), 139-153.

Pardee, D., "Response: The Linguistic Classification of the Deir ʿAllā Text written on Plaster", in J.Hoftijzer and G. van der Kooij (eds.), *The Balaam Text from Deir ʿAllā Re-evaluated: Proceedings of the International Symposium held at Leiden 21–24 August 1989* (Leiden: Brill, 1991), 100-105.

Parker, S.B., *Stories in Scripture and Inscriptions: Comparative Studies on Narratives in Northwest Semitic Inscriptions and the Hebrew Bible* (Oxford: Oxford University Press, 1997).

Patton, C., "'I Myself Gave them Laws that Were Not Good': Ezekiel 20 and the Exodus Traditions", *JSOT* 69 (1996), 73-90.

Peckham, B., "Israel and Phoenicia", in F.M. Cross, W.E. Lemke and P.D. Miller (eds.), *Magnalia Dei: The Mighty Acts of God* (Garden City: Doubleday, 1976), 224-248.

Peltonen, K., *History Debated: The Historical Reliability of Chronicles in Pre-Critical and Critical Research* (2 vols. PFES 64; Helsinki/Göttingen: Finnish Exegetical Society/Vandenhoeck & Ruprecht, 1996).

Penchansky, D., "Up For Grabs: A Tentative Proposal for Doing Ideological Criticism", in D. Jobling and T. Pippin (eds.), *Ideological Criticism of Biblical Texts* (*Semeia* 59; Atlanta: Society of Biblical Literature, 1992), 35-41.

Perdue, L.G., and J. Blenkinsopp, J.J. Collins, C. Meyers, *Families in Ancient Israel* (FRC; Louisville: Westminster John Knox, 1997).

Pfeiffer, R.H., "Three Assyriological Footnotes to the Old Testament", *JBL* 47 (1928), 185.

Picard, C., "Le monument de Nebi-Yunis", *RB* 83 (1976), 584-589.

—"Les représentations de sacrifice Molk sur les ex-voto de Carthage", *Karthago* 17 (1976), 67-138.

—"Les représentations de sacrifice Molk sur les ex-voto de Carthage", *Karthago* 18 (1978), 5-116.

Pippin, T., "Ideology, Ideological Criticism, and the Bible", *CR:BS* 4 (1996), 51-78.

Plataroti, D., "Zum Gebrauch des Wortes *MLK* im ALten Testament", *VT* 28 (1978), 286-300.

Pohl, A., "Zu 4 Könige 17,31", *Bib* 22 (1941), 35-37.

Pope, M.H., "Notes on the Rephaim Texts from Ugarit", in M. de Jong Ellis (ed.), *Essays on the Ancient Near East in Memory of Jacob Joel Finkelstein* (Hamden: Archon, 1977), 163-182.

—*Song of Songs: A New Translation with Introduction and Commentary* (AB 7C; Garden City: Doubleday, 1977).

—"Fertility Cults", *IDB*, vol. 2, 265.

Postgate, J.N., "The Economic Structure of the Assyrian Empire", in M.T. Larsen (ed.), *Power and Propaganda: A Symposium on Ancient Empires* (CSA 7; Copenhagen: Akademisk Forlag, 1979), 193-221.

Prausnitz, M., and E. Mazar, "Achzib", *NEAEHL*, vol. 1, 32-36.

Pritchard, J.B., "The Tanit Inscription from Sarepta", in H.G. Niemeyer (ed.), *Phönizier im Westen* (Madrider Beitrage 8; Mainz: Zabern, 1982), 83-92.

Propp, W.H., "That Bloody Bridegroom", *VT* 43 (1993), 495-518.

Provan, I.W., *Hezekiah and the Books of Kings: A Contribution to the Debate about the Composition of the Deuteronomistic History* (BZAW 172; Berlin: de Gruyter, 1988).

— "Ideologies, Literary and Critical: Reflections on Recent Writing on the History of Israel", *JBL* 114 (1995), 585-606.

Puech, E., 1999, Review of *Aramaic Texts from Deir ʿAlla*, edited by J. Hoftijzer and G. van der Kooij, *RB* 85 (1978), 114-117.

—"Milcom", *DDD*, 575-576.

Pummer, R., *The Samaritans* (Leiden: Brill, 1987).

Rainey, A.F., "Manasseh, King of Judah, in the Whirlpool of the Seventh Century BCE", in *idem*. (ed.), *Kinattutu sa darâti: Raphael Kutscher Memorial Volume* (Tel Aviv: Tel Aviv University, 1993), 147-164.

—"The Chronicler and His Sources—Historical and Geographical", in M.P. Graham, K.G. Hoglund and S.L. McKenzie (eds.), *The Chronicler as Historian* (JSOTSup 238; Sheffield: Sheffield Academic Press, 1997), 30-72.

—"Stones for Bread: Archaeology versus History", *NEA* 64 (2001), 140-149.

Rehm, M., *Das zweite Buch der Könige: Ein Kommentar* (Würzburg: Echter Verlag, 1982).

Reimer, D.J., "The 'Foe' and the 'North' in Jeremiah", *ZAW* 10 (1989), 223-232.

Rendsburg, G., "On the Writing *bytdwd* in the Aramaic Inscription from Tel Dan", *IEJ* 45 (1995), 22-25.

Ribichini, S., "Beliefs and Religious Life", in S. Moscati (ed.), *The Phoenicians* (second edn; New York: Rizzoli, 1997), 120-152.

—"Un 'ipotesi per Milkʿaštart", *RSO* 50 (1976), 43-55.

—and P. Xella, "La Valle dei Passanti (Ezechiel 39.11)", *UF* 12 (1980), 434-437.

Richardson, N.H., "Psalm 106: Yahweh's Succoring Love Saves From the Death of a Broken Covenant", in J.H. Marks and R.M. Good (eds), *Love and Death in the Ancient Near East: Essays in Honor of Marvin H. Pope* (Guildford: Four Quarters, 1987), 191-203.

Richter, W., "Die Überlieferungen um Jephtah. Ri 10,17–12,6", *Bib* 47 (1966), 485-556.

Ringgren, H., "Balaam and the Deir ʿAlla Inscription" in A. Rofé and Y. Zakovitch (eds.), *Isaac Leo Seeligmann Volume: Essays on the Bible and the Ancient World*, vol. 3 (Jerusalem: Rubenstein, 1983), 93-98.

Roberts, J.J.M., "Erra—Scorched Earth", *JCS* 24 (1972), 11-16.

—"The Davidic Origin of the Zion Tradition", *JBL* 92 (1973), 329-344.

—"Zion in the Theology of the Davidic-Solomonic Empire", in T. Ishida (ed.), *Studies in the Period of David and Solomon and Other Essays* (Winona Lake: Eisenbrauns, 1982), 93-108.

—"In Defense of the Monarchy: The Contribution of Israelite Kingship to Biblical Theology", in P.D. Hanson, P.D. Miller, S.B. McBride (eds.), *Ancient Israelite Religion: Essays in Honor of Frank Moore Cross* (Philadelphia: Fortress Press, 1987), 337-396.

Robinson, B.P., "Zipporah to the Rescue", *VT* 36 (1986), 447-461.

Römer, T.C., "Transformations in Deuteronomistic and Biblical Historiography: On 'Book-Finding' and other Literary Strategies", *ZAW* 107 (1997), 1-11.

—"Why Would the Deuteronomists Tell about the Sacrifice of Jephthah's Daughter?", *JSOT* 77 (1998), 27-38.

—"Le sacrifice humain en Juda et Israël au premier millénaire avant notre ère", *AfR* 1 (1999), 16-26.

—"Du Temple au Livre: L'idéologie de la centralisation dans l'historiographie deutéronomiste", in S.L. McKenzie and T. Römer (eds.), *Rethinking the Foundations: Historiography in the Ancient World and in the Bible: Essays in Honour of John Van Seters* (BZAW 294; Berlin/New York, 2000), 207-225.

—"L'école deutéronomiste et la formation de la Bible hébraïque", in T. Römer (ed.), *The Future of the Deuteronomistic History* (BETL 147; Leuven: Peeters, 2000), 179-194.

—"Is There a Deuteronomistic Redaction in the Book of Jeremiah?", in A. de Pury, T. Römer and J.-D. Maachi (eds.), *Israel Constructs Its History: Deuteronomistic Historiography in Recent Research* (JSOTSup 306; Sheffield: Sheffield Academic Press, 2000), 399-421.

—and A. de Pury, "Deuteronomistic Historiography (DH): History of Research and Debated Issues", in A. de Pury, T. Römer and J.-D. Macchi (eds.), *Israel Constructs Its History: Deuteronomistic Historiography in Recent Research* (JSOTSup 306; Sheffield: Sheffield Academic Press, 2000), 9-120.

Rose, M., *Der Ausschliesslichkeitsanspruch Jahwes: Deuteronomische Schultheologie und die Volksfrömmigkeit in der späten Königszeit* (BWANT 106; Berlin: de Gruyter, 1975).

Rösel, H.N., *Von Josua bis Jojachin: Untersuchungen zu den deuteronomistischen Geschichtsbüchern des Alten Testaments* (VTSup 75; Leiden: Brill, 1999).

Rost, L., *Judaism Outside the Hebrew Canon: An Introduction to the Documents* (trans. D.E. Green; Nashville: Abingdon, 1976).

Rouillard, H., "Rephaim", *DDD*, 692-700.

—and J. Tropper, "Vom kanaanäischen Ahnenkult zur Zauberei. Eine Auslegungsgescichte zu den hebräischen Begriffen *'wb* und *yd'ny*", *UF* 19 (1987), 235-254.

Rowley, H.H., Review of *De Molochdienst*, by K. Dronkert, *BO* 10 (1953), 195-196.

—"Sanballat and the Samaritan Temple", *BJRL* 38 (1955–1956), 166-198.

—*Men of God: Studies in Old Testament History and Prophecy* (London: Nelson, 1963).

—*The Origin and Significance of the Apocrypha* (rev. edn; London: SPCK, 1967).

Rudman, D., "A Note on the Personal Name Amon (2 Kings 21,19-26//2 Chr 33,21-25)", *Bib* 81 (2000), 403-405.

Sader, H., "Phoenician stelae from Tyre", *Berytus* 39 (1991), 101-126.

—"Phoenician stelae from Tyre (continued)", *Studi Epigraphici e linguistici sul Vicino Oriente antico* 9 (1992), 53-79.

Sanders, P., *The Provenance of Deuteronomy 32* (OTS 37; Leiden: Brill, 1996).

Sarna, N.M., *Understanding Genesis* (New York: Schocken, 1966).

—*Exodus* (JPSTC; Philadelphia: Jewish Publication Society, 1991), 24-25.

Sass, B., and C. Uehlinger, *Studies in the Iconography of Northwest Semitic Inscribed Seals* (Fribourg: University of Fribourg Press, 1992).

Sawah, F., "Jerusalem in the Time of the Kingdom of Judah", in T.L. Thompson (ed.), *Jerusalem in Ancient History and Tradition* (JSOTSup 381/CIS 13; London: T&T Clark International, 2003), 114-144.

Schaeffer, C.F.A., "Sacrifice à M-l-k, Moloch ou Melek", in C.F.A. Schaeffer and J.C. Courtois (eds.), *Ugaritica IV: Découvertes des XVIIIe et XIXe campagnes, 1951-1955* (Mission de Ras Shamra 15/Bibliothèque archéologique et historique 74; Paris: Imprimerie Nationale, 1962), 77-83.

Schmidt, B.B., *Israel's Beneficent Dead: Ancestor Cult and Necromancy in Ancient Israelite Religion and Tradition* (FAT 11; Tübingen: J.C.B. Mohr, 1994; repr. Winona Lake: Eisenbrauns, 1996).

Schmitt, J.J., "Samaria in the Books of the Eighth-Century Prophets", in S.W. Holloway and L.K. Handy (eds.), *The Pitcher is Broken: Memorial Essays for Gösta W. Ahlström* (JSOTSup 190; Sheffield: Sheffield Academic Press, 1995), 355-367.

Schmitz, P.C., "Topheth", *ABD*, vol. 6, 600-601.

Schniedewind, W.M., "The Source Citations of Manasseh: King Manasseh in History and Homily", *VT* 41 (1991), 450-461.

—"History and Interpretation: The Religion of Ahab and Manasseh in the Book of Kings", *CBQ* 55 (1993), 649-661.

—"History or Homily: Toward Understanding the Chronicler's Purpose", in *Proceedings of the Eleventh World Congress of Jewish Studies* (Jerusalem: World Union of Jewish Studies, 1994), 92-93.

—"A Qumran Fragment of the Ancient 'Prayer of Manasseh'", *ZAW* 108 (1996), 105-107.

—"The Problem with Kings: Recent Study of the Deuteronomistic History", *RSR* 22 (1996), 22-27.

—"Prophets and Prophecy in Chronicles", in M.P. Graham, K.G. Hoglund and S.L. McKenzie, (eds.), *The Chronicler as Historian* (JSOTSup 238; Sheffield: Sheffield Academic Press, 1997), 204-224.

Schramm, B., *The Opponents of Third Isaiah: Reconstructing the Cultic History of the Restoration* (JSOTSup 193; Sheffield: Sheffield Academic Press, 1995).

Schroer, S., "Zur Deutung unter der Grabinschrift von Chirbet el-Qôm", *UF* 15 (1984), 191-199.

Schuller, E.M., *Non-Canonical Psalms from Qumran: A Pseudepigraphic Collection* (HSS 28; Atlanta: Scholars Press, 1986).

Scullion, J.J., "Some difficult texts in Isaiah cc. 55-66 in the light of modern scholarship", *UF* 4 (1972), 105-128.

Seeden, H., "A *tophet* in Tyre?", *Berytus* 39 (1991), 39-82.

—"Le premier cimetière d'enfants à Tyr", *OrEx* (1992), 10-12.

Selman, M. J., *1 Chronicles* (TOTC; Leicester: Inter-Varsity Press, 1994).

Shanks, H., "Who—or what—was Molech? New Phoenician Inscription may Hold Answer", *BAR* 22/4 (1996), 13.

—"Face to Face: Biblical Minimalists Meet Their Challengers", *BAR* 23/4 (1997), 26-42, 66.

—"Is Oded Golan a Forger?", *BAR* 29/5 (2003), 34-37

Shea, W.H., "Sennacherib's Second Palestinian Campaign", *JBL* 104 (1985), 410-418.

—"Sennacherib's Description of Lachish and of its Conquest", *AUSS* 26 (1988), 171-180.

Shemesh, A., "King Manasseh and the Halakhah of the Sadducees", *JJS* 52 (2001), 27-39.

Shiloh, Y., "Jerusalem", *NEAEHL*, vol. 2, 705-708.

Simonetti, A., "Sacrifici umani e uccisioni rituali nel mondo fenicio-punico: Il contributo delle fonti letterarie", *RSF* 11 (1983), 91-111.

Smelik, K.A.D., *Writings from Ancient Israel: A Handbook of Historical and Religious Documents* (trans. G.I. Davies, Edinburgh: T&T Clark, 1991).

—"The Portrayal of King Manasseh. A Literary Analysis of II Kings xxi and II Chronicles xxxiii", in *idem.*, *Converting the Past: Studies in Ancient Israelite and Moabite Historiography* (OTS 28; Leiden: Brill, 1992), 129-189.

—"Moloch, Molekh or Molk-Sacrifice? A Reassessment of the Evidence Concerning the Hebrew Term Molekh", *SJOT* 9 (1995), 133-142.

—"The Representation of King Ahaz in 2 Kings 16 and 2 Chronicles 28", in J. C. de Moor (ed.), *Intertextuality in Ugarit and Israel: Papers read at the Tenth Joint Meeting of the Society for Old Testament Study and Het Oudtestamentisch werkgezelschap in Nederland en Belgie (Oxford 1997)* (OTS 40; Leiden: Brill, 1998), 143-185.

Smend, R., "Das Gesetz und die Völker: Ein Beitrag zur deuteronomistischen Redaktionsgeschichte", in H.W. Wolff (ed.), *Probleme biblischer Theologie: G. von Rad zum 70. Geburtstag* (Munich: Chr. Kaiser Verlag, 1971), 494-509.

Smith, M., "A Note on Burning Babies", *JAOS* 95 (1975), 477-479.

—"The Veracity of Ezekiel, the Sins of Manasseh, and Jeremiah 44:18", *ZAW* 87 (1975), 11-16.

Smith, M.S., "Rephaim", *ABD*, vol. 5, 674-676.

—*The Origins of Biblical Monotheism: Israel's Polytheistic Background and the Ugaritic Texts* (Oxford: Oxford University Press, 2001).

—*The Early History of God: Yahweh and the Other Deities in Ancient Israel* (San Francisco: Harper & Row, 2002).

—and S.M. Olyan, Review of *The Cult of Molek*, by G.C. Heider, *RB* 94 (1987), 273-275.

Snaith, N.H., "The Cult of Molech", *VT* 16 (1966), 123-124.

— *Leviticus and Numbers* (CB; London: Thomas Nelson, 1967).

Soden, W. von, Review of *Molk als Opferbegriff*, by O. Eissfeldt, *ThLZ* 61 (1936), col. 46.

Soggin, J.A., "Child Sacrifice and Cult of the Dead in the Old Testament", in *idem.*, *Old Testament and Oriental Studies* (Biblica et Orientalia 29; Rome: Biblical Institute Press, 1975), 84-87.

—"'Your Conduct in the Valley'. A Note on Jeremiah 2:23a", in *idem.*, *Old Testament and Oriental Studies* (Biblica et Orientalia 29; Rome: Biblical Institute Press, 1975), 78-83 = "'La tua condotta nella Valle', Nota a Geremia ii, 23a", *RSO* 36 (1961), 207-11.

—"The Davidic-Solomonic Kingdom", in J.H. Hayes and J.M. Miller (eds.), *Israelite and Judaean History* (London: SCM Press, 1977), 131-186.

—"King David's State", in W.B. Barrick and J.R. Spencer (eds.), *In the Shelter of Elyon: Essays on Ancient Palestinian Life and Literature in Honor of G. W. Ahlström* (JSOTSup 31; Sheffield: JSOT Press, 1991), 261-275.

—*An Introduction to the History of Israel and Judah* (trans. J. Bowden; third edn; London: SCM Press, 1999).

Solvang, E.K., *A Woman's Place is in the House: Royal Women of Judah and their Involvement in the House of David* (JSOTSup 349; Sheffield: Sheffield Academic Press, 2003).

Spalinger, A.J., "A Canaanite Ritual Found in Egyptian Reliefs", *Society for the Study of Egyptian Antiquities Journal* 8/2 (1978), 47-60.

Spanier, K., "The Northern Israelite Queen Mother in the Judaean Court: Athaliah and Abi", in M. Lubetski, C. Gottlieb and S. Keller (eds.), *Boundaries of the Ancient Near Eastern World: A Tribute to Cyrus H. Gordon* (JSOTSup 273; Sheffield: Sheffield Academic Press, 1998).

Spieckermann, H., *Juda unter Assur in der Sargonidenzeit* (FRLANT 129; Göttingen: Vandenhoech & Ruprecht, 1982).

Spronk, K., *Beatific Afterlife in Ancient Israel and in the Ancient Near East* (AOAT 219; Neukirchen-Vluyn: Neukirchener Verlag, 1986).

Stager, L.E., "Excavations at Carthage 1975. Punic Project: First Interim Report", *AASOR* 43 (1978), 151-190.

—"The Rite of Child Sacrifice at Carthage", in J.G. Pedley (ed.), *New Light on Ancient Carthage* (Ann Arbor: University of Michigan Press, 1980), 1-11.

—"Carthage: A View from the Tophet", in H.G. Niemeyer (ed.), *Phönizier im Westen* (Madrider Beitrage 8; Mainz: Zabern, 1982), 155-166.

—"The Archaeology of the East Slope of Jerusalem and the Terraces of Kidron", *JNES* 41 (1982), 111-124.

—"Merneptah, Israel and Sea Peoples: New Light on an Old Relief", *EI* 18 (1985), 56-64.

—"An *Odyssey* Debate: Were Living Children Sacrificed to the Gods?" *ArchOd* (Nov/Dec 2000), 28-31.

—and S.R. Wolff, "Production and Commerce in Temple Courtyards: An Olive Press in the Sacred Precinct at Tel Dan", *BASOR* 243 (1981), 95-102.

—and S.R. Wolff, "Child Sacrifice at Carthage—religious rite or population control?" *BAR* 10/1 (1984), 31-51.

Steck, O., *Überlieferung und Zeitgeschichte in den Elia-Erzählungen* (WMANT 26; Neukirchen-Vluyn: Neukirchener Verlag, 1968).

Steiner, M., "A Note on the Iron Age Defence Wall on the Ophel Hill of Jerusalem", *PEQ* 118 (1986), 27-32.

—"Redating the Terraces of Jerusalem", *IEJ* 44 (1994), 13-20.

—"Jerusalem in the Tenth and Seventh Centuries BCE: From Administrative Town to Commercial City", in A. Mazar (ed.), *Studies in the Archaeology of the Iron Age in Israel and Jordan* (JSOTSup 331; Sheffield: Sheffield Academic Press, 2001), 280-288.

Stern, E., "Phoenician Masks and Pendants", *PEQ* 108 (1976), 109-118.

—*Archaeology of the Land of the Bible. Volume II: The Assyrian, Babylonian, and Persian Periods, 732–332 BCE* (ABRL; New York: Doubleday, 2001).

Stern, P.D., "Of Kings and Moabites: History and Theology in 2 Kings 3 and the Mesha Inscription", *HUCA* 64 (1993), 1-14.

Sternberg, M., *The Poetics of Biblical Narrative: Ideological Literature and the Drama of Reading* (Bloomington: Indiana University Press, 1985).

Stieglitz, R.R., "Die Göttin Tanit im Orient", *Antike Welt* 21 (1990), 106-109.

Stolz, F., "Monotheismus in Israel", in O. Keel (ed.), *Monotheismus im Alten Israel und seiner Umwelt* (BibB 14; Freiburg: Schweizerisches Katholosches Bibelwerk, 1980).

Stone, M.E., "Apocryphal Notes and Readings", *Israel Oriental Studies* 1 (1971), 123-131.

Sweeney, M.A., *Isaiah 1–39, with an Introduction to Prophetic Literature* (FOTL 16; Grand Rapids: Eerdmans, 1996).

—*King Josiah of Judah: The Lost Messiah of Israel* (Oxford: Oxford University Press, 2001).

Syrén, R., *The Forsaken Firstborn: A Study of a Recurrent Motif in the Patriarchal Narratives* (JSOTSup 133; Sheffield: JSOT Press, 1993).

Tadmor, H., "The Campaigns of Sargon II of Assur: A Chronological-Historical Study", *JCS* 12 (1958), 33-40.

—"The Historical Inscriptions of Adad-nirari III", *Iraq* 35 (1973), 141-150.

Talmon, S., "Polemics and Apology in Biblical Historiography—2 Kings 17:24-41", in *Literary Studies in the Hebrew Bible: Form and Content—Collected Studies* (Leiden: Brill, 1993), 134-159.

Tatum, L., "King Manasseh and the Royal Fortress at Horvat ʿUza", *BA* 54 (1991), 136-145.

Taylor, J.G., *Yahweh and the Sun: Biblical and Archaeological Evidence for Sun Worship in Ancient Israel* (JSOTSup 111; Sheffield: JSOT Press, 1988).

Thiele, R.E., *The Mysterious Numbers of the Hebrew Kings* (third edn; Grand Rapids: Zondervan, 1983).

Thompson, T.L., *Early History of the Israelite People from the Written and Archaeological Sources* (SHANE 4; Leiden: Brill, 1992).

—*The Bible as History: How Writers Create A Past* (London: Pimlico, 2000).

Tigay, J.H., *You Shall Have No Other Gods: Israelite Religion in the Light of Hebrew Inscriptions* (HSS 31; Atlanta: Scholars Press, 1986).

—*Deuteronomy* (JPSTC; Philadelphia: Jewish Publication Society, 1996).

Tomes, R., "The Reason for the Syro-Ephraimite War", *JSOT* 59 (1993), 55-71.

Toorn, K. van der, "Ilib and the 'God of the Father'", *UF* 25 (1993), 379-387.

—"Ancestors and Anthroponyms: Kinship Terms as Theophoric Elements in Hebrew Names", *ZAW* 108 (1996), 1-11.

—*Family Religion in Babylonia, Syria, and Israel* (Leiden: Brill, 1996).

—"Currents in the Study of Israelite Religion", *CR:BS* 6 (1998), 9-30.

—"Yahweh", *DDD*, 910-919.

Trebolle Barrera, J., "La transcripción *mlk* = *moloch*: Historia del texto e historia de lac lengua", *Aula Orientalis* 5 (1987), 125-128.

Tropper, J., *Nekromantie: Totenbefragung im Alten Testament* (AOAT 223; Kevelaer & Neukirchen-Vluyn: Neukirchener, 1989).

—"Wizard", *DDD*, 907-908.

—"Spirit of the Dead", *DDD*, 806-809.

Tsevat, M., "Ishbosheth and congeners: the names and their study", *HUCA* 46 (1975), 71-87.

Turfa, J.M., "Evidence for Etruscan-Punic Relations", *AJA* 81 (1981), 368-374.

Tur-Sinai, N.H., *The Language and the Book*, vol 1 (Jerusalem: Mosad Bialik, 1954). (Hebrew).

Tusa, V., "Sicily", in S. Moscati (ed.), *The Phoenicians* (second edn; New York: Rizzoli, 1997), 231-253.

Uehlinger, C., "Anthropomorphic Cult Statuary in Iron Age Palestine and the Search for Yahweh's Cult Images", in K. van der Toorn (ed.), *The Image and the Book: Iconic Cults, Aniconism, and the Rise of Book Religion in Israel and the Ancient Near East* (Leuven: Peeters, 1997), 97-155.

Ussishkin, D., "Was the 'Solomonic' City Gate at Megiddo Built by King Solomon?", *BASOR* 239 (1980), 1-18.

—*The Conquest of Lachish by Sennacherib* (Tel Aviv: Tel Aviv University, 1982).

—"Jerusalem in the Period of David and Solomon: The Archaeological Evidence" in A. Faust and E. Baruch (eds.), *New Studies on Jerusalem: Proceedings of the Third Conference December 11th 1997* (Ramat-Gan: Bar-Ilan University Faculty of Jewish Studies, 1997), 57-58 (Hebrew).

—"Jezreel, Samaria, and Megiddo: Royal Centres of Omri and Ahab", in J.A. Emerton (ed.), *Congress Volume Cambridge, 1995* (VTSup 66; Leiden: Brill, 1997), 351-364.

Van Seters, J., "The terms 'Amorite' and 'Hittite' in the Old Testament", *VT* 22 (1972), 64-81.

—"The Law on Child Sacrifice in Exod. 22:28B-29", *ETL* 74 (1998), 364-372.

—"The Deuteronomistic History: Can it Avoid Death by Redaction?", in T. Römer (ed.), *The Future of the Deuteronomistic History* (BETL 147; Leuven: Peeters, 2000), 213-222.

Vaughn, A.G., *Theology, History, and Archaeology in the Chronicler's Account of Hezekiah* (Atlanta: Scholars Press, 1999).

Vaux, R. de, Review of *Molk als Opferbegriff*, by O. Eissfeldt, *RB* 45 (1936), 278-282.

—"Bulletin", *RB* 52 (1955), 609-610.

—*Ancient Israel: Its Life and Institutions* (trans. J. McHugh; London: Darton, Longman & Todd, 1961).

—*Studies in Old Testament Sacrifice* (translated from the French; Cardiff: University of Wales Press, 1964).

Veijola, T., *Die ewige Dynastie: David und die Entstehung seiner Dynastie nach der deuteronomistischen Darstellung* (Helsinki: Suomaleinen Tiedeakatemia, 1975).

—*Das Königtum in der Beurteilung der deuteronomistischen Historiographie: Eine redaktionsgeschichtliche Untersuchung* (Helsinki: Suomaleinen Tiedeakatemia, 1977).

Vermes, G., "Leviticus 18:21 in ancient Jewish Bible Exegesis", in J.J. Petuchowski and E. Fleischer (eds.), *Studies in Aggadah, Targum and Jewish Liturgy in Memory of Joseph Heinemann* (Jerusalem: Magnes Press, 1981), 108-124.

Viviano, P., "2 Kings 17: A Rhetorical and Form-Critical Analysis", *CBQ* 49 (1987), 548-559.

Vorländer, H., *Mein Gott: Die Vorstellungen vom persönlichen Gott im Alten Orient und im Alten Testament* (AOAT 23; Neukirchen-Vluyn: Kevelaer, 1975), 218.

Vrijhof, P., and J. Waardenburg (eds.), *Official and Popular Religion: Analysis of a Theme for Religious Studies* (Religion and Society 19; The Hague: Mouton, 1979).

Walker, N., "A New Interpretation of the divine name Shaddai", *ZAW* 72 (1960), 64-66.

Ward, W.A., "The scarabs, scaraboid and amulet-plaque from Tyrian cinerary urns", *Berytus* 39 (1991), 89-99.

Warmuth, G., "*nāqâ*", *TDOT*, vol. 9, 553-563.

Watts, J.D.W., *Isaiah 34–66* (WBC 25; Waco: Word, 1987).

Weinfeld, M., "Cult Centralization in Israel in the Light of a Neo-Babylonian Analogy", *JNES* 23 (1964), 202-212.

—"The Moloch Cult in Israel and Its Background", in *Proceedings of the Fifth World Congress of Jewish Studies* (Jerusalem: World Union of Jewish Studies, 1969), 133-154 (Hebrew), 227-228 (English abstract).

—"The Worship of Molech and of the Queen of Heaven and its Background", *UF* 4 (1972), 133-154.

—"Burning Babies in Ancient Israel: A Rejoinder to Morton Smith's Article in *JAOS* 95 (1975), pp. 477-479", *UF* 10 (1978), 411-413.

Weippert, H., "Die "deuteronomistischen" Beurteilungen der Könige von Israel und Juda und das Problem der Redaktion der Königsbücher", *Bib* 53 (1972), 301-339.

—and M. Weippert, "Die 'Bileam' Inschrift von Tell Deir ʿAlla", *ZDPV* 98 (1982),77-103.

Weippert, M., "Erwägungen zur Etymologie des Gottesnames ʾĒl šaddaj", *ZDMG* 111 (1961), 42-62.

—"The Balaam Text from Deir ʿAllā and the Study of the Old Testament", in J. Hoftijzer and G. van der Kooij (eds.), *The Balaam Text from Deir ʿAllā Re-evaluated: Proceedings of the International Symposium held at Leiden 21-24 August 1989* (Leiden: Brill, 1991), 151-184.

Weise, M., "Jesaja 57,5f.", *ZAW* 72 (1960), 25-32.

Weitzman, S., "Reopening the Case of the Suspiciously Suspended *Nun* in Judges 18:30", *CBQ* 61 (1999), 448-460.

Welten, P., *Geschichte und Geschichtsdarstellung in den Chronikbüchern* (Neukirchen-Vluyn: Neukirchener Verlag, 1973).

Wenham, G.J., *Genesis 16–50* (WBC 2; Dallas: Word, 1994).

Wernberg-Møller, P., "Two Notes", *VT* 8 (1958), 305-308.

Wesselius, J.W., "Thoughts about the Balaam: The Historical Background of the Deir Alla Inscription on Plaster", *BO* 44 (1987), 589-599.

Westermann, C., *Isaiah 40–66* (trans. D.M.G. Stalker; OTL; London: SCM Press, 1969).

—*Die Geschichtsbücher des Alten Testaments: Gab es ein deuterono-mistisches Geschichtswerk?* (Tbü 87; Gütersloh: Chr. Kaiser Verlag, 1994).

Whitelam, K.W., "The Symbols of Power: Aspects of Royal Propaganda in the United Monarchy", *BA* 49 (1986), 166-173.

—*The Invention of Ancient Israel: The Silencing of Palestinian History* (London: Routledge, 1996).

Widengren, G., "The Persian Period", in J.H. Hayes and J.M. Miller (eds.), *Israelite and Judaean History* (London: SCM Press, 1977), 489-538.

Wifall, W.R., "El Shaddai or El of the Fields?", *ZAW* 92 (1980), 24-32.

Wilke, F., "Kinderopfer und kultische Preisgabe im 'Heiligkeitsgesetz'", *Festschrift der 57. Versammlung deutscher Philologen und Schulmänner in Salzburg, 1929* (Vienna: Rudolf M. Rohrer, 1929), 138-151.

Williamson, H.G.M., *Israel in the Books of Chronicles* (Cambridge: Cambridge University Press, 1977).

—"The Death of Josiah and the Continuing Development of the Deuteronomic History", *VT* 32 (1982), 242-248.

—*1 and 2 Chronicles* (NCB; London: Marshall, Morgan & Scott, 1982).

—*Ezra, Nehemiah* (WBC 16; Waco: Word, 1985).

—Review of *Molech: A god of human sacrifice in the Old Testament*, by J. Day, *EpRev* 18 (1991), 92-93.

—"The Temple in the Books of Chronicles", in W. Horbury (ed.), *Templum Amicitiae: Essays on the Second Temple Presented to Ernst Bammel* (JSNTSup 48; Sheffield: JSOT Press, 1991), 15-31.

—"Isaiah 8:21 and a new Inscription from Ekron", *BAIAS* 18 (2000), 51-55.

—"Early Post-Exilic Judaean History", in *idem.*, *Studies in Persian Period History and Historiography* (FAT 38; Tübingen: Mohr Siebeck, 2004), 3-24.

Wilson, R.R., "Who Was the Deuteronomist? (Who Was Not the Deutero-nomist?), Reflections on Pan- Deuteronomism", in L.S. Schearing and S.L. McKenzie (eds.), *Those Elusive Deuteronomists: The Phenomenon of Pan-Deuteronomism* (JSOTSup 268; Sheffield: Sheffield Academic Press, 1999), 67-82.

Wintermute, O.S., "Jubilees", *OTP*, vol. 2, 35-142.

Wiseman, D.J., *1 and 2 Kings* (TOTC; Leicester: Inter-Varsity Press, 1993).

Wolff, S.R., "Archaeology in Israel", *AJA* 98 (1994), 481-519.

Würthwein, E., "Die Josianische Reform und das Deuteronomium", *ZTK* 73 (1976), 365-423.

—*Die Bücher der Könige: 1. Kön. 17–2. Kön. 25* (ATD 11, 2; Göttingen: Vandenhoeck & Ruprecht, 1984).

Wyatt, N., "The problem of the 'God of the Fathers'", *ZAW* 90 (1978), 101-104.

— *Religious Texts from Ugarit: The Words of Ilimilku and his Colleagues* (BS 53; Sheffield: Sheffield Academic Press, 1998).

Xella, P., "Aspekte religiöser Vorstellungen in Syrien nach den Ebla- und Ugarit-Texte", *UF* 15 (1983), 279- 290.

—*Baal Hammon: Recherches sur l'identité et l'histoire d'un dieu phénicio-punique* (SF 32; Rome: Consiglio nazionale delle ricerche, 1991).

Yadin, Y., "Solomon's City Wall and Gate at Gezer", *IEJ* 8 (1958), 82-86.

—(ed.), *Hazor I* (Jerusalem: Magnes Press, 1958).

—"A Note on the Nimrud Bronze Bowls", *EI* 8 (1965), 6.

—"Symbols of Deities in Zinjirli, Carthage, and Hazor", in J.A. Sanders (ed.), *Near Eastern Archaeology in the Twentieth Century: Essays in Honor of Nelson Glueck* (Garden City: Doubleday, 1970), 199-231.

—*Hazor: The Rediscovery of a Great Citadel of the Bible* (New York: Random House, 1975).

Yamada, S., "Aram-Israel Relations as Reflected in the Aramaic Inscription from Tel Dan", *UF* 27 (1995), 611-625.

Yee, G.A., *Poor Banished Children of Eve: Woman as Evil in the Hebrew Bible* (Minneapolis: Fortress Press, 2003).

Yeivin, S., "The Sepulchers of the Kings of the House of David", *JNES* 7 (1948), 30-45.

Yezerski, I., "Burial-Cave Distribution and the Borders of the Kingdom of Judah toward the End of the Iron Age", *TA* 26 (1999), 253-270;

Younger, K.L., "The Deportations of the Israelites", *JBL* 117 (1998), 201-227.

Yurco, F., "Merneptah's Palestinian Campaign", *Society for the Study of Egyptian Antiquities Journal* 8/3 (1978), 70.

Zatelli, I., "Astrology and the Worship of the Stars in the Bible", *ZAW* 103 (1991), 86-99.

Zertal, A., "Israel enters Canaan: Following the Pottery Trail", *BAR* 17/5 (1991), 28-50.

—"'To the Land of the Perizzites and the Giants': On the Israelite Settlement in the Hill-Country of Manasseh", in N. Na'aman and I. Finkelstein (eds.), *From Nomadism to Monarchy* (Jerusalem: Israel Exploration Society, 1994), 37-70.

—"The Heart of the Monarchy: Pattern of Settlement and Historical Considerations of the Israelite Kingdom of Samaria", in A. Mazar (ed.), *Studies in the Archaeology of the Iron Age in Israel and Jordan* (JSOTSup 331; Sheffield: Sheffield Academic Press, 2001), 38-64.

Zevit, Z., "Deuteronomistic Historiography in 1 Kings 12–2 Kings 17 and the Reinvestiture of the Israelian Cult", *JSOT* 32 (1985), 57-73.

—*The Religions of Ancient Israel: A Synthesis of Parallactic Approaches* (London/New York: Continuum, 2001).

—"Three Debates about Bible and Archaeology", *Bib* 83 (2002), 1-27.

Zimmerli, W., *Ezekiel 1* (trans. R.E. Clements; Hermeneia; Philadelphia: Fortress Press, 1979).

Žižek, S. (ed.), *Mapping Ideology* (London: Verso, 1994).

Index of Biblical References

Index of Non-Biblical References

Index of Authors

Subject Index